Network Administration

Author | Author

CENGAGE
Learning™

Australia • Brazil • Japan • Korea • Mexico • Singapore • Spain • United Kingdom • United States

CENGAGE
Learning™

Network Administration

Chuck Easttom/ Bryan
Hoff /Dan DiNicolo/Brian T.
McCann

Executive Editor:
 Maureen Staudt
 Michael Stranz

Senior Project Development Manager:
 Linda de Stefano

Marketing Specialist:
 Sara Mecurio
 Lindsay Shapiro

Production/Manufacturing Manager:
 Donna M. Brown

PreMedia Supervisor:
 Joel Brennecke

Rights & Permissions Specialist:
 Kalina Hintz
 Todd Osborne

Cover Image:
 Getty Images*

For product information and
technology assistance, contact us at **Cengage Learning
Customer & Sales Support, 1-800-354-9706**

For permission to use material from this text or product,
submit all requests online at **cengage.com/permissions**
Further permissions questions can be emailed to
permissionrequest@cengage.com

ISBN-13: 978-1-4240-5900-3

ISBN-10: 1-4240-5900-3

Cengage Learning
5191 Natorp Boulevard
Mason, Ohio 45040
USA

Cengage Learning is a leading provider of customized learning
solutions with office locations around the globe, including
Singapore, the United Kingdom, Australia, Mexico, Brazil, and Japan.
Locate your local office at: **international.cengage.com/region**

Cengage Learning products are represented in Canada by
Nelson Education, Ltd.

For your lifelong learning solutions, visit **www.cengage.com/custom**

Visit our corporate website at **www.cengage.com**

Printed in the United States of America
1 2 3 4 5 6 7 12 11 10 09 08

Contents

1

INTRODUCTION TO WINDOWS SERVER 2003

After reading this chapter and completing the exercises, you will be able to:

Differentiate between the different editions of Windows Server 2003

Explain Windows Server 2003 network models and server roles

Identify concepts relating to Windows Server 2003 network management and maintenance

Explain Windows Server 2003 Active Directory concepts

Windows Server 2003 network administration consists of two major goals. The first is to ensure that network resources such as files, folders, and printers are available to users whenever they need access. The second goal is to secure the network so that available resources are only accessible to users who have been granted the proper permissions.

To acquire the skills needed to meet your network administration goals, you need to understand a number of concepts, from the account creation process to server and resource management. A Windows Server 2003 network administrator also requires an understanding of **Active Directory (AD)** concepts and management, as well as general troubleshooting tools and techniques.

The first section of this chapter explains the main elements of the four Windows Server 2003 editions, including hardware specifications and supported features. Ultimately, the Windows Server 2003 edition best suited to a particular environment or server implementation will depend upon the performance, scalability, and reliability needs of an organization, along with the intended purpose of a particular system. In order to provide you with a better perspective on Windows networking concepts, the second section of this chapter introduces the different logical models used to group network resources, namely workgroups and domains. A look at member servers and domain controllers explains the roles of each type of server in a domain, and why an administrator might choose to configure a server in one role over another.

The third section of this chapter outlines the tasks network administrators are expected to understand and implement as part of managing and maintaining a Windows Server 2003 network. This section provides a basic outline of the concepts and procedures covered in the subsequent chapters of this book.

It is also essential to understand the basic concepts of Windows Server 2003 Active Directory and how it influences network management procedures because most network management tasks take place within domain environments. The final section of this chapter discusses Active Directory concepts and provides a solid foundation on which to build your network administration skills. To become a successful Microsoft Certified Systems Administrator (MCSA) or Microsoft Certified Systems Engineer (MCSE), you need practical, hands-on experience with products like Microsoft Windows Server 2003. This book includes numerous hands-on activities and case studies to help ensure that you not only understand the theory behind the concepts covered but also that you feel comfortable carrying out common system administration tasks. To help simulate a real-world network environment, all of the activities in the book relate to a fictitious multinational organization calif led Dover Leasing Corporation, a property management company with a head office based in Boston. For the purpose of the activities and case projects, you have been hired by Dover Leasing Corporation as a junior network administrator responsible for looking after the day-to-day administration of an Active Directory domain within their Windows Server 2003 network. The scenarios presented are designed to help you relate the concepts that you learn to tasks typically performed by a system administrator in a corporate Windows Server 2003 environment.

WINDOWS SERVER 2003 EDITIONS

Businesses today have a wide variety of needs, making it difficult for a single operating system to include all required features. The Windows Server 2003 product line is divided into four distinct operating system editions. Each edition has similar core capabilities but is differentiated from the others by features (and limitations) that make it suitable for different server environments. This allows businesses to choose the platform that best meets their needs in terms of features, performance, and price.

The Windows Server 2003 operating system comes in the following editions, each of which are discussed in the following sections:

- Windows Server 2003, Standard Edition
- Windows Server 2003, Enterprise Edition
- Windows Server 2003, Datacenter Edition
- Windows Server 2003, Web Edition

Windows Server 2003, Standard Edition

Windows Server 2003, Standard Edition, is designed to meet the everyday needs of small to large businesses. It provides file and print services, secure Internet connectivity, and centralized management of network resources. Windows Server 2003, Standard Edition, provides the logical upgrade path for companies currently running its predecessor, Windows 2000 Server.

This edition of Windows Server 2003 provides basic operating system elements that enable file and printer sharing over a network, along with secure management of resources using NTFS permissions. It supports up to four processors in a symmetric multiprocessor (SMP) system, and up to 4 GB of RAM. Table 1-1 provides an overview of the system requirements and basic feature support for Windows Server 2003, Standard Edition.

Table 1-1   Windows Server 2003, Standard Edition, system requirements and feature support

Specification/Feature	Value
Minimum CPU speed	133 MHz
Recommended minimum CPU speed	550 MHz
Minimum RAM	128 MB
Recommended minimum RAM	256 MB
Maximum RAM supported	4 GB
Multiprocessor support	Up to 4 CPUs
Operating system disk space requirements	1.5 GB Free space
Clustering support	None
Itanium support	None
Active Directory support	Domain controller, Member server
Supported upgrades	Windows NT 4.0 Server (SP5), Windows NT 4.0 Terminal Server Edition (SP5), Windows 2000 Server

Itanium is the name of Intel's line of 64-bit processors aimed at higher-end application, security, and transaction processing servers. Only the Enterprise and Datacenter editions of Windows Server 2003 support these CPUs. For more information on the Itanium processor lines see *http://www.intel.com/itanium*.

Windows Server 2003, Standard Edition is designed to support the everyday business needs of small to medium organizations, or to function as a departmental server in larger environments. Key considerations for companies choosing this edition are the fact that it does not support the Itanium platform or clustering, and that it can only scale to a maximum of four processors and 4 GB of RAM.

Windows Server 2003, Enterprise Edition

Windows Server 2003, Enterprise Edition, is designed to meet the needs of organizations that support higher-end applications that demand better performance, reliability, and availability. Windows Server 2003, Enterprise Edition, supports up to eight processors in an SMP system and is available for both 32-bit x86 and 64-bit Itanium processors. In addition to these features, this platform has the following advantages:

- Supports up to 32 GB of RAM for x86 systems and up to 64 GB for Itanium systems.

- Provides **clustering** capabilities for up to eight nodes. Clustering is the ability to increase access to server resources and provide fail-safe services by linking two or more computer systems so they appear to function as though they are one.

- Supports hot-add memory in which RAM can be added to a system without shutting down the server.

- Provides Non-Uniform Memory Access (NUMA) support for SMP computers, allowing a processor to access memory designated for other processors. Applications can be written so that they take advantage of NUMA capabilities, including faster memory access.

- Supports Microsoft Metadirectory Services to facilitate networks that use multiple directory services to track and manage access to such resources as user accounts, shared folders, and shared printers.

- Provides Windows System Resource Manager (WSRM) to allow administrators to allocate and dedicate CPU and memory resources on a per-application basis.

Table 1-2 provides an overview of the system requirements and basic feature support for Windows Server 2003, Enterprise Edition.

Table 1-2   Windows Server 2003, Enterprise Edition, system requirements and feature support

Specification/Feature	Value
Minimum CPU speed	133 MHz (x86), 733 MHz (Itanium)
Recommended minimum CPU speed	733 MHz
Minimum RAM	128 MB
Recommended minimum RAM	256 MB
Maximum RAM supported	32 GB (x86), 64 GB (Itanium)
Multiprocessor support	Up to 8 CPUs
Operating system disk space requirements	1.5 GB (x86), 2.0 GB (Itanium)
Clustering support	Up to 8 nodes
Itanium support	Yes
Active Directory support	Domain controller, Member server

Table 1-2   Windows Server 2003, Enterprise Edition, system requirements and feature support (continued)

Specification/Feature	Value
Supported upgrades (x86 only)	Windows NT 4.0 Server (SP5), Windows NT 4.0 Terminal Server Edition (SP5), Windows NT 4.0 Enterprise Edition (SP5), Windows 2000 Server, Windows 2000 Advanced Server, Windows Server 2003 Standard Edition

Windows Server 2003, Enterprise Edition, is designed to support the higher-end business needs of medium to large organizations that require support for mission-critical applications. Key considerations for companies choosing this edition are the fact that it does support the Itanium platform and 8-way clustering, can scale to a maximum of eight processors, and supports more RAM than Standard Edition.

Windows Server 2003, Datacenter Edition

Windows Server 2003, Datacenter Edition, is designed for environments with mission-critical applications, very large databases, and information access requiring the highest possible degree of availability. This platform offers support for between eight and 32 processors in an x86 SMP system (64 processors maximum on Itanium systems), along with 8-way clustering. The maximum RAM capabilities for Datacenter Edition are the most robust at 64 GB for x86 systems and 512 GB for Itanium models. Table 1-3 provides an overview of the system requirements and basic feature support for Windows Server 2003, Datacenter Edition.

Table 1-3   Windows Server 2003, Datacenter Edition, system requirements and feature support

Specification/Feature	Value
Minimum CPU speed	400 MHz (x86), 733 MHz (Itanium)
Recommended minimum CPU speed	733 MHz
Minimum RAM	512 MB
Recommended minimum RAM	1 GB
Maximum RAM supported	64 GB (x86), 512 GB (Itanium)
Multiprocessor support	Minimum 8 CPUs required, Maximum 32 CPUs supported (x86), Maximum 64 CPUs supported (Itanium)
Operating system disk space requirements	1.5 GB (x86), 2.0 GB (Itanium)
Clustering support	Up to 8 nodes
Itanium support	Yes
Active Directory support	Domain controller, Member server
Supported upgrades (x86 only)	Windows 2000 Datacenter Server

Windows Server 2003, Datacenter Edition, is the most industrial-strength platform designed for large mission-critical database and transaction processing systems. Unlike the other Windows Server 2003 editions, the Datacenter edition can only be obtained from original equipment manufacturers (OEMs).

Windows Server 2003, Web Edition

Windows Server 2003, Web Edition, is designed for hosting and deploying Web services and related applications. This platform supports up to two processors (x86 only) and a maximum of 2 GB of RAM. It is specifically optimized to run Microsoft Internet Information Services (IIS) 6.0, and provides companies that only need to deploy Web-related services with a more cost-effective solution than the other Windows Server 2003 editions. Table 1-4 provides an overview of the system requirements and basic feature support for Windows Server 2003, Web Edition.

Table 1-1   Windows Server 2003, Web Edition, system requirements and feature support

Specification/Feature	Value
Minimum CPU speed	133 MHz
Recommended minimum CPU speed	550 MHz
Minimum RAM	128 MB
Recommended minimum RAM	256 MB
Maximum RAM supported	2 GB
Multiprocessor support	Up to 2 CPUs
Operating system disk space requirements	1.5 GB
Clustering support	None
Itanium support	None
Active Directory support	Member server only
Supported upgrades	None

Small to large companies, or departments within an organization that develop and deploy Web sites are examples of the intended audience for this platform. One limitation of Windows Server 2003, Web Edition, is that it cannot be configured as a domain controller, a function that is available on all other Windows Server 2003 platforms. You'll learn more about Active Directory later in this chapter.

NOTE   For a complete high-level overview of the features included in the different editions of Windows Server 2003 visit *www.microsoft.com/windows server2003/ evaluation/features/compareeditions.mspx.*

Activity 1-1: Determining the Windows Server 2003 Edition Installed on a Server

Time Required: 5 minutes

Objective: Determine the edition of Windows Server 2003 installed on your server.

Description: The edition of Windows Server 2003 that is installed on a server can be determined in a number of different ways ranging from the operating system selection screen during the boot process to the graphic displayed as part of the logon dialog box. In this exercise you will use the System Properties windows to determine the edition of Windows Server 2003 installed on your server.

1. At the Welcome to Windows dialog box, press **Ctrl+Alt+Delete**.

2. At the Log On to Windows dialog box, type **AdminXX** in the User name text box, where *XX* is your assigned student number. In the Password text box, type **Password01**.

3. Click the **Options** button. Ensure that Domain*XX* is selected in the Log on to drop down box, where *XX* is your assigned student number. Click **OK**.

4. At the Manage Your Server window, check the **Don't display this page at logon** check box, and then close the window.

5. Click **Start**, right-click **My Computer**, and click **Properties**. Notice that the Windows Server 2003 edition installed on your server appears in the System section of the General tab, as shown in Figure 1-1.

6. Click **Cancel** to close the System Properties window.

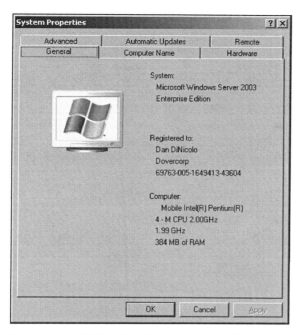

Figure 1-1   Using the General tab of the System Properties window to determine the Windows Server 2003 edition

WINDOWS NETWORKING CONCEPTS OVERVIEW

As part of managing a Windows Server 2003 network environment, a network administrator needs to be familiar with both of the different security models that can be implemented as well as the roles that a server can hold. The two different security models used in Windows network environments are the workgroup model and the domain model. While almost all larger organizations use the domain model (and by extension, Active Directory), the workgroup model is often implemented in smaller environments. As part of understanding a Windows network, you should be familiar with both models, including the benefits and limitations of each.

When a Windows Server 2003 system is deployed, it can participate on the network in one of three major roles. These roles include being configured as a standalone server, member server, and domain controller. The decision as to which role a server should be configured in is a function of the network model in use (workgroup or domain), as well as the types of tasks that the server will be handling. In the following sections you'll learn more about both of the Windows networking models, as well as each Windows Server 2003 server role.

Workgroups

A Windows **workgroup** is a logical group of computers characterized by a decentralized security and administration model. Instead of implementing a server to facilitate functions like centralized authentication, systems in a workgroup rely upon a local account database known as the **Security Accounts Manager (SAM) database**. When a user logs on to their workstation in the workgroup, they are authenticated by the local SAM database on that system. One of the benefits of the workgroup model is that it is simple and does not explicitly require a server at all—users can share resources directly from their desktop systems as necessary.

While this model may initially sound appealing, it does present many limitations. First, a user needs a unique user account to be configured on each and every workstation that they will log on to, rather than a single, centralized account. This may not be difficult in a small environment with only three workstations, but would be very difficult to manage on a larger network. Second, individual users effectively manage their own systems in the workgroup model, which can lead to potential security issues. Finally, the workgroup model is not scalable to very large sizes—as such, it is only recommended for smaller networks. As a general rule, workgroups should only be used in networks with 10 or less client systems, although workgroups up to 20 systems are not uncommon.

Although the workgroup model does not explicitly require a server, a Windows Server 2003 system can still be made part of a workgroup. In the workgroup model, a server would be used for traditional purposes such as providing a centralized location for the storage of user data files or acting as an e-mail server. A Windows Server 2003 system configured as part of a workgroup does not, however, authenticate users in a centralized manner, and configuring security settings (such as file and folder permissions) is more difficult due to the lack of a single user database. When a Windows Server 2003 system is configured as a member of a workgroup, it is properly referred to as a standalone server.

Figure 1–2 illustrates the Computer Name tab of the System Properties window for a server configured as part of a workgroup. Most organizations use the default workgroup name "Workgroup," but any valid NetBIOS name can be chosen to identify the logical group.

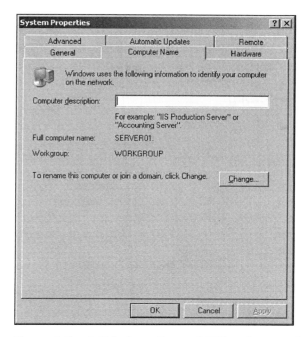

Figure 1-2   A Windows Server 2003 system configured as part of a workgroup named Workgroup

Domains

In contrast to a workgroup, a **domain** is a logical group of computers characterized by centralized authentication and administration. In the domain model, user, group, and computer accounts are stored in a centralized directory database—Active Directory, in the case of Windows Server 2003. While the directory conceptually centralizes both authentication and administration, the database itself is stored on one or more computers configured in a role known as a domain controller. In a Windows Server 2003 environment, a domain controller can be a server running Windows Server 2003, Windows 2000, or even Windows NT 4.0. In order to function as a domain controller, a server must explicitly be configured to hold this role.

The versions of Windows supported as domain controllers in a Windows Server 2003 Active Directory environment depends upon the configured functional level of both the domain and the forest. For more information on domain and forest functional levels see the Windows Server 2003 Help and Support Center.

When a user attempts to log on in a domain environment, they are authenticated by a domain controller rather than by the local SAM database of the workstation under normal circumstances. The authentication request is passed from their workstation to a domain controller where the supplied user name and password are compared to information stored

in the directory database. The obvious benefit of this model is that a user requires only a single account to be created to gain access to the network, rather than an account in the SAM database of many different workstations. By extension, this model also facilitates easier administration of the network since users and their properties can be managed centrally.

The domain model is highly recommended in any environment that consists of more than 10 users or workstations. One drawback of this model is that it requires at least one server to be configured as a domain controller, which means additional expense. Optimally, a domain environment will consist of a minimum of two domain controllers for the purpose of fault tolerance and load balancing. In this case, the second domain controller provides fault tolerance by ensuring that a domain controller is available to service requests should the other fail. Load balancing is achieved by having both domain controllers (rather than just one) handle requests, which results in better performance. Later in this chapter you'll learn more about Windows Server 2003 domains, and specifically Active Directory.

Member Servers

A **member server** is a Windows Server 2003 system that has a computer account in a domain, but is not configured as a domain controller. Member servers are typically used for a wide variety of functions including file, print, and application services. Member servers also commonly host network services such as the Domain Name Service (DNS), Routing and Remote Access Service (RRAS), and others. Each of the four Windows Server 2003 editions can be configured in the role of a member server in a domain environment.

Figure 1-3 illustrates the Computer Name tab of the System Properties window for a member server configured as part of a domain named Domain01.Dovercorp.net.

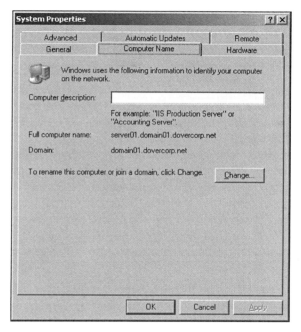

Figure 1-3   A Windows Server 2003 system configured as a member of a domain named Domain01.Dovercorp.net

Domain Controllers

While still a member of a domain, a **domain controller** is a Windows Server 2003 system explicitly configured to store a copy of the Active Directory database, and service user authentication requests or queries about domain objects. While many companies choose to dedicate servers to the role of a domain controller exclusively, other companies will use their domain controllers to also provide file, print, application, and networking services on the network. The main considerations when deciding which additional roles a domain controller should take on are the current utilization of the server, as well as whether sufficient resources (such as memory) are available to handle those roles. Of the four Windows Server 2003 editions, only Windows Server 2003, Web Edition, cannot be configured as a domain controller.

Servers are promoted to the role of a domain controller using either the Active Directory Installation Wizard (DCPROMO.EXE) or the Configure Your Server wizard. The Configure Your Server wizard is illustrated in Figure 1-4.

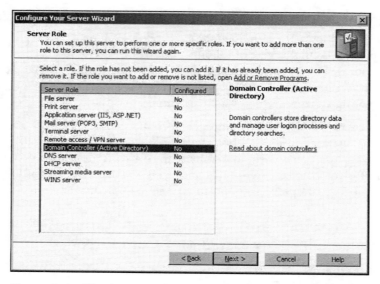

Figure 1-4   The Server Role screen of the Configure Your Server wizard

Activity 1-2: Determining the Domain or Workgroup Membership of a Windows Server 2003 System

Time Required: 5 minutes

Objective: Determine the domain or workgroup membership of a Windows Server 2003 system.

Description: Windows Server 2003 systems can be configured in different roles depending upon the Windows network environment in use and the intended purpose of the server. In this exercise you will use the System Properties window in order to determine the current role of your server as well as domain or workgroup membership settings.

1. Click **Start**, right-click on **My Computer**, and then click **Properties**.

2. Click the **Computer Name** tab. This tab displays both the full computer name of your server along with the domain that it is currently a member of.

3. Click the **Change** button. When the Computer Name Changes dialog box appears, read the message you are presented with and click **OK**. This message appears because your server is currently configured as a domain controller.

4. Notice in the lower portion of the Computer Name Changes window that the Member of section is grayed out and cannot be changed. If your system were not a domain controller, this screen would be used to add the server to a domain or workgroup. Your server is currently configured as a domain controller in domain*XX*.dovercorp.net, where *XX* is your assigned student number.

5. Click **Cancel** to close the Computer Name Changes window.

6. Click **OK** to close the System Properties window.

Computer Accounts

Computers running Windows NT, Windows 2000, Windows XP, or Windows Server 2003 are assigned computer accounts as part of joining a domain. A computer account provides a method to authenticate computers that are members of a domain, as well as audit access to network resources. While systems running Windows 95/98/ME can participate in a domain, these operating systems are not assigned computer accounts.

In an Active Directory environment, computer accounts are represented as computer objects, and can be viewed using administrative tools like Active Directory Users and Computers. In Activity 1-3, you will explore some of the basic properties associated with the computer account for your server. Later in this book you will learn more about the process of creating and managing computer accounts in an Active Directory environment.

Activity 1-3: Viewing and Configuring Computer Account Settings in Active Directory Users and Computers

Time Required: 5 minutes

Objective: Use Active Directory Users and Computers to view and configure computer account settings and properties.

Description: When a Windows Server 2003 system is configured as a member of an Active Directory domain, a computer account is created for the system in the Active Directory database. In this exercise you will use the Active Directory Users and Computers administrative tool to view the location and settings of the computer account associated with your server.

1. Click **Start**, point to **Administrative Tools**, and click **Active Directory Users and Computers**.

2. Click on the **plus sign (+)** next to the domain*XX*.dovercorp.net (where *XX* is your assigned student number) icon to expand it.

3. Click on the **Domain Controllers** folder to view its contents. This object is an organizational unit in the domain*XX*.dovercorp.net domain.

4. Right-click the **Server*XX*** computer object shown in Figure 1-5, and click **Properties**.

5. Review the information provided on the General tab. Notice that this system currently holds the role of Domain controller. In the Description text box, type **Domain Controller for domain*XX*.dovercorp.net**, where *XX* is your assigned student number.

6. Click the **Operating System** tab. This tab displays information about the operating system installed, along with version number and service pack information. Notice, however, that Windows Server 2003 edition information is not provided. Click **OK**. You will review the remaining tabs found in the properties of a computer account in a later chapter.

7. Close Active Directory Users and Computers.

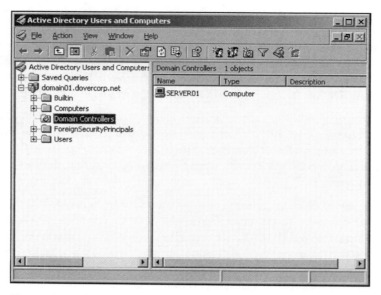

Figure 1-5   Using Active Directory Users and Computers to view a computer object

NETWORK MANAGEMENT AND MAINTENANCE OVERVIEW

Although managing and maintaining a Windows Server 2003 network environment requires an administrator to be familiar with a variety of different tools, concepts, and troubleshooting procedures, most of these tasks can be broadly categorized into one of the following five major focus areas:

- Managing and maintaining physical and logical devices
- Managing users, computers, and groups
- Managing and maintaining access to resources
- Managing and maintaining a server environment
- Managing and implementing disaster recovery

The following sections outline the key tasks associated with each of these five focus areas, which make up the core concepts that a network administrator needs to be familiar with for Microsoft exam 70-290, Managing and Maintaining a Microsoft Windows Server 2003 Environment. Outside of providing a broad overview of each focus area and related tasks, each section also provides details of where these topics are covered within this book.

Managing and Maintaining Physical and Logical Devices

A large part of managing and maintaining any network environment involves ensuring that network hardware is configured and functioning correctly. In a typical environment, a network administrator will be responsible for installing and configuring server hardware devices, managing server disks, and generally ensuring that devices are performing optimally. Key tools that are used to manage server hardware and related settings include various Control Panel applets, Device Manager, and the Computer Management MMC.

A network administrator would typically be responsible for installing new server hardware, such as an additional network adapter card or perhaps a modem. Apart from the physical act of inserting the card in an expansion slot, the administrator needs to be sure that resource settings are configured correctly, the correct driver is installed, and that the installed driver is certified for Windows Server 2003.

As part of managing server disks, an administrator will need to be familiar with the different types of disks available in Windows Server 2003, and how to configure these disks with different logical volumes or partitions. Once partitions or volumes have been created, an administrator will need to manage them to ensure optimal performance using utilities like Disk Defragmenter. In cases where disk redundancy is required, an administrator will need to be familiar with the various fault tolerance techniques available in Windows Server 2003, such as **Redundant Array of Independent Disks (RAID)**.

Although a proactive approach to network management and maintenance will help to ensure that server hardware problems are minimized, there will still be times when problems occur without warning. In these situations, it is imperative that a network administrator be able to identify the problem using the various tools provided in Windows Server 2003 in order to minimize the potential impact to network users.

Managing and maintaining hardware devices and related settings is detailed in Chapter 2. Managing disks and data storage is covered in Chapter 6.

Managing Users, Computers, and Groups

One of the most common day-to-day tasks encountered by a Windows Server 2003 network administrator is the administration of user accounts. New user accounts need to be created, existing settings may need to be changed, and users will invariably forget their passwords from time to time. In large environments, the management and maintenance of user accounts can consume a great deal of time and energy for any administrator.

To help alleviate some of this burden, Windows Server 2003 Active Directory includes a variety of new tools and features that allow an administrator to automate and simplify many account-related tasks. For example, the primary user administration tool, Active Directory Users and Computers, now supports drag-and-drop functionality to make moving objects

easier. Similarly, a number of new command-line utilities are available to help automate the process of adding, changing, and deleting user accounts. These powerful utilities give an administrator more flexibility in effectively managing their user environment. In a similar manner, these same tools can be used to manage the computer accounts required for Windows NT, Windows 2000, Windows XP, and Windows Server 2003 systems that will be part of a domain.

Windows Server 2003 supports a number of different group types and scopes. Groups can be created for the purpose of assigning network rights and permissions to multiple users, as well as to create distribution lists for e-mail. An administrator needs to be familiar with the different group types and scopes available in Windows Server 2003, and, subsequently, how and when each should be used. Group accounts, like user accounts, can also be managed using a variety of new command-line utilities included with Windows Server 2003.

Outside of the creation and management of users, computers, and groups, a network administrator also needs to manage the user desktop environment. In Windows Server 2003, the desktop environment is managed using user profiles. Depending upon the environment and needs of an organization, user profiles may be configured to save settings locally, enforce a standard profile for all users, or follow users to any system that they happen to log on to.

Once network objects are created and settings are configured, an administrator is still responsible for troubleshooting related problems as they arise. In some cases solving these problems may be simple, such as resetting a user's forgotten password. In others, a variety of issues may impact the user's ability to authenticate and access network resources. An administrator must be familiar with the authentication process and the different policy settings that can impact user access to the network.

Managing and maintaining user accounts, computer accounts, profile settings, and troubleshooting authentication issues are looked at in more detail in Chapter 3. The creation and management of group accounts is covered in Chapter 4.

One of the most common tasks for a network administrator involves resetting forgotten user passwords. In Activity 1-4 you will use Active Directory Users and Computers to reset the password associated with your Admin*XX* user account.

Activity 1-4: Resetting a Domain User Account Password Using Active Directory Users and Computers

Time Required: 10 minutes

Objective: Use Active Directory Users and Computers to reset a user password and force the user to change their password the next time they log on.

Description: One of the common tasks of a network administrator is to reset forgotten user passwords. While an administrator can explicitly control the passwords that users will need to provide during the logon process, this is not a common configuration. Instead, when

a user forgets their password, an administrator will typically reset the account password to a temporary value, supply this password to the user, and then force them to change it to a new value during the logon process. In this exercise you will use Active Directory Users and Computers to reset the password associated with your AdminXX account, and then create a new personal password during the logon process.

1. Click **Start**, point to **Administrative Tools**, and then click **Active Directory Users and Computers**.

2. Click the **Users** folder to view its contents. The Users folder is a built-in container in Windows Server 2003 Active Directory environments.

3. Right-click the **AdminXX** user object, where *XX* is your assigned student number. From the shortcut menu, click **Reset Password**.

4. In the Reset Password dialog box displayed in Figure 1-6, type **Password02** in the New password text box and **Password02** in the Confirm password text box.

5. Check the **User must change password at next logon** check box. This will force you to change your password immediately the next time you log on. Click **OK**.

6. When the Active Directory dialog box appears, click **OK**.

7. Close Active Directory Users and Computers.

8. Click **Start**, and then click **Log Off**. In the Log Off Windows dialog box, click the **Log Off** button.

9. Log on using your **AdminXX** account and the password **Password02**. At the Logon Message dialog box, click **OK**.

10. In the Change Password dialog box, type a new password in the New Password text-box and then re-type the new password in the Confirm New Password check box. Click **OK**. If the password you chose does not meet the complexity requirements read the dialog box that appears, click **OK**, and then enter a sufficiently complex password.

11. At the Change Password dialog box, click **OK**.

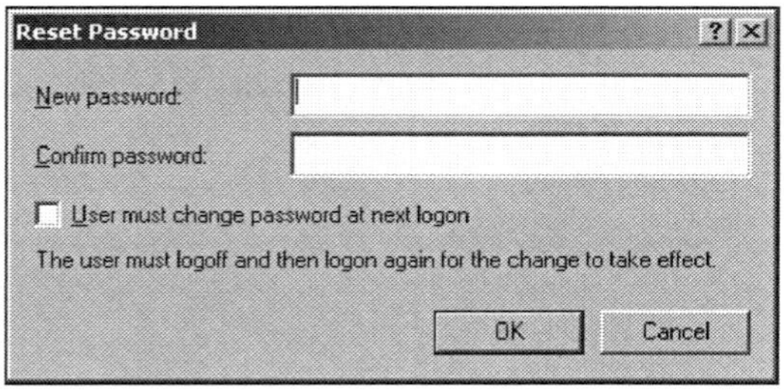

Figure 1-6   The Reset Password dialog box in Active Directory Users and Computers

Managing and Maintaining Access to Resources

The primary reason for implementing a network is to allow users to share resources. Examples of common network resources that users need access to include files saved on network servers and shared network printers. An administrator not only needs to ensure that resources are accessible to users, but also that they are properly secured.

In Windows Server 2003, resources are made available to network users via a technique known as sharing. When a folder or printer is shared over the network it becomes possible for users to connect to and remotely access the resource. The two most common methods of sharing resources are using the Windows Explorer interface and the Computer Management administrative tool. Other methods are also possible including using the command line.

Although sharing resources is the primary reason for implementing a network, it is imperative that resources are properly secured. While it might be fine for all users to access certain network folders or printers, others will need to be restricted to certain users or groups. Windows Server 2003 provides two main methods of securing resources, shared folder permissions and NTFS permissions. Shared folder permissions are only applicable when a user tries to access a resource over a network, while NTFS permissions apply both locally and remotely.

An administrator needs to understand the difference between each type of permission and the effects of combining them in order to properly plan permissions. If these concepts are not correctly understood and accounted for, the security of the network is put at risk, and unauthorized users may be able to access resources they shouldn't be able to.

Windows Server 2003 also includes a service known as **Terminal Services**. Terminal Services allows a user to connect to a central server and access applications as though working from the user desktop. This is a popular method of granting users access to certain applications without the need to deploy those applications to all desktops. Along the same lines, Terminal Services can also be used to give users running different operating systems (such as Windows 98 or Windows NT) the ability to use applications that were designed for Windows Server 2003. Once the decision to use Terminal Services has been made, a network administrator not only needs to ensure that a client can access the environment, but also that the environment is properly secured.

Managing the access to files and configuring security permissions is looked at in more detail in Chapter 5. Terminal Services and related settings are covered in Chapter 10.

Managing and Maintaining a Server Environment

A wide variety of tasks are involved in the general management and maintenance of a Windows Server 2003 server environment. Tasks included in this focus area range from managing server licensing to deploying software updates to managing Web servers. As part

of the day-to-day operations of a network, a network administrator needs to be familiar with a wide variety of software tools and concepts aimed not only at management, but also the monitoring of resources.

Two of the most popular tools used to monitor and troubleshoot a server environment are Event Viewer and System Monitor. Event Viewer handles the primary event logging functions on a Windows Server 2003 system, creating entries when any event of significance occurs. When an error occurs, Event Viewer should be the main tool accessed by a network administrator to gather more information. In cases where the overall performance of a server is in question, the System Monitor tool allows an administrator to gather current performance information that can be compared against the baseline of normal performance. Both tools are key utilities in helping an administrator to identify problem areas or performance issues.

Timely application of software patches and security updates is another key maintenance task for the network administrator. Microsoft typically releases patches for known exploits or issues shortly after they are identified, and then later includes these updates in a Service Pack release. Because managing individual updates for hundreds of computers is time-consuming and difficult, Microsoft has released a tool known as **Software Update Services (SUS)** for managing updates in a centralized manner. Administrators of Windows Server 2003 networks should be familiar with this tool and the capabilities that it provides.

Managing printing is yet another key component of a Windows Server 2003 network. Outside of physically connecting and then sharing printers, an administrator needs to ensure that printers are properly secured, and troubleshoot print queue issues as they arise.

While users should be encouraged to save their data files to a network server, an administrator also needs to prevent misuse of this space. For example, users may begin using their server storage space for non-critical files, such as MP3s. Ultimately such misuse of corporate resources leads to higher costs since additional disk space must consequently be acquired. In order to help control these types of issues, an administrator should be familiar with the disk quota feature of Windows Server 2003, which allows an administrator to control the amount of disk space allocated and available to each user.

Windows Server 2003 also includes Web server software in the form of Internet Information Services (IIS) 6.0. Although not installed by default, a Windows Server 2003 network administrator should be familiar with installing the service, and then subsequently ensuring that it is properly secured.

In order to simplify the administration of Windows Server 2003 servers, a variety of remote administration tools are included. One of these tools, the **Microsoft Management Console (MMC)**, provides an administration framework that allows different tools (known as snap-ins) to be added in custom configurations for different management and maintenance tasks. Almost all MMC snap-ins can be focused locally or remotely, allowing an administrator to manage settings on both local and remote servers from a central location. Another very useful remote management tool included with Windows Server 2003 is Remote Desktop, which allows an administrator to remotely connect to a server and

manage it as though sitting in front of it. Both tools are key components of any Windows Server 2003 remote administration strategy.

Advanced file system management concepts, including the configuration of disk quotas, are looked at in Chapter 7. Implementing and managing printing are detailed in Chapter 8. Software Update Services (SUS) and the remote administration of servers are covered in Chapter 10. Monitoring and managing server performance using tools like Event Viewer and System Monitor is looked at in more detail in Chapter 11. The administration and configuration of Web resources is covered in Chapter 13.

In Activity 1-5 you will create a custom Microsoft Management Console.

Activity 1-5: Creating a Custom Microsoft Management Console

Time Required: 10 minutes

Objective: Create a custom MMC.

Description: The MMC is the common environment in which all of the Windows Server 2003 administrative tools run. Although these tools are individually available from the Administrative Tools section of the Start menu, administrative tasks can be simplified by grouping commonly used tools into a single customized MMC. The IT manager at Dover Leasing has asked you to create and save a custom MMC to access both Event Viewer and Device Manager. In this activity, you will create a custom MMC and save it to your desktop for more convenient access.

1. Click **Start**, click **Run**, and then type **mmc** in the Open text box. Click **OK**. Figure 1-7 shows an empty MMC window.

2. Click the **File** menu, and click **Add/Remove Snap-in**. Figure 1-8 shows an open Add/Remove Snap-in dialog box.

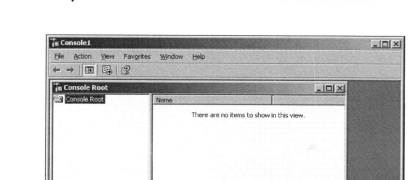

Figure 1-7   An empty MMC

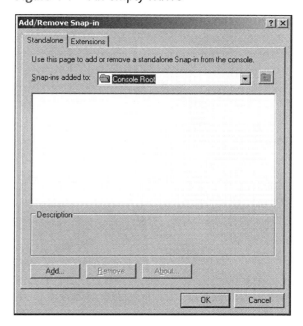

Figure 1-8   The Add/Remove Snap-in dialog box

3. Click the **Add** button to open the Add Standalone Snap-in dialog box listing the available snap-ins, as shown in Figure 1-9.

4. From the list of available snap-ins, click **Event Viewer** and click **Add**. When the Select Computer dialog box opens, make sure that the **Local computer** radio button is selected, as shown in Figure 1-10, and click **Finish**.

Figure 1-9   The Add Standalone Snap-in dialog box

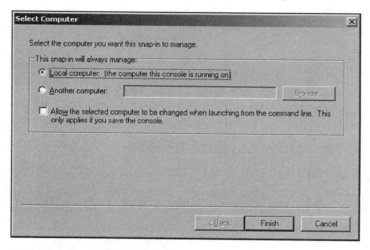

Figure 1-10   Selecting the snap-in focus

5. Click **Device Manager** on the list of available snap-ins and click **Add**. In the Device Manager dialog box, ensure that the **Local computer** radio button is selected and click **Finish**.

6. Click **Close** in the Add Standalone Snap-in dialog box.

7. Click **OK** in the Add/Remove Snap-in dialog box.

8. To save the console, click the **File** menu, and click **Save As**. In the Save in drop-down box, select your desktop, type the file name **My Console** in the File name text box, and click **Save**. Figure 1-11 shows a finished console.

9. Close the My Console window. If prompted to save changes, click **Yes**.

10. Double-click the **My Console** file on your desktop to open the custom console. Notice that it includes both the Event Viewer and Device Manager snap-ins. Close the **MMC**.

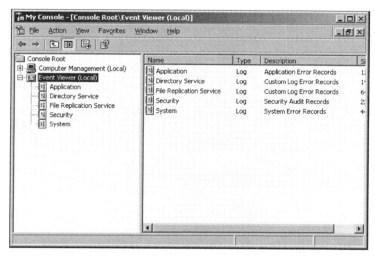

Figure 1-11   A customized MMC

Managing and Implementing Disaster Recovery

The final major focus area for a Windows Server 2003 network administrator is implementing and managing disaster recovery. This focus area concentrates on tasks that ensure both data and system settings are properly backed up and then available in cases like the failure of a server or the accidental deletion of files.

The backup tool provided with Windows Server 2003 is Windows Backup. This tool includes not only a graphical interface where the files to be backed up or restored can be selected, but also a wizard that can be used to simplify the same tasks. A network administrator should be familiar with the different types of backups available using this tool, along with how to schedule backup operations to occur automatically.

The Windows Backup tool can also be used to back up critical system information by selecting the System State option. System State information includes a variety of operating system components, including the Registry and critical system files. An administrator should be familiar with both backing up and restoring System State information using the Windows Backup tool.

Windows Server 2003 also includes a new feature known as Automated System Recovery. This feature, which is accessible from the Windows Backup utility, allows an administrator to create a floppy disk to which critical configuration information will be copied, allowing a server operating system to be restored using a combination of the disk and the Windows Server 2003 installation media. This provides a fast and effective way for an administrator to restore the operating system to a more current configuration rather than reinstalling from scratch.

Finally, another new and important feature in Windows Server 2003 is Shadow Copies of Shared Folders. Shadow Copies of Shared Folders is a feature that maintains previous versions of files on a server in a manner accessible to individual users. In the event that the current copy of a file has been deleted or overwritten, Shadow Copies of Shared Folders allows a user to restore a previous version of the file without having to contact an administrator. Ultimately, this feature can save an administrator a great deal of time and effort traditionally expended restoring individual user files from backup.

Concepts relating to implementing and managing disaster recovery are looked at in more detail in Chapter 12.

Introduction to Windows Server 2003 Active Directory

Active Directory is the native directory service included with Windows Server 2003 operating systems. Active Directory provides the following services and features to the network environment:

- A central point for storing, organizing, managing, and controlling network objects, such as users, computers, and groups
- A single point of administration of objects, such as users, groups, computers, and Active Directory-published resources, such as printers or shared folders
- Logon and authentication services for users
- Delegation of administration to allow for decentralized administration of Active Directory objects, such as users and groups

The Active Directory database is stored on any Windows Server 2003 server that has been promoted to the role of domain controller. Each domain controller on the network has a writeable copy of the directory database. This means that you can make Active Directory changes to any domain controller within your network, and those changes are replicated to all of the other domain controllers. This process is called **multimaster replication**, and provides a form of fault-tolerance. If a single server fails, Active Directory does not fail because replicated copies of the database are available from other servers within the network.

Active Directory uses the **Domain Name Service (DNS)** to maintain domain-naming structures and locate network resources. What this means to a network designer is that all Active Directory names must follow standard DNS naming conventions. An example of a standard DNS naming convention would be *Dovercorp.net*. A child domain of *Dovercorp.net* would add its name as a prefix, such as *Europe.Dovercorp.net*.

Active Directory Objects

Active Directory stores a variety of objects within the directory database. An **object** represents network resources such as users, groups, computers, and printers. When an object is created in Active Directory, various attributes are assigned to it to provide information about the object. For example, Figure 1-12 illustrates creating a new user object and the ability to add various attributes, such as First name, Last name, and User logon name.

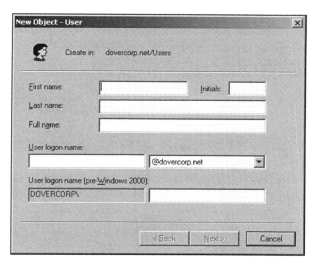

Figure 1-12   Creating a new user object

If you need to locate information about an object from Active Directory, you can perform a search of specific attributes relating to the object. For example, Figure 1-13 shows how you can find the e-mail address of a user object by searching for the specific user name in Active Directory and then viewing the attributes for the object.

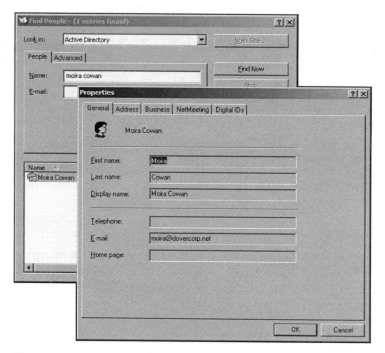

Figure 1-13   Viewing the e-mail address for a user object

Active Directory Schema

All of the objects and attributes that are available in Active Directory are defined in the **Active Directory schema**. In Windows Server 2003, the schema defines the objects for the entire Active Directory structure. This means that there is only one schema for a given Active Directory implementation, and it is replicated among all domain controllers within the network.

The Active Directory schema consists of two main definitions: **object classes** and **attributes**. Object classes define the types of objects that can be created within Active Directory, such as user objects and printer objects. All object classes consist of various attributes that describe the object itself. For example, the user and printer object classes may both have an attribute called description, which is used to describe the use of the object. Attributes are created and stored separately in the schema and can be used with multiple object classes to maintain consistency.

The Active Directory database stores and replicates the schema partition to all domain controllers in an Active Directory environment. Storing the schema within the Active Directory database provides the ability to dynamically update and extend the schema, as well as instant access to information for user applications that need to read the schema properties.

Active Directory Logical Structure and Components

Active Directory is made of several components that provide a way to design and administer the hierarchical, logical structure of the network. The logical components that make up an Active Directory structure include:

- Domains and organizational units
- Trees and forests
- A global catalog

To ensure efficient maintenance and troubleshooting within Active Directory, it is essential that you understand these logical components. The next sections discuss each component in greater detail.

Domains and Organizational Units

A Windows Server 2003 domain is a logically structured organization of objects, such as users, computers, groups, and printers that are part of a network and share a common directory database. Each domain has a unique name and is organized in levels and administered as a unit with common rules and procedures. Windows Server 2003 domains provide a number of administrative benefits including the ability to configure unique security settings, decentralize administration (if necessary), and control replication traffic. By default, members of the Administrators group are only allowed to manage the objects within their own domain. All domain controllers within a single domain store a copy of the Active Directory database, and domain-specific information is only replicated between the domain controllers of the same domain.

An **organizational unit (OU)** is a logical container used to organize objects within a single domain. Objects such as users, groups, computers, and other OUs can be stored in an OU container. For example, you may want to organize your users based upon the department in which they work. You might create a Sales OU to store all of your sales department users and objects and a Marketing OU to store all of your marketing department users and objects. Not only does this make it easier to locate and manage Active Directory objects, but it also allows you to apply **Group Policy** settings to define more advanced features such as software deployment or desktop restrictions based upon department, job function, or perhaps geographic location. Figure 1-14 illustrates an example of a domain with several OUs.

Another main advantage of using an OU structure is the ability to delegate administrative control over OUs. For example, you may want to give a set of users the right to add or remove new users within the Sales OU. You do not have to provide the group with full administrative rights to accomplish this task because Active Directory allows you to delegate very specific tasks, if necessary.

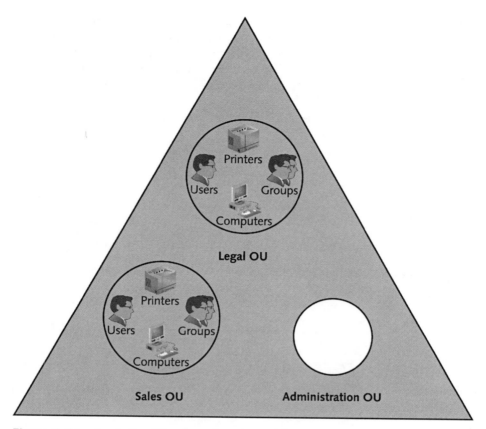

Figure 1-14   An Active Directory domain and OU structure

Trees and Forests

When designing a Windows Server 2003 network infrastructure, there may be times when you are required to create multiple domains within an organization. Reasons for doing this include the following:

- Divisions within the company may be administered on a geographic basis. To make administration easier, a separate domain is created for each division.

- Different password policies are needed between divisions within an organization.

- An extraordinarily large number of objects need to be defined.

- Replication performance needs to be improved.

The first Active Directory domain created in an organization is called the **forest root domain**. When multiple domains are needed, they are connected to the forest root to form either a single **tree** or multiple trees, depending upon the design of the domain name structure. A tree is a hierarchical collection of domains that share a contiguous DNS

namespace. For example, Dover Leasing has its head office in Boston with a forest root domain called *Dovercorp.net*. Dover has two divisions, one located in London and the other located in Hong Kong. Because of geographic and administrative differences, you might decide to create a distinct domain for each division. Two child domains can be created off of the forest root domain. The London domain can be named *Europe.Dovercorp.net*, which follows the contiguous DNS namespace design. Similarly, the Hong Kong domain can be called *Asia.Dovercorp.net*. Figure 1-15 illustrates an example of this structure.

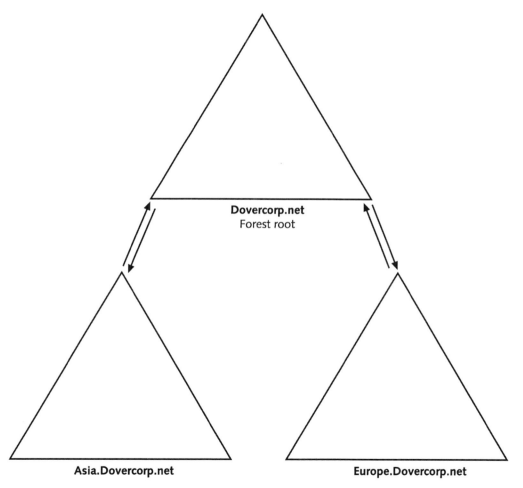

Figure 1-15   The Dovercorp.net domain tree

Whenever a child domain is created, a two-way, transitive trust relationship is automatically created between the child and parent domains. A **transitive trust** means that all other trusted domains implicitly trust one another. For example, because *Europe.Dovercorp.net* trusts the *Dovercorp.net* forest root domain, Europe also implicitly trusts the *Asia.Dovercorp.net*

domain via the *Dovercorp.net* domain. These two–way, transitive trusts allow for resource access anywhere throughout the Active Directory structure. Windows Server 2003 also allows explicit trusts to be created between domains in the same forest, as well as between forests if necessary.

A **forest** is a collection of trees that do not share a contiguous DNS naming structure. For example, Dover Leasing purchases a large international company called Seven Acres Property Management. It may not make sense to make the Seven Acres domain a child of *Dovercorp.net* because of the renaming required to maintain a contiguous naming convention based on *Dovercorp.net*. Instead, you could create a new tree and allow Seven Acres to start its own contiguous naming hierarchy. Both trees make up an Active Directory forest. See Figure 1–16 for an illustration. Although the term "forest" implies a number of trees, an Active Directory forest might consist of only a single domain.

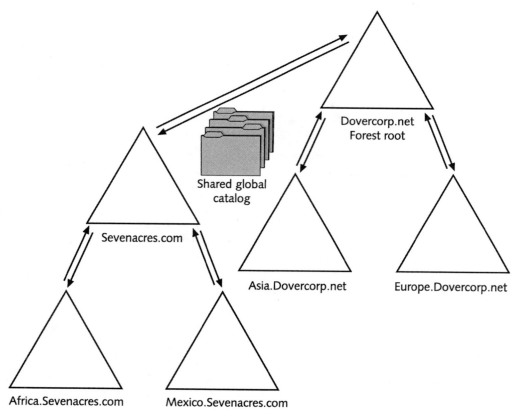

Figure 1-16 Creating an Active Directory forest

Even though the trees within a forest do not share a common namespace, they do share a single Active Directory schema, which ensures that all object classes and attributes are consistent throughout the entire structure. A special group called Enterprise Admins is also

created, which allows members to manage objects throughout the entire forest. The Enterprise Admins group is created within the initial forest root domain and has a scope throughout the entire forest. Another component that is shared throughout the forest is a **global catalog**.

Global Catalog

A global catalog is an index and partial replica of the objects and attributes most frequently used throughout the entire Active Directory structure. Some of the common attributes that are stored in a global catalog include a user's first and last names, logon name, and e-mail address. A global catalog is replicated to any server within the forest that is configured to be a global catalog server.

A global catalog is used primarily for four main functions:

- To enable users to find Active Directory information from anywhere in the forest.

- To provide universal group membership information to facilitate logging on to the network. During the logon process in a multiple-domain environment, a global catalog server is contacted to provide universal group membership information.

- To supply authentication services when a user from another domain logs on using a **User Principal Name (UPN)**. (A UPN is a representation of a user's logon credentials in the form user@domain.com. When a UPN is used, a domain name does not need to be explicitly specified in the Log on to drop-down box.)

- To respond to directory lookup requests from Exchange 2000 and other applications. Global catalog servers also host the Exchange 2000 Global Address List (GAL).

The first domain controller in the forest root domain automatically becomes a global catalog server. To provide redundancy, additional domain controllers can easily be configured to also be global catalog servers. Multiple global catalogs can improve user query and logon authentication performance, especially in Active Directory environments that include geographically distant sites connected by wide area network (WAN) links. Microsoft recommends that each Active Directory site be configured with at least one domain controller acting as a global catalog server.

In cases where placing a global catalog in a specific site is not practical (possibly due to slow WAN links between locations], Windows Server 2003 Active Directory provides a new feature known as universal group caching. Universal group caching allows the domain controllers within a particular site to query a global catalog server in another location for a user's universal group membership information, and then cache that information locally for use in subsequent logons.

Active Directory Communications Standards

As mentioned previously, Active Directory uses the DNS naming standard for hostname resolution and for providing information on the location of network services and resources.

For example, if you need to locate a server called *database.Dovercorp.net*, your workstation first queries a DNS server to resolve the IP address of the database server. Once the IP address is known, a direct communication session can take place.

The same process occurs when you need to log on to the domain. Your workstation queries DNS to find a domain controller to perform authentication. Once the location of a domain controller is known, then the authentication process can take place, thus allowing a user access to network resources.

When users need to access Active Directory, the **Lightweight Directory Access Protocol (LDAP)** is used to query or update the Active Directory database directly. Just as a DNS name contains a specific naming convention (e.g., *Dovercorp.net*), LDAP also follows a specific naming convention. LDAP naming paths are used when referring to objects stored within the Active Directory. Two main components of the naming paths include:

- *Distinguished name*—Every object in Active Directory has a unique **distinguished name (DN)**. For example, the *Dovercorp.net* domain component (DC) has a user object with a common name (CN) of Moira Cowan that is stored within the Marketing OU. The distinguished name for the object would be CN=Moira Cowan, OU=Marketing, DC=Dovercorp, DC=Net.

- *Relative distinguished name*—A portion of the distinguished name that uniquely identifies the object within the container is referred to as the **relative distinguished name (RDN)**. For example, the distinguished name OU=Marketing, DC=Dovercorp, DC=Net would have a relative distinguished name of OU=Marketing. For the distinguished name CN=Moira Cowan, OU=Marketing, DC=Dovercorp, DC=Net, the relative distinguished name would be CN=Moira Cowan.

Active Directory Physical Structure

The Active Directory physical structure relates to the actual connectivity of the physical network itself. Because the Active Directory database is stored on multiple servers, you need to make sure that any modification to the database is replicated as quickly as possible between domain controllers. You must also design your topology so that replication does not saturate the available network bandwidth. One replication problem that you may encounter is when domain controllers are separated over a slow WAN connection. In this scenario, you likely want to control the frequency and the time that replication takes place.

In addition to replication, you may also want to control logon traffic. Referring back to the previous scenario, you generally would not want any user authentication requests to have to cross over slow WAN links during the logon process. Optimally, users should authenticate to a domain controller on their side of the WAN connection.

NOTE Keep in mind that the physical structure of Active Directory is totally separate from the logical structure. The logical structure is used to organize your network resources, whereas the physical structure is used to control network traffic.

You can control Active Directory replication and authentication traffic by configuring sites and site links. An Active Directory **site** is a combination of one or more Internet Protocol (IP) subnets connected by a high-speed connection. It is assumed that domain controllers that belong to the same site all have a common network connection. It is also assumed that any connection between sites that are not reliable at all times must have replication controlled through replication schedules and frequency intervals.

A **site link** is a configurable object that represents a connection between sites. Site links created using the Active Directory Sites and Services snap-in are the core of Active Directory replication. The site links can be adjusted for replication availability, bandwidth costs, and replication frequency. Windows Server 2003 uses this information to generate the replication topology for the sites, including the schedule for replication. Figure 1-17 shows an example of a site structure within a domain. Each site contains domain controllers that share a high-speed connection. Because of a slower WAN connection between Boston, Hong Kong, and London, sites and site links have been defined to better control replication and logon traffic.

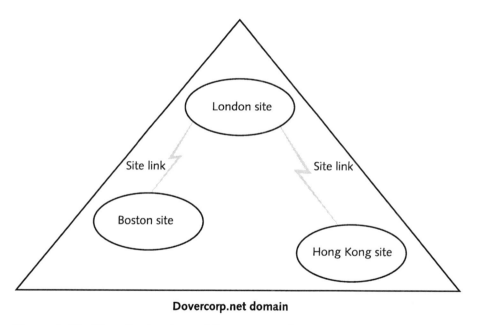

Figure 1-17   The site structure of Dovercorp.net

Replication within a site takes place based on a change notification process. If any change is made within Active Directory, the server waits 15 seconds and then announces the changes to another domain controller. In cases where a domain controller has multiple replication partners within a site, changes are sent out to additional domain controllers at three-second intervals. Replication between sites is initially set at every three hours by default, but can easily be changed by editing the properties of the site link object.

CHAPTER SUMMARY

◻ Windows Server 2003 is available in four different editions—Standard Edition, Enterprise Edition, Datacenter Edition, and Web Edition. The edition chosen for a particular environment or server implementation depends upon the individual performance, scalability, and reliability needs of the business or organization.

◻ Windows networks use one of two models to logically group computers. A workgroup is a model characterized by decentralized authentication and administration, and is typically used on smaller networks. A domain provides centralized authentication and administration, and is more common in larger environments.

◻ Managing and maintaining a Windows Server 2003 environment consists of five major focus areas: managing physical and logical devices; managing users, computers, and groups; managing and maintaining access to resources; managing and maintaining a server environment; and managing and implementing disaster recovery.

◻ Active Directory is the native directory service for Windows Server 2003 operating systems. Active Directory provides a variety of services to a network environment including centralized management and administration, authentication services, and more.

◻ The logical components of Active Directory include domains, organizational units, trees, forests, and the global catalog. The physical components of Active Directory include domain controllers and sites.

KEY TERMS

Active Directory (AD) —The directory service included with Windows Server 2003 that provides a single point of administration, authentication, and storage for user, group, and computer objects.

Active Directory schema — Contains the definition of all object classes and attributes used in the Active Directory database.

attributes — Used to define the characteristics of an object class within Active Directory.

clustering —The ability to increase access to server resources and provide fail-safe services by linking two or more computer systems so they appear to function as though they are one. Clustering is only supported in Windows Server 2003 Enterprise and Datacenter editions.

distinguished name (DN) — An LDAP component used to uniquely identify an object throughout the entire LDAP hierarchy by referring to the relative distinguished name, domain name, and the container holding the object.

domain — A logically structured organization of objects, such as users, computers, groups, and printers, that are part of a network and share a common directory database. Domains are defined by an administrator and administered as a unit with common rules and procedures.

domain controller — A Windows Server 2003 system explicitly configured to store a copy of the Active Directory database, and service user authentication requests or queries about domain objects.

forest — A collection of Active Directory trees that do not necessarily share a contiguous DNS naming convention but do share a common global catalog and schema.

forest root domain — The first domain created within the Active Directory structure.

global catalog — An index of the objects and attributes used throughout the Active Directory structure. It contains a partial replica of every Windows Server 2003 domain within Active Directory, enabling users to find any object in the directory.

Group Policy — The Windows Server 2003 feature that allows for policy creation that affects domain users and computers. Policies can be anything from desktop settings to application assignments to security settings and more.

Lightweight Directory Access Protocol (LDAP) — An access protocol that defines how users can access or update directory service objects.

member server — A Windows Server 2003 system that has a computer account in a domain, but is not configured as a domain controller.

Microsoft Management Console (MMC) — A customizable management interface that can contain a number of management tools to provide a single, unified application for network administration.

multimaster replication — A replication model in which any domain controller accepts and replicates directory changes to any other domain controller. This differs from other replication models in which one computer stores the single modifiable copy of the directory and other computers store back-up copies.

object — A collection of attributes that represent items within Active Directory, such as users, groups, computers, and printers.

object classes — Define which types of objects can be created within Active Directory, such as users, groups, and printers.

Organizational unit (OU) — An Active Directory logical container used to organize objects within a single domain. Objects such as users, groups, computers, and other OUs can be stored in an OU container.

Redundant Array of Independent Disks (RAID) — A collection of hard disks that act as a single unit for the purpose of providing fault tolerance or increasing performance.

relative distinguished name (RDN) — An LDAP component used to identify an object within the object's container.

Security Accounts Manager (SAM) database — The local security and account database on a Windows Server 2003 standalone or member server.

site — A combination of one or more Internet Protocol (IP) subnets connected by a high-speed connection.

site link — A low-bandwidth or unreliable/occasional connection between sites. Site links can be adjusted for replication availability, bandwidth costs, and replication frequency. They enable control over replication and logon traffic.

Software Update Services (SUS) — Microsoft software that allows security patches and updates to be deployed from a centralized server.

Terminal Services — A Windows Server 2003 service that allows a user to connect to and run applications on a server as if sitting at the server console.

transitive trust — The ability for domains or forests to trust one another, even though they do not have a direct explicit trust between them.

User Principal Name (UPN) — A user-account naming convention that includes both the user name and domain name in the format user@domain.com.

workgroup — A logical group of computers characterized by a decentralized security and administration model.

REVIEW QUESTIONS

1. What is the name of the first domain installed within the Active Directory database?

    a. Master root domain

    b. Forest root domain

    c. Main root domain

    d. Tree root domain

2. Assuming a user name of John Doe with a user account located in the Sales OU of the domain *Dovercorp.net*, what would be the object's distinguished name?

    a. OU=Sales, CN=John Doe

    b. CN=John Doe

    c. CN=John Doe, OU=Sales, DC=Dovercorp, DC=Net

    d. DC=Net, DC=Dovercorp, OU=Sales, CN=John Doe

3. In Windows Server 2003, a two-way, transitive trust relationship is maintained between which of the following?

    a. Child and parent forests

    b. Child and parent groups

    c. Child and parent domains

    d. None of the above

4. What is the absolute minimum RAM requirement for Windows Server 2003, Standard Edition?

    a. 64 MB

    b. 128 MB

    c. 256 MB

    d. 512 MB

5. Which of the following are not supported features or configurations for a Windows Server 2003, Web Edition system? (Choose all that apply.)

    a. Standalone server

    b. Domain controller

    c. Member server

6. Which edition of Windows Server 2003 cannot be configured as an Active Directory domain controller?

   a. Windows Server 2003, Web Edition

   b. Windows Server 2003, Standard Edition

   c. Windows Server 2003, Enterprise Edition

   d. Windows Server 2003, Datacenter Edition

7. How often does Active Directory replication between sites take place by default?

   a. Every hour

   b. Every 2 hours

   c. Every 3 hours

   d. Never

8. What is the recommended minimum CPU speed for Windows Server 2003, Enterprise Edition?

   a. 550 MHz

   b. 1 GHz

   c. 733 MHz

   d. 133 MHz

9. How many seconds after a change notification process is triggered does replication between domain controllers occur?

   a. 10

   b. 20

   c. 15

   d. 5

10. The global address list (GAL) for Exchange 2000 e-mail systems is stored on which of the following systems?

    a. All domain controllers

    b. All member servers

    c. All desktop systems

    d. Global catalog server

11. Which group has administrative privileges in all forest domains by default but exists within the forest root domain only?

    a. Administrators

    b. Enterprise Admins

    c. Domain Admins

    d. Forest Admins

12. Which of the following domain controllers will become global catalog servers by default?

    a. First domain controller in all domains

    b. All domain controllers in the forest root domain

    c. First domain controller in the forest root domain

    d. None

13. If a customer network needs to support Windows Server 2003 systems configured in a 4-node cluster, which edition(s) of Windows Server 2003 could be used?

    a. Windows Server 2003, Web Edition

    b. Windows Server 2003, Standard Edition

    c. Windows Server 2003, Enterprise Edition

    d. Windows Server 2003, Datacenter Edition

14. Which of the following operating systems can be upgraded to Windows Server 2003, Standard Edition?

    a. Windows 2000 Server

    b. Windows 2000 Advanced Server

    c. Windows NT Server 4.0 (SP5)

    d. Windows 2000 Datacenter Server

15. Which of the following operating systems can be upgraded to Windows Server 2003, Web Edition?

    a. Windows 2000 Server

    b. Windows NT Server 4.0 (SP5)

    c. Windows 2000 Advanced Server

    d. None of the above

16. Which of the following Windows Server 2003 editions are capable of running on Itanium-based systems?

    a. Windows Server 2003, Web Edition

    b. Windows Server 2003, Standard Edition

    c. Windows Server 2003, Enterprise Edition

    d. Windows Server 2003, Datacenter Edition

17. What is the maximum number of CPUs supported in an SMP configuration on a Windows Server 2003, Datacenter Edition, system running on the x86 platform?

    a. 64

    b. 32

    c. 8

    d. 16

18. Which of the following operating systems can be upgraded to Windows Server 2003, Enterprise Edition?

    a. Windows 2000 Server

    b. Windows Server 2003, Standard Edition

    c. Windows NT Server 4.0 (SP5)

    d. Windows 2000 Advanced Server

19. Which of the following logical Active Directory components is created mainly for the delegation of administrative authority and the implementation of group policy settings?

    a. Tree

    b. Domain

    c. Forest

    d. Organizational unit

20. Which of the following statements best describes an Active Directory forest?

    a. A collection of domains that share a common schema

    b. A collection of organizational units

    c. A collection of trees with different schemas

    d. A collection of users with common settings

CASE PROJECTS

Case Project 1-1

Dover Leasing Corporation has recently implemented Windows Server 2003 and Active Directory. Dover's network consists of three main locations with offices in Boston, Hong Kong, and London. The Boston location is the head office and connects to London via a dedicated T1 WAN link, whereas the Hong Kong location connects to London via a 256-Kbps Frame Relay link. Dover had recently considered opening a new office in San Francisco, which would connect via WAN links to both the Boston and Hong Kong offices. Different password policies need to be implemented in the Boston, Hong Kong, and London locations. Ultimately, the San Francisco office will become the administrative responsibility of IT staff in Boston. Based on what you know of Windows Server 2003 thus far and the information provided above, the IT manager has asked you to assess Dover Leasing's Active Directory design by answering the following questions:

1. Which of the factors listed in the scenario would influence the logical design of Dover Leasing's Active Directory implementation?

2. What type of domain structure would you suggest for Dover Leasing?

3. Based on Dover Leasing's current and future locations, what would be the best naming strategy for their Active Directory domain structure?

4. How many sites would likely be configured as part of Dover Leasing's Active Directory implementation once the San Francisco office opens, and how many site links would be required?

5. Once the San Francisco office is opened, how many global catalog servers should be implemented on the network to ensure adequate performance?

Case Project 1-2

CASE
PROJECTS

Dover Leasing is currently planning the deployment of three new Windows Server 2003 systems in its head office location. The company plans to deploy one server as a dedicated Web server running IIS 6.0. The second server will be used for file and print services, and will be deployed on an SMP system with 4 CPUs and 8 GB of RAM. The last system will be used as a database server, and will be deployed in conjunction with an existing server as part of a 2-way cluster. Based on these configurations, the IT manager at Dover Leasing has asked you to identify the most appropriate Windows Server 2003 edition for each system.

1. Which Windows Server 2003 edition would be most appropriate for the server that will run IIS? Why?

2. Which Windows Server 2003 edition would be most appropriate for the file and print server? Why?

3. Which Windows Server 2003 edition would be most appropriate for the database server? Why?

2

CREATING AND MANAGING USER ACCOUNTS

After reading this chapter and completing the exercises, you will be able to:

Understand the purpose of user accounts

Understand the user authentication process

Understand and configure local, roaming, and mandatory user profiles

Configure and modify user accounts using different methods

Troubleshoot user account and authentication problems

Good management is essential for all modern networks. Active Directory enables you to effectively manage a potentially chaotic group of resources, such as user accounts, shared folders, and shared printers. Active Directory accomplishes this by providing a hierarchy of management elements that allow you to organize resources, control access to them, and advertise their existence—making the lives of users easier.

The most basic unit of any Active Directory environment is a user account. Without a user account object defined in Active Directory, a user cannot log on and gain access to network resources. Aside from being used for authentication purposes, a user account also describes the user associated with that account, including information about that individual and various configuration settings for their working environment.

As part of authenticating a user on a network, Windows Server 2003 uses different authentication types and protocols. This chapter explores the differences between interactive and network authentication, as well as the two primary authentication protocols used in Windows Server 2003 domain environments: Kerberos v5 and the NT LAN Manager (NTLM) protocol.

A user's desktop environment and related settings is known as their user profile. Windows Server 2003 supports three different types of profiles known as local, roaming, and mandatory profiles. The profile type implemented impacts how a

user interacts with their desktop environment, whether their settings followthem to different workstations, and whether they have the ability to customize these settings. Later in this chapter you learn more about each profile type, including how to configure them in a Windows Server 2003 environment.

Although Active Directory Users and Computers is the primary tool used to create and manage domain user accounts, Windows Server 2003 includes a variety of new tools to allow user accounts to be configured and modified from the command line. For administrators looking to import or export user account settings from existing databases or directory services, familiar bulk import and export tools originally introduced in Windows 2000 continue to be supported. This chapter familiarizes you with a variety of tools that can be used to create and manage user accounts.

Finally, there are an array of issues that can impact the user authentication process in a network environment. At the end of this chapter you learn some of the specific settings that impact user authentication, as well as ways to troubleshoot and resolve common user authentication problems.

INTRODUCTION TO USER ACCOUNTS

A **user account** is an object that is stored in Active Directory that represents all of the information that defines a user with access to the network. The information that defines a user may include attributes such as a first and last name, a password, group membership information, as well as a number of other data.

Any person who needs access to resources on the network requires a user account. User accounts can assist in the administration and security of the network by making it possible to:

- require authentication for users connecting to the network
- control access to network resources such as shared folders or printers
- monitor access to resources by auditing actions performed by a user logged on with a specific account

When creating a new user account, it is important that an organization set standards on the various elements of a user object. Some of these standards might include:

- Establishing a naming convention—The user account names within the domain follow a consistent naming convention. Common examples include:
  - First name and last initial—The account name for Kirk Jefferies would be KirkJ
  - First initial and last name—The account name for Karen Armstrong would be Karmstrong
  - Last name and first initial—The account name for Mike Smith would be Smithm; adding additional initials, such as the first letter of a user's middle name, accommodates multiple users with the same name

- Controlling password policy and ownership—The best password policy requires that a password consist of at least eight characters, contain a variety of alphanumeric characters, and have an expiration setting; either the network administrator or the user can control and maintain the password.

- Including additional required attributes— For example, requiring that all phone numbers and e-mail addresses are part of the account information.Keep in mind that every additional attribute requires additional replication bandwidth and storage space within Active Directory.

NOTE   A user logon name is referred to as a User Principal Name (UPN) when combined with the domain suffix (for example, @dovercorp.net). The UPN allows users to log on from any trusted domain within a forest by providing only a UPN name and password at the Windows logon screen.

User Account Properties

The primary tool used to create and manage user accounts in an Active Directory environment is **Active Directory Users and Computers**. Through this interface, a variety of different properties can be configured for a user account. While the configurable settings available represent the most commonly used settings, there remain dozens of other attributes that can be configured for a user account. To open the property page for a user object, simply right-click the object in Active Directory Users and Computers and choose Properties. The window shown in Figure 2–1 appears. You can open the same window by double-clicking a user object, or choosing Properties from the Action menu with the user object selected.

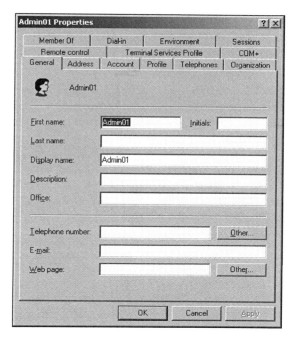

Figure 2–1   Properties of a user account

Although the properties page of a user account displays the most common attributes for a user object, additional attributes can be managed programmatically with code, script, or tools like ADSI Edit.

The number of tabs and the tab headings that appear in this chapter may differ from what you see on your system. Because Active Directory is extensible (that is, the schema can be extended with new attributes and new classes), Active Directory-aware applications may add tabs to the property pages of Active Directory objects such as user accounts. A good example of this is when Microsoft Exchange Server 2000 is installed it adds three new tabs to the user property page.

The following is a brief summary of the account properties that can be set for a user:

- General—Contains personal information about the account holder including the first name, last name, and name as it is displayed in the console, description of the user or account, office location, telephone number, e-mail address, and home page; also provides optional buttons for additional telephone numbers and Web page addresses for the account holder

- Address—Stores information pertaining to the account holder's street address, post office box, city, state or province, postal code, and country or region

- Account—Holds information regarding the logon name, domain name, and account options, such as requiring the user to change a password at next logon, and account expiration date, if one applies; includes a Logon Hours button to set up the account so that the user only logs onto the domain at designated times, such as during backups and designated system work times on the server; also provides a Log On To button to limit from which computer the user can log on to the server or domain

- Profile—Enables the particular profile (discussed later in this chapter) to be associated with the user or a set of users, such as a common desktop; also used to associate the logon script (a file of commands that are executed at logon) and the home folder (a folder that is the users main folder, such as a folder on a particular system)

- Telephones—Stores specific telephone contact numbers for the account holder, which include one or more numbers for home, pager, mobile, fax, and IP

- Organization—Provides a place to enter the account holder's title, department, company name, and the name of the person who manages the account holder

- Member Of—Adds the account to an existing group of users that have the same security and access requirements; also used to remove the account from a group

- Dial-in—Controls remote access from dial-in modems or from virtual private networks (VPNs)

- Environment—Configures the startup environment for accessing one or more servers using terminal services (for running programs on the server)

- Sessions—Configures session parameters for the user utilizing terminal services, such as session time limits, limits on how long a session can be idle, what to do when a connection is broken, and how to reconnect

- Remote control—Sets up remote control parameters for the client using terminal services; enabling the administrator to view and manipulate the client session while it is active in order to troubleshoot problems

- Terminal Services Profile—Sets up the user profile for using terminal services

- COM+—Specifies which COM+ partition set the user is a member of

Some additional tabs available in the properties of a user account are hidden by default. These tabs include Object, Published Certificates, and Security. To view these tabs, click on the View menu item in Active Directory Users and Computers and click Advanced Features. For more information on the purpose of each tab, see the Windows Server 2003 Help and Support Center.

In Activity 2–1 you review the property pages associated with a user account in Active Directory Users and Computers.

Activity 2-1: Reviewing User Account Properties

Time required: 10 minutes

Objective: Review the properties of a user account.

Description: The IT manager at Dover Leasing has recently decided that one of your primary responsibilities will be the configuration of user accounts and related settings for all corporate users. As such, you have decided to familiarize yourself with the configurable elements of a user account in Active Directory Users and Computers. In this activity you review the main tabs associated with configuring the properties of a user account.

1. Click **Start**, select **Administrative Tools**, and click **Active Directory Users and Computers**.

2. Click on the **Users** container located in the left pane to view its contents.

3. Right-click on the **AdminXX account**, where *XX* is your assigned student number, and click **Properties**.

4. Review the configurable settings on the General tab, noting that information such as a telephone number, description, and office can be configured on this screen. Click the **Address** tab.

5. Review the configurable settings on the Address tab. Note the types of information that can be configured on this screen, and click the **Account** tab.

6. Review the settings available on the Account tab, as shown in Figure 2-2 Notice both the user logon name, and the domain name that follows it. Together, these two elements form a UPN, which a user can use to log on to the network. Click the **Logon Hours** button.

7. The Logon Hours for AdminXX appears. This window allows you to configure the days and hours when this user is allowed to log on to the network. By default, a user can log on at any time, as illustrated in Figure 2-3. Click the **Cancel** button to close the Logon Hours for AdminXX window.

8. Click the **Log On To** button. When the Logon Workstations window appears, note that a user can log on to all computers by default. If a user needs to be limited to logging on to specific computers only, this window allows you to configure appropriate settings by computer name. Click the **Cancel** button to close the Logon Workstations window.

9. In the Account options section of the Account tab, review the various configurable properties available, and then click the **Profile** tab.

10. Review the settings available on the Profile tab, noting that it allows you to configure the network path for a user profile, the location of a logon script, and the location of the user's home folder. User profile settings are covered in more detail later in this chapter. Click the **Telephones** tab.

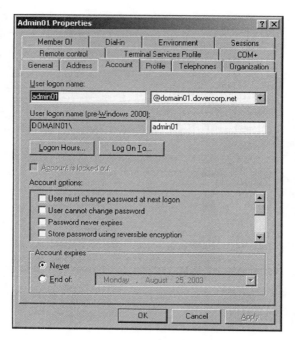

Figure 2-2   The Account tab

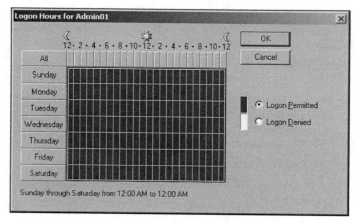

Figure 2-3   The Logon Hours window

11. Review the settings that can be configured on the Telephones tab. The Notes section on the bottom of this page could be used to configure additional information, such as which phone number is preferred for the user. Click the **Organization** tab.

12. Review the settings that can be configured on the Organization tab. Note that information about the user's manager and reporting status within the organization can also be configured on this page. Click the **Member Of** tab.

13. Notice that the Member Of tab displays information about the groups this user is a member of, as shown in Figure 2-4. Users can be added or removed from groups by using the Add and Remove buttons respectively. Group accounts are looked at in more detail in Chapter 4. Click the **Dial-in** tab.

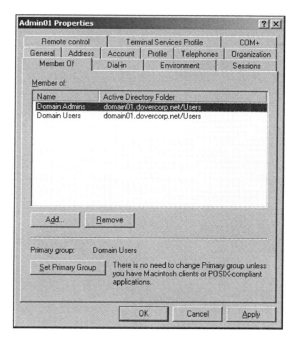

Figure 2-4   The Member Of tab

14. Review the settings that can be configured on the Dial-in tab, as shown in Figure 2-5. Notice that this tab allows you to configure Dial-in and VPN settings for the user, and that remote access permissions are set to the Deny access setting by default. Click on the **Environment**, **Sessions**, **Remote control**, **Terminal Services Profile**, and **COM+** tabs to review their settings as time permits.

15. Click **Cancel** to close the Admin*XX* Properties window.

16. Close Active Directory Users and Computers.

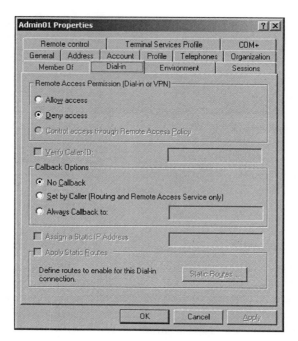

Figure 2-5   The Dial-in tab

User Authentication

In order for a user to gain access to network resources in an Active Directory environment, they must first be authenticated. **Authentication** is the process by which a user's identity is validated and subsequently granted or denied access to network resources. When logging on to the network from a client operating system such as Windows XP or Windows 2000 Professional, a user inputs their user name and password, and then specifies the resource that they wish to log on to (such as a particular domain or the local computer). In an Active Directory environment, a user generally logs on to a domain, where a server configured as a domain controller authenticates the user in a centralized manner. In a workgroup, authentication is handled by the local computer's SAM database. The authentication method used ultimately impacts the manner in which a user interacts with the network and available resources.

Authentication Methods

Authentication in a Windows Server 2003 environment consists of two main processes. The first process is known as interactive authentication, and relates to the act of supplying user account information at the Log On to Windows dialog box. The second process is known as network authentication, and relates to the process by which a user's credentials are

confirmed when they attempt to access a network resource. The following sections define both interactive and network authentication in greater detail.

Interactive Authentication

Interactive authentication is the process by which a user provides their user name and password to be authenticated from the Log On to Windows dialog box. In a Windows Server 2003 Active Directory environment, a user can choose to log on to either a domain or the local workstation as part of this process.

 The option to log on to the local computer is not available on a Windows server configured as a domain controller.

If a user chooses to log on to a domain, the supplied user name and password credentials are compared to information stored on a domain controller in its Active Directory database. If the supplied credentials are correct, the user is validated, and the logon process completes successfully. If the credentials are not correct, the user is not validated, and must supply correct credentials to complete the process. Figure 2-6 illustrates the dialog box encountered when an incorrect user name or password combination is supplied in the Log On to Windows dialog box.

Figure 2-6   The Logon Message dialog box

 Windows Server 2003 also supports interactive authentication using smart cards. When smart cards are configured for users, a user inserts their smart card into a card reader as part of the authentication process. After doing so, the user is prompted to supply a PIN number rather than a password. The need to supply both the physical smart card and associated PIN number as part of the authentication process makes smart card authentication a more secure option than the traditional user name/password combination.

When a user chooses to log on to the local workstation, the supplied user name and password is validated by the local SAM database of the computer rather than by an Active Directory domain controller. In order for this interactive authentication method to successfully validate a user, they must have a configured user account on the computer they are logging on to. If the credentials supplied are correct, the user is validated and the logon

2

process completes successfully. If the credentials are not correct, the user is not validated, and must supply correct credentials to complete the process.

In a domain environment, users normally do not have local user accounts configured on their workstations, so the domain method of interactive authentication is typically used. This method ultimately makes the process of accessing network resources transparent, as you learn in the next section.

Network Authentication

Network authentication is the process by which a network resource or service confirms the identity of a user. For example, when a user attempts to access the contents of a shared folder on the network, their credentials must be validated. The manner in which network authentication occurs is different for a user who chooses to log on to a domain versus a user who logs on to their local computer.

If a user logs on to a domain during the interactive authentication process, the network authentication process is completely transparent. This is because the same credentials that were supplied as part of the interactive authentication process are used to validate their identity when they attempt to access a network resource. For example, if a user logged on interactively using the user name jsmith in the domain*XX*.dovercorp.net domain, these are the credentials that would be supplied to a network server in the event that this user attempts to access a network resource or service. Since the user is already authenticated in the domain, they are not prompted to provide their user name and password again. This makes the process of accessing resources seamless and transparent to an authenticated domain user.

If a user logs on to their local computer during the interactive authentication process, however, that particular computer is the only one to have authenticated them. When a user in this scenario attempts to access network resources such as a shared folder on another computer, they are prompted to supply an appropriate user name and password for that resource. An example of a network authentication dialog box is illustrated in Figure 2-7.

Figure 2-7   A network authentication dialog box

Authentication Protocols

Windows Server 2003 supports two main authentication protocols; **Kerberos version 5 (Kerberos v5)** and **NT LAN Manager (NTLM)**. While Kerberos v5 is the primary authentication protocol used in Active Directory domain environments, it is not supported on all client operating systems. For this reason, Windows Server 2003 also includes support for NTLM authentication, which is the primary authentication protocol of older Microsoft operating systems like Windows NT 4.0 and Windows 98. The following sections reveal more about the Kerberos v5 and NTLM authentication protocols.

Kerberos v5

Kerberos v5 is the primary authentication protocol used in Active Directory domain environments. Microsoft operating system versions that support Kerberos v5 authentication include:

- Windows 2000
- Windows XP
- Windows Server 2003

Although the process used by Kerberos to authenticate users and network services is seamless and transparent in the eyes of the user, it helps to understand the manner in which Kerberos authentication occurs. The following example illustrates the steps involved in the Kerberos authentication process in an Active Directory domain environment.

1. A user logs on interactively from a computer that is a member of a domain by providing a user name/password/domain combination or smart card. The authentication request is passed to a **Key Distribution Center (KDC)**. The KDC in this case is a Windows Server 2003 domain controller.

2. The KDC authenticates the user, assuming they have provided the correct user name and password combination. As part of this process, the KDC creates and issues what is known as a **ticket–granting ticket (TGT)** to the client system. The TGT proves that the client has been successfully authenticated.

3. When a client attempts to access a network resource in the domain, such as a shared folder on another server, the client presents its TGT to the KDC requesting a **service ticket** for the server on which the resource resides.

4. The client then contacts the server hosting the requested network service, and presents the service ticket obtained in Step 3 to this server. This ticket proves the identity of the client to the network service, and proves the identity of the network service to the client. At this point the user can access the requested service on the server, assuming they have appropriate permissions or rights to do so.

The Kerberos v5 process for accessing resources across domains is similar to those listed in the previous steps, but slightly more involved. For more information on the specific Kerberos process for accessing resources in other domains, see the topic "Accessing resources across domains" in the Windows Server 2003 Help and Support Center.

From this example, it should be clear that a KDC is a trusted intermediary (or third party) in the Kerberos authentication process. Every domain controller in a Windows Server 2003 (or Windows 2000) Active Directory environment holds the role of KDC. It is also important to recognize, however, that not all operating systems are capable of functioning as Kerberos clients. Clients not capable of using Kerberos for authentication rely upon NTLM authentication, as looked at in the next section.

NTLM

For clients that do not support Kerberos v5, Windows Server 2003 continues to support authentication using the NTLM protocol. NTLM is a challenge-response protocol that is used for authentication purposes with operating systems running Windows NT 4.0 or earlier (often referred to as "down-level" systems). In cases where Kerberos-based authentication is not possible, Windows 2000 and Windows Server 2003 systems are also capable of using NTLM authentication. NTLM authentication would most commonly be used in conjunction with a Windows Server 2003 system when:

- A Windows Server 2003 system attempts to authenticate to a Windows NT 4.0 domain controller

- A Windows NT 4.0 Workstation system attempts to authenticate to a Windows 2000 or Windows Server 2003 domain controller

The original version of NTLM is sometimes referred to as NTLMv1. A newer version, known as NTLMv2, was introduced in Windows NT 4.0 with Service Pack 4 installed, and offered a variety of security improvements. Operating systems like Windows 95 and Windows 98 can be configured to support NTLMv2 if they have Active Directory Client Extensions software installed.

The following example illustrates the steps involved in the NTLM authentication process between a **down-level operating system** such as Windows NT 4.0 and a domain controller:

1. A user logs on interactively from a computer that is a member of a domain by providing user name, password, and domain information. The client system calculates a cryptographic hash of the supplied password, and then discards the original password information.

2. The client system sends the supplied user name to the domain controller.

3. The domain controller generates a 16-bit random number, and sends it back to the client. This number is known as the "challenge".

4. The client encrypts the challenge with the hash of the user password and sends this value back to the domain controller.

5. The domain controller computes the value that it expects the client to return using the password information stored in the user account database. If the two values match, authentication is successful.

After successful NTLM authentication takes place, a token is generated for the client and attached to their user process. Each time the user attempts to access a resource on the network, their token is checked as part of the authentication process.

 Windows Server 2003 supports a variety of different configuration settings for NTLM security. For more information about configurable NTLM security settings, see the Windows Server 2003 Help and Support Center.

USER PROFILES

Microsoft operating systems since Windows NT 4.0 have automatically stored the unique settings for a user's desktop environment in what is known as a **user profile**. A user profile is simply a collection of settings specific to a particular user. For example, if two users share a PC running Windows XP, each user is provided with their own customizable desktop environment and related settings when they log on using their personal user name and password. In this way, a single system can support the unique desktop settings of many different users.

When a new user logs on to a Windows NT 4.0, Windows 2000, Windows XP, or Windows Server 2003 system for the first time, a new and dedicated user profile is created for that user locally. The default location for all local user profiles is a folder bearing the same name as the user located in the %systemdrive%\Documents and Settings folder, as illustrated in Figure 3-8. User profiles are local by default, and as such do not follow users when they log on to different computers.

Although user profiles are stored locally by default, Windows Server 2003 also supports the ability to have a profile follow a user to different computers with a technique known as a roaming profile. Furthermore, administrators can configure a user profile with a mandatory profile so that a user cannot modify it. Both roaming and mandatory user profiles are covered later in this chapter.

User profiles are often only associated with a user's desktop environment, such as the placement of icons, creation of shortcuts, and the desktop wallpaper that they have chosen. However, a user profile actually consists of a wide variety of items, including a user's My Documents folder, Internet Explorer Favorites menu, and more. Table 2-1 outlines the key folders that make up a user profile, along with the types of information that they store.

2

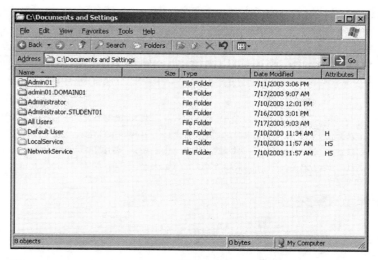

Figure 2-8   The Documents and Settings folder

Table 2-1   User profile folders and contents

Folder Name	Folder Contents
Application Data	Program-specific data such as the data files associated with a particular application
Cookies	Cookie files from visited Web sites
Desktop	User desktop items such as shortcuts, files, and folders
Favorites	Shortcuts to Internet locations
Local Settings	Program data, history information, and temporary files
My Documents	User files and folders
My Recent Documents	Shortcuts to recently used files and folders
NetHood	Shortcuts to items found in My Network Places
PrintHood	Shortcuts to items found in the Printers folder
SendTo	Shortcuts to file-handling utilities, such as the ability to create a desktop shortcut
Start Menu	Shortcuts to programs that appear on the Start Menu
Templates	User templates

Local Profiles

When a user logs on to a Windows Server 2003 system for the first time, a new local user profile is created for them by default. The settings contained in this new profile are copied from a pre-configured profile folder in the Documents and Settings folder named Default User. As its name suggests, the Default User folder contains all of the settings that will be applied to new profiles as they are created. One benefit of this method is that it allows an administrator to edit the contents of the Default User profile such that the default desktop environment applied to users contains specific settings, if these are required.

After a new **local profile** is created for a user, any changes made by the user are saved in their associated profile folder when they log off. For example, if a user logs on, changes their desktop wallpaper, and then logs off, their customized desktop wallpaper settings would be presented the next time they log on to that system. However, if a different user were to log on to that system for the first time, their new profile would consist of the settings found in the Default User folder to begin with.

Although local user profiles are created automatically when a new user logs on to a Windows Server 2003 system for the first time, an administrator can manage various elements of a local user profile. For example, the System program in Control Panel provides access to user profile settings from the Advanced tab, as shown in Figure 2-9.

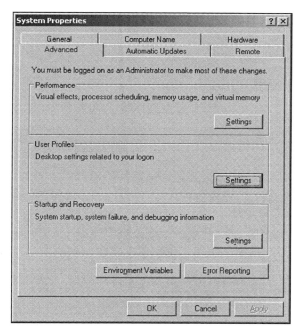

Figure 2-9   The Advanced tab of the System program

Clicking on the Settings button in the User Profiles section opens the User Profiles window, as shown in Figure 2-10. As its name suggests, the Profiles stored on this computer section provides a list of all profiles stored on this computer, including their size, type, status, and last modification date.

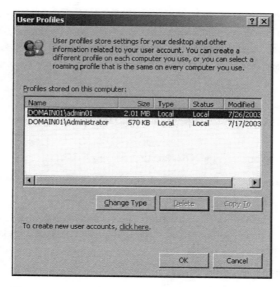

Figure 2-10   The User Profiles window

When an individual profile is selected from the list, one or more of the following three buttons become available:

- Change Type—Allows you to change the type of user profile from local to roaming or vice versa.

- Delete—Allows you to delete a profile if necessary. In some cases, such as when many unnecessary user profiles exist on a system, an administrator may delete old or unused profiles to save disk space.

- Copy To—Allows you to copy a user profile to a different location, such as a central server location. This is useful for maintaining a user's existing desktop settings while switching their profile from local to roaming.

If you select the profile of the currently logged on user in the User Profiles window, both the Delete and Copy To buttons appear unavailable. You can neither delete nor copy the profile of the currently logged on user. To accomplish either of these tasks, you need to log on to the system using a different user account with administrative privileges.

In Activity 2-2 you explore and test local user profile settings on your Windows Server 2003 system.

Activity 2-2: Testing Local Profile Settings

Time required: 10 minutes

Objective: Configure and test a local user profile.

Description: The IT manager at Dover Leasing is currently debating whether Dover would be better served by using local or roaming user profiles for domain users. As part of determining the capabilities of each, he has asked you to explore and test local user profile settings to get a better sense for how they function. In this exercise you create two new user accounts and then test the impact of changing various local user profile settings on your server.

1. Click **Start**, select **Administrative Tools**, and then click **Active Directory Users and Computers**.

2. Right-click on the **Users** container, select **New**, and then click **User**.

3. In the New Object – User window, type **Testuser1** in the First name text box, and type **Testuser1** in the User logon name text box. Click **Next**.

4. In the Password text box type **Password01**, and then type **Password01** in the Confirm password text box. Uncheck the **User must change password at next logon** check box, click **Next**, and then click **Finish**.

5. Right-click on the **Users** container, select **New**, and then click **User**.

6. In the New Object – User window, type **Testuser2** in the First name text box, and type **Testuser2** in the User logon name text box. Click **Next**.

7. In the Password text box type **Password01**, and then type **Password01** in the Confirm password text box. Uncheck the **User must change password at next logon** check box, click **Next**, and then click **Finish**.

8. Close Active Directory Users and Computers, and log off.

9. Log on using the Testuser1 account, using the password Password01. Once the logon process completes, notice that you are presented with the default user desktop environment.

10. Right-click on a blank area of the desktop, and click **Properties**.

11. Click on the **Desktop** tab. In the Background list, click on **Ascent**, and then click **OK**. The Ascent desktop wallpaper will appear on your desktop.

12. Log off, and then log back on using the Testuser1 account with a password of **Password01**. Notice that the Ascent wallpaper appears because it was saved as part of the Testuser1 profile.

13. Log off, and then log back on using the Testuser2 account with a password of **Password01**. Notice that the default user profile appears, because Testuser2 has not logged on to this system before.

14. Log off, and then log on using your Admin*XX* account.

15. Click **Start**, select **Control Panel**, and then click **System**.

16. Click the **Advanced** tab, and then click the **Settings** button in the User Profiles section. Notice that both the Testuser1 and Testuser2 profiles appear on the list as local profiles.

17. In the Profiles stored on this computer section, click **DomainXX\AdminXX** (where *XX* is your assigned student number) to select it if necessary. Notice that both the Delete and Copy To buttons are grayed out because you cannot delete or copy the profiles of the currently logged on user.

18. Click the **DomainXX\Testuser1** profile. Notice that all three buttons are now available.

19. Click the **Change Type** button. Notice that only the Local profile option is available, as shown in Figure 2-11. This is because a roaming profile does not exist for Testuser1. Click **Cancel**.

Figure 2-11   The Change Profile Type window

20. Click the **Delete** button. When the Confirm Delete dialog box appears, click **Yes**. Notice that the Testuser1 profile no longer appears on the list.

21. Click **OK** to close the User Profiles window, and then click **OK** to close the System Properties window.

22. Log off, and then log on using the Testuser1 account with the password **Password01**. Notice that the Ascent wallpaper no longer appears because the previously stored profile for Testuser1 was deleted in Step 20. Because a local profile did not exist, Testuser1 has had a new profile created based on the Default User profile.

23. Click **Start**, and then click **My Computer**.

24. Double-click on drive **C:**, and then double-click on the **Documents and Settings** folder. Double-click on the **Testuser1** folder. A list of some of the folders originally mentioned in Table 2-1 appears.

25. Click the **Tools** menu, and then click **Folder Options**. Click the **View** tab. In the Advanced settings section click the **Show hidden files and folders** radio button, and then click **OK**. Notice that all of the profile folders originally mentioned in Table 2-1 now appear, some of which were previously hidden from view. This is illustrated in Figure 2-12. Close the Testuser1 window.

26. Remain logged on to your server with the Testuser1 account.

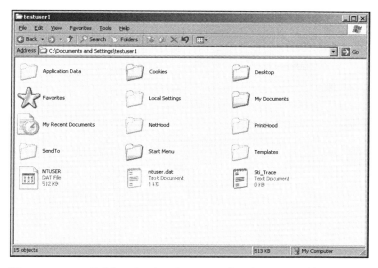

Figure 2-12   Folders in the Testuser1 local user profile

Roaming Profiles

In small and large organizations alike, users sometimes need to log on to different workstations. Although a user in a large organization may use the same workstation every day, a user working in a call center or bank may regularly log on to different computers. Regardless of frequency, the ability of a user's profile to be stored centrally on a server and follow them to different workstations is definitely useful.

In organizations where users always use the same workstation, **roaming profiles** provide the advantage of storing user desktop settings in a single, centralized location rather than locally on many different systems. This provides the advantage of being able to back up user profile settings in a central manner. In cases where users change workstations, the obvious benefit is that their user profile settings will follow them and remain consistent on different computers.

Roaming profiles are configured from the Profiles page of a user account's properties in Active Directory Users and Computers. The location in which the profile is stored is a shared folder on a network server, specified by a Universal Naming Convention (UNC) path such as \\server*XX*\profiles\user name, where *profiles* is a shared folder, and *user name* is the specific folder in which a user's profile will be stored. Typically, roaming profiles are stored in a shared folder that resides on an NTFS partition, so that permissions can be configured such that only a specific user has access to their own profile. You learn more about NTFS permissions later in this book.

The network storage location for roaming profiles can be any Windows server system. There is no requirement to store roaming profiles on a domain controller.

2

Because user profiles are local by default, an administrator needs to give serious consideration to the implementation of roaming user profiles. For example, if a user has been using a local profile for some time, and that profile contains a large number of settings, the user would likely want (or need) to continue using those settings. Because of this, it is generally recommended that an administrator copy a user's existing local profile to a central server location first, and then configure the properties of the user's account to access this profile. This technique helps to ensure that the user's existing profile settings are not lost when a roaming profile is configured.

When a user logs on using a roaming profile for the first time, a copy of this profile is downloaded to the computer they have logged on to. If the user makes any changes to this profile, these changes are saved to the server location when the user logs off. Then, the updated profile settings are available to the user the next time they log on to the same computer or a different computer on the network.

In Activity 2-3 you configure and test roaming profile settings.

Activity 2-3: Configuring and Testing a Roaming Profile

Time required: 15 minutes

Objective: Configure and test a roaming user profile.

Description: The IT manager at Dover Leasing is concerned that local profiles will quickly become unmanageable since so many users at Dover need access to different desktops regularly. In particular, he is concerned about the decentralized nature of local profiles, and backing up user settings. As such, he has asked you to configure and test roaming profile settings on your Windows Server 2003 system. In this activity you create a shared folder in which to store roaming profiles, copy an existing local profile to this shared folder, and then configure the properties of a user account to use this network-based roaming profile.

1. Right-click on a blank area of the desktop, and click **Properties**.
2. Click on the **Desktop** tab. In the Background list, click on **Azul**, and then click **OK**. The Azul desktop wallpaper will appear on your desktop.
3. Log off, and then log back on using the Testuser1 account with a password of Password01. Notice that the Azul wallpaper appears because it was saved as part of the Testuser1 profile.
4. Click **Start**, click **Control Panel**, and then double-click **System**.
5. Click the **Advanced** tab, and then click the **Settings** button in the User Profiles section. Notice that the Testuser1 profile appears on the list as a local profile.

6. Click **Cancel** to exit the User Profiles window, and then click **Cancel** to exit the System Properties window. Close the Control Panel window.

7. Log off, and then log on using your Admin*XX* account.

8. Click **Start**, and then click **My Computer**.

9. Double-click on drive **D** to view its contents. Right-click on a blank area, select **New**, and click **Folder**.

10. Name the new folder **Profiles**. Right-click on the **Profiles** folder and click **Sharing and Security**.

11. On the Sharing tab, click the **Share this folder** radio button. This folder will be used to store roaming user profiles.

12. Click the **Permissions** button. In the Permissions for Profiles window, check the check box next to **Full Control** in the **Allow** column. Click **OK**. Click **OK** again to close the Profiles Properties window.

13. Close the **My Computer** window.

14. Click **Start**, select **Control Panel**, and then click **System**.

15. Click the **Advanced** tab, and then click the **Settings** button in the User Profiles section. Click on the **Domain*XX*\Testuser1** account, and then click the **Copy To** button.

16. In the Copy To window, type **\\Server*XX*\profiles\testuser1** in the Copy profile to text box, where *XX* is your assigned student number, as shown in Figure 2-13.

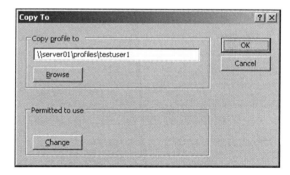

Figure 2-13   Copying a local profile to a network location

17. Click the **Change** button in the Permitted to use section. In the Enter the object name to select text box, type **Domain*XX*\Testuser1**, where *XX* is your assigned student number, and then click **OK**. Click **OK** to close the Copy To window.

18. Click **OK**. Click **OK** again to close the System Properties window. The local profile for Testuser1 has now been copied to the shared location specified.

19. Click **Start**, select **Administrative Tools**, and then click **Active Directory Users and Computers**.

20. Click on the **Users** container to view its contents if necessary.

21. Right-click on the **Testuser1** user account, and click **Properties**.

22. Click the **Profile** tab. In the Profile path text box, type **\\server*XX*\profiles\testuser1**, as shown in Figure 2-14. This is the path from which Testuser1 will obtain their roaming profile the next time they log on. Click **OK**.

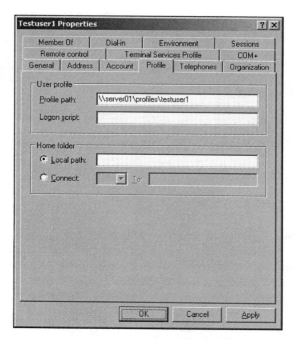

Figure 2-14 Configuring profile path settings in the properties of a user account

23. Close Active Directory Users and Computers, and then log off.

24. Log on using the Testuser1 account with the password Password01. Notice that the Azul wallpaper configured for Testuser1 continues to appear as part of their profile.

25. Click **Start**, click **Control Panel**, and then double-click **System**.

26. Click the **Advanced** tab, and then click the **Settings** button in the User Profiles section. Notice that the Testuser1 user profile now appears as a roaming profile, as shown in Figure 2-15. Click **Cancel** to exit the User Profiles window, and then click **Cancel** again to close the System Properties window. Close the Control Panel window.

27. Log off and then log back on to your server using your Admin*XX* account.

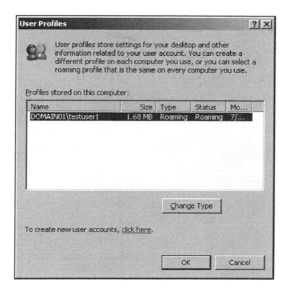

Figure 2-15   Confirming a roaming user profile

Mandatory Profiles

Both local and roaming user profiles allow a user to make changes to their profile settings according to their own preferences by default. For example, a user can change their desktop wallpaper, add additional shortcuts to their desktop, change the placement of desktop icons, add Internet Explorer favorites shortcuts, and more. While this customization provides the user with a flexible desktop environment, it is not suitable in all environments.

Consider the example of a large organization that needs to support many users. Some users may choose to change their wallpaper, delete desktop icons, remove shortcuts, and more. In cases where an organization is trying to standardize a desktop environment for training and support purposes, all users having different desktop environments can lead to increased support costs. Similarly, tellers at a bank probably expect to find applications and related shortcuts in the same desktop location, regardless of which workstation they log on to. If users change their desktop settings, it can ultimately lead to an inconsistent user environment, less efficiency, and increased support costs.

For this reason, Windows Server 2003 supports an alternate type of profile known as a **mandatory profile**. Mandatory profiles allow a user to change their profile while logged on, but the changes are not ultimately saved. For example, if a user is assigned a mandatory profile, they always receive the same profile when logging on. Although they can change or add desktop icons while logged on, any changes made are never saved to their profile when they log off. Because of this, the user always receives a consistent desktop environment at logon.

Both roaming and local user profiles can be configured as mandatory profiles. Changing a profile to be mandatory is not difficult, and simply involves renaming a single file stored in

the profile, namely ntuser.dat. When the ntuser.dat file is renamed to ntuser.man, the settings in the profile become mandatory, and cannot be permanently changed by the user.

In Activity 2-4 you change the roaming user profile assigned to Testuser1 from a normal roaming profile to a mandatory roaming profile.

Activity 2-3: Configuring a Mandatory Profile

Time required: 10 minutes

Objective: Configure and test a mandatory user profile.

Description: The IT manager at Dover Leasing is interested in the possibility of implementing mandatory roaming profiles in order to ensure a consistent desktop environment for support and training purposes. In this activity you configure the roaming user profile for Testuser1 as a mandatory roaming profile.

1. Click **Start**, and then click **My Computer**.

2. Double-click on drive **D:**, double-click on the **Profiles** folder, and then double-click on the **Testuser1** folder.

3. In the Testuser1 folder, locate the file named ntuser.dat. Right-click on the **ntuser.dat** file, and click **Rename**.

4. Rename the ntuser.dat file to **ntuser.man**. The ntuser.man file is illustrated in Figure 2-16.

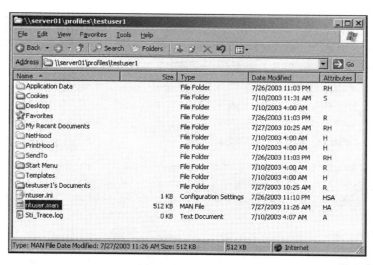

Figure 2-16   Creating a mandatory profile by renaming ntuser.dat to ntuser.man

5. Close the My Computer window.

6. Log off and then log on as Testuser1 with a password of Password01.

7. Right-click on a blank area of the desktop, and click **Properties**.

8. Click on the **Desktop** tab. In the Background list, click on **Autumn**, and then click **OK**. The Autumn desktop wallpaper will now appear on your desktop.

9. Log off and then log back on as Testuser1 with a password of **Password01**. Notice that the Autumn desktop wallpaper does not appear, and that the Azul wallpaper that is part of the mandatory profile is again used. Because the profile for Testuser1 is now mandatory, changes made to the profile are no longer saved when the user logs off.

10. Log off, and then log on using your Admin*XX* account.

CREATING AND MANAGING USER ACCOUNTS

Earlier in this chapter you learned that every user who needs access to a Windows Server 2003 network requires a unique user account. In an Active Directory environment, user accounts are created and stored on domain controllers, in the Active Directory database. Windows Server 2003 supports a number of different methods and tools for creating user account objects. Although the standard tool used for this purpose is Active Directory Users and Computers, Windows Server 2003 also provides a number of command line tools and utilities for adding, deleting, modifying, importing, and exporting user accounts.

This variety of tools allows an administrator to work from whichever environment they feel most comfortable with, or the environment most appropriate to a situation. For example, if an administrator is creating or editing the properties of a single user account, Active Directory Users and Computers would probably be the most logical tool to use. However, in cases where an administrator is creating or managing the properties of multiple users simultaneously, the process might be better undertaken or automated by using some of the command-line tools and utilities available in Windows Server 2003.

In the following sections you learn how to create and manage user accounts using both Active Directory Users and Computers as well as various command line utilities.

Active Directory Users and Computers

The primary tool used to create and manage user accounts in an Active Directory environment is Active Directory Users and Computers. Available from the Administrative Tools menu, it can also be added to a custom Microsoft Management Console (MMC) or opened directly from the Run command by its filename, dsa.msc. This graphical tool makes it easy for administrators to add, modify, move, and delete user accounts as necessary based on the needs of a specific organization. Because Active Directory implementations may ultimately scale to very large sizes with thousands of user objects, this tool also includes the ability to search for user objects based on different settings or criteria.

The version of Active Directory Users and Computers supplied with Windows Server 2003 is functionally very similar to the Windows 2000 version. It has been enhanced, however, to include some additional features, such as the ability to move objects between containers, such

as the Users container and an organizational unit (OU), for example, using common Windows techniques like drag and drop. Another new feature is the inclusion of a node called Saved Queries, which allows an administrator to search for user accounts quickly based on specific settings, such as all users with a particular manager or all accounts that have been disabled. The Active Directory Users and Computers interface is illustrated in Figure 2-17.

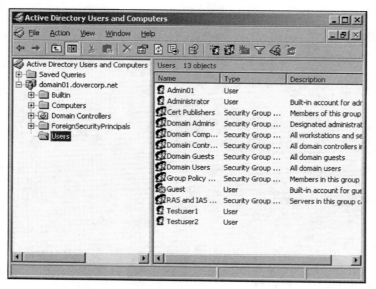

Figure 2-17   Active Directory Users and Computers

As you learned in Activity 2-2, creating user accounts in Active Directory Users and Computers is as simple as right clicking on a particular container (such as Users), selecting New, and then clicking User. This opens the New Object – User window, as shown in Figure 2-18.

Although the built-in Users container may seem like the most logical place to create new user objects, it is not the only place they can be created or located. In larger Active Directory implementations, administrators will typically create additional OU objects to organize users for administration and **Group Policy** application. For example, an OU named Marketing might contain all of the user, computer, and group accounts associated with users in the Marketing department. After a user object is created in one container, it can easily be moved to another, either by selecting the object and then dragging it onto the new destination container, or by right-clicking on the object and selecting Move. The Move window is shown in Figure 2-19.

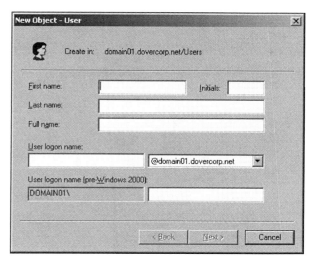

Figure 2-18   The New Object – User window

Figure 2-19   The Move window

In Activity 2-5 you create a number of new user objects using Active Directory Users and Computers.

Activity 2-5: Creating User Accounts Using Active Directory Users and Computers

Time required: 20 minutes

Objective: Use Active Directory Users and Computers to create user accounts.

Description: In the past, Dover Leasing hasn't had a set naming convention for user accounts. Some accounts were created using first names only, while other variations were

used as the company grew larger. Hoping to address some of the scalability issues previously encountered, Dover's IT manager has decided that all corporate user names should follow a convention of first initial and last name. For cases where two users have the same name, the solution will be to use the first initial of subsequent users' middle names to ensure uniqueness. In this activity, you create a number of new user accounts within your dedicated child domain.

1. Click **Start**, select **Administrative Tools**, and click **Active Directory Users and Computers**.

2. Right-click the **Users** container, select **New**, and click **User**.

3. In the New Object – User dialog box, type **John** in the First name text box.

4. Press the **Tab** key twice to reach the Last name text box and type **Smith**. Notice that the Full name text box is populated automatically.

5. Press the **Tab** key twice to reach the User logon name field. Type **jsmith** and press the **Tab** key.

6. In the list box, ensure that your domain name in the form @DomainXX.Dovercorp. net is selected rather than the @Dovercorp.net domain. Click the **Next** button.

7. In the Password text box, shown in Figure 2-20, type **Password01** and press the Tab key. In the Confirm password text box, type **Password01** again.

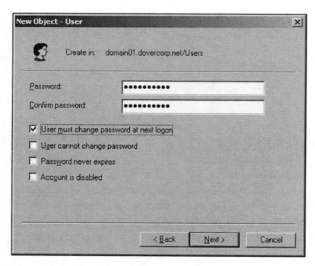

Figure 2-20   Configuring an initial password for a new user object

8. Uncheck the **User must change password at next logon** check box and click **Next**. Click **Finish**.

9. Repeat Steps 2 through 8 to create user accounts for **Mark Manore**, **Frank Adili**, **Christy Jackson**, **John Harold Smith**, **Chris Medved**, **Moira Cowan**, **Mike Aubert**, and **Alan Finn**. Remember to use the user account naming convention originally specified in the description for this activity.

10. When finished, close Active Directory Users and Computers.

The settings configured as part of creating a new user object in Active Directory Users and Computers are fairly limited. Once a new user object has been created, additional attribute settings are configured from the properties of the account, as originally explored in Activity 2-1. From the properties of a user object an administrator can easily add a user to different groups, configure profile settings, and so forth.

Although configuring the properties of each user account individually is possible, it can also be very time consuming, especially when hundreds or even thousands of user accounts need to be created. In many cases, multiple user accounts require the same property settings, and configuring these settings simultaneously can greatly reduce the amount of time and administrative effort required. For this reason, Active Directory Users and Computers includes another new feature in Windows Server 2003, namely the ability to configure the properties of multiple user objects simultaneously. When multiple user objects are selected (by pressing the CTRL key and clicking on different user accounts), accessing the properties of those objects allows you to configure settings on the following tabs once, for all selected accounts:

- General
- Account
- Address
- Profile
- Organization

For example, an administrator could select multiple user accounts and then configure all of them with the same Office setting on the General tab, as illustrated in Figure 2-21.

 TIP One of the benefits of being able to configure settings on multiple user objects simultaneously is that you can take advantage of variables. For example, when configuring the UNC path for a user's profile, you can use the %username% variable in the place of a folder bearing the user's name. This ultimately creates a folder bearing their user name automatically.

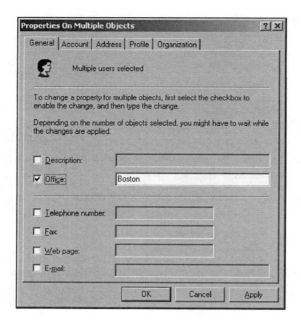

Figure 2-21   Configuring properties for multiple user objects simultaneously

User Account Templates

In order to reduce the time and administrative burden associated with creating new user accounts, many administrators create new user objects by copying a pre-defined template. A **user account template** is simply a user account that is pre-configured with the common settings associated with a particular type of user. For example, when creating new user accounts for users in the Marketing department, a large number of settings are likely to be similar. Because of this, an administrator could create a new user account called Marketing Template, and then populate this account with the common settings required by all marketing users, such as group membership, user profile, and organizational information. Then, when a new user account in the marketing department needs to be created, an administrator can simply copy this account, providing new user name and password information specific to the user.

Only the most common configuration settings are copied to a new user account by default. The settings that are copied when a new user account is created from a template can be controlled by modifying the "Attribute is copied when duplicating user" check box in the Active Directory schema. For more information on the Active Directory schema, see the Windows Server 2003 Help and Support Center.

In Activity 2-6 you configure a new user account template in Active Directory Users and Computers, and then copy that template in order to create a new user account.

Activity 2-6: Creating a User Account Template

Time required: 10 minutes

Objective: Create a user account template and then use that template to create a new user account.

Description: The IT manager at Dover Leasing has asked you to standardize on a method of creating new user accounts. Ultimately, the goal is to reduce the administrative effort and risk of misconfiguration associated with creating new user accounts, especially by junior administrators. In this activity you first create a new user account template, and then copy that template in order to create another new user account.

1. Click **Start**, select **Administrative Tools**, and then click **Active Directory Users and Computers**.

2. Right-click the **Users** container, select **New**, and click **User**.

3. In the New Object – User dialog box, type **_Contractor Template** in the First name text box. Be sure to add the underscore "_" character at the beginning of the name. This will ensure that the template account appears at the top of the user listing when sorted alphabetically by name, making it easier to find when required.

4. Press the **Tab** key four times to reach the User logon name field. Type **contractortemplate** and click **Next**.

5. In the Password text box, type **Password01** and press the **Tab** key. In the Confirm password text box, type **Password01** again. (Passwords are not copied as part of creating a new user account from a template.)

6. Uncheck the **User must change password at next logon** check box and click **Next**. Click **Finish**.

7. Right-click on the **_Contractor Template** user account, and click **Properties**.

8. In the Description text box on the General tab, type **Contractor User**.

9. Click the **Profile** tab. In the Profile path text box, type **\\serverXX\profiles\%username%**. The use of the %username% variable will automatically populate this field with the name of the user account when copied to new accounts.

10. Click the **Member Of** tab. Notice that this account is a member of the Domain Users group by default.

11. Click the **Add** button. In the Enter the object names to select text box on the Select Groups window, type **Domain Guests** and click **OK**. This adds the template account to the Domain Guests group, as shown in Figure 2-22. Click **OK**.

12. Right-click on the **_Contractor Template** user account and click **Disable Account**. User account templates should always be disabled for security purposes. When the Active Directory dialog box appears, click **OK**.

13. Right-click on the **_Contractor Template** user account and click **Copy**.

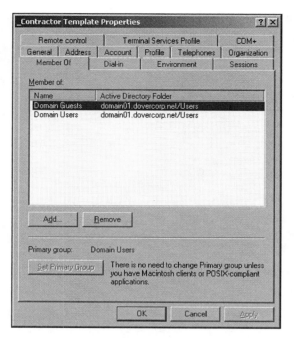

Figure 2-22   The Member Of tab for a user account template

14. The Copy Object – User dialog box appears. Type **Jim** in the First name text box.

15. Press the **Tab** key twice to reach the Last name text box and type **Johnson**.

16. Press the **Tab** key twice to reach the User logon name field. Type **jjohnson** and click **Next**.

17. In the Password text box, type **Password01** and press the **Tab** key. In the Confirm password text box, type **Password01** again. Notice that the Account is disabled check box is checked by default.

18. Uncheck the **Account is disabled** check box, and click **Next**.

19. Review the settings shown in Figure 2-23. Notice that this screen explicitly states that this user is being copied from _Contractor Template. Click **Finish**.

20. Right-click on the **Jim Johnson** user account and click **Properties**. Click on the **General, Member Of,** and **Profile** tabs to confirm that settings configured in the _Contractor Template account have been copied to the Jim Johnson user account. Click **Cancel** once you have confirmed these settings.

21. Close Active Directory Users and Computers.

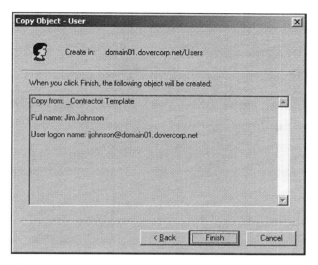

Figure 2-23   Creating a new user by copying a user account template

Command Line Utilities

While Active Directory Users and Computers is the primary tool used to create and manage domain user accounts, Windows Server 2003 includes a variety of new utilities that allow you to create and manage user accounts from the command line. These utilities are aimed at administrators with a preference for working from the command line, or those looking to automate the creation or management of user accounts in a more flexible manner. The command line utilities to be looked at in the following sections include:

- DSADD—Adds objects such as users.
- DSMOD—Modifies object attributes and settings.
- DSQUERY—Queries for objects.
- DSMOVE—Moves objects to different locations within a domain.
- DSRM—Deletes objects from the directory.

DSADD

DSADD allows various object types to be added to the directory. Examples of objects that can be added to the directory with DSADD include computer accounts, contacts, quotas, groups, OUs, and users.

The basic syntax for creating a user account with DSADD is DSADD USER, followed by a variety of different switches that allow you to configure everything from profile paths to group membership information for a single account. The basic syntax for adding a user with the DSADD USER tool consists of only a single piece of information, namely the distinguished name of the account to be created. In Chapter 1 you were introduced to the concept of a distinguished name, which identifies an object in LDAP format.

For example, to create a user account name Mark Jones in the Users container of the domain01.dovercorp.net domain, the correct command syntax would be:

```
dsadd user "cn=Mark Jones,cn=users,dc=domain01,dc=dovercorp,dc=net"
```

In cases where any spaces exist in the distinguished name, the entire name must be enclosed in quotes in a manner similar to this example. If the DSADD USER command completes successfully, a message stating "dsadd succeeded" will be displayed, similar to Figure 2-24.

```
Command Prompt                                          _ □ ×
C:\>dsadd user "cn=Mark Jones,cn=users,dc=domain01,dc=dovercorp,dc=net"
dsadd succeeded:cn=Mark Jones,cn=users,dc=domain01,dc=dovercorp,dc=net

C:\>
```

Figure 2-24   The DSADD USER command

The DSADD account supports a wide variety of switches used to configure different account attributes. The list below provides examples of the more common attributes that might be configured with the DSADD USER command.

- -pwd—Specifies a password for the user account being added.
- -memberof—Specifies groups that the user should be made a member of.
- -email—Specifies the e-mail address of the user.
- -profile—Specifies the profile path for the user.
- -disabled—Specifies whether the account will be initially enabled or disabled.

The following command is an example of creating a new user account named Paul Kohut in the Users container of the domain01.dovercorp.net domain, including values for the switches just explored. Note that the entire command is a single line:

```
dsadd user "cn=Paul Kohut,cn=Users,dc=domain01,dc=dovercorp,dc=net" -pwd
Password01 -memberof "cn=domain
guests,cn=users,dc=domain01,dc=dovercorp,dc=net" -email
paul@dovercorp.net -profile "\\server01\profiles\paul kohut" -disabled no
```

For a complete list of the various switches and options available with the DSADD USER command, see the DSADD topic in Windows Server 2003 Help and Support or type DSADD USER /? at the command line.

NOTE

In Activity 2-7 you create two new user accounts using the DSADD utility.

Activity 2-7: Creating User Accounts Using DSADD

Time required: 10 minutes

Objective: Create new user accounts using the DSADD USER command.

Description: The IT manager at Dover Leasing has asked you to explore different processes for creating user accounts from the command line. Ultimately, the goal is to be able to create user accounts via a telnet session with remote servers when necessary. In this activity you will use the DSADD USER command to create two new user accounts from the command line.

1. Click **Start**, and then click **Run**.

2. In the Open text box, type **cmd.exe**, and click **OK**.

3. At the command prompt window, type **cd ..** and press **Enter**. Type **cd ..** again and press **Enter**. This will help to reduce the on-screen clutter associated with the command prompt path.

4. Type **cls** and press **Enter** to clear the screen.

5. At the command line, type the following, all in one line: **dsadd user "cn=Mark Jones,cn=users,dc=domainXX,dc=dovercorp,dc=net"**, where *XX* is your student number. Press **Enter**. If the dsadd succeeded message appears, the new user account has been created successfully. If you receive an error message, type the command again being careful to avoid errors.

6. Minimize the Command Prompt window.

7. Click **Start**, select **Administrative Tools**, and then click **Active Directory Users and Computers**.

8. Click on the **Users** container to view its contents. Notice that the Mark Jones user account now appears in the container, but that it is disabled by default.

9. Minimize Active Directory Users and Computers, and maximize the Command Prompt window.

10. At the command line, type the following, all in one line: **dsadd user "cn=Paul Kohut,cn=Users,dc=domainXX,dc=dovercorp,dc=net" –pwd Password01 –memberof "cn=domain guests, cn=users,dc=domainXX,dc=dovercorp, dc=net" –email paul@dovercorp.net -profile "\\serverXX\profiles\paul kohut" –disabled no**, where *XX* is your student number. Press **Enter**. If the dsadd succeeded message appears, the new user account has been created successfully. If you receive an error message, type the command again being careful to avoid errors.

11. Close the Command Prompt window, and then maximize the Active Directory Users and Computers window.

12. Right-click on the **Users** container, and then click **Refresh**. Notice that the Paul Kohut user account now appears in the Users container.

13. Right-click on the **Paul Kohut** user account and click **Properties**.

14. On the General tab, confirm that the configured e-mail address is paul@dovercorp.net.

15. Click the **Profile** tab. Confirm the profile path specified in \\server*XX*\profiles\paul kohut, where *XX* is your assigned student number.

16. Click on the **Member Of** tab. Confirm that this account is a member of the Domain Guests group.

17. Click **Cancel**, and then close Active Directory Users and Computers.

DSMOD

DSMOD allows various objects types to be modified from the command line. Examples of directory objects that can be modified with DSMOD include computer accounts, contacts, quotas, groups, OUs, servers, partitions, and users.

The basic syntax for modifying a user account with DSMOD is DSMOD USER, followed by a variety of different switches that allow you to modify everything from profile paths to group membership information for a single account. Since DSMOD USER is used to modify an existing user account, the command requires that you specify the distinguished name of the object to be modified, along with at least one switch (which would specify a particular modification).

For example, to add the description "Marketing Manager" to an existing user account named Mark Jones in the Users container of the domain01.dovercorp.net domain, the correct command syntax would be:

```
dsmod user "cn=Mark Jones,cn=users,dc=domain01,dc=dovercorp,dc=net"
-desc "Marketing Manager"
```

If the DSMOD USER command completes successfully, a message stating "dsmod succeeded" will be displayed, similar to Figure 2-25.

Figure 2-25 The DSMOD USER command

Similarly, the DSMOD USER command can be used to change settings associated with multiple user accounts simultaneously. For example, to change the fax number associated with both the Mark Jones and Paul Kohut user accounts in the Users container of the domain01.dovercorp.net domain, the correct command syntax would be:

```
dsmod user "cn=Mark Jones,cn=users,dc=domain01,dc=dovercorp,dc=net"
"cn=Paul Kohut,cn=users,dc=domain01,dc=dovercorp,dc=net" -fax "800-
555-5555"
```

For a complete list of the various switches and options available with the DSMOD USER command, see the DSMOD topic in Windows Server 2003 Help and Support or type DSMOD USER /? at the command line.

In Activity 2-8 you modify the settings of two user accounts using the DSMOD USER command.

Activity 2-8: Modifying User Accounts Using DSMOD

Time required: 10 minutes

Objective: Modify existing user account properties using the DSMOD USER command.

Description: The IT manager at Dover Leasing has asked you to explore different processes for modifying user accounts from the command line. Ultimately, the goal is to be able to modify user accounts via a telnet session with remote servers when necessary. In this activity you use the DSMOD USER command to modify two existing user accounts from the command line.

1. Click **Start**, and then click **Run**.

2. In the Open text box, type **cmd.exe**, and click **OK**.

3. At the command prompt window, type **cd ..** and press **Enter**. Type **cd ..** again and press **Enter**.

4. Type **cls** and press **Enter** to clear the screen.

5. At the command line, type the following, all in one line: **dsmod user "cn=Mark Jones,cn=users,dc=domainXX,dc=dovercorp,dc=net" –desc "Marketing Manager"**, where *XX* is your assigned student number. Press **Enter**. If the dsmod succeeded message appears, the modification has completed successfully. If you receive an error message, type the command again being careful to avoid errors.

6. Minimize the Command Prompt window.

7. Click **Start**, select **Administrative Tools**, and then click **Active Directory Users and Computers**.

8. Click the **Users** container if necessary to view its contents. Right-click on the **Mark Jones** user account and click **Properties**.

9. On the General tab, confirm that the words Marketing Manager now appear in the Description text box. Click **Cancel**.

10. Minimize Active Directory Users and Computers, and maximize the Command Prompt.

11. At the command line, type the following, all in one line: **dsmod user "cn=Mark Jones,cn=users,dc=domainXX,dc=dovercorp,dc=net" "cn=Paul Kohut,cn=users,dc=domainXX,dc=dovercorp,dc=net" –fax "800-555-5555"**, where *XX* is your assigned student number. Press **Enter**. If the dsmod succeeded message appears, the modification has completed successfully. If you receive an error message, type the command again being careful to avoid errors.

12. Close the Command Prompt window, and then maximize the Active Directory Users and Computers window.

13. Right-click on the **Paul Kohut** user account in the Users container and click **Properties**.

14. Click on the **Telephones** tab to confirm that the fax number configured using the DSMOD command is displayed in the Fax text box. Click **Cancel**.

15. Repeat Steps 13 and 14 to confirm that the fax number has also been configured for the Mark Jones user account.

16. Close Active Directory Users and Computers.

DSQUERY

DSQUERY allows various objects types to be queried from the command line. Examples of directory objects that can be queried for with DSQUERY include computer accounts, contacts, quotas, groups, OUs, servers, partitions, and users. The DSQUERY command also supports the wildcard character (*), effectively allowing it to query for any type of directory object.

At the most basic level, DSQUERY allows you to query the directory for a particular type of object, and return a value. For example, to view all of the user objects in the Users container of the domain01.dovercorp.net domain that are currently disabled, the correct command syntax would be:

```
dsquery user "cn=users,dc=domain01,dc=dovercorp,dc=net" -disabled
```

This command returns a list of the distinguished names of all disabled user accounts in the Users container, as illustrated in Figure 2-26.

Figure 2-26   The DSQUERY USER command

Along the same lines, the DSQUERY USER command can be used to view all of the accounts in a particular domain that have not changed their password in the past 14 days. The correct syntax for this command would be:

```
dsquery user domainroot -name * -stalepwd 14
```

One of the most powerful uses of the DSQUERY command is that its output can be redirected to another command. For example, an administrator might want to automatically disable all of the user accounts that have not changed their password in the last 30 days. Rather than searching for this information using DSQUERY USER and then using DSMOD USER or Active Directory Users and Computers to modify the accounts, the output of the DSQUERY USER command could be piped as input to the DSMOD USER command. In this example, the correct command syntax would be:

```
dsquery user domainroot -name * -stalepwd 30 | dsmod user -disabled
yes
```

The results of piping the output of the DSQUERY USER command to the DSMOD USER command are illustrated in Figure 2-27.

Figure 2-27   Piping the output of the DSQUERY USER command to the DSMOD USER command

 For a complete list of the various switches and options available with the DSQUERY USER command, see the DSQUERY topic in Windows Server 2003 Help and Support or type DSQUERY USER /? at the command line.

DSMOVE

DSMOVE allows various object types to be moved from the object's current location to a new location in the directory, or to rename an object without moving it to a new location.

For example, an administrator might want to move a user account from the Users container into an OU named Marketing. Assuming that the user to be moved is named Paul Kohut and the domain is domain01.dovercorp.net, the correct command syntax to move the user to the new OU would be:

```
dsmove "cn=Paul Kohut,cn=users,dc=domain01,dc=dovercorp,dc=net"
-newparent "ou=marketing,dc=domain01,dc=dovercorp,dc=net"
```

Along the same lines, if Paul Kohut had left the company and was to be replaced by a new user named Johnny Wong, the administrator might chose to simply rename the Paul Kohut user account. Assuming that this account will still exist in the Marketing OU, the correct syntax for this command would be:

```
dsmove "cn=Paul Kohut,ou=marketing,dc=domain01,dc=dovercorp,dc=net"
-newname "Johnny Wong"
```

It is important to understand that the DSMOVE command can only be used to move objects within the same domain. It cannot be used to move an object from one domain to another. If you need to move an object from one domain to another, use the MOVETREE command available when the Windows Server 2003 Support Tools are installed.

NOTE   For a complete list of the various switches and options available with the DSMOVE USER command, see the DSMOVE topic in Windows Server 2003 Help and Support or type DSMOVE USER /? at the command line.

DSRM

The **DSRM** command allows objects to be deleted from the directory. This tool is powerful because it supports the ability to delete not only a single object, but also an entire subtree of objects.

For example, an administrator can specify that only a single object should be deleted by specifying the object's distinguished name. To delete the Mark Jones user account in the Users container of the domain01.dovercorp.net domain, the correct command syntax is:

```
dsrm "cn=Mark Jones,cn=users,dc=domain01,dc=dovercorp,dc=net"
```

After issuing this command, the administrator is prompted to confirm deletion of this object by default, as shown in Figure 2-28.

Figure 2-28   Confirming the deletion of an object with the DSRM command

If the administrator wants to delete the Mark Jones user object without the need to confirm the deletion, the correct command syntax would be:

```
dsrm "cn=Mark Jones,cn=users,dc=domain01,dc=dovercorp,dc=net"
-noprompt
```

The DSRM command can also be used to delete an existing object and its contents if necessary. For example, to delete the Marketing OU (along with all of the objects that it contains) without being prompted to confirm the action, the correct command syntax would be:

```
dsrm –subtree –noprompt –c "ou=marketing,dc=domain01,
dc=dovercorp,dc=net"
```

Conversely, if the administrator wants to delete all of the objects in the Marketing OU, but leave the Marketing OU itself intact, the correct command syntax would be:

```
dsrm –subtree –exclude –noprompt –c "ou=marketing,
dc=domain01,dc=dovercorp,dc=net"
```

Be very careful when using the -noprompt switch with the DSRM command, as you might inadvertently delete required objects.

For a complete list of the various switches and options available with the DSRM USER command, see the DSRM topic in Windows Server 2003 Help and Support or type DSREM USER /? at the command line.

Bulk Import and Export

In large environments, companies may be in the process of transitioning from one directory service to another, or have reams of user data stored in various databases. Rather then manually create hundreds or thousands of user accounts and related objects from scratch, many companies look towards utilities that allow them to import existing stores of data.

Along the same lines, the information stored in a directory service like Active Directory contains a wealth of useful information if properly maintained and kept up-to-date. Companies might be interested in exporting this information for the purpose of populating secondary databases, such as an application used by human resources staff.

To provide administrators with the flexibility to import and export data to or from Active Directory, Windows Server 2003 includes two main utilities, known as **CSVDE** and **LDIFDE**. You learn more about each of these utilities in the following sections.

CSVDE

CSVDE is a command-line tool that supports the bulk export and import of Active Directory data to and from comma-separated value (CSV) files. One of the benefits of the CSV file format is that its structure allows these files to be easily created or opened in a traditional text editor, database program, or spreadsheet application like Microsoft Excel. When data is exported from Active Directory using CSVDE, the first line of the file contains

the name of each attribute being exported, separated by commas. Each subsequent line represents a specific object stored in the directory, with attribute values ordered according to that first line.

For example, CSVDE can be used to export information about all current objects stored in Active Directory to a text file. In the following example, information about objects stored in Active Directory would be exported to a text file named output.csv:

```
csvde -f output.csv
```

Opening the resulting file in a text editor like Notepad would display the exported information in CSV format, as illustrated in Figure 2-29.

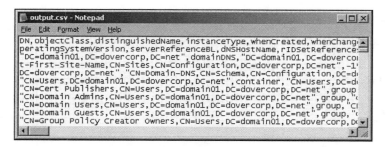

Figure 2-29   Data exported using the CSVDE command

Ultimately, an administrator might choose to import the information stored in the CSVDE file to a different directory or application. In a similar manner, data stored in an existing CSV file, perhaps exported from another LDAP directory, can also be imported into Active Directory to create new objects (such as user accounts) using a bulk process. When importing a file for the purpose of creating new user objects, the key consideration is that the format of the CSV file is correct. For best results, use the first line of an exported CSV file to determine the correct syntax required for such a file to be imported.

For more information about the CSVDE command, see the CSVDE topic in Windows Server 2003 Help and Support Center, or type CSVDE /? at the command line.

LDIFDE

In a manner similar to CSVDE, the LDIFDE utility is a command line tool that can be used to import and export data from Active Directory. Unlike CSVDE, which works with CSV files, LDIFDE uses a file format known as LDAP Interchange Format (LDIF). LDIF is an industry standard method for formatting information imported to or exported from LDAP directories.

Some common uses of LDIFDE and the LDIF file format include extending the Active Directory schema; adding, modifying, and deleting user and group objects; and importing bulk data from an existing directory to populate the Active Directory database.

Unlike a CSV file, where a comma separates every attribute, LDIF files place each attribute and its associated value on a separate line, with a blank line separating individual objects.

The file format associated with LDIFDE is LDF, but these files can be read in any text editor in a manner similar to those created with CSVDE. In Activity 2-9 you export data from Active Directory using the LDIFDE utility.

Activity 2-9: Exporting Active Directory Users Using LDIFDE

Time required: 5 minutes

Objective: Export Active Directory data using LDIFDE.

Description: The IT Manager at Dover Leasing has asked you to determine a way to export Active Directory user account settings to ultimately be imported into another LDAP-compliant application. In this activity you use LDIFDE to export user accounts and selected attributes to an LDF file.

1. Click **Start**, and then click **Run**.

2. In the Open text box, type **cmd.exe**, and then press **Enter**.

3. Type **d:** at the command prompt and press **Enter**.

4. Type the following command, all on one line: **ldifde -f exportusers.ldf -s ServerXX -d "dc=DomainXX,dc=Dovercorp,dc=net" -p subtree -r "(&(objectCategory=person)(objectClass=User)(givenname=*))" -l "cn,givenName,objectclass,samAccountName"**, where *XX* is your assigned student number, and press **Enter**. This will export all user accounts from your domain to the LDIF file named exportusers.ldf. If you receive an error message, type the command again being careful to avoid errors.

5. Close the **Command Prompt**.

6. Click **Start**, and then click **My Computer**.

7. Double-click on drive **D:** to view its contents.

8. Double-click on the **exportusers.ldf** file.

9. At the Windows dialog box, click the **Select the program from a list** radio button, and then click **OK**.

10. At the Open With window, click **Notepad**, and then click **OK**.

11. When the exportusers.ldf file opens in Notepad, scroll through the entries in the file, noticing that each entry corresponds to an Active Directory user account, as shown in Figure 2-30.

12. Close all open windows.

2

```
exportusers.ldf - Notepad                              _ □ ×
File  Edit  Format  View  Help
dn: CN=Admin01,CN=Users,DC=domain01,DC=dovercorp,DC=net
changetype: add
objectClass: top
objectClass: person
objectClass: organizationalPerson
objectClass: user
cn: Admin01
givenName: Admin01
SAMAccountName: admin01

dn: CN=Testuser1,CN=Users,DC=domain01,DC=dovercorp,DC=net
changetype: add
objectClass: top
objectClass: person
objectClass: organizationalPerson
objectClass: user
cn: Testuser1
givenName: Testuser1
SAMAccountName: Testuser1

dn: CN=Testuser2,CN=Users,DC=domain01,DC=dovercorp,DC=net
changetype: add
objectClass: top
objectClass: person
objectClass: organizationalPerson
objectClass: user
```

Figure 2-30   User data exported using the LDIFDE command

NOTE

For more information about the LDIFDE command, see the LDIFDE topic in Windows Server 2003 Help and Support Center, or type LDIFDE /? at the command line.

TROUBLESHOOTING USER ACCOUNT AND AUTHENTICATION ISSUES

Although creating and configuring user accounts is a relatively straightforward process, a number of issues can impact a user's ability to log on to a Windows Server 2003 Active Directory network. Some of these issues are directly related to the configuration of a user account, such as account lockout. In other cases, various policy settings may prohibit a user from being successfully authenticated either interactively or over the network. In the following sections learn some of the key policy settings that can impact the user authentication process, methods of gathering more information about authentication issues, and solutions to common authentication problems.

Account Policies

A variety of configuration settings can and do impact the user authentication process in an Active Directory domain environment. Some of the most important settings to consider are those configured in the Account Policies node of Group Policy objects applied at the domain level. While Group Policy objects and related settings is looked at in more detail in Chapter 9, this section focuses on authentication-related settings, namely those dealing with account lockout, passwords, and Kerberos.

Windows Server 2003 creates a default Group Policy object at the domain level called the Default Domain Policy. Although this object can be configured with a wide variety of different settings, the domain level is the only level at which account lockout, password, and Kerberos settings can be configured for all domain users. The Default Domain Policy can be accessed from Active Directory Users and Computers by right-clicking the domain object, clicking Properties, and then clicking on the Group Policy tab, as shown in Figure 2-31.

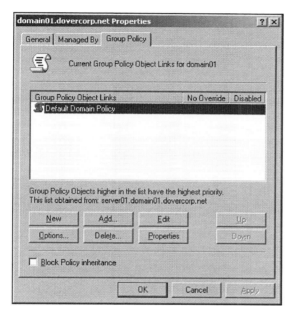

Figure 2-31   The Group Policy tab

Clicking the Edit button opens the Group Policy Object Editor window. The Account Policies node is found in the Computer Configuration section, under Windows Settings – Security Settings – Account Policies, as shown in Figure 2-32.

In the following sections you learn more about each of the three main Account Policies nodes:

- Password Policy
- Account Lockout Policy
- Kerberos Policy

In learning about each node and its configurable settings, pay particular attention to the impact it can have on authentication-related issues.

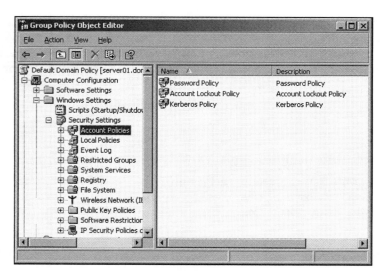

Figure 2-32   The Account Policies node

Password Policy

The Password Policy node contains configuration settings that refer to the required history, age, length, and complexity of user passwords. Settings found in this section don't usually impact a user's ability to authenticate (if they know and submit their current and correct password), but they do impact how often a user must change their password, when their password expires, and so forth. The following list outlines each individual policy item, its default setting, and its intended purpose:

- Enforce password history—Defines the number of passwords that have to be unique before a user can reuse an old password. The default configuration setting is 24 passwords remembered.

- Maximum password age—Defines the number of days that a password can be used before the user is required to change it. The default configuration setting is 42 days.

- Minimum password age—Defines the number of days that a password must be used before a user is allowed to change it. The default configuration setting is one day.

- Minimum password length—Defines the least number of characters required in a password (values can be from 1 to 14 characters); if no password is required, set the value to zero. The default configuration setting is seven characters.

- Passwords must meet complexity requirements—Increases password complexity by enforcing rules that passwords must meet. This setting is enabled by default. A complex password cannot include any portion of the user's account name, must be at least six characters in length, and must include three of the four elements below:

  - English uppercase letters

  - English lowercase letters

  - Numbers

  - Non-alphanumeric (for example, !, $, #)

- Store passwords using reversible encryption—This setting is the same as storing passwords in clear text; this policy provides support for applications using protocols that need the passwords in clear text for authentication purposes. This setting is disabled by default.

Account Lockout Settings

The Account Lockout Policy node contains configuration settings that refer to the password lockout threshold and duration, as well as reset options. Settings configured in this section may impact the user authentication process by locking out user accounts after a specified number of incorrect logon attempts, such as when a user enters an incorrect user name and password combination. The following list outlines each individual policy item, its default setting, and its intended purpose:

- Account lockout duration—Defines the number of failed logon attempts that results in the user account being locked. This setting is not defined by default.

- Account lockout threshold—Defines the number of incorrect logon attempts that must occur before an account is locked out. The default value is zero, meaning that accounts will never be locked out.

- Reset account lockout counter after—Determines the number of minutes that must elapse after a single failed logon attempt before the bad logon counter is reset to zero. This setting is not configured by default.

Kerberos Policy

The Kerberos Policy node contains configuration settings that refer to the Kerberos ticket-granting ticket (TGT) and session ticket lifetimes and time stamp settings. Settings configured in this section may impact both a user's ability to log on to the network, as well as their ability to access network resources. For example, Kerberos relies upon time-stamped tickets in order to ensure that old tickets cannot be reused. If the clock on a user desktop is greatly out of sync with the KDC (a domain controller), the user will not be allowed to log on to the network. The following list outlines each individual policy item, its default setting, and its intended purpose:

- Enforce user logon restrictions—Requires the Key Distribution Center (KDC), a service of Kerberos V5, to validate every request for a session ticket against the user

rights policy of the target computer; if enforced, there may be performance degradation on network access. This setting is enabled by default.

- Maximum lifetime for service ticket—Determines the maximum amount of time, in minutes, that a service ticket is valid to access a resource; the default is 600 minutes (10 hours).

- Maximum lifetime for user ticket—Determines the maximum amount of time, in hours, that a TGT may be used; the default is 10 hours.

- Maximum lifetime for user ticket renewal—Determines the amount of time, in days, that a user's TGT may be renewed; the default is seven days.

- Maximum tolerance for computer clock synchronization—Determines the amount of time difference, in minutes, that Kerberos tolerates between the client machine's clock and the time on the server's clock; the default is five minutes.

Auditing Authentication

Although the auditing feature of Windows Server 2003 is looked at in more detail in Chapter 11, the ability to audit account logon events can provide administrators with useful troubleshooting information relating to authentication.

Windows Server 2003 is capable of auditing one type of event related to users logging on to an Active Directory domain. This setting, known as Audit account logon events, is configured in a Group Policy object linked to the Domain Controllers OU. The name of this policy is the Default Domain Controllers Policy.

By default, a Windows Server 2003 domain controller is configured to audit "success" account logon events only. A success account logon event is related to a user being able to log on to the domain successfully. In cases where user logon is successful, a Windows Server 2003 domain controller will add an event to its Security log, which is accessible in Event Viewer. Administrators should also consider auditing "failure" account logon events for both a higher degree of security and troubleshooting purposes. A failure account logon event would be generated when a user fails to log on successfully, such as if they provided an incorrect user name or password. In cases where you are trying to determine why a user cannot logon, failure events can be a very useful source of information.

While success account logon events are configured by default, failure logon events must be configured manually. To access the Default Domain Controllers Policy, open Active Directory Users and Computers, right-click on the Domain Controllers OU, and click Properties. Click the Group Policy tab to view the Default Domain Controllers Policy, and then click Edit.

To enable the auditing of failure account logon events, access the Audit Policy node, which is available under Computer Configuration – Windows Settings – Security Settings – Local Policies, as shown in Figure 2-33. In the Audit Policy node, double-click on the Audit account logon events policy, check the Failure check box, and then click OK. Domain controllers will now audit both success and failure events related to account logon.

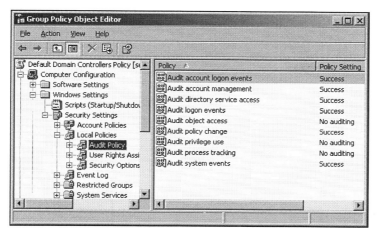

Figure 2-33   The Audit Policy node

Both success and failure account logon events can be viewed using the Security log in the Event Viewer administrative tool. A "key" icon designates success events, while a "lock" icon designates failure events. To open a particular entry in the Security log, simply double-click on it to view more information. Figure 2-34 illustrates a log entry for a failure account logon event. In this case, reading through the information provided makes it clear that the event is a failure event, and that it is related to the user name Admin01. In this case the Event ID listed is 675, which is typically associated with a user providing an incorrect password.

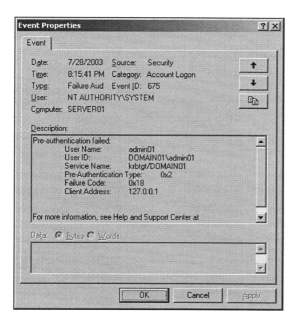

Figure 2-34   A failure event in the Security log

2

When users are unable to log on to an Active Directory domain, failure auditing for account logon events is one of the best sources of information available to an administrator. Although most account logon failure events will fall into Event IDs 675 and 676, the particular Failure Code associated with these errors can vary widely, and provides much more detailed information about the cause of the failure. For more information about Event ID and specific failure codes, your best source of information is the Microsoft Knowledge Base available at *http://support.microsoft.com*.

Resolving Logon Issues

In an Active Directory environment, users may not be able to log on to the domain for a variety of different issues. In some cases, the problem may be as simple as the user forgetting or mistyping their user name or password, while in others network settings may potentially be to blame. The following list outlines some of the more common logon issues that may occur in an Active Directory environment, and how they can be resolved.

- Incorrect user name or password — Most commonly caused by a user forgetting or mistyping their user name or password. The obvious solution to this problem is to reset the user's password using an administrative tool like Active Directory Users and Computers.

- Account lockout — After multiple incorrect logon attempts, a user's account may be locked out, depending on the Account lockout policy settings configured in the domain. User accounts can be unlocked manually from the Account tab in the properties of a user account.

- Account disabled — A user is unable to logon unless their account has been enabled. In some cases, such as when a new user is created based on a template account, their account may not have been enabled. Use Active Directory Users and Computers or the DSMOD USER command line utility to explicitly enable the user's account.

- Logon hour restrictions — A user is having trouble logging on at certain times during the day. Check to ensure that no logon hour restrictions are configured for their account. If a user needs access after normal business hours, ensure that the logon hour restrictions for their account are configured appropriately.

- Workstation restrictions — A user is not able to log on from certain workstations. Check to ensure that workstation restrictions have not been configured in the properties of their user account. Permit their account to log on to additional workstations or all workstations if necessary.

- Domain controllers — Workstations running Windows XP/2000/2003 seem unable to contact a domain controller. Check to ensure that their configured DNS settings are correct. Their operating systems query DNS to find the IP address of a domain controller, and incorrect settings may prohibit them from doing so.

- Client time settings — A user cannot log on to Windows XP, 2000, or 2003 workstations or member servers. Check to ensure that the user's clock is less than five minutes out of sync with the domain controller. Synchronization settings more than five minutes apart will prohibit users from logging on due to Kerberos policy settings.

- Down-level client issues — Down-level clients like workstations running Windows 95/98 and Windows NT are experiencing logon issues. Consider installing the Active Directory Client Extensions software on their systems.

- UPN logon issues — A user cannot log on using their UPN in a multiple-domain environment. Ensure that a Global Catalog server is configured and accessible. Global Catalog servers must be available when a user attempts logon using a UPN.

- Users unable to log on locally — A user needs to log on locally to specific servers or domain controllers. Grant them the right to log on locally in the policy settings on that server.

- Remote access logon issues — A user cannot log on via a dial-up or VPN connection. Be sure that their account is configured to allow access on the Dial-up tab in the properties of their user account.

- Terminal Services logon issues — A user cannot log on to a Terminal Server in the domain. Ensure that the Allow logon to terminal server check box is checked on the Terminal Services Profile tab in the properties of their user account.

CHAPTER SUMMARY

- The two primary authentication protocols used in Windows Server 2003 Active Directory environments are Kerberos v5 and NTLM.

- Windows Server 2003 supports three different types of user profiles; local profiles, roaming profiles, and mandatory profiles.

- The primary tool used to create and manage user accounts in a Windows Server 2003 Active Directory environment is Active Directory Users and Computers. This tool can also be used to configure user templates that can then be copied as a means of simplifying the user account creation process.

- Windows Server 2003 introduces a number of tools to allow user accounts to be created and managed from the command line including DSADD, DSMOD, DSQUERY, DSMOVE, and DSRM.

- The LDIFDE and CSVDE command-line utilities can be used to import and export settings to and from LDIF and CSV text files respectively.

KEY TERMS

Active Directory Users and Computers — An Active Directory MMC tool that allows you to create various objects such as OUs, user accounts, groups, computers, and contacts.

authentication — The process by which a user's identity is validated, which is subsequently used to grant or deny access to network resources.

CSVDE — A command-line utility that can be used to import and export data to and from Active Directory in a comma-separated file format.

down-level operating system — An operating system running Windows NT 4.0 or earlier.

DSADD — A command-line utility used to add objects to Active Directory.

DSMOD — A command-line utility used to modify Active Directory objects.

DSMOVE — A command-line utility used to move or rename Active Directory objects.

DSQUERY — A command-line utility used to query for Active Directory objects.

DSRM — A command-line utility used to delete Active Directory objects.

Group Policy — Enables the centralized management of user desktop settings, desktop and domain security, and the deployment and management of software throughout your network.

interactive authentication — The process by which a user provides their user name and password to be authenticated from the Log On to Windows dialog box.

Kerberos version 5 (Kerberos v5) — The primary authentication protocol used in Active Directory domain environments.

Key Distribution Center (KDC) — An Active Directory domain controller that stores the directory database containing all users and passwords.

LDIFDE — A command-line utility that can be used to import and export data to and from Active Directory using the LDAP Interchange Format file format.

local profile — A user profile stored on a particular computer that doesn't follow a user across the network.

mandatory profile — A user profile with settings that are not changed when a user logs off.

network authentication — The process by which a network resource or service confirms the identity of a user.

NT LAN Manager (NTLM) — The challenge-response protocol that is used for authentication purposes with operating systems running Windows NT 4.0 or earlier.

roaming profile — A user profile stored on a centralized server that follows a user across a network.

service ticket — A Kerberos ticket granted by a KDC allowing a client to gain access to a network resource or service.

ticket-granting ticket (TGT) — A ticket passed to a client system by the KDC once successful authentication occurs.

user account — An object that is stored in Active Directory that represents all of the information that defines a physical user who has access permissions to the network.

user account template — A special user account configured with settings that can be copied in order to simplify the creation of user accounts with common settings.

user profile — The desktop and environment settings associated with a particular user account.

REVIEW QUESTIONS

1. Which of the following tools can be used to modify the properties of existing user accounts from the command line?
   a. DSADD
   b. DSMOD
   c. DSQUERY
   d. DSRM

2. Which of the following tools can be used to create new user accounts?
   a. DSADD
   b. DSMOD
   c. DSQUERY
   d. DSMOVE

3. Which of the following tools can export user objects to a comma-separated text file?
   a. LDIFDE
   b. Active Directory Users and Computers
   c. DSADD
   d. CSVDE

4. Which of the following tools can import settings in LDAP Interchange Format?
   a. LDIFDE
   b. CSVDE
   c. DSRM
   d. DSQUERY

5. Which of the following is not a tool to create user accounts?
   a. DSADD
   b. Active Directory Users and Computers
   c. LDIFDE
   d. DSMOD

6. The Default Domain Policy specifies that a user password must be how long by default?
   a. five characters
   b. six characters
   c. seven characters
   d. eight characters

7. Which of the following is not a required element in a complex password?
   a. Minimum of six characters
   b. Minimum of eight characters
   c. Cannot include the user name
   d. Must include three of four defined character types

8. After how many days must a domain user change their password by default?
   a. 30
   b. 10
   c. 42
   d. 34

9. Active Directory user accounts are configured to lockout after three incorrect logon attempts.
   a. True
   b. False

10. When a user account template is copied, group membership information isalso copied.
   a. True
   b. False

11. How many user passwords are remembered by a domain controller as part of password history setting by default?
   a. 6
   b. 8
   c. 16
   d. 24

12. On which tab of a user account's properties is the user's home directory configured by default?
   a. Home Directory
   b. Profile
   c. Account
   d. General

13. When a new user account is created in Active Directory Users and Computers, which group is it a member of by default?

    a. Domain Admins

    b. Domain Users

    c. Domain Guests

    d. Users

14. Which type of user profile does not save user settings when the user logs off?

    a. Local

    b. Roaming

    c. Null

    d. Mandatory

15. What type of user profile is used by default when a user logs on to a Windows XP system in an Active Directory domain?

    a. Local

    b. Roaming

    c. Null

    d. Mandatory

16. Which authentication protocol do Windows 2000 clients logging on to a Windows Server 2003 domain use?

    a. NTLM

    b. NTLMv2

    c. Kerberos

    d. RADIUS

17. Which authentication protocol is not configured with the Active Directory Client Extensions software used by Windows NT 4.0 clients when logging on to a Windows Server 2003 domain?

    a. NTLM

    b. NTLMv2

    c. Kerberos

    d. RADIUS

18. Logging on to an Active Directory domain from the console of a Windows XP system is referred to as which type of authentication?

    a. Interactive

    b. Network

    c. Domain

    d. Local

19. Which of the following folders in not part of a user profile?

   a. NetHood

   b. PrintHood

   c. My Documents

   d. Networks

20. Creating a mandatory user profile involves renaming which file?

   a. NTUSER.DAT

   b. NTUSER.MAN

   c. NTUSER.PRO

   d. NTUSER.SET

CASE PROJECTS

Case Project 2-1

Dover Leasing currently has information about all users stored in a human resources database application. The IT manager has asked you to explore some of the possible ways that this information could be used to create user accounts and populate the Active Directory database. Which tools could be used to accomplish this, and what are some of the issues involved with using these utilities?

Case Project 2-2

The DSADD command provides an effective method for administrators to create new user accounts from the command line. Use the DSADD utility to create the four new user accounts listed in the table below. All the user accounts should be created in the Users container in your DomainXX.Dovercorp.Net domain. Use the DSADD topic in the Help and Support Center to determine the appropriate switches required to configure these accounts from the command line.

User Name	Group Membership	Title	Pager number	Account Disabled?
Elliot Maxwell	VP Operations		555-1111	Yes
Nick Peers	Domain Guests	Contractor		No
Bob Mackenzie	Domain Admins	Administrator	555-1112	Yes
Doug Mackenzie	Backup Operators	Contractor		Yes

CASE
PROJECTS

Case Project 2-3

In many companies, user account templates are created to help ease the administrative burden of creating many similar accounts. Create an account template called "TempUsers" in the Users container that is made a member of the Guest Users global group and has logon denied on Sundays. After completing the template, use it to create a new user account named "Mary Walsh" and ensure that the properties configured on the template apply to the new user account.

CHAPTER

3

IMPLEMENTING AND MANAGING GROUP AND COMPUTER ACCOUNTS

After reading this chapter and completing the exercises, you will be able to:

Understand the purpose of using group accounts to simplify administration

Create group objects using both graphical and command-line tools

Manage security groups and distribution groups

Explain the purpose of the built-in groups created when Active Directory is installed

Create and manage computer accounts

Although user accounts represent the primary method utilized to identify users on a network, trying to configure permissions or rights for multiple users according to their individual account can quickly become unmanageable, especially in large environments. For this reason, most network operating systems, including Windows Server 2003, include the ability to aggregate user accounts into entities known simply as groups.

Groups help to reduce the administrative effort associated with assigning rights and permissions to users by grouping users with common needs. For example, an administrator might choose to create a group to represent all users in the marketing department, or all users who work in a particular location. Ultimately, groups make administration easier by allowing an administrator to configure rights or permissions for several users at once rather than individually for each user. When a user requires certain rights or permissions, they are simply added to the group to which an appropriate level of access is granted.

In a manner similar to user accounts, Active Directory Users and Computers is the primary tool used to create and manage group accounts in an Active Directory environment. The various directory service command-line tools

introduced in Chapter 3 for creating and managing user accounts can also be used to create and manage groups. You learn more about these methods of group management later in this chapter.

In much the same way that a user object represents an individual user in a domain environment, computer objects represent workstations and servers. In this chapter you also learn how to create and manage computer accounts using both Active Directory Users and Computers, and the DSADD command-line utility.

INTRODUCTION TO GROUP ACCOUNTS

A Windows Server 2003 **group** is a container object that is used to organize a collection of users, computers, contacts, or other groups into a single security principal. You would use a group object to simplify administration by assigning rights and resource permissions to a group rather than to individual users. Groups sound similar to OUs in that both organize other objects into logical containers. The main differences between an OU and a group are as follows:

- OUs are not security principals and as such cannot be used to define permissions on resources or be assigned rights. Active Directory Security Groups are security principals that can be assigned both permissions and rights.

- OUs can only contain objects from their parent domain. Some groups can contain objects from any domain within the forest.

In the following sections you learn more about the different group types and scopes available in a Windows Server 2003 Active Directory environment, as well as the various membership rules that apply to those groups.

Group Types

A group's type is used to define how that group can be used within an Active Directory domain or forest. Windows Server 2003 supports two different group types, known as Distribution Groups and Security Groups. The distinction between each type of group is important, because each is created for a different purpose and has different characteristics. The following sections look at both security and distribution groups in more detail.

Security Groups

Security groups are typically the most popular group type in an Active Directory environment. In a manner similar to a user account, security groups are defined by a Security Identifier (SID) that allows them to be assigned both permissions for resources in **discretionary access control lists (DACLs)**, as well as rights to perform different tasks. When trying to determine whether to create a **security group** or a distribution group, an administrator first needs to consider how that group will be used. Any group that will

ultimately be assigned permissions or rights must be a security group, because distribution groups cannot be assigned permissions and rights.

Although the assignment of permissions and rights is the primary function of security groups, these groups can also be used as e-mail entities. Sending an e-mail message to an Active Directory Security Group (such as when Microsoft Exchange 2000 is installed) sends the message to all of the members of that group.

Distribution Groups

Distribution groups are the other type of group in an Active Directory environment. Unlike security groups, distribution groups do not have an associated SID and therefore cannot be used to assign permissions or rights to members. The primary purpose of a **distribution group** is for use with e-mail applications like Microsoft Exchange 2000, where sending an e-mail message to the distribution group sends the message to all members of that group.

While distribution groups may not seem useful in light of the fact that e-mail messages can also be sent to security groups, they differentiate themselves in an important way. Distribution groups do not have an SID associated with them, therefore they do not impact the user authentication process unnecessarily with excess information not required for security purposes. For this reason, if a group will never be used for security purposes, it should be configured as a distribution group rather than a security group.

Group Scopes

A group's scope refers to the logical boundary within which a group can be assigned permissions to a specific resource within an Active Directory domain or forest. Security and Distribution Groups in Active Directory can be assigned one of three possible scopes:

- global
- domain local
- universal

The following sections explore each group scope in more detail.

Global Groups

Global groups are created for the purpose of logically organizing users, computers, and potentially other groups that exist within the same domain in an Active Directory forest. For example, a **global group** created in Domain A can include objects (such as users) from Domain A, but not from Domain B.

When an administrator creates global groups, it is usually to organize objects associated with a geographic location or job function into logical groups. An administrator might create a global group called Marketing Users that includes all users in the marketing department, for example. Then, when permissions need to be assigned to all users in the Marketing Department for a specific folder or printer, the administrator can assign the permissions once

for the Marketing Users global group, rather than for each user account individually. This obviously helps to reduce the administrative effort associated with configuring security settings like rights or permissions.

The type of objects that can be added to a global group is directly related to the configured functional level of a domain. Windows Server 2003 supports three main domain functional levels in environments that include various combinations of Windows 2000 Server and Windows Server 2003 domain controllers. These include:

- Windows 2000 mixed—This **domain functional level** is the default configured when Windows Server 2003 Active Directory is installed. This level supports a combination of Windows NT Server 4.0, Windows 2000 Server, and Windows Server 2003 domain controllers. Because each type of domain controller is supported, this domain functional level still follows many of the group member-ship rules associated with Windows NT 4.0 domain environments (to be explored shortly).

- Windows 2000 native—This domain functional level supports a combination of Windows 2000 Server and Windows Server 2003 domain controllers only. When configured to this functional level, a domain can support a variety of advanced group membership features, including the ability to nest global groups from the same domain. Supported group membership features at the Windows 2000 native domain functional level is covered shortly.

- Windows Server 2003—This domain functional level supports Windows Server 2003 domain controllers only. When configured to this domain functional level, a domain supports the same group membership features as the Windows 2000 native function level.

As outlined in the previous list, the configured functional level of a domain is directly related to the types of domain controllers present in an environment. For example, a company upgrading an existing Windows NT 4.0 domain needs to exist at the Windows 2000 mixed domain functional level for at least some period of time. Once all of the domain controllers have been upgraded to at least Windows 2000 Server, the domain functional level can be raised to Windows 2000 native. If all domain controllers are ultimately upgraded to Windows Server 2003, the functional level can then be upgraded again. Ultimately, the functional level of a domain impacts much more than group membership rules, but that is beyond the scope of this section.

NOTE   For more information on the different capabilities of different Windows Server 2003 domain functional levels, see the Domain and forest functionality: Active Directory topic in Help and Support Center.

When a domain is configured to the **Windows 2000 mixed** domain functional level, global groups within an Active Directory forest can:

- Contain user accounts from the same domain
- Be added to local groups or domain local groups in any domain

When a domain is configured to the Windows 2000 mixed domain functional level, global groups within an Active Directory forest cannot:

- Be added to universal groups in the forest, since universal groups do not exist at the Windows 2000 mixed domain functional level

When a domain is configured to the **Windows 2000 native** or **Windows Server 2003** domain functional levels, global groups within an Active Directory forest can:

- Contain user accounts or other global groups from the same domain
- Be added to universal groups
- Be added to local groups or domain local groups in any domain

The process of creating different groups and changing the functional level of a domain is looked at in more detail later in this chapter.

Domain Local Groups

Domain local groups are typically created for the purpose of assigning rights and permissions to groups of users in an Active Directory environment. Created on domain controllers, a **domain local group** can be assigned rights and permissions to any resource within the same domain only. However, domain local groups can also contain groups from other domains in addition to users.

For example, a domain local group named Marketing is configured on a domain controller in Domain A. This domain local group is then assigned permissions to a folder on a server in Domain A. Then, instead of assigning permissions on this folder for multiple groups, global groups from Domain A (as well as other trusted domains) can be added to the Marketing domain local group. This ultimately grants users in those global groups the permissions associated with the Marketing domain local group.

In much the same way that the functional level of a domain impacts the membership rules for global groups, the same is true of domain local groups. When a domain is configured to the Windows 2000 mixed domain functional level, domain local groups within an Active Directory forest can:

- Contain user accounts from any domain
- Contain global groups from any domain

When a domain is configured to the Windows 2000 native or Windows Server 2003 domain functional levels, domain local groups within an Active Directory forest can:

- Contain user accounts from any domain
- Contain global groups from any domain
- Contain universal groups
- Contain other domain local groups from the same domain

Groups created on Windows Server 2003 member servers or Windows XP Professional clients are called local groups. Local groups can only be assigned permissions to a resource available on the local machine on which it is created.

Universal Groups

Universal groups are typically created for the purpose of aggregating users or groups in different domains throughout an Active Directory forest. Stored on domain controllers configured as global catalog servers, a **universal group** can be assigned rights and permissions to any resource within a forest. Universal groups can contain not only users and global groups from any domain, but also other universal groups.

For example, a universal group named Enterprise Marketing is configured in a large organization with multiple domains. Then, the Marketing Users global groups from various domains (which contain individual marketing user accounts) is added to the Enterprise Marketing universal group, forming a single group that encompasses all of the marketing users within an organization across domain boundaries. Then, when rights or permissions need to be assigned to all marketing users in the forest, they can be assigned once to the Enterprise Marketing universal group, rather than individual Marketing Users groups from each domain.

Unlike global and domain local groups, which can exist at the Windows 2000 mixed domain functional level, universal groups can only be created once a domain is configured to the Windows 2000 native or Windows Server 2003 domain functional level. When a domain in configured to the Windows 2000 native or Windows 2003 domain functional level, universal groups in an Active Directory forest can:

- Contain user accounts from any trusted domain
- Contain global group accounts from any trusted domain
- Contain other universal groups

TIP Use universal groups with caution. All universal groups along with their memberships are listed in the global catalog. When there is any change to any member of a universal group, this change must be replicated to every global catalog in the forest. Global and domain local groups are also listed in the global catalog but do not have their memberships listed. A best practice is to place individual members within the global groups and then place the global groups within universal groups.

Table 3-1 provides a summary of each group type, its use, and its membership options within an Active Directory forest.

Table 3-1   Windows Server 2003 Group Summary

Group Scope	Usage	Windows 2000 Mixed Domain Functional Level Membership Options	Windows 2000 Native/ Windows Server 2003 Domain Functional Level Membership Options
Local	Assigns permissions to resources on the local computer only	User accounts from any domain; global groups from any domain	User accounts from any domain; global groups from any domain
Domain local	Assigned to resources within local domain	User accounts from any domain; global groups from any domain	User accounts, global groups, and universal groups from any domain; domain local groups from the same domain only
Global	Aggregates individual objects such as user accounts within a domain	User accounts from the same domain only	User accounts and global groups from the same domain only
Universal	Aggregates individual objects such as users or global groups from any domain in a forest	Not available	User accounts, global groups, and universal groups from any domain

CREATING GROUP OBJECTS

Global, domain local, and universal groups are created and stored in the Active Directory database like domain user accounts. Windows Server 2003 supports a number of different methods and tools for creating and managing group account objects. Although the standard tool used for this purpose is Active Directory Users and Computers, Windows Server 2003 also provides a number of command-line tools and utilities for the purpose of managing group accounts from the command line.

This variety of tools allows an administrator to work from whichever environment they feel most comfortable with, or the environment most appropriate to a situation. For example, if

an administrator needs to create or edit the properties of a single group, Active Directory Users and Computers is probably the most logical tool to use. In cases where an administrator needs to create or manage the properties of multiple groups simultaneously, however, using some of the command-line tools and utilities available in Windows Server 2003 is a better, more automated process. Examples include DSADD, DSMOD, DSQUERY, and so forth.

In the following sections you learn how to create and manage group accounts using both Active Directory Users and Computers as well as various command line utilities.

Active Directory Users and Computers

The primary tool used to create group accounts in an Active Directory environment is Active Directory Users and Computers. Fundamentally, creating groups of different types and scopes with this tool is very similar to the process used to create new user accounts.

New group accounts can be created in any of the built-in containers found in Active Directory Users and Computers, as well as in the root of the domain object. For organizational purposes, however, group accounts are often created with custom OU objects. For example, if an administrator creates all user accounts for users in the Marketing Department in an OU named Marketing, it makes sense to also create all marketing-related group accounts in this same OU. However, this method of locating group accounts is not strictly required, and the placement of group objects is at the discretion of the administrator.

Like new user objects, new groups are created in Active Directory Users and Computers by right-clicking on a particular container or OU (such as Users), selecting New, and then clicking Group. Doing so opens the New Object – Group window, shown in Figure 3-1.

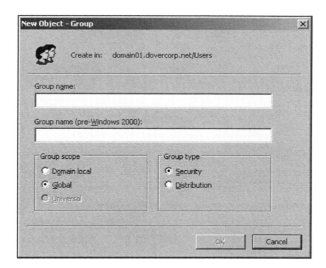

Figure 3-1   The New Object - Group window

Notice in Figure 3-1 that while both group types are available for selection, the Universal group scope option is not. In this case, the universal group option is not available because the functional level of the domain is not yet configured to Windows 2000 native or Windows Server 2003.

Active Directory Users and Computers, like user accounts, can also be used to configure the properties associated with a group account. The properties dialog box for a group account consists of four main tabs:

- General—Allows a description and e-mail address to be configured for the group, and allows the type and scope of a group to be changed.

- Members—Allows members to be added or removed from the group.

- Member Of—Displays any groups that this group is a member of, and allows this group to be added to or removed from other groups.

- Managed By—Displays information about the user or contact responsible for the management of the group object.

When the Advanced Features view is enabled within Active Directory Users and Computers, two additional tabs become visible in the properties of a group account. The Object tab displays information about the properties of the group object, while the Security tab shows the configured permissions for the group object.

In Activity 3-1 you create and add members to global groups using Active Directory Users and Computers.

Activity 3-1: Creating and Adding Members to Global Groups

Time Required: 15 minutes

Objective: Use Active Directory Users and Computers to create global groups.

Description: Having read about the different group types and scopes in Windows Server 2003, you have decided to try and take advantage of some of the reduced administrative effort associated with using groups to manage resource access in an Active Directory environment. In this activity, you create a series of global groups that will be associated with different job functions at Dover Leasing, and then populate these global groups with user accounts.

1. Log on with your Admin*XX* account if you haven't already done so. Click **Start**, select **Administrative Tools**, and click **Active Directory Users and Computers**.

2. Right-click the **Users** container, select **New**, and then click **Group**.

3. In the New Object – Group dialog box, type **Marketing Users** in the Group name text box.

4. Under Group scope, ensure that the **Global** radio button is selected.

5. Under Group type, ensure that the **Security** radio button is selected. Click **OK** to create the group.

6. Repeat Steps 2 through 5 to create global groups named **Help Desk Users**, **Finance Users**, **IT Users**, **Network Support Users**, and **Sales Users** within the Users container.

7. Double-click the **IT Users** global group to view its properties, as shown in Figure 3-2.

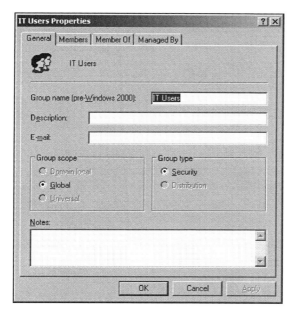

Figure 3-2   The General tab in the properties of a global group

8. Click the **Members** tab.

9. Click the **Add** button. In the Select Users, Contacts, Computers, or Groups dialog box, type **Mark Manore** in the Enter the object names to select text box and click **OK**. The Mark Manore user account should be listed as a member of the group, as shown in Figure 3-3.

10. Click **OK** to close the properties of the IT Users global group.

11. Click the **Moira Cowan** user account to select it. Hold down the **Ctrl** key and click the **John H. Smith** user account. Both accounts should now be selected. Release the **Ctrl** key.

12. Right-click the **John H. Smith** account and click **Add to a group**.

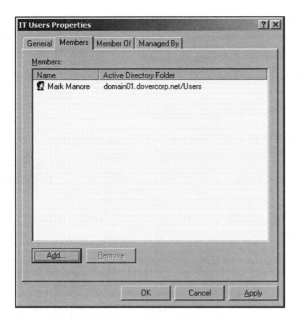

Figure 3-3   The Members tab in the properties of a global group

13. In the Select Group dialog box, type **marketing users** in the Enter the object name to select text box as shown in Figure 3-4, and click **OK**. At the Active Directory dialog box, click **OK**.

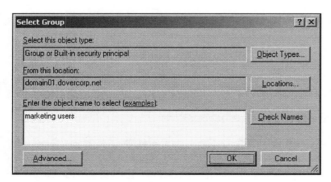

Figure 3-4   The Select Group dialog box

14. Using any combination of the steps outlined here, add the **Chris Medved** account to the Finance Users group, the **Mike Aubert** and **Alan Finn** accounts to the Network Support Users group, the **Frank Adili** and **Christy Jackson** accounts to the Sales Users group, and the **John Smith** account to the Help Desk Users group.

15. Leave Active Directory Users and Computers open.

In Activity 3-2 you create and add members to domain local groups using Active Directory Users and Computers.

Activity 3-2: Creating and Adding Members to Domain Local Groups

Time Required: 10 minutes

Objective: Use Active Directory Users and Computers to create domain local groups.

Description: In this activity, you create a series of domain local groups associated with resource access at Dover Leasing, and then populate these domain local groups with global group accounts.

1. In Active Directory Users and Computers, right-click the **Users** container, select **New**, and then click **Group**.

2. In the New Object – Group dialog box, type **Marketing Resources** in the Group name text box.

3. Under Group scope, click the **Domain local** radio button.

4. Under Group type, ensure that the **Security** radio button is selected. Click **OK** to create the group. Notice that a group's scope and type can be distinguished via the Type header when viewing the contents of a container.

5. Repeat Steps 1 through 4 to create domain local groups named **Help Desk Resources**, **Finance Resources**, **IT Resources**, **Network Support Resources**, and **Sales Resources** within the Users container.

6. Right-click on the **Marketing Resources** domain local group, and then click **Properties**.

7. Click the **Members** tab, and then click the **Add** button.

8. In the Select Users, Contacts, Computers, or Groups window, type **Marketing Users** in the Enter the object names to select text box. Click **OK**.

9. Click **OK** to close the Marketing Resources Properties window.

10. Repeat Steps 6 through 9 to add the **Help Desk Users** global group to the Help Desk Resources domain local group, the **Finance Users** global group to the Finance Resources domain local group, the **IT Users** global group to the IT Resources domain local group, the **Network Support Users** global group to the Network Support Resources domain local group, and the **Sales Users** global group to the Sales Resources domain local group.

11. Leave Active Directory Users and Computers open.

As you learned earlier in this chapter, universal groups cannot be created until the functional level of a domain is set to Windows 2000 native or Windows Server 2003. The functional level of a domain is configured using the Active Directory Users and Computers tool. In

Activity 3–3 you first configure the functional level of your domain to Windows Server 2003, and then create and add members to universal groups.

ACTIVITY

Activity 3-3: Changing the Functional Level of a Domain and Creating and Adding Members to Universal Groups

Time Required: 10 minutes

Objective: Change the functional level of a domain to Windows Server 2003, and use Active Directory Users and Computers to create universal groups.

Description: Because the Dover Leasing Active Directory forest will eventually consist of multiple domains, the IT manager has asked you to determine the process for raising the functional level of a domain and then create and populate universal groups. In this activity you first raise the functional level of your domain to Windows Server 2003, and then create and add a member to a universal group.

1. In Active Directory Users and Computers, right-click the **DomainXX.Dovercorp.net** domain (where *XX* is your assigned student number) and click **Raise Domain Functional Level**.

2. In the Raise Domain Functional Level dialog box, click **Windows Server 2003** in the Select an available domain functional level list box. Note the warning message that appears below the list box, as shown in Figure 3-5.

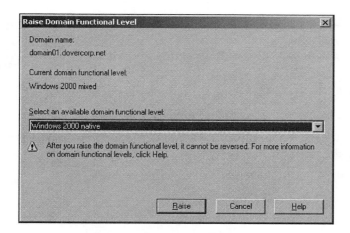

Figure 3-5   The Raise Domain Functional Level dialog box

3. Click the **Raise** button.

4. Click **OK** to confirm that this action will affect the entire domain.

5. Click **OK** when prompted that the functional level was raised successfully, being sure to read the associated message that appears.

6. Right-click on the **Users** container, select **New**, and then click **Group**.

7. In the New Object – Group dialog box, type **Universal Marketing** in the Group name text box.

8. Under Group scope, click the **Universal** radio button, which is now available, as shown in Figure 3-6.

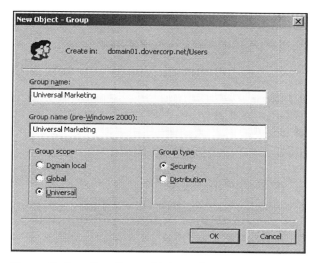

Figure 3-6   Creating a Universal group

9. Under Group type, ensure that the **Security** radio button is selected. Click **OK** to create the group.

10. Right-click on the **Universal Marketing** group, and click **Properties**.

11. Click the **Members tab**, and then click the **Add** button.

12. In the Select Users, Contacts, Computers, or Groups window, type **Marketing Users** in the Enter the object names to select text box. Click **OK**.

13. Click **OK** to close the Universal Marketing Properties window.

14. Leave Active Directory Users and Computers open.

CONVERTING GROUP TYPES

When creating new Active Directory groups, it is important to select the appropriate group type based on how the group will be used. When a group needs to be assigned permissions or rights, you have already learned that security groups are required. It is also conceivable, however, that an administrator might accidentally create a distribution group when a security group is required, or vice versa. For this reason, Active Directory Users and

Computers allows an administrator to change the type of an existing group if required. In order to take advantage of this capability, the domain in which the group account exists must be configured to at least the Windows 2000 native domain functional level. The type of a group cannot be converted if the domain is configured to the Windows 2000 mixed domain functional level.

In Activity 3-4 you use Active Directory Users and Computers to create a new distribution group, and then convert it to a security group.

ACTIVITY

Activity 3-4: Converting Group Types

Time Required: 5 minutes

Objective: Use Active Directory Users and Computers to change group types.

Description: The IT manager at Dover Leasing is worried that new administrators may accidentally create distribution groups where security groups are necessary, and vice versa. He has asked you to test the ability to change the type of groups using the Active Directory Users and Computers tool to be sure that changes to a group's type can be made when necessary. In this activity you first create a new distribution global group and then change the type of the group to security.

1. In Active Directory Users and Computers, right-click on the **Users** container, select **New**, and click **Group**.

2. In the New Object – Group dialog box, type **Testing Type** in the Group name text box.

3. Under Group scope, ensure that **Global** is selected.

4. Under Group type, click the **Distribution** radio button, and then click **OK** to create the group.

5. Verify that the Testing Type group appears as a Distribution Group in the Type column of the Users container, as shown in Figure 3-7.

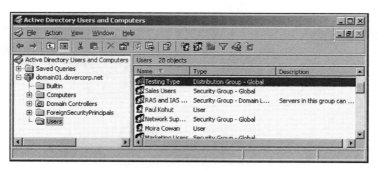

Figure 3-7   Viewing group types in Active Directory Users and Computers

6. Right-click on the **Testing Type** group and click **Properties**. Notice that the group is currently listed as a Distribution group in the Group type section of the General tab.

7. Click the **Security** radio button, as shown in Figure 3-8. Click **OK** to change the type of the Testing Type group from distribution to security, and to exit the properties of the group.

Figure 3-8   Changing a group's type from distribution to security

8. Verify that the Testing Type group now appears as a Security Group in the Type column of the Users container. Leave Active Directory Users and Computers open.

CONVERTING GROUP SCOPES

In much the same way that the type of a group can be changed after it has been created, so can the scope of a group. For example, if an administrator accidentally creates a global group instead of a universal group, the scope of the group can be changed from one to the other, but certain restrictions apply. First and foremost, the functional level of a domain must be configured to at least Windows 2000 native before the scope of a group can be changed. The Windows 2000 mixed domain functional level does not support changing the scope of a group. Additionally, an administrator must consider the membership of a group when attempting to change its scope. The list below outlines the various group scope changes supported in Windows Server 2003 Active Directory, along with restrictions based on group membership:

- Global to universal—This change is supported as long as the global group is not a member of any other global groups. If it were, the result would be a universal group being a member of a global group, which is not supported.

- Domain local to universal—This change is supported as long as the domain local group does not have any other domain local groups as members. If it did, the result would be a domain local group being a member of a universal group, which is not supported.

- Universal to global—This change is supported as long as the universal group does not have any other universal groups as a member. If it did, the result would be a universal group being a member of a global group, which is not supported.

- Universal to domain local—This change is always supported without restrictions.

In Activity 3-5 you attempt to change the scopes of various groups using Active Directory Users and Computers.

ACTIVITY

Activity 3-5: Converting Group Scopes

Time Required: 5 minutes

Objective: Use Active Directory Users and Computers to change group scopes.

Description: The IT manager at Dover Leasing is worried that new administrators may accidentally create groups of the wrong scope when creating new group accounts. He has asked you to test the ability to change the scope of groups using the Active Directory Users and Computers tool to be sure that changes to a group's scope can be made when necessary. In this activity you attempt to change the scope of different groups based on what you have learned about the ability to change group scope relative to the group's existing membership.

1. In Active Directory Users and Computers, right-click on the **Users** container, select **New**, and click **Group**.

2. In the New Object – Group dialog box, type **Testing Scope** in the Group name text box.

3. Under Group scope, ensure that **Global** is selected.

4. Under Group type, ensure that the **Security** radio button is selected, and then click **OK** to create the group.

5. Right-click on the **Testing Scope** group, and click **Properties**.

6. Click the **Members** tab, and then click the **Add** button.

7. In the Select Users, Contacts, Computers, or Groups window, type **Marketing Users** in the Enter the object names to select text box. Click **OK**. This will add the Marketing Users global group to the Testing Scope global group. Click **OK** to close the properties of the Testing Scope group.

8. Right-click on the **Testing Scope** group and click **Properties**.

9. On the General tab, notice that the Group scope section allows you to change the group to the Universal scope. This is because the Testing Scope global group is not a member of any other global groups. Do not make any changes, and click **OK**.

10. Right-click on the **Marketing Users** group, and click **Properties**.

11. On the General tab, notice that the Group scope section allows you to change the group scope to Universal. However, if you select the Universal radio button and click OK, you will receive an error message stating that a global group cannot have a universal group as a member. Click **OK** to close the properties of the Marketing Users group.

12. Right-click on the **Testing Scope** group and click **Properties**.

13. On the General tab, click the **Universal** radio button, and then click **OK**. This will change the scope of the Testing Scope group from global to universal.

14. Close Active Directory Users and Computers.

Command Line Utilities

While Active Directory Users and Computers is the primary tool used to create and manage domain group accounts, Windows Server 2003 also includes a variety of utilities that allow you to create and manage user accounts from the command line. These utilities are aimed at administrators with a preference for working from the command line, or those looking to automate the creation or management of group accounts in a more flexible manner. The command-line utilities to be looked at in the following sections include:

- DSADD—Adds objects such as groups
- DSMOD—Modifies object attributes and settings
- DSQUERY—Queries for objects
- DSMOVE—Moves objects to different locations within a domain
- DSRM—Deletes objects from the directory

DSADD

As you learned in Chapter 3, DSADD is one of the new command-line utilities introduced in Windows Server 2003 to allow various object types to be added to the directory. In much the same way that this utility can be used to add new user accounts to the directory, it can similarly be used to create new group accounts.

The basic syntax for creating a user account with DSADD is DSADD GROUP, followed by a variety of different switches that allow you to configure everything from the members of a scope to its scope and type. The basic syntax for adding a group with the DSADD GROUP tool consists of only a single piece of information, specifically the distinguished name of the group account to be created.

For example, to create a new security global group account named Database Users in the Users container of the domain01.dovercorp.net domain, the correct command syntax would be:

```
dsadd group "cn=Database Users,cn=users,dc=domain01,dc=dovercorp,
dc=net" -secgrp yes -scope g
```

If the DSADD GROUP command completes successfully, a message stating "dsadd succeeded" is displayed, as shown in Figure 3-9.

Figure 3-9   The DSADD GROUP command

The DSADD GROUP command supports a wide variety of switches used to configure different group account attributes. The list below provides examples of the more common attributes that might be configured with the DSADD GROUP command.

- –secgrp:
- –scope:
- –memberof:
- –members:

The following command is an example of creating a new domain local security group account named Archive Resources in the Users container of the domain01.dovercorp.net domain, including values for the switches just explored. Note that the entire command is a single line:

```
dsadd group "cn=Archive
Resources,cn=users,dc=domain01,dc=dovercorp,dc=net"
-secgrp yes -scope l -memberof "cn=Marketing
Resources,cn=users,dc=domain01,dc=dovercorp,dc=net"
-members "cn=Marketing Users,cn=users,dc=domain01,
dc=dovercorp,dc=net"
```

In this example, a new domain local security group named Archive Resources is created. This group has been made a member of the Marketing Resources domain local group, and the Marketing Users global group has been added to it as a member.

For a complete list of the various switches and options available with the DSADD GROUP command, see the DSADD topic in Windows Server 2003 Help and Support or type DSADD GROUP /? at the command line.

In Activity 3-6 you use the DSADD GROUP command to create two new groups from the command line.

Activity 3-6: Creating Groups Using DSADD

Time Required: 10 minutes

Objective: Use the DSADD GROUP command to add groups of different types and scopes.

Description: The IT manager at Dover Leasing has asked you to explore different processes for creating group accounts from the command line. Ultimately, the goal is to be able to create group accounts via a telnet session with remote servers when necessary. In this activity you use the DSADD GROUP command to create two new group accounts from the command line.

1. Click **Start**, and then click **Run**.

2. In the Open text box, type **cmd.exe**, and click **OK**.

3. At the command prompt window, type **cd ..** and press **Enter**. Type **cd ..** again and press **Enter**. This will help to reduce the on-screen clutter associated with the command prompt path.

4. Type **cls** and press **Enter** to clear the screen.

5. At the command line, type the following, all in one line: **dsadd group "cn=Database Users,cn=users,dc=domainXX,dc=dovercorp,dc=net" –secgrp yes –scope g**, where *XX* is your student number. Press **Enter**. If the dsadd succeeded message appears, then the new user account has been created successfully. If you receive an error message, type the command again being careful to avoid errors.

6. Minimize the Command Prompt window.

7. Click **Start**, select **Administrative Tools**, and then click **Active Directory Users and Computers**.

8. Click on the **Users** container to view its contents. Notice that the Database Users group now appears.

9. Minimize Active Directory Users and Computers, and maximize the Command Prompt window.

10. At the command line, type the following, all in one line: **dsadd group "cn=Archive Resources,cn=users,dc=domainXX,dc=dovercorp,dc=net" –secgrp yes –scope l –memberof "cn=Marketing Resources,cn=users, dc=domainXX,dc=dovercorp,dc=net" –members "cn=Marketing Users,cn=users,dc=domainXX,dc=dovercorp,dc=net"**, where *XX* is your student number. Press **Enter**. If the dsadd succeeded message appears, then the new user account has been created successfully. If you receive an error message, type the command again being careful to avoid errors.

11. Close the Command Prompt window, and then maximize the Active Directory Users and Computers window.

12. Right-click on the **Users** container, and then click **Refresh**. Notice that the Archive Resources group now appears in the Users container.

13. Right-click on the **Archive Resources** group and click **Properties**.

14. On the General tab, confirm that the group is of domain local scope and the security type.

15. Click the **Members** tab. Confirm that the Marketing Users group is a member of this group.

16. Click on the **Member Of** tab. Confirm that this group is a member of the Marketing Resources group.

17. Click **Cancel**, and then close Active Directory Users and Computers.

DSMOD

DSMOD is another new utility introduced in Windows Server 2003 that allows various object types to be modified from the command line. In the same way that the DSMOD USER command allows the properties of a user account to be changed, the DSMOD GROUP command allows the properties of a group account to be modified.

The basic syntax for modifying a group account with DSMOD is DSMOD GROUP, followed by a variety of different switches that allow you to modify everything from the type or scope of a group to the group membership. Since DSMOD GROUP is used to modify an existing group account, the command requires that you specify the distinguished name of the object to be modified, along with at least one switch (which would specify a particular modification).

For example, to add the description "Domain01 Marketing Users Global Group" to an existing group account named Marketing Users in the Users container of the domain01. dovercorp.net domain, the correct command syntax would be:

```
dsmod group "cn=Marketing Users,cn=users,dc=domain01,dc=dovercorp,
dc=net" -desc "Domain01 Marketing Users Global Group"
```

If the DSMOD GROUP command completes successfully, a message stating "dsmod succeeded" will be displayed, similar to Figure 3-10.

```
C:\>dsmod group "cn=Marketing Users,cn=users,dc=domain01,dc=dovercorp,dc=net" -d
esc "Domain01 Marketing Users Global Group"
dsmod succeeded:cn=Marketing Users,cn=users,dc=domain01,dc=dovercorp,dc=net

C:\>_
```

Figure 3-10   The DSMOD GROUP command

In a similar manner, the DSMOD GROUP command can also be used to add or remove users from a particular group. For example, to remove the Archive Resources group from the Marketing Resources group, and then subsequently add the Universal Marketing group to Marketing Resources in the domain01.dovercorp.net domain, the correct command syntax would be:

```
dsmod group "cn=Marketing Resources,cn=users,dc=domain01,
dc=dovercorp,dc=net" -rmmbr "cn=Archive Resources,cn=users,
dc=domain01,dc=dovercorp,dc=net" -addmbr "cn=Universal
Marketing,cn=users,dc=domain01,dc=dovercorp,dc=net"
```

> For a complete list of the various switches and options available with the DSMOD GROUP command, see the DSMOD topic in Windows Server 2003 Help and Support or type DSMOD GROUP /? at the command line.

In Activity 3-7 you change the properties of two existing group accounts from the command line using the DSMOD GROUP command.

Activity 3-7: Modifying Groups Using DSMOD

Time Required: 10 minutes

Objective: Use the DSMOD GROUP command to modify group accounts.

Description: The IT manager at Dover Leasing has asked you to explore different processes for modifying group accounts from the command line. Ultimately, the goal is to be able to modify group accounts via a telnet session with remote servers when necessary. In this activity you use the DSMOD GROUP command to modify two existing group accounts from the command line.

1. Click **Start**, and then click **Run**.

2. In the Open text box, type **cmd.exe**, and click **OK**.

3. At the command prompt window, type **cd ..** and press **Enter**. Type **cd ..** again and press **Enter**.

4. Type **cls** and press **Enter** to clear the screen.

5. At the command line, type the following, all in one line: **dsmod group "cn=Marketing Users,cn=users,dc=domainXX,dc=dovercorp,dc=net" –desc "DomainXX Marketing Users Global Group"**,where *XX* is your assigned student number. Press **Enter**. If the dsmod succeeded message appears, then the modification has completed successfully. If you receive an error message, type the command again being careful to avoid errors.

6. Minimize the Command Prompt window.

7. Click **Start**, select **Administrative Tools**, and then click **Active Directory Users and Computers**.

8. Click the **Users** container if necessary to view its contents. Right-click on the **Marketing Users** group and click **Properties**.

9. On the General tab, confirm that the words Domain*XX* Marketing Users Global Group now appear in the Description text box on the General tab. Click **Cancel**.

10. Minimize Active Directory Users and Computers, and maximize the Command Prompt.

11. At the command line, type the following, all in one line: **dsmod group "cn=Marketing Resources,cn=users,dc=domainXX,dc=dovercorp, dc=net" –rmmbr "cn=Archive Resources,cn=users, dc=domainXX,dc=dovercorp, dc=net" –addmbr "cn=Universal Marketing,cn=users,dc=domainXX, dc=dovercorp,dc=net"**, where *XX* is your assigned student number. Press **Enter**. If the dsmod succeeded message appears, then the modification has completed successfully. If you receive an error message, type the command again being careful to avoid errors.

12. Close the Command Prompt window, and then maximize the Active Directory Users and Computers window.

13. Right-click on the **Marketing Resources** group in the Users container and click **Properties**.

14. Click on the **Members** tab to confirm that the Archive Resources group is no longer a member of the group, and that the Universal Marketing group is a member. Click **Cancel**.

15. Close Active Directory Users and Computers.

DSQUERY

As you learned in Chapter 3, DSQUERY is another new utility introduced in Windows Server 2003 that allows various object types to be queried from the command line. In the same way that the DSQUERY USER command is used to query for and return information about user accounts, the DSQUERY GROUP command is used to query for and

return information about groups. Recall that the DSQUERY command also supports the wildcard character (*), effectively allowing it to query for any type of directory object.

At the most basic level, DSQUERY allows you to query the directory for a particular type of object, and return a value. For example, to view all of the group objects in the Builtin container of the domain01.dovercorp.net domain, the correct command syntax would be:

```
dsquery group "cn=builtin,dc=domain01,dc=dovercorp,dc=net"
```

This command would return a list of the distinguished names of all group accounts in the Builtin container, as illustrated in Figure 3-11.

```
Command Prompt                                                    _ □ ×
C:\>dsquery group "cn=builtin,dc=domain01,dc=dovercorp,dc=net"
"CN=Server Operators,CN=Builtin,DC=domain01,DC=dovercorp,DC=net"
"CN=Account Operators,CN=Builtin,DC=domain01,DC=dovercorp,DC=net"
"CN=Pre-Windows 2000 Compatible Access,CN=Builtin,DC=domain01,DC=ne
t"
"CN=Windows Authorization Access Group,CN=Builtin,DC=domain01,DC=dovercorp,DC=ne
t"
"CN=Terminal Server License Servers,CN=Builtin,DC=domain01,DC=dovercorp,DC=net"
"CN=Administrators,CN=Builtin,DC=domain01,DC=dovercorp,DC=net"
"CN=Users,CN=Builtin,DC=domain01,DC=dovercorp,DC=net"
"CN=Guests,CN=Builtin,DC=domain01,DC=dovercorp,DC=net"
"CN=Print Operators,CN=Builtin,DC=domain01,DC=dovercorp,DC=net"
"CN=Backup Operators,CN=Builtin,DC=domain01,DC=dovercorp,DC=net"
"CN=Replicator,CN=Builtin,DC=domain01,DC=dovercorp,DC=net"
"CN=Remote Desktop Users,CN=Builtin,DC=domain01,DC=dovercorp,DC=net"
"CN=Network Configuration Operators,CN=Builtin,DC=domain01,DC=dovercorp,DC=net"
"CN=Performance Monitor Users,CN=Builtin,DC=domain01,DC=dovercorp,DC=net"
"CN=Performance Log Users,CN=Builtin,DC=domain01,DC=dovercorp,DC=net"
C:\>
```

Figure 3-11   The DSQUERY GROUP command

In the same manner as with the DSQUERY USER command, the output of the DSQUERY GROUP command can be piped as input to other directory service command line tools such as DSADD, DSMOD, or DSRM.

NOTE   For a complete list of the various switches and options available with the DSQUERY GROUP command, see the DSQUERY topic in Windows Server 2003 Help and Support or type DSQUERY GROUP /? at the command line.

DSMOVE

The DSMOVE command allows various object types to be moved from the object's current location to a new location in the directory, or an object to be renamed without moving it to a new location. In the same manner that this tool can be used to move or rename user objects, it can also be used to move or rename groups.

For example, an administrator might want to move a group account from the Users container into an OU named Marketing. Assuming that the group to be moved is named Marketing Users and the domain is domain01.dovercorp.net, the correct command syntax to move the user to the new OU would be:

```
Dsmove   "cn=Marketing Users,cn=users,dc=domain01,dc=dovercorp,
dc=net" -newparent "ou=marketing,dc=domain01,dc=dovercorp,dc=net"
```

Along the same lines, if the Marketing Users group was not named according to the correct naming convention and needed to be renamed to Global Marketing Users, the administrator might chose to simply rename the Marketing Users group. Assuming that this account now exists in the Marketing OU, the correct syntax for this command would be:

```
dsmove "cn=Marketing Users,ou=marketing,dc=domain01,dc=dovercorp,
dc=net"-newname "Global Marketing Users"
```

Remember that the DSMOVE command can only be used to move objects within the same domain. To move objects between domains, use the MOVETREE command available when the Windows Server 2003 Support Tools are installed.

NOTE For a complete list of the various switches and options available with the DSMOVE command, see the DSMOVE topic in Windows Server 2003 Help and Support or type DSMOVE /? at the command line.

DSRM

In much the same way that you learned to delete user objects with the DSRM command in Chapter 2, this command can also be used to delete group accounts. For example, if your goal were to delete the Marketing Users global group in the Users container of the domain01.dovercorp.net domain, the correct command syntax would be:

```
dsrm "cn=Marketing Users,cn=users,dc=domain01,dc=dovercorp,dc=net"
```

As when deleting a user account, the DSRM command prompts you to confirm deletion of the specified objects. To delete the Marketing Users group without being prompted, the correct command syntax would be:

```
dsrm "cn=Marketing Users,cn=users,dc=domain01,dc=dovercorp,dc=net"
-noprompt
```

Remember to be very careful when issuing the DSRM command with the –noprompt switch, as this might cause you to accidentally delete required objects.

NOTE For a complete list of the various switches and options available with the DSRM command, see the DSRM topic in Windows Server 2003 Help and Support or type DSRM /? at the command line.

MANAGING SECURITY GROUPS

As you start to implement the use of security groups, a general strategy is to use the acronym A G U DL P. This refers to the following:

1. Create user Accounts (A), and organize them within Global groups (G). Often users are grouped in global groups based on departments in the organization.

2. Optional: Create Universal groups (U) and place global groups from any domain within the universal groups.

3. Create Domain Local groups (DL) that represent the resources in which you want to control access, and add the global or universal groups to the domain local groups.

4. Assign Permissions (P) to the domain local groups.

For example, Dover Leasing has a shared file called Reports. All users in all domains that work in the Marketing Department must have access to the Reports Share. Following the steps previously discussed, this is how you could organize access:

1. In each domain, create a global group called Marketing Users, and add any appropriate user account to the group.

2. Optional: Create a universal group called Dovercorp Marketing, and add all global groups created in Step 1, from all domains to the universal group.

3. Create a domain local group called Reports Share, and add the Dover Marketing universal group to the local group. (If you skipped Step 2, you can add the Marketing Users global group instead.)

4. Assign the Reports Share domain local group to the access control list of the actual share on the network, and specify the appropriate permissions.

If your domain is running in Windows 2000 native mode or the Windows Server 2003 functional level, you can use the option of nesting groups to simplify administrative tasks. For example, Dover Leasing may have three global groups called Help Desk, IT Managers, and Network Support. Together, these three groups of users may represent the Information Technology department of Dover Leasing. You could create the Information Technology global group and put the Help Desk, IT Managers, and Network Support groups into this one group, thus simplifying the assignment of permissions for resources to which all three groups should have access. You do not need to add individuals to the Information Technology group. When you are assigning permissions to resources, assign the permissions to domain local groups.

If you are working in a single domain, you can use global groups or universal groups interchangeably. Choose one of these options to group your users, and then add these groups to the local domain groups.

Determining Group Membership

One of the most important jobs of any Windows Server 2003 network administrator is to ensure that users are members of the correct groups. If not managed effectively, membership (or a lack thereof) in incorrect groups can lead to problems with user access to required resources, or worse still, the ability to access restricted resources.

The easiest method to determine the groups that a user is a member of is via the Member Of tab in the properties of their user account. As you learned earlier in this chapter, this tab lists all of the global, domain local, and universal groups in which a user's account is a member. Unfortunately, the Member Of tab only displays those groups in which a user has been directly added. For example, if a user account is made a member of a global group named Marketing Users, they appear as a member of this group. However, if the same user account is a member of the Marketing Users global group, and the Marketing Users global group is in turn a member of the Marketing Resources domain local group, the Member Of tab displays membership in the Marketing Users group only. This is not a design flaw—instead, the Member Of tab is designed to strictly list the groups in which the user account is directly a member. To dig deeper, an administrator could use the Member Of tab for the Marketing Users global group to gather additional information.

One additional tool that provides an exceptionally easy method of determining a user's group membership from the command line is DSGET. The DSGET command allows you to display the results of a query on-screen, in a manner similar to DSQUERY, but with different switches supported. For example, the DSGET GROUP command could be used to gather information about all the members of the Marketing Users group in the Users container of the domain01.dovercorp.net domain if the following command were issued:

```
dsget group "cn=Marketing Users,cn=users,dc=domain01,cn=dovercorp,
cn=net"-members
```

Similarly, the DSGET GROUP command could also be used to view all of the groups that the Marketing Users group is a member of:

```
dsget group "cn=Marketing Users,cn=users,dc=domain01,cn=dovercorp,
cn=net"-memberof
```

The DSGET USER command can also be used to determine the groups that a specific user is a member of. For example, to view all of the groups that the user Alan Finn in the Users container of the domain01.dovercorp.net domain is a member of, the following command would be issued:

```
dsget user "cn=Alan Finn,cn=users,dc=domain01,cn=dovercorp,cn=net"
-memberof
```

By default, the output of the DSGET command is displayed onscreen. In some situations, however, it might be better for the output of this command to be saved to a text file, perhaps to ultimately be imported to a spreadsheet or database application. This is easily accomplished by using a standard redirect at the command line. For example, issuing the command

below would output a listing of all members of the Marketing Users group to a text file named mktgusers.txt:

```
dsget group "cn=Marketing Users,cn=users,dc=domain01,cn=dovercorp,
cn=net"-members >> mktgusers.txt
```

NOTE For a complete list of the various switches and options available with the DSGET command, see the DSGET topic in Windows Server 2003 Help and Support or type DSGET /? at the command line.

BUILT-IN GROUPS

When Windows Server 2003 Active Directory is installed, a number of built-in local security groups with various pre-assigned rights are created, which you may want to use to allow users to perform certain network tasks. Whenever possible, you should use one of the built-in local groups to assign rights because this eases the implementation of delegation and security rights throughout the network. For example, rather than creating a special group with rights to back up and restore servers, you can use the built-in backup operators group.

The built-in groups created automatically when Active Directory is installed are stored in two different locations, namely the Builtin container and the Users container. The following sections outline the built-in groups found in each location.

The Builtin Container

The Builtin container contains a number of domain local group accounts that are allocated different user rights based on common administrative or network-related tasks. Table 3-2 outlines the name of each of the built-in domain local groups found in this container, as well as a description of the purpose or capabilities of members of the group.

Table 3-2 Domain local groups found in the Builtin container

Group Name	Description
Account Operators	Able to create, delete, and modify user accounts and groups within the domain; they cannot place themselves or anyone else in the administrators group
Administrators	Assigned complete unrestricted access to the domain
Backup Operators	Able to override security restrictions for the purpose of backing up or restoring files
Guests	Have no default permissions or rights (The guests group is a member of the special group named Everyone; this means that any access permissions to the Everyone group gives permission to the Guests group)
Incoming Forest Trust Builders	Able to create one-way incoming trusts to the forest; this group is only available in the forest root domain

Table 3-2   Domain local groups found in the Builtin container (continued)

Group Name	Description
Network Configuration Operators	Able to change TCP/IP settings on domain controllers within the domain
Performance Log Users	Able to remotely access servers to schedule logging of performance counters
Performance Monitor Users	Able to remotely access servers to monitor performance
Pre-Windows 2000 Compatible Access	This group is created to support applications that work with Windows NT 4.0, but may have problems with Windows Server 2003 security; has read access on all users and groups within the domain; used primarily for Windows NT RAS servers that require access to Active Directory
Print Operators	Have all print administration rights
Remote Desktop Users	Able to log on to domain controllers within the domain remotely
Replicator	Used by the File Replication Service
Server Operators	Able to share disk resources, back-up and restore files, and shut down or restart the server
Terminal Server License Servers	Contains computer accounts for all servers configured as Terminal Server License Servers
Users	Have no default permissions, except for permissions assigned by the administrator
Windows Authorization Access Group	Allows members to query user accounts for the group membership information of a user

NOTE Depending upon the services installed and configured on your server, some of the groups listed in Table 3-2 may not appear in the Builtin container.

The Users Container

The Users container contains a number of different domain local and global group accounts. Table 3-3 outlines the name of each of the domain local and global groups found in this container, as well as a description of the purpose or capabilities of members of the group. Note that some of the groups listed are only found in the root domain of an Active Directory forest rather than each individual domain.

Table 3-3   Domain local and global groups found in the Users container

Group Name	Group Scope	Description
Cert Publishers	Domain local	Able to publish certificates in Active Directory
DnsAdmins	Domain local	Able to administer DNS server settings and configuration

Table 3-3   Domain local and global groups found in the Users container (continued)

Group Name	Group Scope	Description
DnsUpdateProxy	Global	Able to perform DNS dynamic updates on behalf of other clients
Domain Admins	Global	Able to perform domain administration tasks
Domain Computers	Global	Contains all workstations and server computer accounts in the domain
Domain Controllers	Global	Contains all domain controller computer accounts in the domain
Domain Guests	Global	Guest accounts in the domain should be added to this group
Domain Users	Global	All domain user accounts are added to this group
Enterprise Admins	Global	Able to perform administrative tasks throughout an Active Directory forest; this group only exists in the forest root domain
Group Policy Creator Owners	Global	Able to modify group policy objects and settings in the domain
RAS and IAS Servers	Global	Servers in this group can access the remote access properties of a user account
Schema Admins	Global	Able to perform administrative tasks related to the Active Directory schema; this group only exists in the forest root domain
WINS Users	Domain local	Allows read-only access to WINS server settings

CREATING AND MANAGING COMPUTER ACCOUNTS

In much the same way that users on a network require user accounts, computers running Windows NT 4.0, Windows 2000, Windows XP, and Windows Server 2003 require computer accounts to be members of an Active Directory domain. While computer accounts can be created in a domain during the operating system installation processes, they can also be added manually after the fact. While the primary tool used to create and manage computer accounts is the familiar Active Directory Users and Computers, computer accounts can also be created from the System applet in Control Panel from the workstation being added to the domain, as long as the user doing so has been granted appropriate privileges in Active Directory.

NOTE

Computers running Windows 95 and Windows 98 do not support advanced security features and, as such, are not assigned computer accounts in a domain.

In the same way that user and group accounts can be created and managed using the various directory service command-line tools looked at earlier in this chapter, so too can computer accounts. For example, the DSADD COMPUTER command can be used to create new computer accounts from the command line, while DSMOD COMPUTER can be used to

change the settings of existing computer accounts. For more information on creating and modifying computer accounts from the command line, see the appropriate command in Windows Server 2003 Help and Support.

In Activity 3-8 you use Active Directory Users and Computers to create a new computer account.

Activity 3-8: Creating and Managing Computer Accounts

Time Required: 10 minutes

Objective: Use Active Directory Users and Computers to create and manage computer accounts.

Description: The IT manager at Dover Leasing has asked you to document the process for creating new computer accounts in Active Directory Users and Computers. In this activity you create and configure the properties of a new computer account.

1. Click **Start**, select **Administrative Tools**, and click **Active Directory Users and Computers**.

2. Right-click the **Computers** container, select **New**, and then click **Computer**. The New Object – Computer window appears, as shown in Figure 3-12.

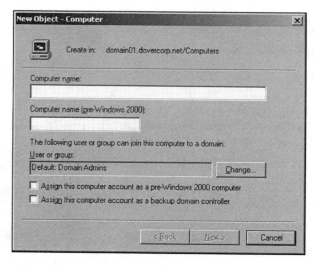

Figure 3-12   The New Object – Computer window

3. In the Computer name text box, type **WorkstationXX**, where *XX* is your assigned student number. Notice that the Computer name (pre-Windows 2000) text box is populated automatically. Click **Next**.

4. At the Managed screen, click **Next**. A managed computer is one associated with the Windows Server 2003 Remote Installation Services (RIS).

5. Click **Finish**. The new computer account will appear in the Computers container.

6. Right-click on **WorkstationXX** and click **Properties**.

7. Review the settings on the General tab, as shown in Figure 3-13. Click the **Operating System** tab.

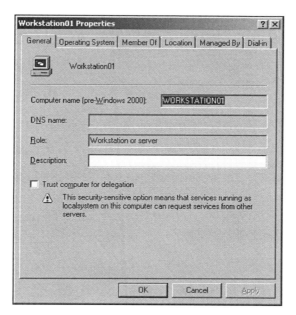

Figure 3-13   The properties of a computer account

8. Notice that no information is available on the Operating System tab. This information would be generated automatically if a computer named WorkstationXX actually existed on the network. Click the **Member Of** tab.

9. Notice that WorkstationXX is a member of the Domain Computers group by default. Click the **Location** tab.

10. In the Location text box, type **Miami**. Click the **Managed By** tab.

11. In a manner similar to a group account, the Managed By tab can be used to configure information about the user responsible for managing the computer. Click the **Dial-in** tab.

12. Review the settings available on the Dial-in tab, and click **OK**.

13. Close Active Directory Users and Computers.

3

Resetting Computer Accounts

Computers that are members of a domain use a secure communication channel known as a secure channel to communicate with a domain controller. A password is associated with this secure channel that is changed every 30 days, and is synchronized automatically with the domain controller and the workstation. In rare cases, such as if a particular computer has not been connected to the network (or turned off) for longer than 30 days or the channel is somehow disrupted, a user logging on to that workstation may not be able to authenticate due to synchronization issues. The error messages associated with this problem are typically listed in Event Viewer as Event IDs 3210 and 5722.

When synchronization problems of this manner occur, an administrator must reset the computer account associated with the workstation. The two primary ways to accomplish this include:

- Using Active Directory Users and Computers
- Using the Netdom.exe command from the Windows Support Tools

To reset a computer account using Active Directory Users and Computers, simply right-click on the computer account object and choose the Reset Account option.

To reset a computer account using Netdom.exe, the following command should be issued from the command line:

```
Netdom reset computername /domain: domainname
```

In this example, computername is the name of the workstation to be reset, and domainname is the domain in which the computer account resides.

Chapter Summary

- The primary purpose of groups in a network environment is to ease the administrative burden associated with assigning rights and permissions to individual user accounts.

- Windows Server 2003 supports two group types, known as security groups and distribution groups. Security groups have an associated SID and can be assigned rights and permissions. Distribution groups are primarily used as e-mail entities and do not include an SID.

- Windows Server 2003 supports three different group scopes, known as global, domain local, and universal. The scope of a group impacts how it can be used in an Active Directory environment. The configured functional level of a domain also impacts the scopes of groups that can be created and associated membership rules.

- The primary tool used to create and manage group accounts in a Windows Server 2003 Active Directory environment is Active Directory Users and Computers. The directory service command-line tools can also be used to manage group accounts, such as DSADD, DSMOD, DSQUERY, DSMOVE, and DSRM.

❑ The most scalable method of managing security groups to assign rights and permissions is A G U DL P. The method provides an administrator with maximum flexibility and a minimal need to assign rights and permissions more often than necessary.

❑ The primary tools used to gather group membership information are the Member Of and Members tabs in the properties of objects, and the DSGET command-line utility.

❑ Windows Server 2003 Active Directory includes a number of built-in global and domain local groups in both the Users and Builtin containers. Many of these groups are pre-assigned rights and permissions to perform common administration-related functions.

❑ Workstations running Windows NT 4.0, Windows 2000, Windows XP, and Windows Server 2003 require computer accounts in Active Directory. Computer accounts are typically created and managed using Active Directory Users and Computers, but can also be created and managed from the command line using tools like DSADD and DSMOD.

KEY TERMS

distribution group — A group that is only used for an e-mail distribution list.

domain functional level — The level at which a Windows Server 2003 domain is configured, such as Windows 2000 mixed mode, Windows 2000 native mode, or Windows Server 2003.

domain local group — A group that can only be assigned permissions to a resource available in the domain in which it is created. However, group membership can come from any domain within the forest. Created on domain controllers within the domain.

global group — A group that is mainly used for organizing other objects into administrative units. A global group can be assigned permissions to any resource in any domain within the forest. The main limitation of a global group is that it can only contain members of the same domain in which it is created.

group — A container object that is used to organize a collection of users, computers, contacts, or other groups into a single object reference.

security group — A group that can be used to define permissions on a resource object.

universal group — A group that can be assigned permissions to any resource in any domain within the forest. Universal groups can consist of any user or group object except for local groups.

Windows 2000 mixed — The default domain functional level for a Windows Server 2003 Active Directory domain. Supports Windows NT Server 4.0, Windows 2000 Server, and Windows Server 2003 domain controllers.

Windows 2000 native — A domain functional level that supports both Windows 2000 Server and Windows Server 2003 domain controllers.

Windows Server 2003 — A domain functional level that supports Windows Server 2003 domain controllers only.

REVIEW QUESTIONS

1. Which of the following are considered group types? (Choose all that apply.)
   a. Global
   b. Domain local
   c. Security
   d. Distribution

2. Which of the following are considered group scopes? (Choose all that apply.)
   a. Global
   b. Universal
   c. Domain local
   d. Distribution

3. Which of the following objects can be added to a global group when a domain is configured to the Windows Server 2003 domain functional level?
   a. Users
   b. Global groups
   c. Domain local groups
   d. Universal groups

4. Which of the following objects can be added to a domain local group when a domain is configured to the Windows 2000 mixed domain functional level?
   a. Users
   b. Global groups
   c. Domain local groups
   d. Universal groups

5. Which of the following group types cannot be created when a domain is configured to the Windows 2000 mixed domain functional level?
   a. Global groups
   b. Domain local groups
   c. Universal groups
   d. None of the above

6. A Windows Server 2003 Active Directory domain is configured to the Windows 2000 mixed domain functional level by default.
   a. True
   b. False

7. When can a domain local group be converted to a universal group?

   a. Always

   b. Never

   c. When the domain local group does not contain any other domain local groups as members

   d. When the domain local group does not contain any global groups as members

8. When can a global group be converted to a universal group?

   a. Always

   b. Never

   c. When the global group does not contain any other global groups

   d. When the global group is not a member of any other global groups

9. When can a universal group be converted to a domain local group?

   a. Always

   b. Never

   c. When the universal group does not contain any other universal groups

   d. When the domain local group does not contain any other universal groups

10. Which of the following command-line utilities is used to convert a group's scope?

    a. DSMOD

    b. DSADD

    c. DSGET

    d. DSRM

11. Which of the following command-line utilities is used to obtain a listing of all group members?

    a. DSMOD

    b. DSGET

    c. DSADD

    d. DSRM

12. Which of the following command-line utilities is used to create new group objects?

    a. DSADD

    b. DSMOD

    c. DSGET

    d. DSMOVE

3

13. Which of the following built-in global groups are all user accounts added to automatically?

    a. Domain Guests

    b. Domain Users

    c. Domain Admins

    d. Schema Admins

14. Which of the following built-in global groups are all workstations and member servers added to automatically?

    a. Domain Computers

    b. Domain Controllers

    c. Domain Servers

    d. Domain PCs

15. Which of the following tools is used to reset a computer account?

    a. Active Directory Users and Computers

    b. NETSH

    c. NETDOM

    d. NETCONF

16. Which of the following group scopes contains global groups as a member in a domain configured to the Windows 2000 mixed functional level?

    a. Domain local groups

    b. Global groups

    c. Universal groups

17. What is indicated when a domain local group cannot be converted to a universal group?

    a. The functional level of the domain is set to Windows 2000 mixed

    b. The functional level of the domain is set to Windows 2000 native

    c. The functional level of the domain is set to Windows Server 2003

18. Which of the following built-in groups is only found in the forest root domain?

    a. Domain Admins

    b. Enterprise Admins

    c. Schema Admins

    d. Domain Guests

19. Which tab in the properties of a user account is used to view that user's group membership information?

    a. Member Of

    b. Members

      c. Policies

      d. Membership

20. Which tab in the properties of a group account is used to view the other groups that are members of this group?

      a. Member Of

      b. Members

      c. Policies

      d. Membership

CASE PROJECTS

Case Project 3-1

Using the information learned in this chapter, create three new security group accounts named Global Test, Domain Local Test, and Universal Test, using the scope designated in their names. For each group scope, attempt to add each of the other two groups to that group as members, and document whether each attempt is successful or not.

Case Project 3-2

The DSADD command provides an effective method for administrators to create new group accounts from the command line. Use the DSADD utility to create the four new groups accounts listed in the table below. All the group accounts should be created in the Users container in your DomainXX.Dovercorp.Net domain. Use the DSADD topic in Help and Support Center to determine the appropriate switches required to configure these accounts from the command line.

Group Name	Group Type	Group Scope	Group Description
Project Users	Security	Global	Project management users
Project Resources	Security	Domain Local	Project management resources
Universal IT Staff	Security	Universal	All Dover Leasing ITstaff
Marketing Distribution	Distribution	Universal	All Dover Leasing marketing staff

Case Project 3-3

The IT Manager at Dover Leasing has asked you to create documentation for the membership of all existing groups at Dover Leasing. Use the DSGET command to create a series of text files that list the membership of all existing groups in the Builtin and Users containers, naming the files according to the names of these groups.

4

MANAGING FILE ACCESS

After reading this chapter and completing the exercises, you will be able to:

Identify and understand the differences between the various file systems supported in Windows Server 2003

Create and manage shared folders

Understand and configure the shared folder permissions available in Windows Server 2003

Understand and configure the NTFS permissions available in Windows Server 2003

Determine the impact of combining shared folder and NTFS permissions

Convert partitions and volumes from FAT to NTFS

The main reason for implementing a network is to allow users to access shared resources. Examples of shared resources commonly found on a network include files, folders, and printers. While the ability to share resources is the primary goal of any network, these resources also need to be properly secured to ensure that they are made available to only those users who require access. Furthermore, the level of access that users need for a particular resource also needs to be considered, since it is likely to be different for different users or groups.

Resources such as files, folders, and printers are secured on a Windows Server 2003 network through the use of permissions. By configuring various permissions on a particular resource, an administrator can limit a certain group of users' ability to read files only, while granting another group complete control. The ability to configure resource permissions in a very granular fashion ultimately gives an administrator a high degree of control over resource access. However, these permissions must be managed carefully. An understanding of how permissions apply in a Windows Server 2003 environment is critical for all network administration staff.

Windows Server 2003 supports two types of permissions in order to secure file and folder resources: NTFS and shared folder. NTFS permissions can be applied to resources that are stored on partitions or volumes formatted with the NTFS file system. Shared folder permissions can be applied to any folder that has been shared to allow access from network workstations. The combination of NTFS and shared folder permissions has often been the basis of intensive troubleshooting tasks for administrators. It is important to understand how permissions are applied to ensure that clients obtain appropriate access to resources. To ensure an understanding of this concept, the integration of NTFS and shared folder permissions is discussed in this chapter, as is monitoring access to folders that are shared on the network.

WINDOWS SERVER 2003 FILE SYSTEMS

Like its predecessor Windows 2000, Windows Server 2003 supports three main file systems, namely File Allocation Table (FAT), FAT32, and NTFS. The file system choice for a particular partition or volume on a Windows Server 2003 system is usually a function of how the system will be used, whether multiple operating systems will be installed on the same system, and the security requirements for the system. For example, if Windows Server 2003 is installed on a system in a lab environment, it might be configured in a dual-boot configuration with another operating system such as Windows 98. Because Windows 98 only supports the FAT and FAT32 file systems, an administrator might not format any partitions or volumes using NTFS, because Windows 98 cannot access this file system locally.

On a production server, however, a dual-boot configuration is exceptionally rare. Because of the security features provided by NTFS, this file system is highly recommended for all partitions on volumes on a Windows Server 2003 system, with very few exceptions. The following sections look at the basic characteristics of the FAT, FAT32, and NTFS file systems.

FAT

FAT is a file system used by MS-DOS and supported by all versions of Windows created since. Although traditionally limited to partitions up to 2 GB in size, the version of FAT included with Windows Server 2003 supports partitions up to 4 GB. The two biggest limitations of the FAT file system are the relatively small supported partition sizes, and the fact that FAT provides no file system security features, such as those available with NTFS. Comparatively speaking, disk space usage on a FAT partition is also poor when compared to both FAT32 and NTFS. For these reasons, most administrators shy away from formatting partitions using the FAT file system on Windows Server 2003 systems.

FAT32

A derivative of the FAT file system, **FAT32** was originally introduced in Windows 95 OSR2. The main difference between FAT32 and the FAT file systems is that FAT32

supports much larger partition sizes, up to 2 terabytes (TB). However, much like the FAT file system, FAT32 does not provide any of the advanced security features of NTFS, namely the ability to configure permissions on file and folder resources.

NTFS

Microsoft introduced a new file system known as **NTFS** beginning with the Windows NT operating system. The current version of NTFS is version 5, which is supported by systems running Windows NT 4.0 (SP5 or later), Windows 2000, Windows XP, and Windows Server 2003. The NTFS file system theoretically supports much larger partition sizes than both FAT and FAT32, since it is capable of addressing up to 16 Exabytes (EB) of disk space. In practice, however, the maximum NTFS partition sizes range from 2 TB up to approximately 16 TB, depending on the disk type and cluster size used.

NTFS is the preferred file system for all partitions and volumes on a Windows Server 2003 system. Some of the advantages of NTFS over both FAT and FAT32 include:

- Greater scalability for large disks, and better performance than FAT-based systems on larger partitions

- Support for Active Directory on systems configured as domain controllers; all domain controllers must have at least one NTFS partition or volume available to hold the Sysvol folder

- The ability to configure security permissions on individual files and folders stored on an NTFS partition or volume

- Built-in support for both compression and encryption

- The ability to configure disk space quotas for individual users

- Support for Remote Storage, the ability to extend disk space using removable media

- Recovery logging of disk activities, allowing information relating to NTFS partitions or volumes to be recovered quickly in the event of system problems

For the purpose of this chapter, the most important consideration when choosing a file system is its ability to support security permissions. In the following sections you learn more about the types of security permissions available on Windows Server 2003 systems.

CREATING AND MANAGING SHARED FOLDERS

Shared folders must be configured with the proper access-control permissions to permit general user access to data on a network. A **shared folder** is a data resource that has been made available over the network to authorized network clients. These clients can then view or modify the contents of the folder, depending upon the level of permissions granted to either the user or group of which the user is a member.

Users are required to have appropriate rights to create shared folders. A member of the Administrators or Server Operators groups has the right to create shared folders within a domain. Members of the Power Users group can also configure shared folders on Windows Server 2003 systems not configured as domain controllers. There are several ways to create shared folders; two of the more popular methods include using the Windows Explorer interface and the Computer Management console. Beyond simply allowing you to create new shared folders, the Computer Management console also allows shared folders to be monitored, as explored later in this section.

Using Windows Explorer

Windows Explorer is the standard method used to create and share folders for all versions of Windows since Windows 95. It can be used to create, maintain, and share folders on any drive connected to the computer. There are many ways to open Windows Explorer. For example, you can click the Windows Explorer icon on the Accessories menu, or you can right-click almost any drive-related object and click the Explore command on the shortcut menu. Figure 4-1 illustrates the Windows Explorer window.

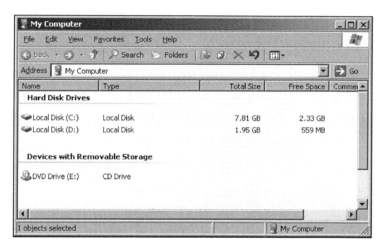

Figure 4-1   The Windows Explorer window

In Activity 4-1 you create a new folder and then share it using Windows Explorer.

Folders are shared in Windows Server 2003 by accessing the Sharing tab of a folder's properties, as illustrated in Figure 4-2.

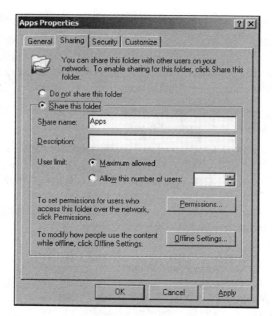

Figure 4-2   The Sharing tab in the properties of a folder

Activity 4-1: Creating a Shared Folder Using Windows Explorer

Time Required: 5 minutes

Objective: Create a shared folder using Windows Explorer.

Description: The IT manager at Dover Leasing has asked you to create a shared folder on a new Windows Server 2003 system that will ultimately be used to store network-accessible applications for users in the Marketing Department. In this activity, you create a new folder called Apps and then share it over the network using Windows Explorer.

1. Log on with your **AdminXX** account, where *XX* is your assigned student number. Click **Start**, select **All Programs**, select **Accessories**, and then click **Windows Explorer**.

2. Click the **plus sign (+)** next to My Computer to expand it, then click drive **D:**. Click **File** on the menu bar, select **New**, and then click **Folder**. Name the new folder **Apps**.

3. Right-click the **Apps** folder and then click **Sharing and Security**.

4. On the Sharing tab, click the **Share this folder** radio button, as shown in Figure 4-2.

5. In the Share name text box, type **Applications**.

6. In the Description text box, type **Applications for Marketing Users**.

7. Click **OK** to share the folder and close the Apps Properties dialog box. Close the Windows Explorer window.

8. To verify that the new shared folder called Applications is available over the network, open a command prompt, and at the command line type **net view \\serverXX**, where *XX* is your assigned student number. Press **Enter**.

9. All of the shared folders available on your server should be visible, including the new Applications folder just created. Close the command prompt window.

10. Click **Start**, and then click **Run**. In the Open text box, type **explorer.exe** and click **OK**. Click the **plus sign (+)** next to My Network Places to expand it. Click the **plus sign (+)** next to Entire Network to expand it. Click the **plus sign (+)** next to Microsoft Windows Network to expand it. Click the **plus sign (+)** next to DomainXX (where *XX* is your assigned student number) to expand it. Click on **ServerXX** to view the shared resources available on your server.

11. Close all open windows.

By default, the shared name of a folder is the same as the actual folder name, but this is not a requirement. It is important to provide a meaningful share name because this is how your users find the share. Be careful of any share names that are longer than eight characters in cases where you have any legacy clients such as Windows 3.1 or DOS that cannot handle long file names.

Windows Explorer indicates a shared folder by placing a hand icon under the folder, as shown in Figure 4-3.

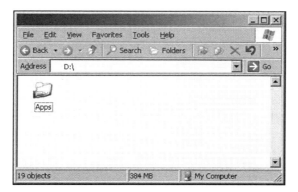

Figure 4-3   Identifying a shared folder by its icon in Windows Explorer

There may be times when you would like to create a shared folder but not have it listed in My Network Places or Network Neighborhood. To hide a shared folder, place a dollar sign ($) after its name. For example, if you create a shared folder called "Salary," you can hide it by giving it the share name "Salary$." To map or connect to a hidden share, a user needs to manually type the share name, including the dollar sign. Windows Server 2003 creates a

number of hidden **administrative shares** by default during the installation process. For example, the Admin$ share allows an administrator to easily connect to the Windows folder on a server or workstation across the network, whereas shares like C$ provide an administrator with easy access to the root of the C drive on a computer. Figure 4-4 illustrates the shared folder name associated with the Windows folder on a Windows Server 2003 system.

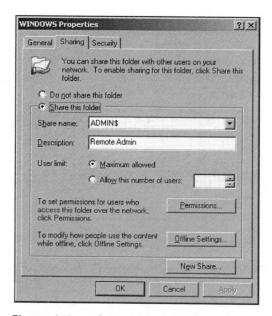

Figure 4-4   The Windows folder is shared as Admin$ by default

Using Computer Management

Another popular method for creating and managing shared folders in Windows Server 2003 is through the use of the **Computer Management console**. Computer Management is a predefined Microsoft Management Console (MMC) application that allows you to perform a variety of administrative tasks, such as sharing and monitoring folders for both local and remote computers.

Shared folders are created in the Shared Folders section of Computer Management using the Share a Folder Wizard. Beyond simply allowing you to create new shared folders, this wizard also allows you to configure shared folder permissions. Three of the choices are preconfigured, whereas the fourth allows custom permissions to be specified. Permission options found in the wizard include:

- All users have read-only access—Grants the Read permission to the Everyone group

- Administrators have full access; other users have read-only access—Grants Full Control permission to the local Administrators group and Read permission to the Everyone group

- Administrators have full access; other users have read and write access—Grants Full Control permission to the local Administrators group and both Read and Change permissions access to the Everyone group

- Use custom share and folder permissions—Allows both share and NTFS permissions to be defined manually

TIP

If you want to stop sharing a folder, the easiest way to do this is via the Shares node in the Computer Management console. The list of shares appears in the details pane of the console. To stop sharing a particular folder, you simply right-click the share that is to be discontinued, and click Stop Sharing on the shortcut menu.

ACTIVITY

Activity 4-2: Creating and Viewing Shared Folders Using Computer Management

Time Required: 10 minutes

Objective: Create and view shared folders using Computer Management.

Description: To streamline the training process for new help desk staff at Dover Leasing, the IT manager has asked you to document the process for using the Computer Management tool to create and view shared folders on network servers. In this activity, you use the Computer Management tool to both view the existing visible and hidden shares, as well as create a new shared folder.

1. Click **Start**, right-click **My Computer**, and click **Manage**. The Computer Management tool opens, as illustrated in Figure 4-5. If necessary, click the **plus sign (+)** next to System Tools to expand it.

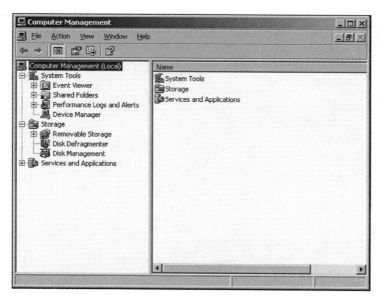

Figure 4-5   The Computer Management console

2. Click the **+ (plus symbol)** next to the Shared Folders node to expand it. The Shares, Sessions, and Open Files nodes appear.

3. Click the **Shares** folder to view its contents, as illustrated in Figure 4-6. Notice that the list includes folders that have been manually created (such as Applications), administrative shares (such as C$), and shared folders used by operating system communication processes (such as IPC$). The Shares node also provides the complete file system path to the shared folder.

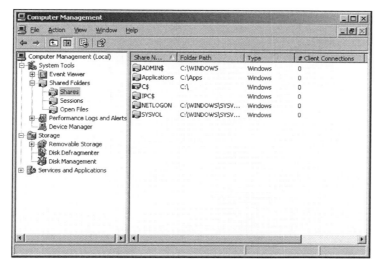

Figure 4-6   Contents of the Shares node

4. Right-click the **Shares** folder and click **New Share**. The Share a Folder Wizard appears. At the welcome screen, click **Next**.

5. At the Folder Path screen, type **D:\mktgdocs** in the Folder path text box, as illustrated in Figure 4-7. Click **Next**.

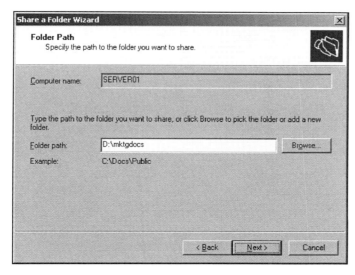

Figure 4-7   Configuring the path for a shared folder

6. When prompted with the dialog box specifying that the folder doesn't exist and asking whether you want to create it, click **Yes**.

7. At the Name, Description, and Settings screen, type **Marketingdocs** in the Share name text box and **All Marketing Documentation** in the Description text box. Click **Next**.

8. At the Permissions screen, select the **Administrators have full access; other users have read-only access** radio button, as shown in Figure 4-8. Click **Finish**.

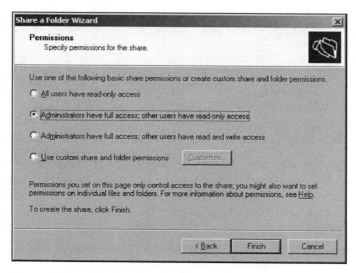

Figure 4-8 Configuring permissions using the Share a Folder Wizard

9. At the Sharing was Successful screen, review the Summary information and then click **Close**.

10. Verify that the new Marketingdocs shared folder is visible in the details pane of the Shares node in Computer Management.

11. To verify that the Marketingdocs folder is accessible over the network, open the Run command and type **\\serverXX\marketingdocs** in the Open text box (where *XX* is your assigned student number) and click **OK**. The Marketingdocs folder should open in a new window.

12. Close all open windows.

TIP

A third method sometimes used to share folders on a Windows Server 2003 system is the NET SHARE command. This command can be used to share an existing folder from the command line. For example, to share the folder C:\testfolder with a share name of test, the correct syntax for the command would be net share test="C:\testfolder".

Monitoring Access to Shared Folders

To assist in maintaining network security and statistics, you may need to periodically monitor shared folder and open-file access. Keeping track of the number of users connected to a specific network share helps you plan for future capacity requirements and fine-tuning of performance levels. In Windows Server 2003, you are able to see how many people are connected to a share, who they are, and what files they have open at any given time. You can also disconnect users from a specific share or send network messages alerting users of pending changes to the server's status, such as a planned reboot.

This Computer Management utility is the tool used to perform shared folder monitoring and management tasks on a Windows Server 2003 network. As with most MMC-based tools, the Computer Management console facilitates the management of both local and remote computers on the network.

The Sessions node in Computer Management provides information about the users currently connected to a server, as illustrated in Figure 4-9.

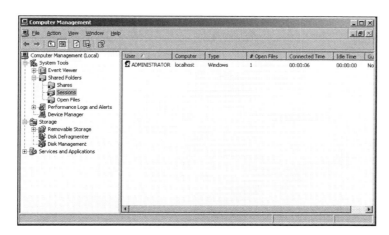

Figure 4-9   The Sessions node under Shared Folders

TIP

To manage a different computer, right-click Computer Management (Local), select Connect to another computer, and then provide the name of the server you wish to manage.

The Open Files node in Computer Management provides information about all of the files that users currently have open. This information can be used to troubleshoot file-access problems, such as when two users attempt to access the same file but one of the users is granted read-access only.

If you want to disconnect an open file connection or session, simply right-click the entry in the details pane, and click Close Open File or Close Session on the shortcut menu. This can assist you in situations where you have changed permissions on a folder or file and you want the new permissions to take effect immediately.

To help prevent data loss, it is always a best practice to send users a warning message before disconnecting sessions or shutting down a server. The Computer Management tool facilitates this by allowing you to send a console message to all users connected to the server. Illustrated in Figure 4-10, the Send Console Message feature allows you to supply a custom warning message that appears as a dialog box on the user's screen.

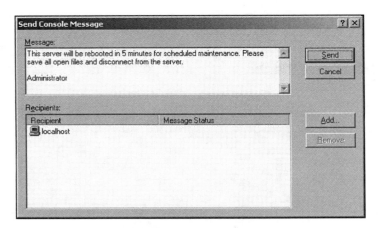

Figure 4-10   The Send Console Message window

MANAGING SHARED FOLDER PERMISSIONS

Each folder that is shared has a **discretionary access control list (DACL)** associated with it. A DACL is part of an object's security descriptor that contains a list of user or group references that have been allowed or denied permissions to the resource. Each user or group name listed in the DACL is referred to as an **access control entry (ACE)**. To access the DACL, click the Permissions button on the Sharing tab of a folder's properties. You can also access it by clicking the Custom button when using the Share a Folder Wizard. Figure 4-8 illustrates the DACL for a shared folder called Apps.

It is important to remember that share permissions only apply to users that connect to a shared folder over the network; they do not apply to a user logged on to the local machine where the shared folder is defined. Windows Server 2003 supports three different share permissions, as explained in Table 4-1.

Table 4-1   Shared folder permissions in Windows Server 2003

Shared Folder Permission	Capabilities
Read	Allows the abilities to browse the file and folder names (including subfolders), read the data in a file, and execute programs
Change	Allows the same abilities as the Read permission, as well as the abilities to add and delete files in the folder, and read and edit the contents of existing files
Full Control	Allows the same abilities as the Read and Change permissions, as well as the ability to change the permissions associated with the folder

Notice that Windows Server 2003 does not include a No Access share permission as found on Windows NT systems. Instead, to deny a user or group access to a shared folder, an administrator must explicitly deny the user that particular permission, as shown in Figure 4-11.

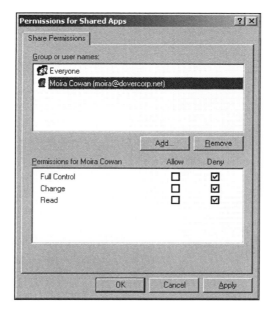

Figure 4-11   Denying permissions for a shared folder

As discussed previously, when a new share is created, the default permission on the shared folder allows the Everyone group read access. One of the first steps an administrator should perform after sharing a folder is to substitute the Everyone group for one that includes authenticated domain users. In many companies, the Users group is given the Full Control shared folder permission, while resources are made more secure through the use of NTFS permissions.

The Everyone group includes all users who have access to the network, regardless of whether they have been authenticated in the domain.

NOTE

When a share is created and a user is assigned permission to that share, the user also has the same level of permissions to all subfolders and files inside that share. In other words, the permissions configured on the shared folder are inherited by all of the objects that it contains. In Activity 4–3, you configure and test the effects of different shared folder permissions.

4

Activity 4-5: Implementing Shared Folder Permissions

ACTIVITY

Time Required: 15 minutes

Objective: Control access to resources using shared folder permissions.

Description: The IT manager at Dover Leasing is very concerned with ensuring that all network resources are properly secured so that only authorized network users can access shared folders and their contents. He has asked you to ensure that only members of the Domain Admins group have Full Control permission for the Marketingdocs shared folder, while members of the Marketing Users group are granted Change permission. All other users should not have access to the folder. In this activity, you configure permissions on the Marketingdocs shared folder to implement the requirements outlined by the IT manager.

1. Open My Computer and access the properties of the D:\mktgdocs folder.

2. Click the **Sharing** tab, and then click the **Permissions** button. The Permissions for Marketingdocs dialog box opens.

3. In the Group or user names list box, ensure that Everyone is selected and click the **Remove** button.

4. Click **Add**. The Select Users, Computers, or Groups dialog box opens.

5. In the Enter the object names to select text box, type **Domain Admins** and click **OK**. Domain Admins should be added to the Group or user names list of the Permissions dialog box, with the configured permission of Allow Read.

6. In the Allow column, check the **Full Control** check box.

7. Click **Add**. In the Enter the object names to select (examples) text box, type **Marketing Users** and click **OK**.

8. Ensure that the Marketing Users group is selected in the Group or user names list box. In the Allow column, check the **Change** box, and then click **OK**. Click **OK** in the mktgdocs Properties dialog box.

9. Close all open windows.

10. Click **Start**, and then click **Run**. In the Open text box, type **serverXX\marketingdocs** (where *XX* is your assigned student number) and click **OK**. The Marketingdocs window opens.

11. Right-click an area of white space in the window, select **New**, and then click **Folder**. Name the folder **July Documents** and then close the window.

12. Log off, and log on again using the **mcowan** account with the password **Password01**.

13. At the Run command, type **serverXX\marketingdocs** (where *XX* is your assigned student number) and click **OK**. The Marketingdocs window opens.

14. Attempt to create a new folder called **August Documents** in the Marketingdocs folder. This will be possible because all members of the Marketing Users group have the Change permission to the shared folder.

15. Close all open windows and log off.

16. Log on as user **mmanore** with the password **Password01**.

17. At the Run command, type **serverXX\marketingdocs** (where *XX* is your assigned student number) and click **OK**. The mmanore account is not able to access the folder because it lacks sufficient permissions.

18. Close all open windows and log off. Log on using your **AdminXX** account.

Shared folder permissions are cumulative. All the permissions assigned to a user, and any group of which the user is a member, are combined and the combination of all the permissions applies. For example, imagine if the user Moira Cowan is a member of both the Marketing and Managers groups. If the Marketing group is assigned the Read permission to a share and the Managers group is assigned Change, Moira's effective permission would be a combination of both, equivalent to Change. A single but important exception to this rule applies: when a user (or a group of which a user is a member) is denied a permission, the denied entry always overrides any permissions that are allowed. So, if the Marketing group were ultimately denied Full Control to the shared folder, Moira would not have access because this permission would override the fact that she is granted the Change permission as a member of the Marketing group.

NTFS PERMISSIONS

Files and folders located on NTFS partitions or volumes can be secured through the use of NTFS permissions. A Windows Server 2003 administrator needs to be familiar with how NTFS permissions are applied, the different standard and special NTFS permissions available, and how the **effective permissions** for a particular user or group can be determined. Each of these concepts is covered in more detail in the following sections.

NTFS Permission Concepts

It is important to understand the different NTFS file and directory permissions that are available, as well as how they are applied. Remember that NTFS permissions can only be applied to files and folders that exist on partitions formatted with the NTFS file system. As such, NTFS permissions cannot be applied to files or folders that reside on partitions formatted using the FAT or FAT32 file systems.

4

- NTFS permissions are configured via the Security tab, which is accessed by right-clicking any file or folder and clicking Properties.

- NTFS permissions are cumulative. If a user is a member of multiple groups that have different permissions, the final permission is the sum of all permissions.

- Permissions that are explicitly denied always override those that are allowed. For example, if the Mark Manore user account is explicitly denied Full Control on a folder through an individual or group permission assignment, this overrides any permissions that Mark may have been allowed via other group memberships.

- NTFS folder permissions are inherited by child folders and files, unless otherwise specified. Clearing the Allow inheritable permissions from the parent to propagate to this object and all child objects check box in the Advanced section of the Security property sheet can prevent the inheritance of NTFS permissions.

- NTFS permissions can be set at a file level, as well as at a folder level.

- When a new access control entry is added to an NTFS file or folder, the default permissions allow the user or group both the Read and the Read and Execute permissions for files, along with the List Folder Contents permission for folders.

- Windows Server 2003 has a set of standard NTFS permissions, as well as special permissions. Figure 4-12 illustrates the standard NTFS permissions available for a folder.

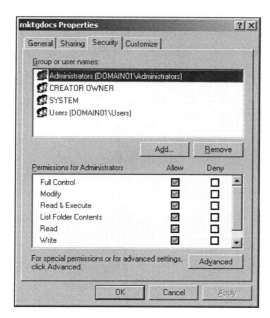

Figure 4-12   Standard NTFS permissions for a folder

Table 4–2 lists and explains the capabilities of **standard NTFS permissions**.

Table 4-2   Standard NTFS permissions in Windows Server 2003

NTFS Permission	Capabilities
Full Control	Allow the user to make any changes to the file or folder; details of the Full Control permission are listed in Table 4-3
Modify	Gives full permissions except the permission to delete subfolders and files, change permissions, and take ownership
Read & Execute	Gives permissions to traverse folders, list folders, read attributes and extended attributes, read permissions, and synchronize; these permissions are inherited by both files and folders
List Folder Contents	Same as Read and Execute permissions, except that the permissions are inherited only by folders and not by files; visible only on folders
Read	Same as Read and Execute, except without the permission to traverse folder; inherited by files and folders
Write	Gives permissions to create files and folders, write attributes and extended attributes, read permissions, and synchronize
Special Permissions	Used to designate that a user has been allowed or denied one or more of the more granular special permissions configured in the Advanced section of the security settings; Special permissions are detailed in Table 4-3

When assigning shared folder or NTFS permissions to users and groups, never grant them a higher level of access than they actually require. For example, if users only need to be able to read (but not change) files, the Read permission would be sufficient. Granting users too liberal a level of access can result in files being accidentally or purposely deleted, changed, and so forth.

In Activity 4-4 you implement standard NTFS permissions.

Activity 4-4: Implementing Standard NTFS Permissions

Time Required: 20 minutes

Objective: Configure and test NTFS permissions on a local folder.

Description: While the IT manager at Dover Leasing is certainly concerned about controlling access to shared folders on network servers, he is equally concerned about controlling access to local files and folders as well. In this activity, you have been asked to implement standard NTFS permission on a folder to review not only the default permissions but also the behavior of permission inheritance.

1. Open My Computer, and double-click on drive **D:**. Right-click an area of white space in the window, select **New**, and then click **Folder**. Name the folder **Test**. Right-click on the **D:\Test** folder and click **Properties**.

2. Click the **Security** tab to view the NTFS permissions assigned to users and groups by default. Click each individual entry in the Group or user names list box to view the properties associated with these accounts. Note that although each group is assigned different permissions to the folder, some assigned permissions appear within a gray box and cannot be changed. This is because these permissions have been inherited from a parent folder, in this case the NTFS permissions assigned to drive D.

3. Access the properties of drive **D:** and click the **Security** tab. Notice that the same NTFS permissions that are applied on the test folder are also applied on the D: drive. The difference is that these permissions were assigned directly to the D: drive by default when the partition was created and can be changed.

4. Click the **Add** button. In the Select Users, Computers, or Groups dialog box, type **moira** in the Enter the object names to select (examples) text box, and click **OK**. Ensure that the Moira Cowan user account is only granted the **Allow Read** permission, and click **OK**. When the Security dialog box appears, click **Yes**.

5. Open the Security tab of the test folder to confirm that the Moira Cowan user account now appears in the list of Group or user names. Click the **Moira Cowan** account to confirm that it has inherited the permissions assigned in the previous step.

6. Click the **Add** button. In the Select Users, Computers, or Groups dialog box, type **Marketing Users** in the Enter the object names to select (examples) text box, and click **OK**. Note that the group is assigned the allow Read & Execute, List Folder Contents, and Read permissions on the folder by default. Click **OK**.

7. Open the D:\Test folder. Right-click an area of white space, select **New**, and then click **Text Document**. Name the file **ntfstest.txt**.

8. Right-click the **ntfstest.txt** file and click **Properties**.

9. Click the **Security** tab to view the NTFS permissions associated with this file. Note that the permissions configured for this file have been inherited from the D:\Test folder.

10. In the Group or user names list box, click **Users** and then click **Remove**. Read the Security dialog box that appears, outlining the fact that the group Users cannot be removed because its settings are inherited from a parent folder. Click **OK**.

11. Click the **Advanced** button. The Advanced Security Settings for test dialog box opens.

12. Uncheck the **Allow inheritable permissions from the parent to propagate to this object and all child objects** check box.

13. When the Security dialog box opens, read its message, click **Copy**, and then click **OK**.

14. Click each user or group in the Group or user names section to view the associated NTFS permissions. Note that permissions are now directly applied to users and groups rather than being inherited. This is a result of clicking the Copy button in the previous step.

15. In the Group or user names list box, click **Users** and then click **Remove**. Notice that this time, the Users group is removed without issue. Close all open windows.

16. Log off and then log on again using the **mcowan** user account.

17. Open My Computer and attempt to create a new text file in the D:\Test folder. Notice that this action is denied because the Moira Cowan user account does not have sufficient permissions for the D:\Test folder as a member of the Marketing Users group.

18. Close all open windows and log off. Log on again using your **AdminXX** account.

Special NTFS Permissions

Windows Server 2003 provides access to 14 individual NTFS permissions that can be used to specify an even more granular level of access to a file or folder. Occasionally, one of the standard permissions may not provide enough control or, conversely, may provide a slightly higher level of access than a user requires. To access the special permissions, click the Advanced button in the Security tab on the Properties dialog box for the folder or file. The

resulting Advanced Security dialog box allows you to assign special permissions to user or group accounts. To view the **special NTFS permissions** assigned to a user or group, click the user or group and then click the Edit button. The Permission Entry dialog box opens, as shown in Figure 4-13.

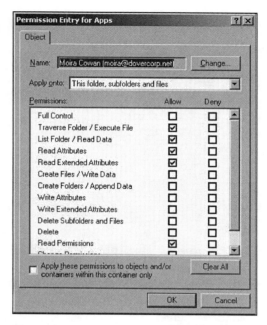

4

Figure 4-13   Viewing special NTFS permissions

The Permission Entry dialog box enables you to assign special NTFS permissions, while also providing a way to control permission inheritance settings. Special permissions can be applied in the following ways, as illustrated in Figure 4-14:

- This folder only
- This folder, subfolders, and files (default)
- This folder and subfolders
- This folder and files
- Subfolders and files only
- Subfolders only
- Files only

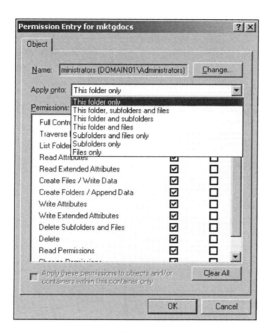

Figure 4-14   Configuring the method in which special permissions will be applied

Table 4-3 shows the special access permissions that you can apply and their functions.

Table 4-3   Special NTFS permissions in Windows Server 2003

Special NTFS Permission	Capabilities
Full Control	Provides the same level of access as the standard Full Control permission, and includes all of the special NTFS permissions listed in this table
Traverse Folder/Execute File	Controls the ability to pass through folders without explicit permission to enter in order to get to an intended folder; for example, a user may not have permission to read the Salesdata folder, but may have Read permission to JuneSales.doc in the Salesdata folder; if the user has traverse folder permissions, the user would be able to open the JuneSales.doc file
List Folder/Read Data	Controls the ability to view the contents of folders and read data files with a folder
Read Attributes	Controls the ability to view the attributes of a file or folder
Read Extended Attributes	Controls the ability to view the extended attributes of a file or folder; extended attributes are additional information attached to a file, as defined by an application
Create Files/Write Data	Controls the ability to create files within a folder (applies to folders only), while also controlling the ability to make changes to files and overwrite any existing content (applies to files only)

Table 4-3   Special NTFS permissions in Windows Server 2003 (continued)

Special NTFS Permission	Capabilities
Create Folders/Append Data	Controls the ability to create additional folders within a folder (applies to folders only), while also controlling the ability to add to the end of the file but not change, delete, or overwrite any existing content (applies to files only)
Write Attributes	Controls the ability to change the attributes of a file or folder, such as read-only or hidden; attributes are defined by NTFS
Write Extended Attributes	Controls the ability to change the extended attributes of a file or folder; extended attributes are defined by programs and can vary
Delete Subfolders and Files	Controls the ability to delete subfolders and files, even if the standard delete permission has not been granted on the sub-folder or file
Delete	Controls the ability to delete a file or folder
Read Permissions	Controls the ability to read the security permissions of a file or folder
Change Permissions	Controls the ability to change the security permissions of a file or folder
Take Ownership	Controls the ability to take ownership of a file or folder

In Activity 4–5 you configure special NTFS permissions.

ACTIVITY

Activity 4-5: Configuring Special NTFS Permissions

Time Required: 15 minutes

Objective: View, configure, and test special NTFS permissions.

Description: Having now used standard NTFS permissions to configure and test file and folder access, you have been asked by the IT manager to test the ability to control resource access using the special NTFS permissions. In this activity, you attempt to deny Marketing users the ability to read the NTFS permissions associated with a file or folder.

1. Open My Computer and create a new folder on drive D: called **Special Permissions**.

2. Open the properties of the Special Permissions folder and click the **Security** tab.

3. Add the **Marketing Users** group to the Group or user names list, granting it the default permissions only. Close all open windows.

4. Log off and then log on again using the **mcowan** user account.

5. Right-click the **D:\Special Permissions** folder, then click **Properties**. Click the **Security** tab to view the permission settings configured for different accounts. Note that while the permissions can be read by the mcowan user account, they cannot be changed. Close all open windows.

6. Log off and then log on again using your **AdminXX** account.

7. Right-click the **D:\Special Permissions** folder, then click **Properties**. Click the **Security** tab, and then click **Advanced**. The Advanced Security Settings for Special Permissions dialog box opens.

8. In the Permission entries list box, click the entry for the **Marketing Users** group and then click **Edit**.

9. In the Permissions section, click the **Read Permissions** check box in the Deny column to specifically disable the ability to read the NTFS permissions associated with this folder. Click **OK** to close the Permission Entry for Special Permissions dialog box, and then click **OK** to close the Advanced Security Settings for Special Permissions dialog box. Click **Yes** in the Security dialog box.

10. In the Group or user names list box, click the **Marketing Users** group account to view its configured security settings. Notice that the Special Permissions Deny column now includes a check mark. Close all open windows.

11. Log off and then log on again using the **mcowan** user account.

12. Attempt to access the Security tab in the Properties dialog box for the **D:\Special Permissions** folder. This tab is no longer available because, as a member of the Marketing Users group, Moira Cowan has been denied the ability to view permission settings.

13. Close all open windows and log off. Log on again using your **AdminXX** account.

Determining Effective Permissions

In versions of Windows prior to Windows Server 2003, one of the more complex and tedious tasks that administrators were often responsible for was determining a user's effective permissions for network resources. Because the permissions that actually apply to a user can be the result of membership on a variety of different groups, this task could often be very complex and involve a great deal of research. In environments that included thousands of users and shared resources, the amount of time and effort required to do this could quickly become unmanageable.

To easily determine the effective NTFS permissions that apply to a user or group, Windows Server 2003 includes the Effective Permissions tab in the Advanced Security Settings dialog box for a file or folder, shown in Figure 4-15. In Activity 4-6, you use the Effective Permissions tab to determine the effective NTFS permissions that apply to a user and group for a specific folder.

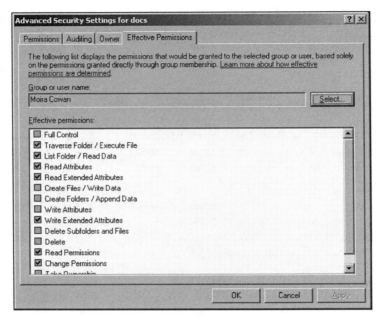

Figure 4-15   The Effective Permissions tab

Activity 4-6: Determining Effective NTFS Permissions

Time Required: 5 minutes

Objective: View effective permissions for a user on an NTFS folder.

Description: Although the IT manager is now convinced of the benefits that NTFS security will provide for Dover Leasing, he is still worried that the application of permissions to many different users and groups may result in mistakes being made with respect to the effective level of permissions assigned to users. In this activity, you use the Effective Permissions tab in the Advanced Security Settings of a folder to view the effective NTFS permissions that apply to both a user and group.

1. Open My Computer and right-click the **D:\Test** folder. Click **Properties** from the shortcut menu, then click the **Security** tab.

2. Click the **Advanced** button to access the Advanced Security Settings for Test dialog box.

3. Click the **Effective Permissions** tab.

4. Click the **Select** button.

5. In the Enter the object name to select (examples) text box, type **Moira** and click **OK**. Review the effective NTFS permissions that apply to the Moira Cowan user account.

6. Click the **Select** button again and, this time, add the **Marketing Users** group. Review the effective NTFS permissions that apply to this group.

7. Close all open windows.

COMBINING SHARED FOLDER AND NTFS PERSMISSIONS

NTFS permissions are often combined with share permissions to provide a strong combination of local and remote security for files and directories. When share and NTFS permissions are combined, the following rules apply:

- When a user is accessing a share across a network and both NTFS and share permissions apply, the most restrictive permission of the two becomes the effective combined permission. For example, if the effective shared folder permission is Full Control, but the effective NTFS permission is Read, then the user will be granted the Read permission to the resource.

- When a user accesses a file locally, only NTFS permissions apply.

In Activity 4-7, you test the impact of configuring both NTFS and shared folder permissions.

Activity 4-7: Exploring the Impact of Combined Shared Folder and NTFS Permissions

Time Required: 10 minutes

Objective: Determine the impact of combining shared folder and NTFS permissions.

Description: Although you understand how both shared folder and NTFS permissions combine, you are worried that the new junior administrators will have difficulty properly configuring these permissions to allow the correct level of user access. You have decided to test the impact of different permission combinations to develop a set procedure to be used by new junior administrators at Dover Leasing. In this activity, you test the impact of combining both shared folder and NTFS permissions for both local and network resource access.

1. Open My Computer and create a new folder on drive D: named **Combined**. Share this folder using the default name.

2. Access the properties of the **Combined** folder. Click the **Security** tab, and then click the **Advanced** button. Uncheck the **Allow inheritable permissions from the parent to propagate to this object and all child objects** check box. When the Security dialog box opens, click **Remove**, and then click **OK**.

3. Read the message in the Security dialog box that opens, and then click **Yes**.

4. Add the **Domain Users** group to the Group or user names list, granting the group the **Allow Modify** permission.

5. Click the **Sharing** tab, and then click the **Permissions** button. Remove the

4

Everyone group from the list, and then add the **Domain Users** group with the **Allow Read** permission. Click **OK**, and then click **OK** again to exit the properties of the Combined folder.

6. Attempt to create a new folder called **Documents** in the D:\Combined folder. This operation should complete successfully because the Domain Users group has the NTFS Modify permission on the folder. Close My Computer.

7. Open the Run command, type **\\serverXX\combined** (where *XX* is your assigned student number), and then press **Enter**. The Combined window should open.

8. Right-click an area of white space in the window and then attempt to create a new folder. When the Unable to create folder dialog box opens, read the message and then click **OK**. You are unable to create a new folder because the share permission is Read, and when the folder is accessed over the network, this is the effective permission that applies because it is more restrictive. Close the \\ServerXX window, and then open **My Computer**.

9. Right-click the **D:\Combined** folder and click **Properties**. Click the **Sharing** tab, click **Permissions** and change the permissions for the Domain Users group to **Allow Full Control**. Click **OK** to exit, and then click **OK** to close the Combined Properties dialog box.

10. Open the Run command again, type **\\serverXX\combined**, then click **OK**. The Combined window should open.

11. Attempt to create a new folder in this window called **Documents2**. The operation should complete successfully because the combination of the Full Control share permission and the Modify NTFS permission make Modify the effective permission on the folder.

12. Close all open windows.

CONVERTING A FAT PARTITION TO NTFS

As you have already learned, the ability to configure files and folders with NTFS permissions requires the volume or partition on which they are stored to be formatted with the NTFS file system. In some environments, it is conceivable that an administrator might have formatted certain partitions with the FAT or FAT32 file system for any number of potential reasons, including accidentally. For the highest degree of security, however, partitions and volumes on a Windows Server 2003 system should always be configured to use the NTFS file system.

Windows Server 2003 provides a command-line utility called CONVERT for the purpose of converting existing FAT or FAT32 partitions and volumes to the NTFS file system. When this utility is used, all existing files and folders on a partition are retained once the conversion process is complete. This is a far more effective method of implementing the NTFS file system than the alternative, which involves formatting the partition.

Although the CONVERT utility can convert existing FAT and FAT32 partitions and volumes to NTFS, the reverse is not true. CONVERT cannot convert an NTFS partition or volume to the FAT or FAT32 file systems; allowing this to occur would potentially represent a serious security risk.

In Activity 4-8 you use the **Disk Management** utility to create a small new FAT32 partition, and ultimately use the CONVERT utility to convert the partition from FAT32 to the NTFS file system.

Activity 4-8: Converting a FAT32 Partition to NTFS

Time Required: 15 minutes

Objective: Convert a FAT32 partition to the NTFS file system.

Description: In the past, one of the administrators at Dover Leasing made the decision to format almost all of the partitions used for storing user data files with the FAT32 file system. The IT manager is interested in converting these partitions to the NTFS file system, but wants to be certain that no existing data files are lost in the process. In this activity you create a small FAT32 partition on your server, create a new folder and file on that partition, and then use the CONVERT utility to convert the partition to the NTFS file system.

1. Click **Start**, right-click **My Computer**, and click **Manage**.

2. Click the **Disk Management** node. Note that you may need to expand the Storage node to access Disk Management.

3. Right-click on an area of free space on Disk 0 and click **New Partition**.

4. At the New Partition Wizard welcome screen, click **Next**.

5. At the Select Partition Type screen, ensure that **Primary partition** is selected, and click **Next**.

6. At the Specify Partition Size Screen, type **50** in the Partition size in MB text box. Click **Next**.

7. At the Assign Drive Letter or Path screen, ensure that drive **F** is selected in the Assign the following drive letter drop down box and click **Next**.

8. At the Format Partition screen, select **FAT32** in the File system drop down box, and check the **Perform a quick format** check box. Click **Next**.

9. Click **Finish** to create the new partition.

10. Close the Computer Management window.

11. Click **Start**, and then click **My Computer**.

12. Double-click on drive **F:** to view its contents.

13. Right-click on a blank area, select **New**, and click **Folder**. Name the folder **permissiontest**.

14. Right-click on the **permissiontest** folder and click **Properties**. Note that the folder does not include a Security tab, since it is stored on a FAT32 partition. Close the permissiontest Properties window.

15. Close the My Computer window.

16. Click **Start**, and then click **Run**. In the Open text box, type **cmd.exe** and click **OK**.

17. Type **convert f: /fs:ntfs** and press **Enter**.

18. At the Enter current volume label for drive F: prompt, type **NEW VOLUME**, and press **Enter**. Note that the conversion process will take a few minutes or more. Once complete, the Conversion complete message appears, as shown in Figure 4-16. When the conversion process is complete, close the command prompt window.

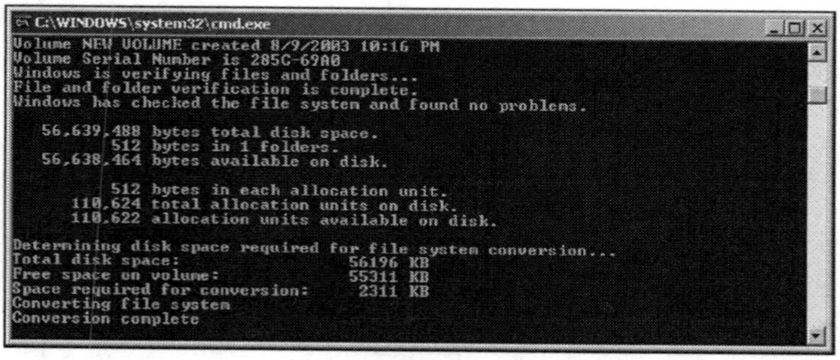

Figure 4-16   Results of the CONVERT command

19. Click **Start**, and then click **My Computer**.

20. Double-click on drive **F:** to view its contents. Notice that the permissiontest folder is still available after the conversion.

21. Right-click on the **permissiontest** folder and click **Properties**. Note that the Security tab is now available.

22. Click on the **Security** tab and review the permissions assigned for the folder. These permissions are inherited from those applied to drive F: by default after the conversion process completed.

23. Click **OK**, and then close all open windows.

CHAPTER SUMMARY

❑ Windows Server 2003 supports the FAT, FAT32, and NTFS file systems. Only the NTFS file system allows local security permissions to be configured.

❑ To create a shared folder, you are required to have the appropriate rights. A domain administrator or server operator has the default rights to create shared folders within a

domain. The primary tools used to create shared folders are Windows Explorer, Computer Management, and the NET SHARE command-line utility.

❑ Windows Server 2003 supports three share permissions: Read, Change, and Full Control. Share permissions are cumulative. If a user is a member of multiple groups that have different permissions, the final permission is the sum of all permissions.

❑ Windows Server 2003 supports both standard and special NTFS permissions. Special NTFS permissions give an administrator a more granular level of control over how permissions are applied.

❑ NTFS permissions are cumulative. If a user is a member of multiple groups that have different permissions, the final permission is the sum of all permissions.

❑ When a shared folder and NTFS permissions are combined, the most restrictive permission applies.

❑ A denied permission always overrides an allowed permission.

❑ Windows Server 2003 provides the CONVERT utility as a way to convert existing FAT or FAT32 partitions to the NTFS file system without losing existing data.

Key Terms

access control entry (ACE) — An entry in an object's discretionary access control list (DACL) that grants permissions to a user or group. An ACE is also an entry in an object's system access control list (SACL) that specifies the security events to be audited for a user or group.

administrative shares — Hidden shared folders created for the purpose of allowing administrators to access the root of partitions and other system folders remotely.

Computer Management console — A predefined Microsoft Management Console (MMC) application that allows administration of a variety of computer-related tasks on the local computer or a remote computer.

discretionary access control list (DACL) — A part of the security descriptor of an object that contains a list of user or group references that have been allowed or denied permissions to the resource.

Disk Management — The Windows Server 2003 utility used to manage disk partitions and volumes.

effective permissions — The permissions that actually apply to a user or group based on the different permissions of the user or groups they are members of on a particular resource.

FAT — A file system supported in Windows Server 2003 but traditionally associated with the MS-DOS operating system. FAT can be used on partitions or volumes up to 4 GB in size.

FAT32 — A derivative of the FAT file system that supports partition sizes up to 2 TB, but provides none of the security features of NTFS.

NTFS — The native file system of Windows Server 2003, provides better scalability and performance than FAT and FAT32, while also providing the ability to configure local security permissions, compression, encryption, and more.

shared folder — A data resource container that has been made available over the network to authorized network clients.

special NTFS permissions — A more granular set of NTFS permissions that allows an administrator a higher degree of control over the abilities assigned to users or groups for a particular resource.

standard NTFS permissions — The permissions available on the Security tab of an NTFS file or folder.

4

REVIEW QUESTIONS

1. What is the default permission assigned to a shared folder?
   a. Allow Full Control to the Everyone group
   b. Allow Read to the Everyone group
   c. Allow Change to the Users group
   d. Deny Read to the Users group

2. Which of the following tools can be used to create shared folders on a Windows Server 2003 system? (Choose all that apply.)
   a. Computer Management
   b. Windows Explorer
   c. Internet Explorer
   d. The NET SHARE command

3. Which of the following are shared folder permissions on a Windows Server 2003 system? (Choose all that apply.)
   a. Read
   b. Modify
   c. Change
   d. Full Control

4. Which of the following shared folders would be hidden in My Network Places?
   a. Documents
   b. Documents$
   c. $Documents
   d. Documents%

5. Assuming that a user is granted the Allow Read shared folder permission as a member of one group and the Deny Full Control permission as a member of another group for the same folder, what is the user's effective permission?

   a. Deny Full Control

   b. Allow Read

   c. Allow Modify

   d. Deny Modify

6. Which of the following are NTFS folder permissions? (Choose all that apply.)

   a. Read & Execute

   b. List Folder Contents

   c. Read

   d. Change

7. Which of the following are NTFS file permissions? (Choose all that apply.)

   a. Read & Execute

   b. List Folder Contents

   c. Read

   d. Modify

8. Which of the following file systems support local security?

   a. NTFS

   b. FAT

   c. FAT32

9. Which of the following commands would be used to convert drive D from FAT32 to NTFS?

   a. Convert fs:ntfs d:

   b. Convert d: ntfs

   c. Convert d: /fs:ntfs

   d. Convert /fs:ntfs d:

10. Which of the following NTFS permissions would allow a user to change the permissions associated with a file?

   a. Full Control

   b. Modify

   c. Read & Execute

   d. Write

11. Which of the following commands would be used to share a folder from the command line?

    a. Net Use

    b. Net Share

    c. Share

    d. Net Config

12. Assuming that a user is granted the Allow Full Control NTFS permission as a member of one group and the Allow Read permission as a member of another group for the same folder, what is the user's effective permission?

    a. Allow Read

    b. Allow Full Control

    c. Allow Modify

    d. Allow Read & Execute

13. Assuming that a user is granted the Allow Modify NTFS permission as a member of one group and the Deny Modify shared folder permission as a member of another group for the same folder, what is the user's effective permission locally?

    a. Allow Modify

    b. Deny Modify

    c. Allow Read

    d. Deny Read

14. Assuming that a user is granted the Allow Full Control NTFS permission as a member of one group and the Allow Read shared folder permission as a member of another group for the same folder, what is the user's effective permission remotely?

    a. Allow Full Control

    b. Allow Read

    c. Allow Modify

    d. Deny Full Control

15. Which of the following file systems allow folders to be shared? (Choose all that apply.)

    a. NTFS

    b. FAT

    c. FAT32

16. Which acronym is used to describe an entry in an access control list?

    a. ACL

    b. DACL

    c. SACL

    d. ACE

17. A denied permission always takes precedence over an allowed permission.

    a. True

    b. False

18. Which tool can be used to determine the ultimate set of permissions that impact a user trying to access resources on an NTFS partition?

    a. The Effective Permissions tab

    b. Active Directory Users and Computers

    c. Active Directory Domains and Trusts

    d. DSADD

19. Which of the following are not standard NTFS permissions on a file? (Choose all that apply.)

    a. Read

    b. Read & Execute

    c. Change

    d. List Folder Contents

20. Which of the following are not standard NTFS permissions on a folder?

    a. Read

    b. List Folder Contents

    c. Change

    d. Modify

CASE PROJECTS

Case Project 4-1

This case project involves configuring share and NTFS permissions. Dover Leasing is in the process of reviewing their current structure and practices. There has been talk of minor security breaches occurring in which users are able to gain access to information they should not be permitted to view. Management would like you to make some recommendations as to how permissions can be changed on specific folders.

1. Two network servers maintain confidential information pertaining to financial data and employee data. Users access the folders both locally and on the network. Only members of the Managers group, Human Resources group, and Accountants group should have access to these folders. Explain how permissions can be implemented, including a short description of how share permissions and NTFS permissions work together.

2. Dover Leasing has recently hired a new server administrator to assist you. He has worked with Windows NT 4.0 in the past and is unfamiliar with Windows Server 2003. Prepare a brief explanation for the new administrator about how to configure share and NTFS permissions.

Case Project 4-2

A new junior administrator at Dover Leasing has just configured a variety of NTFS permissions on a shared folder named Marketing on a newly installed server. After completing his configuration, he notices that some of the Marketing users are having trouble accessing the server with the correct level of access, if at all. What are some of the possible permission-related reasons why users might be having trouble connecting?

Case Project 4-3

To understand how NTFS and share permissions work together, consider the following example and answer the accompanying questions:

Users	Group Membership
User1	Sales, Marketing, domain users
User2	Managers, domain users

Directory Structure	Share Permissions	NTFS Permissions
SalesData	Sales—Full Control	Sales—Modify
	Managers—Read	Marketing—Full Control
CompanyData	domain users—Change	default
HRData	Managers—deny Full Control	default

1. What permissions would User1 have to the SalesData folder if the user were accessing the folder across a network connection?

2. What permissions would User1 have to the SalesData folder if the user were logged on to the computer where the folder was located?

3. What permissions would User2 have to the CompanyData folder if the user were accessing the folder across the network?

4. What permissions would User2 have to the HRData folder if the user were accessing the folder across the network?

5. What permissions would User2 have to the HRData folder if the user were accessing the folder on the computer on which it is located?

5

MANAGING DISKS AND DATA STORAGE

After reading this chapter and completing the exercises, you will be able to:

Understand concepts relating to disk management

Manage partitions and volumes on a Windows Server 2003 system

Understand the purpose of mounted drives and how to implement them

Understand the fault tolerant disk strategies natively supported in Windows Server 2003

Determine disk and volume status information and import foreign disks

Maintain disks on a Windows Server 2003 system using a variety of native utilities

When Intel-based servers first appeared on the scene, disk storage options were limited because disk sizes were relatively small at 20 to 40 MB. At 20 GB and well beyond, disk storage has come a long way and is arguably one of the most important server elements that an administrator needs to configure and maintain. Server activities are typically related to making files, databases, and applications available to network clients, and all of these rely upon disk storage.

In this chapter, you learn the fundamentals of Windows Server 2003 disk management. This begins with a look at the two major types of disks supported on Windows Server 2003 systems, as well as the disk space allocation strategies associated and supported by each type.

Windows Server 2003 also supports a variety of disk fault tolerance features in the form of different Redundant Array of Independent Disk (RAID) strategies. The various RAID levels available in Windows Server 2003, as well as the disk configurations necessary to support them, will also be looked at in this chapter.

While the partitions and volumes implemented on Windows-based systems have traditionally been designated and associated with drive letters, Windows Server 2003 also supports the ability to mount NTFS partitions and volumes to folders, in a manner similar to UNIX- or Linux-based systems. In this chapter you learn the prerequisites for mounting a drive in this fashion, as well as how it is accomplished using tools such as Disk Management.

Although implementing partitions and volumes on the disks of a Windows Server 2003 system is a relatively straightforward process, these resources still must be maintained in order to ensure that they function at an acceptable level. A variety of different utilities are provided in Windows Server 2003 to manage and maintain disks, volumes, and partitions. This chapter ends with a look at the various graphical and command-line tools that you should be familiar with to ensure that hard disk resources are maintained optimally.

DISK MANAGEMENT CONCEPTS

Windows Server 2003 supports two data storage types: basic disks and dynamic disks. A **basic disk** is one that uses traditional disk management techniques and contains primary partitions, extended partitions, and logical drives. A **dynamic disk** is one that does not use traditional partitioning. Dynamic disk architecture provides new flexibility in that there is virtually no restriction to the number of volumes that can be implemented on one disk. Both types of data storage are discussed in more detail in the following sections.

Basic Disks

A basic disk is a hard disk that is divided into primary and extended partitions, where each partition acts as a separate storage unit. You can configure a basic disk with a maximum of four primary partitions, or three primary partitions and one extended partition, as shown in Figure 5-1.

Figure 5-1   Basic disk configurations

Primary partitions on a basic disk are used by default when Windows Server 2003 is installed on a new server. You can format each primary partition with either the FAT, FAT32, or NTFS file systems, and assign that partition a drive letter. Of the primary partitions that are

configured, only one can be marked as the active partition. Also known as the system partition, this is the partition that contains the files required to start the operating system. On Windows operating systems, the system partition is almost always drive C.

> The boot partition is where the operating system files are installed. In a Windows Server 2003 installation, this is the partition where the \WINDOWS folder resides. Unlike the system partition, the boot partition can be located on a primary partition, or on a logical drive in an extended partition.

5

To overcome the limitation of only being able to create four primary partitions on a single basic disk, you also have the option to create up to three primary partitions and one extended partition per disk. An extended partition is created from free hard disk space, but is not formatted or assigned a drive letter. Instead, the space within an extended partition is further divided into logical drives. Each logical drive within the extended partition is formatted and assigned a drive letter.

When you install Windows Server 2003, all disks are automatically initialized as basic disks. You can convert disks from basic to dynamic after the installation, or let them remain as basic if the extended capabilities of dynamic disks are not required. Dynamic disks and their capabilities is explored shortly.

Primary Partitions

A partition can be configured as either primary or extended. A basic disk must contain at least one **primary partition** and can contain a maximum of four primary partitions per disk. A primary partition is one from which you can boot an operating system if required, such as Windows Server 2003. When you boot from a primary partition, it contains the operating system startup files in a location at the beginning of the partition. For example, the startup files for Windows 98 include Io.sys and Msdos.sys. With Windows Server 2003, the startup files include Boot.ini, Ntldr, and Ntdetect.com, for example. At least one primary partition must be marked as active and only one primary partition can be active at a given time. The **active partition** is the partition where your computer looks for the hardware-specific files to start the operating system. Although primary partitions are used to start an operating system when basic disks are used, they can also be used for traditional data storage purposes, such as holding users' home directories.

Extended Partitions and Logical Drives

An **extended partition** is created from space that is not yet partitioned. The purpose of an extended partition is to enable you to exceed the four-partition limit of a basic disk. There can be only one extended partition on a single basic disk. An extended partition is neither formatted nor assigned a drive letter. Once an extended partition is created, the space allocated to it can be further divided into **logical drives**. The logical drives are then formatted and assigned drive letters for the purpose of data storage.

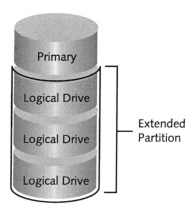

Figure 5-2   An extended partition can be divided into one or more logical drives

Volume Sets and Stripe Sets

On a Windows NT Server 4.0 system you can create multi-disk volumes referred to as volume sets and stripe sets. A volume set consists of two or more partitions combined to look like one volume with a single drive letter. A stripe set consists of two or more disks that combined like a volume set, but that striped for RAID level 0 or RAID level 5 (RAID is discussed later in this chapter). Windows Server 2003 (and Windows 2000 Server) provides backward compatibility with the volume and stripe sets previously created using Windows NT. If you have any of these multi-disk volumes on a computer running Windows NT 4.0, you can still use them after an upgrade to Windows Server 2003, but you cannot create new volume or stripe sets should the disks fail. For this reason, after a Windows NT server is upgraded to Windows Server 2003, you should convert basic disks to dynamic disks in order to implement any new multi-disk volumes.

Dynamic Disks

A dynamic disk is a hard disk that does not use the traditional partitioning strategies of a basic disk. Dynamic disks make it possible to set up a large number of volumes on one disk, while providing the ability to extend volumes onto additional physical disks. Some of the reasons why an administrator might opt to implement dynamic disks include the ability to:

- Extend NTFS volumes
- Configure RAID volumes for fault tolerance or increased performance
- Reactivate missing or offline disks
- Changes disk settings without having to restart the computer

Dynamic disks do not contain primary and extended partitions. Instead, dynamic disks are configured with what are known as volumes. While fundamentally similar in principle to a partition, volumes on dynamic disks provide additional features and capabilities not available

to partitions on a basic disk. The different types of volumes that can be configured on a dynamic disk are in the following sections.

Do not convert basic disks to dynamic disks if the system is configured to dual-boot with other operating systems. Once converted, other operating systems may not have access to the disk.

Dynamic disks are not supported on portable computers, removable disks, detachable disks (such as external USB or IEEE 1394 drives) or disks connected to a shared SCSI bus.

Simple Volume

A **simple volume** is a dedicated and formatted portion of disk space on a dynamic disk. If you do not allocate all available space on a disk to a simple volume, you have the option to later take all or a portion of the unallocated space and add it to an existing simple volume, which is called extending the volume. Only simple volumes formatted with the NTFS file system can be extended. It is important to note that neither the system nor boot volume on a Windows Server 2003 system can be extended.

Spanned Volume

A **spanned volume** consists of space in between two and 32 dynamic disks that is treated as a single logical volume. For example, you might create a spanned volume if you have four separate small hard disks, as shown in Figure 5-3. Another reason to use a spanned volume is if you have several small areas of free disk space scattered throughout a server's disk drives. You might have 600 MB of free space on one drive, 150 MB on another, and 70 MB on a third. All of these free areas can be combined into a single 820 MB spanned volume with its own drive letter, with the advantage that you reduce the number of drive letters needed to make use of the space.

Figure 5-3   Creating a spanned volume using four disks

As you add new disks, the spanned volume can be extended to include each disk. Volumes formatted for NTFS can be extended, but those formatted for FAT16 and FAT32 cannot. The advantage of creating spanned volumes is the ability to maximize the use of scattered pockets of disk space across several disks.

The disadvantage of using a spanned volume is that if one disk fails, the entire volume is inaccessible. Also, if a portion of a spanned volume is deleted, the entire disk set is deleted. For these reasons, avoid placing mission-critical data and applications on a spanned volume.

Striped Volume

A **striped volume** is often referred to as RAID level 0. One reason for implementing a striped volume is to extend the life of hard disk drives by spreading data equally over two or more drives. Spreading the data divides the drive load so that one drive is not working more than any other. Another advantage of striping is that it increases disk performance. Contention among disks is equalized and data is accessed faster for both reading and writing than when it is on a single drive, because Windows Server 2003 can write to all drives simultaneously.

In Windows Server 2003, disk striping requires at least two physical hard disks and can use up to 32. The aggregation of space from the various disks is ultimately called a striped volume. Equal portions of data are written in 64 KB blocks in rows or stripes on each disk. For example, imagine that you have set up a striped volume across five hard disks, and are working with a 720 KB data file. The first 64 KB portion of the file is written to disk 1, the next 64 KB portion is written to disk 2, the third portion is written to disk 3, and so on. After 320 KB are spread in the first data row across disks 1 through 5, the next 320 KB are written in 64 KB blocks in the second row across the disks. Finally, there will be 64 KB in the third row on disk 1 and 16 KB in the third row on disk 2, as shown in Figure 5-4.

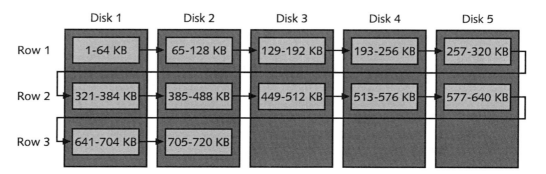

Figure 5-4   Disks in a striped volume

Because of their high performance, striped volumes are useful for storing large databases or for data replication from one volume to another. Striping is not a benefit when most of the data files on a server are very small, such as under 64 KB.

Data can be lost when one or more disks in the striped volume fail, because the system has no automated way to rebuild data. Although often referred to by a RAID-level name, striped volumes do not provide any degree of fault tolerance, and are implemented for performance reasons only.

Windows Server 2003 supports two additional volume types, known as mirrored volumes and RAID-5 volumes. Since both of these volume types provide fault tolerance, they are looked at in more detail in the Fault Tolerant Disk Strategies section later in this chapter.

MANAGING PARTITIONS AND VOLUMES

Disk management tasks are usually performed on a Windows Server 2003 system using the **Disk Management** tool. This tool provides a central facility for viewing disk-related information, and performing tasks such as creating and deleting partitions and volumes. The following sections introduce you to the different tasks you can perform using the Disk Management tool, including viewing disk information, creating and deleting partitions, creating volumes, and converting basic disks to dynamic disks. The Disk Management node of the Computer Management tool is shown in Figure 5-5.

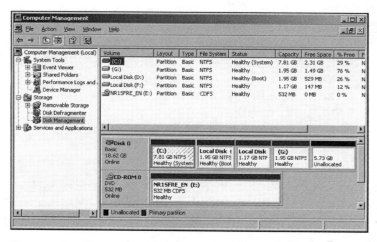

Figure 5-5   The Disk Management node of the Computer Management tool

Managing Disk Properties

Although the Disk Management tool can be added to a custom Microsoft Management Console (MMC), it is most commonly accessed via its node in the Storage section of the Computer Management tool. While primarily used for the creation, deletion, and management of disks, partitions, and volumes the Disk Management tool also provides information about disks, partitions, and volumes that are typically associated with other tools.

5

For example, right-clicking on a specific partition or volume in Disk Management and clicking Properties provides access to the same property sheets for the disk available from within Windows Explorer, as shown in Figure 5-6.

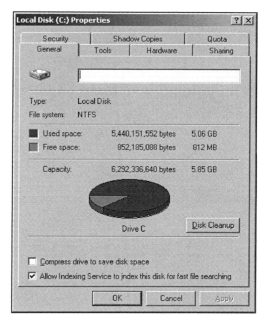

Figure 5-6   The Properties screen for an existing partition

In a similar vein, right-clicking on a disk in the Disk Management tool and clicking Properties opens the same property sheets available from the Device Manager tool for a disk, as shown in Figure 5-7.

In Activity 5-1 you use the Disk Management node of the Computer Management tool to access and view the properties of the hard disk and a partition on your server.

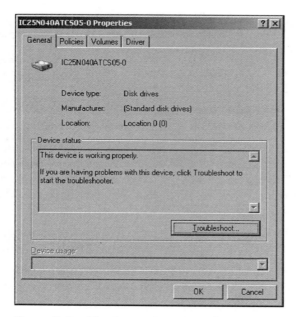

Figure 5-7   The Properties screen for a hard disk

ACTIVITY

Activity 5-1: Viewing and Managing Disk Properties with Disk Management

Time Required: 10 minutes

Objective: Use the Disk Management node of the Computer Management tool to view the properties of a hard disk and partition.

Description: As part of designing a training seminar for new administrators, the IT manager at Dover Leasing would like to include a section on disk management, and specifically on using the Disk Management tool. He has asked you to explore the different property settings for disks and partitions in order to help identify the elements on which new staff should ultimately be trained. In this activity you use the Disk Management node from within the Computer Management tool to view the properties of both your server's hard disk and an existing partition.

1. Log on using your **AdminXX** account. Click **Start**, right-click **My Computer**, and click **Manage**.

2. Click the **+ (plus symbol)** next to Storage to expand it, if necessary.

3. Click the **Disk Management** node to view its contents.

4. In the upper-right pane of the Disk Management node window, right-click on drive **C:** and click **Properties**. The Properties window for drive C: will open, as shown in Figure 5-6.

5. Review the information and settings available on the General tab. Notice that this tab provides an easy way to determine both the capacity and available free space for the partition. Click the **Tools** tab.

6. Review the descriptions of the tools available on this tab. Some of these tools are looked at in more detail later in this chapter. Click the **Hardware** tab.

7. The Hardware tab provides a list of the drives installed in your server, and provides access to both the properties of the drive and a troubleshooting tool. Click the **Sharing** tab.

8. The Sharing tab allows the root of a partition or volume to be shared over the network. Notice that drive C: is shared over the network using the share name C$ by default. The root of all partitions and volumes on a Windows Server 2003 system are shared for administrative purposes. Click the **Security** tab.

9. The Security tab allows NTFS permissions to be configured for the partition or volume, with settings inherited by subfolders and files. Click the **Shadow Copies** tab.

10. The Shadow Copies tab is used to configure the new Shadow Copies feature of Windows Server 2003. This topic is looked at in more detail later in the text. Click the **Quota** tab.

11. The Quota tab allows an administrator to configure disk space quotas for users on individual volumes or partitions. This feature is looked at in more detail later in the text. Click the **Cancel** button.

12. In the lower-right pane of the Disk Management node window, right-click on **Disk 0** and click **Properties**. This opens the property pages for the disk drive, as shown in Figure 5-7.

13. Review the information available on the General tab, noting that it also provides access to a troubleshooting tool. Click the **Policies** tab.

14. The Policies tab is used to configure write caching and safe removal settings for a disk. Review the default settings and available options, and then click the **Volumes** tab.

15. The Volumes tab lists all available partitions (or volumes) currently configured on this disk. Clicking on a partition or volume and then clicking Properties opens the same property sheets for a partition or volume explored at the beginning of this activity. Click the **Driver** tab.

16. The Driver tab allows an administrator to view details about the currently installed driver for the disk, update the driver, roll back the driver, and uninstall the driver, if necessary. Click the **Cancel** button.

17. Leave the Computer Management window open.

CREATING PARTITIONS AND VOLUMES

The Disk Management tool is the primary tool used to create and manage partitions and volumes on a Windows Server 2003 system. In Activity 5-2 you use the Disk Management node of the Computer Management tool to create, and then delete, a new primary partition on Disk 0.

Activity 5-2: Creating and Deleting a Primary Partition

Time Required: 5 minutes

Objective: Create and delete a new primary partition.

Description: In the past, the IT staff at Dover Leasing has always used the FDISK utility to pre-create partitions for servers. However, you have been asked to walk new staff members through the process of creating and managing different partitions, because the IT manager has dictated that all files must be stored on NTFS partitions only. In this activity, you use Disk Management to create, and then delete, a new primary partition on your server.

1. In the Computer Management window, ensure that the **Disk Management** node is selected. Right-click on an area of free space on Disk 0, and click **New Partition**.

2. Click **Next** at the New Partition Wizard welcome screen.

3. At the Select Partition Type screen, ensure that the **Primary partition** radio button is selected, and click **Next**.

4. At the Specify Partition Size screen, type **50** in the Partition size in MB text box. Click **Next**.

5. At the Assign Drive Letter or Path screen, ensure that drive **G** is selected in the Assign the following drive letter drop down box and click **Next**.

6. At the Format Partition screen, ensure that **NTFS** is selected in the File system drop down box, and check the **Perform a quick format** check box. Click **Next**.

7. Click **Finish** to create the new partition. Leave the Computer Management window open.

8. Click **Start**, and then click **My Computer**. Double-click on drive New Volume **G:** to ensure it is accessible. Close the My Computer window.

9. In the Computer Management window, right-click on drive New Volume **(G:)**, and then select **Delete Partition**. Because Disk 0 already contains four primary partitions, this partition must be deleted to make room for an extended partition in the next activity.

10. When prompted to confirm the deletion of the partition, click **Yes**. Notice that the space previously allocated to drive G: is now listed as free space on the disk once again.

11. Leave the Computer Management window open.

In Activity 5-3 you use some of the existing free space on your hard disk to create an extended partition using the Disk Management tool.

Activity 5-3: Creating an Extended Partition

Time Required: 5 minutes

Objective: Create an extended partition.

Description: Although a basic disk supports up to four primary partitions, the IT manager would prefer to have the additional flexibility that implementing a single extended partition per disk provides. In this activity you use Disk Management to create a new extended partition on your server's hard disk.

1. In the Computer Management window, ensure that the Disk Management node is selected. Right-click on an area of free space on Disk 0, and click **New Partition**.

2. Click **Next** at the New Partition Wizard welcome screen.

3. At the Select Partition Type screen, click the **Extended partition** radio button and read the Description section. Notice that the option to create a logical drive is not currently available because an extended partition doesn't currently exist. Click **Next**.

4. At the Specify Partition Size screen, enter **300** in the Partition size in MB text box and then click **Next**.

5. At the Completing the New Partition Wizard screen, click **Finish**.

6. In the Disk Management window, notice the new extended partition that is visible on Disk 0. Note also that because this is an extended partition, it is not formatted and does not have a drive letter assigned to it.

7. Leave the Computer Management window open.

Since an extended partition was created in Activity 5-3, it is now possible to create logical drives within the extended partition. In Activity 5-4 you use the Disk Management tool to create a new logical drive within an extended partition.

Activity 5-4: Creating a Logical Drive

Time Required: 5 minutes

Objective: Create a logical drive from within an extended partition.

Description: In order to use the disk space allocated to an extended partition, logical drives must be defined. In this activity you create a single logical drive that uses all of the space available in the extended partition created in Activity 5-3.

1. In the Computer Management window, ensure that the **Disk Management** node is selected. Right-click within the extended partition on Disk 0, and click **New Logical Drive**.

2. When the New Partition Wizard welcome screen opens, click **Next**.

3. At the Select Partition Type screen, notice that the only available option is to create a logical drive. Click **Next**.

4. At the Specify Partition Size screen, ensure that the Partition size in MB text box matches the value found in the Maximum disk space in megabytes (MB) section and then click **Next**.

5. At the Assign Drive Letter or Path screen, ensure that **G** is selected in the Assign the following drive letter list box and then click **Next**.

6. At the Format Partition screen, ensure that the **Format this partition with the following settings** radio button is selected. In the Volume label text box, type **Logical Drive** and then click **Next**.

7. At the Completing the New Partition Wizard screen, review the summary information provided in the You selected the following settings section and then click **Finish**.

8. After returning to the Disk Management details screen, notice that the Status column of the partition in the upper pane is set to Formatting and provides the percentage information of the format operation currently complete.

9. Once the format operation completes and the new partition's Status is set to Healthy, close Computer Management.

10. Open My Computer and verify that the new logical drive (G:) is now accessible.

11. Close all open windows.

Before you can create any volumes on a Windows Server 2003 system, you must first convert disks from basic to dynamic; otherwise, the only option available is to create traditional partitions. You can convert a basic disk to a dynamic one by using the Disk Management snap-in; right-click the disk you want to convert and then click Convert to Dynamic Disk, as illustrated in Figure 5-8.

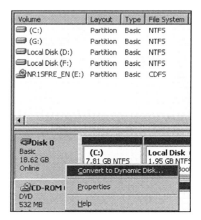

Figure 5-8   Converting a disk from basic to dynamic

Keep the following key points in mind before you upgrade a disk from basic to dynamic:

- You must have administrative privileges to perform the upgrade.

- The disk must contain at least 1 MB of free space for the upgrade to succeed. Windows Server 2003 automatically reserves this space when installed.

- No data is lost when you upgrade from basic to dynamic. To revert back to a basic disk, however, all volumes must first be deleted. You can then restore data from backup once the disk has been reverted to basic.

- Once upgraded, the disk can only be locally accessed by operating systems that support dynamic disks such as Windows 2000, Windows XP, or Windows Server 2003. Converting to a dynamic disk does not affect network access to shared resources on the disk.

- Once upgraded, primary and extended partitions become simple volumes.

To create any new fault-tolerant volumes in Windows Server 2003, such as a mirrored or RAID-5 volume, disks must first be converted to dynamic.

In Activity 5-5 you convert your server's hard disk from a basic disk to a dynamic disk.

Activity 5-5: Converting a Basic Disk to a Dynamic Disk

Time Required: 5 minutes

Objective: Convert a basic disk to a dynamic disk.

Description: While all disks on a Windows Server 2003 system are configured as basic disks by default, the IT manager at Dover Leasing would eventually like to take advantage of the ability to extend existing NTFS volumes, as well as implement fault-tolerant techniques such as RAID 1. Because of this, he has asked you to convert your server's disk from a basic disk to a dynamic disk. In this activity you use the Disk Management tool to convert Disk 0 on your server to a dynamic disk.

1. Click **Start**, right-click on **My Computer**, and click **Manage**.

2. Click on the **Disk Management** node to display its contents, if necessary.

3. Right-click on **Disk 0**, and click **Convert to Dynamic Disk**.

4. In the Convert to Dynamic Disk dialog box, click **OK**.

5. Click the **Convert** button.

6. When the Disk Management dialog box appears, click **Yes**.

7. Click **Yes** to confirm that the file systems on the disk will be dismounted.

8. Click **OK** to reboot the computer when prompted. Once the process completes, log on using your **AdminXX** account.

9. Click **Start**, right-click on **My Computer**, and click **Manage**.

10. Click on the **Disk Management** node to display its contents, if necessary. Notice that Disk 0 is now listed as a dynamic disk. Leave the Computer Management tool open.

There are circumstances when you may need to change a dynamic disk back to a basic disk, such as when you want to implement a dual-boot setup, or when you want to remove Windows Server 2003 from the computer so that a different operating system—such as Windows XP—can be installed. Before reverting back to a basic disk, the disk must be empty; therefore, the data on the disk must be backed up or moved to another disk. A dynamic disk can be converted back to a basic disk by using the following general steps:

1. Back up all data on the dynamic disk volume before you start.

2. Delete all dynamic disk volumes using the Disk Management tool by right-clicking on each volume, and then clicking Delete Volume.

3. Once all volumes on the disk have been deleted, right-click the dynamic disk, and choose Convert to Basic Disk.

4. Use the Disk Management tool to partition and format the disk.

In Activity 5-5 you used the Disk Management tool to covert Disk 0 on your server from a basic disk to a dynamic disk. Once a dynamic disk is available, an administrator can create different types of volumes, as outlined earlier in this chapter. In Activity 5-6 you use the Disk Management tool to create a new simple volume on Disk 0.

Activity 5-6: Creating a Simple Volume

Time Required: 5 minutes

Objective: Create a simple volume.

Description: After converting your hard disk to a dynamic disk in Activity 5-5, you are now capable of creating volumes on the disk. In this activity you create a small simple volume formatted with the NTFS file system.

1. In the Disk Management tool, right-click on an area of free disk space on Disk 0 and click **New Volume**.

2. At the Welcome to the New Volume Wizard screen, click **Next**.

3. At the Select Volume Type screen, ensure that Simple is selected, and click **Next**.

4. At the Specify Volume Size screen, type **50** in the Partition size in MB text box. Click **Next**.

5. At the Assign Drive Letter or Path screen, ensure that drive **I:** is selected in the Assign the following drive letter list box and then click **Next**.

6. At the Format Volume screen, ensure that the **Format this volume with the following settings** radio button is selected. In the Volume label text box, type **New Simple Volume** and then click **Next**.

7. Click **Finish** to create the new simple volume.

8. Close the Computer Management tool.

Extending Volumes

Windows Server 2003 supports the ability to extend NTFS volumes, as long as those volumes are not functioning as the boot or system volume for the system. Although volumes can be extended using the Disk Management tool by right-clicking on a volume and selecting the Extend Volume option, they can also be extended from the command line using the DISKPART utility. In Activity 5-7, you use the DISKPART command-line utility to extend the simple volume created in Activity 5-6. You learn more about the DISKPART command later in this chapter.

Activity 5-7: Extending a Volume Using DISKPART

Time Required: 5 minutes

Objective: Extend an existing volume using the DISKPART command.

Description: In the past, administrators at Dover Leasing have noticed that some servers quickly run out of space in existing partitions. Because NTFS volumes can be extended, you have decided to test this functionality on your server. In this activity, you extend the simple volume created in Activity 5-6 to include additional space by using the DISKPART command–line utility.

1. Click **Start**, and then click **Run**. In the Open text box, type **cmd.exe** and click **OK**.

2. At the command line, type **diskpart** and press **Enter**.

3. At the DISKPART prompt, type **list volume** and press **Enter**.

4. From the list of available volumes, determine the volume number assigned to drive I: in the Volume ### column, and review the volume numbers and letters assigned to other drives.

5. At the DISKPART prompt, type **select volume X**, where X is the number assigned to drive I: on your system. Press **Enter**.

6. At the DISKPART prompt, type **extend size=50** and press **Enter**. This extends the size of drive I: by 50 MB on the same disk.

7. At the DISKPART prompt, type **exit** and press **Enter**. Close the command prompt window.

8. Click **Start**, and then click **My Computer**.

9. Right-click on drive **I:** and click **Properties**. On the General tab, confirm that the size of drive I: is approximately 100 MB, based on the original size of 50 MB, and the extension by another 50 MB.

10. Click **Cancel**, and then close the My Computer window.

Mounted Drives

Windows Server 2003 enables you to mount a drive as an alternative to giving it a drive letter. A **mounted drive** is one that appears as a folder and that is accessed through a path like any other folder. You can mount a basic or dynamic disk drive, a CD-ROM, or a Zip drive. Only an empty folder on a volume formatted for NTFS can be used for mounting a drive.

There are several reasons for using mounted drives, the most apparent being that Windows operating systems are limited to 26 drive letters and mounting drives enables you to reduce the number of drive letters in use, because they are not associated with letters. As server administrator, you might allocate one drive for all user home directories and mount that drive in a folder called Users. The path to this drive might be C:\Users. In another situation, you might have a database that you want to manage as a mounted drive so that it is easier for users to access. Also, by mounting the drive, you can set up special backups for that database by simply backing up its folder.

In Activity 5-8 you use the Disk Management node of the Computer Management tool to mount an existing NTFS volume to a new empty folder on drive D.

Activity 5-8: Mounting an NTFS Volume

Time Required: 5 minutes

Objective: Mount an NTFS volume.

Description: Some of the servers at Dover Leasing contain many disks, each with many partitions. In the past, administrators have been constrained by a lack of available drive letters on some of these servers. Knowing that Windows Server 2003 allows drives to be mounted to an empty folder on an NTFS partition, you decide to test this functionality. In this activity, you use Disk Management to mount drive I to an empty NTFS folder on drive D.

1. Click **Start**, and then click **My Computer**.

2. Double-click on drive **D:** to view its contents.

3. Right-click on an area of blank space, select **New**, and then click **Folder**. Name the new folder **mounted**, and then close My Computer.

4. Click **Start**, right-click on **My Computer**, and click **Manage**.

5. Click on the **Disk Management** node to display its contents, if necessary.

6. Right-click on volume **I:** and click **Change Drive Letter and Paths**.

7. In the Change Drive Letter and Paths for I: (New Simple Volume) window, ensure that drive **I:** is selected, and then click **Add**.

8. In the Add Drive Letter or Path window, ensure that the **Mount in the following empty NTFS folder** radio button is selected, and type **d:\mounted** in the text box. Click **OK**. Drive I: is now accessible both by using its drive letter (I:) and by accessing the d:\mounted folder.

9. Close the Computer Management window.

10. Click **Start**, and then click **My Computer**. Double-click on drive **I:**, and create a new folder named **Test**. Press the **Backspace** button on the keyboard to return to the list of available drives.

11. Double-click on drive **D:** to view its contents. Double-click on the **mounted** folder, noticing that its icon has changed to what appears to be a disk, rather than a folder. The Test folder created in Step 10 appears, since the mounted folder now acts as another entry point to drive I:.

12. Close all open windows.

FAULT TOLERANT DISK STRATEGIES

5

Fault tolerance is the ability of a system to gracefully recover from hardware or software failure. Servers often store critical data that must have high availability. Windows Server 2003 provides a level of fault tolerance through software RAID. RAID is not meant as a replacement for performing regular backups of data, but it increases the availability of disk storage. For example, if a hard disk fails and you have not implemented fault tolerance, any data stored on that disk is lost and unavailable until the drive is replaced and data is restored from backup. With fault tolerance, data is written to more than one drive; in the event one drive fails, data can still be accessed from one of the remaining drives using a combination of other parts of the file, and associated parity information.

RAID Levels

Because hard disk drives are prone to failure, one of the best data security measures is to plan for disk redundancy in servers and host computers. This is accomplished in two ways: by performing regular backups and by installing RAID drives.

Redundant Array of Independent Disk (RAID) strategies is a set of standards for lengthening disk life, preventing data loss, and enabling relatively uninterrupted access to data. There are six basic levels of RAID (other RAID levels exist beyond the basic levels), beginning with the use of disk striping.

The six basic RAID levels are as follows:

- RAID level 0—Striping with no other redundancy features is RAID level 0. Striping is used to extend disk life and to improve performance. Data access on striped volumes is fast because of the way the data is divided into blocks that are quickly accessed through multiple disk reads and data paths. A significant disadvantage to using level 0 striping is that if one disk fails, you can expect a large data loss on all volumes. Windows Server 2003 supports RAID level 0, using between two and 32 disks in a set. In Windows Server 2003, this is called striped volumes, previously referred to as striped sets in Windows NT 4.0.

- RAID level 1—This level employs simple disk mirroring and provides a means of duplicating the operating system files in the event of a disk failure. Disk mirroring is a method of fault tolerance that prevents data loss by duplicating data from a main disk to a backup disk, as shown in Figure 5-9. Disk duplexing is the same as disk mirroring, with the exception that it places the backup disk on a different

controller or adapter than is used by the main disk, as shown in Figure 5-10. Windows Server 2003 supports level 1, but includes disk duplexing as well as mirroring through the fault-tolerance driver Ftdisk.sys. If there are three or more volumes to be mirrored or duplexed, this solution is more expensive than the other RAID levels. When planning for disk mirroring, remember that write access is slower than read access, because information must be written twice, once on the primary disk and once on the secondary disk. Some server administrators consider disk mirroring and disk duplexing to offer one of the best guarantees of data recovery when there is a disk failure.

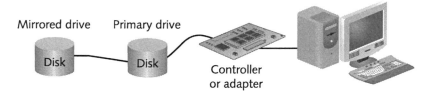

Mirrored drive   Primary drive

Controller or adapter

Figure 6-9   Disk mirroring

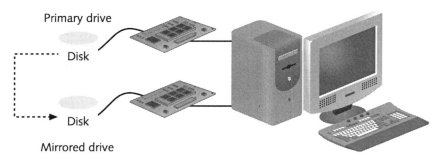

Primary drive

Disk

Disk

Mirrored drive

Figure 5-10   Disk duplexing

- RAID level 2—This uses an array of disks whereby the data is striped across all disks in the array. Also, in this method all disks store error-correction information that enables the array to reconstruct data from a failed disk. The advantages of level 2 are that disk wear is reduced and that data can be reconstructed if a disk fails.

- RAID level 3—Like level 2, RAID level 3 uses disk striping and stores error-correcting information, but the information is only written to one disk in the array. If that disk fails, the array cannot rebuild its contents.

- RAID level 4—This level stripes data and stores error-correcting information on all drives, in a manner similar to level 2. An added feature is its ability to perform checksum verification. The checksum is a sum of bits in a file. When a file is recreated after a disk failure, the checksum previously stored for that file is checked against the actual file after it is reconstructed. If the two do not match, the file may be corrupted. Windows Server 2003 does not support RAID levels 2 through 4.

- RAID level 5—Level 5 combines the best features of RAID, including striping, error correction, and checksum verification. Windows Server 2003 supports level 5, referring to it as a "stripe set with parity on basic disks" or a RAID-5 volume (for dynamic disks), depending on the disk architecture. Whereas level 4 stores checksum data on only one disk, level 5 spreads both error-correction and checksum data over all of the disks, so there is no single point of failure. This level uses more memory than the other RAID levels, with at least 16 MB of additional memory recommended for system functions. In addition, level 5 requires at least three disks in the RAID array. Recovery from a failed disk provides roughly the same guarantee as with disk mirroring, but takes longer with level 5. RAID level 5 can recover from a single disk failure; however, if more than one drive in the array fails, all data is lost and must be restored from backup.

Windows Server 2003 supports RAID levels 0, 1, and 5 for disk fault tolerance (each of these levels is discussed further in the sections that follow), with levels 1 and 5 recommended. RAID level 0 is not recommended in many situations because it does not really provide fault tolerance, except to help extend the life of disks while providing relatively fast access. All three RAID levels support disks formatted with FAT or NTFS. When you decide between using RAID level 1 or RAID level 5, consider the following:

- The boot and system files can be placed on RAID level 1, but not on RAID level 5. Thus, if you use RAID level 5, these files must be on a separate disk or a separate RAID level 1 disk set.

- RAID level 1 uses two hard disks, and RAID level 5 uses from three to 32.

- RAID level 1 is more expensive to implement than RAID level 5, when you consider the cost per megabyte of storage. Keep in mind that in RAID level 1, half of your total disk space is used for redundancy, whereas that value is one-third or less for RAID level 5. The amount of RAID level 5 used for parity is $1/n$ where n is the number of disk drives in the array.

- RAID level 5 requires more memory than RAID level 1.

- Read access is faster in RAID levels 1 and 5 than write access, with read access for RAID level 1 identical to that of a disk that does not have RAID. Because RAID level 5 involves more disks and the read/write heads can acquire data simultaneously across striped volumes, however, RAID level 5 has much faster read access than RAID level 1.

Striped Volume (RAID 0)

As you learned earlier in this chapter, the reasons for using a RAID level 0 or a striped volume in Windows Server 2003 are to:

- Reduce the wear on multiple disk drives by equally spreading the load

- Increase disk performance compared to other methods for configuring dynamic disk volumes

Although striped volumes do not provide fault tolerance, other than to extend the life of the disks, there are situations in which they might be used. Consider, for example, an organization that maintains a "data warehouse" in which vital data is stored and updated on a mainframe; and a copy is downloaded at regular intervals to a server housing the data warehouse. The purpose of the data on the server is to create reports and to provide fast lookups of data, without slowing down the mainframe. In this instance, the goal is to provide the fastest possible access to the data and not fault tolerance, because the original data and primary data services are on the mainframe. For this application, you might create a striped volume on the server used for the data warehouse, because it yields the fastest data access.

To create a striped volume, right-click the unallocated space for the volume, click New Volume, after the New Volume Wizard starts click Next, click the option button for Striped, and complete the remaining steps in the New Volume Wizard.

Mirrored Volume (RAID 1)

Disk mirroring, known as RAID level 1, involves creating a copy of data on a backup disk. Only dynamic disks can be set up as a **mirrored volume** in Windows Server 2003. It is one of the most guaranteed forms of disk fault tolerance because the data on a failed drive is still available on the mirrored drive (with a short down time to make the mirrored drive accessible). Also, disk read performance is the same as reading data from any single disk drive. The disadvantage of mirroring is that the time to create or update information is doubled because it is written twice, once on the main disk and once on the shadow disk. However, writing to disk in mirroring is normally faster than writing to disk when you use RAID level 5. A mirrored volume cannot be striped and requires two dynamic disks.

A mirrored volume is particularly well suited for situations in which data is mission-critical and must not be lost under any circumstances, such as with customer files at a bank. A mirrored volume is also valuable for situations in which a computer system must not be down for long, such as for medical applications or in 24-hour manufacturing. The somewhat slower update time is offset by the assurances that when a disk failure occurs, data will not be lost and the system will quickly be functioning again. However, if fast disk updating is the most important criterion for disk storage, such as when copying files or taking orders over a telephone, then a striped volume may be a better choice than a mirrored volume.

A mirrored volume is created through the Disk Management tool. To create the volume, right-click the unallocated space on one disk, click New Volume, click Next, and choose the Mirrored option in the New Volume Wizard.

RAID-5 Volume

Fault tolerance is better for a RAID-5 volume than for a simple striped volume. A **RAID-5 volume** requires a minimum of three disk drives. Parity information is distributed on each disk so that if one disk fails, the information on that disk can be reconstructed. The parity used by Microsoft is Boolean (true/false, one/zero) logic, with information about the data

contained in each row of 64 KB data blocks on the striped disks. Using the example of storing a 720 KB file across five disks, one 64 KB parity block is written on each disk. The first parity block is always written in row 1 of disk 1, the second is in row 2 of disk 2, and so on, as illustrated in Figure 5-11. (Compare this figure to the striped volume illustrated earlier in Figure 5-4.)

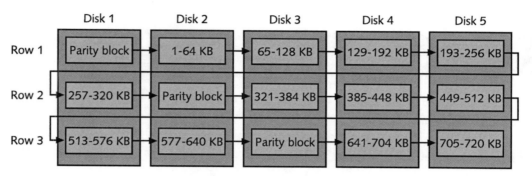

Figure 5-11   Disks in a RAID-5 volume

When you set up a RAID-5 volume, the performance is not as fast as with a striped volume, because it takes longer to write the data and calculate the parity block for each row. However, reading from the disk is as fast as a striped volume. A RAID-5 volume is a viable choice for fault tolerance with mission-critical data and applications where full mirroring is not feasible due to the expense. Also, disk arrays are compatible with RAID level 5. A RAID-5 volume is particularly useful in a client/server system that uses a separate database for queries and report creation, because disk read performance is fast for obtaining data. In applications such as a customer service database that is constantly updated with new orders, disk read performance is slower than with striping without parity.

The amount of storage space used for parity information is based on the formula $1/n$ where n is the number of physical disks in the volume. For example, if there are four disks, the amount of space taken for parity information is 1/4 of the total space of all disk drives in the volume. This means you get more usable disk storage if there are more disks in the volume. A set of eight 2 MB disks yields more usable storage than a set of four 4 MB disks using RAID level 5.

Use the Disk Management tool to create a RAID-5 volume. To start, right-click the unallocated or free space on a disk that is to be part of the volume, click New Volume, click Next, and select the RAID-5 volume option in the New Volume Wizard.

Software RAID and Hardware RAID

Two approaches to RAID can be implemented on a server: software RAID and hardware RAID. Software RAID implements fault tolerance through the server's operating system, such as using RAID levels 0, 1, or 5 through the Windows Server 2003 Disk Management

tool. Hardware RAID is implemented through the server hardware and is independent of the operating system. Many manufacturers implement hardware RAID on the adapter, such as a SCSI adapter, to which the disk drives are connected. The RAID logic is contained in a chip on the adapter. Also, there is often a battery connected to the chip that ensures it never loses power and has fault tolerance to retain the RAID setup even when there is a power outage. Hardware RAID is more expensive than software RAID, but offers many advantages over software RAID, such as:

- Faster read and write response

- The ability to place boot and system files on different RAID levels, such as RAID levels 1 and 5

- The ability to "hot-swap" a failed disk with one that works or is new, thus replacing the disk without shutting down the server (this option can vary by manufacturer)

- More setup options to retrieve damaged data and to combine different RAID levels within one array of disks, such as mirroring two disks using RAID level 1 and setting up five disks for RAID level 5 in a seven disk array (the RAID options depend on what the manufacturer offers)

Monitoring Disk Health and Importing Foreign Disks

The Disk Management tool in Windows Server 2003 provides information on the health of both disks and volumes as a method of allowing administrators to determine the overall health of the disk subsystem. While status messages like Online or Healthy are optimal, it's important to have a basic understanding of the other messages that might appear on disks or volumes.

While monitoring the status of existing disks and volumes is important, Windows Server 2003 also provides the ability to import disks from other servers in the event that another server should fail. Disks that originate from other servers are known as foreign disks, and the process for importing them to another Windows Server 2003 is relatively straightforward.

In the following sections you learn more about both disk and volume status descriptions and the process for importing foreign disks on a Windows Server 2003 system.

Disk and Volume Status Descriptions

Under normal operating conditions, the status associated with a particular hard disk in the Disk Management tool should be "Online", while the status associated with a volume should be "Healthy". These status indicators are listed in the graphical representation of disks or volumes in the Disk Management display, as shown in Figure 5-12.

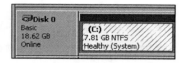

Figure 5-12   Disk and volume status information

Although these status messages are optimal, a variety of additional status messages may appear in their place, and can indicate anything from the failed redundancy of a fault-tolerant volume to different media errors. The most common status messages for a volume are as follows:

- Failed—Indicates that a volume could not be started automatically, or that the disk is damaged. If this status message appears, ensure that the disk is properly connected to the system.

- Failed Redundancy—Indicates that the fault tolerance provided by a RAID-5 or mirrored volume is unavailable because one of the disks in the fault-tolerant volume is not online. Different sub-status messages may appear in parentheses next to the message indicating that the volume at risk is the system or boot volume, holds the paging file, and so forth.

- Formatting—A temporary status message that indicates a format operating is currently being carried out on the volume.

- Healthy—Indicates that a volume is functioning as it should, and no additional actions are required. If this message is followed by a sub-status message in parentheses indicating that the volume is at risk, I/O errors may have been detected, and Check Disk should be run.

- Regenerating—Indicates that a missing disk in a RAID-5 volume has been reactivated and is regenerating its data. Once complete, the status of the volume should return to Healthy.

- Resyncing—Indicates that a mirrored volume is synchronizing information as part of maintaining identical data on both disks. This message may also appear when mirrored disks are imported, or when an offline disk in a mirrored volume is brought back online. Once complete, the status of the volume should return to Healthy.

- Unknown—Indicates that the boot sector for the volume is corrupted, and data on that volume is not accessible.

The most common status messages for a disk are as follows:

- Audio CD—Indicates that an audio CD is located in a CD or DVD drive.

- Foreign—Indicates that the disk is a dynamic disk imported from another computer. To access data on this disk, right-click and select the Import Foreign Disks option.

- Initializing—A temporary status that indicates a basic disk is being converted to a dynamic disk.

- Missing—Indicates that the disk has been removed, is not properly connected, or has been corrupted. If the disk is reconnected, right-click on the disk and choose the Reactivate Disks option to make the disk accessible.

- No Media—Indicates that the CD, DVD, or other removable media drive is empty.

- Not Initialized—Indicates that a new disk has been added to the system without a valid disk signature. To make the disk accessible, right-click on the disk and choose the Initialize Disk option.

- Online—Indicates that the disk is functioning normally, and no additional actions are required.

- Online (Errors)—Indicates that I/O errors have been detected on a dynamic disk. Use the Check Disk utility to scan the disk for errors.

- Offline—Indicates that a disk is no longer accessible. Attempt to fix this problem by right-clicking on the disk and choosing Reactivate Disk. If that doesn't solve the problem, the issue may relate to the connection or a problem with the drive controller.

- Unreadable—Typically indicates I/O errors or corruption on certain portions of the disk. Use the Rescan Disks command to try and bring the disk back online, or try to repair the problem with the Check Disk utility.

For a complete list of the various disk and volume status and sub-status messages available in Windows Server 2003, see the Volume status descriptions and Disk status descriptions topics in Help and Support Center.

Importing Foreign Disks

In cases where a particular server fails, it is conceivable that the data stored on the server's hard disks could still be intact, and need to be made accessible to network users. Windows Server 2003 supports the ability to import dynamic disks from different operating systems, including Windows 2000, Windows XP, and other Windows Server 2003 systems.

When a dynamic disk from another server is connected to a Windows Server 2003 system, the initial status message associated with that disk is Foreign, and the data is inaccessible. To remedy this situation, right-click on the disk and choose the Import Foreign Disks option. This option allows you to choose the disk group to be imported, and display the type, condition, and size of the volumes available on the disk.

If you need to import multiple foreign disks, you should import each disk individually using the Import Foreign Disk command. If more than one disk is used to form a RAID-5 or mirrored volume, fault-tolerance is restored once all disks have been imported. In the case of a spanned volume, all disks that were part of the spanned volume must be imported in order for the data to be accessible. By default, an imported disk attempts to use the same

drive letters assigned to individual volumes from the originating server, but if a conflict exists, the next available drive letters are used instead.

OTHER DISK MAINTENANCE AND MANAGEMENT UTILITIES

Although the Disk Management console is the primary utility used to manage, monitor, and maintain disks on a Windows Server 2003 system, a variety of other disk-related utilities exist. While some of these utilities provide functions or features not available from within the Disk Management interface, others are utilities that allow you to carry out Disk Management-type functions from the command line. The utilities to be explored in this section include:

- Check Disk / CHKDSK
- CONVERT
- Disk Cleanup
- Disk Defragmenter / DEFRAG
- DISKPART
- FORMAT
- FSUTIL
- MOUNTVOL

Check Disk

The Check Disk tool allows you to scan your disk for bad sectors and file system errors. This is a tool that is meant for use when there are no users that need to access the files on the disk you want to check, because the disk is made unavailable during the scan for problems. The Check Disk tool is started from the Properties dialog box for a volume or partition, as shown in Figure 5-13.

There are two options when starting the Check Disk tool, as illustrated in Figure 5-14:

- Automatically fix file system errors—Select this option to have Windows repair any errors in the file system that it finds during the disk-checking process. In order to use this option, all programs must be closed.

- Scan for and attempt recovery of bad sectors—Select this option to have the system find and fix bad sectors and file errors, recovering any information that it can read. Choosing this option also includes the file system fixes that are performed by the Automatically fix file system errors option.

You can also check your disk for errors by running the CHKDSK command (by clicking the CHKDSK command from the command line or Run command). CHKDSK also starts automatically when you boot Windows Server 2003 and the boot process detects a corrupt

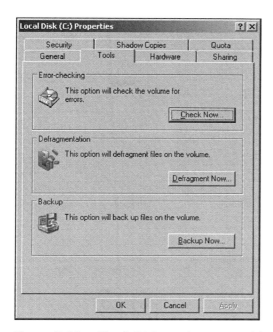

Figure 5-13   Check Disk can be accessed by clicking the Check Now button on the Tools tab in the properties of a volume

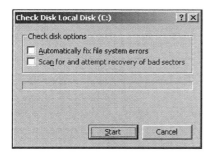

Figure 5-14   The Check Disk tool

file allocation table or corrupted files. In Windows Server 2003, CHKDSK can be used to check FAT16, FAT32, NTFS, or any combination of these (on a dual-boot computer). When the file system is FAT16 or FAT32, the utility checks the file allocation table, folders, files, disk sectors, and disk allocation units. In NTFS, it checks files, folders, indexes, security descriptors, user files, and disk allocation units. The output of the CHKDSK command is illustrated in Figure 5-15.

```
Command Prompt                                    _ □ ×

G:\>chkdsk
The type of the file system is NTFS.
The volume is in use by another process. Chkdsk
might report errors when no corruption is present.

WARNING!  F parameter not specified.
Running CHKDSK in read-only mode.

CHKDSK is verifying files (stage 1 of 3)...
File verification completed.
CHKDSK is verifying indexes (stage 2 of 3)...
Index verification completed.
CHKDSK is verifying security descriptors (stage 3 of 3)...
Security descriptor verification completed.
CHKDSK is verifying Usn Journal...
Usn Journal verification completed.

   4096543 KB total disk space.
   3904616 KB in 12391 files.
      3776 KB in 1117 indexes.
         0 KB in bad sectors.
     63335 KB in use by the system.
     22544 KB occupied by the log file.
    124816 KB available on disk.

      4096 bytes in each allocation unit.
   1024135 total allocation units on disk.
     31204 allocation units available on disk.
```

Figure 5-15   Output from the CHKDSK command

 NOTE
Allow plenty of time for CHKDSK to run on large disk systems, such as a system having over 10 GB. If you have multiple disks, you may want to stagger running CHKDSK on different disks for each week. Also, the presence of some bad sectors is normal. Many disks have a few bad sectors that are marked by the manufacturer during the low-level format and on which data cannot be written.

When CHKDSK finds lost allocation units or chains, it prompts you with the Yes or No question: Convert lost chains to files? Answer Yes to the question so that you can save the lost information to files. The files that CHKDSK creates for each lost chain are labeled Filexxx.chk and can be edited with a text editor to determine their contents.

CONVERT

The primary purpose of the CONVERT command-line utility is to provide a mechanism for converting existing FAT and FAT32 partitions or volumes to the NTFS file system, while leaving existing data intact. This utility was originally explored in Chapter 5, and cannot be used to convert between FAT and FAT32, or from NTFS to either FAT file system. The syntax of the CONVERT command is fairly basic. The example below reiterates the process for converting an existing FAT or FAT32 partition (drive G in this example) to the NTFS file system:

```
convert g: /fs:ntfs
```

Disk Cleanup

Over time, temporary and unnecessary files (such as those placed in the Recycle Bin) can begin to consume very large areas of disk space that could be used for other purposes. The Disk Cleanup utility allows an administrator to quickly determine how much disk space could potentially be freed up on a particular volume or partition by removing unnecessary files. Examples of elements that the Disk Cleanup tool can be used to remove include:

- Temporary Internet files
- Downloaded program files
- Files stored in the Recycle Bin
- Windows temporary files
- Windows components no longer used
- Installed programs no longer used

Additionally, Disk Cleanup can help to increase the amount of disk space made available by compressing files that are seldom used, or removing old catalog files created by the Indexing service. Figure 5-16 illustrates the Disk Cleanup tab of this utility, while Figure 5-17 shows the contents of the More Options tab.

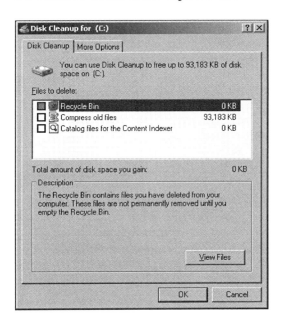

Figure 5-16   The Disk Cleanup utility

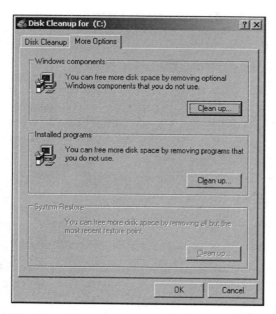

Figure 5-17   The More Options tab in the Disk Cleanup utility

To access the Disk Cleanup tool, right-click the volume or partition and click Properties. On the General tab, click the Disk Cleanup button. The Disk Cleanup utility can also be started from the command line using the CLEANMGR command.

Disk Defragmenter

When you save a file to a disk, Windows Server 2003 saves the file to the first area of available space. The file may not be saved to a contiguous area of free space, and therefore the disk gradually becomes **fragmented**, particularly as more and more files are created and deleted. When your computer attempts to access the file, it may have to be read from different areas on a disk, slowing access time and creating disk wear. The process of **defragmenting** locates fragmented folders and files and moves them to a location on the physical disk so they are in contiguous order.

On a busy server, drives should be defragmented once every week or two. On less busy servers, defragment the drives at least once a month.

In Activity 5-9 you use the Disk Defragmenter utility to analyze and then defragment drive C on your server.

Activity 5-9: Using the Disk Defragmenter Utility

Time Required: 10 minutes

Objective: Defragment a volume using the Disk Defragmenter utility.

Description: In the past, Dover Leasing has always purchased and installed a third-party disk defragmentation utility for all servers. The IT manager at Dover Leasing is exploring ways to help reduce costs, and as such, has asked you to evaluate the Disk Defragmenter tool included with Windows Server 2003. In this activity you use Disk Defragmenter to first analyze and then defragment drive C on your server.

1. Click **Start**, right-click on **My Computer**, and click **Manage**.

2. Click on the **Disk Defragmenter** node to view its contents.

3. Ensure that Volume **C:** is selected, and then click the **Analyze** button.

4. When the Disk Defragmenter dialog box appears, click the **View Report** button.

5. Review the data in the Volume information section, and then click **Close**. The Estimated disk usage before defragmentation bar will be populated with difficult colors to represent fragmented files, contiguous files, unmovable files and free space, as shown in Figure 5-18.

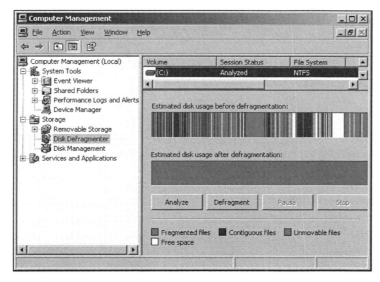

Figure 5-18   Results of analyzing the fragmentation of a volume

6. Click the **Defragment** button to begin the defragmentation process.

7. Once the process completes, click the **View Report** button. After reviewing the report, click the **Close** button.

8. Close the Computer Management window.

Along with the MMC version of the Disk Defragmenter tool, Windows Server 2003 also provides a command-line version of this utility. The DEFRAG command can be used to analyze or defragment an existing volume, partition, or mount point from the command line, and it represents an effective way to schedule disk defragmentation to occur automatically when used in conjunction with a batch file and the Task Scheduler. For example, the following command could be added to a batch file to force a volume (D:) to be defragmented, even if disk space on that volume is low (the disk defragmenter issues a warning when less that 15% of the disk space on a volume is free):

```
defrag d: -f
```

Or, to simply analyze the current fragmentation of drive D from the command line, an administrator could issue the command:

```
defrag d: -a
```

For a list of the complete syntax and switches supported with the DEFRAG command, type DEFRAG /? at the command line and press Enter.

5

DISKPART

The DISKPART command is a powerful utility for managing disks, volumes, and partitions from the command line. Using this tool an administrator can configure the active partition, assign drive letters, control file system mounting, create and extend volumes and partitions, implement fault tolerance schemes, import disks, and more.

One of the most popular uses of the DISKPART utility is to manage disks from within scripts that can be used to automate tasks. For example, the DISKPART tool provides a useful method for creating additional partitions on a system that has been installed using an unattended setup procedure.

For more information on the syntax, commands, and switches available with the DISKPART command, type DISKPART /? at the command line and press Enter.

FORMAT

Users familiar with disk preparation on MS-DOS or Windows 9X systems are likely already familiar with the basic concept of the FORMAT command. Used to implement a file system on an existing partition, the FORMAT command in Windows Server 2003 allows an administrator to not only specify which of the supported file systems should be implemented with the command, but also a variety of advanced settings including the allocation unit (cluster) size. Although the ability to format disks is provided from within the Disk Management console, the command-line version provides administrators with additional flexibility, including formatting partitions from within scripts.

For more information on the syntax, and switches available with the FORMAT command, type FORMAT /? at the command line and press Enter.

FSUTIL

The FSUTIL command is an advanced command-line utility that allows an administrator to gather information and perform tasks relating to FAT, FAT32, and NTFS file systems. Because this utility allows an administrator to control many advanced file system settings and functions, it should only be used by advanced or experienced administrators. Examples of information that can be gathered by the FSUTIL tool include listings of drives, volume information, NTFS-specific data, and so forth. The FSUTIL tool can also be used to manage disk quotas, display the free space available on a volume, and more. For example, to view all of the volumes available on a system, issue the following command:

```
fsutil fsinfo drives
```

To view disk space information about drive C, including the amount of free space and total disk space available, issue the following command:

```
fsutil volume diskfree c:
```

The FSUTIL command supports a variety of sub-commands and switches. For detailed information on the capabilities of the FSUTIL command, see the FSUTIL topic in Help and Support Center.

MOUNTVOL

Although Windows Server 2003 allows NTFS volumes to be mounted to an empty folder from within the Disk Management console, the MOUNTVOL command can also be used to create, delete, or list volume mount points from the command line. Unfortunately, one of the parameters associated with mounting a new volume is VolumeName, and this value is specified using a globally unique identifier (GUID) value that can be exceptionally long. Thankfully, issuing the MOUNTVOL /? command and pressing Enter will not only list the various switches associated with the command, but also the GUIDs of existing volumes and partitions.

For example, the command to mount a volume with the GUID ced284f1-6962-11d7-8400-806d6172696f to an empty NTFS folder named D:\mountpoint would be:

```
mountvol d:\mountpoint \\?\volume{ced284f1-6962-11d7-8400-
806d6172696f}\
```

Although the length of the GUID complicates the task of adding a new mount point, existing mount points can be easily deleted using the command. For example, the mount point created in the previous example would be deleted by issuing the following command:

```
mountvol d:\mountpoint /d
```

For more information on the syntax, and switches available with the MOUNTVOL command, along with the VolumeName values for existing volumes and partitions, type MOUNTVOL /? at the command line and press Enter.

CHAPTER SUMMARY

- Windows Server 2003 supports both basic and dynamic disks. Basic disks consist of primary and extended partitions, as well as logical drives. Dynamic disks allow volumes to be created and fault-tolerant disk strategies to be implemented.

- Basic disks can support up to four primary partitions, or three primary and one extended partition. Extended partitions can be further divided into logical drives.

- Dynamic disks can support simple, spanned, striped, mirrored, and RAID-5 volumes.

- Disk Management is the primary tool used to manage disks, partitions, and volumes on a Windows Server 2003 system.

- Windows Server 2003 supports two main fault-tolerance techniques for hard disks. Mirrored volumes, also known as RAID 1, mirrors the contents of one volume to another disk. RAID-5 volumes use disk striping with parity to allow continued operation of a volume in the event that a single disk in that volume should fail.

- Windows Server 2003 provides a number of tools for managing, maintaining, and monitoring disks and partitions from the command line including CHKDSK, DISKPART, DEFRAG, FORMAT, FSUTIL, and MOUNTVOL.

- The Disk Cleanup utility allows Administrators to remove unnecessary files and applications from a partition or volume, as well as save space by compressing seldom-used files.

- The Disk Defragmenter tool is used to optimize the performance of a partition or volume by moving fragmented files back into contiguous blocks of disk space.

KEY TERMS

active partition — The partition from which an operating system begins the boot process. Typically drive C: is configured as the active partition on a Windows Server 2003 system.

basic disk — In Windows Server 2003, a partitioned disk that can have up to four partitions and that uses logical drive designations. This type of disk is compatible with MS-DOS, Windows 3.x, Windows 95, Windows 98, Windows NT, Windows 2000, Windows XP, and Windows Server 2003.

defragmenting — A process by which fragmented files are rearranged into contiguous areas of disk space, improving file access performance.

Disk Management — An MMC snap-in used to manage and monitor disks, volumes, and partitions.

dynamic disk — A disk in Windows Server 2003, that does not use traditional partitioning, meaning there are no restrictions on the number of volumes that can be set up on one disk or the ability to extend volumes onto additional physical disks. Dynamic disks are only compatible with Windows Server 2003, Windows 2000, and Windows XP Professional systems.

extended partition — A partition on a basic disk that is created from unpartitioned free disk space, and is not formatted with a file system. Space in an extended partition is allocated to logical drives.

fault tolerance — Techniques that employ hardware and software to provide assurance against equipment failures, computer service interruptions, and data loss.

fragmented — A normal and gradual process in which files become divided into different areas of disk space in a volume, resulting in slower file access.

logical drives — Dedicated and formatted portions of disk space created within an extended partition on a basic disk.

mirrored volume — A fault-tolerant disk strategy in which a volume on one dynamic disk has its contents mirrored to a second dynamic disk.

mounted drive — A partition or volume accessible via an empty folder on an existing NTFS partition. Often implemented to circumvent the need to assign the volume or partition of a drive letter.

primary partition — A dedicated portion of a basic disk that is potentially bootable, and formatted with a file system. A basic disk can support a maximum of four primary partitions.

RAID-5 volume — A fault-tolerant disk strategy that consists of creating a single volume across anywhere between three and 32 dynamic disks. RAID-5 volumes use disk striping with parity to allow the volume to remain accessible in the event that a single disk with the volume should fail.

Redundant Array of Independent Disks (RAID) — Disk performance and fault tolerance strategies that can be implemented on a Windows Server 2003 system with multiple hard disks installed.

simple volume — A dedicated and formatted portion of disk space on a dynamic disk.

spanned volume — Dedicated and formatted space on between two and 32 dynamic disks that is treated as a single logical volume.

striped volume — Dedicated and formatted space on between two and 32 dynamic disks that is treated as a single logical volume, with data striped across the disks in the volume in 64 KB blocks.

Review Questions

1. What is the maximum number of primary partitions that a basic disk can support?

   a. 1

   b. 2

   c. 3

   d. 4

2. What is the maximum number of extended partitions that a basic disk can support?

   a. 1

   b. 2

   c. 3

   d. 4

3. Which of the following can be created on a dynamic disk?

   a. Simple volume

   b. Spanned volume

   c. Primary partition

   d. Extended partition

4. What term is used to describe an installed dynamic disk that originated from another server?

   a. Foreign disk

   b. External disk

   c. Dynamic disk

   d. Basic disk

5. If only one hard disk is installed on a Windows Server 2003 system, what disk number will it be assigned?

   a. 0

   b. 1

   c. 2

   d. 01

6. Which of the following can be created on a basic disk?

   a. RAID-5 volume

   b. Spanned volume

   c. Primary partition

   d. Logical drive

7. RAID-5 volumes can be created on a basic disk.

   a. True

   b. False

8. Which of the following volumes cannot be extended on a Windows Server 2003 system?

   a. System volume

   b. Boot volume

   c. All volumes can be extended on a Windows Server 2003 system, as long as the file system used is NTFS

9. Which of the following file systems supports the ability to extend existing volumes?

   a. FAT

   b. FAT32

   c. NTFS

10. What is the minimum number of hard disks required for implementing a RAID-5 volume?

    a. 2

    b. 3

    c. 4

    d. 5

11. What is the maximum number of hard drives supported for a striped volume on a Windows Server 2003 system?

    a. 3

    b. 6

    c. 16

    d. 32

12. What term is used to describe disk mirroring when each drive is connected to its own hard disk controller?

    a. Disk mirroring

    b. Disk duplexing

    c. Shadowing

    d. Controller mirror

13. What term is used to describe the volume the Windows folder is located on?

    a. Boot volume

    b. System volume

    c. Dynamic disk

    d. Basic disk

14. How many partitions can be marked active on a Windows Server 2003 system at any point in time?

    a. 0

    b. 1

    c. 2

    d. 3

15. Which of the following RAID levels provides no fault tolerance?

    a. RAID level 0

    b. RAID level 1

    c. RAID level 4

    d. RAID level 5

16. All access to a spanned volume is lost if one disk on which the spanned volume resides fails.

    a. True

    b. False

17. Which of the following tools can be used to view and remove unnecessary files on a particular partition or volume?

    a. Disk Cleanup

    b. Check Disk

    c. MOUNTVOL

    d. DISKPART

18. Which of the following command-line utilities can be used to defragment files?

    a. DISKPART

    b. DEFRAG

    c. DEFRAGMENT

    d. DF

19. An extended partition is formatted with a file system.

    a. True

    b. False

20. A volume can be mounted to an empty folder on a drive formatted with the FAT32 file system.

    a. True

    b. False

5

CASE PROJECTS

Case Project 5-1

The IT manager at Dover Leasing wants all administrative staff to be capable of managing disks from the command line. Using the details provided in Help and Support Center, use the DISKPART command to create a new simple volume using the remaining disk space on DISK 0. Use the FORMAT command to format this new partition with the NTFS file system. Finally, use the MOUNTVOL command to mount the new partition to an empty folder named Newmount on drive D.

Case Project 5-2

Dover Leasing is interested in implementing a disk-management strategy that will allow them to use the fault-tolerance features of Windows Server 2003. Outline each of the fault-tolerant disk methods available on Windows Server 2003, how they work, and the requirements for implementation.

6

ADVANCED FILE SYSTEM MANAGEMENT

After reading this chapter and completing the exercises, you will be able to:

Understand and configure file and folder attributes

Understand and configure advanced file and folder attributes

Implement and manage disk quotas

Understand and implement the Distributed File System

Managing resources such as files and folders on a Windows Server 2003 system consists of a variety of tasks. In Chapter 5 you learned about how file resources are shared and then secured using both shared folder and NTFS permissions. While the configuration of file and folder permissions is a critical part of an administrator's overall security strategy, administrators also need to be familiar with other tasks and capabilities relating to managing these resources.

Since the days of MS-DOS, Microsoft operating systems have used file and folder attributes as a method of "describing" and even securing files. Windows Server 2003 supports the four standard file and folder attributes available since MS-DOS, namely the Archive, Hidden, Read-only, and System attributes. An understanding of how these attributes impact files and folders is an important part of any file management strategy. In this chapter you learn how to utilize and configure standard attributes using both the Windows graphical interface as well as command-line utilities.

When a volume or partition is formatted with the NTFS file system, Windows Server 2003 also supports a number of advanced file system attributes. For example, a feature of the NTFS file system known as the Encrypting File System (EFS) allows an administrator to further secure files by encrypting their contents. Another advanced attribute, known as compression, allows an administrator to reduce the amount of disk space occupied by files on an NTFS partition by compressing the contents of selected files and folders. Although

other advanced attributes are also discussed, encryption and compression are looked at in detail in this chapter.

In many network environments, the amount of server disk space consumed by user files can quickly fill existing disk space, especially in cases where users are saving non-work-related files to locations such as their home directory. While features like compression can help to reduce the amount of disk space consumed by files, Windows Server 2003 provides administrators with a more granular level of control over how disk space is allocated to users via the disk quotas feature. When implemented, an administrator can control the amount of disk space allocated to users for particular NTFS partitions and volumes. Later in the chapter you learn about how disk quotas are implemented, as well as how they are managed in Windows Server 2003 environments.

As any network environment grows, users may need to access various shared folders on a variety of different servers. Although techniques such as mapping network drives help to make shared folders more easily accessible, shared resources can still be difficult to find. To help account for this, Windows Server 2003 supports a feature known as the Distributed File System (DFS). If correctly designed and implemented, DFS allows an administrator to create a single logical directory structure for shared folders on different servers throughout a network environment, allowing them to appear as though they are simply sub-folders or a single directory tree. Ultimately, the implementation of DFS can make accessing resources spread across multiple servers much simpler for users, and reduce costs associated with time wasted searching for resources.

FILE AND FOLDER ATTRIBUTES

Microsoft Operating systems since MS-DOS have included the ability to apply attributes to files and folders. Broadly speaking, attributes are used to describe files, folders, and their characteristics. On a Windows Server 2003 system, file and folder attributes can be viewed and configured using both graphical tools as well as the ATTRIB command.

The four standard file and folder attributes that have been available since MS-DOS include:

- Read-only
- Archive
- System
- Hidden

Each of these attributes is looked at in more detail in the following sections.

Read-only

As its name suggests, the **read-only attribute** designates that the contents of a file cannot be changed. The read-only attribute provides a degree of security that helps to ensure that files are not accidentally changed or deleted, and is available regardless of the file system in

use. For example, attributes can be configured for files located on FAT, FAT32, or NTFS partitions and volumes.

Although the read-only attribute suggests that it provides a degree of security, the level of security associated with the attribute depends upon the file system on which the file resides. For example, setting the read-only attribute on a file stored on a FAT or FAT32 volume will indeed make the contents of that file read-only, but any user could change the attribute, effectively disabling the setting. When attributes are configured on a file stored on an NTFS volume, only users with at least the Allow Modify NTFS permission (or those users who have been explicitly granted the Write Attributes special NTFS permission) have the ability to change attributes. In this way, attributes configured on an NTFS volume can be effectively secured, while attributes configured for files stored on a FAT or FAT32 volume are inherently insecure.

The read-only attribute can be configured for a file or folder from the General tab of its Properties dialog box, as shown in Figure 6-1. When the read-only attribute is configured for a folder, the attribute doesn't apply to the folder itself, but rather the files it contains. For example, checking the read-only attribute for a folder will automatically configure all of the files in that folder as read-only, while unchecking the read-only attribute will remove this attribute for all files within the folder. If the read-only check box on the General tab of a folder appears as solid gray, it means that some, but not all of the files within the folder have their read-only attribute set.

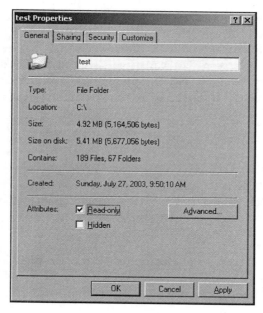

Figure 6-1   Configuring the read-only attribute for a folder

While any user can open a file configured with the read-only attribute, attempts to save changes to this file will result in a warning dialog box similar to the one illustrated in Figure 6-2.

Figure 6-2   The result of trying to save changes to a file configured with the read-only attribute set

Archive

The main purpose of the **archive attribute** is to provide a method for both administrators and applications to determine which files and folders have recently been created or changed. When a new file is created, or an existing file has been changed, the archive attribute for that file is turned on, marking the file as "ready for archiving". The status of the archive attribute is particularly important to backup programs, where different backup methods will manipulate the attribute as part of different backup schemes.

For example, if an administrator uses the Windows Backup utility to perform a full back up on all files on drive C, the archive attribute is cleared on files as part of the process. Then, as new files are created or existing files changed, the archive attribute for these files would be turned out. Ultimately, this allows the backup utility to determine which files are new (or have changed) since the last full backup, and makes it possible to selectively back up only these new files. The various backup techniques used by programs like Windows Backup (and their impacts on the archive attribute) is looked at in more detail in Chapter 10.

When a file or folder is stored on a FAT or FAT32 partition or volume, the archive attribute can be configured from the General tab in the properties of the file or folder, as shown in Figure 6-3.

Configuring the archive attribute using Windows Explorer for files and folders stored on NTFS partitions and volumes is looked at in the Advanced Attributes section later in this chapter.

Determining whether the archive attribute is set or cleared for a particular file is possible by using both Windows Explorer and command-line utilities such as DIR (used to view directory listings) and the ATTRIB command. Both are looked at in more detail later in this chapter.

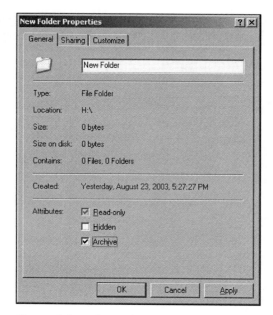

Figure 6-3   The archive attribute can be configured from the General tab of a file or
folder residing on a FAT or FAT32 partition or volume

System

Although originally designed to identify operating system files in MS–DOS, the actual application of the **system attribute** has never been entirely consistent or well documented. On a Windows Server 2003 system, a number of files and folders have their system attribute configured, usually in conjunction with the hidden attribute. When both the system and hidden attributes are configured for a file or folder, that file or folder is considered "super hidden", and is not displayed in the Windows Explorer interface, even when the option to show hidden files is configured. Instead, files or folders with both the hidden and system attributes configured are treated as "protected operating system files", which have their own specific display options. You learn more about the display options associated with hidden files in the next section.

The system attribute is not configurable from the General tab in the properties of a file or folder in a manner similar to the read-only and hidden attributes. The system attributes can be manipulated using the ATTRIB command, as outlined later in this section.

Hidden

As a method of protecting certain files and folders from being visible to users from Windows Explorer or the command line, another attribute appropriately named hidden is available. In

much the same way that a file can be configured as read-only from the General tab of it's properties, the **hidden attribute** can be configured in a similar manner, as shown in Figure 6-4.

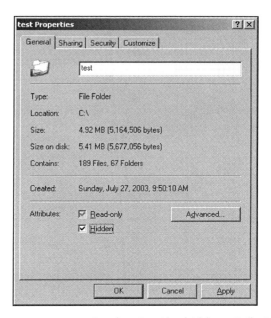

Figure 6-4   Configuring the hidden attribute for a file

Although the name hidden seems to suggest that a file cannot be viewed using a tool like Windows Explorer, the default configuration setting in Windows Server 2003 displays files configured with the hidden attribute using a semi-transparent icon. By default, the only hidden files that do not appear in the Windows Explorer interface by default are those with both their hidden and system attributes configured. The degree to which hidden files and folders are visible from within the Windows Explorer interface is configurable from the View tab of the Folder Options program available from the Tools menu in Windows Explorer, as shown in Figure 6-5.

The two most relevant settings on this tab and their capabilities are as follows:

- Hidden file and folders—When the Show hidden files and folders option is selected (it is not selected by default), hidden files and folders appear in the Windows Explorer interface using transparent icons. When the Do not show hidden files and folders option is selected, any file with its hidden attribute configured is not displayed in the Windows Explorer interface.

- Hide protected operating system files (Recommended)—When this option is selected (the default setting), all files with both their hidden and system attributes set are completely hidden in the Windows Explorer interface. When deselected, all files with the hidden and system attributes configured are visible from Windows Explorer.

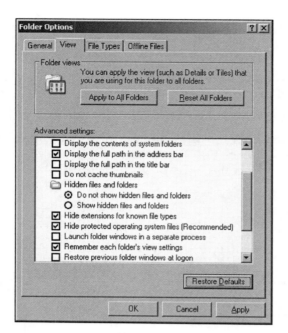

Figure 6-5   Configuring display settings for hidden files and folders

In Activity 6-1 you use Windows Explorer to view and configure attributes, as well as change the display settings for Hidden files and folders.

Activity 6-1: Viewing and Configuring File and Folder Attributes Using Windows Explorer

Time Required: 10 minutes

Objective: Use Windows Explorer to view and configure file and folder attributes.

Description: NTFS permissions are the primary method used to secure files and folders on Dover Leasing's Windows Server 2003 systems. However, the IT manager is also interested in taking advantage of file system attributes for their ability to control which files are included in backup processes, and which files are visible to users, including junior administrators. In this activity you use the Windows Explorer interface to view and configure attribute settings on your server.

1. Log on using your **AdminXX** account (where *XX* is your assigned student number). Click **Start**, and then click **My Computer**.

2. Double-click on drive **C:** to view its contents.

3. Click the **View** menu, and then click **Details**. This view displays the Name, Size, Type, Date Modified, and Attributes associated with files and folders. Review the letters listed in the Attribute column for the files and folders displayed. Each letter

listed represents configured attributes for that folder. For example, the letters RHSA would designate a file or folder that has its read-only (R), hidden (H), system (S), and archive (A) attributes configured.

4. Double-click the **Documents and Settings** folder to view its contents. Make note of the folders that are visible in the Documents and Settings folder by default.

5. Click the **Tools** menu, and then click **Folder Options**. Click the **View** tab.

6. In the Advanced settings section, click the **Show hidden files and folders** radio button, as displayed in Figure 6-6. Click **OK**. Notice that a folder named Default User now appears on the list, and that this folder has its hidden attribute configured.

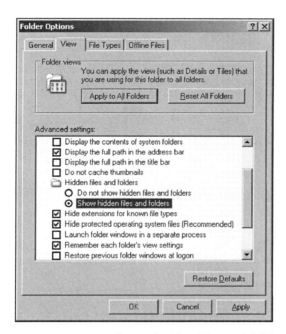

Figure 6-6   Displaying hidden files and folders

7. Press the **Backspace** button on the keyboard to return to the contents of drive C:. Note that no additional files or folders appear in this list as a result of showing hidden files.

8. Click the **Tools** menu, and then click **Folder Options**. Click the **View** tab.

9. In the Advanced settings section, uncheck the **Hide protected operating system files (Recommended)** check box. When the Warning dialog box shown in Figure 6-7 appears, read the message it displays, and click **Yes**. Click **OK**.

10. Review the additional files and folders now displayed in the Windows Explorer interface, noting that each of the new files and folders now visible has its system and hidden attributes configured.

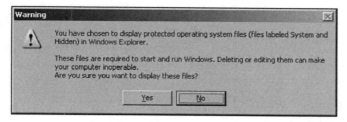

Figure 6-7 Warning message when choosing to view protected operating system files

6

11. Right-click on the **NTDETECT** file, and click **Properties**. On the General tab, notice that the Read-only check box is checked and can be changed, but that the hidden attribute is checked and cannot be changed. The fact that the Hidden check box is not configurable is a function of the fact that this file also has its System attribute configured. Click **Cancel**.

12. Press the **Backspace** button to view the contents of My Computer. Double-click on drive **D:** to view its contents.

13. Click the **File** menu, select **New**, and then click **Text Document**. Name the new file **attribute-test**.

14. After creating the file, notice that it is automatically assigned the archive attribute by default.

15. Right-click on the **attribute-test** file and click **Properties**.

16. On the General tab, check both the **Read-only** and **Hidden** check boxes, and click **OK**.

17. Notice that the Attribute column now displays RHA, because the read-only, hidden, and archive attributes are configured for the file. Close all open windows.

The ATTRIB Command

ATTRIB is a command-line utility that can be used to add or remove any of the four main attributes to or from files and folders. Although Windows Explorer allows you to configure the read-only and hidden attributes using a graphical interface, the system attribute can only be configured from the command line when necessary. The ATTRIB command can also be used to view the configured attributes for a file or folder. For example, to view the attributes associated with a file named text.txt in the D:\docs directory, the correct syntax would be:

```
D:\>attrib d:\docs\test.txt
```

The basic syntax used to change attributes with the ATTRIB command is outlined below. In the first example, the archive, system, hidden, and read-only attributes are configured for a file named test.txt in the D:\docs directory. In the second command, these same attributes are removed.

```
D:\>attrib +A +S +H +R d:\docs\test.txt
```

```
D:\>attrib -A -S -H -R d:\docs\test.txt
```

One of the major advantages of using the ATTRIB command is that it supports wildcards, allowing the attributes for multiple files and folders to be changed simultaneously. For example, the following command would configure the hidden attribute for all files stored in the D:\docs folder that end in a .TXT extension:

```
D:\>attrib +H d:\docs\*.txt
```

In Activity 7-2 you use the ATTRIB command to view and change file attributes from the command line.

Activity 6-2:   Changing File Attributes Using the ATTRIB Command

Time Required: 10 minutes

Objective: View and change file attributes from the command line.

Description: While Windows Explorer provides a simple method to configure attributes for files and folders, this can also be accomplished using the ATTRIB command. In this activity you use the ATTRIB command to view and change the attributes associated with files from the command line, and then view those changes in Windows Explorer.

1. Click **Start**, and then click **Run**. In the Open text box, type **cmd.exe** and click **OK.**

2. At the command line, type **d:** and press **Enter.**

3. Type **mkdir attributes** and press **Enter** to create a new directory called attributes. Leave the command prompt window open.

4. Click **Start**, and then click **My Computer**. Double-click on drive **D:** to view its contents, and then double-click on the **attributes** folder to open it. Create three new text files in the folder named **file1.txt**, **file2.txt**, and **file3.txt**. Once complete, close the My Computer window.

5. In the command prompt window, type **cd attributes** and press **Enter.**

6. Type **attrib file1.txt** and press **Enter**. Notice that the output of the command displays the letter A (meaning the archive attribute is set) and the path to the file, as shown in Figure 6-8.

7. Type **attrib −A file1.txt** and press **Enter**. This removes the archive attribute from file1.txt.

8. Type **attrib file1.txt** and press **Enter**. Notice that the output no longer displays any attributes for file1.txt.

9. Type **attrib +A +H +R +S file1.txt** and press **Enter**. This command adds the archive, hidden, read-only, and system attributes to file1.txt. Close the command prompt window.

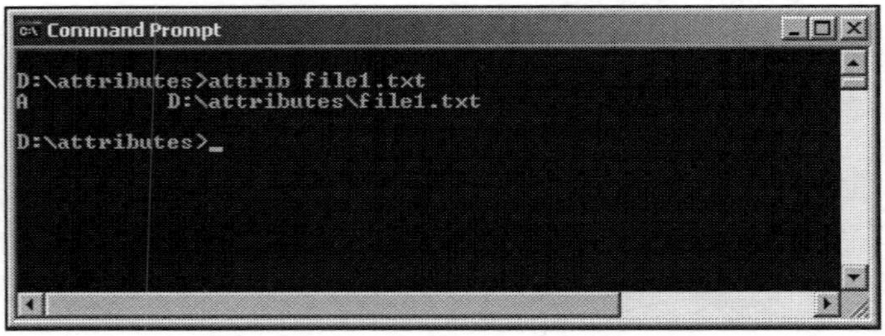

Figure 6-8   Viewing file attributes with the ATTRIB command

6

10. Click **Start**, and then click **My Computer**. Double-click on drive **D:** to view its contents, and then double-click on the **attributes** folder to open it. Notice that all three files are visible in the Windows Explorer interface, along with their associated attributes. Notice also that file1.txt uses a transparent icon, since its hidden attribute is set.

11. Click the **Tools** menu, and then click **Folder Options**. Click the **View** tab.

12. In the Advanced settings section, check the **Hide protected operating system files (Recommended)** check box, and click **OK**.

13. Notice that file1.txt no longer appears in the list of files in Windows Explorer. This is because file1.txt has both the system and hidden attributes set, and as such is hidden from display because it is treated like a protected operating system file as configured in Step 12.

14. Close the My Computer window.

ADVANCED ATTRIBUTES

In addition to the standard file and folder attributes outlined in the previous section, Windows Server 2003 also supports a number of advanced attributes for files or folders stored on NTFS partitions or volumes. Advanced attributes are accessible by clicking the Advanced button on the General tab in the properties of a file or folder that resides on an NTFS partition or volume. This opens the Advanced Attributes window, as shown in Figure 6-9.

The Archive and Index attributes section of the Advanced Attributes windows consists of the following two options for a file:

- File is ready for archiving—Configures the archive attribute for the file.
- For fast searching, allow Indexing Service to index this file—Indexes the contents of the file, allowing searches to be performed within the text and according to properties such as configured attributes, modification dates, and so forth.

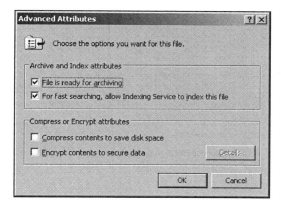

Figure 6-9   The Advanced Attributes configuration window for a file

The Advanced Attributes window for a folder contains similar options, but will set the archiving or indexing attributes for an entire folder (and potentially its contents) rather than just a single file. For example, when the indexing option is changed for a folder it sends a prompt inquiring whether the indexing status should also be changed for subfolders and files, as illustrated in Figure 6-10.

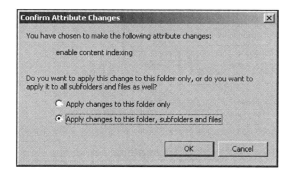

Figure 6-10   The Confirm Attribute Changes window

The Compress or Encrypt attributes section of the Advanced Attributes window consists of the following two options:

- Compress contents to save disk space—Compresses the file or folder to reduce the amount of space that it occupies on the disk.

- Encrypt contents to secure data—Encrypts the contents of a file to secure it. When configured for a folder, new files saved to this folder (and potentially existing files) are encrypted as well.

Compression and encryption settings are only applicable to files and folders residing on NTFS partitions or volumes. Both the compress and encrypt attributes are mutually exclusive. In other words, you cannot encrypt and compress a given file or folder at the same time.

Both the compression and encryption features of Windows Server 2003 are looked at in more detail in the following sections.

File Compression

On volumes that are formatted with NTFS, you can enable **compression** to reduce the amount of disk space that folders and files take up, thus allowing more data to be stored on the volume. Once a volume, folder, or file is compressed, you do not need any additional utilities to uncompress it. When a user accesses the file, it is automatically uncompressed in a manner completely transparent to the user.

Configuring compression is as simple as enabling or disabling the compression attribute of a file or folder within Windows Explorer. Checking the Compress contents to save disk space check box enables compression, as illustrated in Figure 6-11.

Figure 6-11   Configuring compression settings for a folder

After a folder or file has been compressed, it is displayed in a different color within Windows Explorer (making it easy for an administrator to identify what is and is not compressed). Compressed folders and files are displayed in blue by default, though you can change this option from the View tab in the Folder Options dialog box.

The compression attribute can be affected when copying and moving files. Keep the following points in mind when using the compression attribute:

- If a file is copied to another folder within the same NTFS volume, it automatically inherits the compression attribute of the destination folder.

- If a file or folder is moved within the same NTFS volume, it retains its compression attribute.

- If a file or folder is copied between NTFS volumes, the file or folder inherits the compression attribute of the destination folder.

- If a file or folder is moved between NTFS volumes, the file or folder inherits the compression attribute of the destination folder.

Although the previous points specifically list the impact of moving or copying compressed files within or between NTFS volumes or partitions, the same rules apply to moving or copying encrypted files, as well as any NTFS permissions applied to files. For example, if an encrypted file is copied to another folder (with its encryption attribute configured) on the same NTFS volume, it inherits the encryption attribute of the target folder. The configuration of encryption settings is looked at in more detail later in this section.

In Activity 6-3 you will use the compression feature to compress a folder stored on an NTFS volume on your server.

Activity 6-3: Configuring Folder Compression Settings

Time Required: 5 minutes

Objective: Configure a folder to compress its contents.

Description: Both the Legal and Marketing Departments at Dover Leasing generate enormous quantities of data over the course of a year. Although much of the old marketing data can be deleted after this time, all files belonging to the Legal Department must be archived indefinitely. Because of the large amount of disk space that this data occupies, the IT manager has asked you to evaluate ways in which the amount of disk space used by these files can be reduced. In this activity, you test the impact of using the NTFS compression attribute to save disk space.

1. Open My Computer, and then browse to drive **D:**. Create a new folder called **Compress** and then copy the setup.bmp file from the C:\WINDOWS\System32 folder into this new folder.

2. Right-click the **Compress** folder and click **Properties**. Note both the Size and Size on disk information provided on the General tab.

3. Click the **Advanced** button to open the Advanced Attributes dialog box.

4. In the Compress or Encrypt attributes section, click the **Compress contents to save disk space** check box and then click **OK**.

5. Click **OK** to exit the properties of the Compress folder.

6. When the Confirm Attribute Changes dialog box opens, ensure that the **Apply changes to this folder, subfolders and files** radio button is selected and then click **OK**.

7. In the My Computer interface, notice that the Compress folder is now listed in blue text, which designates it as having its compression attribute set.

8. Open the **Compress** folder, right-click on the **setup.bmp** file, and click **Properties**. Notice that while the Size value has not changed, the Size on disk value is now significantly reduced from its original value, as shown in Figure 6-12.

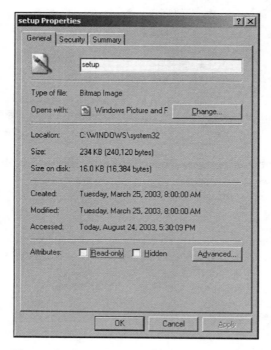

Figure 6-12   Viewing the Size and Size on disk settings for a compressed file

9. Close all open windows.

COMPACT

Windows Server 2003 includes a utility named COMPACT to allow the compression attribute of files and folders to be changed from the command line. When issued without any switches, the COMPACT command will display compression settings for the contents of the current directory, as shown in Figure 6-13.

The most common switches used in conjunction with the COMPACT command are /c (to compress files and folders) and /u (to uncompress files and folders). For example, to compress a single file named setup.bmp in the C:\WINDOWS\system32 directory, the correct syntax would be:

```
C:\WINDOWS\system32>compact /c setup.bmp
```

```
Command Prompt                                              _ □ ×

D:\attributes>compact

 Listing D:\attributes\
 New files added to this directory will not be compressed.

          0 :          0 = 1.0 to 1   file1.txt
          0 :          0 = 1.0 to 1   file2.txt
          0 :          0 = 1.0 to 1   file3.txt
     787512 :     559616 = 1.4 to 1 C test.bmp

Of  4 files within 1 directories
1 are compressed and 3 are not compressed.
787,512 total bytes of data are stored in 559,616 bytes.
The compression ratio is 1.4 to 1.


D:\attributes>_
```

Figure 6-13   Viewing compression information for the current directory using the COM-
             PACT command

Similarly, if you wanted to remove the compression attribute from all files and subfolders of the directory C:\compressed, but not change the compression attribute of the C:\compressed folder itself, the correct syntax would be:

```
C:\>compact /u c:\compressed
```

Because the COMPACT command requires the NTFS file system to function, it cannot be used to compress files or folders stored on FAT or FAT32 partitions or volumes.

For a complete list of the switches supported with the COMPACT command, type COMPACT /? at the command prompt, or view the Compact: Command-line reference topic in Help and Support Center.

File Encryption

Another method to secure files and folders is to use encryption. The ability to encrypt files adds another level of protection on top of setting share or NTFS permissions. The **Encrypting File System (EFS)** uses public key cryptography to transparently encrypt folders and files.

File and folder encryption is implemented using two main types of encryption keys. When a file is configured for encryption, EFS encrypts the data using a special session key known as a **file encryption key (FEK)**. The FEK is added to a header attached to the encrypted data known as the **data decryption field (DDF)**. The DDF is subsequently encrypted using the user's public key, so only they can decrypt it using their corresponding private key.

The main challenge associated with using encryption to secure file resources is that if a user were to leave the company, all data that had been encrypted with their public key would be inaccessible by other user accounts. One exception to this is when an administrator renames

the user account to which the private key is associated. In this case, the new user would be able to access data encrypted by the private key because only the username associated with the account has changed.

For data recovery purposes, Windows Server 2003 includes a special role known as a **data recovery agent**. In the event that a user encrypts data and then leaves the company or loses their private key, the user designated as the recovery agent can recover the encrypted data. When data is encrypted using EFS, the FEK of the data recovery agent is also stored in a second header called the **data recovery field (DRF)**. This key is encrypted using the data recovery agent's public key, thus making the data recovery agent capable of decrypting or recovering EFS-encrypted files and folders. By default, the local administrator of a standalone workstation or member server is designated as the recovery agent. In a domain environment, the domain administrator account is configured as the only data recovery agent by default, though additional recovery agents can be designated using Certificate Services and Group Policy. Windows Server 2003 also includes a new feature that allows EFS-encrypted files to be shared with other users, which you learn about later in this section.

EFS encryption for a file or folder is configured using advanced attributes in Windows Explorer. The advanced attribute settings for a folder are shown in Figure 6-14.

Figure 6-14   Viewing the encryption settings for a folder

Before using EFS to encrypt data, keep the following in mind:

- If you set the encryption attribute on a folder, the folder itself is not actually encrypted, only the contents of the folder
- Once a folder's encryption attribute is set, any data saved in the folder, or copied or moved into the folder, is encrypted

- If an encrypted file is copied or moved into a folder that is not encrypted, the file retains its encryption attribute as long as the file system is NTFS; encrypted files moved to a FAT partition are automatically decrypted

- Encryption and compression are mutually exclusive; you cannot encrypt and compress data at the same time

In Activity 6-4 you configure a folder to encrypt files using EFS and then attempt to access an encrypted file using different user accounts.

Activity 6-4: Encrypting Files Using Windows Explorer

Time Required: 10 minutes

Objective: Implement and test file encryption security using EFS.

Description: Dover Leasing is interested in having its laptop users utilize EFS to better protect corporate data on these machines should they be lost or stolen. In this activity, you configure a folder to use EFS encryption and then attempt to access files within the folder using different user accounts.

1. Open My Computer and create a new folder on drive D: named **Encrypted**.

2. Right-click the **Encrypted** folder and click **Properties**.

3. On the General tab, click the **Advanced** button to open the folder's advanced attributes settings.

4. Check the **Compress contents to save disk space** check box, and then check the **Encrypt contents to secure data** check box. Notice that only one of these two options can be selected at any time.

5. Click **OK** to exit the Advanced Attributes window, and then click **OK** again to exit the properties of the Encrypted folder. Notice that the text in the name of the Encrypted folder changes to the color green. This is to help easily identify encrypted folders and files.

6. Open the Encrypted folder and create a new text file within it called **encrypted.txt**. In the encrypted.txt file, type **this is an encrypted file**, then save your changes and close the file. Access the Advanced Attributes of this file to ensure that the Encrypt contents to secure data check box is checked. Close the Advanced Attributes dialog box and the encrypted Properties dialog box.

7. Close all open windows and then log off. Log on as the user **mmanore** with the password **Password01**.

8. Open My Computer and attempt to open the D:\Encrypted folder. Remember that although EFS will mark a folder with the encryption attribute, the folder itself is not encrypted. As such, it opens without issue.

9. Attempt to open the **encrypted.txt** file by double-clicking on it. Notice that access is denied, as shown in Figure 6-15, because Mark Manore does not have the private key necessary to decrypt the file. Close all open windows.

Figure 6-15   Attempting to open a file encrypted by another user

6

10. Log off and then log on again as **Administrator** with the password **Password01**.

11. Open the D:\Encrypted folder and attempt to open the file **encrypted.txt**. Notice that the file opens because the domain Administrator account is the default recovery agent. Close all open windows.

12. Log off and then log on again using your **AdminXX** account.

Sharing Encrypted Files

On Windows 2000 systems, EFS used only the public keys of both the user encrypting a file and the data recovery agent to encrypt the file encryption key used to secure the file. As such, the contents of an encrypted file were only accessible to these two users by default, and all other users would be denied access if they attempted to access the file.

In order to allow users to share EFS-encrypted files, Windows Server 2003 supports a new feature to provide this functionality. When accessing the Advanced Attributes window for an encrypted file, clicking the Details button opens the Encryption Details window, as shown in Figure 6-16.

From this window, the Add button can be used to allow other users to access the file, effectively using that user's public key to encrypt the FEK that was originally used to encrypt the file. If you plan to use this feature, the following issues must be kept in mind:

- EFS sharing can only be configured for files, not folders.
- You can only share EFS-encrypted files with users, not groups.
- Users who are being granted access to the file must have a certificate located on the computer.
- Users granted access to the file must also have appropriate NTFS permissions to access the file.

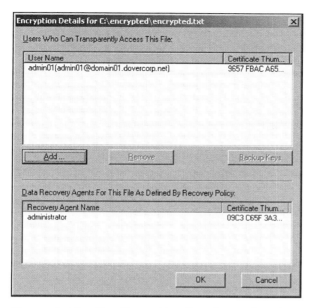

Figure 6-16   The Encryption Details window for an EFS-encrypted file

The management and configuration of user certificates is beyond the scope of this text. For more information on user certificates, see the Certificates overview: Certificates topic in Help and Support Center.

The CIPHER Command

In much the same way that the COMPACT command can be used to compress files or folders from the command line, the CIPHER command allows an administrator to encrypt the contents of files stored on NTFS partitions and volumes. When issued without any switches, the CIPHER command will display encryption settings for the contents of the current directory, as shown in Figure 6-17.

The most common switches used in conjunction with the CIPHER command are /e (to encrypt files and folders) and /d (to decrypt files and folders). CIPHER will only set the encryption attribute on folders by default unless the /a switch is also specified. For example, to encrypt a single file named test1.txt in the C:\encrypted directory, the correct syntax would be:

```
C:\encrypted>cipher /e /a test1.txt
```

One of the most popular uses of the CIPHER utility is to perform bulk encryption from the command line. For example, to encrypt all of the files with a .DOC extension in the C:\encrypted folder, the correct command syntax would be:

```
C:\encrypted>cipher /e /a *.doc
```

Because the CIPHER command requires the NTFS file system to function, it cannot be used to encrypt files or folders stored on FAT or FAT32 partitions or volumes.

The CIPHER command cannot encrypt files with their read-only attribute set.

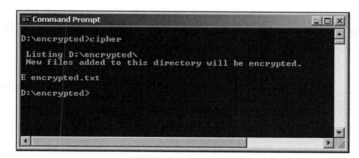

Figure 6-17   Viewing encryption information for the current directory using the CIPHER command

In Activity 6-5 you use the CIPHER command to encrypt files stored in a directory on your server.

Activity 6-5: Encrypting Files Using the CIPHER Utility

Time Required: 5 minutes

Objective: Encrypt and decrypt files using the CIPHER utility.

Description: Although encryption settings can be easily configured from the properties of a file or folder in the Windows Explorer interface, the CIPHER command presents an excellent alternative, especially in cases where large numbers of files need to be encrypted simultaneously. In this activity you use CIPHER to view encryption settings and configured encryption for multiple files simultaneously.

1. Click **Start**, and then click **My Computer**.

2. Double-click on drive **D:** to view its contents.

3. Click the **File** menu, select **New**, and then click **Folder**. Name the new folder **ciphertest**.

4. Double-click the **ciphertest** folder.

5. Click the **File** menu, select **New**, and then click **Text Document**. Name the file **file1.txt**. Repeat this step to create additional files named **file2.txt** and **file3.txt**. Close the My Computer window.

6. Click **Start**, click **Run**, and in the Open text box type **cmd.exe**. Click **OK**.

7. Type **d:** and press **Enter**.

8. Type **cd ciphertest**, and press **Enter**.

9. Type **cipher** and press **Enter**. All files in the ciphertest folder should currently be listed as unencrypted, as designated by the letter U that precedes their file names.

10. Type **cipher /e /a file1.txt** and press **Enter**. This action encrypts file1.txt only.

11. Type **cipher** and press **Enter**. Notice that file1.txt is now preceded with the letter E, meaning the file is encrypted.

12. Type **cipher /e /a *.txt** and press **Enter**. This command encrypts all currently unencrypted text files in the ciphertest folder.

13. Type **cipher** and press **Enter** to confirm that all files in the folder are currently encrypted.

14. Close the command prompt window.

DISK QUOTAS

In all server environments, available disk space eventually becomes an issue. This is often a result of users storing large data files or archiving e-mail messages (which may include attachments) in their home directories. Depending on the number of users on the network and the amount of data they are storing, disk space can easily become scarce and needs to be managed.

Windows Server 2003 uses **disk quotas** as a means of monitoring and controlling the amount of disk space available to users. Administrators can use disk quotas as a capacity-planning tool or as a way of managing data storage.

Using disk quotas has the following advantages:

- Prevents users from consuming all available disk space
- Encourages users to delete old files as they reach their disk quota
- Allows an administrator to track disk usage for future planning
- Allows administrators to track when users are reaching their available limits

You can enable disk quotas on any NTFS volume, but they are disabled by default. By enabling disk quotas on a volume, you can see the amount of disk space that is being consumed by users, allowing you to use them as a capacity-planning tool. To use disk quotas as a management tool, you can set default quotas that specify the maximum amount of space allocated to network users. This is particularly useful for volumes hosting home folders, which tend to consume a lot of disk space. For example, many organizations establish a default quota of 10 to 100 MB per user on home folder volumes. The default quota prevents a few users from occupying disk space that is needed for all users, while also encouraging users to save only essential information and delete files and folders that are no longer needed.

TIP

Disk quotas can be implemented only on NTFS volumes, and they are set on a per-user/per-volume basis.

To configure disk quotas, access the properties of a volume and click the Quota tab, as shown in Figure 6–18.

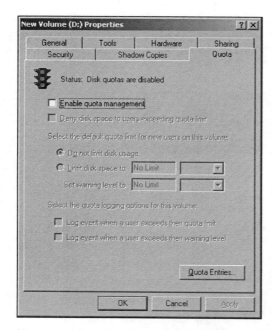

Figure 6-18   The Quota tab in the properties of a volume or partition

Table 6–1 summarizes the options available on the Quota tab of an NTFS volume.

Table 6-1   Disk quota configuration parameters

Parameter	Description
Enable quota management	Tracks disk space on the volume and allows for the configuration of disk quotas
Deny disk space to users exceeding quota limit	Once users reach their quota limit, they are denied access to additional disk space
Do not limit disk usage	Tracks disk usage, but does not limit disk space to users
Limit disk space to	Sets the default amount of disk space that is available to users
Set warning level to	Sets the default amount of disk space that a user can consume before a warning message is sent to the user stating that the quota is being reached
Log event when user exceeds their quota limit	Causes an event to be entered in the System log to notify the administrator that the user has reached their quota

Table 6-1   Disk quota configuration parameters (continued)

Parameter	Description
Log event when a user exceeds their warning level	Causes an event to be entered in the system log to notify the administrator that the user is approaching their quota

Exceptions can be created for users who require more disk space than others. You can set disk quotas for specific user accounts by clicking the Quota Entries button on the Quota tab, and then clicking New Quota Entry on the Quota menu. This allows you to choose the user account for which you want to establish a quota and configure appropriate quota limits for that user. This updates the Quota Entries dialog box to reflect the quota for that user account, as shown in Figure 6-19.

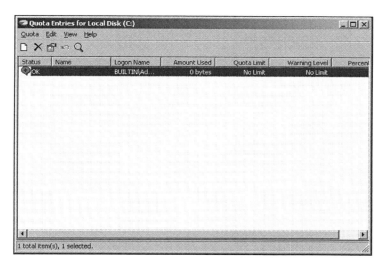

Figure 6-19   The Quota Entries window

It is important to keep in mind that the amount of disk space a user is currently occupying changes when ownership of files transfers from one user account to another. For example, imagine if Moira creates a database called Clients.mdb that occupies 1022 KB on a volume with disk quotas enabled. After Moira creates and saves the database, her available disk space is decreased by 1022 KB. If Moira later changes job roles within the company and John takes ownership of the database, Moira's available disk space would increase by 1022 KB, while John's would be decreased by the same amount.

At any time, you can click the Quota Entries button to view both the disk quota limit and warning level configured for any account, as well as the amount of disk space currently being used by an account.

In Activity 6-6 you configure a disk quota for a volume on your server as well as a quota entry for a specific user.

Activity 6-6: Configuring and Managing Disk Quotas

Time Required: 10 minutes

Objective: Enable and manage disk quotas settings.

Description: The IT manager at Dover Leasing is very concerned about the amount of disk space that users are allocated to store their personal files. In the past, users were told that they could use a maximum of 40 MB of disk space in their home folder, but a third-party quota-management system was never implemented. As such, many users simply ignored the directive, and available disk space is constantly an issue on Dover's servers. Understanding that Windows Server 2003 allows you to configure disk quotas for users on a partition-by-partition basis, the IT manager has asked you to test the implementation of quotas to determine whether or not they will meet Dover's needs.

1. Open My Computer.

2. Right-click drive **D:** and then click **Properties**.

3. Click the **Quota** tab. Notice that the status notice and icon both point out disk quotas are currently disabled for the partition.

4. Click the **Enable quota management** check box.

5. Click the **Limit disk space to** radio button, then type **100** in the text box and select **MB** in the drop-down box.

6. In the Set warning level to text boxes, type **80** and select **MB**.

7. Check the **Log event when a user exceeds their quota limit** check box.

8. Check the **Log event when a user exceeds their warning level** check box.

9. Review all of the choices selected. Notice that although quota information is tracked for this volume, the option to Deny disk space to users exceeding quota limit was not selected. As such, these quotas settings would be considered "soft" because they do not actually deny disk space to users and would instead be used for monitoring purposes. Click **OK**.

10. When the Disk Quota dialog box opens, read the message and then click **OK**. Allow a few minutes for the disk to be rescanned and quota information gathered if necessary.

11. Open the Properties of drive **D:** and click the **Quota** tab. Notice that the Disk quota system is now active and that the quota icon has changed.

12. Click the **Quota Entries** button.

13. In the Quota Entries dialog box, double-click the entry that appears for the Administrator user account to view its properties. Note the quota used and quota remaining information provided.

14. Change the quota entry for Administrator such that the quota limit and warning level are both set to **1 KB**. Click **OK**. Notice that the icon next to the quota entry changes to a warning because this user is now over their quota limit.

15. Close all open Windows.

Managing Disk Quotas from the Command Line

Windows Server 2003 also provides the ability to manage disk quotas from the command line with the FSUTIL utility. The FSUTIL QUOTA command provides six different sub-commands that allow an administrator to disable, enforce, modify, query, and track quota information, as well as report quota violations.

For example, to enable disk quotas on drive E using the FSUTIL QUOTA command, the correct syntax would be:

```
fsutil quota enforce e:
```

To display disk quota information for a particular partition or volume with quotas enabled, the command would be:

```
fsutil quota query e:
```

Example output from the FSUTIL QUOTA QUERY command is shown in Figure 6-20.

Figure 6-20   Using FSUTIL to query a volume or partition for quota information

The FSUTIL quota command can also be used to configure quota entries for individual users. For example, to create a new quota entry on drive E for the Mark Manore user

account that limits disk space to 100 MB and issues a warning at 80 MB, the correct command syntax would be:

```
fsutil quota modify e: 80000 100000 mmanore
```

When a quota is created or modified using the FSUTIL QUOTA command, the warning threshold and limit values are specified in bytes.

TIP

As a method of helping to keep administrators informed of disk quota violations, Windows Server 2003 writes events to the System log (accessible via Event Viewer) periodically. Quota violations for users are written to the system log every hour by default. In some cases, administrators might want to change the interval associated with these events being written to the System log, especially if the log files are filling up too quickly or becoming unmanageable. The FSUTIL BEHAVIOR command can be used to change the interval associated with these events. For example, to change the default notify interval from the default of one hour (3600 seconds) to once every three hours (10800 seconds), the correct command syntax would be:

```
fsutil behavior set quotanotify 10800
```

For a complete list of the sub-commands and capabilities associated with both the FSUTIL QUOTA and FSUTIL BEHAVIOR commands, see the Fsutil : quota : Command-line reference and Fsutil : behavior : Command-line reference topics in Help and Support Center.

NOTE

DISTRIBUTED FILE SYSTEM

The **Distributed File System** allows administrators to simplify access to multiple shared-file resources by making it appear as though multiple shared-file resources are stored in a single hierarchical structure. For example, if the network has eight Windows Server 2003 systems that provide a variety of shared folders to network users, DFS can be set up so that users do not have to know which specific server offers which shared folder. All of the folders can be set up to appear as though they are on one server and under a single folder structure. This eliminates the need for users to have to browse the network looking for shared resources. DFS also makes managing folder access easier for server administrators.

DFS is configured using the Distributed File System console in the Administrative Tools menu, as illustrated in Figure 6-21.

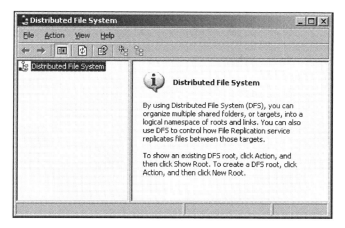

Figure 6-21   The Distributed File System console

A DFS share resembles a tree structure and consists of a root and DFS links. When configuring DFS, the root is configured first, then the DFS links. The DFS root is at the top of the tree structure and is the container for DFS links. The DFS links point to shared folders throughout the network, as illustrated in Figure 6-22.

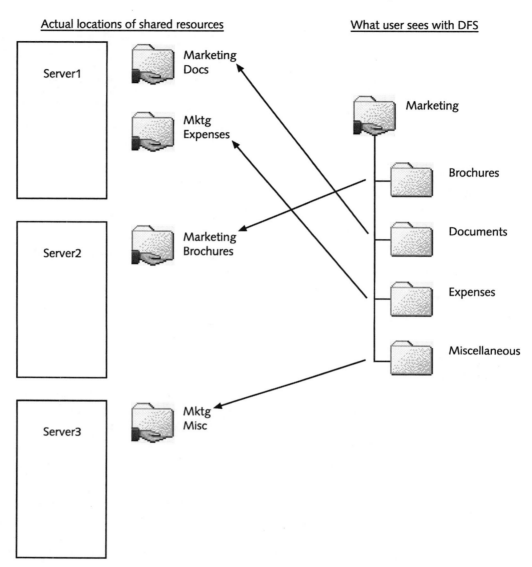

Figure 6-22   Shared folders organized using DFS

DFS Models

There are two models for implementing DFS: the **standalone DFS model** and the **domain-based DFS model**. The standalone DFS model offers limited capabilities compared to the domain-based model. Table 6-2 summarizes the two models.

Table 6-2   Standalone DFS and domain-based DFS

DFS Model	Description
Standalone DFS	DFS information is stored on the local server where DFS is configured. This model offers no fault tolerance.
Domain-based DFS	DFS information is stored within Active Directory. Links can be configured to point to multiple copies of a share for fault tolerance. DFS root must be on an NTFS partition.

NOTE

To access Windows Server 2003 DFS resources, clients must be running DFS client software. Although new Windows versions such as Windows 2000 and XP include this ability by default, older versions such as Windows 98 or NT 4.0 must have the Active Directory client extensions installed to access resources through DFS. You can download the Active Directory client extensions from the Microsoft Web site.

The hierarchical structure of DFS in the domain-based model is called the DFS topology or logical structure. There are three elements to the DFS topology:

- The DFS root
- The DFS links
- Servers on which the DFS shared folders are replicated as replica sets

A **DFS root** is a main container that holds links to shared folders that can be accessed from the root. The server that hosts the DFS root is called the host server. When a network client views the shared folders under the DFS root, all of the folders appear as though they are physically located in one main folder on the DFS root computer, even though the folders may actually reside on many different computers in the domain.

A **DFS link** is a pointer to the physical location of shared folders that are defined in the root. DFS links can also be made to another DFS root on a different computer or to an entire shared volume on a server.

A **replica set** is a set of shared folders that is replicated or copied to one or more servers in a domain. Configuring a replication set includes establishing links to each server that participates in the replication, as well as setting up synchronization so that replication takes place among all servers at a specified interval, such as every 15 minutes.

The first step in creating a DFS is to configure a DFS root of either the standalone or domain-based variety. Once the root is configured, you can create DFS links that point to the actual physical location of the shared files and folders. In Activity 6-7, you create a new domain-based DFS root along with multiple DFS links.

Activity 6-7: Implementing Domain-Based DFS and Creating Links

Time Required: 15 minutes

Objective: Create a new domain-based DFS root and add DFS links.

Description: The IT manager at Dover Leasing has recognized that based on the large number of servers that the company plans to implement, users may have difficulty finding the resources that they most commonly need access to. Because of this, he has asked you to investigate whether or not the distributed file system will help to make resource access easier for users. In this activity, you create a new domain-based DFS root and then add DFS links for shared folders on multiple servers.

1. Click **Start**, select **Administrative Tools**, and then click **Distributed File System**.

2. Right-click the **Distributed File System** icon and then click **New Root**. The Welcome to the New Root Wizard screen appears. Click **Next**.

3. At the Root Type screen, ensure that the **Domain root** radio button is selected and click **Next**.

4. At the Host Domain screen, ensure that your domain is selected on the Trusting domains list and then click **Next**.

5. At the Host Server screen, click the **Browse** button. In the Find Computers screen, select your server and then click **OK**. Click **Next** to continue.

6. At the Root Name screen, type **dfsroot** in the Root name text box and click **Next**.

7. At the Root Share screen, type **d:\dfsroot** in the Folder to share text box and click **Next**. When asked whether you want to create the folder, click **Yes**.

8. Click **Finish** to close the New Root Wizard.

9. Right-click your new DFS root and then click **New Link**.

10. In the New Link dialog box, type **Marketing Applications** in the Link name text box.

11. In the Path to target (shared folder) text box, type **\\serverXX\applications** (where *XX* is your student number), and then click **OK**. The new link appears under your DFS root, as shown in Figure 6-23.

6

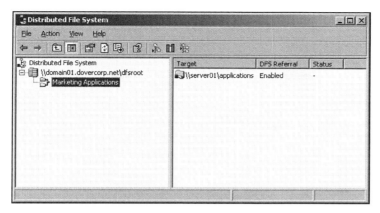

Figure 6-23   A DFS link named Marketing Applications

12. Open My Computer, and create a new shared folder on your D: drive called **partner**. Ensure that the shared folder permissions on this folder are set to allow the Everyone group the Read permission at a minimum.

13. In the Distributed File System window, add another DFS link named **Partner**, specifying the path to the partner folder on your partner's server in the Path to target (shared folder) text box.

14. To test whether the DFS root functions correctly, open the **Run** command, type **\\domainXX.dovercorp.net\dfsroot** (where *XX* is your assigned student number), and click **OK**. Ensure that both the Marketing Applications and Partner folders appear beneath as the contents of the dfsroot folder.

15. Right-click the **Partner** folder in the dfsroot window and click **Properties**. Notice the Location path specified on the General tab.

16. Click the **DFS** tab. Notice that the actual path to the shared folder on your partner's server is listed in the Referral list.

17. Close all open windows.

Managing DFS

After a new DFS root system is set up, there are several tasks involved in managing the root including:

- Deleting a DFS root
- Removing a DFS link
- Adding root and link replica sets
- Checking the status of a root or link

Each of these tasks is described in the following paragraphs.

After a DFS root is created, it is possible to delete it—when you want to configure it differently, for example. To delete a DFS root, open the Distributed File System console, and right-click the root you want to delete. You can then click Delete Root on the shortcut menu.

To remove a link from the DFS root, right-click the link in the details pane, and then click Delete Link on the shortcut menu.

One of the features of a domain-based DFS is that an entire DFS root or specific DFS links in a root can be replicated on servers other than the one that contains the master folder. The replication capability is what enables you to provide fault tolerance as well as load balancing of requests between servers. On a network in which there are multiple servers, replication can prove to be a vital service to provide uninterrupted access for users, in case the computer with the master folder is inaccessible. Load balancing also is vital as a way to provide users with faster service and better network performance by enabling users to access the nearest server containing the DFS shared folders. DFS takes advantage of Active Directory sites by ensuring that users are forwarded to a replica within their own site, if one exists. You can set up a DFS link for replication by right-clicking the link and selecting the Configure Replication option. This opens a wizard that walks you through the various DFS replication options and topologies available. In order to configure a new replica, at least one additional server in the same domain is required.

 You can configure replication to occur manually or automatically. If you choose to use automatic replication, ensure that the File Replication Service is started and set to start automatically because automatic DFS replication relies on this

NOTE service. For more information on configuring DFS replication, see the Configuring Replication option in Help and Support Center.

The most common problem associated with DFS shared folders is that one or more DFS links are inaccessible because a particular server is disconnected from the network, shut down, or has failed. You can quickly check the status of a DFS root, link, or replica by right-clicking it in the right pane of the Distributed File System management tool, and then clicking Check Status. A DFS root, link, or replica that is working and fully connected has a green check mark in a white circle through its folder icon, as shown in Figure 6-24. One that is disconnected has a white "x" in a red circle through its folder icon.

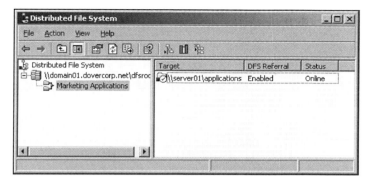

Figure 6-24   Viewing the status of a DFS link

Chapter Summary

❑ The four standard file and folder attributes supported by Windows Server 2003 are archive, hidden, read-only, and system. Attributes can be configured using Windows Explorer and the ATTRIB command-line utility.

❑ Windows Server 2003 supports advanced attributes on NTFS partitions including archiving, indexing, compression, and encryption settings.

❑ NTFS includes built-in support for compression, allowing individual files or the contents of directories to be compressed to save disk space. Compression can be configured from the properties of a file or folder, or by using the COMPACT command-line utility.

❑ NTFS also includes support for the encrypting file system (EFS), a public key cryptography method for providing additional security for sensitive files. EFS can be configured from the properties of a file or folder, or by using the CIPHER command-line utility.

❑ Administrators can implement disk quotas to control the amount of disk space a user's files can consume on a particular NTFS partition or volume.

❑ The Distributed File System (DFS) provides a method to make shared folders on different servers appear to be part of a single logical hierarchy. Windows Server 2003 supports two models known as standalone and domain-based DFS.

Key Terms

archive attribute — A standard attribute used to determine the backup status of a file or folder.

compression — An advanced attribute of the NTFS file system used to reduce the amount of space that files and folders occupy on a partition or volume.

data decryption field (DDF) — The storage location for the file encryption key (FEK) is an EFS-encrypted file.

data recovery agent — A user account capable of gaining access to EFS-encrypted files encrypted by other users. In a domain environment, the domain Administrator account is the default data recovery agent.

data recovery field (DRF) — The storage location for the file encryption key (FEK) encrypted by the data recovery agent.

disk quotas — A Windows Server 2003 feature that is used as a means of monitoring and controlling the amount of disk space available to users.

Distributed File System (DFS) — A system that enables folders shared from multiple computers to appear as though they exist in one centralized hierarchy of folders instead of on many different computers.

domain-based DFS model — A DFS model that uses Active Directory and is available only to servers and workstations that are members of a particular domain. The domain-based model enables a deep root-based hierarchical arrangement of shared folders that is published in Active Directory. DFS shared folders in the domain-based model can be replicated for fault tolerance and load balancing.

Encrypting File System (EFS) — An advanced attribute of NTFS that enables a user to encrypt the contents of a folder or a file so that it can only be accessed via private key code by the user who encrypted it or a data recovery agent by default.

file encryption key (FEK) — The session key used to encrypt the contents of a file when EFS encryption is used.

hidden attribute — A standard attribute that controls the visibility of files and folders.

read-only attribute — A standard attribute, that when configured, does not allow the contents of a file or folder to be changed.

standalone DFS model — A DFS model in which there is no Active Directory implementation to help manage the shared folders. This model provides only a single or flat level share.

system attribute — A standard attribute typically associated with critical operating system files.

REVIEW QUESTIONS

1. Which of the following is not a standard attribute?
   a. Hidden
   b. System
   c. Compressed
   d. Read-only

2. Which of the following attributes can be configured from the properties of a folder residing on a FAT32 volume?

   a. Hidden

   b. System

   c. Read-only

   d. Archive

3. Which of the following attributes combined to make a file or folder "super hidden"? (Choose all that apply.)

   a. Hidden

   b. System

   c. Read-only

   d. Archive

4. When a folder's encryption attribute is configured, which of the following cannot be configured at the same time?

   a. Read-only

   b. System

   c. Hidden

   d. Compression

5. Which of the following is used to encrypt a file encryption key with EFS?

   a. A user's public key

   b. A user's private key

6. Which of the following users can access an EFS-encrypted file by default?

   a. The user who encrypted the file

   b. Any users in the same group as the user who encrypted the file

   c. The data recovery agent

   d. All users

7. Which of the following file systems support the ability to implement disk quotas?

   a. FAT

   b. FAT32

   c. NTFS

8. Which of the following tools can be used to encrypt files from the command line?

   a. COMPACT

   b. COMPRESS

   c. CIPHER

   d. ENCRYPT

9. Which of the following tools can be used to compress files from the command line?

    a. COMPACT

    b. COMPRESS

    c. CIPHER

    d. ENCRYPT

10. Which of the following tools can be used to review disk quota settings from the command line?

    a. QUOTAUTIL

    b. QUOTA

    c. FSUTIL

    d. COMPACT

11. What would be the result of issuing the command attrib –s –h file1.txt from the command line?

    a. File1.txt will have the system attribute added

    b. File1.txt will have the hidden attribute added

    c. File1.txt will have the system attribute removed

    d. File1.txt will have the hidden attribute removed

12. Which of the following are DFS models supported in Windows Server 2003? (Choose all that apply.)

    a. Domain-based DFS

    b. Standalone DFS

    c. Enterprise DFS

    d. Limited DFS

13. What term is used to describe alternative copies of a DFS link stored on other servers?

    a. Copy

    b. Replica

    c. Match

    d. Mount

14. A standalone DFS root is not fault tolerant.

    a. True

    b. False

15. Which of the following file systems are capable of natively supporting both encryption and compression? (Choose all that apply.)

   a. FAT

   b. FAT32

   c. NTFS

16. What is the result of copying a compressed file to another folder on the same NTFS volume?

   a. The file inherits the compression attribute of the target folder.

   b. The file retains its compression attribute.

17. What is the result of copying an EFS-encrypted file to a folder on a FAT32 partition?

   a. The copied file remains encrypted.

   b. The copied file is decrypted.

18. What happens when the COMPACT command is issued in a directory without any additional switches specified?

   a. All files in the directory are compressed.

   b. All files and subfolders in the directory are compressed.

   c. The compression attributes of files are listed.

19. The disk quota feature in Windows Server 2003 allows disk quotas to be configured on a server-wide basis.

   a. True

   b. False

20. Disk quotas can be configured according to group membership.

   a. True

   b. False

CASE PROJECTS

CASE
PROJECTS

Case Project 6-1

Management has expressed a concern over disk usage because of the number of support calls indicating that server volumes are full. You have been sending memos asking users to delete any temporary or old files. Discuss how Dover Leasing can use disk quotas to limit usage and plan for future storage capacity requirements.

Case Project 6-2

Many of the executives at Dover Leasing have expressed concerns that even though NTFS permissions control user access to files, junior administrators could potentially grant themselves permissions to read sensitive documents. What solution could be implemented to help mitigate this risk?

Case Project 6-3

Users at Dover Leasing have been complaining that as additional servers are added to the network, shared file resources are becoming confusing. Some users consistently save files to the wrong folders because they forget to use the designated folder on a new server. Also, some users have been upset because certain folders have periodically not been accessible due to maintenance issues. What can be done to solve this issue?

6

7

IMPLEMENTING AND MANAGING PRINTERS

After reading this chapter and completing the exercises, you will be able to:

Understand Windows Server 2003 printing terms and concepts

Install and share printer resources

Configure and manage installed printers

Publish printers in Active Directory

Troubleshoot printer problems

The concept of sharing resources among many different users is a primary reason why companies implement networks today. Networks have evolved from simple peer-to-peer arrangements where users would share files from their local workstations, to large and complex entities that may include hundreds, if not thousands, of interconnected and shared resources. This evolution means that an administrator is not only responsible for ensuring that shared resources are available to users but also that these resources are monitored and managed effectively.

Although sharing file resources is still the most common reason to implement a network, sharing access to print devices is probably a close second. Windows Server 2003 includes the ability to act as a print server, allowing both locally attached and network-interface print devices to be installed and shared amongst network users. In this chapter, you learn how to install and share print resources, and how to configure permissions to control printer access. Some of the more advanced configuration features of print devices in a Windows Server 2003 environment are also discussed.

Once you have created and shared file and print resources on your network, users may need a simple and effective way to search for these objects. Publishing resources into Active Directory allows any Active Directory-aware client to perform a simple search on the network. This chapter illustrates how to configure resource publishing and perform Active Directory searches.

The chapter closes with a look at some of the most common problems that may arise with respect to printers, and troubleshooting techniques that can be used to solve these problems.

WINDOWS SERVER 2003 PRINTING CONCEPTS

Managing a Windows Server 2003 network includes configuring and maintaining an efficient network of shared printers. You need to know how to install and configure these printers to ensure that users have an appropriate level of access when needed. One of the most common troubleshooting tasks for any network administrator is ensuring the continued availability of the shared network printers.

To successfully configure and troubleshoot Windows Server 2003 printing, you should be aware of very specific terms used to define the components of the printing system.

- Print device—The actual hardware device that produces the printed document. There are two main types of print devices: a **local print device** and a **network print device**. Local print devices are connected directly to a port on the print server or workstation. A network print device connects to a print server through its own network adapter and connection to the network.

- Printer—A configurable object in Windows Server 2003, the **printer** controls the connection to the print device.

- Print driver—Files that contain information Windows Server 2003 uses to convert raw print commands to a language that the printer understands; a specific **print driver** is needed for each print device model used and for each type of operating system in place.

- Print server—The computer in which the printers and print drivers are located; the **print server** is usually where you set up and configure the shared printing system.

- Print client—The computer from which a particular print job originates.

To set up an efficient printing environment, it is also important to make sure that your network meets the following hardware requirements:

- One or more computers to act as print servers—Although both Windows Server 2003 and Windows XP Professional can be used as print servers, Windows XP Professional only supports a maximum of 10 simultaneous client connections. This makes XP an inappropriate choice as a print server in all but the smallest network environments.

- Sufficient space on the hard drive for the print server—This is very important because Windows Server 2003 uses space on the hard drive to queue and buffer documents as they are being directed to the print device.

■ Sufficient RAM beyond that of the minimum Windows Server 2003 requirements—This is critical if you expect to have a large number of print jobs and still wish to maintain an acceptable performance level.

Understanding Network Printing

When a user sends a print job to a locally attached printer, the job is spooled on the local machine, and ultimately directed to a particular port, such as LPT1. When a user attempts to print a document to a network printer, however, the process is somewhat more involved. Both the **print client** and the print server run specific processes to deliver a print job to a network printer.

1. A print file is generated by the software application at the print client.

2. The application communicates with the Windows **graphics device interface (GDI)** as it creates the print file. The GDI integrates information about the print file—such as word-processing codes for fonts, colors, and embedded graphics objects—with information obtained from the printer driver installed at the client for the target printer, in a process that Microsoft calls rendering.

3. The print file is formatted with control codes to implement the special graphics, font, and color characteristics of the file. At the same time, the software application places the print file in the client's spooler by writing the file, called the spool file, to a subfolder used for spooling. In the Windows 95, 98, NT, 2000, XP, and 2003 operating systems, a **spooler** is a group of dynamic-link libraries, information files, and programs that processes print jobs for printing.

4. The remote print provider at the client makes a remote procedure call to the network print server to which the print file is targeted, such as a Windows Server 2003 print server. If the print server is responding and ready to accept the print file, the remote printer transmits that file from the client's spooler folder to the Server service on Windows Server 2003.

5. The network print server uses four processing elements to receive and process a print file; router, print provider, print processor, and print monitor. The router, print provider, and print processor are all pieces of the network print server's spooler.

6. The Server service calls its router, the Print Spooler service, once the remote print provider at the client contacts it. The router then directs the print file to the print provider, which stores it in a spool file until it can be sent to the printer.

7. The print provider works with the print processor to ensure that the file is formatted to use the right data type, such as **TEXT** or **RAW**, while the file is spooled.

8. The print monitor pulls it from the spooler's disk storage and sends it to the printer, when the spool file is fully formatted for transmission to the printer.

Ultimately, the final step in the printing process should result in the production of the intended file. In the following sections you learn more about the main administrative tasks associated with installing, configuring, and troubleshooting printing on Windows Server 2003 systems.

INSTALLING AND SHARING PRINTER RESOURCES

In order to allow users on a network to gain access to shared printer resources, printers must first be connected and installed, and then shared. In the following sections you learn more about installing a local printer, sharing it for access to network users, and then connecting to an existing network printer using different methods.

Adding a Printer as a Local Device

Smaller networks may have workstations or servers that share print devices connected directly to a local port on the computer. To add and share a local print device, you need to have administrator privileges on the computer that acts as the print server. Use the Add Printer Wizard to install and configure printers on systems running Windows Server 2003. Access this tool from the Printers and Faxes program (available on the Start menu), as illustrated in Figure 7-1.

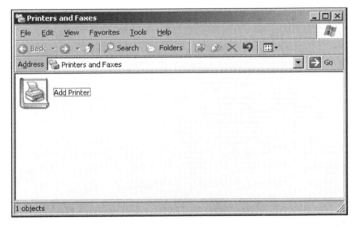

Figure 7-1   The Add Printer shortcut in the Printers and Faxes tool

The Add Printer Wizard provides access to all of the necessary configuration options to get a local printer up and running. As with Windows 2000, the Windows Server 2003 Add Printer Wizard lets you detect printers via Plug and Play. Conversely, the Wizard also allows you to manually configure printers by make and model, allowing you to add a manufacturer's driver from a supplied disk if necessary, as shown in Figure 7-2.

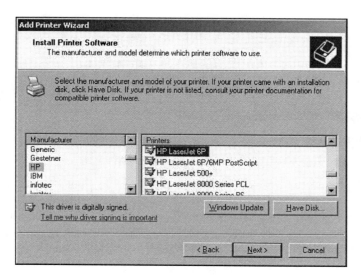

Figure 7-2   Manually configuring a printer

Additional configuration options specified during the local printer installation process include the port that the print device connects to, as illustrated in Figure 7-3.

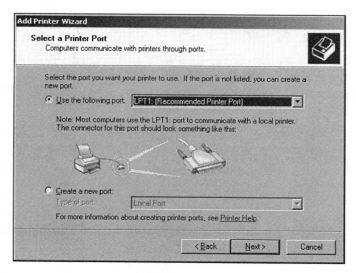

Figure 7-3   Configuring printer port settings

The Add Printer Wizard also allows you to specify if the device serves as the Windows default printer and whether the printer should be shared to provide network access. More advanced options, such as configuring printer permissions, priorities, and features such as

print pooling, are handled once the printer is already installed by accessing its properties. Configuring additional printer settings is looked at later in this section.

In Activity 7-1 you install a local printer using the Add Printer Wizard accessible from the Printers and Faxes tool.

Activity 7-1: Installing a Local Printer

Time Required: 10 minutes

Objective: Use the Add Printer Wizard to install a local printer.

Description: The IT manager at Dover Leasing is interested in migrating all corporate printers from various platforms to Windows Server 2003-based print servers. He has asked you to begin the testing process by installing and configuring a locally connected print device that will eventually be shared for access by network users. In this activity, you install and configure a new local printer using the Add Printer Wizard from the Printers and Faxes tool.

1. If necessary, log on using your **AdminXX** account. Click **Start**, and then click **Printers and Faxes**.

2. In the Printers and Faxes window, double-click the **Add Printer** icon to start the Add Printer Wizard. At the Welcome screen click **Next**.

3. At the Local or Network Printer screen, ensure that the **Local printer attached to this computer** radio button is selected. Uncheck the **Automatically detect and install my Plug and Play printer** check box. Click **Next**.

4. At the Select a Printer Port screen, ensure that **LPT1: {Recommended Printer Port}** is selected in the Use the following port list box and click **Next**.

5. At the Install Printer Software screen, click **HP** in the Manufacturer list. In the Printers list, click **HP LaserJet 6P** and click **Next**.

6. At the Name Your Printer screen, type **HPLaserJet-ServerXX** in the Printer name text box (where *XX* is your assigned student number). Click **Next**.

7. At the Printer Sharing screen, select the **Do not share this printer** radio button and click **Next**.

8. At the Print Test Page screen, select the **No** radio button and click **Next**.

9. At the Completing the Add Printer Wizard screen, review the stated configuration information and then click **Finish**.

10. Verify that the new printer appears in the Printers and Faxes windows with a check mark icon specifying that it is the default printer. Close the **Printers and Faxes** window.

In order to allow other users on a network to access a printer, the printer must be shared in a manner similar to a folder. In Activity 7-2 you share the local printer created in Activity 7-1, making it accessible to network users.

Activity 7-2: Sharing a Local Printer for Network Access

Time Required: 5 minutes

Objective: Share an installed printer to allow network access.

Description: Having created a local printer in the previous activity, you now decide to share this printer to allow network clients to print to it. In this activity, you access the properties of the printer to configure sharing.

1. Click **Start**, and then click **Printers and Faxes**.

2. Right-click the **HPLaserJet–ServerXX** icon and then click **Properties**.

3. On the General tab, type **Marketing Laser Printer** in the Comment text box.

4. Click the **Sharing** tab, and then click the **Share this printer** radio button. In the Share name text box, type **MarketingLaser** (as shown in Figure 7-4) and then click **OK**.

Figure 7-4   Sharing an existing printer

5. When the Printer Properties dialog box opens, read the message about access from MS-DOS workstations and then click **Yes**. Notice that a hand icon appears under the printer in the Printers and Faxes windows, designating it as a shared resource.

6. Click **Start**, and then click **Run**. In the Open text box, type **\\ServerXX** (where *XX* is your assigned student number), and then click **OK**.

7. When the \\Server*XX* window opens, look for the MarketingLaser printer icon as shown in Figure 7-5. Notice that it also includes the description specified in Step 3.

8. Close all open windows.

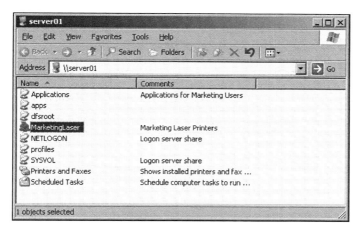

Figure 7-5   Viewing shared resources on Server01

TIP

In the same way that you can hide a shared folder by appending the $ symbol to the end of its share name, this method can also be used to stop printers from being displayed in lists of shared resources.

Adding a Printer as a Network Device

Many corporate print devices have integrated network interface cards that do not require a direct connection to the computer acting as the print server via a parallel port or USB connection. These network print devices use TCP/IP or other protocols to allow communication over the network.

You can also use the Add Printer Wizard to add network print devices to your network. The main difference is that instead of choosing to configure the device using a local port, you need to create a new TCP/IP port to facilitate communication directly over the network. To create this new TCP/IP port, click the Create a new port radio button on the Select a Printer Port screen, and then click the Standard TCP/IP Port option. Ultimately, doing this opens the Add Standard TCP/IP Printer Port Wizard, as illustrated in Figure 7-6. Once the configuration of the TCP/IP port is complete, the Add Printer Wizard continues as it does for any local printer.

In Activity 7-3 you install a network printer using two different methods.

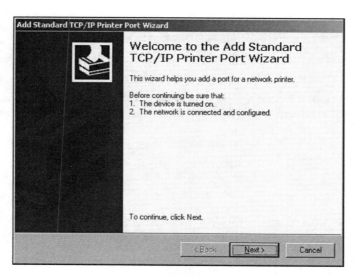

Figure 7-6   The Add Standard TCP/IP Printer Port Wizard

Activity 7-3: Installing a Network Printer

Time Required: 10 minutes

Objective: Install a network printer using the Add Printer Wizard and by browsing the network.

Description: After successfully sharing a printer over the network, you decided to explore some of the methods used to install network printers. In this activity, you install a network printer connected to your partner's server using both the Add Printer Wizard and by browsing the network.

1. Click **Start**, and then click **Printers and Faxes**.

2. Double-click the **Add Printer** icon to open the Add Printer Wizard. At the Welcome screen, click **Next**.

3. At the Local or Network Printer screen, click the **A network printer, or a printer attached to another computer** radio button, and click **Next**.

4. At the Specify a Printer screen, click the **Connect to this printer** radio button and then type **\\serverXX\MarketingLaser** in the Name text box (where *XX* is your *partner's* student number). Click **Next**. Select the **No** radio button on the Default Printer screen, then click **Next**.

5. Click **Finish** to close the Add Printer Wizard.

6. Verify that the new network printer appears in the Printers and Faxes window. Notice that the icon used to represent a network printer is different from the one used to represent a local printer.

7. In the Printers and Faxes window, right-click your partner's network printer and click **Delete**. When the Printers dialog box opens, click **Yes**.

8. Click **Start**, and then click **Run**. In the Open text box type **\\ServerXX** (where *XX* is your *partner's* student number), and then click **OK**.

9. In the list of shared resources that appears, right-click the **MarketingLaser** icon and then click **Connect**, as shown in Figure 7-7. This installs the printer on your computer.

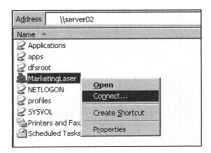

Figure 7-7   Connecting to an existing network printer

10. Verify that the MarketingLaser printer installed in the previous step appears in the Printers and Faxes window.

11. Close all open windows.

CONFIGURING AND MANAGING PRINTER RESOURCES

Although the basic settings encountered in the Add Printer Wizard can provide a suitable configuration to allow users to access shared printer resources, the properties of an installed printer provide access to many additional configuration settings. In the following sections you learn more about some of the settings and features involved with configuring and managing printers installed on a Windows Server 2003 system.

Configuring an Existing Printer

Once you have a printer installed, you may want to modify some of the configuration options such as sharing, permissions, and other advanced settings. To modify these options, right-click the printer icon and click Properties to access the properties of the printer. Figure 7-8 illustrates some of the configuration options and tabs available in the properties of a printer.

Figure 7-8   The properties of an existing printer

In Activity 7-4 you explore the properties of an existing local printer installed on your server.

Activity 7-4: Exploring Printer Properties

Time Required: 15 minutes

Objective: Explore the configurable properties for an installed printer.

Description: The IT manager at Dover Leasing has given you the responsibility of configuring the properties of all printers to be installed on the network. You decide to explore the property settings associated with a printer to better prepare yourself. In this activity, you open and explore the properties of the printer originally installed in Activity 7-1.

1. Click **Start**, and then click **Printers and Faxes**.

2. Right-click the **HPLaserJet-ServerXX** icon (where *XX* is your assigned student number), and then click **Properties**.

3. On the General tab, click the **Printing Preferences** button. This opens the Printing Preferences dialog box for the printer, allowing you to configure settings such as paper layout and quality settings. Browse through the configurable settings and then click **OK**.

4. Click the **Sharing** tab, as originally seen in Figure 7-4. Notice that this tab is used to configure sharing settings, as well as to specify whether this printer should be listed in the directory. Click the **Additional Drivers** button, noting that this dialog box shows you which drivers are currently installed, while also allowing you to install additional drivers. Click **Cancel** to close the Additional Drivers dialog box.

5. Click the **Ports** tab. Notice that this tab is used to configure printer port settings, as well as enable settings like printer pooling.

6. Click the **Advanced** tab. Notice that this tab allows you to configure settings such as the availability of the printer as well as the printer spooling options. Click the **Separator Page** button, and then click the **Browse** button. This allows you to configure a separator page to be printed before a user's print job. Click **Cancel** twice to return to the printer properties dialog box.

7. Click the **Security** tab. Notice that this tab allows you to configure security settings for the printer.

8. Click the **Device Settings** tab. Notice that this tab allows you to configure properties specific to the printer model, such as the types of paper used in various trays and the amount of physical memory installed in the print device, as shown in Figure 8-9.

9. Click **Cancel** to close the printer properties dialog box, and then close the Printers and Faxes window.

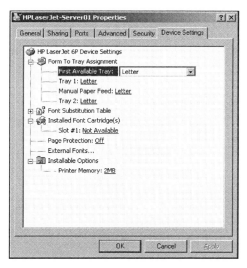

Figure 7-9   The Device Settings tab

Two of the most important configuration options for printers are the Sharing and Security tabs. The Sharing tab allows you to enable or disable printer sharing and Active Directory publishing, as well as install additional drivers for other operating systems that may need to use the printer. The Security tab allows you to control **printer permissions**, in much the same way that this tab is used to control NTFS permissions for files and folders. There are three main levels of print permissions, as well as the ability to configure more granular special permissions. Print permissions are outlined in Table 7-1.

Table 7-1   Printer permissions

Permission	Description
Print	Allows connection to a printer, printing of documents, and editing a user's own print jobs; the Everyone group has this permission by default
Manage Documents	Allows all of the Print permissions with the addition of controlling document print jobs for all users; the Creator Owner group has this permission by default
Manage Printers	Allows all of the Print and Manage Documents permissions and also allows sharing, modification, and deletion of printers and their properties; the Administrators, Print Operators, and Server Operators have this permission by default
Special Permissions	Much like NTFS special permissions these provide a more granular level of control over printer security including: controlling user ownership of a printer, viewing printer permissions, and changing printer permissions

NOTE

Like NTFS and shared-folder permissions, printer permissions are cumulative.

In Activity 7-5 you configure security permissions for an existing printer installed on your server.

ACTIVITY

Activity 7-5: Configuring Printer Permissions

Time Required: 15 minutes

Objective: Configure printer security permissions.

Description: Dover Leasing has a number of different printers scattered through a variety of departments and business units. Because each department is responsible for paying maintenance costs associated with their printers, the department heads want to ensure that only users within their own departments have the ability to print to these printers. The IT manager at Dover Leasing has asked you to ensure that all printers are properly secured according to this requirement. However, he also wants to ensure that members of the Help Desk group have the ability to manage documents, while all domain administrators are granted the Manage Printers permission. In this activity, you configure permissions on the Marketing Department's laser printer.

1. Click **Start**, and then click **Printers and Faxes**.

2. Right-click the **HPLaserJet-ServerXX** icon (where *XX* is your assigned student number), and click **Properties**.

3. Click the **Security** tab, as shown in Figure 7-10.

4. In the Group or user names list, click the **Everyone** group, and then click **Remove**.

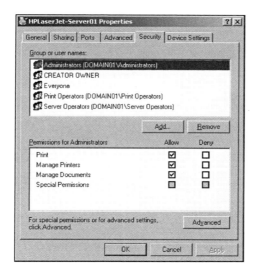

Figure 7-10   The Security tab for a printer

5. Click the **Add** button. In the Select Users, Computers, or Groups dialog box, type **Marketing Users** in the Enter the object names to select text box, and then click **OK**. Notice that once added, the Marketing Users group is granted the Allow Print permission by default.

6. Click the **Add** button. In the Select Users, Computers, or Groups dialog box, type **Help Desk Users** in the Enter the object names to select text box, and then click **OK**. In addition to the Allow Print permission, grant the Help Desk Users group the **Allow Manage Documents** permission.

7. Click the **Add** button. In the Select Users, Computers, or Groups dialog box, type **Domain Admins** in the Enter the object names to select text box, and then click **OK**. In addition to the Allow Print permission, grant the Domain Admins group the **Allow Manage Printers** permission.

8. Click **OK** to close the Properties dialog box.

9. Open the **Run** command and in the Open text box type **notepad.exe** and press **Enter**. This opens Notepad. In the Notepad window, type **testing**. Click **File** on the menu bar, and then click **Print**.

10. In the Print dialog box, ensure that the default printer is selected and then click **Print**. Close Notepad, click **No** when asked to save the changes.

11. In the Printers and Faxes window, double-click the **HPLaserJet-ServerXX** icon (where *XX* is your assigned student number). This displays the print queue for the HPLaserjet-Server*XX* printer, including the print job that you just sent. Close the HPLaserjet-Server*XX* and the Printers and Faxes windows.

12. Log off and then log back on as the user **cmedved** with the password **Password01**.

13. Open **Notepad**, type some text, and then attempt to print the document to the HPLaserJet–Server*XX* printer. Notice that it doesn't appear in the list of available printers because the Chris Medved user account is not a member of a group with sufficient permissions to print to the device.

14. Close all open windows and log off. Log on using your **AdminXX** account.

Windows Server 2003 also lets you determine a user's effective printer permissions via the Effective Permissions tab in the Advanced Security Settings of a printer, as shown in Figure 7-11.

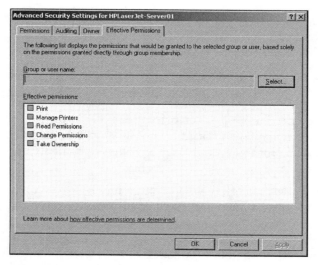

Figure 7-11   The Effective Permissions tab in the Advanced Security Settings of a printer

Printer Pools and Priorities

Some advanced features of Windows Server 2003 printing include setting up printer pools and configuring printer priorities.

A **printer pool** consists of a single printer that is connected to a number of print devices. The advantage of a printer pool is that it allows many physical print devices to function as a single logical printer, thus providing better document distribution in high-volume environments while reducing the time that users must wait for documents to print. One cautionary note is that all print devices configured to be part of the same printer pool must be capable of using the same print driver, or output problems will almost certainly occur. A printer pool is configured by clicking the Ports tab and then placing a check mark in the box next to the Enable printer pooling command, as shown in Figure 7-12.

Figure 7-12   Enabling printer pooling

There may be times when you need to set **printer priorities** for different groups of users. For example, you may want to configure your print environment to give precedence to any printouts from the CEO of the company, even if there are other documents already ahead of it in the print queue.

Print priorities are especially useful in cases where you want different groups of users to have different levels of priority to a limited number of print devices. To configure printer priorities, install two printers on the print server and connect them both to the same print device. Configure the priority of each printer by clicking the Advanced tab and then adjusting the Priority to a number between 1 and 99, with 1 being the lowest priority and 99 being the highest priority, as shown in Figure 7-13. Again, higher priority printers print first.

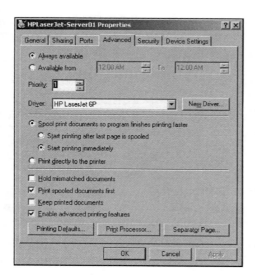

Figure 7-13 Printer priority settings

The next step in configuring print priorities is to only allow specific users to print to a specific printer. For example, if you want the CEO to always have first priority at printing, only allow the CEO to print to the printer with the higher priority setting. All other users print to the printer with the lower priority setting. To do this, configure the printer security settings, as discussed earlier in this section.

In Activity 7-6 you configure a printer pool on your server.

Activity 7-6: Configuring Printer Pooling

Time Required: 10 minutes

Objective: Configure two printers to use the printer pooling feature in Windows Server 2003.

Description: The Marketing Department creates the largest volume of documents on a regular basis at Dover Leasing. Although the department is planning to upgrade all print devices later in the year, they currently have a number of spare HP LaserJet 6P units that they would like to better utilize. Because you are aware of the fact that Windows Server 2003 provides the printer pooling feature, you decide to configure printer pooling for two units in the Marketing Department. In this activity, you install an additional HP LaserJet 6P printer and then configure printer pooling with the original printer installed in Activity 7-1.

1. Click **Start**, and then click **Printers and Faxes**.

2. In the Printers and Faxes window, double-click the **Add Printer** icon to start the Add Printer Wizard. Click **Next** at the Welcome screen.

3. At the Local or Network Printer screen, ensure that the **Local printer attached to this computer** radio button is selected. Uncheck the **Automatically detect and install my Plug and Play printer** check box if necessary. Click **Next**.

4. At the Select a Printer Port screen, select **LPT2: {Printer Port}** in the Use the following port list box and click **Next**.

5. At the Install Printer Software screen, ensure that **HP** is selected in the Manufacturer list, and that **HPLaserJet 6P** is selected in the Printers list. Click **Next**.

6. At the Use Existing Driver screen, ensure that **Keep existing driver (recommended)** is selected, then click **Next**.

7. At the Name Your Printer screen, type **HPLaserJet2-ServerXX** in the Printer name text box (where *XX* is your assigned student number). In the Do you want to you use this printer as the default printer section, click the **Yes** radio button and click **Next**.

8. At the Printer Sharing screen, ensure that the **Do not share this printer** radio button is selected and click **Next**.

9. At the Print Test Page screen, ensure that the **No** radio button is selected and click **Next**.

10. At the Completing the Add Printer Wizard screen, review the stated configuration information and then click **Finish**.

11. Right-click the **HPLaserJet2-ServerXX** icon and then click **Properties**.

12. Click the **Ports** tab. Click the **Enable printer pooling** check box in the lower left of the window. If necessary, click the check box next to **LPT2** in the Port: column. Check the check box next to **LPT1**, then click **OK**. This allows documents sent to the HPLaserJet2-Server*XX* printer to print from both printers as availability dictates.

13. Close all open windows.

Setting Up and Updating Client Computers

Once the printer is added and configured, you must next set up the client computers to be able to print to the print server. If there is a mix of client operating systems throughout the network, a different version of the print driver is needed for each operating system that is connected to the print server.

Any client computers that run Windows 2000, Windows Server 2003, or Windows XP automatically download the print driver when they initially connect to the printer. Windows 95, Windows 98, Windows ME, and Windows NT 4.0 clients also automatically download the print driver, but only if there is a copy of the appropriate driver on the print server. Install additional print drivers by accessing the Additional Drivers dialog box from the Sharing tab, as shown in Figure 7-14.

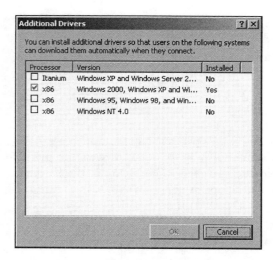

Figure 7-14   The Additional Drivers dialog box

If you have any older Windows clients on your network such as Windows 3.x, or non-Microsoft clients such as Macintosh or UNIX clients, you must manually install the necessary print driver. Non-Microsoft clients may also require additional print services such as Print Services for Macintosh or UNIX to be installed on the print server.

In Activity 7-7 you install additional print drivers for an existing printer.

Activity 7-7: Installing Additional Print Drivers

Time Required: 5 minutes

Objective: Install additional print drivers for the Windows 98 operating system.

Description: Although Dover Leasing has almost fully migrated all of their existing workstations to Windows XP, a number of Windows 98 clients continue to exist and will for the foreseeable future. The IT manager at Dover Leasing has asked you to ensure that the appropriate drivers for Windows 98 are installed on the server in addition to the default drivers. In this activity, you install additional drivers for Windows 98 in the properties of the HPLaserJet2-Server*XX* printer.

1. Click **Start**, and then click **Printers and Faxes**.

2. Right-click the **HPLaserJet2-Server*XX*** icon (where *XX* is your assigned student number), and then click **Properties**.

3. Click the **Sharing** tab, and then click the **Additional Drivers** button.

4. In the Additional Drivers dialog box, click the check box next to **x86** for **Windows 95**, **Windows 98**, and **Windows Millennium Edition** and then click **OK**.

5. When prompted for the location of the driver files, type the path **D:\Source\I386** in the Copy files from text box and then click **OK**.

6. Click **Close** to close to properties of the printer.

7. Close all open windows.

Managing Print Queues

Once users have sent print jobs to a printer from a particular application, these jobs are queued while waiting to be output. The most common way for a user to view the **print queue** for a particular printer is to simply double-click on that printer's icon in the Printers and Faxes tool. This displays the current contents of the print queue, as shown in Figure 7-15.

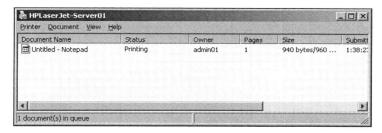

Figure 7-15   Viewing the contents of a print queue

Once a print job has been queued, a user with the Print permissions can pause, resume, restart, or cancel the printing of their own documents by clicking on the document in the queue and then selecting the appropriate option from the Document menu. Users cannot pause, resume, restart, or cancel print jobs belonging to other users unless they have the Manage Documents permission for that printer. In some cases, problems with the printer might be stopping the printer from physically printing the required documents. This might be a result of the physical printer being offline, the Print Spooler service stalling or hanging, or the printer having simply run out of paper. Troubleshooting printing issues is looked at in more detail later in this chapter.

Internet Printing Protocol

In addition to the standard method of configuring and gaining access to printers via the Printers and Faxes tool, Windows Server 2003 also supports the **Internet Printing Protocol (IPP)** specification, which allows printers to be managed via a Web browser, and print jobs to be submitted to a URL. Although IPP support is built into Windows Server 2003, Internet Information Services (IIS) must be installed on a print server to take advantage of it (IIS is not installed by default with Windows Server 2003).

Once enabled, IPP allows an administrator to connect to and manage the printers on a Windows Server 2003 system using a Web browser like Internet Explorer. The URL to access the management interface is in the form http://*printservername*/printers. Connecting in this method provides a list of all of the configured printers on the server, their status, location, jobs, and model, as shown in Figure 7–16.

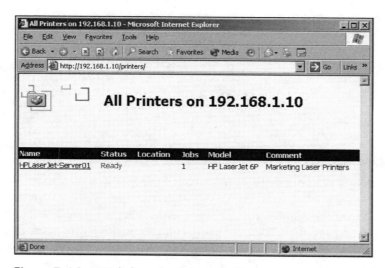

Figure 7-16   Web-based printer management

Clicking on the hyperlink for a particular printer allows an administrator to view and control print jobs currently queued, to pause and resume them, and to print documents, as well as install a printer if necessary, as shown in Figure 7-17. Normal users can also utilize this interface, although their configured permissions will limit the capabilities they have access to.

Figure 7-17   Viewing a print queue using Web-based printer management

Once IPP is installed and configured on the print server, clients running Windows 2000, Windows XP, and Windows Server 2003 can easily connect to existing printers using either the Web interface just discussed, or using the Add Printer Wizard. The URL used to connect to a printer using the Add Printer Wizard is *http://printservername/printers/printername/ .printer*, as shown in Figure 7-18.

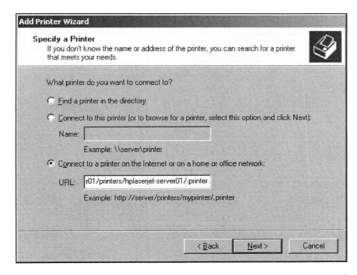

Figure 7-18   Specifying a URL in the Add Printer Wizard

One of the main benefits of using IPP is that it greatly simplifies the ability of an administrator to manage printers from any system on the network, without requiring those printers to be installed on the local client system. Another benefit is the fact that IPP can be used to print to other locations over the Internet, allowing users a method to easily gain access to remote printers using the standard HTTP protocol.

Printer Command-Line Utilities

Along with the Printers and Faxes tool and Web-based printer management, Windows Server 2003 also provides a number of built-in VBScript files that allow printers and related properties to be managed from the command line. These commands include:

- Prncnfg.vbs—configures a printer or displays configuration information for a printer

- Prndrvr.vbs—adds, deletes, or lists printer drivers

- Prnjobs.vbs—views existing print jobs, as well as pauses, resumes, and cancels print jobs in a queue

- Prnmngr.vbs—adds, deletes, or lists printers and related connections, as well as sets and displays the default printer

- Prnport.vbs—creates, deletes, or lists standard TCP/IP printer ports, as well as displays or changes the configuration of an existing port

- Prnqctl.vbs—pauses or resumes a printer, cancels all jobs queued for a particular printer, and prints a test page

Because the files listed in the preceding bullet points are VBScripts rather than standard executables, they must be invoked from the command line using the **Windows Script Host (WSH)**. WSH serves as a controller for the ActiveX scripting engines, and is provided in both Windows-based and command-line versions. The Windows-based version is named Wscript.exe, and the command-line version is Cscript.exe. As such, when you wish to access a VBScript file from the command line, the correct syntax first issues the Cscript command (from the WINDOWS\system32 directory), followed by the name of the appropriate script, and any necessary switches. For example, the following command would display the current configuration of a printer named HPLaserJet-Server01 on the local system:

```
C:\WINDOWS\system32>cscript prncnfg.vbs -g -p hplaserjet-server01
```

The output from the preceding command is shown in Figure 7-19.

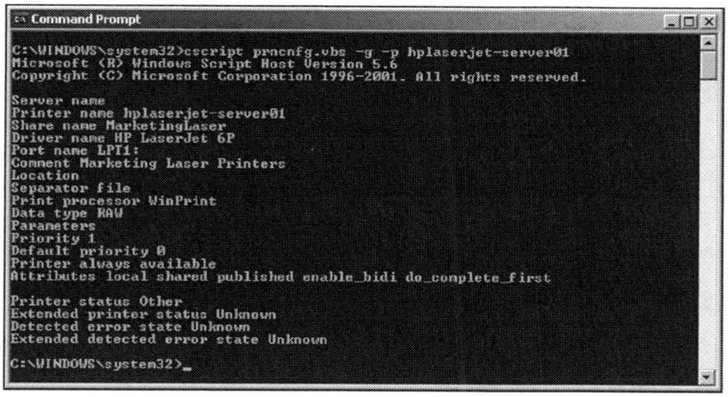

Figure 7-19   Listing the configuration of a local printer using the `Prncnfg.vbs`
command

> For more information on the capabilities of WSH, see the topic Windows Script
> Host overview in Help and Support Center. For a complete list of the switches
> and options supported with the various command-line printing utilities, search
> for the command by name in Help and Support Center.

NOTE

Print Spooler

As users send print jobs to a printer, they are spooled on the hard disk of the print server by default. On a Windows Server 2003 system, spooling occurs in the WINDOWS\system32\spool\PRINTERS folder by default. Although the default location of the print spool folder is generally sufficient for low-volume printing, it is not optimal for higher-volume requirements, mainly a result of it being located in the same volume as the Windows operating system files. Ultimately, leaving the spool folder in the default location can lead to printing delays, especially on busy systems.

For best performance, Microsoft recommends moving the print spool folder to a different partition, preferably one located on a disk that has its own controller. For example, many companies will set up dedicated print server systems running Windows Server 2003, and dedicate an entire second hard disk to print spooling.

In Activity 7-8 you move the print spool folder from its current location to a dedicated folder on drive D on your server.

Activity 7-8: Changing the Location of the Spool Folder

Time Required: 5 minutes

Objective: Move the print spool folder to a different volume to improve printing performance.

Description: Having learned that placing the spool folder on a different volume can help to improve printing performance, the IT manager has asked you to test the process. In this activity you move the spool folder from its default location to a folder named Spool on drive D on your server by reconfiguring the print server's properties.

1. Click **Start**, and then click **Printers and Faxes**.

2. Click the **File** menu, and then click **Server Properties**.

3. Click the **Advanced** tab, as shown in Figure 7-20. In the Spool folder text box, type **D:\Spool**, and then press **OK**.

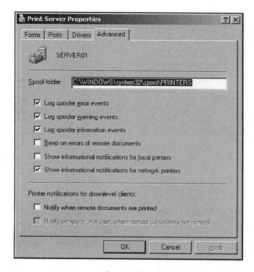

Figure 7-20   The Advanced tab of the Print Server Properties window

4. When the Print Server Properties dialog box appears, read the message that appears, and then click **Yes**.

5. Complete the process of moving the spool folder location by restarting your server, and then logging on using your Admin*XX* account. This step can also be substituted with restarting the Print Spooler service, which is looked at in Activity 7-10.

PUBLISHING PRINTERS IN ACTIVE DIRECTORY

Shared printers can be published into Active Directory to help users find network printer resources. In fact, any Windows Server 2003- or Windows 2000-compatible printer that is installed on a domain print server is automatically **published** into Active Directory during installation. By default, published printer objects are hidden in the Active Directory Users and Computers interface.

To view the published printers in Active Directory Users and Computers, click View on the menu bar, and click Users, Groups, and Computers as containers. This option modifies the view to show objects that are associated with a user, group, or computer object. Printer objects are associated with the computer object that acts as its print server. When the container in which the print server is located is expanded, computer objects can also be expanded to view the printer objects associated with them, as shown in Figure 7-21.

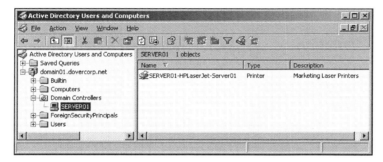

Figure 7-21   Viewing published printers in Active Directory Users and Computers

Printer shares that are created on pre-Windows 2000 print servers are not published into Active Directory by default. However, these printers can be added manually to the directory by creating new published printer objects in Active Directory Users and Computers. Like shared folder objects, these printers can be published in whichever container makes the most sense, based on environment and administrative goals. The New Object – Printer dialog box is illustrated in Figure 7-22.

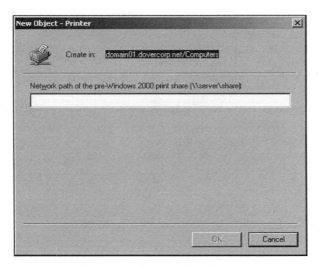

Figure 7-22   The New Object - Printer dialog box

In Activity 7-9, you will publish a printer to Active Directory.

Publishing printers into Active Directory manually can involve a great deal of administrative effort in large environments. To help ease this burden, a script called Pubprn.vbs in the WINDOWS\system32 directory can be used to help automate the process. View the header of the Pubprn.vbs script (right-click on the script file and choose the Edit option to open it in Notepad) for more information on its configuration.

Activity 7-9: Publishing Printers in Active Directory

Time Required: 10 minutes

Objective: Configure printer publishing settings and publish printers manually in Active Directory.

Description: Dover Leasing's network includes such a wide variety of printers connected to different operating systems, that the IT manager has asked you to explore how printers can be made easier to find in Active Directory. Although he wants most printers to be published in the directory, he is also concerned with users finding and attempting to access the printers belonging to the Marketing Department. In this activity, you browse existing published printers, manually publish a fictitious printer object in Active Directory, and then manually disable the publishing of printers belonging to the Marketing Department.

1. Click **Start**, select **Administrative Tools**, and then click **Active Directory Users and Computers**.

2. Click **View** on the menu bar, and then click **Users, Groups, and Computers as containers**.

3. Click the **plus signs (+)** next to the Domain*XX*.Dovercorp.net icon and the Domain Controllers OU to expand their contents.

4. Click the **Server*XX*** icon (where *XX* is your assigned student number) to view the new objects that are now visible. Notice that the shared printer created earlier in the chapter is now visible as a published object in Active Directory.

5. Right-click the **SERVER*XX*-HPLaserJet-Server*XX*** printer icon listed and click **Properties**. Notice that searchable features of the printer including its description and ability to print in color are configurable from this interface.

6. Click the **Color** check box and then click **OK**.

7. Click **Start**, and then click **Search**.

8. In the Search Companion pane, click **Other search options**, click **Printers, computers, or people** and then click **A printer on the network**.

9. In the Find Printers window, ensure that your domain is selected in the In list box. Click the **Features** tab, check the **Can print color** check box, and then click the **Find Now** button. The HPLaserJet-Server*XX* printer configured in Step 5 should appear in the Search results pane, as shown in Figure 7-23.

10. Right-click **HPLaserJet-Server*XX*** listed in the Search results pane to view the available options. Notice that a user can install a printer from this interface by choosing the Connect option.

11. Close the Find Printers window and the Search Results window.

12. Click **Start**, and then click **Printers and Faxes**.

13. Right-click the **HPLaserJet-Server*XX*** icon, and then click **Properties**.

14. Click the **Sharing** tab, uncheck the **List in the directory** check box, and then click **OK**.

15. Open the Search program from the Start menu and then attempt to search for a printer that is capable of printing in color again (see Steps 7-9 for explicit steps). Note that the HPLaserJet-Server*XX* printer is not found because it is no longer published in Active Directory.

16. Close all open windows.

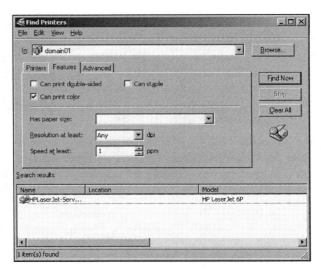

Figure 7-23   Searching for a printer based on its capabilities

TROUBLESHOOTING PRINTER PROBLEMS

Because printers installed on a Windows Server 2003 system include a wide variety of configurable options and settings, problems eventually can (and probably will) occur. The most common printing problems that you are likely to encounter and their appropriate solutions include:

- Print jobs will not print—Print jobs may not physically print from a particular print device for a variety of reasons. The most common causes include the print device being off-line, there not being enough hard disk space available to spool the job, or the print device simply being out of paper. To fix these problems, ensure that the print device is online, consider moving the spool folder to a different location (or free up disk space on the current volume), or add more paper to the device, respectively.

- Printer output appears garbled—Printed output may appear garbled or not print complete pages. The usual source of this problem is that an incorrect driver for the device is installed. Download the correct drivers from the manufacturer's Web site for the appropriate platforms, and then reinstall these drivers on the print server.

- Users receive an Access Denied message when attempting to print—An Access Denied message is received when attempting to send a job to a printer from a particular application. This message usually indicates incorrectly configured permissions. Review and correct permissions for the printer from the Security tab in the printer's properties to solve the problem.

- Users cannot find an existing printer when searching Active Directory—If a user cannot find an existing printer by searching Active Directory, begin by ensuring

that the printer is still published. If it is not, publish the printer manually using Active Directory Users and Computers, or the PUBPRN.VBS script.

- Printer only works at certain times of the day—Windows Server 2003 allows schedules to be configured to control printer availability by the time of day. If a printer is not available during certain times, either change the availability from the Advanced tab of the printer's properties, or direct the user towards another configured printer that allows printing at those times.

- Windows 95/98/ME users cannot connect to a printer—When a printer is installed on a Windows Server 2003 system, drivers for Windows 95/98/ME are not installed by default. If users on these platforms require access to the printer, make the required drivers available from the Sharing tab of the printer's properties.

- Print jobs become stuck in the print queue—Some documents may appear in the print queue, but they do not print, and they cannot be deleted. To fix this problem, on the print server, open the Services console on the Administrative Tools menu, right-click the Print Spooler service, and then click Restart. Note that any print jobs that are in the queue are deleted.

- Print device failure—A print device may fail because of a paper jam, hardware failure, or a stuck print job. Any documents that are behind the current document in the queue can be redirected to a new print device. To redirect the print jobs, access the properties of the printer that is connected to the failed print device. Click the Ports tab, and then click the port to another printer assigned on the print server. If you need to redirect to another print server, click the Add Port button to add a local port that is directed to the IP address and share name of the other print server.

In Activity 8-10 you review the properties of the Print Spooler service, and use the Services console to restart the service.

Activity 7-10: Configuring the Spooler Service

Time Required: 10 minutes

Objective: View and configure properties of the spooler service.

Description: Dover Leasing's IT manager informs you that in the past printers have stopped printing due to the Print Spooler service hanging. Because of this, he has asked you to familiarize yourself with stopping and restarting the spooler service. In this activity, you use the Services node in the Computer Management console to view Print Spooler service settings and restart the service.

1. Click **Start**, right-click **My Computer**, and then click **Manage**.

2. In the Computer Management window, click the **plus sign (+)** next to the Services and Applications node to expand it.

3. Click the **Services** node to view it contents.

4. Scroll through the list of services until you find the Print Spooler service.

5. Double-click **Print Spooler** to view its properties. Notice that the service is configured to start automatically when Windows Server 2003 starts.

6. Click the **Log On** tab. Notice that the Print Spooler service is enabled as part of the only existing hardware profile.

7. Click the **Recovery** tab. Notice that when the service fails, it is configured to restart automatically.

8. Click the **Dependencies** tab. Notice the services upon which the Print Spooler service depends in order to function correctly. In this case, if the Remote Procedure Call is not running, the Print Spooler service cannot function.

9. Click **OK** to close the properties window of the Print Spooler service.

10. Right-click the Print Spooler service in the list of services and then click **Restart**. Notice the dialog box indicating that the service is restarting.

11. Close all open windows and log off.

CHAPTER SUMMARY

- Windows Server 2003 printing has its own unique terminology, and understanding this terminology is critical towards understanding how print devices function in a Windows environment.

- Printers are configurable objects that ultimately represent an interface to a print device. The primary tool used to install printers is the Add Printer Wizard, available from the Printers and Faxes tool.

- In order for a printer to be made available to network users, it must be shared in a manner similar to a shared folder.

- Printer permissions can be used to control user access to printers and the manner in which users can interact with a printer. Printer permissions follow the same general concepts as NTFS permissions.

- Printers on a Windows Server 2003 system can be configured with different priorities to control the order in which print jobs will be queued before being output to a particular print device.

- Printer pooling can be used to increase the speed and availability of a printer by making use of multiple physical print devices.

- Additional drivers can be installed from the properties of a printer in order to allow access to clients running different operating systems such as Windows 95/98/ME to gain access to a printer.

- The Internet Printing Protocol (IPP) allows printers to be managed via a Web browser, and allows users to print using the HTTP protocol.

- For best performance, the print spool folder should be located on its own dedicated partition, preferably on a separate disk than the Windows Server 2003 operating system files.

- Printer publishing allows users to query Active Directory for a list of available printers based on different criteria, such as a printer's ability to print in color.

- Common printer problems encountered on Windows Server 2003 systems include the print device being off-line, misconfigured printer permissions, the Print Spooler service hanging, or incorrect drivers being installed.

Key Terms

graphics device interface (GDI) — An interface on a Windows network print client that works with a local software application, such as Microsoft Word, and a local printer driver to format a file to be sent to a local printer or a network print server.

Internet Printing Protocol (IPP) — A specification supported by Windows Server 2003 that allows printers to be managed from a Web browser, and print jobs to be sent to a printer using the HTTP protocol.

local print device — A printer, such as a laser printer, physically attached to a port on the local computer.

network print device — A printing device, such as a laser printer, connected to a print server through a network.

print client — Client computer or application that generates a print job.

print driver — Files that contain information that Windows Server 2003 uses to convert raw print commands to a language that the printer understands.

print queue — A stack or lineup of all requested print jobs waiting to be sent from the spooler to the printer.

print server — The computer in which the printers and print drivers are located. This is usually where you set up and configure the shared printing system.

printer — A configuration object in Windows Server 2003 that controls the connection to the print device.

printer permissions — Security permissions that allow an administrator to control access to printer resources, in a manner similar to NTFS permissions.

printer pool — Consists of a single printer that is connected to a number of print devices.

printer priorities — Configuring multiple printers to print to the same print device. One printer is then configured to print before any of the other printers by adjusting the priority setting from 1 (lowest priority) to 99 (highest priority).

published — An Active Directory object that represents a link to or direct information on how to use or connect to the shared resource.

RAW — A data type often used for printing MS-DOS, Windows 3.x, and UNIX print files.

spooler — In the Windows 95, 98, Me, NT, 2000, XP, and 2003 environment, a group of DLLs, information files, and programs that process print jobs for printing.

TEXT — A data type used for printing text files formatted using the ANSI standard that employs values between 0 and 255 to represent characters, numbers, and symbols.

Windows Script Host (WSH) — A controller for the ActiveX scripting engines provided in both Windows-based and command-line versions.

REVIEW QUESTIONS

1. Which of the following is not a print permission in Windows Server 2003?
   a. Print
   b. Full Control
   c. Manage Documents
   d. Manage Printers

2. Which of the following permissions allows a user to pause not only their own print jobs, but also those of other users?
   a. Print
   b. Manage Documents
   c. Full Control
   d. Change

3. Printers installed on a Windows Server 2003 system are published to Active Directory by default.
   a. True
   b. False

4. Which of the following must be used to invoke the Prncnfg.vbs command from the command line?
   a. Cscript
   b. Wscript
   c. Script
   d. Vbscript

5. Which of the following is the highest printer priority on a Windows Server 2003 system?
   a. 100
   b. 99
   c. 1
   d. 0

6. Which of the following scripts can be used to publish printers in Active Directory?

   a. Pubprn.vbs

   b. Prncnfg.vbs

   c. Publish.vbs

   d. Pub.vbs

7. When a new printer is installed, drivers will be made available for which of the following operating systems by default?

   a. Windows 2000

   b. Windows Server 2003

   c. Windows 95

   d. Windows 98

8. What term is used to describe a printer that can send output to more than one print device?

   a. Printer pooling

   b. Multithreaded

   c. Multihomed

   d. Dual-port

9. The output from a configured printer is garbled. What is most likely the cause of the problem?

   a. The printer priority is incorrect

   b. The wrong driver is installed

   c. The print device is malfunctioning

   d. The wrong port is configured

10. When documents appear to be stuck in the print queue, which of the following services should be restarted?

    a. Print Spooler

    b. Server

    c. Workstation

    d. Plug and Play

11. What is the default printer permission assigned to the Administrators group on a Windows Server 2003 system?

    a. Print

    b. Manage Documents

    c. Manage Printers

    d. Full Control

12. A page that contains user information and prints before a user's print job is called what?

    a. Separator page

    b. Split page

    c. Document handle

    d. Outline document

13. In order to use the Internet Printing Protocol (IPP), which of the following services must be installed?

    a. Clustering

    b. Internet Information Services

    c. Network Load Balancing

    d. Routing Information Protocol

14. Which of the following represents the correct URL syntax to connect to a printer named Printer1 on Server01?

    a. http://server01/printers/printer1/.printer

    b. http://server01/.printer

    c. http://printer1/printers/server01/.printer

    d. http://server01/.printer/printer1

15. The printer spool folder is located on the same partition or volume as the WIN-DOWS folder by default.

    a. True

    b. False

16. In order for a printer to be made available to network users, it must be shared.

    a. True

    b. False

17. Only the drivers supplied with Windows Server 2003 can be used when installing a printer.

    a. True

    b. False

18. Which of the following script files is used to view the print jobs queued on a printer?

    a. Pubprn.vbs

    b. Prncnfg.vbs

    c. Prnmngr.vbs

    d. Prnjobs.vbs

7

19. Which of the following script files is used to set the default printer on a Windows Server 2003 system?

   a. Prnmngr.vbs

   b. Pubprn.vbs

   c. Prnjobs.vbs

   d. Prndrvr.vbs

20. Only one printer can be designated as the default printer at any point in time on a Windows Server 2003 system.

   a. True

   b. False

CASE PROJECTS

CASE
PROJECTS

Case Project 7-1

Dover Leasing is in the process of adding two new print devices to the network. One is for the Managers group and the other is for the Sales and Accountants groups. Both printers are identical and are connected to two separate servers. You have been asked to advise the Help Desk users about how to set up the printers.

1. How should the new print devices be configured to ensure that network users can connect to them?

2. What permissions should be assigned to those users responsible for managing the printers?

3. Explain how printer permissions are configured so the appropriate groups have access to the printers.

CASE
PROJECTS

Case Project 7-2

To understand how printer permissions work, consider the information provided in the table below, and then answer the questions that follow.

Users / Printers	Group Memberships / Permissions
User1	Sales Users, Marketing Users, Managers, Domain Users
User2	Help Desk Users, Managers, Domain Users, Domain Admins
User3	Accounting Users, Domain Users, Project Planners
LaserJetA	Sales Users – Print Managers – Manage Documents Domain Users – Print Everyone – Print Domain Admins – Manage Printers
LaserJetB	Domain Users – Manage Documents Domain Admins – Manage Printers Help Desk Users – Print
LaserJetC	Accounting Users – Print Project Planners – Print Everyone – Deny Print Help Desk Users – Manage Documents

1. What permissions would User1 have to the LaserJetA printer?
2. What permissions would User2 have to the LaserJetC printer?
3. What permissions would User3 have to the LaserJetB printer?
4. What permissions would User1 have to the LaserJetB printer?
5. What permissions would User2 have to the LaserJetA printer?
6. What permissions would User3 have to the LaserJetC printer?

8

IMPLEMENTING AND USING GROUP POLICY

After reading this chapter and completing the exercises, you will be able to:

Create and manage Group Policy objects to control user desktop settings, security, scripts, and folder redirection

Manage and troubleshoot Group Policy inheritance

Deploy and manage software using Group Policy

An important part of your Windows Server 2003 management skills is the ability to effectively incorporate Group Policy into your Active Directory structure. Group Policy allows you to easily manage and control various configurations, such as user desktop settings, desktop and domain security, as well as deploy and manage software.

Another important aspect of Group Policy involves understanding how to control the inheritance and application of Group Policies throughout the Active Directory hierarchy. The following sections discuss these concepts as well as basic Group Policy troubleshooting techniques.

INTRODUCTION TO GROUP POLICY

Group Policy enables the centralized management of user and computer configuration settings throughout your network. A **Group Policy object (GPO)** is an Active Directory object that is used to configure and apply policy settings for user and computer objects. It performs a variety of administrative tasks, including:

- Configuring desktop settings using administrative templates
- Controlling security settings for users and computers
- Assigning scripts to run when a user logs on or off, or when a computer is started up or shut down
- Redirecting folders, such as the My Documents folder, out of a user's local profile to a different network location
- Automating software distribution and maintenance to computers throughout the network

To implement Group Policy, you must first create a GPO or modify one of the default GPOs to meet the company requirements.

There are two default GPOs created when Active Directory is installed. The first GPO is linked to the domain container and is called the **Default Domain Policy**. The second is linked to the domain controllers organizational unit (OU) and is called the **Default Domain Controllers Policy**.

Once a GPO is created, you can then link it to a site, domain, or OU. When you link a GPO to one of these container objects, its policy settings are applied to all users and computers in the container, including those within child OUs.

 Group Policy can only be applied to computers running Windows Server 2003, Windows 2000, and Windows XP. If you still have down-level clients, such as those running Windows NT or Windows 9x, you must use system policies to control environment settings.

Creating a Group Policy Object

You can create a GPO in two different ways: use the Group Policy standalone Microsoft Management Console (MMC) snap-in, or use the Group Policy extension in Active Directory Users and Computers. In Activity 8-1 you create a new GPO by adding the Group Policy Object Editor snap-in to an empty MMC.

Activity 8-1: Creating a Group Policy Object Using the MMC

Time Required: 10 minutes

Objective: Use the Group Policy Object Editor MMC snap-in to create GPOs.

Description: The IT manager at Dover Leasing has decided that the company will use GPOs for the purpose of configuring a standard user desktop environment, as well as the deployment of software applications and updates. You have been asked to explore some of the different ways in which GPOs can be created from a Windows Server 2003 system. In this activity, you create a new GPO using the Group Policy Object Editor MMC snap-in.

1. Log on with your **AdminXX** account (where *XX* is your assigned student number).

2. Click **Start**, and then click **Run**. In the Open text box, type **mmc** and press **Enter**.

3. Click **File** on the menu bar, and click **Add/Remove Snap-in**.

4. Click **Add**. In the Add Standalone Snap-in dialog box, click **Group Policy Object Editor** as shown in Figure 8-1 and click **Add**.

8

Figure 8-1   Adding a standalone snap-in

5. In the Select Group Policy Object dialog box, click **Browse**.

6. In the Browse for a Group Policy Object dialog box, click the **All** tab to display a list of all GPOs that currently exist.

7. In the All Group Policy Objects stored in this domain section, right-click a blank area and click **New**.

8. Rename the new GPO using the name **Test Policy** and press the **Enter** key. Click **OK**, and then click **Finish**.

9. Click **Close** at the Add Standalone Snap-in window, and click **OK** at the Add/Remove Snap-in window.

10. Close the MMC window without saving your changes.

Group Policy objects can be applied to Active Directory sites, domains, and organizational units. In Activity 8-2 you create a number of new OU objects, and then move some existing user accounts into these OUs. Ultimately, these OUs will be used to test the application of Group Policy settings in activities later in the chapter.

Activity 8-2: Creating OUs and Moving User Accounts

Time Required: 10 minutes

Objective: Create new OUs and then move existing user accounts into those OUs.

Description: The IT manager at Dover Leasing would eventually like to take advantage of using OUs as a method of controlling the application of Group Policy settings. In this activity you create a number of new OUs, and then move some existing user accounts out of the Users container and into these new OUs.

1. Click **Start**, select **Administrative Tools**, and click **Active Directory Users and Computers**.

2. Right-click on the **DomainXX.Dovercorp.net** domain object, select **New**, and click **Organizational Unit**.

3. In the New Object – Organizational Unit window, type **Marketing** in the Name text box, and click **OK**. This creates a new OU named Marketing.

4. Right-click on the **DomainXX.Dovercorp.net** domain object, select **New**, and click **Organizational Unit**.

5. In the New Object – Organizational Unit window, type **Information Technology** in the Name text box, and click **OK**. This creates a new OU named Information Technology.

6. Right-click on the **DomainXX.Dovercorp.net** domain object, select **New**, and click **Organizational Unit**.

7. In the New Object – Organizational Unit window, type **Sales** in the Name text box, and click **OK**. This creates a new OU named Sales.

8. Click the **Users** container to view its contents. Right-click on the **Moira Cowan** user account, and click **Move**. In the Move window, click on the **Marketing** OU, and click **OK**. Click on the **Marketing** OU to confirm that the Moira Cowan user account has been moved.

9. Repeat Step 8 to move the John H. Smith user account to the Marketing OU, and the Mark Manore user account to the Information Technology OU.

10. Close Active Directory Users and Computers.

In Activity 8-3 you create a new Group Policy object and browse through various Group Policy settings.

Activity 8-3: Creating a Group Policy Object and Browsing Settings Using Active Directory Users and Computers

Time Required: 15 minutes

Objective: Use Active Directory Users and Computers to create a GPO.

Description: While the Group Policy Object Editor MMC snap-in provides one method used to create new or edit existing GPOs, you have learned that another alternative is to create and edit these objects from within the Active Directory Users and Computers tool. Because this tool is the primary administrative application in use at Dover Leasing, you have decided to explore its integrated GPO management features. In this activity, you create a new GPO and explore some of the settings that can be configured through the use of Group Policy.

1. Click **Start**, select **Administrative Tools**, and click **Active Directory Users and Computers**.

2. Click the **plus sign (+)** next to the **DomainXX.Dovercorp.net** domain object to view its contents, if necessary.

3. Right-click the **Marketing** OU and click **Properties**.

4. Click the **Group Policy** tab.

5. Click **Add**. The Add a Group Policy Object Link window opens. Click the **All** tab.

6. In the All Group Policy Objects stored in this domain section, click **Test Policy** and click **OK**. Notice that the GPO named Test Policy now appears in the list of Current Group Policy Object Links for Marketing.

7. Click the **New** button, type **Marketing Policy**, then press **Enter** to create a new GPO. This new GPO is now linked to the Marketing OU.

8. Ensure that **Marketing Policy** is selected and click **Edit**. The Group Policy Object Editor opens to allow the configuration settings of the Marketing Policy to be viewed and configured, as shown in Figure 8-2.

9. In the User Configuration section, click the **plus sign (+)** next to **Administrative Templates** to expand its contents, and then click the **Start Menu and Taskbar** icon.

10. Double-click **Remove My Documents icon from Start Menu**. Notice that the configuration settings include Not Configured, Enabled, and Disabled. Do not change any configuration settings at this point.

11. Click the **Explain** tab, and read the purpose and notes associated with this setting. Click **OK** to close the window.

12. As time permits, browse through additional Group Policy settings in both the User Configuration and Computer Configuration sections. Do not configure any settings during this exercise.

8

13. Close the Group Policy Object Editor window when you are finished, along with the properties of the Marketing OU. Leave Active Directory Users and Computers open.

Figure 8-2   Viewing a Group Policy object

Editing a GPO

After a GPO has been created, it needs to be edited to control specific user or computer settings that should be applied. Table 8-1 lists the configuration categories available in both the Computer Configuration and User Configuration sections of a GPO.

Table 8-1   Configuration categories available for GPOs

Configuration Category	Explanation
Software Settings	Centralizes the management of software installation and maintenance; the installation, upgrading, and removal of applications can be controlled from one central location
Windows Settings	Manages the deployment and oversight of scripts, security settings, Internet Explorer settings, and features such as Remote Installation Services and folder redirection
Administrative Templates	Sets registry-based settings to configure application and user desktop settings; this includes access to the operating system components, access to Control Panel settings, and configuration of offline files

To enable a particular setting as you create or edit a GPO, choose the appropriate configuration category in the left console pane of the MMC snap-in and then, in the details pane, right-click the specific configuration setting, and click Properties.

Figure 8-3 shows the User Configuration\Administrative Templates\Control Panel category selected and the properties of the option to hide specified control panel applets. The Setting tab allows you to enable or disable the setting, as well as set any parameters that may be needed. The Explain tab provides information on what the effect of applying that setting is.

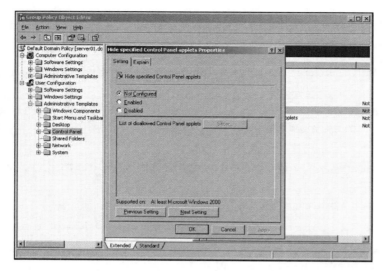

Figure 8-3   Configuring a Group Policy setting

When a GPO is created, the GPO content is stored in two different locations on the server:

- **Group Policy container (GPC)**—An Active Directory container that stores information about the GPO and includes a version number that is used by other domain controllers to ensure that they have the latest information. The version number is also used to make sure that the Group Policy template is synchronized. The GPC is located in Active Directory Users and Computers\System\Policies.

The Advanced Features view must be enabled in Active Directory Users and Computers to view the GPC.

NOTE

- **Group Policy template (GPT)**—The GPT contains the data that makes up the Group Policy. The template includes all the settings, administrative templates, security settings, software installation settings, scripts, and so forth. The registry changes are stored in a configuration file named Registry.pol. A configuration file is stored for both the user settings and computer settings. The GPT is stored in the %systemroot%\Sysvol\<Domain Name>\Policies folder.

The GPC and GPT are identified by a unique 128-bit number known as a **globally unique identifier (GUID)**, which is assigned to the object upon creation. GUIDs are guaranteed to be unique for the entire forest. When a computer accesses the GPO, it uses the GUID to distinguish between GPOs.

In Activity 8-4, you permanently delete an existing GPO.

Activity 8-4: Deleting Group Policy Objects

Time Required: 5 minutes

Objective: Use Active Directory Users and Computers to permanently delete a GPO.

Description: Having learned how to create new GPOs, you are interested in learning what happens if you attempt to delete one of these objects when it has been linked to one or more containers. In this activity, you attempt to delete a linked GPO to learn more about the options presented to you.

1. In Active Directory Users and Computers, right-click the **Marketing** OU and click **Properties**.

2. Click the **Group Policy** tab.

3. Ensure that the **Test Policy** GPO is selected and press the **Delete** button.

4. In the Delete dialog box, click the **Remove the link and delete the Group Policy Object permanently** radio button and click **OK**.

5. When the Delete Group Policy Object dialog box opens, click **Yes**. Notice that the Test Policy GPO is removed from the list.

6. Click **Add** and click the **All** tab to confirm that the Test Policy GPO has been deleted. Click **Cancel**.

7. Click the **Close** button to close the Marketing Properties window, leaving Active Directory Users and Computers open.

Application of Group Policy

GPOs can apply a variety of configuration options to the local computer, site, domain, and OU. There are two main categories to a Group Policy:

- Computer Configuration—Any configuration settings set within this category affect computers located in the container to which the GPO is linked.

- User Configuration—Any configuration settings set within this category apply to any user objects located in the container to which the GPO is linked.

When a computer is started and a user logs on, the following process takes place:

1. A Windows 2000, Windows XP, or Windows Server 2003 computer in a domain starts up. The client computer queries the domain controller for a list of GPOs that it needs to apply. The domain controller examines all of the GPOs to see

which policies apply to the computer. Policies that are executed on the computer include the computer settings and startup scripts.

2. The domain controller presents the client with the list of GPOs that apply to it in the order that the GPOs need to be processed. The computer contacts the domain controller and extracts the Group Policy templates from the Sysvol share, then applies the settings and runs the scripts.

3. When the user logs on, the same process happens again, except this time the user settings, logon scripts, and software policies are applied.

Controlling User Desktop Settings

Companies spend a lot of time and money designing standard computer installation configurations only to have users change settings, thus resulting in nonstandard configurations and increased calls to the help desk. Group Policy helps reduce administrative costs by allowing the enforcement of standard computer configurations, limiting user access to various areas of the operating system, and ensuring that users have their own personal desktop and application settings. Administrative templates consist of a number of administrative configurations, which can be used to apply these settings.

Administrative templates are basically registry settings that can be configured to manage computer and user desktop settings. There are seven main categories of configuration settings that can be applied to either the computer or user section of a GPO.

Table 8-2 explains each of the main categories of configuration settings for administrative templates and the section of the GPO to which each can be applied.

Table 8-2   Configuration categories of administrative templates

Configuration Category	Explanation	Configuration
Windows Components	Configures settings for applications such as Internet Explorer, NetMeeting, Task Scheduler, and the Microsoft Management Console	User and computer
System	Configures settings related to Group Policy, disk quotas, logons, and code signing	User and computer
Network	Configures settings for off-line files and network and dial-up connections	User and computer
Printers	Configures settings related to installing, publishing, and maintaining printers	Computer
Start menu and taskbar	Configures settings related to options available on the Start menu and taskbar	User
Desktop	Configures user desktop settings such as wallpaper, display of icons, and Active Desktop	User
Control Panel	Restricts various icons and applets within Windows Control Panel	User
Shared Folders	Configures shared folder and DFS root publishing settings	User

8

In Activity 8–5, you create a new GPO that assigns desktop settings to users in the Marketing OU.

Activity 8-5:   Configuring Group Policy Object User Desktop Settings

Time Required: 15 minutes

Objective: Configure and test the application of Group Policy settings.

Description: The IT manager at Dover Leasing has asked you to test the use of GPO settings for the purpose of controlling the user desktop environment. In this activity, you attempt to remove the Recycle Bin icon, as well as restrict access to Control Panel for users whose accounts exist within the Marketing OU.

1. Using Active Directory Users and Computers, access the configuration settings of the **Marketing Policy** GPO. See Activity 8-3 for details, if necessary.

2. Under the User Configuration settings section, click the **plus sign (+)** next to **Administrative Templates** to view its contents.

3. Click the **Desktop** folder to view its contents. Double-click the **Remove Recycle Bin icon from Desktop** item to view its properties.

4. Click the **Enabled** radio button as shown in Figure 8-4, and click **OK**.

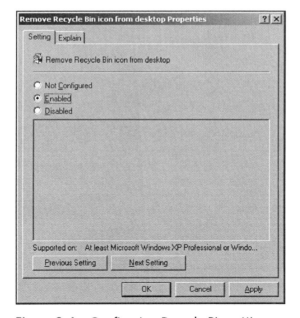

Figure 8-4   Configuring Recycle Bin settings

5. Click the **Start Menu and Taskbar** folder to view its contents. Double-click the **Remove Run menu from Start Menu** item to view its properties.

6. Click the **Enabled** radio button and click **OK**.

7. Click the **Control Panel** folder to view its contents. Double-click the **Prohibit access to the Control Panel** item to view its properties.

8. Click the **Enabled** radio button and click **OK**.

9. Close the Group Policy Object Editor window, close the properties window of the Marketing OU, and then close Active Directory Users and Computers.

10. Log off and then log on as the Marketing OU user **mcowan**, using the password **Password01**.

11. Confirm that the Recycle bin does not appear on the user desktop. Click **Start** to confirm that both the Run command and access to Control Panel are unavailable.

12. Log off and log back on using your **AdminXX** account.

Managing Security Settings with Group Policy

Windows Server 2003 allows an administrator to control a number of security settings using Group Policy. In Chapter 2, you learned that a variety of Group Policy settings could only be configured in GPOs assigned to domain objects, namely Password Policy, Account Policy, and Kerberos Policy settings.

The other nodes under the Security Settings category can be applied to both the domain and OU levels. Here is a summary of the functions of each node:

- Local Policies—Applies security settings to the local account database of the workstation or server; settings may be overwritten at the site, domain, or OU level but remain in effect if there are no other policies at those levels

  There are three subcategories of Local Policies that can be configured:

  - Audit Policy—Defines various successful or unsuccessful events that can be audited and recorded in the event logs

  - User Rights Assignment—Controls local computer rights that may be assigned to users or groups (e.g., the right to log on locally or shut down the computer)

  - Security Options—Defines a wide variety of configuration settings that adjust the registry (e.g., logon banner configurations, restricting floppy or CD-ROM access, and removing the last logged-on user name from the logon screen)

- Event Log—Defines configuration settings for event log size, retention period, and access restrictions

- Restricted Groups—Gives the administrator the ability to control who is a member of any security group; each time the policy is refreshed, any users that have been added to the group by any means other than the security template are

removed automatically; can also control the other groups to which a particular security group belongs

- System Services—Allows an administrator control over service startup mode, disabling of a service, permissions to edit the service mode, and auditing of the service

- Registry—Defines security and auditing access control list (ACL) settings for Registry keys and subkeys; allows an administrator to control who has the ability to change or overwrite various registry settings

- File System—Defines and maintains NTFS security permissions and auditing permissions for any folder or file listed in the policy; files or folders must reside on an NTFS partition

- Wireless Network (IEEE 802.11) Policies—Defines security settings for wireless networks, including which wireless networks a client can connect to, whether access points should be used, and the data encryption settings

- Public Key Policies—Defines configuration settings for different public key-based applications like the Encrypting File System (EFS), certificate auto-enrollment settings, and Certificate Authority (CA) trusts

- Software Restriction Policies—Defines security settings for the deployment of software, such as the ability to manually define which file extensions are considered executable, control security settings of software-related Registry paths, and over-ride software settings from other GPOs

- IP Security Policies on Active Directory—Defines different IP Security settings based on the role of a server or workstation; three default policies exist, but none are applied by default

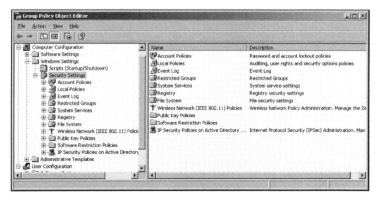

Figure 8-5   Viewing configuration areas under Security Settings

In Activity 8-6 you configure security settings for an existing GPO.

Activity 8-6: Configuring Group Policy Object Security Settings

Time Required: 10 minutes

Objective: Use Group Policy settings to configure a logon banner for domain users.

Description: Windows Server 2003 enables you to configure a variety of different security settings using GPOs. The IT manager at Dover Leasing is concerned about legal issues relating to the fact that the user authentication process does not include any type of warning message about which users are authorized to access Dover's computers. In this activity, you configure and test Group Policy settings to require that users accept the parameters of a warning message before logging on.

1. Using Active Directory Users and Computers, access the configuration settings of the **Default Domain Policy** GPO. (See Activity 8-3 for details, if necessary.)

2. In the Computer Configuration section, click the **plus signs (+)** next to **Windows Settings**, **Security Settings**, and **Local Policies** to expand them.

3. Click **Security Options** to view its settings.

4. Double-click **Interactive logon: Message text for users attempting to log on** to view its properties.

5. Click the **Define this policy setting in the template** check box. In the text box, type **Only authorized users of Dover Leasing are permitted to log on** as shown in Figure 8-6, and click **OK**.

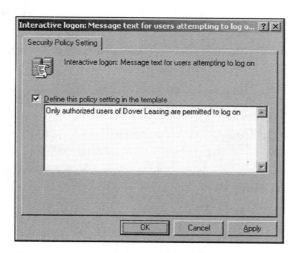

Figure 8-6   Configuring an interactive logon message

6. Double-click **Interactive logon: Message title for users attempting to log on** to view its properties.

7. Click the **Define this policy setting** check box. In the text box, type **Dover Corporate Security Policy** and click **OK**.

8. Close the Group Policy Object Editor window, as well as the properties of Domain*XX*.Dovercorp.net.

9. Close Active Directory Users and Computers and restart your server.

10. Press **Ctrl+Alt+Delete** to begin the logon process. The Dover Corporate Security Policy window opens. Click **OK**.

11. Log on using your **AdminXX** account.

In Activity 8-7 you configure file system security settings using Group Policy.

Activity 8-7: Configuring File System Security Using Group Policy Settings

Time Required: 15 minutes

Objective: Use Group Policy settings to configure security permissions on a file or folder.

Description: Users in the Marketing Department at Dover Leasing use a custom application requiring that a folder named Reports be present on their D: drive. The security requirements of this application dictate that only users in the Marketing Department should have access to the folder. The IT manager at Dover Leasing has asked you to attempt to find a way to use Group Policy settings to configure the necessary folder security, to avoid the need to manually configure each and every computer. In this activity, you test the ability to control file and folder permissions through the use of Group Policy file system settings.

1. Click **Start**, click **My Computer** and then double-click drive **D:** to view its contents.

2. Right-click in a blank area, select **New**, and click **Folder**.

3. Name the new folder **Reports**, and then close My Computer.

4. Open Active Directory Users and Computers and access the configuration settings of the **Marketing Policy** GPO. (See Activity 8-3 for details, if necessary.)

5. In the Computer Configuration section, click the **plus signs (+)** next to **Windows Settings** and then **Security Settings** to expand it.

6. Right-click **File System** and click **Add File**, as shown in Figure 8-7.

7. In the Add a file or folder dialog box, browse to the **Reports** folder on drive **D:** and click **OK**. The Database Security for D:\Reports window opens.

8. Click **Add**. In the Enter the object names to select text box, type **Moira** and click **OK**.

9. In the Permissions for Moira Cowan section, click the **Allow** check box next to the **Full Control** permission and click **OK**. When the Add Object dialog box opens, read the available options and then click **OK**.

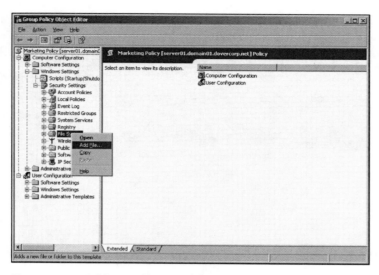

Figure 8-7   Adding a file to configure security settings

10. Close the Group Policy Object Editor window, as well as the properties of the Marketing OU.

11. Click **Start**, and then click **Run**. In the open text box, type **gpupdate.exe** and click **OK**. This will update Group Policy settings on your server.

12. Open My Computer and browse to the **D:\Reports** folder. Right-click the folder and click **Properties**. Click the **Security** tab, making note of the fact that no permissions for the Moira Cowan user account are explicitly defined. Close the Reports Properties window, then close My Computer.

13. Close Active Directory Users and Computers and restart your server.

14. Log on as the user **mcowan** using the password **Password01**.

15. Open My Computer and browse to the **D:\Reports** folder. Right-click the folder and click **Properties**. Click the **Security** tab, making note of the fact that permissions for the Moira Cowan user account are now explicitly defined, as per the GPO linked to the Marketing OU.

16. Log off and log back on using your **AdminXX** account.

Assigning Scripts

Most administrators are familiar with the application of various types of scripts or files that incorporate a number of commands used to automate routine operations. Logon scripts were most popular in the past and used to automate such tasks as drive mapping or application updates.

Windows Server 2003 can use scripts to perform tasks at various times during the logon or logoff process. Group Policy allows you to configure computer startup and shutdown scripts, which are configured in the computer section of a GPO, as shown in Figure 8-8. The user section of a GPO can be accessed to configure logon and logoff scripts.

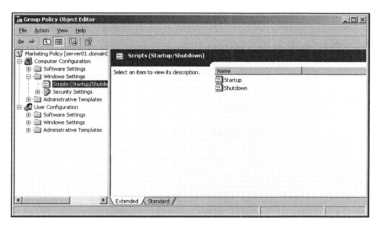

Figure 8-8   Viewing the startup and shutdown script configuration icons

If you assign multiple logon/logoff or startup/shutdown scripts to the configuration containers, each script is run synchronously in order from top to bottom. You can modify the order by selecting the script and clicking the Up or Down buttons in the Properties dialog box. In addition to modifying the order, other policy settings for groups allow you to specify script time-outs, change the running of the scripts to asynchronous, and specify whether scripts are hidden when they are executed.

In Activity 8-8 you assign a logon script to users using Group Policy.

Activity 8-8: Assigning Logon Scripts to Users Using Group Policy

Time Required: 15 minutes

Objective: Use GPOs to assign logon scripts to domain users.

Description: Dover Leasing has traditionally used logon scripts to easily define user environment settings, such as mapped network drives, printers, and so forth. Although the logon scripts in use at Dover currently meet all requirements, they have become very long and difficult to manage based on the specific requirements of users from different departments. Because of this, the IT manager at Dover Leasing has asked you to evaluate the ability to deploy logon scripts using GPO settings. In this activity, you deploy a logon script that maps a drive for Marketing users only through the use of a GPO.

1. Open My Computer, click **Tools** on the menu bar, and then click **Folder Options**.

2. Click the **View** tab. In the Advanced settings section, ensure that the **Hide extensions for known file types** check box is unchecked, and click **OK**.

3. Open drive D: and create a new folder called **Scripts**.

4. Open the Scripts folder. Right-click an area of free space, select **New**, and then click **Text Document**.

5. Double-click **New Text Document.txt** to open it.

6. In the first line of the file, type **net use x: \\instructor\shared**. Save the file and then close it.

7. Right-click **New Text Document.txt** and click **Rename**. Rename the file to **logon.bat** and press **Enter**. When prompted, click **Yes** to confirm the change.

8. Right-click the **logon.bat** file and click **Copy**. Close My Computer.

9. Open Active Directory Users and Computers and access the configuration settings of the **Marketing Policy** GPO.

10. Under User Configuration, click the **plus sign (+)** next to **Windows Settings** to expand it and then click **Scripts (Logon/Logoff)**.

11. Double-click **Logon** to access its properties. Click the **Show Files** button.

12. In the new window that opens, right-click an area of free space, click **Paste**, and then close the window.

13. In the Logon Properties window, click **Add**. In the Add a Script window, click **Browse** and then double-click **logon.bat**. Click **OK** to close the window, and then click **OK** again to close the Logon Properties window shown in Figure 8-9.

8

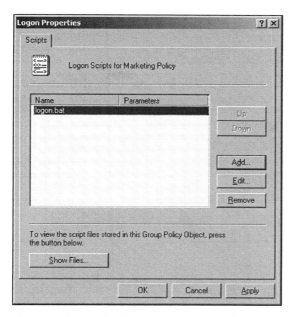

Figure 8-9   Assigning a startup script in group policy

14. Close the Group Policy Object Editor window, close the properties of the Marketing OU, and then close Active Directory Users and Computers.

15. Log off and then log back on as the user **mcowan** using the password **Password01**.

16. Open My Computer and verify that drive **X** has been mapped to the \\instructor\shared folder. Close My Computer.

17. Log off and then log back on using your **AdminXX** account. Open My Computer to verify that drive X has not been mapped because the AdminXX account does not fall under the scope of the Marketing Policy GPO.

18. Close My Computer.

Redirecting Folders

Folder redirection is a Group Policy feature that enables you to redirect the following contents of a user's profile to a network location:

- Application data
- Desktop
- My Documents
- Start menu

Some of the reasons why you would want to redirect the folders out of a user's profile include:

- Storing the folders on the network ensures that user information is backed up at all times, as opposed to being stored on the local workstation.
- User logon time is reduced because the contents of the folder do not have to be copied from the workstation to the server each time the user logs on or off.
- Folder redirection allows you to create a standard desktop for multiple users.

The Settings tab has a number of options that control the behavior of folder redirection. Table 8-3 describes each setting.

Table 8-3   Folder redirection settings

Configuration Setting	Description
Grant the user exclusive rights to <folder name>	This setting makes sure that only the individual user that owns the folder has access; this is enabled by default.
Move the contents of <folder name> to the new location	This setting moves the contents of the folder to the new location specified; if this check box is cleared, the contents of the folder before the redirection are not moved to the new location (this is enabled by default).
Policy removal	When a folder redirection policy is removed, by default the redirected folder remains in the redirected location; you can choose to redirect the folder back to the user's profile if the policy is removed.

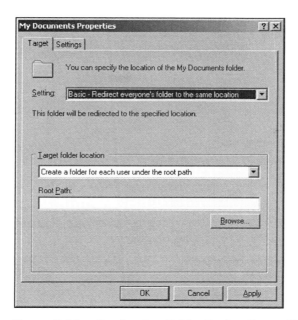

Figure 8-10   Configuring Folder Redirection settings

MANAGING GROUP POLICY INHERITANCE

As a Windows 2000, Windows XP, or Windows Server 2003 computer starts, GPOs are applied in the following order:

1. Local computer
2. Site
3. Domain
4. Parent OU
5. Child OU

All of the individual GPO settings are inherited by default. For example, a Group Policy setting on a parent container is also applied to child containers and, therefore, to all the users and computers in the child containers. One computer or user can process many policies during startup and logon.

At each level, more than one GPO can be applied. If there is more than one GPO per container, the policies are applied in the order that they appear on the Group Policy tab for the container, starting with the bottom GPO first.

Be careful about the number of GPOs that are applied. Computer startup and logon performance can be affected if a large number of GPOs need to be applied to the user or workstation.

Because of the multiple policies that can be applied to a user or computer, there is the chance of a conflict in the settings between policies. The computer uses the following steps to determine which policy to apply:

1. If there is no conflict, then both policies are applied. For example, if a policy at a domain level enables a certain setting and the policy at an OU level has that setting set as "Not Configured," then the domain policy is applied.

2. If there is a conflict, later settings overwrite earlier settings. If both a domain-level policy and an OU-level policy configure the same setting differently, then the OU-level policy is applied.

3. If computer and user policy settings directly conflict, computer policies usually override user policies.

After a user has logged on, the computer refreshes its policies every 90 minutes plus a random number of minutes (no more than 30) so that all the computers don't contact the DC to refresh at the same time. If a user does not shut down his computer, or a setting has changed in the Group Policy, then refreshing the policy ensures that the computer and user settings are up-to-date. Domain controllers refresh their policy settings for groups every five minutes.

You can refresh Group Policy settings manually by running GPUPDATE.EXE from the command prompt. The SECEDIT.EXE command used with Windows 2000 has been replaced with GPUPDATE.EXE in Windows Server 2003.

As mentioned previously, GPOs can be linked to site, domain, or OU containers in Active Directory. This allows the administrator maximum flexibility when applying Group Policies in the domain. There are a number of possibilities for how to apply Group Policy settings in a domain, as outlined in the following list:

- Certain policies that apply to everyone in a physical location can be applied at the site level. Other settings can be configured at a domain level. Some policy settings, such as account policy, can only be set at the domain level. If account policies are set at levels other than the domain level, they apply to local computer accounts and local user accounts on those systems only. Very specific policies can then be set based on OUs.

8

- Multiple Group Policies can be assigned to one container. Several GPOs can be created that define different settings and then link all of them to a specific container. For example, you might want to create a policy that defines security settings and another that defines user desktop settings, and then link both of them to the same container.

- The same Group Policy can be used to link it to multiple containers. A policy can then be created once and used for different containers. For example, you may create a policy for software distribution and then link that policy to the OUs where the policy should be applied.

In Activity 8-9 you link a Group Policy object to multiple containers.

Activity 8-9:   Linking a Group Policy Object to Multiple Containers

Time Required: 10 minutes

Objective: Link a single GPO to multiple containers.

Description: As part of planning the deployment of GPOs for the *DomainXX.Dovercorp.net* domain, you have recognized that there are some cases where users in different departments (but not the entire domain) require the same configuration settings. Instead of configuring multiple GPOs that contain identical settings, you have decided that a smaller number of more generic policies linked to multiple containers might better meet your needs. In this activity, you create a new GPO that removes the Run command from user Start menus and then links that policy to multiple containers.

1. Open Active Directory Users and Computers, if it is not already opened.

2. Expand the **DomainXX.Dovercorp.net** domain if necessary, right-click on the **Information Technology** OU, and click **Properties**.

3. Click the **Group Policy** tab and then click **New**. Type **Remove Run Command**, then press **Enter** to name the new GPO.

4. Click **Edit** to access the properties of the Remove Run Command GPO.

5. Under User Configuration, click the **plus sign (+)** next to **Administrative Templates** to expand it, and then click **Start Menu and Taskbar** to view its settings.

6. Double-click the **Remove Run menu from Start Menu** icon to access its properties, as shown in Figure 8-11. Click the **Enabled** radio button, and then click **OK**.

7. Close the Group Policy Object Editor window and then close the properties of the Information Technology OU.

8. Right-click the **Sales** OU and then click **Properties**.

9. Click the **Group Policy** tab and then click **Add**.

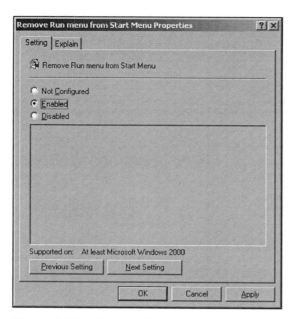

Figure 8-11   Viewing the Remove Run menu from Start Menu Properties

10. In the Add a Group Policy Object Link window, click the **All** tab. Click the **Remove Run Command** GPO and then click **OK**. The Remove Run Command GPO is now linked to both the Information Technology OU as well as the Sales OU.

11. Close the properties of the Sales OU, but leave Active Directory Users and Computers open.

Configuring Block Policy Inheritance, No Override, and Filtering

By default, all policy settings for groups are inherited from parent containers. However, there are several ways to change this default behavior, as outlined in the following sections.

Blocking Group Policy Inheritance

If you do not want any of the higher-level settings to be applied to a particular child container, then check the Block Policy inheritance check box on the Group Policy tab for the container properties. Figure 8-12 shows the interface.

Checking this option means that all higher-level policies for other containers are blocked. For example, if the properties of the Marketing OU were set to block Group Policy inheritance, then GPOs from the site or domain levels would not be applied. Blocking Group Policies can be very useful if you have one OU that has very different policy requirements than all of the other OUs, or if the OU must be separately managed.

8

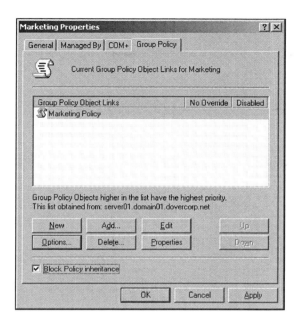

Figure 8-12   Blocking Group Policy inheritance

Configuring No Override

If you want a particular GPO's settings to always be enforced, you can configure the policy using the No Override option, as shown in Figure 8-13.

This results in the policy being enforced even if a lower-level policy that is processed later tries to change a setting. The No Override setting also enforces a policy on a container that has Block Policy inheritance set. Use this option if there is a particular group of settings that must be enforced in the entire network and then link this policy to the domain or site level so that it applies to all containers.

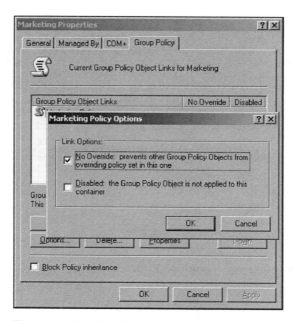

Figure 8-13   Configuring No Override on a Group Policy Object

Filtering Using Permissions

Another way of controlling the inheritance of Group Policies is to prevent policy settings from applying to a particular user, group, or computer within a container. For example, the Marketing OU may have a GPO linked to it, but you don't want the settings from the GPO to apply to the Marketing Vice President. To filter the Marketing Vice President so that she does not have the GPO applied, you could access the security settings associated with the GPO and deny the Read and Apply Group Policy permissions for the Marketing Vice President user account only. This would prevent the Group Policy from being applied to the Marketing Vice President, while the settings would still affect all other users within the OU.

In Activity 8–10 you configure Group Policy inheritance settings for existing GPOs.

Activity 8-10: Configuring Group Policy Object Inheritance Settings

Time Required: 20 minutes

Objective: Configure Group Policy inheritance settings.

Description: As part of his decision to deploy configuration settings using GPOs, the IT manager at Dover Leasing has identified a number of potential issues about how GPOs are processed in Active Directory environments. In particular, the IT manager is concerned that if administration is ultimately decentralized, administrators responsible for a particular OU might configure policy settings that override those configured at the domain level. You have been asked to configure and test Group Policy inheritance settings that ensure settings

configured at the domain level can not be overwritten by OU-level configurations. In this activity, you configure and test the Group Policy No Override setting.

1. Open Active Directory Users and Computers (if necessary) and then access the configuration settings of the **Default Domain Policy** GPO.

2. Under the User Configuration settings section, click the **plus sign (+)** next to **Administrative Templates** to expand it, and then click **Start Menu and Taskbar** to view its settings.

3. Double-click **Remove Run menu from Start Menu**, click the **Enabled** radio button, and then click **OK**. This will disable the Run command for all domain users.

4. Close the Group Policy Object Editor window, and close the properties of the Domain*XX*.Dovercorp.net domain.

5. Access the configuration settings of the **Marketing Policy** GPO.

6. Under the User Configuration settings section, click the **plus sign (+)** next to **Administrative Templates** to expand it, and then click **Start Menu and Taskbar** to view its settings.

7. Double-click **Remove Run menu from Start Menu**, click the **Disabled** radio button, and then click **OK**. This will stop the removal of the Run command for all users in the Marketing OU.

8. Close all open windows and log off.

9. Log on using your **AdminXX** account, noting that the Run command is no longer available. Log off.

10. Log on using the **mcowan** account with the password **Password01**. Note that the Run command is now available because OU-level policies are applied after domain-level policies.

11. Log off and then log on using your **AdminXX** account.

12. Open Active Directory Users and Computers and then access the properties of the **DomainXX.Dovercorp.net** domain.

13. Click the **Group Policy** tab and ensure that the **Default Domain Policy** is selected. Click the **Options** button. Under Link Options, check the **No Override** check box and then click **OK**. Notice the check mark next to the Default Domain Policy in the No Override column. This will prevent settings in the Default Domain Policy from being overridden by policy settings applied at the OU level.

14. Close all open windows and log off.

15. Log on as user **mcowan** using the password **Password01**.

16. Click **Start** to verify that the Run command no longer appears.

17. Log off and then log back on using your **AdminXX** account. Remove the **No Override** setting from the **Default Domain Policy** GPO. Close all open windows.

In Activity 8-11 you use security permissions to filter the application of GPO settings.

ACTIVITY

Activity 8-11: Filtering Group Policy Objects Using Security Permissions

Time Required: 10 minutes

Objective: Use security permissions to filter and control the application of Group Policy settings.

Description: Although the OU structure in place in the *DomainXX.Dovercorp.net* domain was designed with network administration issues in mind, the IT manager is concerned about the fact that in some cases he does not want Group Policy settings to apply to all users. For example, in some departments he would rather not restrict the desktop settings of managers, many of whom find it intrusive. In this activity, you configure and test the ability to filter the application of Group Policy settings through the use of security permissions.

1. In Active Directory Users and Computers, access the properties of the **Marketing** OU.

2. Click the **Group Policy** tab, ensure that the **Marketing Policy** is selected, and then click **Properties**.

3. Click the **Security** tab, and review the permissions associated with the Authenticated Users group. Note that this group has both the Read and Apply Group Policy permissions set to allow.

4. Click **Add**. In the Enter the object names to select text box, type **Moira** and then click **OK**.

5. Ensure that the Moira Cowan user account is selected and then note the permissions associated with the account. Check the **Deny** check box for the **Apply Group Policy** permission. This will stop settings in the Marketing Policy GPO from applying to Moira Cowan. Click **OK**. Click **Yes** in the Security dialog box.

6. Close all open windows and log off.

7. Log on as the user **jhsmith** with the password **Password01**. Click the **Start** menu to confirm that the Run command is available for jhsmith as per the Marketing Policy GPO setting. Log off.

8. Log on as the user **mcowan** with the password **Password01**. Click the Start menu to confirm that the Run command is not available for mcowan because the Marketing Policy GPO does not apply due to permission filtering. As such, the policy settings applied by the Default Domain Policy are applied to the mcowan user account.

9. Log off and then log back on using your **AdminXX** user account.

8

Troubleshooting Group Policy Settings

There may be times when a GPO does not work as expected. For example, restrictions may not be enforced as configured, or may be too restrictive and thus interfere with user productivity.

A careful inspection of the Active Directory hierarchy could possibly uncover the reasons for a Group Policy not working correctly. Do not forget the order of Group Policy processing: local computer, site, domain, and OU. Be sure to inspect all containers above and below the OU that is causing the problem. In some cases, improper use of No Override or Block Policy inheritance settings can cause problems. Another area to be aware of is the Group Policy's Security tab. Make sure that the user or group has been assigned the Read and Apply Group Policy permissions.

Group Policy settings are refreshed every five minutes on domain controllers by default. User and computer Group Policy settings are refreshed every 90 minutes, with a 30-minute maximum offset. Group Policy settings can be refreshed immediately by issuing the GPUPDATE command.

Windows Server 2003 also includes two main utilities that allow you to view the effective Group Policy settings that have been applied to a particular user or computer in the form of the command-line **GPRESULT** tool and the graphical **Resultant Set of Policy (RSoP)** tool. These utilities are useful because they can be used to discover Group Policy-related problems and to illustrate which GPOs were applied to a user or computer. GPRESULT also lists all group memberships of the user or computer being analyzed, along with information about any GPOs that may have been filtered using security permissions.

If you are experiencing performance problems that relate to the processing of GPOs, you may want to disable the unused portion of the computer or user section of the policy. For example, if a particular GPO is only used to apply computer-related settings, then disabling the user configuration section of the policy would improve group policy processing performance. To disable processing of the computer or user configuration section of a policy, access the policy's properties and choose the appropriate setting, as shown in Figure 8-14.

Figure 8-15 shows the output of the GPRESULT command for a specified user.

Figure 8-14   Disabling a section of a Group Policy Object

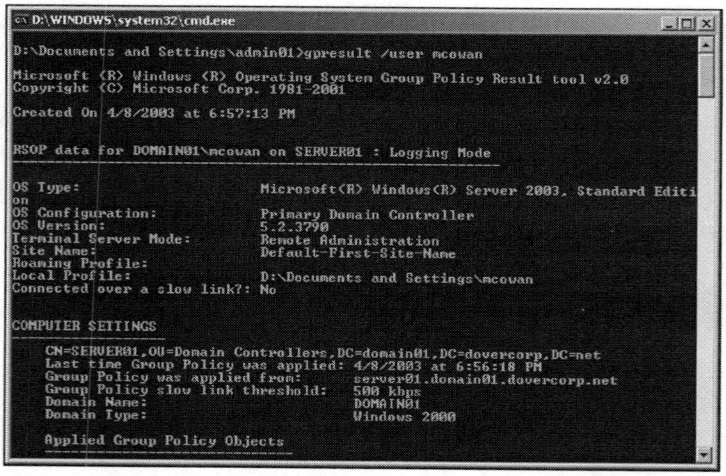

Figure 8-15   Using the GPRESULT tool

In Activity 8-12 you use the RSoP tool to view resultant Group Policy settings for a user on a particular computer.

Activity 8-12:   Determining Group Policy Settings Using the Resultant Set of Policy Tool

Time Required: 10 minutes

Objective: Use RSoP to determine effective Group Policy settings.

Description: Although GPRESULT.EXE provides all of the information necessary to troubleshoot effective Group Policy settings, you have decided that the data it provides can be overwhelming from the command line. As an alternative, you have decided to try the graphical Resultant Set of Policy (RSoP) tool. In this activity, you again evaluate the effect of Group Policy settings for a domain user but this time using the RSoP tool.

1. Open Active Directory Users and Computers and then access the configuration settings of the **Default Domain Policy** GPO.

2. Under the User Configuration settings section, click the **plus sign (+)** next to **Administrative Templates** to expand it, and then click **Start Menu and Taskbar** to view its settings.

3. Double-click **Remove Run menu from Start Menu**, click the **Disabled** radio button, and then click **OK**. This will once again enable the Run command for all domain users.

4. Close the Group Policy Object Editor window, and close the properties of the Domain*XX*.Dovercorp.net domain. Close Active Directory Users and Computers.

5. Log off, and then log on again using your **Admin*XX*** account.

6. Open a new MMC and add the **Resultant Set of Policy** snap-in. (Refer to Activity 8-1 for details on opening an MMC console if necessary.)

7. Right-click the **Resultant Set of Policy** icon and click **Generate RSoP Data**, as shown in Figure 8-16.

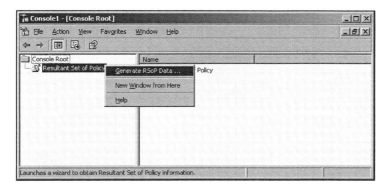

Figure 8-16   Generating RSoP data

8. At the Resultant Set of Policy Wizard welcome screen, click **Next**.

9. At the Mode Selection window, ensure that the **Logging mode** radio button is selected and click **Next**.

10. At the Computer Selection window, ensure that the **This computer** radio button is selected, and click **Next**.

11. At the User Selection window, click the **Select a specific user** radio button. Click the **DOMAINXX\mcowan** user account and then click **Next**.

12. At the Summary of Selections window, click **Next** to begin the analysis process.

13. Click **Finish** to complete the Resultant Set of Policy Wizard.

14. Click the **plus sign (+)** next to **mcowan on ServerXX – RSOP**. Under the Computer Configuration section, click the **plus signs (+)** next to **Windows Settings**, **Security Settings**, and **Local Policies** to expand them. Click **Security Options** to view its settings.

15. Scroll through the list to view the Security Options that are applied to the Moira Cowan user account as a result of Group Policy settings.

16. If time permits, browse through additional sections to view other policies that have been applied to the Moira Cowan user account via GPO settings.

17. Close the MMC without saving changes.

8

DEPLOYING SOFTWARE USING GROUP POLICY

In addition to managing user desktops, maintaining security, applying scripts, and redirecting folders, Group Policy can also help you deploy and maintain software installations throughout the domain. There are a variety of applications that can be deployed using Group Policy, including business applications such as Microsoft Office, utilities such as anti-virus software, and software updates such as service packs.

When a company rolls out a new software application, there are four main phases that are addressed:

- Software preparation
- Deployment
- Software maintenance
- Software removal

Software Preparation

The first phase of software deployment is to prepare the software for distribution. Windows Server 2003 Group Policy uses a special installation file called a **Microsoft Windows installer package (MSI)**. An MSI file contains all of the information needed to install an application in a variety of configurations. Many software vendors are starting to include

preconfigured MSI packages with their applications to enable administrators to take advantage of the features provided by Windows Server 2003 Group Policy. For older applications, you can create your own MSI packages using third-party utilities, such as a program called WinINSTALL from Veritas.

After you obtain or create an MSI package file, place the file, along with any related software installation files, in a shared folder on the network. You configure Group Policy to access this shared folder so that a successful installation is ensured.

If an MSI package is not available for an application, and you cannot repackage the application using an application like WinINSTALL, you have the option to use another file type called a **ZAP file**. A ZAP file is a text file that can be used by Group Policy to deploy an application. However, applications deployed using the ZAP file:

- Can only be published and not assigned
- Are not resilient and do not repair themselves automatically
- Usually require user intervention and require the user to have the proper permissions to install applications on their local computer

For more information on creating a ZAP file, consult KB article 231747 on the Microsoft Web site.

Deployment

Using Windows Server 2003 Group Policy, applications can be deployed in one of two ways:

- Assigning applications
- Publishing applications

Assigning Applications

When you create a policy to assign an application, any user to which the policy applies has a shortcut to the application advertised on the Start menu. The application is installed when a user clicks the shortcut for the first time or double-clicks a document that is associated with the application. If the user does not click the shortcut, the application is not installed, which saves space on the hard drive.

If the policy was configured in the computer section of the Group Policy, any computer to which the policy applies has the application automatically installed the next time that the computer is started.

One other advantage to assigned applications is that these applications are resilient, meaning that if files were to become corrupted, the application would automatically reinstall itself.

Publishing Applications

When a policy is created to publish an application, the application is not advertised on the Start menu. Users can install published applications by accessing the Add/Remove Programs applet in Control Panel or by double-clicking a document associated with the application. Applications can only be published to users and not to computers.

Configuring the Deployment

Configuring the deployment of the software package involves creating or editing a GPO and then specifying application deployment options. For example, an administrator might choose to assign a certain application to all computers at the domain level, which would automatically install the application the next time individual computers were started. Similarly, a different application might be published to members of the Marketing OU only, allowing users to whom this policy applies to install the application, if necessary, at their own discretion.

In Activity 8-13 you publish an application to users using Group Policy.

Activity 8-13: Publishing an Application to Users Using Group Policy

Time Required: 15 minutes

Objective: Publish an application using Group Policy settings.

Description: Dover Leasing has traditionally used Microsoft's System Management Server to deploy software packages and updates to domain users. Although the system is effective, the IT manager at Dover has found it both difficult and expensive to train system administrators in the use of this product. Understanding that Windows Server 2003 Group Policy includes features associated with software deployment, the IT manager has asked you to evaluate the ability to make software available for installation by users without administrative privileges. In this activity, you publish an application to users in the Information Technology OU.

1. Click **Start**, and then click **My Computer**. Double-click on drive **D:**, right-click an area of blank space, select **New**, and then click **Folder**. Name the new folder **shared**.

2. Right-click on the **shared** folder and click **Properties**. Click the **Sharing** tab. Click the **Share this folder** radio button, and then click **OK**.

3. Double-click the **D:\Source\SUPPORT\TOOLS** folder to open it. Copy the files named **suptools.msi** and **support.cab** to the **D:\shared** folder.

4. Open Active Directory Users and Computers and create a new GPO named **Support Tools Publishing** linked to the **Information Technology** OU.

5. Click **Edit** to access the configuration settings of the **Support Tools Publishing** Group Policy Object.

6. Under User Configuration, click the **plus sign (+)** next to **Software Settings** to expand it.

7. Right-click **Software installation**, click **New**, and then click **Package**, as shown in Figure 8-17.

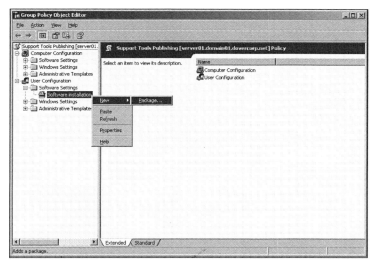

Figure 8-17   Configuring software deployment via Group Policy

8. In the Open dialog box, type **\\serverXX\shared\suptools.msi** (where *XX* is your assigned student number) in the File name text box and click **Open**.

9. In the Deploy Software dialog box, ensure that the **Published** radio button is selected and click **OK**. Click on the **Software installation** icon. Notice that the Windows Support Tools application, source folder, and deployment option information is now listed, as illustrated in Figure 8-18.

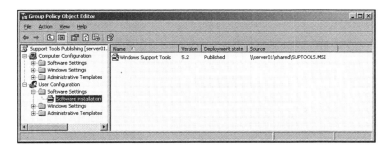

Figure 8-18   Viewing a published application

10. Close all open windows, log off, and then log back on as **mmanore** using the password **Password01**.

11. Click **Start**, click **Control Panel**, and then double-click **Add or Remove Programs**. Click the **Add New Programs** button. Notice that the Windows Support Tools are now available for installation by the mmanore user account.

12. Close all open windows, log off, and then log back on using your **AdminXX** account.

13. Open Active Directory Users and Computers and delete the **Support Tools Publishing** GPO (the entire GPO, not just the link) from the properties of the **Information Technology** OU. Close the properties of the Information Technology OU, but leave Active Directory Users and Computers open.

In Activity 8-14 you assign an application to users using Group Policy.

Activity 8-14: Assigning an Application to Users Using Group Policy

Time Required: 10 minutes

Objective: Assign an application using Group Policy settings.

Description: Having now seen the results of publishing applications to users, the IT manager at Dover Leasing has asked you to evaluate whether it is possible to ensure that the Windows Support Tools are always available for all users in the Information Technology OU without the need for them to manually install the application. In this activity, you configure and test a GPO designed to assign the Windows Support Tools to users in the Information Technology OU.

1. In Active Directory Users and Computers, create a new GPO named **Support Tools Assignment** linked to the **Information Technology** OU.

2. Click **Edit** to access the configuration settings of the **Support Tools Assignment** GPO.

3. Under User Configuration, click the **plus sign (+)** next to **Software Settings** to expand it.

4. Right-click **Software installation**, click **New**, and then click **Package**.

5. In the Open dialog box, type **\\serverXX\shared\suptools.msi** (where *XX* is your assigned student number) in the File name box and click **Open**.

6. In the Deploy Software dialog box, ensure that the **Assigned** radio button is selected and click **OK**. Click on the **Software installation** icon. Notice that the Windows Support Tools application, source folder, and deployment option information is now listed. Close all open windows.

7. Restart your server, and then log back on as **mmanore** using the password **Password01**.

8. Click **Start**, select **All Programs**, select **Windows Support Tools**, and then click **Command Prompt**. The Windows Support Tools install, and the Command Prompt opens.

9. Close all open windows, log off, and then log on using your **AdminXX** account.

Software Maintenance

After an application has been deployed, there are various types of maintenance tasks that usually need to be performed. Most vendors provide periodic updates and service patches to fix reported problems with their applications. You have the task of keeping the deployed software updated with the latest service releases. If vendors release new versions of the software, your users may want to transition slowly to the new version. You may want to allow the users to use both the old and new versions of the software.

When deploying application patches or upgrades, you have three choices for how the deployment is performed:

- A mandatory upgrade
- An optional upgrade
- Redeploying an application

A mandatory upgrade automatically replaces the old version of the software with the new version that is being deployed. Figure 8-19 shows the Upgrades tab found in the properties of a deployed application.

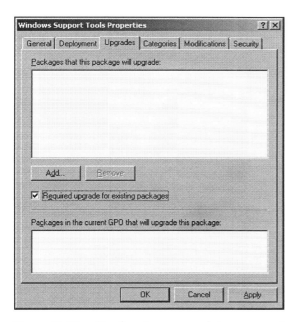

Figure 8-19   Configuring a mandatory upgrade

If the original package and the updated package are both native Windows installer files, the update automatically knows that it is to replace the original package; just the mandatory selection box needs to be configured.

To perform an optional upgrade, do not check the Required upgrade for existing packages option. If the user has installed the original application, all shortcuts still open the first version of the program. To install the upgrade, the user has to access Add or Remove Programs from Control Panel and choose to install the upgrade. If the original version was never installed, clicking the advertised icons invokes an installation of the updated version.

Redeployment of a package means to force an application to reinstall itself everywhere that it is already installed. You may have to do this if you need to deploy an application service pack or hot fix. The main requirement for redeployment is that the patch has to come with an MSI file. To configure redeployment, place the update in the same installation folder as the original application. Open the original GPO that deployed the package, right-click the application, and click All Tasks, Redeploy application.

Software Removal

The final phase of an application life cycle is the removal process. When you need to remove an application that you no longer want to deploy in the organization, Group Policy can save a great amount of time and money. The only caution is that the application must have been originally installed using a Windows installer package.

When removing an application, you are given two choices about how the removal process takes place:

- A forced removal
- An optional removal

A forced removal automatically uninstalls the application from all computers and prevents the software from being reinstalled. The removal takes place either the next time the computer restarts (for computer-based policies) or when the user logs on (for user-based policies).

An optional removal does not remove any of the installed copies of the software, but it does prevent any future installations from taking place. If users remove the application, they are not able to reinstall it.

CHAPTER SUMMARY

❏ Group Policy enables the centralized management of user and computer settings throughout the network. GPOs can be used to perform a variety of administrative tasks, including configuration of desktop settings, control of security settings for users and computers, assignment of scripts, the redirection of folders, and the automation of software distribution on computers throughout the network.

❏ Group Policy is applied in the following order: local computer, site, domain, OU, child OU.

❏ Group Policy is automatically inherited from parent containers to child containers. This can be modified by applying Block Policy inheritance, No Override, or by filtering the policy for specific users.

❏ When deploying software, Group Policy uses an MSI file to determine the installation options.

❏ Applications can either be assigned or published within a GPO. Assigned applications are advertised for users and automatically installed for computers. Published applications appear in the Add/Remove Programs applet for users. Computers cannot have applications published.

KEY TERMS

Default Domain Policy — The name of the GPO that is linked to the domain container in Active Directory; used primarily for configuration of domain-wide password policies.

Domain Controllers Policy — The name of the default GPO that is linked to the domain controllers OU. Used primarily for configuration of policy settings that are only to be applied to the domain controllers in the domain (i.e., auditing).

Folder redirection — A Group Policy feature that enables you to redirect the contents of the Application Data, Desktop, My Documents, My Pictures, and Start menu folders from a user's profile to a network location.

globally unique identifier (GUID) — A unique 128-bit number assigned to the object when it is created.

GPRESULT — This utility can be used to discover Group Policy-related problems and to illustrate which GPOs were applied to a user or computer. GPRESULT also lists all group memberships of the user or computer being analyzed.

Group Policy — Enables the centralized management of user desktop settings, desktop and domain security, and the deployment and management of software throughout your network.

Group Policy container (GPC) — An Active Directory container that stores information about the GPO and includes a version number that is used by other domain controllers to ensure that they have the latest information.

Group Policy object (GPO) — An Active Directory object that is configured to apply Group Policy and linked to either the site, domain, or OU level.

Group Policy template (GPT) — The GPT contains the data that makes up the Group Policy. The template includes all the settings, administrative templates, security settings, software installation settings, scripts, and so forth.

Microsoft Windows installer package (MSI) — A file that contains all of the information needed to install an application in a variety of configurations.

Resultant Set of Policy (RSoP) — A graphical utility included with Windows Server 2003 that enables you to review the aggregated Group Policy settings that apply to a domain user or computer.

ZAP file — A text file that can be used by Group Policy to deploy an application; it has a number of limitations compared to an MSI file.

REVIEW QUESTIONS

1. Which of the following MMC snap-ins is used to configure Group Policy settings?
   a. Group Policy Object Editor
   b. Disk Management
   c. Disk Defragmenter
   d. Active Directory Domains and Trusts

2. Which command-line tool can be used to view effective Group Policy settings?
   a. GPRESULT
   b. GPUPDATE
   c. SECEDIT
   d. SFC

3. Joe attempts to publish an application to a computer, but the publish setting is disabled. What is wrong?
   a. Applications can only be published to users
   b. The GPO is corrupted
   c. Applications can only be published to computers
   d. The user is not logged on

4. What is the order in which GPOs are applied?
   a. Local, Domain, Site, OU
   b. Local, Site, Domain, OU
   c. Local, OU, Site, Domain
   d. Domain, Site, OU, Local

8

5. Group policy settings cannot be applied to which of the following?

    a. Users

    b. Computers

    c. Security groups

    d. Distribution groups

6. Which of the following permissions should be applied to ensure that GPO settings apply to users?

    a. Apply Group Policy

    b. Read

    c. Write

    d. Modify

7. Two user accounts in a certain OU need to be configured without a GPO application, while the remaining users still need restrictions. How can this be accomplished?

    a. Allow the Apply Group Policy permission for these users

    b. Block inheritance for the policy

    c. Configure No Override for the policy

    d. Deny the Apply Group Policy permission for these users

8. Published applications are resilient in that they reinstall automatically if any files become corrupt.

    a. True

    b. False

9. Assigned applications are added to Add or Remove Programs, allowing them to be installed by a user if necessary.

    a. True

    b. False

10. When a GPO is created, its content is actually stored in which two locations on the server? (Choose two.)

    a. The Group Policy container within the Active Directory database

    b. The Group Policy container in the Sysvol folder

    c. The Group Policy template within the Active Directory database

    d. The Group Policy template in the Sysvol folder

11. You have created a GPO that removes the Run command and have linked it to the domain level. At the OU level, you have created a GPO to enable the Run command. Which GPO takes effect for a user in this OU?

    a. The GPO applied to the domain

    b. The GPO applied to the OU

   c. Both settings

   d. Neither setting

12. You have just made a change to the computer portion of a Windows Server 2003 GPO and want to manually refresh the policy settings. Which command accomplishes this?

   a. GPREFRESH

   b. SECEDIT

   c. GPUPDATE

   d. GPREF

13. A GPO can use a ZAP file to publish an application for which an MSI file is not available.

   a. True

   b. False

14. If an application has been assigned to a computer using Group Policy, when is the application installed?

   a. When a user logs on

   b. The next time the computer is restarted

   c. The next time the computer is shut down

   d. When a user logs off

15. A user has accidentally deleted a required file on his local machine for an application that you had previously assigned to the domain using an MSI file and Group Policy. What must you do to make sure that the application continues to function?

   a. Redeploy the application using the original GPO and MSI file.

   b. Do nothing; the application automatically fixes itself.

   c. Publish the application to the domain.

   d. Reinstall the application locally on the user's machine using a CD-ROM or the installation point.

16. Which removal option allows users to continue to work with an installed application but prevents any new installations?

   a. Forced removal

   b. Optional removal

   c. Installation removal

   d. None of the above

17. In which folder do scripts have to be stored to ensure proper functioning and replication to all domain controllers?

   a. The temp folder

   b. The sysvol folder

   c. The replication folder

   d. The system32 folder

18. For Group Policy settings to apply to a user, that user must be a member of a group with both the Read and Apply Group Policy permissions set to Allow.

   a. True

   b. False

19. You need to redirect the My Documents folder to a server location based upon security group memberships. Which setting do you choose?

   a. Basic

   b. Advanced

   c. None of the above

20. Both the GPRESULT and Resultant Set of Policy tools can be used to view the aggregated Group Policy settings that apply to a user.

   a. True

   b. False

CASE PROJECTS

Case Project 8-1

A fellow administrator is having problems with GPOs not being applied as expected. List five troubleshooting methods that you would use to diagnose problems with GPOs.

Case Project 8-2

Dover Leasing has decided to implement GPOs to configure different settings for all users within the Information Technology OU and its child OUs. All Information Technology users should have the Windows Server 2003 Administrative Tools installed regardless of the workstation that they log on to and have the Run command enabled. Users in the Network Support OU only should have the ability to install the Windows Support Tools if necessary. Finally, all users in the Help Desk OU should have access to the Microsoft Management Console in user mode only. Given these requirements, what OUs should be created and which settings should they contain to deploy Group Policy in the most efficient manner possible?

Case Project 8-3

Dover Leasing has decided to deploy GPOs for the purpose of controlling desktop settings for users in the Marketing OU of the *DomainXX.Dovercorp.net* domain. Although these settings should apply to almost all marketing staff, the IT manager has decided that the new settings should not apply to three marketing executives. Given these requirements, how should Group Policy settings be applied so that only the required marketing users are affected by the new settings?

8

9

MONITORING SERVER PERFORMANCE

After reading this chapter and completing the exercises, you will be able to:

Identify the importance of monitoring server performance

Use Task Manager to monitor server performance and resource usage

Use Event Viewer to identify and troubleshoot problems

Use the Performance console to monitor server performance using both System Monitor and Performance Logs and Alerts

Optimize server performance through the configuration of service settings

Many businesses today rely heavily on their servers for day-to-day operations. Expectations are set for network server availability and performance. When a server goes down or starts to perform poorly, many routine functions are affected and the complaints soon filter in. This means that as a network administrator, you need to ensure that a server is capable of meeting performance expectations and that server downtime is minimal.

Windows Server 2003 includes a variety of tools that can be used to monitor server performance, and potentially troubleshoot problems as they arise. For example, the Windows Task Manager utility provides administrators with a snapshot of current CPU and memory performance information, as well as data about the CPU utilization and memory usage of running processes. Although the information that Task Manager provides allows an administrator to obtain a real-time snapshot of system performance, it is rather limited, and is generally used as a starting point before gathering additional information using other tools and utilities. This chapter begins with a look at the Task Manager utility.

Event Viewer is another invaluable server monitoring tool; logging errors, caution messages, and general information about both operating system processes and applications. A proactive server management strategy involves checking the Event Viewer log files regularly as a method of trying to identify small issues and problems before they have a larger impact on server availability and performance. Both the Event Viewer system and application logs are looked at in this chapter.

One of the most robust tools that can be used to monitor server performance is the Performance console, which includes both the System Monitor and Performance Logs and Alerts tools. These tools are both capable of monitoring and logging data from countless different objects ranging from memory to processor utilization to the performance of various applications. This tool also provides a great deal of flexibility, allowing data to be represented both graphically or logged in files for export to other analysis applications. The Performance console is covered in detail in this chapter.

Windows Server 2003 performance is mainly impacted by the hardware resources installed in the server, and the various processes that are running at any given point in time. Examples of processes include not only applications, but also the various services that run in the background. This chapter closes with a look at how unnecessary services can be disabled to reduce resource usage, and how service settings can be configured such that different actions are taken when an error occurs.

INTRODUCTION TO MONITORING SERVER PERFORMANCE

Maintaining a server is similar to maintaining an automobile. When you purchase a new automobile, it must be serviced on a regular basis to ensure its performance over time. Many of the new cars and trucks today also come with tools that can alert you to problems when they occur. Server maintenance is similar. Often, administrators configure servers for network use, while not realizing that over time, server performance can deteriorate for a number of reasons.

One of the more important reasons for monitoring the health of your server is that it can help alert you to problems before they occur or become more serious. Over time, networks change; the demands placed on a server can vary or increase. Monitoring server performance can help you determine what normal behavior is for your server under the current demands and alert you to any performance issues that may be occurring if the normal behavior changes. This normal behavior is known as **baseline** performance.

Windows Server 2003 comes with several built-in tools that can be used to monitor server health and performance, including:

- Task Manager
- Event Viewer
- Performance console

The following sections introduce you to these tools, providing you with a description of how they can be used to monitor your server and how to use them.

TASK MANAGER

Although Windows Server 2003 provides a variety of tools that can be used to monitor and manage server performance, one of the fastest ways to obtain a snapshot of system performance is via the **Task Manager** tool. While the information provided by Task Manager is rather high-level in nature, it provides an effective method to quickly gauge server performance.

The Windows Task Manager interface can be accessed using a variety of different methods, such as by right-clicking on the Windows taskbar and clicking the Task Manager shortcut, or by pressing the Ctrl+Alt+Delete key combination and clicking the Task Manager button in the Windows Security dialog box. Once opened, Windows Task Manager consists of five main tabs, each of which provides different information and capabilities. These tabs are:

- Applications
- Processes
- Performance
- Networking
- Users

Each of the tabs found in the Windows Task Manager interface are looked at in more detail in the following sections.

Monitoring and Managing Applications

You can use Task Manager to view applications running on the server by pressing Ctrl+Alt+Del while logged on as Administrator or as a member of the Administrators group. Click the Task Manager button, which displays a dialog box with five tabs: Applications, Processes, Performance, Networking, and Users. An alternate way to start Task Manager is to right-click an area of open space on the Windows taskbar, and click the Task Manager shortcut item.

When you select the Applications tab, a list of all foreground software applications is displayed, as shown in Figure 9-1. To stop an application, select it from the list and click the End Task button. If an application is listed as Not Responding (no longer responding to user input), you can select that application and press End Task to stop the program, thus freeing up server resources such as memory and CPU cycles. The Switch To button brings the highlighted application to the foreground, and the New Task button enables you to start another application at the console, in a manner similar to the Run command.

Figure 9-1   The Task Manager Applications tab

If you right-click a particular task, several active options appear in a shortcut menu, as follows:

- Switch To—Takes you into the highlighted program
- Bring To Front—Brings the highlighted program to the foreground, but leaves the focus on Task Manager
- Minimize—Causes the program to be minimized
- Maximize—Causes the program to be maximized, but leaves you in Task Manager
- End Task—Stops the highlighted program
- Go To Process—Takes you to the Processes tab and highlights the main process associated with the program

Monitoring and Managing Processes

The Task Manager Processes tab lists all of the processes in use by applications and services, including those running in the background, as shown in Figure 9-2. Besides allowing you to right-click on a process to end it, the Processes tab also displays important information about each running process, as summarized in Table 9-1.

Figure 9-2   The Task Manager Processes tab

Table 9-1   Information provided by the Task Manager Processes tab

Process Information	Description
Image Name	The process name, such as winword.exe for Microsoft Word
User Name	The user account under which the process is running
CPU	The percentage of CPU resources currently used by the process
Mem Usage	The amount of memory currently used by the process

In Activity 9-1 you use Task Manager to manage applications on your Windows Server 2003 system.

Activity 9-1:   Using Task Manager to Manage Applications and Processes

Time Required: 10 minutes

Objective: Use Task Manager to manage applications and processes.

Description: The IT manager at Dover Leasing wants all junior administrators to be able to identify tasks and processes running on all Windows Server 2003 systems with minimal effort. He has asked you to explore the settings available on the Task Manager Applications and Processes tab in order to train the junior staff. In this activity you use Task Manager to identify running tasks, determine the process associated with a task, and then end the task from the Task Manager interface.

1. If necessary, log on using your **AdminXX** account (where *XX* is your assigned student number).

2. Press **Ctrl+Alt+Delete**. At the Windows Security dialog box, click the **Task Manager** button.

3. If necessary, click the **Applications** tab. Assuming that you have no foreground applications running, this tab should not currently list any running tasks.

4. Click **Start**, and then click **Run**. In the Open text box, type **calc.exe** and click **OK**. This opens the Calculator program, which is now listed on the Applications tab with a status of Running.

5. Click on the **Calculator** icon on the Applications tab to select it, and then click the **Switch To** button. This minimizes Task Manager and brings the Calculator program to the foreground.

6. Click on **Windows Task Manager** on the taskbar to restore it.

7. Right-click on the **Calculator** icon on the Applications tab to view the items available on the shortcut menu that appears. Click **Go To Process**. Notice that this action switches focus to the Processes tab, with the process calc.exe highlighted. Review the User Name, CPU, and Mem Usage columns associated with the process.

8. Right-click on the **calc.exe** process to view the items available on the shortcut menu that appears. Click **End Process**.

9. At the Task Manager Warning dialog box, read the message that appears, and click **Yes**. Notice that the Calculator window closes, and that the calc.exe process no longer appears on the Processes tab.

10. Click the **Applications** tab and confirm that the Calculator task is no longer present.

11. Close the **Windows Task Manager** window.

Outside of providing an excellent snapshot of how resources like memory and CPU cycles are currently being consumed by running processes, the Processes tab also allows you to configure the priority associated with a process. By default, processes run under the Normal priority, meaning that all running processes are granted the same level of access to system CPU resources. In some cases, an administrator might want to grant certain processes a higher or lower level of access to these resources, based on their perceived importance or for performance-tuning purposes. For example, on a Windows Server 2003 system running a time-critical application, an administrator might choose to run the associated process at a higher priority to ensure it gains access to the processor immediately when necessary. To change the priority of a running process, right-click on a selected process in the Image Name column, select Set Priority, and then click the priority level required for the process.

Use the Realtime priority with caution. If assigned to a process, that process may completely monopolize the server's CPU resources, preventing necessary access by any other processes.

Monitoring Real-Time Performance

The Task Manager Performance tab shows vital CPU and memory performance information through bar charts, line graphs, and performance statistics, as shown in Figure 9-3. The CPU Usage and PF Usage bars show the current use of CPU and page file use. To the right of each bar is a graph showing the immediate history statistics. The bottom of the Performance tab shows more detailed statistics, which are described in Table 9-2. Typically, an administrator uses the Performance tab of Task Manager to gain a quick snapshot of the current performance of a Windows Server 2003 system, and then uses a more detailed tool like System Monitor (looked at later in this chapter) to gather more detailed information.

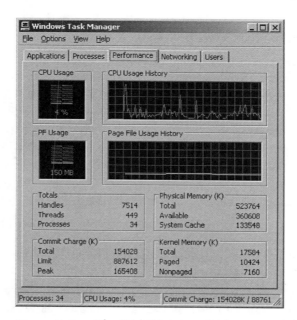

Figure 9-3   The Task Manager Performance tab

Table 9-2   Information provided by the Task Manager Performance tab

Performance Information	Description
CPU Usage/CPU Usage History	Shows the percentage of CPU being used and graphs both current and historical CPU usage
PF Usage/Page File Usage History	Shows the amount of page file usage and graphs historical page file usage
Totals	Displays the total number of handles, threads, and processes

Table 9-2   Information provided by the Task Manager Performance tab (continued)

Performance Information	Description
Physical Memory	Displays the total amount of memory, how much is available, and the amount of memory used for the system cache
Commit Charge	Displays the amount of memory that has been committed to all applications currently running
Kernel Memory	Displays the amount of memory that has been allocated to kernel functions, the amount of memory that could be paged to disk, and the amount of nonpaged memory

In Activity 9-2 you explore information on the Task Manager Performance tab.

Activity 9-2:   Using Task Manager to Monitor Performance

Time Required: 5 minutes

Objective: Use Task Manager to monitor server performance.

Description: Some of the users at Dover Leasing have been complaining that server performance seems sluggish at different times during the day. As a first-level response, the IT manager would like junior administrators to quickly gauge server CPU and memory performance prior to passing this information off to network engineering staff. In this activity you review server performance using the Task Manager Performance tab.

1. Press **Ctrl+Alt+Delete**. At the Windows Security dialog box, click the **Task Manager** button.

2. Click the **Performance** tab. Review the information provided on this tab, such as CPU Usage, CPU Usage History, PF Usage, and Page File Usage History.

3. Leave the Windows Task Manager window open. Click **Start**, and then click **Run**. In the **Open** text box, type **wmplayer.exe** and click **OK**. Review the CPU Usage History graph on the Performance tab. A small spike should be visible at the point when Windows Media Player 9 Series was opened.

4. Click the **Applications** tab. In the Task list, click the **Windows Media Player 9 Series** icon, and then click **End Task**. This closes the Windows Media Player 9 Series program.

5. If time permits, open additional applications to view the impact on both CPU and Page File usage. As more applications are opened and active, these counters should increase, at least temporarily.

6. Close all open windows, and then close **Windows Task Manager**.

Monitoring Network Performance

The Task Manager Networking tab allows you to monitor network performance of all network cards installed on a Windows Server 2003 system. The graphical interface on this tab displays total network utilization information, which is roughly the percentage of the network bandwidth in use.

The lower portion of the Networking tab displays network performance data for each installed network card, as shown in Figure 9-4. It lists the name of the adapter (or connection), the network utilization detected by the adapter (from 0% to 100%), the speed of the network link, such as 10 Mbps, and the operational state of the adapter. This information can be valuable if you suspect there is a problem with a NIC in the server and you want an immediate determination if it is working. The information on the tab also can be an initial warning that something is causing prolonged high network utilization—80% to 100%, for instance.

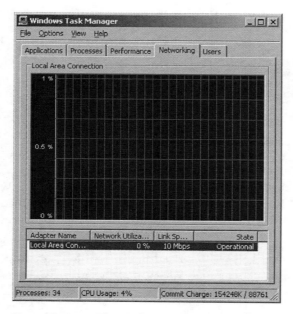

Figure 9-4   The Task Manager Networking tab

Monitoring Users

The Task Manager Users tab provides a listing of the users currently logged on to a system, including network clients with connections to the system. You can log off a user by selecting user and clicking the Logoff button (this ensures that any open files are closed before the user is logged off), or select the Disconnect option to disconnect a user's session (usually if that session is hung or cannot be logged off). Other options available from this tab include the

ability to send a network message to a connected user, or connect to another user's session. The Users tab is shown in Figure 9-5.

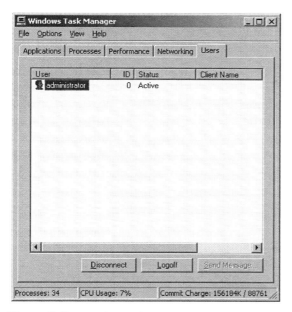

Figure 9-5   The Task Manager Users tab

EVENT VIEWER

Perhaps the most common and effective monitoring and troubleshooting tool in Windows Server 2003 is **Event Viewer**. You can use Event Viewer to gather information and troubleshoot software, hardware, and system problems. Figure 9-6 shows the Event Viewer console.

Events that occur on a system are tracked and recorded in different log files. You can use Event Viewer to view the contents of the log files. For example, you can use Event Viewer to view the contents of the **system log** to determine when, and possibly why, a specific service failed to start.

Whenever you are troubleshooting a problem with a server, one of the first places to look to gather information about the cause is Event Viewer. Entries in the log files can alert you to warnings and errors that are occurring, the component or application that is generating the message, and possibly why the problem is happening. Most entries also include an event ID that you can research on Microsoft's Support Web site (or the vendor's Web site in the case of third-party counters) to gather more detailed information on the problem and find a possible solution.

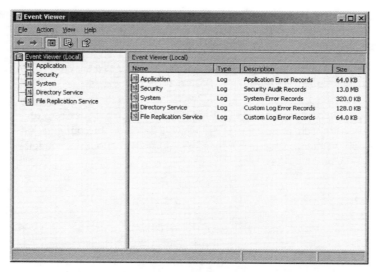

Figure 9-6   The Event Viewer console

Events are typically written to one of three log files:

- Application log — Information, warnings, and errors generated by programs installed on the system are written to the **Application log**.

- Security log — Events pertaining to the audit policy are written to the **Security log**. For example, if the audit policy is tracking failed logon attempts, an event is written to the security log each time a user is unsuccessful in logging on. By default, security logging is disabled until an audit policy is configured.

- System log — Information, warnings, and errors generated by Windows Server 2003 system components, such as drivers and services, are written to the System log.

 A domain controller has two additional logs: the directory service log, which records events logged by Active Directory, and the file replication service log, which logs file replication events. A server installed with the DNS service also includes the DNS server log, which records events related to the DNS server service.

By default, any user can view the contents of the application and system log. Only administrators can view the security log, as well as those users who have been assigned the Manage Auditing and Security Log right.

The system and application logs display the following types of events:

- Information — When a component or application successfully performs an operation; information events are identified by an "I" icon.

- Warning — When an event occurs that may not be a problem at the current time, but may become a problem in the future; an exclamation point icon indicates warnings.

- Error — When a significant event has occurred, such as a service failing to start or a device driver failing to load, an "x" icon indicates errors.

There are two other types of events that are logged. These are successes and failures of actions that are performed on the network based on the configuration of an audit policy. Refer to Chapter 11 for more information about the configuration of security audit policies.

Interpreting Events

When you click a log file within Event Viewer, the details pane lists all the events that have occurred and provides general information about each one, such as:

- Type of event (information, warning, or error)
- The date and time that the event occurred, along with associated user information
- The source of the event (the component or application that logged the event)
- The category and event ID
- The computer on which the event occurred

An example of an event message is shown in Figure 9-7.

The header for an event provides the same information listed above. The event description provides an administrator with a description of what occurred and why the event is significant, which is usually the most useful information.

The data field of an event displays information that is generated by the program or component. It contains binary data that can be used by support technicians to troubleshoot the problem.

In Activity 9-3, you explore events in your server's system and application logs.

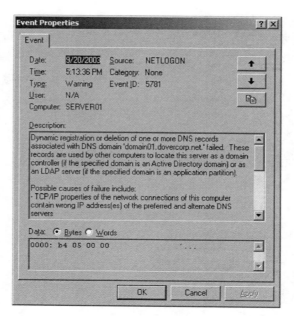

Figure 9-7   Viewing the details of a specific event

Activity 9-3:   Viewing Event Viewer System and Application Log Events

Time Required: 10 minutes

Objective: View events in the Event Viewer system and application logs.

Description: The IT manager at Dover Leasing has decided that all IT staff needs to be familiar with using the Windows Server 2003 Event Viewer tool to monitor system and application events on corporate servers. In this activity, you explore events in both the Event Viewer system and application logs.

1. Click **Start**, select **Administrative Tools**, and then click **Event Viewer**.

2. Click the **Application** icon to view the contents of the application log.

3. Double-click the first **Information** event found in the list to view its properties. The Event Properties dialog box opens, similar to the one shown in Figure 9-8.

4. Read the information contained in the event header and Description fields, and then click the **down arrow** button. The next event in the application log is displayed.

5. Click the **Cancel** button.

6. Click the **System** icon to view the contents of the system log.

7. Double-click the first **Error** event found in the list to view its properties. Read through the details of the event header and Description fields.

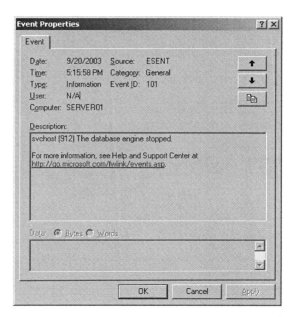

Figure 9-8   Viewing the properties of an Information event

8. Scroll to the bottom of the description field, if necessary, and then click the hyper-link at the bottom of the section to visit the Microsoft events Web site. Click **Yes** in the Event Viewer dialog box. The site opens in the Help and Support Center win-dow automatically.

9. Close all open windows.

PERFORMANCE CONSOLE

Although Task Manager provides administrators with an easy way to quickly gauge server performance, Windows Server 2003 also includes an administrative tool known as the **Performance console** that allows more detailed information to be gathered using various methods. The Performance console consists of two different tools – System Monitor, and Performance Logs and Alerts. System Monitor allows an administrator to view data gathered from a wide variety of counter objects in real time, usually by viewing a graphical representation of collected data. Performance Logs and Alerts allows an administrator to gather similar information, but periodically log samples to a data file to be imported into other applications (such as Microsoft Excel or SQL Server), or to generate alerts when certain configured thresholds are met. The Performance console is displayed in Figure 9-9.

The following sections take a look at both the System Monitor and Performance Logs and Alerts components of the Performance console in more detail.

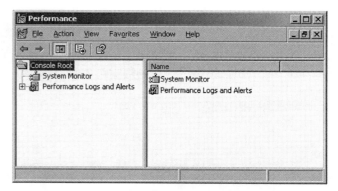

Figure 9-9   The Performance console

System Monitor

System Monitor is one of the most useful tools for collecting data on real-time server performance. As part of the Windows Server 2003 Performance MMC, this tool allows you to track how system resources are being used and how they are behaving under the current workload. System Monitor collects data that you can use for the following tasks:

- Server performance — If you use System Monitor on a regular basis, it can help you understand how the server performs under the current workload.

- Problem diagnosis — You can use the data that is collected to diagnose server components that may not be performing optimally, causing a bottleneck within the server.

- Capacity planning — You can use the information to see how server usage is changing over time and plan ahead for future upgrades.

- Testing — If configuration changes are made, you can use the data to observe the impact that the changes have on the server.

Using System Monitor, you can define the components you want to monitor and the type of data you want to collect. You choose the performance objects you want to monitor, such as memory, and the specific type of performance counters or data associated with the object for which you want to gather data. You can further customize the data you want to capture by specifying the source or computer you want to monitor. You can use System Monitor to gather data from the local computer or from a network computer for which you have appropriate permissions. Although the System Monitor tool includes a number of performance objects and associated counters to monitor by default, additional objects and counters are added when various services and applications are added to a server, such as DNS or Microsoft SQL Server.

Using System Monitor

When you first open the Performance tool, System Monitor automatically begins displaying performance data. By default, the tool displays data related to the memory, processor, and physical disk objects for the local computer, as displayed in Figure 9-10.

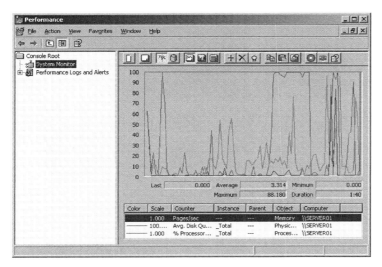

Figure 9-10   The default display of System Monitor

The information that System Monitor captures can be displayed in one of three views:

- Graph — Displays counter information as a continuous graph updated onscreen in real time
- Histogram — Displays counter information as a histogram, with information updated onscreen in real time
- Report — Displays a text-based report view of counters, with information updated onscreen in real time

The System Monitor interface provides a number of options for viewing performance data, including the ability to add additional performance counters as required, switch between display views, highlight a selected counter, copy and paste selected information, and freeze the display for analysis purposes. The System Monitor toolbar, found at the top of the details pane in System Monitor, allows you to easily control these functions. In Activity 9-4, you explore the various settings of the System Monitor tool.

Activity 9-4:   Exploring System Monitor Settings

Time Required: 10 minutes

Objective: Explore Windows Server 2003 System Monitor settings.

Description: The IT manager at Dover Leasing has informed you that all corporate servers will eventually be monitored for performance purposes using the Windows Server 2003 System Monitor utility. He has asked you to become familiar with the tool and explore its various features because all networking-related staff will eventually need to be trained on this tool. In this activity, you explore the various features of System Monitor.

1. Click **Start**, select **Administrative Tools**, and click **Performance**. The Performance console opens and System Monitor begins running automatically using the three default counters.

2. Click the **View Histogram** button on the toolbar at the top of the System Monitor details pane, as shown in Figure 9-11.   This illustrates the same counter information as a histogram.

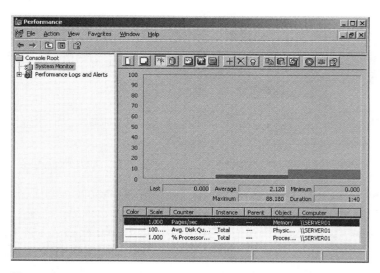

Figure 9-11   Viewing System Monitor data as a histogram

3. Click the **View Report** button on the System Monitor toolbar. This shows the same counter information using the report view.

4. Click the **View Graph** button to return to the original graph view.

5. Click the **% Processor Time** counter at the bottom in the details screen, and then click the **Highlight** button. Notice that the % Processor Time counter in the graph now appears as a thick white line to make it easier to distinguish from the other counters. Click the **Highlight** button again to remove highlighting from the counter.

6. Right-click on any area within the counter listing at the bottom of the details pane and click **Properties**.

7. In the System Monitor Properties dialog box, click **\Processor(_Total)\% Processor Time** if necessary, and then click on the largest line thickness in the **Width** list box, as shown in Figure 9-12. Click **OK**. The % Processor Time counter now appears as a thick red line on the graph.

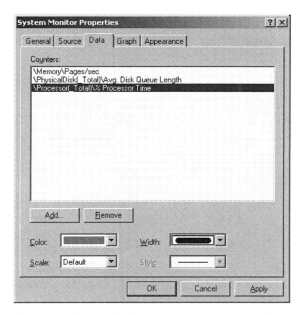

Figure 9-12   Configuring counter properties

8. Click the **Freeze Display** button on the System Monitor toolbar. This pauses the System Monitor view until the button is pressed again.

9. Click the **Update Data** button four or five times to allow the graph to move forward. This button allows you to update the onscreen data manually.

10. Click the **Freeze Display** button again to allow data to be gathered.

11. Click the **Clear Display** button on the System Monitor toolbar to clear and restart all onscreen counters.

12. Leave the Performance console window open.

Performance Objects and Counters

Monitoring performance on your server should be a regular maintenance task. The information you gather can help to establish a baseline of server performance and identify what is considered normal server performance under typical operating conditions. As you continue to monitor your server over time, you can compare the data against the baseline to

identify how performance is changing as the network changes and workloads increase. Doing so allows you to pinpoint bottlenecks, such as components that may be hindering server performance, before they become a serious problem.

 Any time you upgrade or add a component to a system, whether it is a hardware or software component, you should run System Monitor to determine the effect the change has on server performance.

When monitoring server performance, there are a few performance objects that should be included, as well as specific performance counters associated with each one.

- % Processor Time—This processor counter measures the percentage of time that the processor is executing a non-idle thread. If the value is consistently at or above 80%, a CPU upgrade may be required.

- % Interrupt Time—This processor counter measures hardware interrupts. If you experience a combination of Processor Time exceeding 90% and % Interrupt Time exceeding 15%, check for malfunctioning hardware or device drivers.

- Pages/Second—This memory counter measures the number of pages read in or out to disk to resolve hard page faults. If this number exceeds 20 page faults per second, add more RAM to the computer.

- Page Faults/Second—This memory counter measures the number of hard and soft page faults per second. A hard page fault refers to a request that requires hard disk access, whereas a soft page fault refers to a request found in another part of memory.

- % Disk Time—This physical and logical disk counter measures the percentage of elapsed time that the selected disk drive is busy. If this is above 90%, try moving the page file to another physical drive or upgrading the hard drive.

- Avg. Disk Queue Length—This physical and logical disk counter measures the average number of requests currently outstanding for a volume or partition. If averaging over two, then drive access may be a bottleneck. You may want to upgrade the drive or hard drive controller. Implementing a Stripe Set with multiple drives may also fix this problem.

 In Windows NT, all disk counters were turned off by default. In Windows 2000, the physical disk object is turned on by default and the logical disk object is turned off by default. In Windows Server 2003, all disk counters are enabled by default. Disk counters can be turned on or off by using the DISKPERF –Y and DISKPERF –N commands, respectively.

In Activity 9–5 you add various counters to the System Monitor interface.

Activity 9-5: Adding Counters to System Monitor

Time Required: 10 minutes

Objective: Add object counters to the System Monitor tool.

Description: After exploring the various features of the System Monitor interface, you decide to add various counters to the tool to get a better sense of server performance and the purpose of the various counters. In this activity, you add counters to the System Monitor interface, explore the Explain feature for counter objects, and view the counter results using the graph, histogram, and report views.

1. In the Performance console, click the **New Counter Set** button on the System Monitor toolbar. Notice that all counters are removed from the System Monitor details pane.

2. Click the **Add** button on the System Monitor toolbar. The Add Counters dialog box opens, as shown in Figure 9-13.

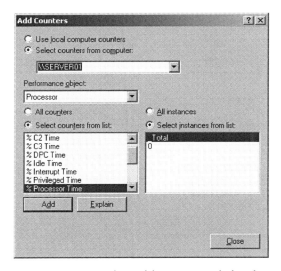

Figure 9-13   The Add Counters dialog box

3. In the Performance object list box, click **PhysicalDisk**.

4. In the Select counters from list list box, click **% Disk Read Time**. In the Select instances from list list box, click the first entry under **_Total**, and then click **Add**.

5. In the Performance object list box, click **Memory**.

6. In the Select counters from list list box, click **Available MBytes**. In the Select instances from list list box, click **_Total** if possible.

7. Click the **Explain** button. This opens a window that explains the purpose of the selected counter, as shown in Figure 9-14.

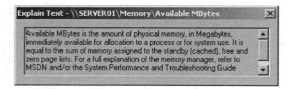

Figure 9-14   Using the Explain button to view the purpose of a selected counter

8. Close the **Explain Text** window.

9. Click the **Add** button to add the counter to System Monitor.

10. In the Performance object list box, click **Network Interface**.

11. Click the **All counters** radio button, and then click **Add**. This adds all of the performance counters for the Network Interface object to the graph.

12. Click **Close**.

13. Notice that the number of counters now available on the graph has increased dramatically. Click the **View Histogram** button to view the counter data using that method, and then click the **View Report** button.

14. Click the **New Counter Set** button to clear all counters from System Monitor.

15. Close the **Performance** console window.

Gathering data with a tool like System Monitor is the easy part. The more difficult part is interpreting the information to determine which component is affecting performance. The difficulty lies in the fact that the performance of some components can affect other components. It may appear from the data that one component is performing poorly when this can be the result of another component performing poorly, or even too well. For example, if you determine that your processor is running over 80%, your first instinct may tell you to upgrade the processor or install multiple processors if the motherboard supports it. Through further analysis by monitoring the Pages / Second Memory counter, however, you may find a lack of memory is the bottleneck causing excess paging. Thus, monitoring multiple components on a regular basis should give you an idea of how they perform together and make troubleshooting server performance that much easier.

The System Monitor tool provides a number of alternatives in terms of saving or viewing historical performance data. One particularly interesting feature is the ability to save System Monitor data to an HTML file. This allows an administrator to post performance data on a Web server, such that it could subsequently be easily viewed and retrieved. When System Monitor data is saved in this format, many of the control functions of the tool are still available through the Web interface. In other words, the data presented is not a simple graphics file, but rather an interactive interface.

The System Monitor tool is also capable of displaying older data that may have been saved to a log file or database using the **Performance Logs and Alerts** tool. This tool is looked at in more detail in the next section.

In Activity 9-6, you use the System Monitor tool to save and view a System Monitor graph.

Activity 9-6:   Saving and Viewing System Monitor Data

Time Required: 10 minutes

Objective: Explore options for saving System Monitor data.

Description: Although the IT manager at Dover Leasing is aware of the fact that multiple servers can be monitored on a single System Monitor graph, he has asked you to explore the possibility of making counter data available via a Web browser for those users who will not have access to the MMC. In this activity, you save the output of various System Monitor counters to an HTML file and then access that HTML file using Internet Explorer to monitor your server.

1. Click **Start**, select **Administrative Tools**, and then click **Performance**.

2. Allow the System Monitor graph to gather information until the end right side of the window is almost reached, and then click the **Freeze Display** button.

3. Right-click on an area within the graph and click **Save As**.

4. In the Save As dialog box, click the **D:** drive in the Save in list box.

5. In the File name text box, type **sysmon**, and then click the **Save** button.

6. Click **Start**, and then click **My Computer**. Browse to the **D:** drive, and then double-click the file **sysmon.htm**.

7. The sysmon.htm file opens in Internet Explorer and displays the System Monitor details pane, as shown in Figure 9-15.

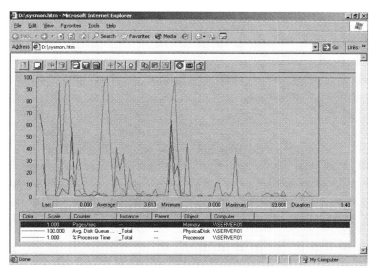

Figure 9-15   Viewing System Monitor data in a Web browser

8. In the Internet Explorer window, click the **Avg. Disk Queue Length** counter at the bottom of the window, and then click the **Highlight** button. Notice that even though the System Monitor information is displayed in a Web browser, some of its ordinary functions are still available.

9. Click the **View Histogram** button, and then click the **View Report** button. Notice that both of these functions are also supported from the Web browser interface. Click the **View Graph** button.

10. Click the **Freeze Display** button in the Internet Explorer window to deselect it. When the System Monitor Control dialog box opens, click **Yes**. Notice that the Web page automatically begins updating counter data again.

11. Close **Internet Explorer**.

12. In the Performance window, click the **New Counter Set** button to clear all counters from System Monitor.

13. Close the **Performance console** window, and close all open windows.

Performance Logs and Alerts

Another tool available within the Performance console is Performance Logs and Alerts. This tool allows you to automatically collect data on the local computer or from another computer on the network, and then view it using System Monitor or another program such as Microsoft Excel or a relational database such as Microsoft SQL Server.

Performance Logs and Alerts allows you to perform the following tasks:

- Collect data in a binary, comma-separated, tab-separated format, or SQL Server database format; the binary versions of the log files can be read with System Monitor, but comma- and tab-separated data can easily be imported into another program for analysis

- View data both while it is being collected and after it has been collected

- Configure parameters such as start and stop times for log generation, file names, and file size

- Configure and manage multiple logging sessions from a single console window

- Set up alerts so a message is sent, a program is run, or a log file is started when a specific counter exceeds or drops below a configured value

You can access Performance Logs and Alerts through the Performance console. There are three options available under Performance Logs and Alerts:

- Counter Logs
- Trace Logs
- Alerts

Counter logs take the information that you view using System Monitor and save it to a log file. One of the main advantages of using counter logs is that you can configure logging to start and stop at different intervals. **Trace logs** are similar to counter logs but are triggered to start when an event occurs. You can use **Alerts** to configure an event to occur when a counter meets a predefined value. For example, you might choose to run a specific program or utility automatically when a certain threshold is reached, or send a message to a network administrator.

Configuring Alerts

Logging does increase overhead on a server, so it is generally not something you want to have running all the time. It is essential that you set up a regular schedule for collecting data, and then review this data regularly as part of a proactive server monitoring strategy. Because logging should not be running constantly, alerts should be set up to notify you of a potential problem. For example, you can configure an alert to monitor processor usage, and notify you if it exceeds 80%.

Table 9-3 summarizes the available options on the Action tab, as illustrated in Figure 9-16.

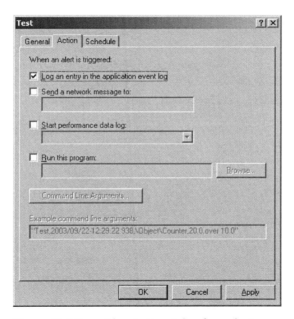

Figure 9-16   The Action tab of an alert

Table 9-3   Actions that can be taken when an alert is triggered

Action	Description
Log an entry in the application event log	An entry is added to the application log when the event is triggered
Send a network message to	Messenger service sends a message to the specified computer when the alert is triggered
Start performance data log	Counter log is run when the alert is triggered
Run this program	Specified program is run when the alert is triggered
Command Line Arguments	Specified command line arguments are copied when the Run this program option is used

In Activity 9-7, you configure Performance Logs and Alerts settings on your Windows Server 2003 computer.

ACTIVITY

Activity 9-7:   Configuring Performance Logs and Alerts

Time Required: 15 minutes

Objective: Configure performance logging and alerts.

Description: Although the servers at Dover Leasing are monitored regularly during business hours, the company still does not have staff on hand outside of business hours to monitor system performance. Because of this, the IT manager has asked you to look into features of the Performance console that will allow data to be gathered after hours. Similarly, he would also like to have alerts configured such that an administrator would receive an onscreen message in the event that a critical server threshold is reached. In this activity, you will explore and configure various logging options as well as configure alerts using Performance Logs and Alerts.

1. Click **Start**, select **Administrative Tools**, and then click **Performance**.

2. Click the **plus sign (+)** next to **Performance Logs and Alerts** to expand its contents.

3. Click the **Counter Logs** icon to view its contents. Notice that a single sample log exists by default with the name System Overview.

4. Double-click the **System Overview** icon to view its properties. The System Overview Properties dialog box opens, as shown in Figure 9-17.

5. Notice the log file name associated with the log, the counters that the log includes, and the interval at which data is being gathered.

6. Click the **Log Files** tab.

7. Click the **Log file type** list arrow to view all of the different log type options available, as illustrated in Figure 9-18.

8. Click the **Schedule** tab. This tab allows you to schedule stop and start times for the log if necessary.

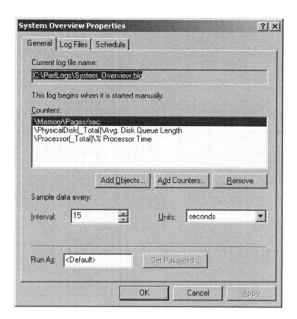

Figure 9-17   The System Overview Properties dialog box

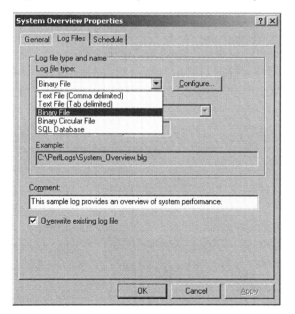

Figure 9-18   Configuring Log type options

9. Click **Cancel**.

10. Right-click the **System Overview** icon and click **Start**. Notice that the icon turns from red to green.

11. Wait approximately two minutes, and then right-click the **System Overview** icon and click **Stop**.

12. Click the **System Monitor** icon. On the System Monitor toolbar, click the **View Log Data** button.

13. When the System Monitor Properties dialog box opens, click the **Log files** radio button, and then click **Add**.

14. In the Select Log File dialog box, browse to **C:\PerfLogs**, click the **System_Overview.blg** file to select it, click **Open**, and then click **OK**. This loads the data stored in the System_Overview.blg log file into the System Monitor window.

15. Under Performance Logs and Alerts, click the **Alerts** icon to view its contents. There are no alerts configured by default.

16. Click **Start**, select **Administrative Tools**, and then click **Services**.

17. Right-click the **Alerter** service icon and click **Properties**.

18. In the Startup type list box, click **Automatic**. Click **OK**.

19. Right-click the **Alerter** service and click **Start**.

20. Right-click the **Messenger** service icon and click **Properties**.

21. In the Startup type list box, click **Automatic**. Click **OK**.

22. Right-click the **Messenger** service and click **Start**.

23. In the Performance window, right-click **Alerts** and click **New Alert Settings**.

24. In the New Alert Settings dialog box, type **CPU Utilization** in the Name text box and click **OK**.

25. On the General tab of the CPU Utilization dialog box, click the **Add** button.

26. In the Add Counters dialog box, click the **Add** button to add the % Processor Time counter, and then click **Close**.

27. Type **30** in the Limit text box to have the alert triggered when CPU utilization reaches a value over 30%, as illustrated in Figure 9-19.

28. In the **Interval** spin box, type **1**.

29. Click the **Action** tab. Click the check box next to **Send a network message to** and then type **Admin01** in the associated text box. Click **OK**.

30. Click **Start**, click **Run**, and type **wmplayer.exe** in the Open text box. Click **OK**. The Windows Media Player opens, which usually increases the CPU utilization for brief periods.

31. When the Messenger Service dialog box opens onscreen, as illustrated in Figure 9-20, read its contents and click **OK**.

32. Close all open windows.

9

Figure 9-19   Configuring alert settings

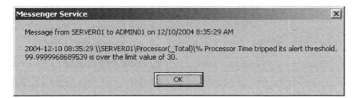

Figure 9-20   The Messenger Service dialog box, triggered by an alert

CONFIGURING AND MANAGING SERVICES

When it comes to optimizing and securing your server, one of the first things you can do is disable any unnecessary components, such as services. When a service is unnecessarily installed during setup or is no longer used, it should be disabled. Running unnecessary services consumes additional system resources such as memory and CPU, thus adding overhead to a system. For example, if you have installed Internet Information Services on a server for testing purposes and then no longer require it, the service should be uninstalled, or associated services should be disabled via the Services MMC. If not, it continues to run in the background and consumes resources, even though it may not be performing any valuable system function.

The services that you disable depend on the role the server plays on the network. For example, a Web server requires different services than a print server. Another consideration is service dependencies. Before you stop or disable a service, check to see if there are any

other services running that depend on the service. Use the Dependencies tab of a service to view the other services it depends upon to function correctly. Use this tab in the properties of a service to view the other services that are dependent upon the one you are disabling. Figure 9-21 illustrates the Dependencies tab of the Messenger service.

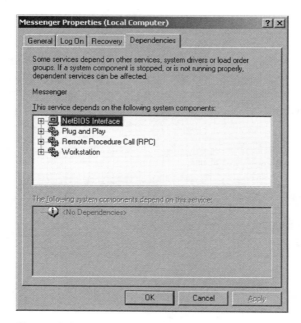

Figure 9-21   Viewing the Dependencies tab for the Messenger service

The Services MMC allows you to configure a variety of settings related to how services function and respond to potential problems on a Windows Server 2003 system. The properties of a service include four different configuration tabs, as follows:

- General — Displays a service's name, description, the path to the executable file, service startup parameters, and buttons allowing you to start, stop, pause, and resume a service

- Log On — Allows you to specify the user name that a service runs as, along with the hardware profiles for which the service is enabled

- Recovery — Allows you to configure the computer's response when a service fails, including different actions depending on the number of failures; also allows you to specify a program that should be run when a service failure occurs

- Dependencies — Specifies the services that a service depends upon to function correctly, as well as the services that depend on this service to function

In Activity 9–8, you configure the properties of various services on your server.

Activity 9-8:   Configuring Windows Server 2003 Services

Time Required: 10 minutes

Objective: Configure the startup properties and settings of Windows Server 2003 services.

Description: The IT manager at Dover Leasing is very concerned about the levels of resource utilization of corporate servers, including the impact that this ultimately has on performance for users. He is also concerned about the security risks associated with having unnecessary services running on various servers throughout the organization. In this activity, you configure service startup settings, as well as other configuration options, such as how a service reacts to a failure.

1. Click **Start**, select **Administrative Tools**, and then click **Services**. The Services MMC opens, as illustrated in Figure 9-22.

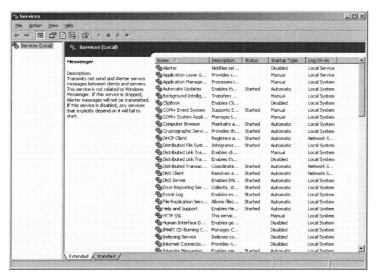

Figure 9-22   The Services MMC

2. Right-click the **Remote Desktop Help Session Manager** service icon, and then click **Properties**. The Remote Desktop Help Session Manager Properties dialog box opens, as shown in Figure 9-23.

3. In the Startup type list box, click **Automatic**. This sets the Remote Desktop Help Session Manager service to start automatically the next time the computer restarts.

4. Click the **Apply** button, and then click the **Start** button. This manually starts the Remote Desktop Help Session Manager service.

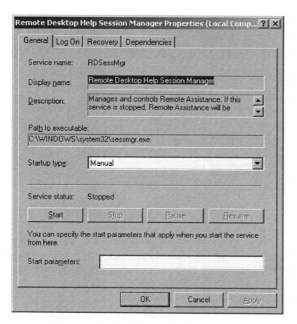

Figure 9-23   The General tab in the properties of a service

5. Click the **Log On** tab. This displays the properties of the account under which the Remote Desktop Help Session Manager service will run, as shown in Figure 9-24.

6. Click the **Recovery** tab.

7. In the First failure list box, click **Restart the Service**.

8. In the Second failure list box, click **Run a Program**, as shown in Figure 9-25.

9. In the Program text box, type **cmd.exe**. This causes the Command Prompt program to start in the event that the Remote Desktop Help Session Manager service fails for a second time.

10. Click the **Dependencies** tab. Review the list of services that the Remote Desktop Help Session Manager service depends upon. Click **OK**.

11. Right-click the **Messenger** icon and click **Properties**.

12. In the Startup type list box, click **Disabled**. This prevents the Messenger service from starting the next time the computer reboots. Click **OK**.

13. Close all open windows.

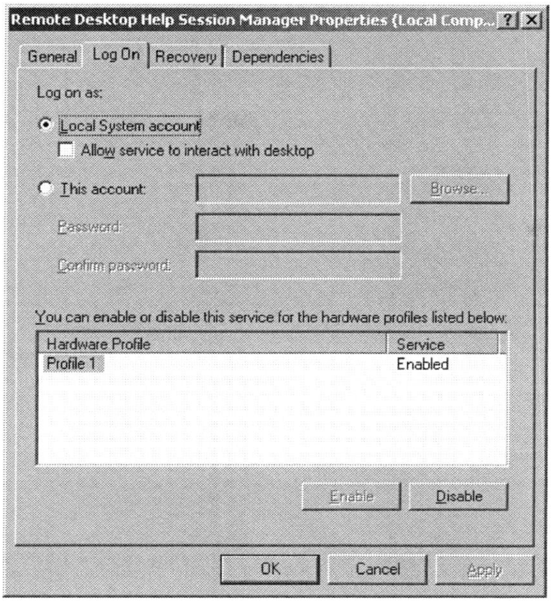

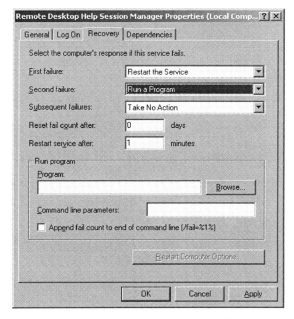

Figure 9-24   The Log On tab in the properties of a service

Figure 9-25   The Recovery tab in the properties of a service

CHAPTER SUMMARY

◻ The Windows Task Manager utility can be used to view and control running applications and processes, obtain basic performance information, view network utilization information, and view connected users.

◻ The Event Viewer tool is used to view information, warning, and error events relating to the operating system and installed applications. All Windows Server 2003 systems include system, security, and application logs. Additional logs may also be present based on the role of the server, such as in the case of a domain controller.

◻ The Performance console is the primary server monitoring utility provided with Windows Server 2003. It consists of two main tools: System Monitor and Performance Logs and Alerts.

◻ System Monitor is a Windows Server 2003 performance-monitoring utility that allows various server resources to be monitored graphically or in a report view. Monitoring can be configured for a combination of local and remote systems in a single graph, histogram, or report.

◻ Performance Logs and Alerts is another Windows Server 2003 performance-monitoring utility that allows data about server resources to be collected for additional analysis. Both counter and trace logs can be configured with this tool, and alerts can be configured to identify when performance moves outside of predefined parameters.

◻ A number of background services run on a Windows Server 2003 system by default, with the exact services dependent upon the applications and server services installed on the system. Disabling unnecessary services, or uninstalling unnecessary applications can help to optimize a server.

KEY TERMS

Alert — An alert performs a specified action once a counter meets the specified setting. Once an alert is triggered, a message can be sent, a program can be run, a counter log started, or an event can be written to the application log.

Application log — Where applications that are written to Microsoft standards record event information. The application developer determines the type of information an application writes to the log file.

baseline — A performance benchmark that is used to determine what is normal server performance under a specific workload.

counter logs — Performance data that is collected into a comma-separated or tab-separated format.

Event Viewer — A utility used to view the contents of the system, security, and application logs.

Performance console — A pre-defined MMC that includes both the System Monitor and Performance Logs and Alerts tools.

performance counters — Data items associated with a particular performance object used to measure a certain aspect of performance.

Performance Logs and Alerts — A tool included with Windows Server 2003 that enables you to create counter logs, trace logs, and configure alerts.

performance objects — System components that you can monitor using System Monitor.

Security log — The spot where events pertaining to the audit policy are written. By default, security logging is disabled until an audit policy is configured.

System log — The spot where system components such as services and device drivers record information, warnings, and errors.

System Monitor — A tool that allows you to gather and view real—time performance statistics of a local or network computer.

Task Manager — A tool used to view the processes and applications currently running on a system. Also provides basic resource usage statistics.

trace logs — Where data provider collects performance data when an event occurs.

REVIEW QUESTIONS

1. Which of the following Task Manager tabs allows the priority of a running process to be configured?

   a. Applications

   b. Processes

   c. Performance

   d. Users

2. Which of the following methods can be used to access the Task Manager utility?

   a. Press Ctrl+Alt+Delete, then click Task Manager

   b. Press Ctrl+T

   c. Right–click on the taskbar, click Task Manager

   d. Click Start, click Task Manager

3. Which of the following are logs found in Event Viewer on a Windows Server 2003 system?

   a. system log

   b. application log

   c. security log

   d. program log

4. Which of the following Task Manager tabs can be used to view the current status of a foreground program?

   a. Processes

   b. Applications

   c. Users

   d. Networking

5. Operating system events are always written to the application log in Event Viewer.

   a. True

   b. False

6. Which of the following tools is included in the Performance console?

   a. System Monitor

   b. Task Manager

   c. Performance Logs and Alerts

   d. Computer Management

7. Which of the following is not an action associated with an alert?

   a. Send a network message to

   b. Start performance data log

   c. Run this program

   d. Disable a service

8. Which of the following counters is displayed by default in the System Monitor display when the Performance console is opened?

   a. Pages/sec

   b. Avg. Disk Queue Length

   c. % Memory Time

   d. % Processor Time

9. What term is used to describe a service that must be running in order for another service to function?

   a. Dependency

   b. Dedicated

   c. Process

   d. Processor

10. Windows Server 2003 systems will only log information events in the system log in Event Viewer by default.

   a. True

   b. False

11. System Monitor can be used to monitor performance information on a remote computer.

   a. True

   b. False

12. Disk performance counters are enabled by default on a Windows Server 2003 system.

   a. True

   b. False

13. Which command is used to enable or disable disk counters on a Windows Server 2003 system?

   a. DISKPERF

   b. DISKPART

   c. DISKPARK

   d. DISKLOT

14. Which of the following is not a type of event stored in the system log in Event Viewer?

   a. information

   b. warning

   c. error

   d. success

15. The data displayed on the Task Manager Performance tab can be exported to a text file.

   a. True

   b. False

16. Which of the following is a valid Recovery action in the event of a service failure?

   a. Take No Action

   b. Restart the Service

   c. Run a Program

   d. Stop the Service

17. Which of the following are available views in the System Monitor tool? (Choose all that apply.)

   a. Report

   b. Histogram

   c. Graph

   d. Pie Chart

18. The CPU column on the Task Manager Processes tab displays point-in-time CPU usage information.

   a. True

   b. False

19. Which of the following are valid performance objects in System Monitor on a Windows Server 2003 system? (Choose all that apply.)

   a. Memory

   b. Processor

   c. Server

   d. System

20. It is not possible to monitor objects on more than one server at the same time using System Monitor.

   a. True

   b. False

9

CASE PROJECTS

CASE
PROJECTS

Case Project 9-1

You are responsible for the administration of three Dover Leasing servers. You have recently installed a new service on your server. The service is set to start automatically and run continuously to service user requests. Your manager is concerned about server performance after the service is installed, and you assure him that performance should not suffer. Answer the following questions based on the scenario.

1. After you install the service, what is one of the first things you should do?

2. During peak hours, your manager stops in to see how the server is performing under the added workload. What tool can you use to quickly show your manager the current processor usage on the server?

3. You have a slight concern that the service may indeed have an impact on the amount of time the processor is utilized. The % utilization was running at times near 50% before the service was installed. You would like to be notified if the processor utilization exceeds 60%. Explain how this can be done. What other actions can be configured if this occurs?

4. Because the server is working under an increased workload, you want to disable any unnecessary services to eliminate the overhead associated with running them. What should you consider before disabling any services on the server?

Case Project 9-2

The IT manager at Dover Leasing is looking for a quick way for junior administrators to monitor the performance of Windows Server 2003 systems on the network from any internal desktop system. Given that desktops are running a range of operating systems including Windows 98, Windows 2000, and Windows XP, what would be the best way to accomplish this?

Case Project 9-3

The development staff at Dover Leasing is in the process of developing an SQL Server-based application for the purpose of monitoring historical server performance and baseline data. Which Windows Server 2003 tool and specific data gathering option would be best suited to obtaining this information?

MANAGING AND IMPLEMENTING
BACKUPS AND DISASTER RECOVERY

After reading this chapter and completing the exercises, you will be able to:

Plan for disaster recovery of Windows Server 2003 systems

Back up and restore data

Implement shadow copy volumes

Understand the purpose of the Automated System Recovery feature

Understand Windows Server 2003 advanced startup options

Install and use the Recovery Console

One of the most important roles of any network administrator is to ensure that systems and user data remain available, even under adverse circumstances. Part of ensuring server availability involves implementing and maintaining an effective backup and disaster recovery strategy such that when issues arise, they can be dealt with quickly and effectively.

Windows Server 2003 includes a number of different tools, utilities, and features that can be used as part of a backup and disaster recovery strategy. Throughout this chapter you not only learn about how to use the various tools and utilities effectively, but also how to plan and implement an effective disaster recovery strategy using both traditional methods and new features introduced in Windows Server 2003.

PLANNING FOR DISASTER RECOVERY

Although the accidental deletion of user data files is far more common than a full server failure, administrators still need to be prepared in case disaster strikes. When such issues do arise, an administrator should be prepared to get systems up and running again as quickly as possible, ensuring that all necessary data is also available. To make this easier, Windows Server 2003 includes a number of different features:

- The Backup utility—This backs up and restores operating system, application, and user data files. The Backup utility included with Windows Server 2003 allows backup jobs to be scheduled, critical System State information to be backed up and restored, and provides access to the Automated System Recovery feature.

- Shadow Copies of Shared Volumes—A new feature that allows users to access previous versions of files in shared folders when older versions need to be restored, when a file is accidentally deleted, or when they simply want to compare the current version of a file to an older version. Ultimately, this feature helps to reduce administrative burden by providing users with access to previous versions of files, without the need to contact an administrator to manually restore that file from backup.

- Automated System Recovery (ASR)—Another new feature that provides a mechanism for recovering a server from configuration information stored on floppy disks when used in conjunction with the Windows Server 2003 CD-ROM. Although this feature helps an administrator to restore the operating system and configuration settings quickly, applications need to be reinstalled and data needs to be restored from backup, since ASR handles neither process.

- Advanced startup options—These include familiar startup methods such as Safe Mode, Last Known Good Configuration, and others. These different modes allow an administrator to attempt to boot Windows Server 2003 when recent configuration settings make a normal boot unavailable.

- The Recovery Console—A command-line environment into which an administrator can boot a server in order to troubleshoot or make configuration changes when the operating system will not boot normally.

Each of the tools, utilities, and features listed here are looked at in more detail in subsequent sections.

Backing Up and Restoring Data

Windows Server 2003 includes a backup utility that allows you to restore an operating system or data in the event of a total hardware or storage media failure. The Windows Server 2003 Backup utility builds on the backup utility originally introduced in Windows 2000 and represents a significant improvement over backup utilities included with previous versions of Windows. Using the Windows Server 2003 Backup utility, you can perform a variety of tasks, including:

- Back up and restore files and folders
- Schedule a backup
- Back up Windows 2003 System State data
- Restore all or a portion of the Active Directory database
- Create an Automated System Recovery (ASR) backup

The Windows Server 2003 Backup utility also supports a wide variety of storage devices and media, such as tape drives, recordable CD-ROM drives, logical drives (such as local partitions and volumes), and removable disks.

Backup and Restore Concepts

The main reason for backing up both operating system and user data files is to ensure that both are available in the case of accidental deletion by users, or when some type of server failure occurs. A primary goal of any network administrator is to ensure that in the event of accidental deletion or failure, data can be restored (and made available to users) as quickly as possible. To meet this goal, data backup processes must be performed regularly, or the possibility exists that newer or updated files will not be available when a restoration process is necessary. Thankfully, the Backup utility included with Windows Server 2003 provides administrators with a great deal of flexibility when it comes to performing backups, allowing different types of backups to be performed according to the needs and requirements of an organization. Each of the backup types supported with this utility is looked at later in this section.

In many corporate environments, the amount of data that needs to be backed up regularly varies greatly. For example, a small organization may be able to simply back up user data files to a dedicated partition or volume on a server, since the total size of user files may be relatively small. In larger organizations, however, many servers may be present, and hundreds of gigabytes of backup storage space may be required. In these situations, companies typically invest in dedicated tape backup devices, ranging from simple single-tape hardware devices on individual servers to large centralized (and potentially automated) storage systems. The biggest single issue that determines the backup hardware and software implemented is usually the amount of user and application data present on network systems. However, operating system files are also typically backed up to ensure that these files can also be restored when necessary.

10

One key consideration that should be part of any backup strategy is determining which users should (or should not) have the ability to back up files and folders. In order to perform a backup, certain rights and permissions are required. By default, members of the following local groups can back up any files and folders on a member server running Windows Server 2003:

- Administrators
- Backup Operators
- Server Operators

In a domain environment, an administrator might instead choose to grant certain users the ability to back up any files and folders on all domain systems. Members of the Administrators, Backup Operators, or Server Operators domain local groups on a domain controller can back up any files or folders on any system within a domain.

Users who are not members of the Administrators or Backup Operators groups (on either their local system or a domain controller) are limited in terms of the files and folders that they can back up. In order for these users to back up files, they must either be listed as the owner of the file, or have one or more of the following NTFS permissions:

- Read
- Read and execute
- Modify
- Full Control

The primary purpose of limiting the files and folders that a normal user can back up is to ensure proper security. In cases where users need to be able to back up files and folders belonging to other users, they should be granted membership in the Backup Operators group, assigned at least the read permission for the files and folders in question, or granted the appropriate rights.

Two main rights are associated with the ability to back up and restore files and folders. These settings are configured via Group Policy, in the Computer Configuration > Windows Settings > Security Settings > Local Policies > User Rights Assignment section, as shown in Figure 10-1. The two main settings that impact the ability to back up and restore files are the Back up files and directories and Restore files and directories rights, respectively. If granted in a Group Policy object applied to the Domain Controllers OU, these rights apply to all domain systems. However, these settings can also be configured locally, or in a Group Policy object. When applied in a Group Policy object at the site, domain, or OU level, systems that fall under the scope of these policies have the settings applied. Figure 10-2 illustrates the Back up files and directories Properties dialog box as configured in the Default Domain Controllers Policy.

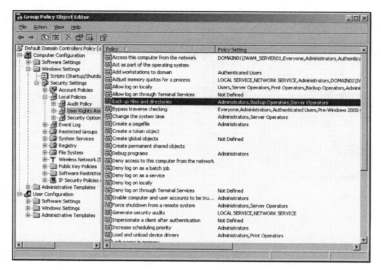

Figure 10-1   The Back up files and directories right in the Default Domain Controllers Policy

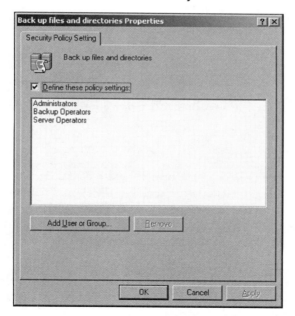

Figure 10-2   The Back up files and directories Properties window

The Windows Server 2003 Backup utility also provides additional security for any backup jobs created by selecting the Allow only the owner and the Administrator access to the backup data check box in the Backup Job Information dialog box, as shown in Figure 10-3. When selected, only the person who created the backup or an administrator has the ability to restore the backup, regardless of which users have the rights or permissions to restore files.

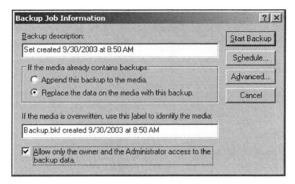

Figure 10-3   The Backup Job Information dialog box

Backup Types

Like most major backup programs, the Windows Server 2003 Backup Utility supports a variety of backup types, including:

- Normal backup
- Incremental backup
- Differential backup
- Daily backup
- Copy backup

Each of these backup methods and their impact on backup procedures are looked at in the following sections.

Normal Backup

The most common (and default) type of backup performed by the Backup utility is known as a **normal backup**. When chosen, this backup type backs up all selected files and folders, and clears the archive attribute on these files and folders. The purpose of clearing the archive attribute is to mark files as having been backed up, an important distinction when a normal backup is used in conjunction with some of the other backup methods outlined in this section.

Although the normal backup type backs up all selected files and folders, it is not always the best choice for backup jobs. For example, if an administrator were to specify a normal backup for Monday, and then complete another normal backup of the same files and folders for Tuesday, all files would be backed up again, regardless of whether any changes had taken place. This would result in larger-than-necessary backups, and duplicate copies of identical files being stored. While there is nothing explicitly wrong with this, it can be very inefficient. In most situations, administrators will begin the week with a normal backup of all necessary files, and then use either incremental or differential backups on subsequent days. Both incremental and differential backups, along with their impacts on backup processes, are looked at shortly.

Incremental Backup

The **incremental backup** type is significantly different from a normal backup. Instead of backing up all selected files and folders, it only backs up those files that have changed since the last normal or incremental backup took place. In a similar manner to a normal backup, an incremental backup also clears the archive attribute associated with any files and folders that it does back up.

The main purpose of an incremental backup is to reduce the overall size of backup jobs. For example, let's say that an administrator creates a normal backup of selected files and folders on Monday. If an incremental backup is then performed on these same files and folders on Tuesday, only those files that have changed since Monday will be backed up. Then, if another incremental backup is performed on Wednesday, only those files that have changed since Tuesday will be backed up, and so on. This method ensures that backups created after the initial normal backup take as little time as possible.

While an incremental backup strategy ensures that backups take the least time possible, they do result in a more involved restore process. For example, let's say that a folder containing user data is accidentally deleted on Thursday morning. In order to restore this data completely, an administrator needs to first restore the normal backup from Monday, and then the incremental backups from both Tuesday and Wednesday. This ensures that all files that have been backed up since Monday are again available.

Figure 10-4 illustrates the backup and restore processes for a folder named Data using a combination of normal and incremental backup types.

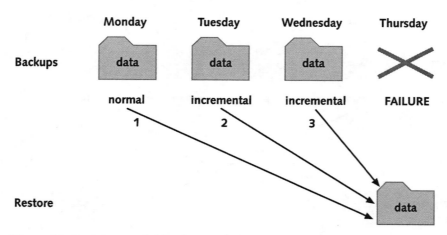

Figure 10-4   Incremental backup and restore operations

Differential Backup

The **differential backup** type is different from both a normal and incremental backup. Instead of backing up all selected files and folders, it only backs up those files that have changed since the last normal or incremental backup took place. In contrast to a normal or incremental backup, a differential backup does not clear the archive attribute associated with any files and folders that it backs up.

The main purpose of a differential backup is to reduce the overall size of backup jobs, although not to the same degree as an incremental backup. For example, let's say that an administrator creates a normal backup of selected files and folders on Monday. If a differential backup is then performed on these same files and folders on Tuesday, all files that have changed since Monday are backed up. Then, if another differential backup is performed on Wednesday, again all files that have changed since Monday are backed up, and so on.

While a differential backup strategy ensures that the restore process is less involved, they do result in a more involved backup process. For example, let's again say that a folder containing user data is accidentally deleted on Thursday morning. In order to completely restore this data, an administrator would need to first restore the normal backup from Monday, and then only the differential backup from Wednesday. Because the differential backup performed on Wednesday includes all changes to files since Monday, this ensures that all files that have been backed up since Monday are again available.

Figure 10-5 illustrates the backup and restore processes for a folder named Data using a combination of normal and differential backup types.

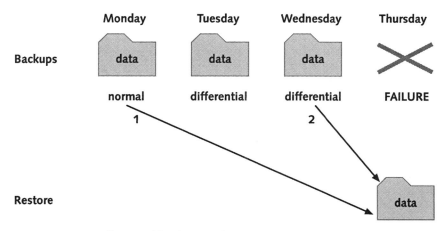

Figure 10-5   Differential backup and restore operations

Daily Backup

Unlike the other backup types explored already, the **daily backup** backs up selected files or folders that have been created or changed on the day that the backup takes place. When this method is used, the archive attribute is not changed, and, as such, it does not interfere with any existing backup procedures that may already be in place.

Copy Backup

In the same way that a normal backup backs up all selected files and folders, a **copy backup** does the same. However, a copy backup doesn't change the archive attribute associated with a backed up file or folder to mark it as having been backed up. The main purpose of a copy backup is to create the equivalent of a normal backup (perhaps for a backup tape to ultimately be stored offsite) without interrupting any other backup procedures in place.

Using the Backup Utility

The most common use of the Windows Server 2003 **Backup utility** is to back up critical data and operating system files to ensure that recovery is possible in the event that files are accidentally deleted or a disaster occurs. The Backup utility can be used in two different modes, known as Wizard mode and Advanced mode. As the name suggests, Wizard mode walks you step-by-step through the process of creating a backup or restoring files, while Advanced mode provides complete control over the file and folder selection process through a standard graphical interface. The Backup or Restore Wizard interface is show in Figure 10-6.

10

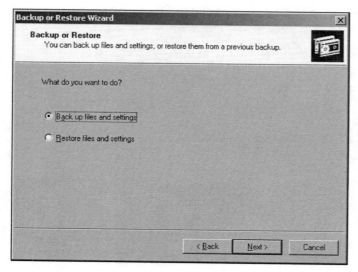

Figure 10-6   The Backup or Restore Wizard

As outlined earlier in this section, the Backup utility allows you to back up and restore files, schedule backups if necessary, back up critical operating system information known as System State data, restore Active Directory or related objects, and access the Automated System Restore (ASR) feature. In Activity 10-1 you use the Backup utility to back up the contents of a folder on your server using Advanced mode.

Activity 10-1: Backing Up Files and Folders Using the Backup Utility

Time Required: 15 minutes

Objective: Back up files and folders using the Windows Server 2003 Backup utility.

Description: The IT manager is currently in the process of trying to select a backup software solution for all Windows Server 2003 systems at Dover Leasing. You have been asked to test the capabilities of the Backup utility included with Windows Server 2003 as part of this process. In this activity you use the Backup utility to back up a folder and the files that it contains on your server.

1. Click **Start**, select **All Programs**, select **Accessories**, select **System Tools**, and then click **Backup**.

2. In the Backup or Restore Wizard dialog box that opens, click the **Advanced Mode** link to access the complete functionality of the Backup program. The Backup utility window appears, as shown in Figure 10-7.

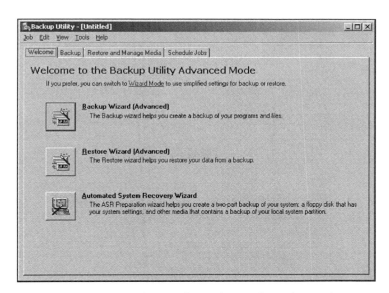

Figure 10-7   The Backup Utility Advanced Mode window

3. Click the **Backup** tab.

4. Click the **plus sign (+)** next to **Local Disk (C:)** to expand its contents.

5. Click the **plus sign (+)** next to **WINDOWS** to expand its contents.

6. Click the **plus sign (+)** next to **system32** to expand its contents.

7. Click the **config** folder to view its contents. Click the check box next to **config** to select the entire folder for backup, as illustrated in Figure 10-8.

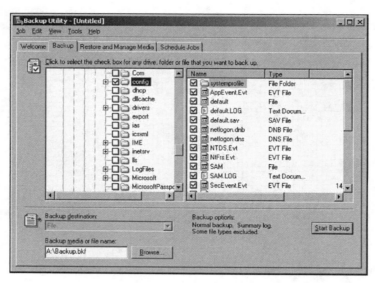

Figure 10-8   Selecting a folder to be backed up

8. In the Backup media or file name text box, type **d:\backup-config.bkf**, and then click the **Start Backup** button.

9. In the Backup Job Information dialog box, review the details provided, and then click the **Advanced** button.

10. In the Advanced Backup Options window, check the **Verify data after backup** check box, as shown in Figure 10-9. Click the **Backup Type** drop-down menu to view available backup options, but be sure that settings are left in the Normal configuration setting. Click **OK**.

11. Click the **Start Backup** button.

12. Once started, the Backup Progress window appears. Once the backup is complete, click the **Report** button, shown in Figure 10-10.

13. Close the **backup01.log** window (the number following the name of your log file may be different).

14. Close the Backup Progress window, and then close the Backup Utility window.

In Activity 10-2 you restore the files that you backed up in Activity 10-1.

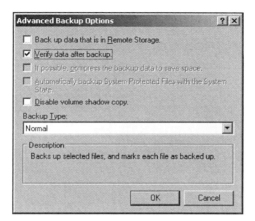

Figure 10-9   The Advanced Backup Options dialog box

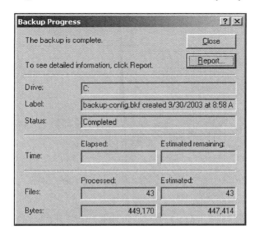

Figure 10-10   The Backup Progress dialog box

Activity 10-2: Restoring Files and Folders Using the Backup Utility

Time Required: 10 minutes

Objective: Restore files and folders using the Windows Server 2003 Backup utility.

Description: Having used the Backup utility to back up a folder and its contents in the previous activity, you decide to test the restore capabilities of this program. In this activity you restore a folder using the Backup utility Advanced Mode interface.

1. Click **Start**, and then click **Run**. In the Open text box type **ntbackup.exe** and click **OK**.

2. In the Backup or Restore Wizard dialog box that opens, click the **Advanced Mode** link to access the complete functionality of the Backup program.

3. Click the **Restore and Manage Media** tab. The backup job just created is listed, as shown in Figure 10-11.

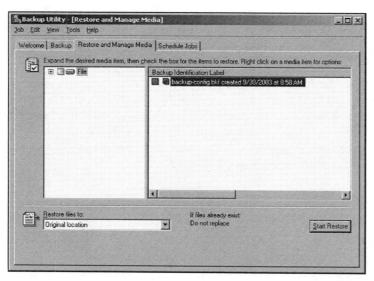

Figure 10-11   The Restore and Manage Media tab

4. Click the **plus sign (+)** next to the **File** icon to expand its contents.

5. Click the **plus sign (+)** next to **backup-config.bkf** to expand its contents.

6. Click the **plus sign (+)** next to **C:** to expand its contents.

7. Click the **plus sign (+)** next to **WINDOWS** to expand its contents.

8. Click the **plus sign (+)** next to **system32** to expand its contents.

9. Click the **config** folder to view the contents of the backup file. Check the check box next to the **config** folder.

10. In the Restore files to list box, click **Alternate location**.

11. In the Alternate location text box, type **D:\configbackup** and click the **Start Restore** button. Ultimately, this restores the contents of the backup–config.bkf file to the configbackup folder.

12. In the Confirm Restore dialog box, click **OK**.

13. After the Restore process is complete, click the **Close** button in the Restore Progress screen.

14. Close the Backup Utility window.

15. Click **Start,** and then click **My Computer**. Double-click drive **D:,** and then double-click the **configbackup** folder.

10

16. Double-click the **WINDOWS**, **system32**, and **config** folders to view their contents, confirming that the contents of the backup file were restored to an alternate location.

17. Close all open windows.

Scheduling Backups

In order to ensure that backups are completed without any interaction from an administrator, the Windows Server 2003 backup utility also supports the ability to schedule configured backups to take place according to the customer needs and requirements. For example, backups can be scheduled to take place daily, weekly, or monthly, at predefined times, or on predefined days. Figure 10-12 illustrates the Schedule Job dialog box from the Advanced settings of the Backup or Restore Wizard.

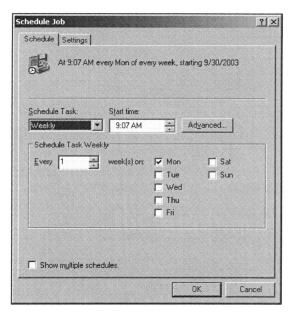

Figure 10-12   Scheduling backups

In Activity 10–3 you use the Backup or Restore Wizard to create and then schedule a backup operation on your server.

ACTIVITY

Activity 10-3: Scheduling Backup Operations Using the Backup Utility

Time Required: 10 minutes

Objective: Schedule a backup using the Windows Server 2003 Backup utility.

Description: Having manually created a backup of a folder and its files in Activity 12-1, you decide to test the ability to have this folder backed up automatically using the scheduling feature of the Windows Server 2003 backup utility. In this activity you use the Backup or Restore Wizard to define a new backup job, and then schedule this backup job to occur daily.

1. Click **Start**, and then click **Run**. In the Open text box type **ntbackup.exe** and click **OK**.

2. In the Backup or Restore Wizard dialog box that opens, click **Next**.

3. At the Backup or Restore screen, ensure that **Back up files and settings** is selected, and click **Next**.

4. At the What to Back Up screen, click the **Let me choose what to back up** radio button, and click **Next**.

5. At the Items to Back Up screen, click the **plus sign (+)** next to **My Computer** in the Items to back up section. Click the **plus signs (+)** next to **Local Disk (C:)**, **WINDOWS**, and **system32** to view their contents. Check the check box next to the **config** folder, and then click **Next**.

6. At the Backup Type, Destination, and Name screen, click the **Browse** button.

7. At the Save As dialog box, select drive **D:** in the Save in drop-down menu and click **Save**.

8. In the Type a name for this backup text box, type **ScheduledBackup** and click **Next**.

9. At the Completing the Backup or Restore Wizard screen, click the **Advanced** button.

10. At the Type of Backup screen, click **Next**.

11. At the How to Back Up screen, check the **Verify data after backup** check box, and click **Next**.

12. At the Backup Options screen, click the **Replace the existing backups radio** button, and then check the **Allow only the owner and the Administrator access to the backup data and any backups appended to this medium** check box. Click **Next**.

13. At the When to Back Up screen, click the **Later** radio button, as shown in Figure 10-13. Click the **Set Schedule** button.

14. In the Schedule Job window, select **Daily** in the Schedule Task drop-down menu, and select a Start time approximately 10 minutes after the current time. Click **OK**.

15. In the Set Account Information dialog box, type your **AdminXX password** in both the Password and Confirm password text boxes. Click **OK**.

10

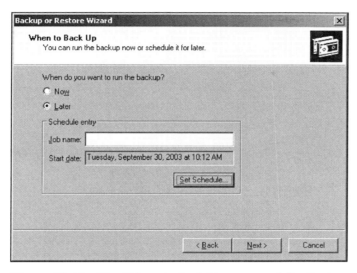

Figure 10-13   The When to Back Up screen of the Backup or Restore Wizard

16. At the When to Back Up screen, type **ScheduledBackup** in the Job name text box, and click **Next**. The Set Account Information dialog box opens again. Enter **your AdminXX password** in both the Password and Confirm password text boxes, then click **OK**.

17. At the Completing the Backup and Restore Wizard screen, click **Finish**.

18. Click **Start**, select **Control Panel**, and then double-click **Scheduled Tasks**. In the Scheduled Tasks window, confirm that a task named ScheduledBackup exists. Close the Scheduled Tasks window.

19. Once the 10 minutes since completing Step 14 has passed, click **Start**, and then click **My Computer**. Double-click on drive **D:** and confirm that a file named ScheduledBackup.bkf exists. This is the backup created automatically as part of the scheduled backup process.

20. Close all open windows.

Backing Up and Restoring System State Data

Besides the ability to back up normal data files and folders, the Windows Server 2003 Backup Utility also provides the ability to back up what is referred to as **System State** data. Backing up the System State data on a Windows Server 2003 system includes the following elements:

- Registry (always)
- COM+ Class Registration database (always)
- Boot files (always)

- Certificate Services database (if Certificate Services is installed)

- Active Directory (only on domain controllers)

- SYSVOL directory (only on domain controllers)

- Cluster service (if the server is part of a cluster)

- IIS Metadirectory (if IIS is installed)

- System files (always)

You should also back up these components regularly with your standard backup schedule. In the event of an Active Directory or system startup failure, the most common solution is to restore the System State data.

One limitation to the Windows Server 2003 Backup utility is that you cannot back up individual components of the System State data. Third-party backup applications, like Veritas Backup Exec, often allow individual component backups.

If you are restoring the System State because of a corrupt Active Directory database, you must restart the computer and choose the Directory Services Restore Mode advanced startup option. You can then use the backup utility to restore the latest System State data from backup. After you restart the computer and Windows Server 2003 starts normally, Active Directory is automatically reindexed and updates Active Directory and the file replication service.

10

In the event that you are attempting to restore a portion of the Active Directory tree, a few additional steps may be required. For example, if an OU was inadvertently deleted by an administrator, you can still use the Windows Server 2003 Backup Utility to restore the System State in an attempt to restore the deleted OU. One problem with this scenario is that when an Active Directory object is restored from backup, the other domain controllers still think that the object should be deleted. When replication takes place with the other domain controllers, the newly restored object is again deleted.

This problem can be overcome by performing an authoritative restore. An authoritative restore marks specific objects in the Active Directory as the master copy and forces the other domain controllers to receive the change.

To perform an authoritative restore, restart the computer in directory service restore mode, restore the most recent System State from backup, and then run the NTDSUTIL utility at a command prompt in authoritative restore mode.

For more information about the NTDSUTIL utility and its syntax, see the Windows Server 2003 Help and Support Center.

In Activity 10-4, you use the Windows Server 2003 Backup Utility to back up System State data on your server.

Activity 10-4: Backing Up System State Data

Time Required: 15 minutes

Objective: Back up the System State data on a Windows Server 2003 domain controller.

Description: Because your server is also a domain controller, the IT manager at Dover Leasing has asked you to explore the capabilities of the Backup Utility in terms of backing up System State data, including individual components. Ultimately, this will be an important consideration in whether the IT manager decides to rely on the Backup Utility or a third-party alternative. In this activity, you back up the System State data for your server.

1. Click **Start**, click **Run**, and in the Open text box type **ntbackup** and press **Enter**. Click the **Advanced Mode** link in the Backup or Restore Wizard screen.

2. In the Backup Utility window, click the **Backup** tab.

3. Click the **System State** icon to view its contents. Notice that the individual check boxes are grayed out because individual System State components cannot be backed up by this utility.

4. Click the check box next to the **System State** icon, as illustrated in Figure 10-14.

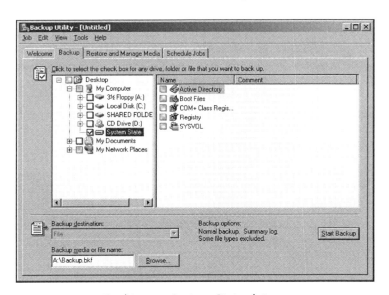

Figure 10-14   Backing up System State data

5. In the Backup media or file name text box, type **d:\systemstate.bkf** and click the **Start Backup** button.

6. In the Backup Job Information dialog box, click the **Start Backup** button.

7. After the Backup process is complete, click the **Close** button in the Backup Progress screen.

8. Click **Start**, and then click **My Computer**. Double-click on drive **D:** to view its contents.

9. Right-click on the file **systemstate.bkf** and click **Properties**. From the General tab, review the size of this file to get a better sense of how large a System State backup of your system is.

10. Close all open windows.

SHADOW COPIES OF SHARED FOLDERS

Windows Server 2003 introduces a new feature to help make the recovery of user data files stored in shared folders easier than ever before. Traditionally, if a user were to accidentally delete a file from a shared folder, an administrator would need to be contacted in order to restore the file from a previously created backup. Although this method is tried and tested, it does result in obvious inefficiencies. Firstly, the user needs to contact an administrator, which may result in delays, and lost user productivity. Secondly, the administrator has to take time from their schedule to find the backup media that contains a backed up version of the file, and restore it. The **Shadow Copies of Shared Folders** feature was designed to make recovering previous versions of files stored in shared folders simple for users, without the need for intervention from an administrator.

 The Shadow Copies of Shared Folders feature is not intended for use as a replacement for or alternative to creating regular backups. Regular backups should be performed normally in order to ensure that all data is available in the case of accidental deletion or some other disaster.

Implementing the Shadow Copies of Shared Folders feature on a Windows Server 2003 system allows users three main advantages:

- restoration of files that they accidentally delete
- recovery of previous versions of files when necessary
- comparison of the current version of a file to a previous version

The Shadow Copies of Shared folders feature is not enabled on a Windows Server 2003 system by default. When required, this feature is enabled on a volume-by-volume basis from the Shadow Copies tab of the properties of a drive, as shown in Figure 10-15.

Once enabled, the Shadow Copies of Shared Folders feature periodically creates shadow copies of all files stored in shared folders on that particular volume. It cannot be individually enabled or disabled for certain folders—the setting is volume-wide. By default, shadow copies of files are created according to a pre-defined scheduled, every Monday through

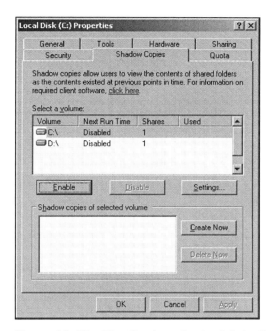

Figure 10-15   The Shadow Copies tab in the properties of a volume or partition

Friday at 7:00 a.m. and 12:00 p.m.. This schedule can be changed, but Microsoft recommends that shadow copies be created no more than once per hour at a maximum.

By default, the Shadow Copies of Shared Folders feature uses 10% of the available disk space on a volume for storing shadow copies, with a minimum of 100 MB allocated for this purpose. When space limits are reached, the older shadow copies are deleted, and a maximum of 64 shadow copies are stored per volume. As more shadow copies are created, the oldest ones are deleted to make way for newer versions.

In Activity 10-5, you enable and configure the Shadow Copies of Shared Folders feature for your server's D: drive.

ACTIVITY

Activity 10-5: Enabling and Configuring Shadow Copies of Shared Folder Settings

Time Required: 15 minutes

Objective: Enable and configure the Shadow Copies of Shared Folders feature for a selected volume.

Description: The IT manager at Dover Leasing is concerned about the amount of time lost and productivity wasted when users accidentally delete a file or need a previous version restored from backup. Because of this, he has asked you to test the Shadow Copies of Shared

Folders feature in Windows Server 2003. In this activity you enable and configure Shadow Copy settings for drive D: on your server.

1. Click **Start**, and then click **My Computer**.

2. Double-click on drive **D:** to view its contents. Right-click on an area of blank space, select **New**, and then click **Folder**. Name the new folder **shadow**.

3. Right-click on the **shadow** folder and click **Properties**. Click on the **Sharing** tab, and then click the **Share this folder radio** button. Click the Permissions button. Check the **Full Control** check box in the Allow column, and then click **OK**.

4. Click the **Security** tab. Click on the **Users** group, and then check the **Full Control** check box in the Allow column. Click **OK**.

5. Double-click on the **shadow** folder to open it. Right-click on an area of blank space, select **New**, and then click **Text Document**. Name the new text document **test.txt**.

6. Double-click on the **test.txt** document to open it in Notepad. Type **Testing shadow copies**, click **File**, and then click **Save**. Close Notepad.

7. Click **Start**, then click **My Computer**. Right-click on drive **D:** and then click **Properties**.

8. Click the **Shadow Copies** tab. In the Select a volume section, click on volume **D:**, and then click **Enable**.

9. When the Enable Shadow Copies dialog box appears, read the message and then click **Yes**. Note that enabling shadow copies for the volume may take a minute or more. Once complete, notice that a new shadow copy is listed in the Shadow copies of selected volume section.

10. Click the **Settings** button. This opens the Settings window, as shown in Figure 10-16. This screen allows you to change the volume where shadow copy files are stored, the amount of disk space allocated to shadow copy storage, and so forth.

11. Click the **Schedule** button. Click the drop-down menu at the top of the window to view the currently configured schedule for creating new shadow copies. By default, new shadow copies are created at 7:00 a.m. and 12:00 p.m., Monday through Friday.

12. Click **New** to add a third schedule to the list. Use the Start time spin box to set the schedule for this new task to **4:00 PM**. This adds one additional shadow copy creation task at 4:00 p.m. each day. Click **OK**.

13. Click **OK** to close the Settings window, and then click **OK** to close the properties windows of drive D:.

14. Double-click on drive **D:** to view its contents, and then double-click on the **shadow** folder to open it.

10

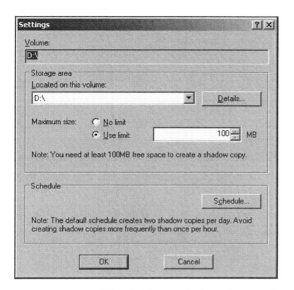

Figure 10-16   The Settings window for a volume with shadow copies enabled

15. Double-click on the **test.txt** file to open it in Notepad. Highlight the text in the document, press the **Backspace** key, and then type **Second shadow copy test**. Click **File**, and then click **Save**. Close the Notepad window.

16. Close all open windows.

Previous Versions

In order for network users to be able to access previous versions of files via the Shadow Copies of Shared Folders feature, additional software must be installed on their systems. The client software can be found on a Windows Server 2003 system in the %systemroot%\system32\clients\twclient\x86 folder for Intel-based systems. The client software is provided in MSI format, meaning that an administrator can install it manually, or deploy it using methods like Group Policy. Once installed, this software adds an additional tab to the Properties pages of files stored in shared folders called Previous Versions. This name was chosen to make it easier for users to understand the purpose of the tab, and the functions it allows them to carry out.

In Activity 10-6 you install the **Previous Versions Client** software on your server and explore settings on the Previous Versions tab in the properties of a file.

Activity 10-5: Installing and Using the Previous Versions Client

Time Required: 10 minutes

Objective: Install and use the Previous Versions Client and then view and restore a previous copy of a file.

Description: Having configured Shadow Copies on drive D:, you decide to install and test the Previous Versions Client as part of trying to determine how users will interact with the Shadow Copies of Shared Folders feature enabled in the previous activity. In this activity you first install the Previous Versions Client software, and then use the functionality that it provides to restore a previous version of the test.txt file created in the last activity.

1. Click **Start**, and then click **Run**. In the Open text box, type **%systemroot%\system32\clients\twclient\x86** and click **OK**. This opens the x86 folder in Windows Explorer.

2. Double-click on the **twcli32.msi** file to launch the installer.

3. Once the installation is completed, click **Finish**.

4. At the Installer Information dialog box, click **Yes** to restart your server if necessary. Once the reboot is complete, log on with your **AdminXX** account.

5. Click **Start**, and then click **Run**. In the Open text box, type **\\serverXX** (where XX is your assigned student number) and click **OK**.

6. Double-click on the **shadow** folder to view its contents. Double-click on the **test.txt** file to open it, confirming that it contains the text Second shadow copy test. This is the most recent version of the file. Close Notepad without making or saving any changes.

7. Right-click on the **test.txt** file and click **Properties**. Notice that the properties of this file now includes a tab named Previous Versions.

8. Click the **Previous Versions** tab, as shown in Figure 10-17.

9. In the File versions list, review the Time information next to the test.txt file, and click **View**. This opens the previous version of the test.txt file. Close Notepad.

10. With the test.txt file still selected, click **Copy**. This allows you to save this copy of the file to an alternate location, if necessary. Click **Cancel**.

11. With the test.txt file still selected, click **Restore**. This restores the previous version of the test.txt file to the folder. When the Previous Versions dialog box appears, click **Yes**.

12. Close all open windows.

10

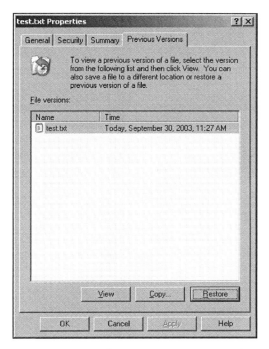

Figure 10-17   The Previous Versions tab in the properties of a shared file

AUTOMATED SYSTEM RECOVERY

Windows Server 2003 introduces a powerful new utility for the purpose of restoring system configuration information. The **Automated System Recovery (ASR)** feature allows you to restore system configuration settings in the event that a system cannot be repaired using the various safe-mode startup options or the last known good configuration feature.

ASR consists of two different elements on a Windows Server 2003 system. The first is the ASR backup, which you access from the Backup Utility. The second is a floppy disk that contains information about the backup, disk configuration information, and how the restore should be performed.

The main purpose of the ASR feature is to restore a Windows Server 2003 system to a functional state. However, ASR is only used to back up and restore system configuration information and not data files. You should back up any user data files separately before initiating ASR and then restore them once the ASR process is complete, using a tool such as the Windows Server 2003 Backup utility.

You should create a new ASR backup any time the system configuration of a server running Windows Server 2003 is changed.

If an ASR backup exists, you can restore system configuration settings by booting from the Windows Server 2003 CD and then selecting the Repair option. The information stored on the ASR floppy disk and in the ASR backup is then used to restore appropriate settings.

You create an ASR backup set using the Automated System Recovery Wizard, which you access from the Windows Server 2003 Backup Utility Advanced Mode Welcome tab. The Automated System Recovery Preparation Wizard Backup Destination screen is shown in Figure 10-18.

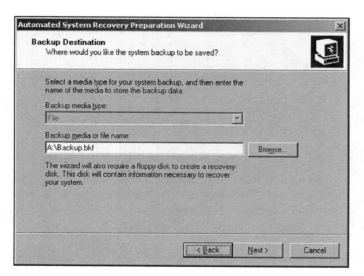

Figure 10-18 The Automated System Recovery Preparation Wizard Backup Destination screen

Both Windows NT Server 4.0 and Windows 2000 included a system-restore feature known as an Emergency Repair Disk (ERD). ASR replaces the ERD feature on Windows Server 2003 systems.

For more information on using the Automated System Recovery feature, see the topic of the same name in the Windows Server 2003 Help and Support Center.

10

Advanced Startup Options

Several things can cause a system not to start, such as the installation of new software or device drivers, or changes made to the system's configuration. If your computer fails to start, you can try using one of the advanced startup options to troubleshoot the problem. For example, you can start the computer in **safe mode**, which only loads the default Windows Server 2003 settings and the device drivers necessary to start the operating system. If you have installed new software that you think is causing the problem, you can uninstall it once in safe mode.

You can access the Windows Advanced Startup Options screen during system startup by pressing F8 while viewing the Boot Loader Operating System Selection menu. The screen that appears (see Figure 10-19) presents you with a list of eight advanced startup options, summarized in Table 10-1.

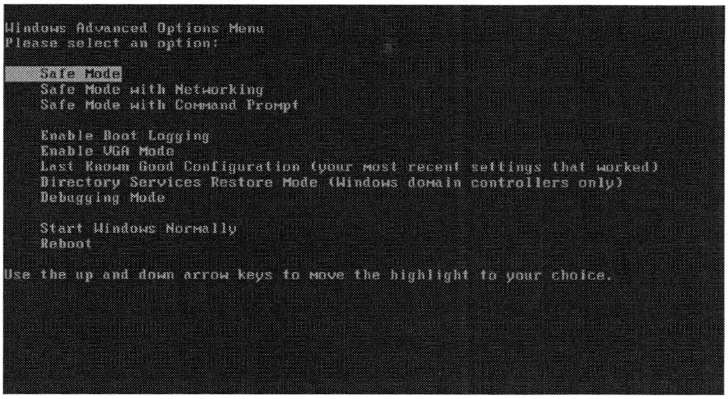

Figure 10-19   The Windows Advanced Startup Options screen

Table 10-1   Advanced startup options

Startup Option	Description
Safe Mode	Only the basic files and drivers required to start Windows Server 2003 are loaded. The default Windows Server 2003 settings are used. This option is useful when an application or component that is causing a problem needs to be uninstalled or disabled.
Safe Mode with Networking	This option starts the computer the same as in safe mode, but provides network connectivity. Use this option if you need access to the network to repair the problem.
Safe Mode with Command Prompt	This option starts the computer the same as in safe mode, but provides access to the Windows Server 2003 command line rather than the graphical user interface.

Table 10-1   Advanced startup options (continued)

Startup Option	Description
Enable Boot Logging	This option starts Windows Server 2003 while creating a log file that lists all the installed drivers and services that were loaded or not loaded. Use this option to determine the exact cause of startup problems. The file is called ntbtlog.txt and is stored in the %systemroot% folder.
Enable VGA Mode	This option starts Windows Server 2003 with the basic VGA driver for the video card. This is useful if you've installed a new video driver that is causing Windows Server 2003 not to start.
Last Known Good Configuration	This option starts Windows Server 2003 using registry information saved after the last successful logon. This option is useful if incorrect configuration changes have been made and you need to return to the computer's previous configuration.
Directory Services Restore Mode	This option enables you to restore the Sysvol and Active Directory Services on a domain controller. The system must be a domain controller to have this option available.
Debugging Mode	Debugging information is sent to another computer via a serial cable connection when Windows Server 2003 boots. Use this option to provide software developers with detailed debugging information about the problem.

10

In Activity 10-7 you explore some of the various advanced startup options on your Windows Server 2003 system.

Activity 10-7: Viewing and Testing Advanced Startup Options

Time Required: 20 minutes

Objective: View and Test Windows Server 2003 Advanced Startup Options.

Description: Based on his experiences in troubleshooting problems in Windows 2000, the IT manager at Dover Leasing has asked you to familiarize yourself with the advanced startup options that can be used to repair a Windows Server 2003 server if necessary. In this activity, you access the advanced startup options menu and then boot your server using the Safe Mode and Safe Mode with Command Prompt advanced options.

1. Click **Start**, and then click the **Shut Down** button. In the What do you want the computer to do? list box, click **Restart**. In the Comment text box, type **testing advanced startup options**, and click **OK**.

2. At the operating system selection screen, press the **F8** key to access the Windows Advanced Options Menu. If your system is not configured to dual boot, press **F8** prior to the Windows Server 2003 boot screen appearing.

3. Select **Safe Mode** on the list of available options, and press **Enter**.

4. If the operating system selection screen appears, select **Windows Server 2003, Enterprise** (or **Standard** if applicable) if necessary, and press **Enter**. If prompted to select a hardware profile, select **Profile1** and press **Enter**.

5. Log on using the **Administrator** user account with the password **Password01**.

6. When the Desktop dialog box opens, read the message it provides and click **OK**.

7. Click **Start**, click **Run**, and then type **cmd.exe** in the Open text box. Click **OK**.

8. At the command line, type **ping www.course.com** and press **Enter**. Notice that the ping fails because network functionality is disabled in Safe Mode.

9. Restart your server, and access the Windows Advanced Options Menu as outlined in Step 2.

10. Select **Safe Mode with Command Prompt** on the list of available options, and press **Enter**.

11. At the operating system selection screen, select **Windows Server 2003, Enterprise** (or **Standard** if applicable) if necessary, and press **Enter**. If prompted to select a hardware profile, select **Profile1** and press **Enter**.

12. Log on using the **Administrator** user account with the password **Password01**. Notice that the Command Prompt opens as the Windows shell environment.

13. At the command line, type **ping www.course.com**. Notice that this command also fails because Safe Mode with Command Prompt also provides no networking support.

14. Press **Ctrl+Alt+Delete** to access the Windows Security dialog box.

15. Click the **Shut Down** button, and then reboot your server normally, logging on with your **AdminXX** account.

Last Known Good Configuration

The **last known good configuration** allows you to recover your system from failed driver and registry changes. For example, installing a device driver that is incorrect for your hardware can cause a system to fail on startup. The last known good configuration information is stored in the registry and is updated each time the computer restarts and the user successfully logs on.

Normally when a computer is restarted, any configuration changes made before the reboot process was initiated are used. Each time you make configuration changes, these changes are copied to the default configuration that will be used the next time the computer is restarted. If these changes damage the default configuration, your computer may not be able to boot successfully. For example, the installation of new device drivers may cause the computer to stop responding and, ultimately, result in stop errors during the boot process, also known as the "Blue Screen of Death" (BSoD).

The last known good configuration can be thought of as a backup that can be used to restart the system in the event that the current configuration fails.

Because the last known good configuration is updated each time you log on, make sure you do not log on to your server if problems are evident during the boot process. Once you do, the last known good configuration is updated with the incorrect configuration changes.

The last known good configuration is useful in situations where Windows Server 2003 configuration changes have been made that negatively impact the system. However, it cannot resolve problems such as missing or corrupt files, or if you restart and log on after the configuration changes have been made. Additional tools for system recovery are discussed later in this chapter.

In Activity 10-8, you test the use of the last known good configuration advanced startup option on your server.

Activity 10-8: Testing Last Known Good Configuration

Time Required: 15 minutes

Objective: Test the last known good configuration advanced startup option.

Description: Because any change to a server can severely impact user productivity if it results in system failure, the IT manager at Dover Leasing has asked you to familiarize yourself with the process for using the last known good configuration feature of Windows Server 2003. In this activity, you simulate errors by disabling both your network adapter card and DVD/CD-ROM drive, and then restore a previous server configuration by using the last known good configuration feature.

1. Click **Start**. Right-click the **My Computer** icon and click **Properties**.

2. In the System Properties dialog box, click the **Hardware** tab.

3. Click the **Device Manager** button.

4. In the Device Manager window, click the **plus sign (+)** next to the **Network adapters** icon to expand it.

5. Right-click your computer's network adapter, and click **Disable**. When prompted, click the **Yes** button.

6. In the Device Manager window, click the **plus sign (+)** next to the **DVD/CD-ROM drives** icon to expand it.

7. Right-click your computer's CD-ROM or DVD drive, and click **Disable**. When prompted, click the **Yes** button.

8. Click **Start**, and then click **Run**. In the Open text box, type **cmd** and press **Enter**.

9. At the command line, type **ping www.course.com** and press **Enter**. The ping fails because your network adapter has been disabled.

10

10. Click **Start**, and then click the **Shut Down** button. In the Shut Down Windows dialog box, choose **Restart**, type **Testing LKGC** in the Comment text box, and click **OK**.

11. At the operating system selection screen, press **F8**. If your system is not configured to dual boot, press **F8** prior to the Windows Server 2003 boot screen appearing.

12. On the Windows Advanced Options menu, select **Last Known Good Configuration** and press **Enter**.

13. At the operating system selection screen, select **Windows Server 2003, Enterprise** (or **Standard** if applicable) if necessary and press **Enter**. If prompted to select a hardware profile, select **Profile1** and press **Enter**.

14. When prompted, log on with your **AdminXX** account.

15. Click **Start**. Right-click the **My Computer** icon and click **Properties**.

16. In the System Properties dialog box, click the **Hardware** tab.

17. Click the **Device Manager** button.

18. Click the **plus signs (+)** next to both the **Network adapters** icon and the **DVD/CD-ROM drives** icon to expand them and verify that these devices are no longer disabled.

19. Close all open windows.

THE RECOVERY CONSOLE

Another Windows Server 2003 tool that can be used for system recovery is the **Recovery Console**. The Recovery Console is an advanced tool for experienced administrators, allowing them to gain access to a hard drive on computers running Windows Server 2003. It can be used to perform the following tasks:

- Start and stop services
- Format drives
- Read and write data on a local hard drive
- Copy files from a floppy or CD to a local hard drive
- Perform administrative tasks

Installing the Recovery Console

You can start the Recovery Console in one of two ways. The first option is to run it from the Windows Server 2003 CD once a serious error occurs by booting from the CD. The second option is to install it on your computer permanently before you need it to resolve a problem. Once you have installed the Recovery Console, it is listed as an option from the list of available operating systems during the initial boot process. You can then start the Recovery Console by selecting it on the boot loader menu, as shown in Figure 10-20.

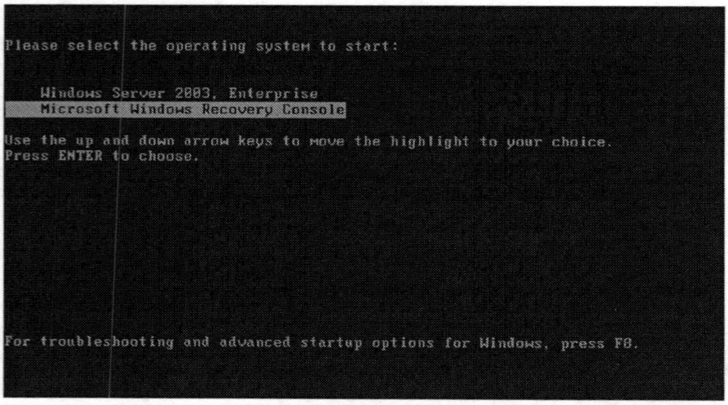

```
Please select the operating system to start:

    Windows Server 2003, Enterprise
    Microsoft Windows Recovery Console

Use the up and down arrow keys to move the highlight to your choice.
Press ENTER to choose.




For troubleshooting and advanced startup options for Windows, press F8.
```

Figure 10-20   Accessing the Microsoft Windows Recovery Console

If you choose not to install the Recovery Console on your system, you can start by booting your system from the Windows Server 2003 CD. Instead of choosing to reinstall the operating system, you would initiate the recovery process by selecting the option to repair using the Recovery Console.

You must be an administrator to run the Recovery Console, so accessing the console requires users to provide the correct local administrator's password for the system.

There are a variety of commands available through the Recovery Console. The following list includes some of the common commands that are used. For a complete list of commands that are available, use the Help command from within the console.

- Copy—Copies a file from removable media to the system folders
- Disable—Disables a system service or a device driver
- Enable—Enables or starts a system service or a device driver
- Exit—Closes the Recovery Console and restarts your computer
- Fixboot—Writes a new partition boot sector onto the system partition
- Fixmbr—Repairs the master boot record of the boot partition
- Listsvc—Lists all the services on the computer

In Activity 10-9, you first install and then use the Windows Server 2003 Recovery Console.

Activity 10-9: Installing and Using the Recovery Console

Time Required: 20 minutes

Objective: Install and use the Recovery Console.

Description: The IT manager has mandated that the Windows Server 2003 Recovery Console should be installed on all corporate servers to provide an alternate troubleshooting and repair environment in cases where the last known good configuration feature fails to fix an issue. In this activity, you first install and then test the Recovery Console to become familiar with the basic operation of its interface.

1. Click **Start**, and then click **Run**. In the Open text box, type **D:\SOURCE\ i386\winnt32.exe /cmdcons** and click **OK**.

2. In the Windows Setup dialog box, as illustrated in Figure 10-21, click **Yes**.

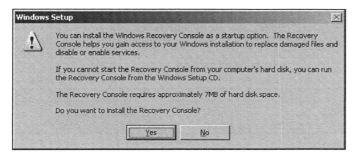

Figure 10-21   Installing the Recovery Console

3. Press **ESC** to cancel the dynamic update. Click **Yes**. Select the **Skip this step and continue installing Windows** radio button, then click **Next**.

4. In the Windows Server 2003, Enterprise Edition Setup dialog box, click **OK**.

5. Click **Start**, and then click the **Shut Down** button. In the Shut Down Windows dialog box, click **Restart**, and then type **Recovery Console Test** in the Comment text box. Click **OK**.

6. At the operating system selection screen, select the **Microsoft Windows Recovery Console** option, and press **Enter**.

7. When the Which Windows installation would you like to log onto prompt appears, type **1** and press **Enter**.

8. At the Type the administrator password prompt, type **Password01** and press **Enter**. This brings you to the C:\WINDOWS prompt.

9. Type **help** and press **Enter**. This displays a list of commands available via the Recovery Console. Press the **spacebar** to scroll though the remainder of the list and return to the command prompt.

10. Type **listsvc** and press **Enter**. This lists all of the services on the server, along with information about their status, as shown in Figure 10-22.

11. Press the **spacebar** until the RemoteAccess service is visible onscreen. Notice that its status is set to Disabled.

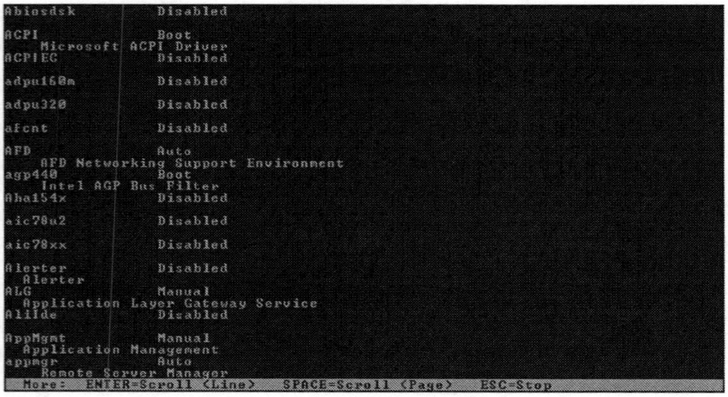

Figure 10-22   Viewing the results of the Recovery Console LISTSVC command

12. Press the **spacebar** until you return to the command prompt.

13. Type **enable RemoteAccess SERVICE_AUTO_START** and press **Enter**. This will configure the Remote Access service to start automatically once the server reboots.

14. Type **listsvc** and press **Enter**. Press the **spacebar** until the RemoteAccess service is visible. Notice that its status is now set to Auto.

15. Press the **ESC** key to return to the command line.

16. Type **exit** and press **Enter**. This exits the recovery console and initiates a reboot of the server.

17. Boot your server normally, and log on using your **AdminXX** account.

CHAPTER SUMMARY

- One of the most critical roles of any network administrator is to be able to restore a server and related data quickly in the event of failure or accidental deletion. Windows Server 2003 includes a variety of tools and utilities to restore a server to a previous configuration, undo problematic configuration changes, and back up and restore operating system, application, and user data files.

- In order to ensure that operating system, application, and user data files are not lost in the event of a server failure or accidental deletion, critical files and folders can be backed up and restored using the Windows Server 2003 Backup utility. This tool provides the option of using a wizard interface to perform these tasks along with what is known as Advanced mode.

- The Windows Server 2003 Backup utility supports five different types of backups including normal, incremental, differential, copy, and daily backups.

◻ As part of ensuring that critical operating system files are available in the event of a server failure or accidental deletion, the Windows Server 2003 Backup utility provides the ability to back up this information via a single element known as System State.

◻ Shadow Copies of Shared Folders is a new feature in Windows Server 2003 that allows an administrator to make previous versions of files available to users for the purpose of restoring a previous version, restoring a file that has been accidentally deleted, or to compare versions of files. This feature allows users to access these previous versions without the intervention of an administrator, or the need to restore data from backup.

◻ Automated System Recovery (ASR) is another new feature in Windows Server 2003 that allows an administrator to quickly recover from a server failure by storing server configuration information on floppy disks. These disks are used in conjunction with the Windows Server 2003 installation CD to restore a server to a previous configuration state, although it does not restore applications or user data files.

◻ Windows Server 2003 supports a variety of different advanced startup options that can be used to attempt to boot a server in the event that the normal boot process will not complete correctly. Examples of these options include Safe Mode and Last Known Good Configuration.

◻ The Windows Server 2003 Recovery Console provides administrators with an alternate environment into which a server can be booted to make various configuration changes if necessary. This tool is useful when a server will not boot due to errors or other incorrect configuration settings.

Key Terms

Automated System Recovery (ASR) — A new Windows Server 2003 feature that allows an administrator to restore server configuration settings in the event that a system cannot be repaired using other methods such as safe mode or last known good configuration. This technique involves creating floppy disks that include system configuration information, and then using these in conjunction with the Windows Server 2003 installation CD to restore a server to its previous configuration. ASR does not restore applications or user data files.

Backup utility — The tool included with Windows Server 2003 used to back up and restore files and System State information.

copy backup — A backup type that backs up all selected files and folders, but does not change the archive attribute setting. This allows a copy backup to be performed without interrupting any other backup processes currently in place.

daily backup — A backup type that backs up selected files or folders than have been created or changed on the day that the backup takes place.

differential backup — A backup type that only backs up those files that have changed since the last normal or incremental backup took place, but does not clear the archive attribute associated with those files.

incremental backup — A backup type that only backs up those files that have changed since the last normal or incremental backup took place and clears the archive attribute associated with those files.

last known good configuration — An advanced startup option that you can use to recover a system from failed Windows Server 2003 configuration changes.

normal backup — A backup type that backs up all selected files and folders, and clears the archive attribute on these files and folders.

Previous Versions Client — The client software component that allows users to access the Previous Versions tab to view or restore previous versions of files stored on a volume with Shadow Copies of Shared Folders enabled.

Recovery Console — A command-line interpreter that you can use to gain access to a local hard drive in the event that the system fails to boot.

safe mode — An advanced boot option that allows a Windows Server 2003 system to be booted with minimal services or drivers loaded, typically used for troubleshooting or diagnostic purposes.

Shadow Copies of Shared Folders — A new feature in Windows Server 2003 that can be enabled on a volume-by-volume basis to allow a user to view or recover previous versions of files stored in shared folders. In order to access this feature, user systems must have the Previous Versions Client software installed.

System State — A group of critical operating system files and components that can be backed up as a single group on a Windows Server 2003 system. System State data always includes the Registry, COM+ Registration database, boot files, and system files. On a domain controller, it also includes Active Directory and the SYSVOL directory. Other components that are included (assuming their associated services are installed) include the Certificate Services database, the Cluster Service, and the IIS Metadirectory.

10

REVIEW QUESTIONS

1. Which of the following backup types backs up all selected files and folders and changes their archive attribute?

   a. Normal

   b. Incremental

   c. Differential

   d. Daily

2. Which of the following backup types backs up all files that have changed since the last incremental or normal backup?

   a. Normal

   b. Incremental

   c. Differential

   d. Daily

3. Which of the following backup types backs up only the selected files and folders that have changed since the last differential or normal backup and does not change their archive attribute?

    a. Normal

    b. Daily

    c. Incremental

    d. Differential

4. Which of the following backup types backs up only the selected files and folders that have changed since the last incremental or normal backup and changes their archive attribute?

    a. Normal

    b. Copy

    c. Daily

    d. Incremental

5. Which of the following backup types only backs up the selected files and folders that have changed on the current day?

    a. Daily

    b. Normal

    c. Copy

    d. Incremental

6. Which of the following backup types backs up all selected files and folders and does not change their archive attribute so as not to interfere with any existing backup process?

    a. Daily

    b. Copy

    c. Differential

    d. Normal

7. Members of which of the following groups can back up any files and folders on a Windows Server 2003 domain controller?

    a. Administrators

    b. Backup Operators

    c. Server Operators

    d. Users

8. Which of the following permissions allows a user to back up files and folders that they do not own?

    a. Read

    b. Read and Execute

    c. Full Control

    d. Modify

9. Individual users can be granted rights that allow them to back up and restore files on a Windows Server 2003 system if necessary.

    a. True

    b. False

10. Having only the Read permission to a file is sufficient to allow a user to back up that file.

    a. True

    b. False

11. Which of the following advanced startup options allows a user to access the network on a Windows Server 2003 system?

    a. Safe Mode

    b. Safe Mode with Command Prompt

    c. Safe Mode with Networking

    d. Enable Boot Logging

10

12. What must be installed on a client workstation in order for a user to access previous versions of files in shared folders?

    a. Shadow Copies Client

    b. Previous Versions Client

    c. Automated System Recovery

    d. Windows Backup utility

13. Which of the following features allows an administrator to create floppy disks that can be used in conjunction with the Windows Server 2003 CD to restore a server?

    a. Automated System Restore

    b. Recovery Console

    c. Last Known Good Configuration

    d. Shadow Copies of Shared Folders

14. Which of the following advanced startup options boots Windows Server 2003 using a basic video driver?

    a. Safe Mode

    b. Safe Mode with Networking

    c. Enable VGA Mode

    d. Enable Boot Logging

15. The Backup utility included with Windows Server 2003 allows backup jobs to be scheduled.

    a. True

    b. False

16. How much disk space is required to enable the Shadow Copies of Shared Folders feature for a particular volume?

    a. 10 MB

    b. 100 MB

    c. 1 GB

    d. 10 GB

17. Which of the following options are available to a user from the Previous Versions tab in the properties of a file stored in a shared folder? (Choose all that apply.)

    a. View

    b. Copy

    c. Restore

    d. Delete

18. A normal user cannot restore a file from the Previous Versions tab without the intervention of an administrator.

    a. True

    b. False

19. Which of the following switches is used in conjunction with the WINNT32 command to install the Recovery Console?

    a. /recovery

    b. /console

    c. /cmdcons

    d. /conscmd

20. Any user can log on to a Windows Server 2003 installation using the Recovery Console.

    a. True

    b. False

CASE PROJECTS

Case Project 10-1

The IT manager at Dover Leasing has asked you to design a new backup strategy for Windows Server 2003 systems. Each server has a tape backup drive attached, and the IT manager wants backups performed each evening, Monday through Friday. Because of the large amount of user data to be stored on each server, a normal backup should be performed on Monday evenings, and then a less intensive option should be chosen for Tuesday through Friday. Assuming that the IT manager would like to be able to restore from backup as quickly as possible, what backup method would you suggest for these other days?

Case Project 10-2

A new administrator has been hired at Dover Leasing to work during evenings and weekends under your direction. One evening he decides to install a new device driver on one of the servers to enhance performance. Before checking with you or any other administrators on staff, he installs the device driver. You receive a call that upon restart the new administrator discovered that the server no longer boots successfully. The server needs to be available to users in the morning.

10

1. What options in Windows Server 2003 are available to recover from a failed reboot? What is each option used for?

2. What recovery tool would be appropriate for this situation?

3. You noticed after the server is recovered that the Recovery Console was not listed as an option during the operating system selection. It is company policy that this tool be installed on all servers. How can the tool be installed? If you needed to use the Recovery Console and it wasn't installed, how could you start it?

Case Project 10-3

After a serious server failure at Dover Leasing, you decide to attempt to restore the server using the Automated System Recovery (ASR) feature. Although the server now boots, users are calling to complain that their files are no longer accessible on the server. What is the cause of this, and what can you do to remedy the situation?

11

WINDOWS SERVER 2003 SECURITY FEATURES

After reading this chapter and completing the exercises, you will be able to:

Identify the various elements and techniques that can be used to secure a Windows Server 2003 system

Use Security Configuration and Analysis tools to configure and review security settings

Audit access to resources and review Security log settings

One of the most important roles of any network administrator is to ensure that servers and the data they hold are properly secured. In practice, implementing proper security is a far-reaching endeavor that varies from organization to organization. Considerations not only include the various security features and capabilities of an operating system like Windows Server 2003, but also the various policies and procedures of an organization. Although securing a server to the greatest possible extent might seem like the most logical choice in the eyes of an administrator, in practice the ability for users to access systems in a timely and straightforward manner also needs to be considered. Implementing security always involves finding the right balance between both business and technical factors. In other words, there is more to implementing sound security practices than often meets the eye, especially for inexperienced administrators.

Windows Server 2003 includes a number of different security features and capabilities, many of which have been looked at in previous chapters. This chapter begins with a basic review of the key security features of Windows Server 2003, and then takes a closer look at two additional capabilities not yet explored, namely Security Configuration and Analysis tools, as well as the auditing capabilities that allow administrators to review various security-related events.

SECURING YOUR WINDOWS 2003 SYSTEM

Windows Server 2003 includes a number of different security-related features and tools that help an administrator to properly secure both server and desktop systems. Although a wide variety of tools and features exist, they can generally be categorized into one of the following areas:

- Authentication
- Access control
- Encryption
- Security policies
- Service packs and hot fixes

The following sections provide an overview of each security category, and how various features and tools relate to these categories.

Authentication

Authentication is a concept at the heart of any network security strategy. At the most basic level, Windows Server 2003 authentication processes require a user to submit a valid user name and password combination to gain access to desktop systems (such as those running Windows NT, Windows 2000, and Windows XP) or domain environments.

In a domain environment, a Windows Server 2003 system configured as a domain controller handles authentication functions in a centralized manner. In a workgroup environment, users are authenticated by the local Security Accounts Manager (SAM) database on the computer they are logging on to. In both cases, the end result is the same—the user's identity is confirmed, and this confirmation later serves to dictate which resources a user can and cannot access on either their local computer or the network. This identification process is a critical element of security in any network environment.

In the same way that users can be authenticated to their local computer or a domain controller in their home domain, trust relationships extend this process to other domains, and possibly other forests. Ultimately, this means that users in domain environments can authenticate themselves a single time, and then potentially access resources across many domains and forests without the need to authenticate again.

Other Windows Server 2003 services support additional authentication methods. One example is Internet Information Services (IIS), which provides a variety of authentication methods for users accessing resources stored on a Web server. These authentication methods make it possible to not only authenticate internal netework users, but also users from the Internet when necessary.

For the highest degree of security possible, all network users should be required to authenticate themselves. While it is possible to allow users access to a network without authentication, this is inherently insecure and should be avoided whenever possible.

 Windows Server 2003 user authentication methods were originally explored in Chapter 2.

Access Control

In order to secure resources like files, folders, and printers, Windows Server 2003 also supports another key security capability known as access control. As the name suggests, access control literally controls which users, groups, and computers can access resources, along with the level of access granted. For example, NTFS permissions are used to provide access control to resources stored on NTFS partitions and volumes such as the ability to read, write, or modify a file. Shared folder permissions allow an administrator to control who can access the files and subfolders or a shared folder, and to what extent. Similarly, printer permissions extend the concept of access control to printers and associated print devices.

As a general rule, users should only be granted the lowest level of access to resources that they require to carry out necessary functions. For example, if a user only needs to be able to read a file and not make changes, they should be granted no more than the Read permission to that file. This concept is known as the "principal of least privilege". Although the concept is fundamentally sound, implementing it is often easier said than done, since the effective permissions of a user are impacted by the permissions directly applied to them, as well as any groups they are members of. For this reason, Windows Server 2003 includes features like the Effective Permissions tab in the properties of resources, allowing an administrator to quickly determine the impact of these combined permissions for an individual user, group, or computer.

11

 Shared folder and NTFS access control permissions were explored in detail in Chapter 4.

In the same way that access control is used to control access to traditional network resources like files, folders, and printers, permissions can also be used to control access to Active Directory objects. For example, using techniques like the Delegation of Control Wizard or by explicitly configuring permissions on the Security tab of objects like a user account, an administrator can control what level of access users have to that particular object. In a manner similar to file, folder, and printer permissions, the principle of least privilege should be followed when applying access control settings to Active Directory objects.

Encryption

In order to further protect data on a server beyond what access control settings provide, Windows Server 2003 also supports the ability to encrypt confidential files. This capability is provided via the Encrypting File System (EFS), which uses a combination of private and public keys to encrypt and decrypt the symmetric files encryption key that was used to actually encrypt the contents of a file. EFS is only available for use with files stored on NTFS partitions and volumes, and only encrypts files locally. In other words, EFS does nothing to encrypt files or folders as they traverse a network. In a Windows Server 2003 environment, the encryption of network data is handled by a protocol known as IPSec.

The Encrypting File System (EFS) was looked at in detail in Chapter 6.

NOTE

IPSec is an open-standard security protocol used to encrypt the contents of packets sent across a TCP/IP network. When implemented between network clients and servers, IPSec is running in what is known as transport mode, and can fully secure communications sessions across a network based on rules defined by an administrator. For example, an administrator might choose to encrypt the contents of all communications between the desktops of all executives and their local file servers, while maintaining unsecured communications for all other users. IPSec can also be used in a second mode known as tunnel mode, where data is secured between two pre-defined endpoints only. Such a configuration is common when a company wants to connect two LANs over an intermediate public network, such as the Internet.

IPSec should be implemented on networks that require a high degree of security for the transmission of sensitive data. This technique makes it extraordinarily difficult for hackers or other rogue users to capture network data packets and view their contents using network monitoring or packet capturing tools like Sniffer or Network Monitor.

IPSec is beyond the scope of Microsoft exam 70-290. For more detailed information on Windows Server 2003 IPSec functions and features see the Help and Support Center.

NOTE

Security Policies

Security policies allow an administrator to control a wide range of security settings on Windows Server 2003, Windows 2000, and Windows XP standalone and domain systems. The tools that can be used to configure these settings include the Local Security Policy and the Group Policy Object Editor MMC snap-ins. In domain environments, these security settings are most easily applied via Group Policy, where settings can be configured once in a centralized manner, and then be applied to different domain systems.

Beyond the tools used to configure security policy settings, Windows Server 2003 also includes tools that allow an administrator to analyze policy settings to those stored in a number of pre-configured security templates. The two main tools for this purpose are the Security Configuration and Analysis MMC snap-in and the command-line SECEDIT utility. Later in this chapter you learn more about using the various Security Configuration and Analysis tools provided with Windows Server 2003.

 Group Policy objects and related settings were looked at in detail in Chapter 8.

NOTE

Service Packs and Hot Fixes

Although not explicitly considered a security feature, an important part of any security strategy involves ensuring that all network systems have critical updates and security patches applied as they are released. In the Microsoft world, updates are released as "hot fixes" when a security flaw or other issue is identified and corrected, effectively acting as a "patch" when applied. Over time, **hot fixes** and other updates are combined and released in a single **service pack**. A service pack includes all previous updates, and is always cumulative. In other words, applying Service Pack 2 to a Windows Server 2003 would also include all of the updates originally included in Service Pack 1, and any hot fixes released since Service Pack 1. Applying service packs and hot fixes helps to ensure that a Windows Server 2003 system is not susceptible to any security vulnerabilities that may have been identified.

Service packs and hot fixes can be downloaded and installed via Windows Updates and by downloading the individual executables from the Microsoft Web site. Microsoft never sends updates to customers as e-mail attachments. As such, any attachments in messages that appear to be from Microsoft should never be installed—more than likely, these attachments contain a virus or other malicious code.

In environments that include many internal systems running operating systems like Windows Server 2003, Windows 2000, and Windows XP, an update solution like Microsoft Software Update Services can help an administrator to automate and better control the process of distributing updates.

11

USING SECURITY CONFIGURATION MANAGER TOOLS

In the past, as network systems increased in size and complexity, administering security across the enterprise also became increasingly complex. Windows NT did not provide adequate tools or utilities to implement and manage an effective network security policy. For example, if administrators wanted to implement security auditing on a particular group of workstations, either they would have to visit each machine individually or try to find adequate third-party tools to assist in the configuration.

Another common problem with managing security policies in Windows NT involves maintaining the configuration. If a company or department has more than one administrator in charge of applying and maintaining the security settings, it can be difficult to keep track of configuration changes to the policy. Without proper documentation and good communication between the administrators, a great deal of time may be spent figuring out which auditing and security settings each administrator has changed.

Windows Server 2003 makes significant changes to how security configurations can be maintained. Tools included for this purpose are collectively referred to as the **Security Configuration Manager tools**. This tool set, together with Windows Server 2003 Group Policies, allows an administrator to configure a specific group of security settings to form a **Security Policy template**. This template can then be administered centrally and applied throughout Active Directory.

To assist with security policy changes, the Security Configuration Manager tools can also be used to analyze and implement security settings on a computer system. In the analysis, a comparison can be made between a computer system's security settings and a previously defined security template file. Differences between the computer system and the policy template can then be viewed and reported, and action can then be taken to change the settings on the computer to the desired settings.

For example, your security plan may provide detailed information on the security settings for the company's computers. Creating the design is only the first step, however. You also need to implement the design, which could mean making changes to every computer on the network. The Security Configuration Manager tools are designed to make the implementation of the security policy much easier. When the security policy has been designed and approved, the settings can then be defined in a security template. This template can then be compared to the current settings on the network by using the Security Configuration and Analysis tool. This shows which current settings match the security policy and which do not. You can then apply and implement the new settings with a simple command.

The Security Configuration Manager tools are also useful in maintaining security settings. In addition, it is easy to check the security settings for the network on a regular basis and reapply any settings that may have been changed.

The Security Configuration Manager tools consist of the following core components:

- Security templates
- Security settings in Group Policy objects
- Security Configuration and Analysis tool
- SECEDIT command-line tool

Security Templates

An administrator uses a security template to define, edit, and save baseline security settings to be applied to computers with common security requirements to meet organizational security standards. Templates help ensure that a consistent setting can be applied to multiple machines and be easily maintained.

The templates are text-based files that can be read but should not be changed or edited using any text editor. Be sure to use the Security Templates snap-in to create and edit the templates. The Security Templates snap-in is illustrated in Figure 11-1.

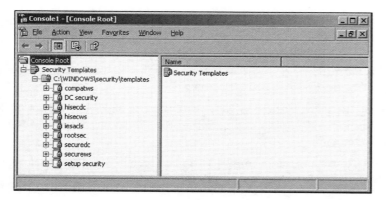

Figure 11-1 The Security Templates MMC snap-in

In Activity 11-1 you browse some of the default security templates provided with Windows Server 2003.

Activity 11-1: Browsing Security Templates

Time Required: 10 minutes

Objective: Exploring settings associated with built-in security templates.

Description: Windows Server 2003 includes a number of pre-defined templates that can be used to configure security settings on domain workstations and servers. The IT manager at Dover Leasing is interested in evaluating the potential impact of using these settings but wants to be sure that increasing the overall level of security will not render certain systems unable to communicate. In this activity, you browse through some of the default security templates included with Windows Server 2003 to evaluate their configuration settings.

1. If necessary, log on using your **AdminXX** account, where *XX* is your assigned student number.

2. Click **Start**, and then click **Run**. In the Open text box type **mmc** and then click **OK**.

3. Click **File** on the menu bar, click **Add/Remove Snap-in**, and then click **Add**.

4. In the Add Standalone Snap-in window, click **Security Templates** and click **Add**.

5. Click **Close** to close the window, and then click **OK**.

6. Click the **plus sign (+)** next to **Security Templates** to expand it, and then click the **plus sign (+)** next to **C:\WINDOWS\security\templates** to view the available templates.

7. Click the **plus sign (+)** next to **hisecdc** to view its contents.

8. Click the **plus sign (+)** next to **Account Policies**, and then click **Password Policy**. Browse through the password settings associated with the hisecdc security template.

9. Click **Account Lockout Policy** to view the template's associated settings. Click the **plus sign (+)** next to **hisecdc** to hide its contents.

10. Click the **plus sign (+)** next to the **securedc** template to expand it, and then click the **plus sign (+)** next to **Account Policies**.

11. Click **Account Lockout Policy** to view its settings, as shown in Figure 11-2. Compare the account lockout settings configured in the hisecdc template to those found in the securedc template.

12. As time permits, browse through some additional security templates to compare differences between settings configured in the various security templates.

13. Leave the MMC open.

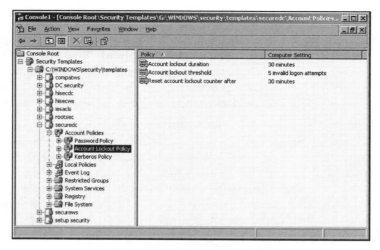

Figure 11-2   Account Lockout Policy settings in the securedc template

Analyzing the Pre-configured Security Templates

The first step in configuring and implementing security templates is to sort the network computers into three main categories: workstations, servers, and domain controllers. These three categories relate to the default security templates included with Windows Server 2003, although an administrator can also design custom templates. Keep in mind that only computers running Windows Server 2003, Windows XP, and Windows 2000 can take advantage of security template configurations and deployments.

The Default Template

When Windows Server 2003 is installed, the default security settings applied to the computer are stored in a template called **Setup Security.inf**. The contents of this template will be different depending upon the original configuration of the computer, such as whether the operating system was freshly installed or upgraded from a previous version of Windows. The purpose of this template is to provide a single file in which all of the original computer security settings are stored. If the security settings of a computer are ever changed and an administrator wishes to easily return the system to its original settings, the Setup Security.inf template could simply be reapplied.

The Setup Security.inf template should never be applied using Group Policy because it contains a large number of settings that can seriously degrade Group Policy processing performance.

Incremental Templates

If the basic security settings do not meet your security needs, you can apply various additional security configurations using **incremental templates**. These templates modify security settings incrementally. However, these templates should only be applied to machines already running the default security settings because they do not include any of the initial configurations that the template created during the initial installation.

- Compatws.inf—This template can be applied to workstations or servers. Windows Server 2003 has increased the default security considerably over previous versions like Windows NT. In some cases, this increased security brings application compatibility problems, especially for non-certified applications that require user access to the registry. One way to run these applications is to make the user a member of the Power Users group, which has a higher level of rights and permissions than a normal user. Another option is for the administrator to increase the security permissions for the Users group. The Compatws.inf template provides a third alternative by weakening the default security to allow legacy applications to run under Windows Server 2003.

- Securews.inf and Securedc.inf—These templates provide increased security for areas such as account policy, auditing, and registry permissions. The securews template is for any workstation or server, whereas the securedc template should only be applied to domain controllers.

- Hisecws.inf and Hisecdc.inf—These templates can be incrementally applied after the secure templates have been applied. Security is increased in the areas that affect network communication protocols through the use of such features as packet signing. These templates should only be applied to client computers running Windows 2000 or higher, and all domain controllers must be running Windows 2000 or Windows Server 2003. If used, these templates should be applied to all computers on the network to ensure proper connectivity. The hisecws template is for workstations or servers, whereas the hisecdc template should only be applied to domain controllers.

- Iesacls.inf—This template contains settings to lock down Internet Explorer security settings.

- DC Security.inf—This template is applied automatically whenever a Windows 2000 or Windows Server 2003 member server is promoted to a domain controller. This is available to give the administrator the option to reapply the initial domain controller security settings if the need arises.

- Rootsec.inf—This template specifies the original permissions assigned to the root of the system drive. The main purpose of this template is for use in reapplying security permissions to resources on the system drive that have been changed, whether intentionally or accidentally.

The security templates included in Windows Server 2003 provide the administrator with acceptable security configurations for a variety of situations. If there is a unique situation

where a pre-configured template is not suitable, you also have the ability to create a custom template to meet your needs.

 You can also use a pre-configured template as a baseline and save any changes to a new template. To do this, right-click a pre-configured template, and then choose Save As.

Applying Security Templates

Security templates can be applied to either the local machine or the domain via GPOs. To apply a security template to a local machine, open the Local Security Settings MMC snap-in by running SECPOL.MSC. Right-click Security Settings in the console pane, and choose Import Policy. You can then select the template file to be imported, as shown in Figure 11-3.

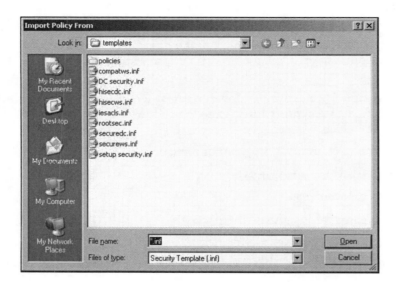

Figure 11-3   Importing settings from a security template

Security settings that are applied using Group Policy will always override local settings. Group Policy security settings are refreshed any time the machine is rebooted, at 90-minute intervals (with a maximum 30-minute offset) for servers and workstations, and every five minutes on domain controllers. Even if there have been no changes, the security settings are refreshed every 16 hours.

In Activity 11-2 you use the Security Templates MMC snap-in to create a custom security template.

Activity 11-2: Creating a Security Template

Time Required: 10 minutes

Objective: Define a new security template to meet custom requirements.

Description: Although the default security templates include a variety of different settings that can be used to increase the security level of Dover Leasing's servers and workstations, the IT manager has decided to explore the possibility of defining a custom template containing settings specific to Dover's requirements. Ultimately, a custom template will be defined that can be distributed to other Dover business units to standardize the security process if necessary. In this activity, you explore the process of defining a custom security template based on some of Dover's specific requirements.

1. In the MMC with the Security Templates snap-in added, right-click **C:\WINDOWS\security\templates** and click **New Template**.

2. In the Template name text box, type **dovercorptest**. In the Description text box, type **Test security template for the DomainXX.Dovercorp.net domain**. Click **OK**.

3. Browse through the configuration settings of the new dovercorptest security template. Notice that because the template is new, no settings have yet been configured.

4. Click the **plus sign (+)** next to the **dovercorptest** template to expand it, click the **plus sign (+)** next to **Account Policies** to expand it, click **Password Policy**, and configure the following settings:

    - Enforce password history – 5 passwords remembered

    - Maximum password age – 20 days

    - Minimum password age – 19 days

    - Minimum password length – 6 characters

    - Password must meet complexity requirements – Enabled

5. Click on **Account Lockout Policy** and then configure the following settings:

    - Account lockout duration – 30 minutes

    - Account lockout threshold – 3 invalid logon attempts

    - Reset account lockout counter after – 30 minutes

6. Right-click the **dovercorptest** security template and click **Save**. Close the MMC. Click **No** in the Microsoft Management Console dialog box.

7. Open My Computer and browse to **C:\WINDOWS\security\templates**. Double-click the **dovercorptest.inf** file to open it in a text editor, as shown in Figure 11-4. Notice that the settings originally configured in the Security Templates tool now appear in the text file.

8. Close the dovercorptest.inf file, and then close My Computer.

```
[Unicode]
Unicode=yes
[Version]
signature="$CHICAGO$"
Revision=1
[Profile Description]
Description=Test security template for the Domain01.Dovercorp.net domain
[System Access]
MinimumPasswordAge = 19
MaximumPasswordAge = 20
MinimumPasswordLength = 6
PasswordComplexity = 1
PasswordHistorySize = 5
LockoutBadCount = 3
ResetLockoutCount = 30
LockoutDuration = 30
[Registry Values]
```

Figure 11-4   Viewing template settings using Notepad

In Activity 11-3 you apply the custom security template created in Activity 11-2 to the Default Domain Policy on your server.

Activity 11-3: Applying Security Template Settings to Group Policy Objects

Time Required: 10 minutes

Objective: Deploy security template settings using Group Policy.

Description: Although security templates allow you to configure security settings directly on a local computer, their settings can also be imported into GPOs to facilitate easier deployment. The IT manager at Dover Leasing has asked you to explore the possibility of using Group Policy to deploy settings configured in the template defined as part of the previous activity. In this activity, you import the security settings of a security template into an existing GPO.

1. Click **Start**, select **Administrative Tools**, and then click **Active Directory Users and Computers**.

2. Right-click the **DomainXX.Dovercorp.net** icon (where *XX* is your assigned student number) and click **Properties**.

3. Click the **Group Policy** tab, ensure that **Default Domain Policy** is selected, and then click **Edit** to view its settings.

4. In the Computer Configuration section, click the **plus sign (+)** next to **Windows Settings** to expand it.

5. Right-click **Security Settings** and click **Import Policy**.

6. In the Import Policy From window, click **dovercorptest.inf** and click **Open**.

7. After importing the security template settings to the Default Domain Policy, browse through the Password Policy and Account Lockout Policy sections. Verify that the settings from the dovercorptest security template have been imported into the GPO.

8. Close the Group Policy Object Editor window, as well as the properties of the DomainXX.Dovercorp.net domain. Close Active Directory Users and Computers.

Security Configuration and Analysis

The **Security Configuration and Analysis** snap-in illustrated in Figure 11-5 allows administrators to compare current system settings to a previously configured security template. The comparison identifies any changes to the original security configurations and any possible security weaknesses that may be evident when compared to a stronger security baseline template.

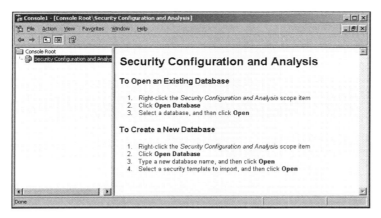

Figure 11-5   The Security Configuration and Analysis snap-in

The Security Configuration and Analysis tool uses a container, also referred to as a database, to store imported templates to be compared to the current system. The administrator imports a template into the database and then compares the template settings to the actual computer settings. If desired, the administrator can import more than one template to compare the effects of combining templates on the current settings. Once a combined template has been created, it can be saved and exported for future analysis, or it can be used to configure working computer systems.

After the analysis process is complete, the security categories appear. As each node is expanded, you can see the comparison between the database (imported templates) and the computer's current configuration. A green check mark indicates that the two settings match; a red "x" indicates a mismatch. You can make changes by double-clicking any configuration entry and selecting the desired configuration.

In Activity 11-4 you compare the current configuration of your domain controller with the settings found in the built-in hisecdc.inf security template.

Activity 11-4: Analyzing Security Settings Using Security Configuration and Analysis

Time Required: 15 minutes

Objective: Use the Security Configuration and Analysis tool to compare Group Policy and security template settings.

Description: As part of a new security initiative, the IT manager at Dover Leasing has decided that a mechanism must exist to allow systems to be periodically evaluated to ensure that they meet Dover's defined security-setting requirements. You have been asked to evaluate the Security Configuration and Analysis tool to determine whether or not this application will meet the stated requirements. In this activity, you compare the current configuration of your domain controller with the settings found in the built-in hisecdc.inf security template.

1. Open a new MMC and add the **Security Configuration and Analysis** snap-in. Follow the instructions in Activity 11-1 if necessary.

2. Right-click the **Security Configuration and Analysis** icon and click **Open Database**.

3. In the Open database window, type **SecurityTest** in the File name text box, as illustrated in Figure 11-6, and then click **Open**.

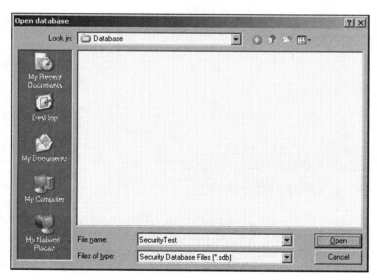

Figure 11-6   Opening a new database

4. In the Import Template window, click **hisecdc.inf** and click **Open**.

5. Right-click the **Security Configuration and Analysis** icon and click **Analyze Computer Now**.

6. In the Perform Analysis dialog box, click **OK** to accept the default log file location. The Analyzing System Security dialog box opens, as shown in Figure 11-7.

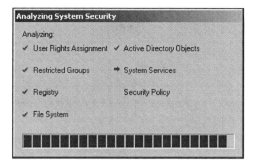

Figure 11-7   The Analyzing System Security dialog box

7. Click the **plus sign (+)** next to **Security Configuration and Analysis** and **Account Policies** to expand them, and then click **Password Policy**. An example of this screen is shown in Figure 11-8.

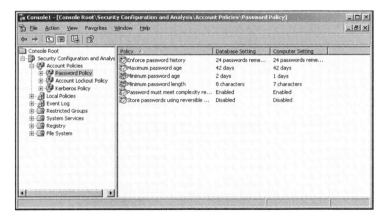

Figure 11-8   Reviewing Password Policy settings

8. Review both the Database Setting column and the Computer Setting column. The first column outlines the settings found in the database that relate to the template, whereas the second column outlines the settings currently configured on your server. Note that the icons displayed as part of each setting outline whether or not your server's current configuration meets or exceeds the settings outlined in the security database.

9. As time permits, browse through additional settings such as those found in the Account Lockout Policy, User Rights Assignment, and Security Options sections.

10. Close the MMC without saving any changes.

SECEDIT Command-Line Tool

SECEDIT.EXE is a command-line tool used to create and apply security templates, as well as analyze security settings. This tool can be used in situations where Group Policy cannot be applied, such as in workgroup configurations. SECEDIT, along with the Task Scheduler, can ensure that every computer in the workgroup maintains consistent security-policy settings. The SECEDIT command uses six main switches, as shown in Figure 11-9:

- /analyze—Analyzes database settings and compares them to a computer configuration

- /configure—Configures a system with database and template settings

- /export—Exports database information to a template file

- /import—Imports template information into a database file for analysis purposes

- /validate—Verifies the syntax of a template

- /GenerateRollback—Generates a template that saves the current security settings of a system; this template can be used to return to previous security settings in the event that settings are changed

Figure 11-9   The SECEDIT command

The Windows Server 2003 version of SECEDIT.EXE no longer includes the /refreshpolicy switch that was used to manually refresh computer and user Group Policy settings in Windows 2000. Refreshing Group Policy settings is now accomplished using the command-line tool GPUPDATE.EXE.

11

AUDITING ACCESS TO RESOURCES AND ANALYZING SECURITY LOGS

Monitoring network events is an increasingly critical and important facet of any network security strategy. Monitoring helps detect potential threats, increases user accountability, and provides evidence of security breaches if or when they occur. Monitoring can also be used for resource planning. Auditing specific resources, such as printer and file shares, can tell you how often users are accessing them. For example, if you determine through auditing that a specific share is heavily used by users on the network, you may need to create another instance of the share on another server, or physically move it to a system that is more capable of handling the required workload.

Auditing in Windows Server 2003 is used to monitor and track activities on a network. You can specify which events to monitor based on your security or resource planning requirements. When an audited event does occur, a record of it is written to the **security log**. The audit entry in the security log provides you with information such as the user who performed the action, the specific action that was performed (for example, a logon attempt), and whether it was a success or failure. **Event Viewer** is used to view the audit entries stored in the security log.

Before you can begin auditing security events or the access of network resources, you must first set up an audit policy. An **audit policy** defines the events on a network that Windows Server 2003 records in the security log as they occur. For example, if you choose to monitor failed logon attempts, when a user attempts to log on with an invalid user name and/or password, an event is written to the security log. Keep in mind that an event is not written to the security log on the local computer; rather, the event is written to the security log on the domain controller that attempted to validate the user. In other words, events are stored in the security log of the computer on which the event transpires.

When implementing an audit policy, you need to determine those events you wish to track, along with whether you want to track the successes and/or failures. The audit policy settings available in Windows Server 2003 are illustrated in Figure 11-10. You explore these settings in Activity 11-5.

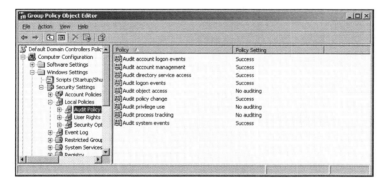

Figure 11-10   Windows Server 2003 Audit Policy settings

Activity 11-5: Exploring Default Auditing Settings

Time Required: 10 minutes

Objective: Explore the default audit settings configured on a Windows Server 2003 domain controller.

Description: Having read about Windows NT 4.0 in the past, you understand that by default, no auditing settings were configured on these servers. To verify whether this is still the case with Windows Server 2003, you decide to explore the default auditing settings

configured on your domain controller. In this activity, you explore the properties of the default domain controller Group Policy object to view its default settings.

1. Click **Start**, select **Administrative Tools**, and then click **Active Directory Users and Computers**.

2. Right-click the **Domain Controllers** OU and click **Properties**.

3. Click the **Group Policy** tab. Ensure that **Default Domain Controllers Policy** is selected on the Group Policy Object Links list, and then click the **Edit** button.

4. In the Computer Configuration section, click the **plus signs (+)** next to **Windows Settings**, **Security Settings**, and **Local Policies** to expand them.

5. Click the **Audit Policy** node to view its contents. Notice the nine policy settings and their configured default values in the Policy Setting column.

6. Double-click the **Audit account logon events** icon to view its configured settings. Notice that the policy setting is enabled but that only success events are being audited by default, as shown in Figure 11-11.

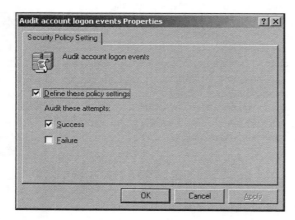

Figure 11-11   The Audit account logon events window

7. Browse through additional policy settings as time permits, but make no changes.

8. Close all open windows.

Table 11–1 outlines the different types of events that can be monitored in a Windows Server 2003 environment.

Table 11-1   Auditing events that can be monitored

Event	Explanation of Event
Audit account logon events	Activated when a user logs onto a computer; account logon events are generated where the user account is located (such as on the local computer or a domain controller), whereas logon events (outlined later in this table) are generated where the logon event occurs.
Audit account management	Activated whenever a user or group is created, deleted, or modified; this category also tracks successful or unsuccessful password changes.
Audit directory service access	Activated when an Active Directory object is accessed; the specific Active Directory object that is to be audited must also have auditing enabled.
Audit logon events	Activated when a user logs on or off a local computer or Active Directory; audits logon failures to find out if password hacking is taking place.
Audit object access	Activated when an object such as a folder or printer is accessed; the administrator must also configure the specific object for audit successes and failures.
Audit policy change	Activated when a policy that affects security, user rights, or auditing is changed.
Audit privilege use	Activated whenever a user uses an assigned right, such as changing the system time, or taking ownership of a file.
Audit process tracking	Activated any time an application process takes place; can assist developers in discovering which files or registry settings an application accesses when executing a command.
Audit system events	Activated when a system event takes place, such as the computer restarting.

Configuring Auditing

Once you have determined the events that need to be audited based on the security requirements of your network, you are ready to configure an audit policy. The following section outlines the requirements of which you should be aware, the steps in configuring an audit policy, and some general guidelines.

How you configure an audit policy is determined by the role of the computer on the network. If the computer is a member server or workstation in a domain, an audit policy can be implemented using Group Policy objects assigned to the domain or different OUs. For domain controllers, audit policy settings are implemented via the Default Domain Controllers Policy applied to the Domain Controllers OU. For non-domain standalone workstations and servers, audit settings can be defined by using the Local Security Policy tool on a system-by-system basis.

Requirements

The following requirements must be met to configure an audit policy:

- You must be a member of the Administrators group or be assigned the Manage auditing and security log user right.

- If you are auditing files and folders (via the audit object access setting), these files and folders must reside on an NTFS volume (auditing is not available on FAT volumes).

Configuring an Audit Policy

To set up an audit policy, you must first choose the events you wish to monitor and then decide whether to monitor the successes and/or failures of these events, as illustrated in Figure 11-12. However, if you are auditing access to files, folders, printers, and Active Directory objects, you also need to configure auditing settings on the specific resources for which you want to monitor access. Configuring object access auditing settings is looked at later in this section.

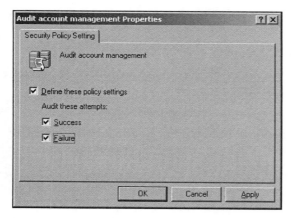

Figure 11-12   Configuring audit policy settings

In Activity 11-6 you configure and test new audit policy settings on your Windows Server 2003 system.

Activity 11-6: Configuring and Testing New Audit Policy Settings

Time Required: 10 minutes

Objective: Configure and test new audit policy settings.

Description: The IT manager at Dover Leasing has informed you that he wants to implement a new corporate security policy that will not only log all failed domain logon attempts, but that will also provide the capability to log different types of object access

events. In this activity, you make changes to the default auditing policy such that all unsuccessful logon attempts are audited and the ability to audit object access is enabled.

1. Use Active Directory Users and Computers to open and view the settings of the Default Domain Controllers Policy GPO auditing settings, as described in Activity 11-5.

2. Double-click the **Audit account logon events** icon to view its properties.

3. In the Audit these attempts section, click the **Failure** check box and click **OK**.

4. Double-click the **Audit object access** icon to view its properties.

5. In the Audit these attempts section, click both the **Success** and **Failure** check boxes and click **OK**.

6. Close the Group Policy Object Editor window, the Domain Controllers Properties dialog box, as well as Active Directory Users and Computers.

7. Click **Start**, and then click **Run**. Type **gpupdate.exe**, then press **Enter**.

8. Log off.

9. Attempt to log on as the user **AdminXX** with the password **pass**. This logon attempt fails.

10. Log on as the user **AdminXX** with your correct password.

11. Click **Start**, select **Administrative Tools**, and click **Computer Management**. Click the **plus sign (+)** next to **Event Viewer** to view its contents.

12. Click the **Security** icon to view the contents of the security log.

13. Search through the security log for a Failure event in category Account Logon that uses the event ID number 675. Double-click this Failure event to open it and view its details, as shown in Figure 11-13.

14. Read through the information provided by the event and then close all open windows.

Windows Server 2003 will automatically refresh audit policy settings every 90 minutes (with a maximum 30-minute offset) on a workstation or server and every five minutes on a domain controller as per normal Group Policy processing. If no changes occur, these settings are also refreshed every 16 hours by default. If you want to apply the changes immediately, you can do one of the following:

- Restart the computer
- At the command prompt, issue the GPUPDATE.EXE command

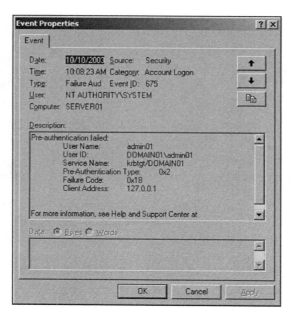

Figure 11-13   Viewing a failed logon event

NOTE Remember that Group Policy settings are applied in the order Local, Site, Domain, and Organizational Unit. As such, auditing settings configured at one level may be overridden by settings configured at another. Refer back to Chapter 8 for an overview of Group Policy processing settings.

Auditing Object Access

If your files and folders reside on an NTFS volume, you can set up auditing to monitor user access. For example, some information such as employee records or financial data may be confidential. To maintain a high level of security for this information, you need to enable auditing to detect any attempted or successful security breaches. This is especially useful if you want to track which users are attempting to access files or folders that contain sensitive data.

TIP Auditing object access can result in a very large number of events being logged to the Security log. This can have a detrimental impact on system performance, and should be used sparingly.

To configure auditing settings for specific files or folders, access the Advanced Security Settings on the particular resource. Figure 11-14 illustrates the Auditing Entry dialog box for a folder called Accounting. Notice that the interface allows you to configure different types of access attempts, including whether these attempts were successful or failed.

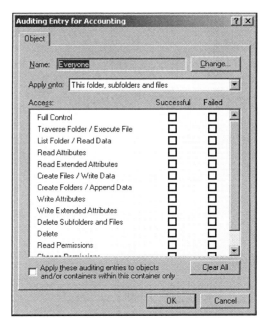

Figure 11-14.   The Auditing Entry window

TIP

When configuring auditing of object access, you should generally audit access by the Everyone group to ensure that all access attempts, including those by unauthenticated users, are recorded.

Auditing can also be configured for objects that are stored within Active Directory. The process is very similar in that the audit policy is first configured, then auditing is enabled for individual objects within Active Directory such as computers, users, groups, and OUs.

In Activity 11-7 you configure auditing settings for a folder located on an NTFS volume on your server.

ACTIVITY

Activity 11-7: Configuring Auditing on an NTFS Folder

Time Required: 10 minutes

Objective: Audit failed and successful access to an NTFS folder.

Description: Although Dover Leasing has decided to implement NTFS security on all files and folders stored on corporate servers, the IT manager is still very interested in gathering information about which users are attempting to access restricted resources. In this activity, you configure object access auditing settings to track attempted access to a secured folder.

1. Click **Start**, and then click **My Computer**.

2. Double-click on drive **D:**, click **File** on the menu bar, select **New**, and then click **Folder**. Name this new folder **Accounting**. Secure this folder with NTFS permissions such that only the **Domain Admins** account has **Full Control** of the folder for the time being. Leave the properties dialog box of the folder open once complete.

3. On the Security tab, click the **Advanced** button, and then click the **Auditing** tab.

4. Click the **Add** button. In the Select User, Computer, or Group dialog box, type **Everyone** in the Enter the object name to select text box and click **OK**.

5. In the Auditing Entry for Accounting dialog box, click the **Failed** check box next to **List Folder / Read Data** along with the **Failed** check box next to **Delete** and then click **OK**.

6. Click **OK** to exit the Advanced Security Settings for Accounting dialog box, and then click **OK** again to close the properties dialog box of the Accounting folder.

7. Log off and then log back on using the **mcowan** user account with the password **Password01**.

8. Open My Computer, browse to drive **D:**, and then attempt to open the Accounting folder. Access should be denied according to the NTFS permissions you configured in Step 1.

9. Right-click the **Accounting** folder and click **Delete**. When asked if you're sure you want to delete the folder, click **Yes**.

10. When the Error Deleting File or Folder message appears, click **OK**.

11. Log off and then log back on using your **AdminXX** account.

12. Click **Start**, select **Administrative Tools**, and then click **Computer Management**. Click the **plus sign (+)** next to **Event Viewer** if necessary to expand it, and then click on the **Security** log icon to view its contents. Search for Failure events that use the event ID 560.

13. Double-click any event using ID **560** to view its contents, as shown in Figure 11-15. View additional 560 events as time permits.

14. Close all open windows.

11

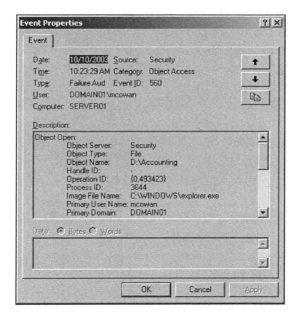

Figure 11-15   Viewing the properties of a failure event

Best Practices

To implement an audit policy that effectively meets your security requirements, it is a good idea to take some time to properly plan the implementation. Planning includes determining the computers for which auditing should be configured, what objects need to be audited, the type of events to audit, and whether to audit the successes, failures, or both. An audit policy can quickly become unmanageable and provide you with information that is of no use. By the same token, excessive auditing can seriously degrade the performance of network servers and workstations. Only choose to audit those events that are going to provide you with valuable information about your network. Here are some general guidelines that you should follow when you are planning your audit policy:

- Only enable auditing for those events that can provide you with useful information. Auditing unnecessary events increases overhead and fills up the security log with information that is not useful.

- Review the audit entries in the security log on a regular basis so you are aware of any security issues.

- Enable auditing for sensitive and confidential information.

- Audit the Everyone group instead of the Users group because the Everyone group includes unauthenticated users.

- Audit the use of user rights assignment so that administrative users are more accountable for their actions.

■ Always audit the Administrators group so you can track changes made by users who are members of this group.

Analyzing Security Logs

Once an audit policy has been created, an entry is written to the security log each time an event occurs that is defined within the policy. For example, if you enable auditing for object access and then audit all successful and failed read attempts on a folder called Accounting Docs, when a user opens the folder or attempts to open it, an entry would be written to the security log. You can then use Event Viewer to examine the contents of the log. All information written to the log is a result of the audit policy that you configure.

 For security purposes, only administrators and those users assigned the Manage Auditing and Security Log user right can view the contents of the security log.

To open Event Viewer and view the contents of the security log, access Event Viewer from the Administrative Tools menu, or from the Computer Management MMC. The contents of the security log are displayed in the details pane, providing a summary of each audit entry, including the date and time that the event occurred and the user who performed the action, as shown in Figure 11-16. A key icon represents a successful event, and unsuccessful events (failures to perform a specific action) are represented by lock icons. Double-click an event to provide detailed information about the specific event, as illustrated in Figure 11-17.

11

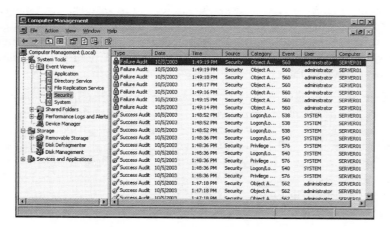

Figure 11-16   Viewing the contents of the Security log in Event Viewer

 By default, the security log shows events that occurred on the local computer. You can also use Event Viewer to view the security log on a remote computer by right-clicking Event Viewer (Local), and then clicking Connect to another computer.

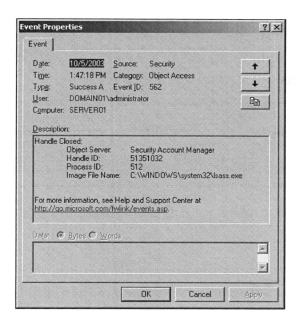

Figure 11-17   Viewing the properties of a success event

Depending on the number and type of events you choose to audit, the security log can quickly grow in size, making it difficult to pick out certain events. Fortunately, Event Viewer has a Find option that allows you to search through the security log to locate specific events. You can search for specific event types such as successful events or unsuccessful events, but you can also do a more detailed search by providing an event ID, category of event, or even a user logon name. To use the Find option, click the Security Log within the Event Viewer console, click View on the menu bar, and click the Find option. The Find in local Security dialog box opens, as shown in Figure 11-18.

Events in the security log can also be filtered so only those events matching your criteria are displayed in the details pane. This is useful if you have a large number of audit entries in the log and want to view entries based on event type or entries that occurred during a specific date and time. Similar to the Find option, you can also filter events based on event ID, category, user logon name, and computer name. To use the filter command, click the security log within the Event Viewer console, and click the Filter option located on the View menu. The Filter tab is shown in Figure 11-19.

Figure 11-18   The Find in local Security dialog box

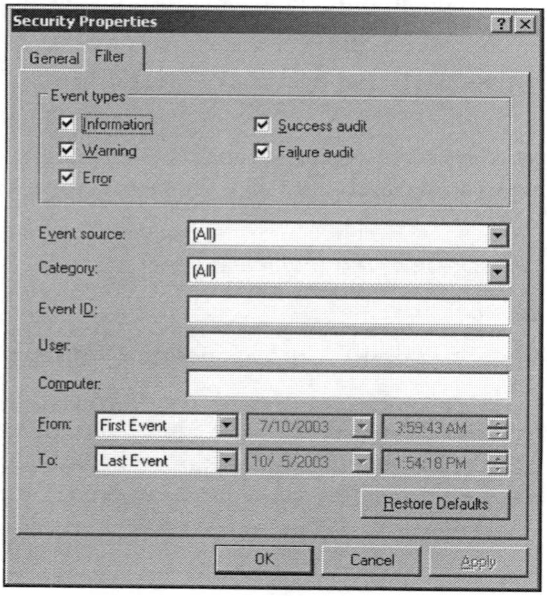

Figure 11-19   Use the Filter tab to filter events by various criteria

11

You may have noticed a number of other logs available within Event Viewer. The application and system logs are found on all computers running on Windows Server 2003. The application log contains information such as warnings and error messages generated by any programs coded to write events to this log. The system log contains information such as warnings and error messages that are generated by the operating system. Other logs, such as directory service, DNS server, and file replication service logs are only displayed in Event Viewer if the server is running their associated services. For example, all DNS servers include the DNS server log to track DNS-specific error and information messages.

In Activity 11–8 you configure the properties of the Event Viewer Security log.

Activity 11-8: Configuring Event Viewer Log Properties

Time Required: 10 minutes

Objective: Configure properties for log files in Event Viewer.

Description: After viewing the extremely large number of events that are found in the security log with only a very basic audit policy applied, you decide to look into alternative methods to quickly search for and find events. In this activity, you use both the find and filter features in Event Viewer to sort through log file entries.

1. Click **Start**, select **Administrative Tools**, and then click **Computer Management**.

2. Click the **plus sign (+)** next to **Event Viewer** to expand its contents if necessary, and then click the **Security** log to view all events. Click the first event in the list to highlight it.

3. Right-click the **Security** log, select **View**, and then click **Find**.

4. In the Event source list box, click **Security**.

5. In the Category list box, click **Logon/Logoff**. Uncheck both the **Information** and **Success audit** check boxes.

6. In the User text box, type **AdminXX**, and then click the **Find Next** button a number of times. Notice that the event highlighted in the background continues to change as the Find command moves through the list of events in the log that meet the criteria specified.

7. Click the **Close** button.

8. Right-click the **Security** log icon, select **View**, and then click **Filter**. The properties dialog box of the Security log opens to the Filter tab.

9. Repeat Steps 4 to 6 above to provide the information that should be used to filter the log. Click **OK** once complete.

10. Notice that the security log is now filtered to display only those events that have met the specified criteria.

11. Double-click any of the events listed to view its properties. Notice that the source, category, and user sections meet the criteria that you specified in Step 9. Click **OK** to close the Event Properties dialog box.

12. Right-click the **Security** log, select **View**, and then click **All Records**. Notice that all events now appear in the security log once again.

13. Close all open windows.

Configuring Event Viewer

In the past, one of the problems with auditing a large number of events was that the security log becomes full very quickly. By default, the security log of a Windows 2000 server was set to a maximum default size of 512 KB and once it reached this size, logging stopped. This has been changed in Windows Server 2003, where the default initial security log size is 16 MB. However, this should not be used as an excuse to prolong checking the security log on a regular basis because events may be overwritten once the maximum log file size is reached depending on configured settings. One way to avoid this problem, as previously mentioned, is to audit only those events that are essential. Another way is to change the default settings or properties of the security log. Ideally, making a point to review and archive the security log files on a regular basis is the best administrative strategy.

To configure the properties of the security log, in Event Viewer, right-click the Security log and click Properties. The Security Properties dialog box opens, as illustrated in Figure 11-20. Table 11-2 summarizes the configuration options available.

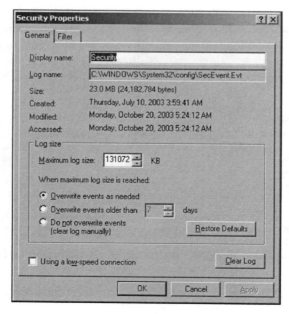

Figure 11-20   Configuring the properties of the Security log

Table 11-2   Security log configuration options

Option	Description
Log name	Changes the name and location of the log
Maximum log size	Specifies the size of the log file; the default is 128 MB
Overwrite events as needed	All new events overwrite the oldest events when the log file becomes full; if you plan to use this option, check the log file at regular intervals
Overwrite events older than X days	Sets the number of days before a log is overwritten (between 1 and 365)
Do not overwrite events (clear log manually)	Events in the log are not overwritten and when the log becomes full new events are discarded until the log is manually cleared
Using a low-speed connection	Specifies whether the log is located on another computer and whether you are connected using a low-speed device (such as a modem)

In Activity 11-9 you edit Security log settings and learn how to save the contents of an Event Viewer log file.

ACTIVITY

Activity 11-9: Editing Security Log Settings and Saving Events

Time Required: 10 minutes

Objective: Edit security log settings and save events for archiving purposes.

Description: The IT manager at Dover Leasing has asked you to implement a process to ensure that security log settings are never overwritten. Based on the large number of servers that will ultimately need to be managed at Dover, he has asked you to configure the security log settings to a maximum size of approximately 200 MB. Because log files must be emptied manually to ensure that events are not overwritten, he has also asked you to save the security log files using a date-related format. In this activity, you configure the properties of the security log to meet the requirements outlined by the IT manager.

1. Click **Start**, select **Administrative Tools**, and then click **Computer Management**. Click the **plus sign (+)** next to **Event Viewer** to expand it, if necessary.

2. Right-click the **Security** log and then click **Properties**.

3. In the Log size section, type **250000** in the Maximum log size text box.

4. In the When maximum log size is reached section, click the **Do not overwrite events (clear log manually)** radio button and then click **OK**.

5. A message appears telling you that the log file size must be an increment of 64K. Click **OK** to continue.

6. Click the **Security** log. Click **Action** on the menu bar, and then click **Save Log File As**.

7. In the File name text box, type **seclog-MM-DD-YY** using today's date for the file-name variables.

8. Click the **Save as type** list arrow to view the different formats in which a log file can be saved. On this list, click **Event Log (*.evt)**, and then click the **Save** button.

9. Note that the security log events are not cleared as part of a save operation. It's worth noting that you are prompted to save events when you attempt to clear an event log, however.

10. Right-click the **Security** node and click **Clear all Events**. When prompted with whether you want to save the security log, click **No**. This empties the security log with the exception of any new events.

11. Right-click the **Security** node and click **Open Log File**. Click the log file saved in Step 7 and then click **Security** in the Log Type list box. Click **Open**. Notice that the contents of the saved log now appear in the security log.

12. Close all open windows.

CHAPTER SUMMARY

□ Windows Server 2003 includes a number of security-related features that can be used to ensure a high level of system security. The general areas that these features fall into include authentication, access control, encryption, security policies, and service packs and hot fixes.

□ Security policies provide administrators with a way to configure a variety of security-related settings on Windows Server 2003, Windows 2000, and Windows XP systems.

□ The primary tools used to configure security policy settings include the Local Security Policy and Group Policy Object Editor MMC snap-ins. Security settings can also be imported from pre-defined or custom security templates.

□ Security Configuration and Analysis tools allow an administrator to compare the current security policy settings of a server to those stored in security templates. Both the Security Configuration and Analysis MMC snap-in and the SECEDIT command-line utility allow an administrator to compare, analyze, import, export, and configure security policy settings.

□ Auditing is a Windows Server 2003 feature that allows an administrator to track a wide range of security-related events. Examples include the use of user rights, logon events, object access, system events, and more.

□ The Event Viewer Security log is used to view the events relating to audit settings. A success event is depicted with a key icon in the log, while a lock icon represents a failure event.

11

Key Terms

audit policy — Defines the events on the network that Windows Server 2003 records in the security log as they occur.

Auditing — The process that tracks the activities of users by recording selected types of events in the security log of a server or a workstation.

Event Viewer — A component you can use to view and manage event logs, gather information about hardware and software problems, and monitor security events. Event Viewer maintains logs about program, security, and system events.

hot fixes — Interim updates to Windows Server 2003 that are released between major service pack releases. These are used to fix operating system bugs and security issues.

incremental templates — A set of text-based security template files that you can use to apply uniform security settings on computers within an enterprise. The templates modify security settings incrementally and do not include the default security settings.

IPSec — An open-standard security protocol used to encrypt the contents of packets sent across a TCP/IP network.

SECEDIT.EXE — A command-line tool used to create and apply security templates, as well as analyze security settings.

Security Configuration and Analysis — An MMC snap-in that allows an administrator to compare the configuration of a Windows Server 2003 system to settings stored in a security template and to apply template settings if necessary.

Security Configuration Manager tools — A security toolset consisting of security templates and utilities that can be used to analyze and apply security configurations.

security log — A Windows Server 2003 event log used to record security events such as auditing information.

Security Policy template — A template used to apply various security settings to an Active Directory container or object.

service pack — Periodic updates to the Windows Server 2003 operating system to fix reported bugs and security issues.

Setup Security.inf — The security template applied to Windows Server 2003 systems during the installation process.

Review Questions

1. Which of the following Event Viewer log files are success and failure events written to?
   a. DNS
   b. Security
   c. System
   d. Application

2. What is the default size of the Security log on a Windows Server 2003 system?

   a. 512 KB

   b. 8 MB

   c. 16 MB

   d. 32 MB

3. Which of the following is not a default security template included with Windows Server 2003?

   a. Hisecdc.inf

   b. Securedc.inf

   c. Rootsec.inf

   d. Secureserver.inf

4. Which of the following audit settings should be configured to audit access to files and folders?

   a. Audit account logon events

   b. Audit policy change

   c. Audit object access

   d. Audit system events

5. Which of the following audit settings should be configured to audit server reboots?

   a. Audit system events

   b. Audit policy change

   c. Audit logon events

   d. Audit object access

6. Which of the following audit settings should be configured to audit the creation of group objects?

   a. Audit system events

   b. Audit account management

   c. Audit policy change

   d. Audit logon events

7. Which of the following audit settings should be configured to audit successful password changes?

   a. Audit account management

   b. Audit object access

   c. Audit policy change

   d. Audit logon events

11

8. No auditing settings are configured for domain controllers by default on Windows Server 2003 systems.

   a. True

   b. False

9. Which of the following security features is used to encrypt data as it is transmitted over a TCP/IP network?

   a. IPSec

   b. EFS

   c. Access Control

   d. Software Update Services

10. Which of the following security features is used to encrypt files and folders stored on an NTFS volume?

    a. IPSec

    b. EFS

    c. Access control

    d. Service packs

11. Which of the following security features is used to validate the identity of a user on a Windows Server 2003 network?

    a. IPSec

    b. Authentication

    c. EFS

    d. Hot fixes

12. Which of the following security features is used to secure files and folders on an NTFS partition?

    a. Access control

    b. IPSec

    c. Service packs

    d. Software Update Services

13. Which of the following security templates contains the default security settings applied to a Windows Server 2003 system by default?

    a. Setup Security.inf

    b. Secure.inf

    c. Setup.inf

    d. Hisecdc.inf

14. Security template settings can be applied via Group Policy.

    a. True

    b. False

15. Which of the following command-line tools can be used to create and apply security templates?

    a. GPUPDATE

    b. SECEDIT

    c. SECCONFIG

    d. GPREFRESH

16. Which of the following is not a supported switch with the SECEDIT command in Windows Server 2003?

    a. /configure

    b. /analyze

    c. /export

    d. /refresh

17. Where are security templates stored by default on a Windows Server 2003 system?

    a. C:\Windows

    b. C:\Windows\Security

    c. C:\Windows\security\templates

    d. C:\Templates

18. Which of the following MMC snap-ins can be used to compare current server security settings to those stored in a security template?

    a. Security Configuration and Analysis

    b. SECEDIT

    c. Active Directory Users and Computers

    d. Active Directory Sites and Services

19. Which security template is automatically applied to a Windows Server 2003 system when it is promoted to the role of domain controller?

    a. DC Security.inf

    b. Secdc.inf

    c. Securedc.inf

    d. Dcsec.inf

20. It is possible to configure access control settings on Active Directory objects such as user accounts.

    a. True

    b. False

11

CASE PROJECTS

Case Project 11-1

The IT manager at Dover Leasing is looking for a way to ensure that Windows Server 2003 systems have consistent security settings configured according to the role of the server. For example, he would like all file servers throughout the enterprise to have consistent security settings. Having analyzed all of the default built-in security templates provided with Windows Server 2003, he has decided that custom settings need to be applied. Based on these needs, which tool can first be used to create a new template? Once the template is defined, what would be the most efficient way of distributing these security settings to network servers?

Case Project 11-2

Dover Leasing is in the process of reviewing their current structure and practices. Management would like to know if there is a way to track user access so that if a security breach does occur, there is a record of it. Once the appropriate permissions have been established, you want to be able to track user access to various folders. Explain how you can use auditing and the general steps that you need to complete to implement an audit policy.

EXAM OBJECTIVES TRACKING FOR MCSE CERTIFICATION EXAM #70-290 MANAGING AND MAINTAINING A MICROSOFT WINDOWS SERVER 2003 ENVIRONMENT

Exam #70-290: Managing and Maintaining a Microsoft Windows Server 2003 Environment

Managing and Maintaining Physical and Logical Devices

Objective	Chapter: Section	Activities
Manage basic disks and dynamic disks.	Chapter 5: Managing Disks and Data Storage	Activity 5-1 Activity 5-2 Activity 5-3 Activity 5-4 Activity 5-5 Activity 5-6 Activity 5-7 Activity 5-8
Optimize server disk performance. • Implement a RAID solution. • Defragment volumes and partitions	Chapter 5: Managing Disks and Data Storage	Activity 5-9

Managing Users, Computers, and Groups

Objective	Chapter: Section	Hands-on Activity(s)
Managing local, roaming, and mandatory user profiles.	Chapter 2: Creating and Managing User Accounts	Activity 2-2 Activity 2-3 Activity 2-4
Create and manage computer accounts in an Active Directory environment.	Chapter 2: Creating and Managing User Accounts	Activity 3-8
Create and manage groups. • Identify and modify the scope of a group. • Find domain groups in which user is a member • Manage group membership • Create and modify groups by using the Active Directory Users and Computers Microsoft Management Console (MMC) snap-in. • Create and modify groups using automation.	Chapter 3: Implementing and Managing Group and Computer Accounts	Activity 3-1 Activity 3-2 Activity 3-3 Activity 3-4 Activity 3-5 Activity 3-6 Activity 3-7

Objective	Chapter: Section	Hands-on Activity(s)
Create and manage user accounts. • Create and modify user accounts by using the Active Directory Users and Computers MMC snap-in. • Create and modify user accounts by using automation • Import user accounts	Chapter 2: Creating and Managing User Accounts	Activity 2-1 Activity 2-5 Activity 2-6 Activity 2-7 Activity 2-8 Activity 2-9
Troubleshoot computer accounts • Diagnose and resolve issues related to computer accounts by using the Active Directory Users and Computers MMC snap-in • Reset computer accounts	Chapter 3: Implementing and Managing Group and Computer Accounts	Discussed in Chapter 3
Troubleshoot user accounts • Diagnose and resolve account lockouts • Diagnose and resolve issues related to user account properties	Chapter 2: Creating and Managing User Accounts	Discussed in Chapter 2
Troubleshoot user authentication issues	Chapter 2: Creating and Managing User Accounts	Discussed in Chapter 2

Managing and Maintaining Access to Resources

Objective	Chapter: Section	Hands-on Activity
Configure access to shared folders • Manage shared folder permissions	Chapter 4: Managing File Access Chapter 6: Advanced File System Management	Activity 4-1 Activity 4-2 Activity 4-3 Activity 6-7
Configure file system permissions • Verify effective permissions when granting permissions. • Change ownership of files and folders	Chapter 4: Managing File Access	Activity 4-4 Activity 4-5 Activity 4-6 Activity 4-7
Troubleshoot access to files and shared folders.	Chapter 4: Managing File Access Chapter 6: Advanced File System Management	Discussed in Chapter 4 Activity 6-4

Managing and Maintaining a Server Environment

Objective	Chapter: Section	Hands-on Activity
Monitor and analyze events. Tools might include Event Viewer and System Monitor.	Chapter 11: Windows Server 2003 Security Features	Activity 11-5 Activity 11-6 Activity 11-7 Activity 11-8 Activity 11-9
Troubleshoot print queues	Chapter 7: Implementing and Managing Printers	Activity 7-1 Activity 7-2 Activity 7-3 Activity 7-4 Activity 7-5 Activity 7-6 Activity 7-7 Activity 7-8 Activity 7-9 Activity 7-10
Monitor system performance	Chapter 9 : Monitoring Server Performance	Discussed in Chapter 9
Monitor file and print servers. Tools might include Task Manager, Event Viewer, and System Monitor • Monitor disk quotas • Monitor print queues • Monitor server hardware for bottlenecks	Chapter 6: Advanced File System Management Chapter 9 : Monitoring Server Performance	Activity 6-6 Activity 9-1 Activity 9-2 Activity 9-3 Activity 9-4 Activity 9-6
Monitor and optimize a server environment for application performance. • Monitor memory performance objects • Monitor network performance objects • Monitor process performance objects • Monitor disk performance objects	Chapter 9 : Monitoring Server Performance	Activity 9-5 Activity 9-7

Managing and Implementing Disaster Recovery

A

Objective	Chapter: Section	Hands-on Activity
Perform system recovery for a server • Implement Automated System Recovery (ASR) • Restore data from shadow copy volumes • Back up files and System State data to media • Configure security for backup operations	Chapter 10: Managing and Implementing Backups and Disaster Recovery	Activity 10-4 Activity 10-5 Activity 10-6 Activity 10-10
Manage backup procedures • Verify the successful completion of backup jobs • Manage backup storage media	Chapter 10: Managing and Implementing Backups and Disaster Recovery	Activity 10-1
Recover from server hardware failure	Chapter 10: Managing and Implementing Backups and Disaster Recovery	Discussed in Chapter 10
Restore backup data	Chapter 10: Managing and Implementing Backups and Disaster Recovery	Activity 10-2

Objective	Chapter: Section	Hands-on Activity
Schedule backup jobs	Chapter 10: Managing and Implementing Backups and Disaster Recovery	Activity 10-3

APPENDIX
B

DETAILED LAB SETUP GUIDE

HARWARE

Classroom PCs should be configured as follows:

- Pentium 233–MHz processor or faster
- At least 128 MB of RAM
- At least 1.5 GB of available hard disk space
- CD-RW or DVD-RW drive
- Keyboard and mouse or some other compatible pointing device
- Video adapter and monitor with Super VGA (800 × 600) or higher resolution
- Sound card for the Instructor PC
- Self powered/amplified speakers for the Instructor PC
- Internal or external fax/modem
- Ethernet network interface controller
- 3.5–inch disk drive
- An Ethernet hub or switch with at least as many ports as there are PCs in the classroom
- One twisted–pair, Category 5 straight–through cable per PC

Other equipment that may be needed:

- An additional Instructor PC to act as an additional domain controller
- A generic printer

Consumable items that students should bring to class:

- Five blank CD-R disks
- Five blank 3.5–inch disks

SOFTWARE

The following software is needed:

- Microsoft Windows Server 2003 Enterprise Edition operating system (one CD media per student)
- Adobe Acrobat Reader (version 4 or later)
- Latest version of Software Update Services (SUS) (*www.microsoft.com/windows serversystem/sus*)
- Microsoft Virtual PC (*www.microsoft.com/windows/virtualpc*) (optional)

Setup Instructions

To work on the material in this book, students need to have administrative privileges over their respective PCs. In a classroom setting, students should have the freedom to make administrative-level configuration errors. Normally such errors can render a PC unbootable or otherwise unusable for participation in the classroom. However, a student's mistakes should never impede completion of lab assignments. In this light, the lab should have a data recovery system and working backups that are both easy to use and reliable.

The most straightforward method of data recovery is the reinstallation of the operating system from the Microsoft factory CDs. However, having to reinstall the operating system from the factory CD every time a student corrupts his or her system can be time consuming and frustrating. There are no activities in the book that go over a Windows Server 2003 install. This leaves some flexibility for the instructor to decide how the students should install Windows Server 2003. Therefore, to ensure rapid and reliable data recovery, consider the following guidelines when setting up the lab:

- Microsoft's Virtual PC provides quick access to an operating system from a previous state. The ability to use undoable disks gives students the opportunity to restore their computers to the state before the lab. Students must Save State in Virtual PC after each successful lab. Virtual PC is very resource intensive and the student computers should exceed the hardware requirements if used.

- If using an imaging product, such as Norton Ghost, a single image file that contains all of the data stored on the reference installation is created. This image file even contains the partition table of the hard disk drive along with the master boot record. Restoring data from such an image brings the machine back to its original state at the time the backup was created.

- When creating a reference image file, it is important to remember that the image file will be an exact copy of the reference PC's hard disk drive. This means that data such as NetBIOS computer names and SIDs (security identifiers) are preserved as they were on the reference PC. This also means that unless further steps are taken, all PCs that are imaged from this reference image will have the *same* NetBIOS computer name, SIDs, and perhaps even IP address (if the IP addresses are set up statically). However, you do *not* want a classroom where all the PCs have the same NetBIOS name or IP address because such duplication can cause conflicts throughout the class. You may be able to get away with all the SIDs being the same for a while, but this should not be a permanent state. You especially do not want identical SIDs in an environment that employs Active Directory domains.

- To make a classroom of uniquely identifiable PCs, utilities such as Microsoft sysprep, Norton Ghost Walker, or REMBO Toolkit (the NTChangeName command) may be executed on each PC. The easiest to use is Ghost Walker; it is an MS-DOS program that not only changes the NetBIOS computer name but also creates a randomly generated SID in one easy step. If you don't feel the need to change the SID, you can manually change the NetBIOS name by simply right-clicking the My Computer icon, clicking Properties, clicking the Computer

Name tab, clicking the Change button, and typing the desired NetBIOS computer name in the Computer name field. Click OK when finished.

Keep the following in mind if imaging or Virtual PC is not available:

- The instructor needs to decide on the following key points and make them available to all students during their installs:
  - Computer naming convention
  - IP addressing (default gateways, DNS, and WINS, if necessary)
  - Workgroup/domain names
- Students should install Windows Server 2003 Enterprise Edition from the CD.

C

EXPANDED CHAPTER SUMMARIES

Chapter 1 Summary

Windows Server 2003 has four editions that are targeted for different roles. They are the Web, Standard, Enterprise, and Datacenter Editions.

Web Edition is optimized to run Web applications and for hosting multiple Web sites on Internet Information Services 6.0. It is a more cost-effective solution than all other editions of the Windows Server 2003 family. A major feature that is missing from Web Edition is that you cannot configure it as a domain controller.

Standard Edition is the next step up from Web Edition. It includes all of the features that you get from Web Edition with the addition of Active Directory and other critical services that can be installed. Microsoft has targeted small to midsized businesses to use Standard Edition for File and Print services and even as Active Directory domain controllers. It is critical that you know what type of hardware you can put into a server running Standard Edition. Standard Edition can have a total of four physical processors and up to 4 GB of RAM.

Enterprise Edition is geared for midsized to large companies looking for servers that require additional hardware and better reliability. It includes all of the features from Standard Edition and adds the capability of 8-node clustering. That feature alone makes this operating system a more reliable one. Enterprise Edition supports up to eight physical processors and a maximum of 32 GB of RAM. The minimum system requirements for Enterprise Edition are exactly the same as Standard Edition.

The Web, Standard, and Enterprise Editions all have the same system requirements. Here are the minimum system requirements for the main system components:

- *Processor*—133 MHz
- *RAM*—128 MB
- *Disk space*—1.5 GB

The Datacenter Edition is designed for mission-critical applications and large databases. It includes the features from the previous editions. Datacenter Edition can support up to 32 processors and an amazing 64 GB of RAM. Here are the minimum system requirements for the main system components:

- *Processor*—400 MHz
- *RAM*—512 MB
- *Disk space*—1.5 GB

Windows Server 2003 was built to work within a network and to be able to communicate with other computers. There are two choices for how your server interacts with networks: workgroups or domains. Workgroups are great if you have a small number of computers that need to share resources. The one big problem in a workgroup is that each computer stores its own Security Accounts Manager (SAM). Accounts are stored in the SAM database, which means if you want to have an account for all the computers in your workgroup, you have to

C

create one on each local computer. The other option is to join your computer to a domain or create your own Active Directory domain. This way, all of the accounts are stored in a centralized database called Active Directory that runs on your Windows Server 2003 server. Having the accounts stored in this manner allows for centralized management.

Windows Server 2003 can be configured as either a member server or a domain controller. Member servers are part of a domain and provide key services such as file, print, application, RRAS, and DNS. Domain controllers provide authentication for clients within a domain. It is very common to have domain controllers function in other roles that a member server would take. Web Edition is the only server that cannot become a domain controller. To promote a server to a domain controller, run the Active Directory Wizard.

A big part of a network administrator job is to manage and maintain the server hardware, as in adding new expansion cards to configuring fault tolerance through a Redundant Array of Independent Disks (RAID). Another common task would be to manage user and group accounts. Tasks such as creating new users, modifying existing users, and resetting passwords are not uncommon. By managing groups, an administrator can add users to groups to assign them permissions to resources and to grant them system rights.

An administrator can make resources, such as folders and printers, available over the network by sharing them. To properly secure shared resources, an administrator needs to assign permissions locally and remotely. Terminal Services allows users to connect to remote servers to access applications.

When a server needs monitoring, there are several tools available. One of those tools, System Monitor, allows an administrator to compare results against a baseline. Event Viewer, which is another tool, is the primary logging feature in Windows Server 2003. By applying patches and security updates, you can help secure your servers. The Software Update Service allows for centralized management of updates. The Backup utility allows an administrator to create new backups and restore old ones.

Active Directory domains contain objects such as users, computers, and printers. As an Active Directory administrator, you will be creating many of the objects within your domain.

Every object that is created in Active Directory has additional attributes that are associated with it. For example, a User object has attributes such as First Name, Middle Initial, Last Name, Address, Home Phone, and Manager. These objects and attributes are defined in what is known as the Active Directory schema.

Active Directory gives you the ability to logically organize your objects in what are known as organizational units (OUs). You place objects such as user accounts in these OUs. You can create your OU structure based on location, departments, or any other combination. These objects may initially seem like folders to you, but as your knowledge expands, you will see that they also have a crucial role in the management of your users and computers within Group Policy.

A powerful feature that senior-level Active Directory administrators will enforce is delegation. They delegate control of certain tasks, such as resetting passwords, to OU admins. That way, those OU admins can reset passwords for the users within the OU over which they have been granted control.

Trees and forests are also part of the logical structure of Active Directory. A tree is one or more domains with a contiguous namespace. A forest is one or more domains that have a noncontiguous namespace. The first domain you create in Active Directory is known as your forest root domain.

When users of a domain want to search for attributes in Active Directory, they search a domain controller with a special role known as the global catalog. Using the global catalog is much like dialing 411 to look for a phone number. If you want to look for users with last names that started with "McC," you would put that text into your search. The global catalog would perform the query.

Your network infrastructure is something that you must plan accordingly. You will be configuring Active Directory sites to conform to your current networks. Try to remember these two facts about sites: a site is one or more well-connected IP networks, and a site can have more than one network, but a network can be a member of only one Active Directory site.

CHAPTER 2 SUMMARY

Each user account has dozens of attributes (also known as properties) that you can configure. Some of the common properties you may configure are group membership, profile settings, account settings, and address information.

The main tool you use to manage users accounts is called Active Directory Users and Computers. Every user account has properties that can be configured, and certain applications can add additional properties. These tabs can include a lot of additional information about the user, such as office location, telephone number, address, group membership, and terminal services settings—to name just a few.

Authentication is needed to grant users access to resources in an Active Directory environment. A user must log on with a valid user account and password. In a domain environment, this user account and password exists in Active Directory; however, in a workgroup, it is stored in the Security Accounts Manager (SAM) database. When a user logs on to a computer using the Log On to Windows dialog box, the logon is considered interactive authentication. If a user decides to connect to a network resource, the user uses network authentication.

Users who log on to an Active Directory domain use an authentication protocol called Kerberos v5. Kerberos v5 is a protocol that provides authentication services for computers in an Active Directory domain. Only computers running Windows 2000, Windows XP, and Windows 2003 can use Kerberos. This authentication protocol is an improvement in security from what NT domains used, which was either NTLM or NTLM v2. The NTLM authentication protocol is used by down-level clients running Windows NT 4.0 and Windows 9x.

The first time a user logs on to a computer, he or she creates a new user profile based on the Default User profile. A user profile stores settings specific to that user and includes the following:

- Application data
- Desktop settings
- Favorites
- Cookies

- Desktop
- Start menu

When the user logs off, those changes the user has made are saved to his or her unique profile, which is stored in the C:\Documents and Settings folder. This profile is known as a local profile and is stored only on that machine.

Users of domain accounts can have their profiles follow them from computer to computer. These profiles are called roaming profiles and are set up within the Domain Account properties. This allows for centralized backups of user profiles. The first time a user logs on to a computer with a roaming profile, the profile is copied to the local machine. Any changes that are made are then copied back to the server when the user logs off.

Administrators can force all the domain accounts to fit a specific profile by forcing the use of a mandatory profile. Administrators can create one by modifying an existing roaming profile. To create a mandatory profile, you need to change the name of the ntuser.dat file to ntuser.man. When you do this, users who get this profile can make changes, but the next time they log on, those changes revert to whatever was set up by the administrator.

Active Directory Users and Computers is available on the Administrative Tools menu, or you can add it to a custom MMC. The version that comes with Server 2003 is slightly different than the version that came with Windows 2000. This version gives you the ability to drag and drop, and it gives you a node called Saved Queries. This node allows administrators to quickly search for objects based on specific settings.

If you have been tasked with creating user accounts that have many of the same account properties, you should consider using a template account. A template account is a user account that you can create and configure with common attributes. With the templates feature, if you had 10 accounts that needed to be created for new sales employees, you would first create a sales template. In that template, you would define all the groups in which these new users would exist. As a best practice, you should start the name of this account with a symbol such as an underscore. When you do this, the template account is always going to be listed first in Active Directory Users and Computers and be easy to find. Now all you have to do is right-click your template account and select Copy. This requests a new user name and password and then copies most of the settings from the template account.

Windows Server 2003 has added command-line tools so that you can easily script accounts through the command line. The new command-line tools are:

- *DSADD*—Adds objects
- *DSMOD*—Modifies objects
- *DSQUERY*—Queries for objects
- *DSMOVE*—Moves objects
- *DSRM*—Deletes objects

You can also take advantage of bulk importing and exporting of accounts. The two supported formats are LDIFDE and CSVDE.

All accounts that you create follow certain guidelines set up in the domain account policy. Account policies include settings on user account passwords, such as the length, age, and complexity. Account Policies also define settings that lock out users from logging on to an account after a specified number of invalid logon attempts. Finally, your account policy helps with the configuration of your Kerberos settings. All of these account policies are defined in the default domain group policy and must be configured at the domain level for domain accounts. You can also set up auditing to check for the success or failure of an event such as account logons. The results of auditing are stored in the security log in Event Viewer.

CHAPTER 3 SUMMARY

A group is an object that you use to organize other objects, such as users, computers, contacts, or other groups. Groups sometimes seem like the same thing as OUs, but they are very different from each other. With groups, you can assign permissions to resources; you cannot do that with OUs. With OUs, you can link group policies, but you cannot link a group policy to a group.

There are two types of groups that you can create in an Active Directory domain: security groups and distribution groups. These two types have very different uses and should be used appropriately. Security groups are the most popular types of groups because they give you the ability to have a Security Identifier (SID) that can be assigned to resources. Thus, when you have a group that needs to be granted access to a folder, you create that group as a security group. In addition, a security group can be used as an e-mail entity. This means you could send an e-mail to that group, and it would be delivered to all of the members. Distribution groups can be used only as e-mail entities.

Once you decide the type of group you want to create, you then need to decide what type of scope this group will have. There are three group scopes from which to choose:

- Global
- Domain local
- Universal

Global groups are created for organizing users, computers, and other groups. Thus, when you have users that belong to the same department, you should create a global group and place those users into that global group. The membership of a global group is limited to user accounts only from its domain. If your Active Directory is in native mode, then you can also nest global groups into other global groups from the domain.

Domain local groups are primarily used for assigning permissions to resources such as files, folders, or printers. As their name states, they are local to their domain and can be assigned permissions only for resources in their domain. A domain local group can have users,

computers, and global groups as members while in mixed mode. If you increase your domain mode from mixed mode to anything higher, such as native mode, you could have other domain local groups and universal groups as members.

Universal groups are primarily used in a multiple domain forest in which administrators want to aggregate users or other groups. You can use universal groups only while your domain is in native or Windows Server 2003 functional level. Universal groups can be members of domain local and other universal groups from any domain that is trusted. In addition, universal groups can have global, domain local, and universal groups—as well as users and computers—as members. Universal groups should be used with caution because certain membership changes with them increase your global catalog replication traffic. To cut down on this, make sure to place groups—and not individual user accounts—inside your universal group.

The primary tool used to create groups is called Active Directory Users and Computers. Using Active Directory Users and Computer, you can also manage group memberships and alter properties. If a group is accidentally created as the wrong group scope, it can be easily converted to another, as follows:

- Global to universal
- Domain local to universal
- Universal to global
- Universal to domain local

As with user accounts, you can also use the DSADD command utility to create new group objects. You can also manage groups by using these additional command-line utilities:

- *DSMOD*—Modifies objects
- *DSQUERY*—Queries for objects
- *DSMOVE—Moves objects*
- *DSRM*—Removes objects

Microsoft has included a number of groups that you can use for specific rights and tasks. These are known as built-in groups and you can find them in the Builtin container or the Users container. You can add users to these groups instead of creating a new group that does the same task if there is a task you want them to be able to accomplish.

Of course, there may be times where you have to create a new group and give it specific permissions because there is no default group. As an example of creating a custom group, consider that Backup Operators is a default group that gives members the right not only to back up files and folders but also the right to restore files. If you need a group that does only backups and another that does only restores, you would do better to create two new groups, assign those rights to the groups, and then add members to those groups.

Computers running Windows NT, 2000, XP, and 2003 all need valid computer accounts in your Active Directory domain. You can create these computer accounts much the same way you have created users and groups—with Active Directory Users and Computers or DSADD.

CHAPTER 4 SUMMARY

One of an administrator's most important jobs is to manage access to resources. For the most part, the management of those resources concerns access to files and folders over the network. Your primary task will be to ensure that users, groups, or computers have been granted the appropriate permissions to resources they access.

The FAT file system was developed long ago to support DOS. FAT was included in Windows Server 2003 only for backward compatibility and has some very serious limitations, such as no folder- or file-level security. It also supports volumes only up to 4 GB.

FAT32 is an enhancement that was released with Windows 95 OSR2 that overcame the 4 GB limitation and bumped this limitation up to 2 TB in Windows Server 2003. There is still no file- or folder-level security with FAT32.

NTFS was released with Windows NT 4.0 and has evolved to the version that is included with Windows Server 2003. This version supports volumes up to 16 EB, file- and folder-level security, quotas, and compression.

When you want to make a folder accessible over a network, you need to share an existing folder. This allows others to see that folder when they access your computer over the network.

You can create shared folders by using multiple methods, but the two most common methods are through Windows Explorer or the Computer Management console. With either method, the share name does not have to match the name of the folder; however, you will want to keep a couple of best practices in mind when you create a share:

- Older clients may have a difficult time connecting to names that are longer than 8.3 characters.

- You should make the name intuitive for users to connect.

- If you have a share that you want to keep hidden from users, you must append a $ to the share name. This makes it hidden to all users, including administrators, so you need to make sure that you remember the share name. Even though it is hidden, you still need to assign the appropriate permissions.

When you create a shared folder, users must connect to that share through a Universal Naming Convention (UNC) path. A UNC is a string of text that you type into the Run dialog box. UNC paths allow you to connect to a computer that has shares. You could also just connect with the computer name. Connecting in this manner would show you a list of all the shares on that computer. Remember that you must have the appropriate permissions to access those resources.

Shared folders have a simple set of permissions, as follows:

- Read
- Change
- Full Control

Share permissions apply only to shared folders and take effect only over the network. If you want to secure local files and folders and lock down access to resources over the network even more, you have to use NTFS permissions. NTFS has standard and special permissions. The standard permissions are as follows:

- Full Control
- Modify
- Read & Execute
- List Folder Contents (only on folders)
- Read
- Write
- Special Permissions

As an administrator, you have the ability to grant users, groups, or even computers access to specific files and folders stored on that computer. The special NTFS permissions are just subsets of the standard permissions. For example, Read is more than just read. There are special NTFS permissions that combine to make the Read permission. The special NTFS permissions that make up the Read permission are read attributes and read extended attributes.

Determining effective permissions to a resource is critical to resource administration. If you are a user in multiple groups who has been granted shared folder permission, then your effective permission is those cumulative shared permissions. The same goes for NTFS. If you are a member of multiple groups that have each been granted different access, then you just add up the permissions for the groups of which your account is a member. There is one exception to this rule: deny overwrites all other permissions.

On each file or folder that is created on an NTFS volume, you can use the Effective Permission tab. On this tab, you enter a user or group for whom you would like to see the effective permission. Note that this shows only the effective *NTFS* permission. When you have a shared folder that has both NTFS and shared folder permissions, it gets a little bit more difficult to find out the effective permission. The effective permission to that resource is going to be the permission that is common between the NTFS and shared folder permissions. For example, if you have Full Control as a shared permission and Read as an NTFS permission, then your effective permission is Read. You get this result because Read is also part of Full Control, and the permission that is common between the two types of permissions is Read.

CHAPTER 5 SUMMARY

Traditionally, operating systems use basic disks for storage. With basic disks, you can create partitions. There are two types of partitions: primary or extended. A primary partition can be marked active, which means that you can boot an operating system from it. You are limited to four primary partitions per system. If you need to have more than four partitions, then you have to create extended partitions. Extended partitions cannot be marked as active, and you must create logical drives inside extended partitions.

By default, when you install Windows Server 2003, it installs into a single partition, which is the C: drive. During the setup, you have the option to change where Windows Server 2003 is going to be installed. The default directory is C:\Windows. This directory is called the boot partition, and it contains system files. The root of the C:\ drive is known as the system partition, and it contains boot files.

Windows Server 2003 also has support for what are known as dynamic disks. These are the same type of disks as basic disks, except Windows Server 2003 views them differently. For a disk to become a dynamic disk, you must convert the entire disk through the Disk Management tool.

With dynamic disks, you are able to create three types of volumes. The tools that you use to manage these volumes are either the Disk Management MMC or the command-line utility DISKPART. The Windows Server 2003 supported volumes are as follows:

- Simple
- Spanned
- Striped

A simple volume is a single area of space that is formatted on a dynamic disk. This truly is the simplest and easiest type of volume to create. If the volume is formatted with NTFS, then you can extend it in the future if you need additional space. However, you cannot extend a simple volume that is either the boot or system partition.

Spanned volumes contain between two and thirty-two dynamic disks that are treated as a single volume. Collectively, they are used to create a larger volume than the actual size of any single dynamic disk. The spanned volume fills up disk space one disk at a time. Just as with simple volumes, you can extend spanned volumes on NTFS partitions only. If one of your spanned volumes fails, then there is no fault tolerance feature that allows users to still connect and access data on the spanned volume. For that reason, do not place mission-critical data on spanned volumes.

Striped volumes are also known as RAID level 0. Unlike every other type of RAID volume, this one provides no fault tolerance. A striped volume contains between two and thirty-two physical hard disks. The striped volume appears as one volume; however, unlike spanned volumes, a striped volume stripes data across all disks evenly. Because of the striping, your disk performance increases for both reads and writes. Be aware that stripe sets provide no fault tolerance, so do not place mission-critical data on them.

The most common tool used for disk management is the Disk Management tool that resides inside the Computer Management console. Disk Management allows you to perform these management tasks:

- Manage disk properties
- Create new partitions and volumes
- Extend NTFS volumes
- Mount drives

Windows Server 2003 has the ability to support fault-tolerant drives. This is done through what is known as Redundant Array of Independent Disks (RAID). Windows Server 2003 can use software- or hardware-based RAID solutions. Windows Server 2003 supports only RAID 0, 1, and 5 for software-based solutions.

Striped volumes are known as RAID level 0 and provide no fault tolerance. They can be used to reduce the amount of wear on disks and increase disk performance. A minimum of two disks is needed.

A mirrored volume is a combination of two dynamic disks. One of the disks is the primary disk that is used by the system and users, and the other is used as a backup. Every time you write something to the primary disk, it mirrors that information on the other disk. Mirrored volumes are known as RAID level 1 and *do* provide fault tolerance. Mirrored volumes are a great place to install the system and boot partitions for a Windows Server 2003 server.

Stripe sets with parity are known as RAID level 5. They contain anywhere from three to thirty-two dynamic disks. They function much like stripe sets in that they stripe data across drives evenly. The big difference is that they also stripe parity information that can be used to rebuild data if one of the drives fails.

Disk management includes checking the health of disks. Status messages appear in the Disk Management tool to help show if there are any problems with disks. Common status messages you may encounter for volumes are as follows:

- Failed
- Failed Redundancy
- Formatting
- Healthy
- Regenerating
- Resyncing
- Unknown

Besides the Disk Management tool, there are several other command-line tools that allow you to perform disk management tasks. For instance, Check Disk allows you to scan a disk for bad sectors. The Convert command-line tool converts FAT16 or FAT32 partitions or volumes to NTFS. Disk Cleanup removes temporary and unnecessary files. Over time, as

data is written to a disk, it eventually becomes fragmented. Windows Server 2003 includes a built-in disk defragmenter that can organize data that is stored on the disk. DISKPART allows administrators to create and extend volumes and partitions, import disks, and much more. You also can use the FORMAT command to format disks. FSUTIL is a command-line utility that gathers information about disks. MOUNTVOL is a tool that allows an administrator to use the command line to create mount points.

CHAPTER 6 SUMMARY

Each file and folder stored on a disk has attributes that can be configured. One of those attributes is the read-only attribute. As the name of this attribute implies, it makes all the files or folders with that attribute read-only. On a FAT volume, this can easily be unchecked because there is no local security for the FAT file system.

The archive attribute allows administrators to mark a file or folder as changed. When certain backups run, the backup program checks to see if a file has changed by looking at its archived attribute.

The system attribute is commonly used with the hidden attribute. The hidden attribute marks files or folders as hidden. With this attribute checked, normal users cannot see the files or folders and so are unable to harm them. When both of these attributes are checked, they can be an effective way to hide files and folders. Even if you select that you want to view hidden files in the Folder Options dialog box, they remain hidden. You must also choose to view system files be able to view the hidden files. So, in effect, using both the hidden and system attribute is like a doubly hidden attribute.

Windows Server 2003 supports advanced attributes. If an administrator wants to configure the archive attribute for a file or folder, it can be done within the advanced attributes. The advanced attributes is also where an administrator can go to index a file to help with searches. Windows Server 2003 also has the ability to compress files and folders. By using compression, you can save some space on your servers. This option is available only on volumes formatted with NTFS. Once you compress a file or folder, the text used for the name is displayed as blue instead of the default black.

There are two rules to remember when moving and copying files and folders:

- Moving a file or folder in the same volume retains the file or folder's attributes.
- Every other operation inherits the permission of its new parent folder.

These two rules work not only with the compression attribute, but also with NTFS permissions and EFS.

You can secure file and folder resources by using NTFS permissions, but there are times when an additional layer of security is needed. Consider this situation: You travel frequently with a laptop and you store sensitive documents on it. Laptops can easily be misplaced or stolen, and there are third-party tools that can be used to bypass NTFS security if someone were to gain

physical access to the disk. Fortunately, Encrypting File System (EFS) can be used to add the additional layer of security needed. EFS encrypts the file or folder with a special session key known as a file encryption key (FEK). Once the encryption is done, the FEK is copied to a secured area on the file header called the data decryption field (DDF). That DDF is also encrypted by the user's public key. The entire encryption/decryption process is transparent to the user except when a user initially configures a file or folder for EFS.

When a user wants to decrypt the encrypted file or folder, he or she opens up the folder normally. However, it is a completely different story behind the scenes. Windows Server 2003 uses his or her private key to unlock the data recovery field (DRF). Depending on how the administrator sets up the DRF policy, that policy may automatically include the domain administrator account for recovery purposes. With the administrator added to the DRF, an administrator can always recover data that has been encrypted by any user.

Windows Server 2003 includes the option for users to add other users' private keys into the DDF. This is a common method for sharing access to an encrypted file or folder. In this way, only the users who were included can decrypt the file or folder. EFS and NTFS compression are mutually exclusive of each other, so you cannot encrypt *and* compress a file.

NTFS also allows you to limit how much space users can utilize on your file servers. This feature is called disk quotas and can be a lifesaver on file servers. You can assign disk quotas only to user accounts and not to groups. This can make it a little more difficult to set up for a large domain. You set this up per volume and not per disk. You can also set it up to warn users when they are getting close to their limits.

Another valuable feature of Windows Server 2003 for file servers is the distributed file system (DFS). DFS allows administrators to have multiple shared folders from multiple servers appear as if they are all under the same share hierarchy. There are two DFS models that you can configure. Standalone DFS provides no fault tolerance, and everything is stored on one server. Domain-based DFS stores information in Active Directory and can be configured to point to multiple copies of the shared folder to provided fault tolerance. This makes it extremely easy to perform maintenance on a file server because users are redirected to another server that has the same resources available.

CHAPTER 7 SUMMARY

Printing is an extremely important part of an administrator's responsibilities in almost every organization. There are few aspects of the job as widespread as printing. The first step in understanding printing in Windows is to understand Microsoft's perspective on terminology. The following are some of the most common terms encountered and their meanings:

- *Print device*—A print device is the actual hardware used for printing documents. There are two general types of print devices: a local print device, which is directly connected to a port on the print server or workstation, and a network print device, which connects to a print server through its network adapter.

C

- *Printer*—This is the software interface between the hardware print device and the user. It is configurable and controls the connection to the print device.

- *Print driver*—These are files that are used by Windows Server 2003 to send a raw print job to the print device in a language it understands. These are hardware specific, designed for a specific print device based on its model.

- *Print server*—This is a computer with one or more print devices connected to it, and which acts as a central server where end users can send print jobs.

- *Print client*—This is the computer that sends a job to the print device.

It is important to have an efficient printing environment. Such an environment would have the following:

- *One or more computers designated as print servers*—Both Windows Server 2003 and Windows XP Professional can act as a print server; however, Windows XP Professional has a limitation of 10 simultaneous client connections. This makes Windows XP a poor choice as a print server in most network environments.

- *Sufficient space on the hard drive for the print server*—Setting up print jobs for printing can be disk-space intensive; therefore, plenty of hard drive space is needed, preferably on a drive where the operating system files are not located. The space is used to queue and buffer documents in preparation to be sent to the print device.

- *Sufficient RAM beyond that of the minimum Windows Server 2003 requirements*—This allows a server to handle large jobs with greater ease; otherwise, several large print jobs may negatively impact the server's performance.

From a user's perspective, the printing process is fairly straightforward and can be initiated by a single press of a button. However, the actual process behind the scenes is much more complicated:

1. A print file is created by a software application on the print client.

2. The software communicates with the Windows graphics device interface (GDI) during creation of the print file. The GDI integrates characteristics of the print job—colors, fonts, and embedded graphics—with information provided by the print driver installed on the client for the target printer. This process is referred to as rendering.

3. The file is formatted with control codes that allow special graphics, fonts, and color information to be printed. The application places the print file in the client's spooler, which is a subfolder used for spooling.

4. The client's remote print provider uses a remote procedure call to the network print server where the file is being delivered. If the print server responds and is ready to accept the file, the remote printer sends the file to the Server service on the server.

5. The network print server has four different processing elements that receive and process a print file. These are the router, print provider, print processor, and print monitor. They are all pieces of the network print server's spooler.

6. The Server service calls its router, the Print Spooler service, once the remote print provider at the client contacts it. The router then directs the print file to the print provider, which stores it in a spool file until it can be sent to the printer.

7. The print provider works with the print processor to ensure that the file is formatted to use the right data type, such as TEXT or RAW, while the file is spooled.

8. When the spool file is fully formatted for transmission to the printer, the print monitor pulls it from the spooler's disk storage and sends it to the printer.

A printer can be added as a local device. This may require administrative privileges, depending on your network. This is most easily accomplished using the Add Printer Wizard.

Printers can also be network devices. When they are network devices, printers can use TCP/IP, and network print devices can include their own network card. To add network devices, you can use the Add Printer Wizard. When adding a printer, you define the Standard TCP/IP Port option with the TCP/IP address of the network device. Print jobs can then be sent directly to the print device.

The following printer permissions can be set to manage a user's control over specific printers:

- *Print*—This permission permits connection to a printer, the printing of documents, and the editing of a user's own print jobs. The Everyone group has this permission by default.

- *Manage Documents*—This permission grants all capabilities of the Print permission, plus it allows the controlling of document print jobs for all users. The Creator Owner group has this permission by default.

- *Manage Printers*—This permission grants all the capabilities of Print and Manage Documents. In addition, it allows sharing, modification, and deletion of printers and their properties. The Administrators, Print Operators, and Server Operators groups have this permission by default.

- *Special Permissions*—This permission is similar to NTFS special permissions. Special permissions allows a granular level of control over printer security, including controlling user ownership of a printer, viewing printer permissions, and changing printer permissions.

A printer pool consists of a single printer that is connected to a number of print devices. The advantage of a printer pool is that it allows many physical print devices to function as a single logical printer, thus providing better document distribution in high-volume environments while reducing the time that users must wait for documents to print.

C

Printer priorities allow you to grant some groups of users a higher priority to a print device than other users. For example, you may want to configure your print environment to give precedence to any printouts from the CEO of the company, even if there are other documents already ahead of the CEO's documents in the print queue.

If you need to manage your environment through scripts, the following are provided for you:

- *Prncnfg.vbs*—This file either configures a printer or displays configuration information about a printer.

- *Prndrvr.vbs*—This script can add, delete, or list printer drivers.

- *Prnjobs.vbs*—This script allows you to view existing print jobs. It can also pause, resume, and cancel jobs that are in the queue.

- *Prnmngr.vbs*—This script is used to add, delete, or list printers and related connections. It also can set a printer as default.

- *Prnport.vbs*—This script allows standard TCP/IP ports to be shown. In addition, you can create or delete ports, or change their current configurations.

- *Prnqctl.vbs*—This script allows you to pause or resume a printer, cancel all of the jobs currently queued for a printer, or print a test page.

The print spooler stores the spooled print jobs on the hard drive. By default, this location is in the WINDOWS\system32\spool\PRINTERS folder. You may need to change this location if the print server handles several print jobs. Ideally, it should be moved away from the Windows operating system files.

To make printers easy to locate in Active Directory, they can be published. This process adds information regarding the printer into Active Directory so that users can find it by searching.

Windows Server 2003 simplifies managing printers and enables you to effectively manage your printing environment. Through permissions, printer pools, priorities, and command-line utilities, there are a variety of ways for you to effectively manage and deploy print servers in your Windows environment.

CHAPTER 8 SUMMARY

Windows Server 2003 supports Group Policy Objects. GPOs are an Active Directory feature, so they are available only in a domain environment. When used effectively, group policies enhance an administrator's ability to manage the network and its policies. Group policies can be thought of as groups of policies, or rules, that can be applied to user accounts. User accounts with similar management needs can be grouped together in an organizational unit, or OU. Then, a GPO can be applied to the OU, defining sets of rules for objects, such as user or computer accounts, contained in the OU.

A Group Policy Object (GPO) is used to configure and apply policy settings for user and computer objects. It performs a variety of administrative tasks, including:

- Configuring a user's desktop settings using predefined templates
- Controlling desktop and domain security settings for users and workstations
- Creating and assigning scripts that run for particular users and computers during logging, starting up, or shutting down
- Redirecting folders, such as the My Documents folder, to a network location
- Automating the distribution of software and its maintenance to computers throughout the network

Group policies can also contain multiple categories. The policies controllable by a GPO can be broken into the following three categories:

- *Software settings*—These centralize software installation maintenance and management, including the installation, upgrading, and uninstallation of applications.
- *Windows settings*—These settings are for the management of scripts, security settings, Internet Explorer settings, and other features such as Remote Installation Services and folder redirection.
- *Administrative templates*—These enable defining registry-based settings to configure application and user desktop settings. Additional settings include those granting access to operating system components, Control Panel settings, and offline file configuration.

When a GPO is created, it can be located in two main locations. The first location is a Group Policy container (GPC). This is an Active Directory container located in the Active Directory Users and Computers console. The second is the Group Policy template (GPT). The template contains all the settings, administrative templates, security settings, software installation settings, and scripts. Note that the configuration file Registry.pol stores the registry changes. A configuration file defines settings for both users and computers. The template is stored in the Sysvol folder, which is located under the %systemroot%\Sysvol\ <*Domain Name*>\Policies folder.

GPOs can define a variety of settings. Administrators can assign a group policy to multiple locations, such as the local computer, site, domain, and OUs. Group policies have two main categories: computer configuration and user configuration.

Active Directory applies group policies as the computer starts up. The process of applying Group Policy is as follows:

1. A Windows 2000, Windows XP, or Windows Server 2003 computer in a domain boots and queries the domain controller for a list of GPOs that apply to it. The domain controller checks the GPOs to find policies that apply to the computer. Policies that are executed on the computer include the computer settings and startup scripts.

C

2. The domain controller gives clients the list of GPOs that apply to the client in the order that the GPOs must be processed. The client contacts the domain controller and pulls down the Group Policy templates from the Sysvol share. Next, it applies the settings and runs the scripts.

3. At user logon, the process is repeated, except that this time user settings are processed and user policy settings, such as scripts and software policies, are applied.

When editing GPOs, the manageable settings are broken down into nodes. These nodes are applicable to policies set at the domain and OU levels. The node functions are as follows:

- *Local Policies*—These apply settings to the local account database of the workstation or server.

- *Event Log*—These settings set configuration settings for event log size, retention period, and access restrictions.

- *Restricted Groups*—These settings grant the administrator the ability to control who is a member of any security group.

- *System Services*—These allow an administrator control over service startup mode, disabling of a service, permissions to edit the service mode, and auditing of the service.

- *Registry*—This group of settings sets security and auditing access control list (ACL) settings for registry keys and subkeys.

- *File System*—These manage and maintain NTFS permissions and auditing permissions for any folder or file listed in the policy. To be effective, the files or folders must reside on an NTFS partition.

- *Wireless Network (IEEE 802.11) Policies*—These policies define settings that govern wireless networks, including to which wireless networks a client can connect, whether access points should be used, and the data encryption settings used.

- *Public Key Policies*—These options govern configuration settings for different public key-based applications. These include the encrypting file system (EFS), as well as certificate autoenrollment settings and certificate authority (CA) trusts.

- *Software Restriction Policies*—These settings control software deployment. They include the ability to manually define which file extensions are considered executable, control security settings of software-related registry paths, and override software settings from other GPOs.

- *IP Security Policies on Active Directory*—These define different IP security settings based on the role of a server or workstation; three default policies exist, but none are applied by default.

Other options include the capability to force storage of user documents to a server. This option enables an administrator to ensure that documents are properly backed up. This policy is known as folder redirection. It is a Group Policy feature that enables you to redirect the following contents of a user's profile to a network location:

- Application data
- Desktop
- My Documents
- Start menu

Because Group Policy can be applied at multiple levels, it is important to understand the processing order of group policies. In a Windows 2000, Windows XP, or Windows Server 2003 computer, GPOs are applied in the following order:

1. Local computer
2. Site
3. Domain
4. Parent OU
5. Child OU

Note the following:

- If you do not want any of the higher-level settings to be applied to a particular child container, then check the Block Policy inheritance check box on the Group Policy tab for the container properties.
- If a conflict exists between policies at different levels, the last policy implemented applies. However, this behavior can be modified by blocking the inheritance of policies and by using the No Override option.
- If you want a particular GPO's settings to always be enforced, you can configure the policy using the No Override option.

Group Policy also includes the ability to install software across the network. This is done using a Microsoft Windows installer package (MSI). If an MSI package is not available, a ZAP file, created with a tool such as WinINSTALL, can be used.

Deployment can be accomplished using either of two methods: assigning applications or publishing applications. Assigning applications to a user advertises the program in the Start menu. The program is installed when a user clicks the shortcut or opens an associated file. If it is assigned to a computer, the next time the computer starts, the software is installed.

Publishing applications is an alternate method of deploying them. Published applications can be installed via the Add/Remove Programs applet in Control Panel.

You can also maintain and manage deployed applications. During maintenance, you can force upgrades for software, make them optional, and even redeploy an application.

CHAPTER 9 SUMMARY

A benchmark of a good administrator includes the ability to troubleshoot and maintain systems to perform optimally. If a system is performing poorly, several problems can result. Productivity can decrease when a system is not performing well, and users cannot accomplish their jobs. Windows Server 2003 includes several tools that make resolving performance issues, identifying bottlenecks, and tuning performance an easier task.

The first step in performance tuning is establishing a baseline. A baseline is a standard against which you can measure the system's performance. A baseline includes recorded observations regarding a computer system's behavior. Having a baseline allows you to identify bottlenecks, or areas of the system that slow the overall performance of the operating system.

Windows Server 2003 comes with several built-in tools that can be used to monitor server health and performance, including:

- Task Manager
- Event Viewer
- Performance console

Task Manager is a versatile and underutilized utility in troubleshooting a variety of performance-related issues. Task Manager includes several tabs to assist an administrator:

- The Applications tab displays information regarding currently running programs and allows you to start applications as well as end applications. It also informs you if a program appears to be unresponsive to the operating system.

- The Processes tab gives a detailed view of the processes running in the background on your system. Information includes the Process ID number, CPU usage, CPU time, and Memory Usage. Additional information can be added along with these default options. In addition, processor affinity can be set here. Processor affinity allows the user to assign a process to a single CPU, or multiple CPUs on a multiprocessor system.

- The Performance tab gives a graphical view of CPU and memory utilization. It includes graphical displays and real-time measurements of system performance and resource usage. The information includes:

  - *CPU Usage/CPU Usage History*—This shows the usage level of the CPU.

  - *PF Usage/Page File Usage History*—This shows the usage level of the page file and historical graphs.

  - *Totals*—This displays the count of all the handles, threads, and processes.

  - *Physical Memory*—This shows the entire amount of memory, the amount available, and the amount used by the system cache.

  - *Commit Charge*—This is the amount of memory committed to all running applications.

  - *Kernel Memory*—This is the amount of memory set aside for kernel functions.

- The Network tab displays information regarding the network adapter's utilization, showing the information in a real-time graph.

- The User's tab provides information regarding the currently logged-in users.

Events affecting performance may be recorded in Event Viewer, in one of three standard logs. Additional logs may be present depending on the services installed. The three logs are as follows:

- *Application log*—This log records information, warnings, and errors created by applications installed on the system.

- *Security log*—Security-related events are recorded in the security log. These are created in accordance with the audit policy.

- *System log*—This log contains information, warnings, and errors that have been logged by Windows Server 2003 system components, including drivers and services.

When viewing a log, different types of information may be recorded. In the system and application event logs, the following entries may be included:

- *Information*—These events are recorded when a component or application successfully performs an action.

- *Warning*—Warnings are recorded when an event may not require immediate attention; however, the event may eventually become a problem.

- *Error*—This event type indicates a significant problem. A service may not have started in a timely fashion, or a device driver may not have loaded.

In addition, the security log entries include success and failure entries. These are successes and failures of actions that are performed on the network based on the configuration of an audit policy.

For in-depth performance monitoring, System Monitor is the tool of choice. It is the standard on Windows Server 2003 for collecting data on real-time server performance. System Monitor facilitates the information gathering performed by administrators. It allows you to monitor how the system is performing under the current workload. You are also able to diagnose performance problems such as bottlenecks. You can use the information you gather to plan for growth, and you can also test changes on the server and observe their impact on the server's performance.

Performance Logs and Alerts, an additional performance monitoring tool in Windows Server 2003, provides useful analyses of your systems and includes the ability to alert you based on a system's performance compared to threshold values. Performance Logs and Alerts provides the ability to capture data in a variety of formats, such as binary, comma-separated, tab-separated, and a format compatible with SQL Server databases. Data can be viewed while it is being monitored, or administrators can view all of the collected data. Parameters can be set that govern the data collection, including start and stop times for logs, filenames, and file sizes. Multiple logging sessions can be managed from a single management console. Alerts that are sent when thresholds have been exceeded can also be created, and thresholds can be defined by the administrator.

The cumulative tools provided by Windows Server 2003 for performance tuning allow an administrator to maximize a company's hardware investment. By optimizing and tuning servers, the administrator can ensure maximum system performance. In addition, the administrator can troubleshoot bottlenecks and identify other performance issues, and he or she can wisely recommend upgrades and resolutions to performance-related problems.

CHAPTER 10 SUMMARY

Even in the best-managed networks, things go wrong. From power outages to equipment failure to natural disasters, administrators are tasked with insulating the corporate network infrastructure from a variety of calamities. An effective administrator plans for these events and has a contingency plan to mitigate negative effects. Windows includes a variety of tools to assist an administrator in these endeavors:

- *The Backup utility*—This utility allows an administrator to back up and restore the operating system, software applications, and user data files. Backup jobs can be scheduled.

- *Shadow Copies of Shared Volumes*—This new feature keeps previous versions of files in shared folders so that if a user needs to restore an older version, it is accessible. This gives end users a simple method to restore their own data, reducing an administrator's workload.

- *Automated System Recovery (ASR)*—This new feature allows the recovery of a server from configuration information stored on disks. It allows for a quick reinstall; however, applications still need to be reinstalled and data must be restored from backups.

- *Advanced startup options*—These options allow an administrator to control how the system boots, giving access to different methods of starting up that allow trouble-shooting and diagnostic steps. Modes available include Safe Mode, Last Known Good Configuration, and others.

- *Recovery Console*—This is a command-line environment to which an administrator can boot on a server. It allows the administrator to troubleshoot and make configuration changes when the system will not boot as expected.

One of the most important parts of your plan is the backup plan. By default, members of the following local groups can back up any files and folders on a member server running Windows Server 2003:

- Administrators
- Backup Operators
- Server Operators

If users are not members of the local groups in the preceding list, they cannot by default back up files. Instead, for users to back up files, the users must either be listed as the owner of the file or have one or more of the following NTFS permissions:

- Read
- Read and Execute
- Modify
- Full Control

The most common type of backup is the Backup utility's normal backup. This backup method backs up all files selected and clears the archive attribute on the selected files and folders. By clearing the archive attribute, any subsequent file changes are marked for backup during a subsequent backup.

The incremental backup type is another backup method. This method backs up all files that have changed since the last normal or incremental backup, and it clears the archive attribute.

Another backup type is the differential backup type. Unlike the first two backup types, the differential backup type does not reset the archive attribute. It backs up all files that have changed since the last normal backup, regardless if a differential has been performed since the last normal backup ran.

The preceding three types of backups are the most common. However, there are two additional backup types with which you should be familiar: daily backups and copy backups. Daily backups back up files that have changed on the day the backup is scheduled. The archive attribute is not modified, so other backup types remain unaffected.

A copy backup backs up all files and folders that are selected, and, as with the daily backup, the archive attribute is not modified. The copy backup is similar to a normal backup, except the archive attribute is not modified, so other backup types aren't interfered with.

In defining what to back up, you can select files and folders. In addition, you have an option to back up the System State data. Backing up the System State data on a Windows Server 2003 system includes the following choices:

- Registry (always)
- COM+ Class Registration database (always)
- Boot files (always)
- Certificate Services database (if Certificate Services is installed)
- Active Directory (only on domain controllers)
- Sysvol directory (only on domain controllers)
- Cluster service (if the server is part of a cluster)
- IIS Metadirectory (if IIS is installed)
- System files (always)

Another feature is Shadow Copies of Shared Folders. This feature allows for:

- Restoration of files that users accidentally delete
- Recovery of previous versions of files when necessary
- Comparison of the current version of a file to a previous version

The Automated System Recovery feature in Windows Server 2003 is another administrative tool that can assist you when a system cannot be repaired. This powerful new utility can restore system configuration information. The Automated System Recovery (ASR) feature is used to restore an operating system's configuration settings during a reinstallation, if a system cannot be repaired or otherwise restored to a normal running state.

The advanced startup options allow a number of ways to start the system in an attempt to diagnose or troubleshoot problems. Last Known Good Configuration boots the system with the registry information from the last successful logon. This allows registry changes to be undone so that the system can be restored to an operable state.

Recovery Console is an option that allows an administrator to boot into a command-line environment. In this environment, an administrator is able to manage files and services and make modifications to the operating system from a command prompt. Recovery Console can be used to fix more serious errors where one of the other advanced startup methods fails.

CHAPTER 11 SUMMARY

Various security features are built into Windows Server 2003. The available features can be broken down into these categories:

- *Authentication*—Ensures authorized access by requesting credentials before granting access to the system.

- *Access control*—Controls access to resources by allowing administrators to define levels of access.

- *Encryption*—Grants confidentiality by encrypting sensitive information so that it cannot be viewed by unauthorized users.

- *Security policies*—Allows granular definition and implementation of a company's desired security goals.

- *Service packs and hot fixes*—These are rollups of bug fixes and security flaws issued by Microsoft to ensure the stable and secure functioning of the operating system.

The Security Configuration Manager tools with Windows Server 2003 include these core components:

- Security templates
- Security settings in Group Policy objects
- Security Configuration and Analysis tool
- Secedit command-line tool

Security templates are primary tools for an administrator. They grant the ability to define, edit, and save baseline security settings to be applied to computers with common security requirements to meet organizational security standards. Several templates are included with Windows Server 2003, and it is important to be familiar with them.

The first template is the default template. This template is created when Windows Server 2003 is initially installed. The default security settings that are applied are stored in a template known as Setup Security.inf. These templates vary by installation, as the original configuration of the computer can alter them, especially when the initial installation is a fresh install or an upgrade. This file provides a single template that allows an administrator to restore the original computer security settings.

The next template category contains the incremental templates. Each incremental template has a specific level of security. To achieve the desired level of security within Windows, all templates up to the desired level of security must be applied. That is, each template builds on the templates that have lower security. You should apply these templates only to those machines already running the default security settings because they do not include any of the initial configurations created during the initial installation.

C

The incremental templates are as follows:

- *Compatws.inf*—This template is intended for either workstations or servers. Windows Server 2003 is more secure by default than earlier Windows versions because the default security is set to a higher level. However, this may cause problems with older applications, but this template might lower the security to enable the older applications to run successfully.

- *Securews.inf and Securedc.inf*—These templates increase the level of security for account policies, auditing, and registry permissions. The latter template is for domain controllers only; the former can be used for either a server or workstation.

- *Hisecws.inf and Hisecdc.inf*—These templates are intended to greatly increase security, especially in the area of network communications.

- *Iesacls.inf*—This template has settings designed to increase the security of Internet Explorer.

- *DC Security.inf*—This template is applied to Windows 2000 or Windows Server 2003 servers that are promoted to domain controllers. It allows an administrator to redeploy the initial security settings.

- *Rootsec.inf*—This template defines the original permissions assigned to the root of the system drive and can be used to reapply the settings if necessary.

Security templates can be applied to the local machine, or they can be applied across computers in the domain through a Group Policy Object (GPO).

The Security Configuration and Analysis snap-in enables administrators to compare configured, effective computer settings to a predefined template. This allows an administrator to compare the current policy to the desired policy. Differences between the actual policy and the desired policy are designated in the console tool so that the administrator can make appropriate corrections. In addition, the administrator can configure the computer with the desired settings.

Secedit.exe is a command-line tool used to create and apply security templates, as well as analyze security settings. This tool can be used in workgroups in which GPOs are not applied. The following switches can be used with this tool to define its behavior:

- */analyze*—Analyzes and compares security settings between the database and computer configuration

- */configure*—Implements the settings in the desired template

- */export*—Exports the current database information to a template file

- */import*—Imports a template file's information into a database file that can be used for analysis purposes

- */validate*—Verifies that a template has the correct syntax

- */GenerateRollback*—Creates a template with the current security settings of a system, which can be used to restore the settings in case the results of a change are undesirable

Auditing is a tool administrators can use to monitor and track activities on the network. Auditing should follow a defined security plan and meet specific needs. Auditing can be resource intensive, so it should be carried out with a definite plan. Audit information is logged in Event Viewer's security log and can include who performed an action, what the action was, and the result of the action.

Auditing can record these types of events:

- *Audit account logon events*—Indicate when a user logs onto a computer.

- *Audit account management*—Indicates when a user or group account is created, deleted, or modified. In addition, it also records successful or unsuccessful password changes.

- *Audit directory service access*—Indicates the access of an Active Directory object.

- *Audit logon events*—Indicate when a user logs on or off either a local computer or Active Directory.

- *Audit object access*—Indicates when objects, such as a file, folder, or printer, have been accessed.

- *Audit policy change*—Indicates when a policy that affects security, user rights, or auditing is modified.

- *Audit privilege use*—Indicates when a user invokes a right or privilege. Rights and privileges are actions, such as changing the system time or taking ownership of a file.

- *Audit process tracking*—Indicates that an application process has taken place.

- *Audit system events*—Indicates that a system event, such as a computer restart, has occurred.

To configure an audit policy, the following conditions must be met:

- Your user account must be a member of the Administrators group, or it must be granted the right to manage auditing and the security log.

- If auditing includes monitoring file and folder access, then the files and folders must be on an NTFS-formatted partition.

Setting up an audit policy includes two steps. You must first choose the events you wish to monitor and then decide whether to monitor the successes and/or failures of these events as the first step. If you are auditing access to files, folders, printers, and Active Directory objects, a second step is required. You need to configure auditing settings on the specific resources for which you want to monitor access.

If policies have been modified, you can apply changes immediately if necessary. To do so, either restart the computer, or, at a command prompt, issue the Gpupdate.exe command.

When configuring auditing, carefully consider what will actually be monitored. Auditing unnecessary items creates additional overhead and creates more log entries to filter. You should monitor log entries on a regular basis. It is typically a good idea to monitor sensitive and confidential information. Monitoring the Everyone group as opposed to Users includes unauthenticated users.

Event Viewer in Windows 2000 Server had a maximum default of 512 KB allotted for logging, and once it reached this limit, logging stopped. Windows Server 2003 has increased the log size to 16 MB. Depending on configuration, events may be overwritten when the maximum size has been reached, so it is important to only audit critical events and to monitor the log regularly.

C

12 Making the Move from Windows to Linux

In This Chapter

■ What Is Linux?
■ Where Did Linux Come From?
■ How Does Linux Compare to Windows?
■ Where Is Linux Going?

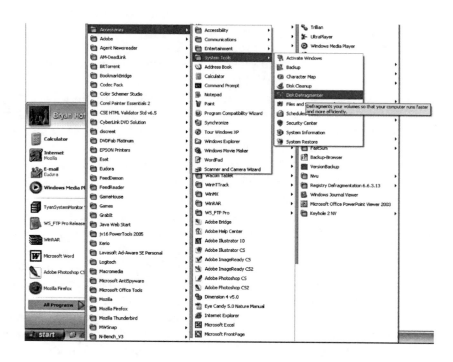

INTRODUCTION

If you're reading this book, you're probably a Microsoft® Windows® user who is considering switching to Linux®. You might be considering this change for any number of factors. Perhaps your employer is starting to use Linux, or maybe you're intrigued by all the media attention Linux has received recently. Whatever your reasons for considering moving from Windows to Linux, it's likely that you're contemplating this change with a fair amount of trepidation. You've probably grown quite comfortable with Microsoft Windows, and regardless of any advantages Linux might have or how curious you might be, you probably have a lot of questions. Will the transition be difficult? Will you be able to do all the things you want to do with your computer? Will you need to be a complete computer geek to understand and use Linux?

The answers to those questions, in order, are no, yes, and no. It won't be difficult. You will be able to do all the things you want to do. The best part about transitioning to Linux is that you don't have to be a computer wizard or a computer professional to be able to do so. In fact, this book simply assumes that you're a relatively experienced computer user with some exposure to Microsoft Windows, the Internet, and some office applications such as word processors and spreadsheets. The reader for whom this book was designed is a competent and experienced computer user, one who is comfortable with some basic configuration tasks such as changing screen resolution, finding items in the Control Panel, and perhaps even adding some extra hardware. Perhaps the best description for the target audience of this book would be a Windows *power user*.

One common misconception about Linux is that it is hard to understand and difficult to use. This simply isn't true. Contrary to what you may have heard, Linux is no more difficult to use than Windows or Mac OS X®. It just takes a little guidance, which this book will endeavor to provide, and some patience on your part. The purpose of this book is to answer your questions about Linux and ease you through that transition. This chapter is the beginning of your journey.

It's designed to introduce you to the world of Linux, which means that this chapter is a sort of smorgasbord of Linux concepts and terminology. These concepts are introduced here briefly and expounded upon in more depth later in the book. The purpose of this chapter is to give you an initial overview of Linux. That means a few advanced topics are touched upon in this chapter. If you feel that some topic in this chapter is still not completely clear to you, don't worry—it will be explained in much more detail in a later chapter.

The following pages take you through the fundamental concepts of Linux. You find out what Linux is and what it is not. You also are introduced to a brief history of Linux and a few thoughts on its future. Some of the information in this chapter might already be familiar to you, but it's hoped that you learn a few new things

about Linux. This material sets the stage for subsequent chapters. Therefore, it is imperative that you thoroughly master the fundamentals before proceeding with subsequent topics.

WHAT IS LINUX?

Linux is one of the hottest buzzwords in the world of computers, but beyond that, what is it? Simply put, Linux is an operating system. Which, of course, begs the question, "what is an operating system?" In simple terms, an operating system is software that runs your PC. Microsoft Windows is another operating system, as is the Apple OS X®. Of course, you're familiar with the various applications you run on your PC, such as word processors, graphics utilities, spreadsheets, and even games. An operating system is like these other applications, except that rather than create a document or play a game, it actually runs your PC. When you move a file, delete a file, create a directory, load software, and so on, your operating system performs all of these tasks. Without an operating system, your PC is really just a pile of useless circuits, worth less to you than a toaster. The operating system runs your machine. In addition to communicating with your printer, displaying output to your monitor, and running your CD, it has other functions. Your operating system provides a context within which your applications run. For example, your favorite word processor must run within the context of your computer's operating system. When you print, your word processor talks to the operating system, which in turn handles the printing. The operating system is, essentially, the soul of your computer.

Other operating systems are available for you to use. You are probably familiar with Microsoft Windows (Windows 98, 2000, or XP). Windows is a very popular operating system for home users and small businesses. In fact, in its various versions, Windows is the predominant desktop operating system. It's hard to find a modern office without computers running Windows. Most home users have a Windows PC. This is obvious when you go to any store that sells computer software. Most commercial software stores carry predominantly Windows software, with only a small selection of titles for other operating systems. Another popular operating system is Apple Macintosh OS. As of this writing, the Macintosh OS is up to version 10, popularly referred to as OS X. Macintosh is easy to use and has been particularly popular with the graphics and computer animation industries. Many very high-end computer graphics companies use Apple computers. Many of the special effects you see in movies were probably created, or at least augmented, with Apple computers. Another operating system generally used for high-end servers, not for desktops, is Unix, which is known for its stability and security, but also for its expense.

Linux is a variant of Unix. In fact, many people now use the term *nix* to refer to Unix and its variants. Linux is an operating system with some unique features. First, it's very stable and robust, being based on the time-honored Unix operating system (more on that in the next part of this chapter). Second, it's distributed under an open source license. Open source licensing is rather simple, yet elegant. *Open source* means that after you obtain a piece of software, it is yours to do with as you please. Would you like to make a copy or change the source code? Under open source, the source code of the software is open to the public. In case you did not realize it, this is radically different from Microsoft, Oracle®, Sun®, and most commercial software. For example, when you buy Microsoft Windows, the manufacturer's licensing agreement that comes with the product places rather significant restrictions on what you can do with that product. Violating that license agreement can result in losing the license to that software and, in some extreme cases, in lawsuits. Each vendor's licensing agreement stipulates what is acceptable use of its software and what is not. Most commercial vendors don't allow you to alter their software, nor do they allow you to have access to the source code for the software. Most vendors also don't allow you to make or distribute copies of their software after you purchase it. One example of software licensing restrictions is that if you purchase a computer that comes with Windows, you can't later sell that copy of Windows, even if you have disposed of the machine. Several eBay® sellers have been shut down by Microsoft for just that sort of activity. Also, you most certainly don't have access to its source code. With open source software, you can do anything you want with the software after you get it, and you have complete access to the source code.

For those readers who may not know what source code is, it's the programming commands that were written to create a piece of software. With commercial software, source code is usually carefully guarded. With open source software, it is freely distributed.

Access to source code might not be particularly intriguing to many readers. You have to be a rather highly skilled programmer to make much use of it. However, if you have skilled programmers on staff, they can take the Linux source code and make modifications to customize the operating system for your particular needs.

One note of caution is in order. What you can do with open source software is not completely unlimited. For example, you can't put your own label on open source software and resell it. The open source license doesn't give you this right. If you put SuSE® Linux and your name on a CD and then started selling copies, you might find yourself the target of litigation and possible criminal charges. The authors don't claim to be attorneys and recommend that with any software, you read the licensing agreement carefully. Open source software has the least restrictive li-

censing of any software you can find—far less restrictive than commercial software. However, there are still some limitations. It's recommended that you visit *www.opensource.org/* to see a wealth of information and links on open source software.

One advantage of an open source operating system is that much of the software written for the operating system is also open source. This means that, although the software selection for Linux in an average retail store might be slim, the selection of freely downloadable software on the Internet is vast.

You'll also find that the Linux community is rather supportive of itself. You will find several links in the appendices of this book, and it's even possible that you might find a Linux users' group in your area, especially if you live in a major metropolitan area. These people can be quite helpful to the Linux novice.

WHERE DID LINUX COME FROM?

Linux is essentially a clone of the Unix operating system. This means that its commands, file structure, and behavior are a lot like Unix. In fact, in many cases they are exactly like Unix.

Unix was the creation of the legendary Bell Laboratories, which is famous for a plethora of technological and scientific breakthroughs, including the discovery of the first evidence of the Big Bang, inventing the transistor, and the creation of the C programming language. At the time Unix was developed (circa 1969), operating systems were written for a specific machine's hardware. This meant that even if you were an expert on a given operating system, the odds were that your expertise would not transfer to other machines. Unix was an attempt to create an operating system that could run on various hardware, and it turned out to be an unequivocal success. Unix was first released in 1971, and more than 30 years later it's still a top-notch operating system. In the world of computing, five years is often considered woefully out of date, and any technology a decade or more old is likely to be considered a quaint antique. For an operating system to survive and flourish for more than 30 years speaks volumes about its stability and functionality. Unix is used around the world, particularly on high-end systems that must service a large number of users. It's renowned for its efficiency and stability. Most experts agree that even today, there is no operating system more stable than Unix. Unfortunately, Unix is also known for its high cost. A Sun Solaris® Unix machine or an SCO® Unix machine is quite expensive.

SCO and Solaris are simply brand names for individual companies' versions of Unix. SCO is an acronym for Santa Cruz Operation, and Solaris is made by Sun Microsystems, which also created the Java programming language.

Sun Solaris machines cost from $3,000 to more than 1 million dollars. That's a lot more expensive than your standard Windows PC or even a high-end Windows server. Of course, Sun Microsystems would probably like to point out that their higher-end Unix servers are in a completely different class than a Windows server running on a standard PC. They're able to handle much more work than any Windows/PC server. These Unix servers are designed for very intensive projects, thus their expense.

This cost, combined with the perceived complexity of Unix, prevented it from becoming a player in the desktop operating system market. Unix was primarily an operating system for high-end servers. The advent of the open source movement would eventually change this. Open source, briefly described earlier, was first brought to the public forefront by Richard Stallman, who in 1985 published his famous *GNU Manifesto*, a document outlining the parameters for open source licensing. Stallman had begun working on his own operating system in 1983. He called this system GNU (GNU is *not* Unix). His goal was to create an open source version of Unix. Stallman's Free Software Foundation later created the GNU General Public License, which today allows Linux and other software to remain completely free. This open source movement was the start of a really big idea with which others picked up and ran.

In 1987, Andrew S. Tanenbaum created Minix, an operating system quite similar to Unix. Minix was a fairly stable and functional system and a reasonably good Unix clone. Although Minix failed to gain the popularity of some other Unix variants, it was an inspiration for the creator of Linux.

The story of the Linux operating system starts with a young computer science graduate student named Linus Torvalds. Torvalds was introduced to Minix and, while still in graduate school, decided to create his own open source Unix clone. Torvalds found many things he liked about the Minix operating system, but he believed he could make a better Unix variant. He chose the name Linux, as a combination of his first name and the end of the word Unix. He began by posting the operating system code on an Internet discussion board, allowing anyone to use it, play with it, or modify it. Finally, he released Linux 0.01 on the Internet under a GNU public license. Torvalds not only released the operating system for free, he released the source code and even invited other programmers to lend a hand in making the system more workable.

Over the years, Linux's popularity has grown. It's moved from a hobby operating system for computer enthusiasts to a full-fledged business operating system. Vendors like Red Hat, SuSE, and Xandros have released popular distributions of Linux that bundle the operating system with useful programs and a graphical user interface (GUI). You can find out more about the history of Linux at any of these Web sites:

- *http://ragib.hypermart.net/linux/*
- *www.li.org/linuxhistory.php*
- *http://www.linux.org/info/*

You might be wondering how these vendors make money. If the operating system can be downloaded for free from the Internet, it would seem that any Linux company would have a very narrow profit margin. The first way they make money is by selling their operating systems in neatly packaged boxes with manuals and easy-to-install CDs. If you download a free version of Linux from the Internet, you don't get any manuals or CDs, installation can sometimes be tricky, and the download time will severely tax even a high-speed cable connection. These vendors also make money by selling support for Linux. If you purchase SuSE Linux, you also can call their support line for help on a fee-per-call basis.

HOW DOES LINUX COMPARE TO WINDOWS?

Since you've used Windows and are now at least thinking about moving to Linux, it might be prudent to compare the two operating systems. What does one offer that the other does not? What do they have in common? Why would you move from Windows to Linux? First set aside some of the operating system wars that you find in Internet discussions. Those of you who are not familiar with the raging Internet debates between proponents of different operating systems are probably fortunate. Many an Internet discussion group or chat room has become bogged down with proponents of Linux/Unix and proponents of Microsoft hurling accusations and insults at each other. At times these arguments get quite nasty. The purpose of this book is not to bash one operating system or to exalt another. Both Windows and Linux have their place. One author has both a Windows XP machine and a Red Hat Linux machine at home and a dual boot on his laptop (*dual boot* means you have both operating systems installed, and at startup you are prompted to pick the one you want to use). The other author dual boots between Windows XP and SuSE Linux 9.3. Some people seem to have an almost religious fervor regarding their operating system of choice. That's not the tone of this book. Still, there are significant differences in the two operating systems; differences that should be examined thoroughly.

Advantages of Linux over Windows

First, take a look at the advantages of using Linux as opposed to Microsoft Windows. The most obvious advantage is cost. If you purchase a commercial version of Linux, you can expect to spend about $100 for SuSE 9.3 Professional, as opposed to about $200 for Windows XP Home Edition or $300 for Windows XP Professional

Edition. You also can download several versions of Linux for free from the Internet. Simply by purchasing Linux rather than Microsoft Windows, you immediately save money. You also don't have to worry about licensing fees. If you're using a Windows 2003 server in your small business, you're required to purchase a license for each machine that will connect to it—something that gets many small businesses in trouble. With Linux, the number of machines you connect is irrelevant—you don't need any licenses. If you set up a Windows server and connect 10 employees to it, you're supposed to purchase 10 licenses. If you don't, you're in violation of copyright laws and subject to criminal and civil penalties. With a Linux server, you can connect as many machines as you want.

You also can install your copy of Linux on multiple machines. This isn't the case with Windows. When you buy any version of Windows, it's illegal to install it on more than one machine at a time. Linux has no such restriction; you can install it on every machine in your office if you want.

To continue our scenario of an office with 10 machines and one server; this could all be done for about $100 with Linux. With Windows, you need 10 copies of Windows XP Pro at $300 each, one copy of Microsoft Windows Server™ 2003, Standard Edition with 10 client licenses for the 10 machines to connect to the server at $1,200.00. You need well over $4,000 worth of software and licenses! That's a lot of money; probably as much as you spent for the computers themselves or very close to it. Clearly, using Linux saves you money.

You also save money on applications. After you have purchased Microsoft Windows, you'll then need to pay for a variety of applications to run on it. You'll need to purchase Microsoft Office (about $500) in order to do word processing, spreadsheets, presentations, small database work, and so on. If you need large-scale databases, you have to first purchase Microsoft Windows XP Server instead of the Home or Professional edition, and then purchase Microsoft SQL Server® for about $1,500. With SuSE Linux 9.3, you get Open Office® for free. Open Office has a complete office suite, including word processor, spreadsheet, and presentation tools. You also get MySQL®, which is a complete large-scale database server. You can purchase Star Office® for $60. It would seem that even after buying the operating system, you save yet more money on applications with Linux. Linux is the most cost-effective solution for the home user or small business operator.

Saving money is obviously a good thing, but it's certainly not the only criterion you should consider when choosing an operating system. Another consideration is the operating system's stability, which includes a number of factors, the most obvious of which is uptime. How much of the time is the operating system actually running and performing useful work, versus downtime due to crashing? The Linux operating system is stable. Will it work when you need it to? The answer is a resounding yes. In fact, by every standard, both Unix and Linux are far more stable

than Windows. You can have a Linux machine running for months and never need to reboot it or defragment it.

Some readers might wonder what is meant by defragmenting a hard drive. You might have heard this process called optimizing a drive, and it's periodically necessary because of the way files are stored. Your hard drive has multiple spinning platters, and when you save a file, segments are saved to the hard drive. These segments may not be contiguous. This leads to file fragmentation, which means that a single document might be found in pieces scattered all over your hard drive. This fragmentation can make your computer run much more slowly because it must search throughout all of your hard drive's platters to find all the pieces of the document, rather than finding them all in one place. When you defragment your hard drive, you'll often find that it will run faster.

The way in which an operating system handles the files on the computer depends entirely on the file system used by the operating system. A file system is exactly what its name implies, a system for storing and accessing files. Put another way, a file system organizes the files on your computer. You have lots of files of different types on your PC. You have saved documents, spreadsheets, programs, and so on. All of these are files. The problem for the computer is organizing them in such a way that you can easily find them. This is where the file system comes in. It's simply the method the computer uses to organize the files stored on your computer. The file systems used by Linux, Extended File System (ext) and ReiserFS, are more robust than the systems used by Windows (FAT, FAT32, and NTFS) and don't need defragmenting.

In Windows you would go to the Start menu, choose Programs, select Accessories, then go to System Tools, where you would find the defragmentation tool, as shown in Figure 12.1.

All of the aforementioned file systems for Microsoft operating systems work on a table that relates specific file segments with addresses on the hard drive. The first of these is File Allocation Table (FAT). Windows 2000 and XP use a significantly enhanced file system called New Technology File System (NTFS).

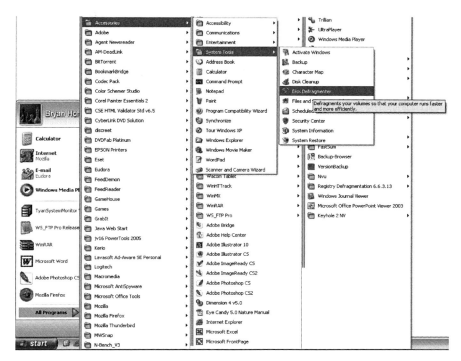

FIGURE 12.1   Finding the Windows defragmentation tool.

Disadvantages of Linux Compared to Windows

It appears that there are some significant advantages to using Linux. It's a very stable operating system that's also very cheap. There also are a few disadvantages to using the Linux operating system, the first being the availability of software. You can get office products such as Star Office and Open Office, which will be explored later in this book, beginning in Chapter 9, "Moving from Microsoft Word to Open Office Writer." You can find robust graphics programs such as The GIMP® (GNU Image Manipulation Program, also explored in this book). You can even purchase a few games for Linux. However, you can't get Microsoft Office®, Adobe Photoshop®, or many other popular applications for Linux—at least not yet. You'll be able to do all the tasks you're used to, but you might need to do them with new software. You'll probably have to seek out alternative applications for some of the products with which you're used to working. Fortunately, many of these alternative applications are also open source. In fact, SuSE 9.3 includes several of these on the installation disks. Even if you're not using SuSE 9.3, you'll find many of these alternative applications are available as free downloads from the Internet. We'll also explore

Wine, a program that allows you to run some (but unfortunately not all) Windows and DOS applications under Linux.

In addition to learning some new software applications, you'll find that some applications simply can't be found for Linux, and no suitable Linux analog exists. For example, many games have not been ported to Linux. This is changing, but you'll still find a great many games that don't have Linux versions. You'll also find that some hardware doesn't have a Linux driver. Most standard CD-ROMs, printers, network interface cards (NICs), and such will work under Linux, but more obscure brands might not. If you're using fairly common hardware, this shouldn't be a problem.

One significant disadvantage for small businesses using Linux is finding appropriate technical staff. Most computer companies that do outsourcing of PC support and repair are trained in Windows, not in Linux. It's also likely that most of your employees have significant Windows experience but little or no Linux experience. This might necessitate retraining your staff in the use of Linux (of course, you could start by simply buying them all copies of this book!). In plain terms, competent technical personnel trained in Windows are quite easy finding, whereas competent Linux technical support can be a little more difficult to find. This sometimes (although not always) leads to Linux professionals commanding a somewhat higher salary.

WHERE IS LINUX GOING?

Now that you know where Linux came from and what you can do with it, the next question is, where is it going? Linux is gaining a large share of the Web server market. The fact that it's very inexpensive and comes with both Web server and FTP server software makes it very attractive to people running Web servers. More businesses are turning to Linux for Web servers, file servers, and other servers. America Online and Amazon.com book sellers both use Linux servers. Windows is still king of the home and business desktops, but this is changing. Business owners are tired of paying exorbitant licensing fees for proprietary products. More and more small businesses are looking to Linux and open source software as a low-cost alternative. Clearly, a growing market share of the home and small business community is in Linux's future.

Linux is also becoming popular with makers of high-tech appliances, such as the television viewing product TiVo®. The low cost and lack of licensing restrictions make it ideal for such operations. It is clear that Linux is growing in popularity and will be taking a growing portion of the market over the next few years.

Recently, Linux has made some fascinating inroads into very high-end computing. Many scientific research endeavors require computing power well beyond

the capabilities of any standard server—Windows, Unix, or Linux. This leads some research facilities to purchase supercomputers that often cost millions of dollars. A supercomputer is a very powerful computer. A normal computer running Unix or Windows might have one, two, or four processors. A supercomputer is essentially a multiprocessor machine, running hundreds or even thousands of processors. All of those processors need very specialized cooling that is quite expensive. In the past few years, some researchers have linked dozens and even hundreds of old PCs with Linux on them, making them work in concert and essentially mimicking the power of a supercomputer. This setup is referred to as a *cluster*, and usually depends on old, often discarded PCs running a free version of Linux. Thus, the only cost is that of connecting the PCs and powering them. This is yet one more way that Linux is making its mark on the world of computing.

SUMMARY

Linux is a powerful and inexpensive operating system that provides a very user-friendly graphical user interface and provides access to a number of software applications. Linux is an open source Unix clone, which means that much, if not most, of what you do in Linux is identical to what you can do in Unix (and if you've used applications such as Firefox and Thunderbird, you can get Linux versions of those as well—there's even a version of OpenOffice for Windows). Its price and stability are attracting a growing number of users, but there are still a number of applications that have no corresponding Linux version. It's also important to note that more obscure hardware might not have a Linux driver.

REVIEW QUESTIONS

1. What operating system are both Minix and Linux based on?
2. What does GNU stand for?
3. Who invented Linux?
4. List two advantages of Linux over Windows.
5. List two advantages of Windows over Linux.
6. What file system(s) does Linux use by default?
7. What file system does Windows XP use by default?

13 Linux Distributions

In This Chapter

- The Concept of Distros
- What's Available
- Other Distributions
- File Migration

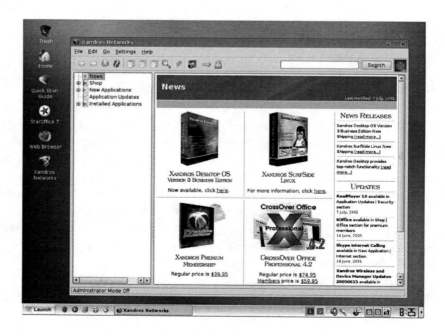

THE CONCEPT OF *DISTROS*

This book deals with SuSE Linux. However, a number of other brand names are associated with Linux. It's important that you know the similarities and differences between these brands. To begin with, they're usually referred to as *distributions*. These distributions have much more in common than they have differences. The various desktops (such as KDE and GNOME), shells, commands, and administrative tasks you'll learn in this book apply to all Linux distributions.

You might be wondering what's different about them. Each distribution, or *distro*, while still distributing Linux on CDs, DVDs, or online as a burnable ISO file, creates its own installation routine and decides which additional programs will be bundled with it. In other words, the real difference between distros amounts to the installation process and the different applications that will be installed with the operating system. SuSE Linux, for example, ships with the popular graphics program GIMP, a complete office suite, and a plethora of other applications. A few distros ship with special extras like Star Office, Crossover Office (a commercial version of Wine), or a custom desktop theme.

The most important thing to keep in mind is that the actual operating system is the same for all distros. That means that what you learn in this book will carry over into other Linux distros such as Fedora Core, Mandriva, Linspire, and Xandros.

WHAT'S AVAILABLE

Many Linux distributions are available today, and we're about to take a closer look at six of them. They all ship with office productivity software like Open Office or Star Office 7, email software, Web browsers, and most even include server software in case you want to host your own Web or FTP servers. Pricing varies between distributions, with some being available online for free and others offering only retail versions. Many are readily available for download as ISO files; disk images that you burn to a CD or DVD and install on your computer. Depending on your situation and your requirements, you should be able to find a Linux distribution in the following list. The main things they have in common is the fact that they're all relatively easy to use and update and are ideal for home and office use. Of course, some are stronger in certain areas, and weaker in others.

SuSE

As mentioned earlier, SuSE is the distribution we'll be working with throughout this book (see Figure 13.1). It's one of the most elegant, easy-to-use distributions available today and includes a full complement of server and workstation tools.

Whether you want a personal computing setup or to serve Web pages, SuSE has something to offer everyone.

FIGURE 13.1   SuSE Professional 9.3 with KDE desktop.

With its Yet another Setup Tool (YaST) backbone, it's easy to install and update software, and to configure hardware, as shown in Figure 13.2. YaST makes it simple to update software, install new packages, and otherwise configure SuSE. SuSE also offers the latest versions of the KDE and GNOME window managers and the latest Linux kernel and includes Firefox for Web browsing and the Evolution email and calendar application. SuSE's productivity software includes the Open Office suite, and the OS might be used for workstation and server applications. SuSE Professional 9.3 retails for $99.95 and offers a free, fully functional evaluation version. Check out SuSE at *www.novell.com/products/linuxprofessional/* for more information.

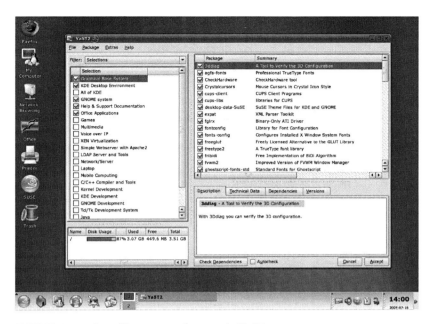

FIGURE 13.2 Installing new software via YaST.

Fedora Core

Fedora Core is currently at version 4 and is a completely free and open source Linux project sponsored by Red Hat (see Figure 13.3). Even if you're new to Linux, you've probably heard the name Red Hat and might be aware that they're a big player in the Linux industry. One interesting feature of Fedora is that it uses open source software exclusively; it doesn't ship with commercial software like RealPlayer.

Like SuSE, Fedora Core includes a full arsenal of applications for desktop and server, and ships with the GNOME and KDE desktops, plus the latest Linux kernel. Fedora Core's default Web browser is also Firefox, and just like SuSE, it uses Evolution for organizing appointments and sending and receiving email. SuSE and Fedora Core both use Red Hat Package Manager (RPM) files for updating and installing new software. RPM is a means for installing, updating, uninstalling, and verifying software. Instead of using YaST, Fedora Core uses the Red Hat up2date application for software updates (see Figure 13.4). If you're interested in a Linux distro that has frequent updates, a wide user base, and you don't mind downloading and burning your own CDs or DVDs, Fedora Core might be for you. It's available for download from *http://fedora.redhat.com/download/*.

FIGURE 13.3 Fedora Core 4 with default GNOME desktop.

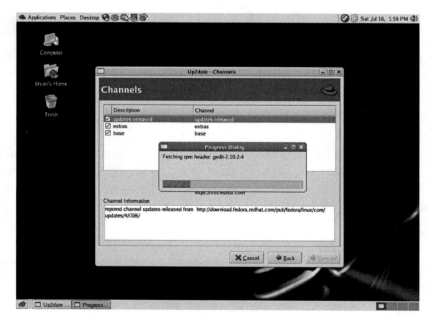

FIGURE 13.4 Updating Fedora Core 4 with up2date.

Mandriva

Mandriva is the new name for Mandrake Linux, and the software is currently at version 10.2. Mandriva is an extremely popular Linux distro with users all over the world (see Figure 13.5). You can opt to join the Mandriva Club on a monthly or yearly basis, purchase a packaged version of the software, or download disk images for free.

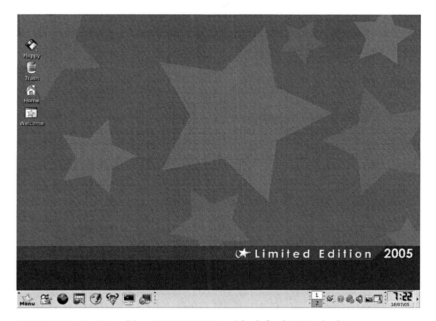

FIGURE 13.5 Mandriva 10.2 LE 2005 with default KDE desktop.

Mandriva also uses Firefox and Evolution as its default Web browsing and email software, but unlike SuSE and Fedora, it doesn't ship with the very latest KDE or GNOME desktop versions. Software is RPM-based and updates and installs are handled by Mandrakelinux Control Center (see Figure 13.6). Mandriva uses KDE by default. Visit *www.mandrivalinux.com/en-us/* for more information.

Linspire

Linspire is a low-cost Linux distribution based on Debian Linux, a product known for its stability and community support. Linspire Five-0 was released recently, and the software has an interesting pricing structure (see Figure 13.7). You can purchase the OS itself starting at $49.95 for the digital edition and then purchase a yearly membership to Linspire's Click-and-Run (CNR) Warehouse starting at an additional $29.95 per year.

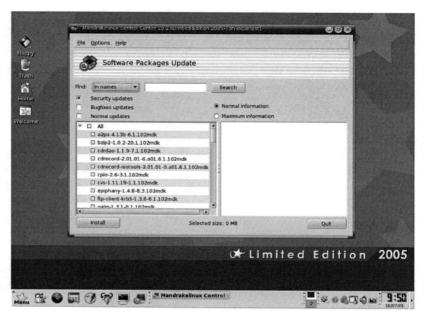

FIGURE 13.6   Updating Mandriva with Mandrakelinux Control Center 10.2.

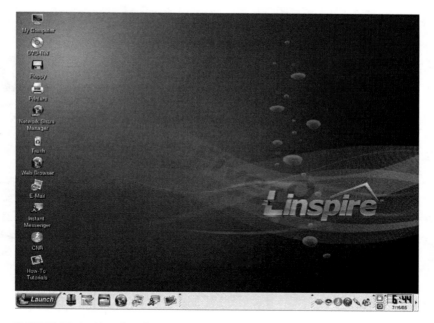

FIGURE 13.7   Linspire Five-0.

CNR is where you download all of your software packages, ensuring the simplicity of one-click installation and complete compatibility with your OS. You can also buy the packages together for $89.95. Linspire is the only distro that offers a retail DVD player option. You can also purchase other software through CNR such as Linspire's VirusSafe and Sun's Star Office 7. Unlike the other distros we've looked at, Linspire uses the Mozilla suite of applications for Web browsing and email and only includes the KDE desktop environment. It includes its own Lassist software for managing your calendar and address book.

One interesting feature is the ability to boot the Linspire installation CD as a "Live CD"; a version of the OS that runs completely from CD and doesn't install anything to your hard drive. Live CDs are ideal for evaluating Linux distros without committing to installing them. Linspire doesn't ship with any server software, but it's possible to install applications like Apache and MySQL through CNR (see Figure 13.8). Linspire claims to be "The World's Easiest Desktop Linux;" see their home page at *www.linspire.com/*. It's certainly one of the easier distros to use, and if you don't want to be bothered with the inner workings of your software, it might be the right choice for you. Visit Linspire's home page at *www.linspire.com/*.

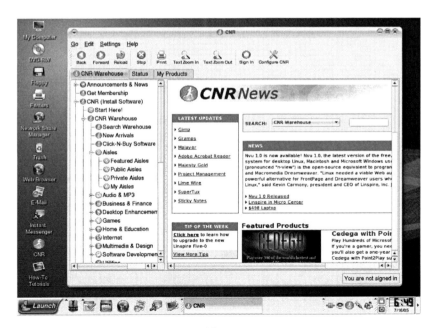

FIGURE 13.8 Updating Linspire with CNR.

Xandros

Xandros Linux, currently at version 3, is geared more toward the workstation crowd. Also built on Debian, Xandros has a package manager similar to Linspire's CNR, called Xandros Networks, available as part of the purchase price, with the option to purchase additional software like Star Office 7 through this service's Shop (see Figure 13.9).

FIGURE 13.9   Xandros Desktop OS Version 3 Business.

Xandros Desktop OS Version 3 Business includes Crossover office, Codeweavers' retail software that runs many Windows applications within Linux and Star Office 7, Sun Microsystems's Open Office-based commercial office application. You can also purchase a Premium membership to Xandros Networks, which entitles you to discounts in the Xandros Networks Shop (see Figure 13.10). Like Linspire, Xandros doesn't offer the GNOME desktop. However, it does include antivirus software as part of the package. It also boasts seamless file sharing on Windows networks and compatibility with Windows server software. Like the others, it uses Firefox and Evolution as its default Web browser and email/calendar applications. The Business edition is priced at $129, which is reasonable considering the inclusion of antivirus, Crossover Office, and Star Office 7. There's also a free downloadable version called Open Circulation Version 3, which obviously doesn't

include all the bells and whistles. Xandros Desktop OS Version 3 Business is a serious contender for Windows desktop replacement. Visit *www.xandros.com/* for details.

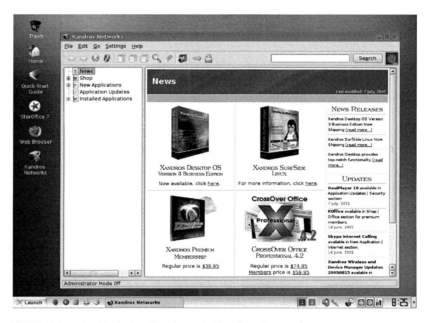

FIGURE 13.10   Updating Xandros via Xandros Networks.

Java Desktop System

Java Desktop System is actually based on SuSE Linux. Currently at version 2, version 3 has recently been released for Sun's Solaris 10 operating system. Unlike the other offerings, JDS2 is based on the older Linux 2.4.x kernel and offers only the GNOME desktop (see Figure 13.11). And unlike the other distros, JDS2 doesn't ship with Apache or MySQL server software, although it's possible to find versions compatible with JDS2.

For email and calendar tasks, JDS2 includes Evolution and Mozilla for browsing the Web. Sun also bundles Star Office 7 with JDS2. As is the trend with older Linux distros, the firewall is disabled by default. Since JDS2 is based on SuSE, it's not surprising that software installation is handled by YaST (see Figure 13.12). The software retails for $100, and no free version is available. If you're interested in SuSE Linux but want Star Office included in the price, Java Desktop System may be a good choice. Visit *www.sun.com/software/javadesktopsystem/* for details.

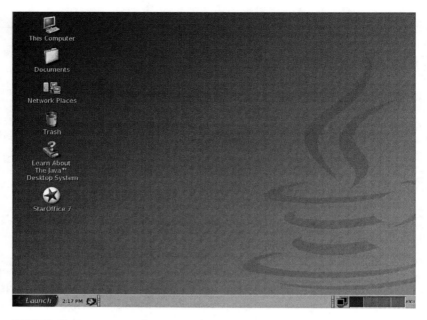

FIGURE 13.11   Java Desktop System 2.

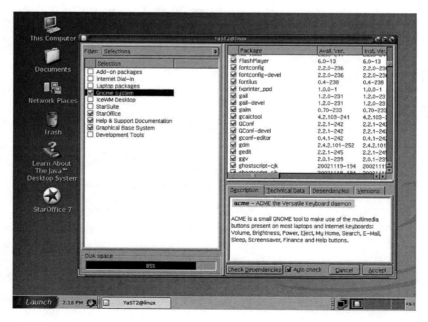

FIGURE 13.12   Updating JDS2 with YaST.

OTHER DISTRIBUTIONS

Literally hundreds of Linux distributions are available today. If you consider the fact that some distros are based on others and some come in more than one flavor, there are still about 300 distributions from which to choose. So how do you choose? You could start at DistroWatch (*http://distrowatch.com/*), which keeps track of the various Linux distributions, sorts them by popularity, and keeps a listing of major distributions. You'll notice that several of the distributions discussed here are included in the top 10. There are plenty of other popular distros in this list.

Although not a distro per se, Debian is a very popular version of the Linux operating system. The name is pronounced "Deb-Ian" and is a combination of the names of founder Ian Murdock and his wife Debra. Debian Linux uses the Advanced Packaging Tool (APT), while the packages themselves are called *Debs*. The advantage of using APT is that it automatically takes care of file dependencies so your applications always work. Another very popular distro based on Debian is Ubuntu Linux. It's completely free and has a growing user base. They'll even ship CDs to you for free! Slackware is one of the older Linux distributions and also has a large following. Gentoo Linux uses an advanced package manager called Portage.

We briefly looked at Linux Live CDs with our Linspire coverage. One of the most popular Linux Live CDs is Knoppix. Files are decompressed on-the-fly, with CDs holding as much as 2 gigabytes of data. If you want to have Linux without the commitment, a Live CD is the way to go. Live CDs are available for Linspire, Mandriva, and SuSE, among others.

- *www.debian.org/*
- *www. ubuntulinux.org/*
- *www.slackware.com/*
- *www.gentoo.org/*
- *www.knoppix.com/*

FILE MIGRATION

After you've made the move to Linux, you'll probably want to migrate all of your files and settings over from Windows. This includes documents, email, bookmarks, and even desktop wallpapers among other familiar things. One solution is to create a CD containing all of your files and copy those files to your Linux home folder. Then, you can go about importing email messages, setting your desktop wallpaper and otherwise organizing things the way you like them. It's kind of a brute force approach, but it gets the job done. Unfortunately, there's no easy way to migrate user profiles from Windows to Linux. It's easy enough to copy the contents of your Doc-

uments and Settings folder but finding saved emails, address book entries, and other settings might be more difficult. File extensions to watch out for while searching for your documents include doc, rtf, ppt, xls, and txt. To migrate your email, it's best to use your Windows email program's Export option and save the files to a location where you can easily find them. One trick is to install the Mozilla Thunderbird email client under Windows, and then use its import tools to create new versions of your Outlook, Outlook Express, or Eudora mail or address books. You can do similar things with your Web browser's bookmarks. Freeware programs are available for exporting Internet Explorer Favorites to an HTML format that can be read by Firefox or Mozilla.

Another option—depending on your distro—is to use software like Resolvo's $20 MoveOver (*www.resolvo.com/products/moveover/*), which migrates all of your Windows environment settings for you. If you don't mind spending money or using commercial software, it could be the simplest option for you.

SUMMARY

In this chapter, we examined the plethora of Linux distributions and options available. We learned about sources for downloading the different distros and obtaining information about them. We explored some of the similarities and differences between Linux distributions, such as that all distros include office productivity software, a Web browser, email software, and, in the case of the distros, we looked at, some sort of package management and installation software. Finally, we considered the options available for migrating files and settings.

REVIEW QUESTIONS

1. What's a "distro?"
2. Which distro includes Crossover Office?
3. Which distros include Star Office?
4. Which distros are based on Debian Linux?
5. What's a Live CD?
6. Do all Linux distros have their firewalls enabled by default?

14 Installing Linux

INTRODUCTION

We've now taken a broad overview of the world of Linux, including a brief history and an examination of the advantages and disadvantages Linux versus Windows. However, we won't be able to do much with Linux unless we install it. Although this isn't a particularly difficult process, you should realize that installing any operating system is a very important step.

The manner in which you install the operating system and the options you select during installation will determine what features your operating system has and, to some extent, how it behaves on your machine. For this reason, you must pay very close attention to this process. This process is critical, but it's not particularly difficult if you proceed carefully; still, there are pitfalls you will need to avoid. Read this entire chapter before attempting the install. You shouldn't simply start at the be-

ginning of the chapter and follow along as you read. Read through the entire chapter one time, making certain that you understand all the issues involved, and then go through the chapter a second time while you actually perform an installation. Pay particular attention to any Notes in the text. These Notes are designed to highlight potential problems or specific issues that will require particularly close attention on your part. That way, you'll be aware of any potential problems before you start the installation process. You should also read the installation instructions that came with your version of Linux. After you carefully read this chapter and are certain you understand the material, then simply pay attention to the installation process itself, and you should do just fine, especially since the installation instructions that come with your distro might differ from what's described in this book.

It might seem odd to recommend that you pay attention to the installation process, but this warning comes from long experience. It's not uncommon for beginners to rush through parts of the install and end up doing some things very wrong. If you simply pay careful attention to each screen and read any instructions, you should be fine. The install process is not that difficult; in fact, it's no more difficult than installing Windows and, in some ways, even less difficult. Of course, in the worst-case scenario, if you should totally botch the installation, you can simply reinstall the operating system. You can't damage the hardware by doing a bad installation.

> *If you really botch the installation, you'll have to repartition your hard drive and reinstall the operating system. This chapter discusses the process of partitioning a hard drive. It's a very good idea either to perform your first Linux installation on an old machine that doesn't have any important data on it, or to make sure you've made backups of all your data before beginning the installation process. In fact, if you aren't using an old machine that has no data, it's absolutely critical that you back up all data before starting. Failing to do so can lead to a loss of all of your data.*

However, for those readers who just don't want to try the installation, a number of major computer stores offer PCs that come with Linux already installed. Usually they are much cheaper than a Windows PC. You can always purchase one of those and skip the installation process. Be sure to read the most up-to-date installation instructions—those usually ship with the software.

This book uses SuSE Linux for all examples; however, the installation of other distributions such as Fedora or Mandrake will have a great many similarities. In fact, the installation process of any Linux distribution is likely to have more similarities than differences. If you're using one of the other major Linux distributions, don't worry. The material in this chapter, combined with the documentation that came with your particular Linux distribution, should still be enough for you to in-

stall Linux. Also keep in mind that when you're through the installation, many of the other tasks in this book are common to all major Linux distributions.

Before you embark on the installation of SuSE 9.3, or any software for that matter, you should make sure that your system will support it. The minimum hardware specifications to run a particular software package are also referred to as its *system requirements*. These minimum requirements are usually determined by the operating system vendor. System requirements are yet another reason to consider moving to Linux. The Linux operating system doesn't require an expensive high-end PC in order to run. In fact, Linux has been successfully installed and run on machines that were literally thrown away by small businesses, since each new version of Windows requires more and more power to run properly. SuSE puts the minimum specifications for its Professional Edition at a Pentium I or faster processor, 128 megabytes of RAM, 500 megabytes of hard drive space, and a CD-ROM drive. To give you a perspective on how low these system requirements are, remember that these are Pentium I machines—Pentium IV is the current model of Intel processor as of this writing. You would also have a difficult time finding a new computer that had less than 128 megabytes of RAM. In fact, even new low-end PCs tend to have 256 megabytes of RAM and at least 10 gigabytes of hard drive space. If you purchased a new machine anytime in the last 18 months, Linux probably will install and run just fine on it. In fact, Linux will work on machines so old and outdated that they are not even sold in stores any longer and have not been for several years. This means that you don't need an expensive PC to run Linux, or even a new machine.

It's critical that you realize that the manufacturer's minimum recommended hardware is just that, a bare minimum. If you choose to use a PC that only has the bare minimum, you will find that it performs quite sluggishly, although it will work. You'll usually want more than the minimum requirements for any software you use. Fortunately, any system purchased new in the last two years is likely to be more than enough for Linux. However, the authors' personal recommended minimums, which exceed the manufacturer's minimum standards, are a Pentium III 500, 256 megabytes of RAM, and a 5-gigabyte hard drive. Fortunately, the machine just described would have been considered new in about 2001, which means you still won't need to purchase an expensive new computer to run Linux. The rule of thumb on any PC, however, is that there is no such thing as too much power. Today, you can purchase a brand new Pentium IV with 512 megabytes of RAM and a 60-gigabyte hard drive for less than $600 from virtually any major computer store.

You can obtain Linux from a variety of sources. Most local computer stores such as Best Buy™ and Microcenter™ carry the major distributions of Linux. You can also order or download Linux from several Web sites, some of which are listed here. Some of these sites offer a Linux distribution for free, and others for a small fee.

These are various distribution Web sites:

- *www.novell.com/linux/suse/index.html*
- *http://fedora.redhat.com/*
- *http://fedora.redhat.com/download/*
- *www.mandriva.com/*
- *www.linspire.com/*
- *www.xandros.com/*
- *www.debian.org*
- *www.slackware.com*

These are generic Linux Web sites:

- *http://linux.tucows.com/*
- *www.linux.com*
- *http://freshmeat.net/*

These sites offer very inexpensive or free Linux CDs:

- *www.cheapbytes.com/*
- *http://freelinuxcd.org/*

Unless you're a particularly savvy reader, it's recommended that you purchase a commercial version of Linux, such as SuSE 9.3 Professional, or you can just install the Evaluation Edition from the DVD included with this book! The Evaluation Edition is exactly the same as the Professional Edition, but with fewer extras such as browsers or desktop managers. Be assured, though, you *will* get KDE, GNOME, and all of the most popular browsers including Firefox and Konqueror. The installation is much easier, and there is extensive documentation included. If you download, you'll have a more complicated time with the installation. You might need to transfer the installation files to one or more CDs before beginning the installation.

The installation described in this chapter was done with a commercial version of SuSE 9.3, or optionally purchased for about $100 at one of the major computer stores (*www.novell.com/products/linuxprofessional/pricing_us.html*). There was nothing special purchased or added. The author simply installed SuSE 9.3 Professional Edition, exactly the same version as you'd have bought off the shelf, and extremely similar to the Evaluation Edition included with this book. However, it should be stressed that this installation can be done with Linux versions obtained from other sources, and anywhere you obtain SuSE Linux, the installation should be much the same. Even other Linux distributions such as Mandriva, Debian, and Fedora should be very similar.

GETTING STARTED

Most computers today can *boot* (start up) from the CD or DVD-ROM drive. This means that if you put the SuSE installation disk into your DVD drive and *reboot* (restart) your machine, it should start the Linux installation. However, if it does not, the reason is probably that your PC isn't booting through the DVD drive. Don't worry, most PCs have their floppy drive somewhere in the boot sequence, so we can start the installation process from a floppy.

> *We're assuming that you're going to install SuSE from the included DVD, but if you don't have a DVD-ROM drive, you'll need to download the appropriate CD images or use the CDs included with the retail version of SuSE 9.3 Professional. You can find a CD image—called an ISO—at ftp://ftp.suse.com/pub/suse/i386/ 9.3/iso/. The file's name is SUSE-Linux-9.3-mini-installation.iso, and it includes only the files necessary to do a base install of the software. But don't worry—you can use YOU, SuSE's online update software—to install more software later.*

Making a Bootable Floppy Disk

If your PC boots through the DVD drive, you can skip this part; it's for those readers whose machines will not boot through the CD drive. (You might be able to press Esc or another key to bring up a menu of drives from which to boot. Check your computer's documentation to find out whether that's possible and which key to press.) This process is not particularly complicated. Your first step is to find a working PC that you can use to create the bootable disk. If you find a machine with Windows like the one on which you are about to install Linux, that would be perfect. Unfortunately, SuSE no longer ships with boot floppy images, but they're still available online at *ftp://ftp.suse.com/pub/suse/i386/9.3/boot*. You'll want the three files named bootdsk1, bootdsk2, and bootdsk3. Just download them to your desktop for now, adding the file extension .img to the end of each file to make it easier to find in RawWriteWin. Next, simply place the DVD-ROM (or the first CD-ROM of your installation set) into the DVD/CD drive and place a blank floppy into your floppy drive. Using either My Computer or Windows Explorer, find the folder located on your DVD that's named \dosutils\rawritewin. If you're using My Computer, you should see something much like what's shown in Figure 14.1A. If you prefer to use Windows Explorer™, your screen will appear much like what's shown in Figure 14.1B.

FIGURE 14.1A The DOS utilities via My Computer.

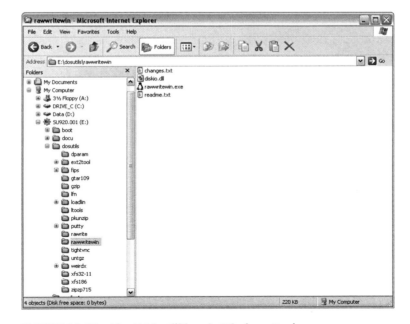

FIGURE 14.1B The DOS utilities via Windows Explorer.

You should notice a file named `rawwritewin.exe`. This program is going to make the blank disk you put into your floppy drive into a boot disk for the Linux install. When you launch this application (by double-clicking on it), you should see something very much like what is shown in Figure 14.2.

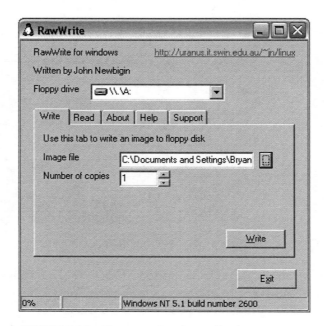

FIGURE 14.2 The rawwritewin application.

RawWriteWin is actually a Windows wrapper for an old Unix/Linux utility called RawWrite, which utility is used to write material to disks.

You now have to use the small button next to the text box titled "Image file" to select the image you want to place on the disk. When you press that button, you will be presented with a standard dialog box that enables you to select a particular file from a specific folder. Navigate to your Desktop or wherever your boot files directory is located, and you'll see several files with the extension .img. These are *images*, and each is used to create a boot disk. You should select the `bootdsk1.img` file, as shown in Figure 14.3. On some Linux distribution disks, the file is called `boot.img`, so if you don't see `bootdsk1.img`, select `boot.img`.

FIGURE 14.3 Selecting the boot.img file.

Now you simply press the button labeled Write, and a boot disk will be created for you. Repeat the preceding steps for images 2 and 3. Now you're done. You have bootable disks. These disks will boot your PC and start the installation process. It will then turn over installation to the DVD or CD, so you'll need both the DVD/CD and the floppy disks to install. Place the first boot disk into the floppy drive of the machine you want to install SuSE Linux on and put the DVD or the first of your installation CDs into the CD drive. Then, reboot your PC, and the install process will start.

The installation described in this chapter makes some specific choices, which will install specific applications. These applications will be covered later in this book. If you do not follow this installation process exactly as it is detailed in this book, you might not be installing all the applications we will be covering later.

INSTALLING SUSE 9.3

Now we're ready to install SuSE Linux. Simply place the DVD or disk one in the CD drive and restart your PC (unless you were using a floppy disk install, in which case your floppy disk and your CD should already be in their respective drives, and remember that you might need to press Esc or another key to bring up a menu of

drives to boot from). After it boots up, you will see the Welcome screen and then be taken to the Installation screen. There is very little information on this screen; it simply offers various installation, boot, and repair options.

If you've ever watched a Microsoft Windows machine boot up, you will notice that the Linux bootup shows a lot more information. What you are seeing is virtually every detail of the boot process.

This screen offers you various ways to proceed with the installation. You'll want to select the Installation option. You can select this option by using the arrow keys on the keyboard to move to this option and then press the Enter key, which loads the Linux kernel and starts YaST, SuSE's graphical installer.

On the next screen, you'll find the Novell Software License Agreement in a window above the YaST Base Installation screen. Click I Agree to continue. If this is your first time installing Linux, it's recommended that you carefully examine the screen that's revealed after the License Agreement is dismissed before pressing the Accept button at the bottom of the screen. It will give you an overview of what the installation process will be doing.

The first screen is very simple; it asks what language you want to use. Select your language from the options provided and then click Accept. This step is shown in Figure 14.4. It's interesting to note the plethora of languages from which you have to select. Linux is now available to users in a variety of nations, using a wide range of languages.

YaST now probes your hardware, and you arrive at the Installation Settings dialog. On the left it shows the steps the installation process will take you through. On the right, you'll see a list of Installation Settings you're able to change. By clicking on the title of each item in the list, you're taken to a configuration screen that displays an explanation of each setting on the left and the setting's options on the right. We'll go through each item one at a time to see what each setting does.

The first item in the list is System. Clicking on it takes YaST into hardware detection mode, where it lists your CPU, memory, hard drive, video card, mouse, keyboard, and so on. Check to make sure that your hardware has been recognized, and move on to the next section (see Figure 14.5).

The next section is Mode, and it brings up a mini dialog that allows you to choose the type of installation you're doing, along with a description of each installation type (see Figure 14.6). It's a good idea to double-check everything here to make sure your hardware was detected properly. We'll leave it set to the default of New installation, and then click OK to move on. If you ever need to update or repair your installation, this is where you'll do so.

As you'd expect, Keyboard Layout allows you to set your keyboard's configuration. Click on it, select your language, and click Accept.

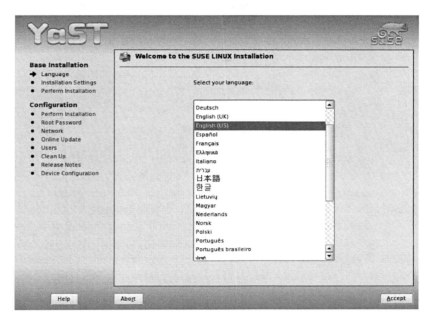

FIGURE 14.4 Choosing a language.

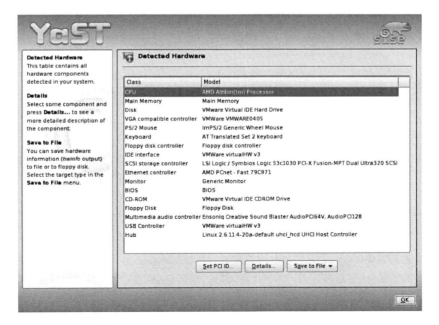

FIGURE 14.5 The Detected Hardware section under System.

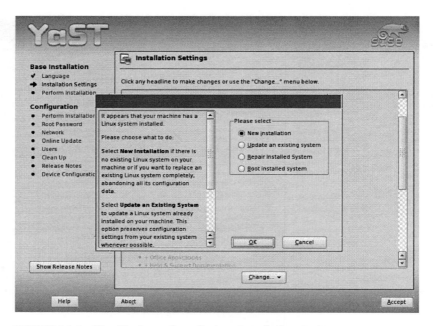

FIGURE 14.6 The Mode section displays installation options.

The Mouse heading, shown in Figure 14.7A, allows you to choose and configure your mouse. If you don't see your model, select either IntelliMouse Explorer (PS2) or IntelliMouse Explorer (USB), and then click Accept. SuSE does a pretty good job of identifying your mouse, so you can probably leave it at the default setting shown in the System settings section.

If your mouse connector (the end that connects to the PC) is a small round plug, it's a PS2 connector. If it's a horizontal plug with several pins (usually there are nine pins), it's a serial connector. If you're unfamiliar with mice and connectors, read Appendix E, "PC Hardware," before continuing with this book. It will give you a brief crash course in PC hardware. For readers who don't know how to tell what type of mouse they have, a picture of the connector for each of the three major types is shown in Figures 3.7B, 3.7C, and 3.7D.

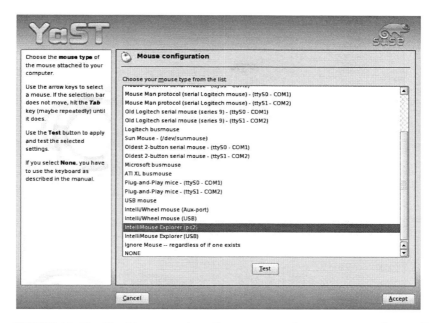

FIGURE 14.7A   The Mouse section allows you to select your mouse from a list.

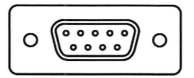

FIGURE 14.7B   A serial mouse connector.

FIGURE 14.7C   A PS2 mouse connector.

FIGURE 14.7D A USB mouse connector.

DISK PARTITIONING

If the machine you're installing on already has a previous version of Linux on it, you'll be asked whether you want to wipe out the old installation completely and start from scratch or simply upgrade. This is shown in Figure 14.8.

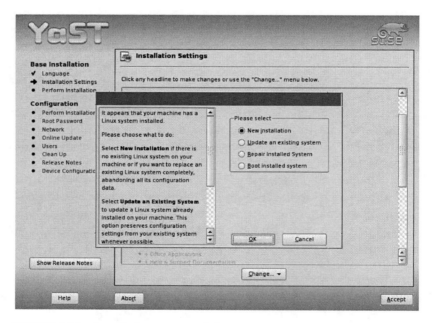

FIGURE 14.8 Installation or upgrade?

The first question you might be asking at this point is: what, exactly, is a disk partition? Partitioning is literally the process of dividing your hard drive into one or more useable segments. Simply put, you can divide your hard drive into several *logical drives*. A logical drive is simply a part of your hard drive that is treated as if it were a separate drive. In other words, you can treat your hard drive as if it were several different hard drives. This is particularly useful for very large hard drives, and in cases where people want to organize their computers more efficiently. You might have one partition that's designated for business and another for home use

or entertainment. A partition that's created to look like a separate hard drive is called a *logical drive*. Your computer might have only one actual hard drive, but several logical drives. Partitions and logical drives are not applicable only to Linux. All operating systems have partitions and can be divided into logical drives. Even if you aren't going to partition your hard drive into multiple logical drives, you'll still need to partition it. The only difference is that you'll partition it into a single logical drive.

This brings us to the topic of partitioning a hard drive that will run Linux. Your hard drive must have at least one main partition. This primary partition is the starting point when your computer turns on, and is called the *root partition*. It must also have one swap partition. This brings us to the questions: what is a swap partition, and why do you need one? A swap partition is a pretty incredible innovation. Essentially, it's a small segment of your hard drive that's set aside as a sort of backup for your PC's memory. The way it works is rather simple. As you open up programs, they're loaded into memory. So, as you open more programs, you utilize more and more of your memory, and there's less free memory for other programs to use. When a program has been idle for a while, the program is taken out of memory and moved to this swap file. If you later activate that program, for instance by clicking on it, it's moved from the swap file portion of the hard drive back into memory. By placing it into a special segment of the hard drive, it can be more quickly reloaded into memory than if you simply loaded it off the normal hard drive partition. Thus, the name *swap*, since it swaps programs from memory to a special segment of the hard drive.

All operating systems support swap partitions. The swap partition's size should be at least equal to the amount of RAM your machine has, but no more than two and one half times the RAM. That means if you have 128 megabytes of RAM, your swap partition should be at least 128 megabytes in size but no more than 320 megabytes.

> *Although YaST's partitioner makes partitioning an existing Windows formatted drive easy, it's strongly recommended that you make a backup of your files before you install SuSE. It's also necessary that you defragment your Windows drive before allowing YaST to repartition it. Failing to do so might cause partitioning to fail and could result in loss of data or at the very least slow the partitioning process significantly. When setting aside space for Linux, try to leave at least 10 to 15 percent for Windows. Dual booting is useful, as it leaves Windows on your system and allows you to choose whether you want to boot into Windows or Linux.*

Now that you understand disk partitions, at least in a rudimentary fashion, you're ready to partition your hard drive. You'll notice that the SuSE Linux installation gives you three options. The first is to partition your hard drive automatically. You can choose this option if you have no intention of dual booting your

machine, if you've already created a Linux partition on your drive, or if you're willing to accept SuSE's automatic drive resizing suggestion as-is. Usually, this involves SuSE claiming some of the free drive space on a Windows partition and reformatting it for Linux. Assuming that you're not dual booting, you'll want to allow YaST to automatically partition the drive for you. This is the simplest setup and is highly recommended for beginners. If you're dual booting, you might want the next option, which allows you to create a Linux partition that co-exists with your Windows partition.

> *If you choose to automatically partition, all existing Linux partitions will be erased and one root partition, one boot partition, and one swap partition will be created. If you're installing SuSE on a drive with an existing Windows istallation, a boot partition won't be created.*

If you want more space left over for Windows to use, you should select the Base partition setup on this proposal option. This will open YaST's Expert Partitioner, where you can select the existing Windows NTFS or FAT/FAT32 formatted drive and resize it as you desire.

The final option is to select Create Custom Partition Setup, which allows you to select from multiple hard drives installed in your system (if you have more than one) and manually modify partitions. Whether you choose either the Base partition setup on this proposal or Create custom partition setup, clicking the Resize button will allow you to set how much space is used for the Linux partition and how much is left for Windows. Click OK to accept your changes and then click Finish to return to the Base Installation screen where we'll continue preparing to install SuSE.

> *If you're uncomfortable allowing YaST to partition your hard drive and would rather use a Windows tool, one of the easiest and relatively least expensive routes is to obtain a utility such as Partition Magic, install it in Windows, and resize your partitions as you see fit, assigning a Linux-friendly formatting such as ext3 to the new partition. Then, when you reboot and install Linux, the partitions will already be set up for you.*

SOFTWARE

The next step is to select packages. A *package* is a logical grouping of a number of separate applications. The various applications that you can install with Linux are grouped so you can easily pick the set of applications you are most likely to need, depending on how you intend to use the machine. Your choice of packages will determine what software gets installed on your PC. SuSE breaks the installation

options down into four selections that can then be customized by selecting the Detailed selection button:

- Minimum system
- Minimum graphical system (without KDE/GNOME)
- Standard system with GNOME
- Standard system with KDE

Each of these is designed for a specific use. These various configurations are summarized in Table 3.1.

TABLE 3.1 Installation Packages

Configuration	Contents/Purpose
Minimum system	This includes a bare-bones Linux installation, excluding a graphical interface. You probably don't want to select this one!
Minimum graphical system	This is intended for users who want the bare essentials plus a graphical interface. It's serviceable, but not very pretty.
Standard system with GNOME	This option is for users who want a standard workstation installation, including office applications, games, and the GNOME graphical interface.
Standard system with KDE	This option is for users who want a standard workstation installation including office applications, games, and the KDE graphical interface. This is the default installation for systems with enough hard drive space.

Each of these configurations is provided to make installation simple for a certain type of machine or user. However, this simplicity comes at a cost. If you choose any of the preceding selections, you won't be installing the Web server, FTP server, or other server packages by default. And obviously, if you select either of the first two selections, you won't get GNOME or KDE, not to mention even a basic graphical interface with the minimum system. Since each of the preset options has some limitations, for our purposes we'll leave the software selection at the default setting of Standard system with KDE and then select the Detailed selection button to add more packages (see Figure 14.9).

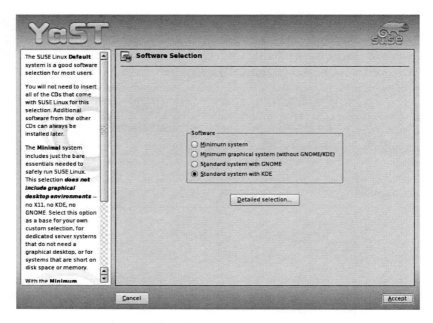

FIGURE 14.9   Software Selection screen.

Choosing Additional Packages

What packages you choose to install is a very important topic. Next to partitioning, this is probably the most important part of the installation. There are a number of packages you could select, each with a different purpose. They're divided into categories such as Graphical Base System, Games, Multimedia, and Network/Server. The categories we're concerned with will be explored in this part, and specific package groups will be explained. At the end of this section is a list of the packages it's recommended you select. The Selections screen is shown in Figure 14.10.

Linux Graphical Desktops

You can use Linux in a simple command-line mode (also called shell mode). This means that you type in everything on a plain black screen, but why would you want to? As a Windows user, you're used to a rich graphical interface, and you probably want to continue using such an interface. Linux not only provides you with a very easy-to-use graphical interface, it provides you with more than one to choose from. There are three package groups listed in this section: Graphical Base System, which includes the X Window System, KDE (K Desktop Environment), and GNOME system (GNU Object Model Environment). Each of these is a complete graphical window interface that operates in a fashion similar to Microsoft Windows. Which

one you choose is a matter of preference. In this book, we'll use the KDE user interface. Whether you choose KDE or GNOME, it should be chosen in conjunction with X Window System. To follow along with this book, you should select GNOME, KDE, and Graphical Base System.

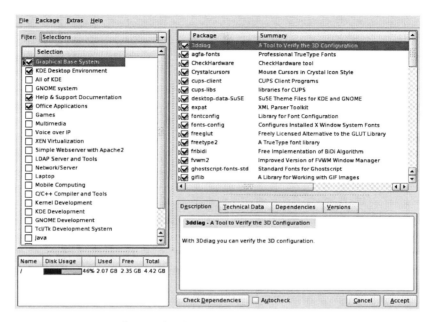

FIGURE 14.10   Package selection.

Office Applications, Games, Multimedia, and More

This part is going to be very important to you. It lists the various types of applications Linux can install. Most of it is self explanatory. For example, the Office Productivity package includes word processors, spreadsheets, and so on. The Games and Entertainment package includes games for Linux. A complete list, with explanation, is provided in Table 3.2.

Servers

A number of different server-related packages are available under the Simple Webserver with Apache2 and Network/Server selection groups. These include Web servers, database servers, and mail servers. Some of these packages will apply only to network servers, but some might be applicable to small business and personal use. The individual packages are described in Table 3.3.

TABLE 3.2 Application Packages

Package	Purpose
Office Applications	This selection installs The Java Runtime Environment, The Open Office suite (including a word processor, spreadsheet, presentation tool, and more), and Wine (for running Windows programs under Linux).
Games	SuSE includes many games, but not all of them are installed by default. Installed games include Freeciv, Frozen-Bubble, GL-117 (flight simulator), and Supertux.
Multimedia	This package selection includes software for viewing videos and TV, listening to music, and importing images from digital cameras. You can also select *xmms*, a nice and compact MP3 player.
Laptop	Check this selection if you're installing SuSE on a laptop computer.

TABLE 3.3 Server Packages

Package	Purpose
Simple Webserver with Apache2	This selection group includes the Apache2 Web server, MySQL server, and additional tools.
LDAP Server and Tools	This will install Lightweight Directory Access Protocol that email programs use.
Network/Server	This collection contains the IMAP mail server, DHCP server, and various networking tools.

Development

If you're a programmer, you'll absolutely love SuSE 9.3 and Linux in general. It offers a wide range of development tools you can install for free. You'll have everything you need to develop your own Linux software of your own. SuSE even includes Mono, software for .NET development. The individual packages are described in Table 3.4.

TABLE 3.4   Development Packages

Package	Purpose
Kernel Development	This selection set contains the tools and the code to the Linux kernel. If you are a skilled programmer and want to alter the Linux operating system, you can.
KDE Development	This selection group has everything you need to develop software that runs with KDE.
GNOME Development	This selection group includes everything you need to develop software to run with GNOME.
Tcl/Tk Development	This selection group contains software necessary to install the Tool Command Language development system.
Java	This selection of packages installs Java development tools.

Different Linux users will find different combinations of packages to their liking. However, this book concentrates on certain applications that you must install. For that reason, please ensure that you select everything in Table 3.5.

TABLE 3.5   Recommended Selections

Selection	Packages
Graphical Base System	All packages
KDE Desktop Environment	All packages
GNOME system	All packages
Office Applications	All packages
Games	Default selection (add more if you want a larger selection)
Multimedia	Default selection plus the xmms MP3 player
Simple Webserver with Apache2	Default selection plus Apache2 and MySQL
Network/Server	Default selection plus Very Secure FTP Daemon (vsftpd)
Development	None
All others	Leave at default

This selection of packages is a good mix of server, workstation, and personal options. You have the office productivity of a business workstation, the entertainment and graphics of a personal workstation, and the Web and FTP server software of a server. Together, these packages, many of which will be covered in this book, will give you a wide range of applications you can choose from. However, if your hard drive is significantly larger than 5 gigabytes, as many current ones are, you would be well advised to place a check mark in all the selections and install every package. Of course, this will make your installation take longer, since you're installing more than 6 gigabytes worth of files.

Even if you don't place a check next to every selection, it's important to note that some packages within each selection group will still be selected. Explicitly checking the box next to a selection group will install *all* of the files within that selection group. It's also very important to note that packages can be added and removed after Linux is in operation. The procedure to add or remove packages will be described later in this book. Chapter 15, "Miscellaneous Linux Applications," includes a section on adding and removing packages.

> *As you go through this book, you'll be introduced to various applications that are used in Linux. If you don't include the appropriate packages, you won't have those applications on your machine. However, you can either add a package or download the application from a Web site. In most cases, you're given the Web site address when you're first introduced to the product. It's also possible that readers using a different Linux distribution or a different version of SuSE won't have all of the applications installed.*

After you click Accept you'll see an information dialog warning that YaST needs to install other packages that will resolve dependencies. In other words, the packages we added require other packages to be installed so they'll function properly (you can always remove packages later using YaST). Click Continue to install these additional packages and be returned to the Installation Settings screen.

CONTINUING WITH THE INSTALLATION

Once you've finished package selection, there are still some steps to take before installation is complete. The Booting section will list the operating systems on your PC. If you aren't dual booting, you should see just one—Linux. If you are dual booting, you can select which operating system you want to be the default. Highlight Default Section in the list and click Edit where you can arrange the order of listed operating systems and choose which one will be booted by default. This is shown in Figure 14.11. Click Finish to return to the Installation Settings screen.

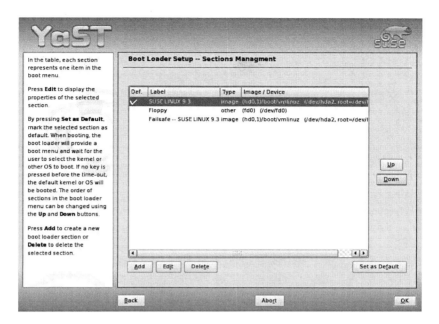

FIGURE 14.11   Selecting an operating system.

When your machine first starts, you'll be shown a display listing these operating systems, and you'll have a few moments to select one. If you don't make a selection, the default will be selected for you. You should note that this screen is configuring your *boot loader*, which is just a small program that loads the operating system into memory. During your boot phase, it loads the operating system, thus the name boot loader. Many Linux distributions use the Linux load (LILO) boot loader software. SuSE 9.3 uses a newer boot loader, GRand Unified Boot loader (*GRUB*). Among other things, GRUB makes dual booting much easier.

The Time Zone setting allows you to set your clock and time zone configuration. Language sets your keyboard to your primary language, and Default Runlevel ensures your computer boots into graphical mode. Leave this setting as-is.

The next phase begins after you click Accept. This begins the installation process along with formatting of the hard drive partitions. Click to accept any licensing agreements and then click Install to get things underway. Now you can sit back and watch a SuSE slideshow and a progress meter that shows how much time remains on the DVD (or on each CD). You can also click the Details tab to see what's being installed. After the first CD is installed (if you install from a set of CDs rather than a DVD), the system will start up momentarily and then return you to the Package Installation screen where you'll be prompted to insert CD 3. Obviously, if you install from DVD, you won't need to insert extra media.

When you're finished installing, the next step is to enter an Administrator password. Clicking the Expert Options button allows you to select the type of encryption used. We'll leave that at the default Blowfish (see Figure 14.12).

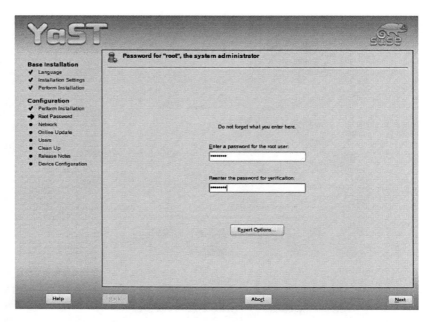

FIGURE 14.12   Setting the root password.

This is critical. In Linux and Unix, root is like the system administrator in Windows. Anyone who logs on to your PC as root can do anything to the machine. This means you must select a good password. It should be at least eight characters in length and contain a combination of letters and numbers. Make certain you write it down somewhere. If you forget it, you are in really deep trouble. Your only option will be to reinstall completely and wipe out the previous Linux installation.

Since it's possible to damage your Linux installation when logged in as root, it's best to create a default user account and log in with that whenever you're working with Linux. We use examples with the user logged in as root to simplify the steps you need to take when administering Linux, but we cannot warn you enough to practice safe Linux computing! Consider the fact that you're likely always logged in as administrator (the Windows equivalent of root) when using Windows. That's how many viruses get spread, because you have full access to everything, and so do the viruses!

Now it's time to configure your network. This screen is sort of a mini version of the Installation Settings screen, where you'll set up your firewall, network, and Internet connection. The network adapter, also called an network interface card (NIC), is simply the card into which you plug a network cable. If this is a standalone home machine, leave the default settings shown in Figure 14.13.

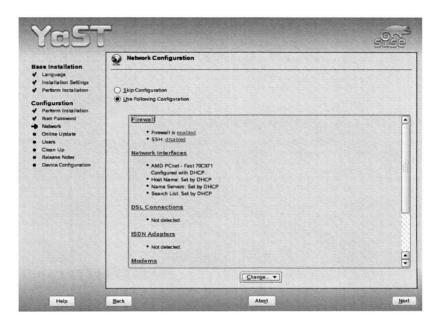

FIGURE 14.13 Network configuration.

If this isn't a standalone machine but instead is a machine that will be used on a network, you'll need to set the IP address assigned to you by your network administrator.

If you aren't on a network but are going to log on to the Internet, the chances are that your Internet service provider (ISP) assigns you an IP each time you log on (this is referred to as a dynamic IP). This is the default setting for Linux, so you should be fine. If your ISP assigns you a static IP, a rather unusual step for an ISP to take, it will have to tell you what that IP address is.

An IP address consists of four numbers, each between 0 and 255 and separated by periods. An example of an IP address is 10.32.0.43.

Don't worry if you either don't know the proper network settings right now or put them in wrong. You can change them at any time, once you have Linux up and running. Chapter 5, "System Configuration in KDE," shows you in detail exactly how to do so.

After you've configured your network card, you can set up your firewall. The firewall is enabled by default, but you can set it to allow FTP and Web servers by clicking Firewall and then Allowed Services. In case you're wondering what a firewall is, it's a barrier between your computer and the outside world. It's your first line of defense against hackers. A firewall can be a separate device (such as a router or another PC) or software that filters incoming packets. In this case, it's software that filters incoming packets. If you don't have extensive knowledge of firewalls, your best bet is to leave the default settings for now. This firewall, however, is one more of the many strengths of SuSE and many other Linux distributions. It's bundled with and installs a firewall, and that makes your PC much more secure from the various dangers posed by the Internet.

The NICs in your PC are listed in order as eth0, eth1, and so on. eth is short for Ethernet. Most home PCs have only one card.

After you've finished configuring your network settings, the next screen tests your Internet connection and, if successful, offers to install any available updates. It's a good idea to allow your software to be updated to the latest versions. If you say yes to updating your system, YaST Online Update (YOU) is started. Choose an Installation source near you from the list and click Next to choose update files. Security updates are red; recommended updates are blue; and optional updates are black. Security and Recommended updates are selected by default. Select any Optional updates you want to install and click the Accept button. When the updates are installed, click Finish to move to the final stages of installation.

The next few screens are very simple. In fact, they're pretty self explanatory, but we'll discuss them briefly. The very next screen has you add user accounts. These are important because you can define users with specific permissions, allowing them to do only the tasks you want them to do. It's a good idea to take a minute and add a user account for yourself. That way, you can log on without needing to do so as root. Leave the Authentication Method at the default of Local and then click Next. Enter your user information and password here. A common system for usernames is to use the first initial of the first name with the last name. For example, one of the authors' usernames might be bhoff. You can also click the Receive System Mail box, which will email any system messages to you.

It's usually unwise to simply log on as root every time you use your PC. The reason is that root has complete and unfettered access to the entire system. However, in this book we'll be covering some basic administrative duties that will require you to log on as root. It's recommended that you log on as the username you just created anytime you're just using your Linux machine, but log on as root when trying the administrative exercises found later in this book.

Now you're shown SuSE 9.3 release notes. Read through them before moving on to hardware configuration.

In normal operations, it's not recommended that you log on as the root user. Remember that the root is the same thing as an administrator in Windows. However, for the purposes of this book, you should log on as root. That way, you'll have access to all the features of Linux, including administrative tools. This will be critical when we cover administrative tools later in this book.

COMPLETING THE INSTALLATION

The final step before rebooting your system and starting SuSE for the first time is the Hardware Configuration screen. If all hardware listed on this screen looks OK, you can simply leave Use Following Configuration selected and move on. If not, you'll need to make a few adjustments. It's not a good idea to choose the Skip Configuration option.

The first item listed is Graphics Cards. Clicking this opens SaX2, YaST's Extended X11 Configuration module. Here you can set select your video card, monitor, color depth, and resolution. Choose your monitor and video card from the provided lists, selecting generic options if necessary. Select a resolution and refresh rate that you know both your monitor and video card can handle and then click Finalize. You can select Test to make sure everything's performing as expected and then save your settings. After this, you can configure and test your printer and sound card, and configure any TV cards and Bluetooth devices you might have. Clicking Next will finalize your device settings and take you to the Installation Completed screen, where you can select Finish to restart your system and try SuSE for the first time!

INSTALLING FEDORA CORE

To install Fedora Core, simply place disk one in the CD drive and restart your PC (unfortunately, Fedora Core no longer ships with floppy images, just a 6 MB image

that you can install to a USB thumb drive, but chances are if you can't boot from CD you won't be able to boot from a thumb drive, either). After it boots up, you'll be taken to the opening screen. There is very little information on this screen; it simply notifies you that you are ready to start the installation.

You're asked how you wish to proceed with the installation. You almost always will want to choose the first option, Install or upgrade in graphical mode. You can select this option by simply pressing the Enter key. In fact, the only good reason not to use graphical mode would be if your PC were so outdated that it couldn't support a graphical installation. Of course, if your machine doesn't support a graphical installation, it might not support most of the really cool graphical Linux products such as KDE, GNOME, GIMP, and Open Office. If you will recall our earlier discussion about system requirements, consider that one of the authors has personally installed Red Hat 9.0 with all options in graphical mode on a Pentium II 233MHz with only 64 megabytes of memory. (However, it should be noted that the machine *didn't* perform as well as one might like, and that Red Hat 9.0 is a slightly older version of Fedora Core Linux, but still in use today.) To put this in perspective, a machine like the one just described has not been sold new in stores since about 1998. This means that you probably have a machine that is more than capable of using graphical mode and running everything Linux has to offer.

This is another strong point in favor of Linux. Unlike Microsoft Windows, it's not resource intensive. Fedora Core 4 will run on machines that don't support later versions of Windows, such as Windows XP.

You'll be asked next whether you want to test your CD. If you purchased a packaged version of Linux, then this is probably unnecessary. If you downloaded Fedora Core Linux onto your own CDs, you'll probably want to select Yes. The reason for this is simple. If you copied downloaded install files to a CD using your own CD burner, a variety of things may have gone wrong, and it's possible that the CD is not in proper working order. If you're using a packaged installation purchased commercially, it's very unlikely that the CD has any damage. You can use the keyboard's arrow and Enter keys to make your selection.

You may notice in the following screen that Fedora's system installer Anaconda briefly probes for video card, monitor type, and mouse type.

On the next screen, you'll find an introduction to Fedora Core Linux. It will explain what is going to happen and tell you a little about Red Hat and Fedora. If this is your first time installing Linux, it's recommended that you carefully read this screen before pressing the Next button at the bottom of the screen. It will give you an overview of what the installation process will be doing.

The next two screens are very simple, they ask what language you want to use and what keyboard setup you want. Select your language from the options provided. These steps are shown in Figures 3.14 and 3.15. It's interesting to note the plethora of languages from which you have to select. Linux is now available to users in a variety of nations, using a wide range of languages.

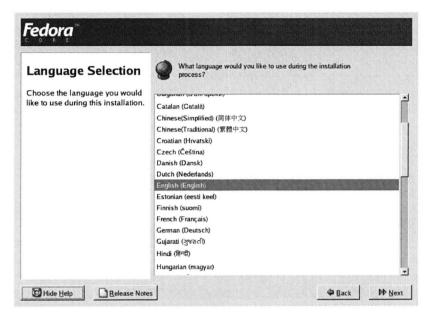

FIGURE 14.14   Choosing a language.

If the machine you're installing on already has a previous version of Linux on it, you'll be asked whether you want to wipe out the old installation completely and start from scratch or simply upgrade. This is shown in Figure 14.16.

The next step is to select packages. A *package* is a logical grouping of a number of separate applications. The various applications you can install with Linux are grouped so you can easily pick the set of applications you're most likely to need, depending on how you intend to use the machine. Your choice of packages will determine what software gets installed on your PC. The options are:

- Personal Desktop
- Workstation
- Server
- Custom

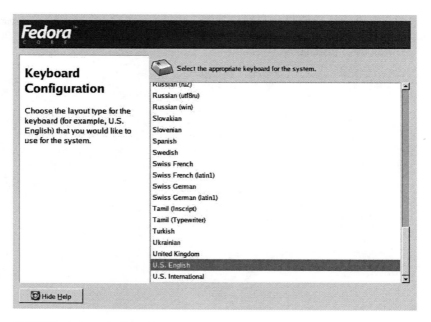

FIGURE 14.15   Keyboard setup.

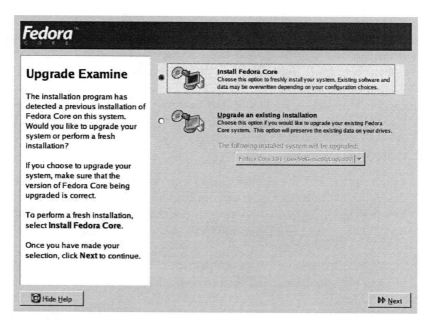

FIGURE 14.16   Installation or upgrade?

Each of these is designed for a specific type of user, are summarized in Table 3.6.

TABLE 3.6 Installation Packages

Package	Contents/Purpose
Personal Desktop	This includes things the average home user would want, including Internet software such as Web browsers and email clients. It also includes graphics programs and games.
Workstation	This is intended for the business user and includes productivity tools such as Open Office.
Server	This option is for servers. It will install a Web server, an FTP server, an email server, and other server software.
Custom	This option allows you to pick any packages you want to install.

Each of these packages is provided to make installation for a certain type of machine simple. However, this simplicity comes at a cost. If you choose Personal Desktop or Workstation, you won't be installing the Web server, FTP server, or other server packages. Conversely, if you select Server, you won't be installing many personal use items such as games. Since each of the preset options has some limitations, for our purposes we'll choose Custom because we want several elements drawn from more than one package. When you select Custom, you'll be prompted during the installation to select individual packages and applications to install. Later in this section we'll cover the options you should select. For now, select Custom. This screen is shown in Figure 14.17.

Disk Partitioning

You'll notice that the Fedora Core Linux installation gives you two options. The first is to partition your hard drive automatically. You can choose this option if you have no intention of dual booting your machine. It's also the easiest method if you don't want to bother with mount points and other esoteric Linux issues.

If you choose to automatically partition, all existing partitions will be erased and one root partition, one boot partition, and one swap partition will be created.

The second option is to use Disk Druid, which is a graphical disk partitioning program designed specifically for Linux.

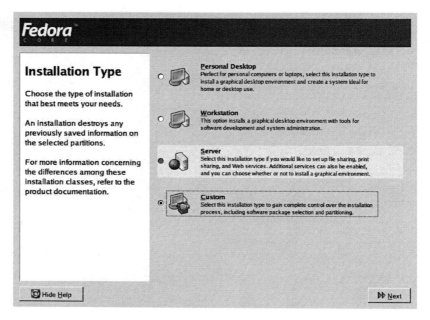

FIGURE 14.17   Selecting packages.

If you select Disk Druid, you'll be taken to a screen displaying your current partitions. There are two courses of action you might take. First, if you're not going to dual boot your system (have more than one operating system on it), it's probably best to highlight each partition, one by one, and delete it. Then, you can start fresh. Next, you will choose the New button, which will take you to a screen where you can set the parameters for this new drive. This is shown in Figure 14.18A.

You're also taken to this screen if you choose to edit an existing partition.

If you're planning to dual boot with an operating system that's already installed—for example, should you want to install Linux on your Windows machine and keep both operating systems—you will *not* delete all the existing partitions. You'll delete all partitions except for the one that contains Windows. This means that when we're done, you'll have one Windows partition and one Linux partition. The important point to remember is that you should leave the partition that has Windows on it completely untouched. The real question is, how do you know which partition has Windows? Linux and Disk Druid identify partitions differently than Windows does, but both Disk Druid and Windows list the size of the partition. The trick is to boot up your system before you begin the install and use My Computer to note the size of the partition you want to install Linux on. For example, consider Figure 14.18B.

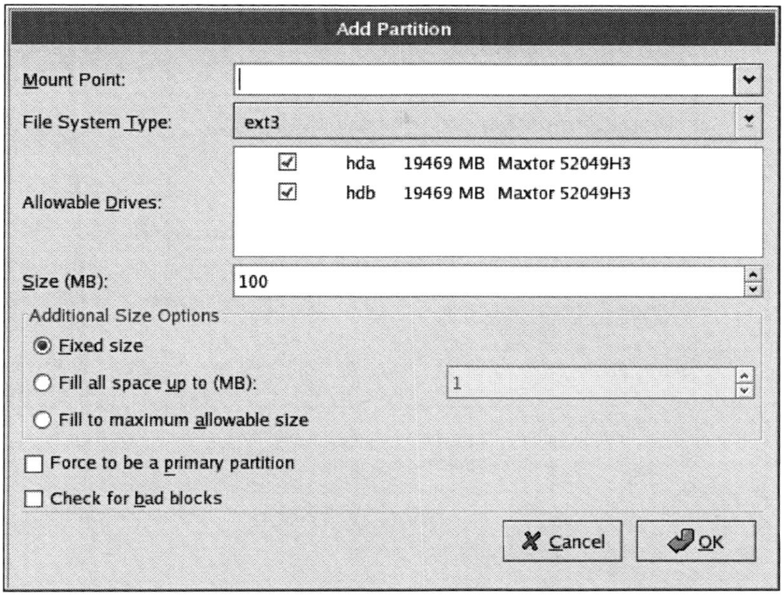

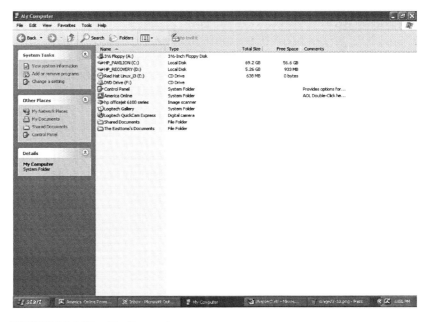

FIGURE 14.18A Setting up partitions.

FIGURE 14.18B My Computer.

This is one more reason why you were advised to read this entire chapter before attempting to perform the installation.

Here we see there's a single large partition of 13.6 gigabytes, and it's called the C drive. When you start the Linux install and get to Disk Druid, you won't see a drive labeled C, but you will see a drive that is about 56.6 gigabytes in size.

The best way to do a dual boot with Windows is to have a separate partition created to hold Linux. This partition should be created before you begin the Linux installation. If you're uncomfortable with partitioning your hard drive, you might consider using a commercial product such as Partition Magic™, available from www.symantec.com/partitionmagic/. If that were present on the machine depicted in Figure 14.19A, you'd also see a D or an E drive (unless you formatted the space using ext3 or another Linux file system, which will also be easier to identify within Disk Druid). Also note that it's much simpler to have one operating system per machine. In other words, it's easier and simpler to have separate Linux and Windows PCs than to try to install both on one machine.

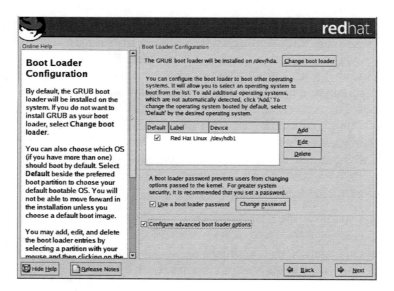

FIGURE 14.19A   A partition created to hold Linux.

One significant problem with Disk Druid is that it can be difficult to resize partitions. If your machine already has two partitions of about the right size to handle

Windows and Linux, then this is fine. If it doesn't, you could be in for a problem. As we already discussed, one of the easiest and relatively least expensive routes is to obtain some utility such as Partition Magic, install it in Windows, and resize your partitions as you see fit. Then, when you reboot and install Linux, the partitions will already be set up for you. If you want to repartition your machine manually so you can dual boot, the best option for you is to follow Microsoft's recommendations. The Microsoft Web site *www.microsoft.com/exchange/techinfo/ tips/StorageTip2.asp* might be of some help to you.

Another option is to use the FDisk utility, previously mentioned, to repartition your drive. FDisk doesn't actually allow you to resize your partitions as you need to. However, it does let you delete one partition and create one or more partitions from that freed space. One of the best Web pages on the Internet on the FDisk utility can be found at *www.computerhope.com/fdiskhlp.htm*. You can also access the Linux FDisk manual at *www.die.net/doc/linux/man/man8/fdisk.8.html*. FDisk is more versatile, but also more complex. For this reason, this book will focus on Disk Druid. Readers who want to learn more about FDisk are encouraged to use the Web sites previously mentioned and perhaps do a search in their favorite search engine for FDisk for even more resources.

Assuming that you aren't dual booting, you'll probably want to use Disk Druid to create only two partitions: a swap partition, described earlier, and a single large partition for your operating system. This is the simplest setup and is highly recommended for beginners. Once you have made those selections, you click to tell Disk Druid that you're done. You can also select a check box indicating that you want the installation process to check the actual physical disks before creating the partitions. This is a very good idea. It's time consuming, but it ensures that you won't be installing Linux on a bad hard drive. Fedora Core requires a minimum of 100 megabytes for the /boot partition. The /boot partition should also be the first partition on an older system that has 2 gigabyte BIOS limitations on hard drive size.

Continuing with the Installation

After you've finished with Disk Druid, there are still some steps to take before installation is complete. The next screen will list the operating systems on your PC. If you're not dual booting, you should see just one—Linux. If you're dual booting, you can select which operating system you want to be the default. This is shown in Figure 14.19B.

When your machine first starts, you'll be shown a display listing these operating systems, and you'll have a few moments to select one. If you don't make a selection, the default will be selected for you. You should note that this screen is configuring your boot loader. A boot loader is just a small program that loads the operating system into memory. During your boot phase, it loads the operating system, thus the name boot loader. Many Linux distributions use the LILO (Linux

load) boot loader software. Fedora Core uses a newer boot loader, GRUB (Grand Unified Boot Loader). Among other things, GRUB makes dual booting much easier.

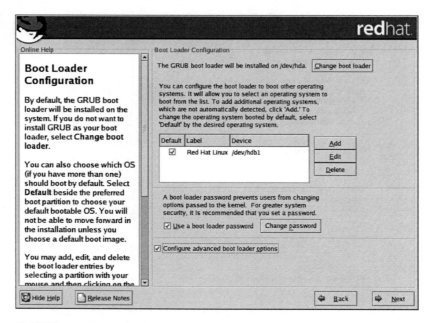

FIGURE 14.19B   Selecting an operating system.

The next stage of the installation is to configure your network adapter. If this is a standalone home machine, leave the default settings shown in Figure 14.20.

If this isn't a standalone machine but instead is a machine that will be used on a network, you'll need to set the IP address assigned to you by your network administrator.

If you're not on a network but are going to log on to the Internet, the chances are that your ISP assigns you an IP each time you log on (this is referred to as a dynamic IP). This is the default setting for Linux, so you should be fine. If your ISP assigns you a static IP, a rather unusual step for an ISP to take, it will have to tell you what that IP address is.

An IP address consists of four numbers, each between 0 and 255 and separated by periods. An example of an IP address is 10.32.0.43.

Don't worry if you either don't know the proper network settings right now or put them in wrong. You can change them at any time, after you have Linux up and running.

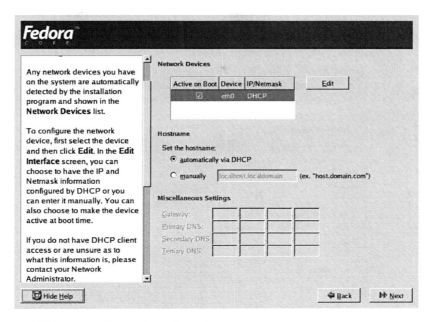

FIGURE 14.20   Network configuration.

Chapter 5 shows you in detail exactly how to do it. After you've configured your network card, the next phase is to set up the firewall. The default configuration is shown in Figure 14.21. On this screen you can also allow access to services such as mail and FTP servers and enable Security Enhanced Linux (SELinux), which is a highly secure Linux kernel.

The very next screen has you select your time zone. If you get this wrong, don't worry; as with the network configuration, you can reconfigure this after your PC is up and running. You can see the time zone screen in Figure 14.22.

The next screen is simple but important. Here you set the root password. The main action taken at this point and depicted in Figure 14.23 is to set the root password.

This is critical. In Linux and Unix, root is like the system administrator in Windows. Anyone who logs on to your PC as root can do anything to the machine. This means you must select a good password. It should be at least eight characters in length and contain a combination of letters and numbers. Make certain you write

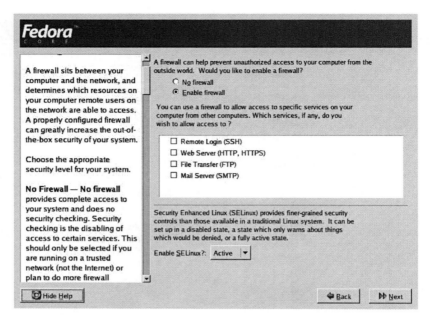

FIGURE 14.21   Firewall configuration.

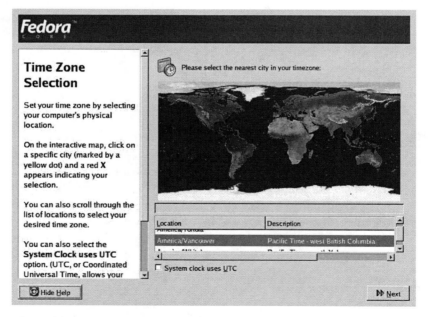

FIGURE 14.22   Selecting the time zone.

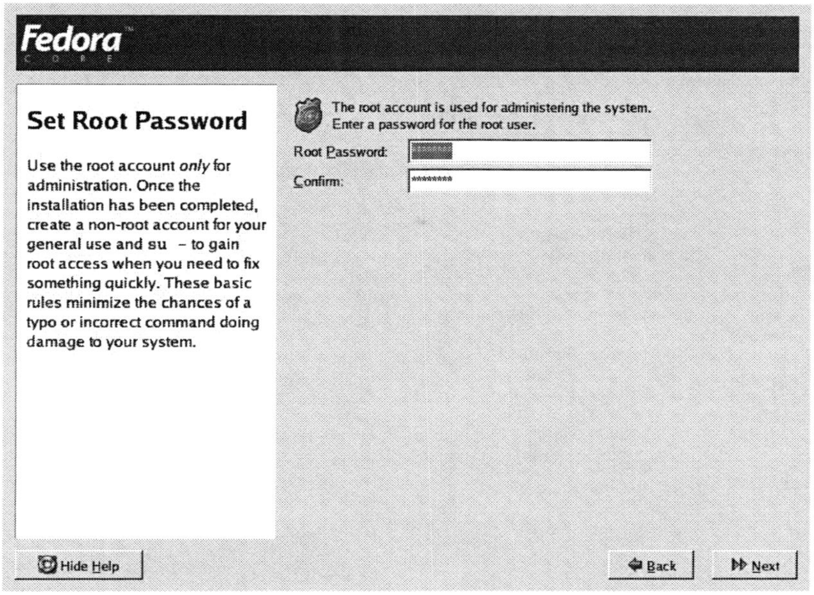

FIGURE 14.23 Setting the root password.

it down somewhere. If you forget it, you're in really deep trouble. Your only option will be to reinstall completely and wipe out the previous Linux installation.

Next, you'll choose packages. This is a rather lengthy topic in itself and will be covered in the next section. You're now, however, done with the essential configuration of your PC and have reached a significant milestone in the installation process.

CHOOSING PACKAGES

Next to the Disk Druid, this is probably the most important part of the installation. There are a number of packages you could select, each with a different purpose. They're divided into categories such as desktops, servers, and development. Each of those categories will be explored in this part, and specific package groups will be explained. At the end of this section is a list of the packages it's recommended you select. The Package Group Selection screen is shown in Figure 14.24.

Desktops

You can use Linux in a simple command-line mode (also called shell mode). There are three packages listed in this section: X Window System, GNOME (GNU Object

Model Environment), and KDE (K Desktop Environment). Each of these is a complete graphical window interface that operates in a fashion similar to Microsoft Windows. Which one you choose is a matter of preference. In this book, we'll use the KDE user interface. Whether you choose KDE or GNOME, it should be chosen

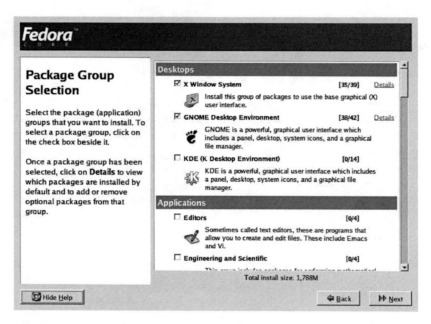

FIGURE 14.24   Package selection.

in conjunction with X Window System. To follow along with this book, you should select GNOME, KDE, and X Window System.

Applications

This part is going to be very important to you. It lists the various types of applications Linux can install. Most of it is self explanatory. For example, the Office Productivity package includes word processors, spreadsheets, and so on. The Games and Entertainment package includes games for Linux. A complete list, with explanation, is provided in Table 3.7.

TABLE 3.7 Application Packages

Package	Purpose
Editors	This package provides a variety of text editors, many of which have functionality far beyond text editors such as Notepad, which you may have used.
Engineering and Scientific	This package contains a number of programs for scientists and engineers.
Graphical Internet	Including this package will provide you with access to a variety of Internet tools, including a Web browser, chat software, and email clients.
Text-Based Internet	You'll need this package only if you'll be running without a desktop graphical user environment. It will allow you to check email and do some Internet activities.
Office Productivity	This package includes a wide array of word processors, spreadsheets, presentation tools, and more.
Sound and Video	Installing this package gives you access to several programs used to record sound and video, play video, and more.
Authoring and Publishing	These programs are specifically for desktop publishing and Web page development.
Graphics	In this package you will find applications for image manipulation. Some of these applications are on a par with commercial products such as Adobe Photoshop.
Games and Entertainment.	Fedora Core 4 comes with several games you can play to amuse yourself.

Different Linux users will find different combinations of packages to their liking. However, this book concentrates on certain applications you must install. For that reason, please ensure that you select everything in Table 3.8.

This set of packages is a good mix of server, workstation, and personal options. You have the office productivity of a business workstation, the entertainment and graphics of a personal workstation, and the Web software of a server

TABLE 3.8   Recommended Packages

Part	Packages
Desktops	X Window System GNOME KDE
Applications	Editors Graphical Internet Office Productivity Sound and Video Graphics Games and Entertainment
Servers	Server and Configuration Tools Web Server PostgreSQL Database MySQL Database
Development	None
System	Administration Tools System Tools Printing Support
Miscellaneous	Java (Optional)

It's also very important to note that packages can be added and removed after Linux is in operation. The procedure to add or remove packages will be described later in this book. Chapter 15 includes a section on adding and removing packages.

> As you go through this book, you'll be introduced to various applications that are used in Linux. If you don't include the appropriate packages, you won't have those applications on your machine. However, you can either add a package or download the application from a Web site. In most cases, you're given the Web site address when you're first introduced to the product. It's also possible that readers using a different Linux distribution or a different version of Fedora/Red Hat won't have all of the applications installed.

You must set a root password before leaving this screen, but adding users can be done later if you prefer. In fact, many Linux administrators add users after the machine is fully installed and configured. However, you do have the option of adding user accounts now if you so desire.

Completing the Installation

At this point, the installation will run unattended for several minutes. Depending on the speed of your PC's processor and the number of packages you selected, this could take anywhere from a few minutes to 30 minutes or more. At some point, the CD-ROM door will open and you will be prompted to insert disk two. When that disk is

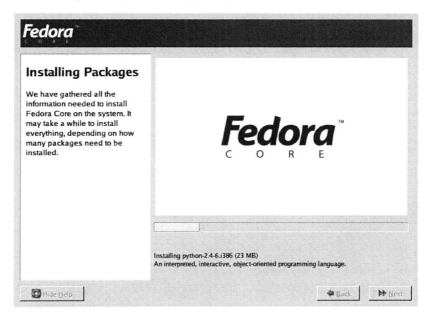

FIGURE 14.25 Installation progress.

done, you might be prompted to insert a third disk, and then there are just a few basic configuration items you need to take care of. As your disk is installing, you'll see a screen displaying the progress of the installation. That screen is shown in Figure 14.25.

The more packages you select, the longer the installation will take. An installation that includes all available packages can take over two hours.

When package installation is complete, you'll be prompted to reboot your computer, where you'll be greeted by a Welcome screen. You'll need to agree to the License Agreement and then you'll be given an opportunity to set the date and time. You can choose whether you want to have your computer's clock set via Network Time Protocol, which will synchronize your time with one of several atomic clocks. Just select the check box, choose a server, and then click Next. Now you can

configure your video display, including resolution and color depth. Choose something that both your video card and monitor can handle and then click Next. On the next screen, you can add user accounts. These are important because you can define users with specific permissions, allowing them to do only the tasks you want them to do. It's a good idea to take a minute and add a user account for yourself. That way, you can log on without needing to do so as root. A common system for usernames is to use the first initial of the first name with the last name. For example, one of the authors' usernames might be bhoff. Next, you'll have the opportunity to test your sound card and then install any additional software you might need. After this, your system will reboot and you can log in with your username and password. You've successfully installed Linux and are ready to start using it.

> *In normal operations it's not recommended that you log on as the root user. Remember that the root is the same thing as an administrator in Windows. However, for the purposes of this book, you should log on as root. That way, you'll have access to all the features of Linux, including administrative tools. This will be critical when we cover administrative tools later in this book.*

A BRIEF LOOK AT INSTALLING OTHER DISTROS

Due to the fact that we're going to focus mainly on SuSE Linux 9.3 in this book, we'll just have a brief look at the installation process for Mandriva, Linspire, and Xandros Linux.

Mandriva

Upon inserting the first Mandriva CD, you're greeted with a screen containing several options. Choose the Press <Enter> to install or upgrade option, which begins loading the Linux kernel and probing for devices. You now arrive at the System installation section. Here you'll see a list of steps on the left. The first step is Language selection, followed by the License Agreement. Next is the Security screen, where you'll choose your desired security level from a drop-down list that includes Standard, High, Higher, and Paranoid, and a slot below it for the email address of a Security Administrator. Partitioning is next. Mandriva uses the DrakX Partitioning wizard, which offers the options Use free space and Custom disk partitioning. As you'd expect, the Use free space option uses free disk space, while Custom allows you to choose or create a swap partition and main file partition, plus the file type (Ext2, Ext3, Reiser, and so on). After making your selections, formatting begins. Following formatting is the Install System screen, including Package Group Selection, where you should check Game station, uncheck Development, check

Web/FTP and Database under Server, and check GNOME Workstation under Graphical Environment. There's also a checkbox for Individual package selection. You'll need to check this in order to select all the necessary packages listed in the previous SuSE and Fedora sections. At this point, installation begins, and you'll need to agree to installing servers. Now you're treated to a slideshow that displays info about GNU, Joining the Mandriva Community, Mandriva Products, and so on. When complete, the system reboots and finishes the installation process by moving to the System configuration section where you'll enter the Root password and add a user. Next comes the Summary screen, which includes keyboard, mouse, time zone, hardware setup, plus setting of networking, security, and boot preferences. Finally, Mandriva installs updates, after which you can exit the installation and restart the system.

Linspire Five-0

At the initial boot screen, choose INSTALL or UPDATE Linspire on this computer's hard drive (you can also run it as a Live CD without installing anything, or go to ADVANCED Options. Linspire begins loading and you see the Welcome screen. Clicking Next takes you to Keyboard Layout where you choose your language. Next is the Install or Update? screen. Choose Install and click Next, at which time you'll be taken to the Installation Method screen where your options are Take over an entire hard disk or Advanced Install. You can take over an entire drive or use Advanced to choose a pre-formatted partition. On the next screen you'll see headings for Computer Name, which is for networking, and Password to set up an Administrator password. Setup Confirmation is next. Click Yes I'm Sure to move to the Installing Linspire screen, which shows information about Linspire's features and a progress bar. Note there are no options for selecting packages; you do this through the CNR Warehouse. This way, Linspire can be provided on a single install CD. Click OK to continue with the installation process. Once finished, the CD is ejected and you're prompted to remove it and restart your system by pressing Enter. You'll see a loading screen and then be prompted for the Administrator password. You're actually logged in at this point, but there are still a few more steps to take. A License Agreement appears. Click I Agree and then Next. Now you'll set the sound volume, then the date, time, and time zone. Next comes Advanced Settings. Here you can add a user account, Set Display Resolution and Configure Network Settings, among other things. Add a user account now. If you bought the boxed copy of Linspire, you may have a Linspire Extras CD. You can add extras from the CD at this point. Click Finish. A Flash tutorial automatically starts; watch any tutorial you like. You can start CNR (the little green sphere with the white running man on it), set up and sign in to your CNR account, and download the packages necessary to follow along with this book. Note that some packages may not be available to you under Linspire but most should be.

Xandros 3.0

Upon inserting the single installation CD you're presented with a splash screen. After a short time, you see the messages Preparing Default Setup, loading kernel, hardware detection, and Configuring hardware. Soon the Xandros Installation Wizard begins and you're greeted by a Welcome screen. Click Next, accept the License Agreement, and click Next again. This is the Installation Selection screen, where you can choose Express install or Custom install. Express install uses the default settings chosen by Xandros, and Custom install allows you to choose your settings and packages. You should choose Custom. You're taken to the Software Selection screen where you should select Complete Desktop from the list. Click Next to move to the Disk Configuration screen. Here your choices are Use free space, Take over disk or partition, Resize a Windows partition (may be grayed out), Replace existing Xandros OS (may be grayed out), and Manage disks and partitions (recommended for experts only). You're shown a summary screen. Clicking Manage allows you to alter partition settings. Click Next to move to the Network Connection Configuration screen. Adjust your settings as necessary, then click Next to move to Administration Configuration where you'll enter an Administrator password and Computer name, and then set security options. Next comes the User Account Configuration screen. Click Add to create a user account and password. Clicking Next takes you to the Installation Summary screen. Click Finish at which time installation begins and your hard drive is prepared. You'll see a slideshow describing Xandros and its features. When finished you're asked if you want to create a rescue boot disk. Click Create or Exit. You're told to remove the CD and press Enter to restart your computer. At the bootloader screen you can press Enter to start Xandros Desktop 3.0 or wait for it to start automatically. Once Xandros is loaded, the First Run Wizard starts, allowing you to configure your mouse, Regional Settings (keyboard and language), Date and Time, printers, System Behavior (theme), and to register your copy of Xandros. It then offers to let you open the Control Center (to configure video and other settings) and Xandros Networks (for software updates and downloads). You'll be able to add packages like MySQL through Xandros Networks, but may have problems trying to install GNOME, and other packages.

SUMMARY

This chapter walked you through the installation of SuSE Linux 9.3 and Fedora Core 4 and looked at the basic steps for installing Mandriva, Linspire, and Xandros. You were shown the steps needed to install Linux successfully. This chapter also explained the concept of partitioning and gave suggestions as to how you should partition your drive. Finally, each of the major packages was explained, and you were

given a list of what packages you should consider installing (most Linux distributions install similar software with similar functionality). It's recommended that you read this chapter carefully before attempting to install Linux on your PC.

The installation process requires some practice. Chances are that when your PC is up and running with Linux, you won't have occasion to install Linux again for quite some time. In fact, you might not install Linux again unless someone asks you to help him install it. For this reason, it's a good idea for you to repeat the entire installation process once or twice. When your PC is in use, you'll have data on it that would be wiped out by a reinstallation. If you want to practice the installation a few more times, do it now, before you personalize your PC or begin to save any data. If you choose not to practice the installation, you should at least read this chapter once thoroughly before you install and review it again after the installation. This will help to ensure that you have a firm understanding of the installation process.

REVIEW QUESTIONS

1. What are the four options for selecting packages?
2. If your PC has two NICs, what would the second one be named when you look at firewall or network configuration?
3. What is Disk Druid?
4. What is the minimum size for your swap partition?
5. What is the maximum size for your swap partition?
6. What is GRUB?
7. What is LILO?
8. What is a NIC?
9. What is RAM?

15 Basics of the Linux Operating System

In This Chapter

- Desktops and Shells
- Shell Basics
- Moving around in KDE

INTRODUCTION

Now that you've made it through the installation of Linux, you're probably anxious to begin using it. This chapter is sort of a tour of Linux basics. Many useful features and some fundamental concepts and terms are introduced here. The primary goal of this chapter, however, is simply to get you comfortable with Linux. With that in mind, it's recommended that you read this chapter and do some exploring. When you see something, play with it a little. The goal is that at the end of this chapter—and this part—you'll be comfortable with Linux.

You'll see a wide range of topics in this chapter. Each is introduced and explained briefly. You might feel that some topics are given too brief an explanation and that you're not getting enough detail. Don't let this trouble you. Each of these topics will be expanded upon in subsequent chapters.

This chapter also marks the end of Part I, "Linux Fundamentals." By the time you've completed this chapter and this section, you should be familiar with simple Linux concepts, know how to maneuver in the Linux graphical user environment, and have a basic understanding of Linux terminology. You won't be a guru, and you probably should refrain from applying for a job as a Linux system administrator, but you should be comfortable and ready to move deeper into the world of Linux.

DESKTOPS AND SHELLS

If you followed the instructions in Chapter 3, "Installing Linux," chances are that you're working from within the KDE desktop. If you aren't in KDE, or aren't sure, you can right-click the panel at the bottom of the screen (what's referred to as the taskbar in Windows) and you'll see either About Panels or Help. Clicking on About Panels will bring up an About the GNOME Panel dialog, and clicking on Help will display a list that includes About KDE Panel. If you see About KDE Panel, you're already in KDE. If you see About the GNOME Panel, you'll need to exit the current session and restart it as a KDE session. To do this, click the text that says Desktop at the top left of the screen, then select Log Out from the menu that appears. Click OK to proceed with logging out. Now you're taken to the login screen. When you first boot up SuSE, you're logged in automatically. However, if you go to the login screen, there are several words at the bottom, such as Session Type. If you click on these you'll see that they also have menus. You can go to the Session Type menu and select the desktop environment you want to use. If you followed the instructions in Chapter 3, you'll have other desktop options, such as GNOME. You should select the KDE environment. Throughout most of this book, we'll be working with the KDE environment.

Before we begin exploring desktops and shells, it would be prudent to get a firm grasp of exactly what a shell is and what a desktop environment is. A desktop environment is simply a graphical environment such as Windows. This means that your interaction with the computer is done via a graphical interface. You push buttons, click drop-down menus, and do most of your maneuvering with a mouse or similar pointing device. It might never have occurred to you that there are other ways to interact with your computer. For most PC users, the graphical Windows interface is the only thing they have known since the early 1990s.

Even after the discovery of an alternative means of interacting with a computer, most people prefer the graphical environment because it's more intuitive and user friendly. The earliest versions of Linux suffered from the lack of a graphical interface. Fortunately, that's no longer the case. Linux has several desktop environments to choose from and has offered a GUI for at least 10 years. It also has a

command-line environment that's superior to Windows. We'll delve into desktops later in this chapter, and much of this book will concern itself with using desktop environments and some of the applications you can run in the Linux desktop environment.

A shell is simply a command-line interface. A command-line interface is one in which you type commands, and the operating system types out responses. The interface is text only, often a simple black font on a white background. There are no user-friendly graphics, no buttons or drop-down menus. If you've ever used the DOS prompt in Windows 95 or 98 or the command prompt in Windows NT, 2000, or XP, then you've used a command-line interface. During the early years of computing, the command-line interface was the only way to work with any computer. In fact, Microsoft originally used a command-line interface—based on an operating system called Microsoft DOS® (disk operating system). Unix originally worked only via command-line interface as well. Apple was the first company to bring graphical desktop environments to the public, and Microsoft soon followed with Windows. Many people have become so accustomed to using a rich graphical environment that they're not even aware of command-line interfaces. You might think that such an interface is now outdated and of no use. Although it's true that most users and even many administrators prefer the easy-to-use graphical interface, it's not true that the command-line interface has no use.

Now that you know what a shell is, you might wonder why anyone would ever choose to use one when there's a rich graphical desktop environment available. There are several reasons to use a command-line interface instead of a graphical user interface. One is that the command-line interface uses less of your computer's resources. Since the command-line interface isn't creating a graphical user interface, it doesn't require as much memory or processor power. Displaying all those colorful and easy-to-use graphical elements (such as buttons, toolbars, and drop-down menus) takes memory and processor speed. If you're working on an older machine that has limited resources, you may choose not to use a graphical user interface. With Linux, you can dispense with the graphical user interface altogether and use only the command line, if that's what you want.

Another reason you might consider working with the command-line interface is that it's more streamlined. You can do anything with a command typed in directly. You don't need to go through a series of graphical steps such as selecting a drop-down menu, then a submenu, then choosing an option. You simply enter the appropriate command. A person who knows the proper commands can often accomplish a task faster in the command-line interface than via a graphical interface. This is especially useful for carrying out repetitive tasks. It's also true that command-line interfaces, while less user friendly, are far more stable. In essence, they almost never crash or freeze up.

Linux has a command-line interface called a shell, which looks very similar to the DOS prompt or command prompt from Windows. However, Linux takes the command-line interface to a whole new level. With Windows you have a single command-line interface that has a limited repertoire of commands. With Linux you have several different shells you can use and a host of commands to work with. Each shell looks pretty much the same, and the vast majority of shell commands work in any shell. We'll examine many of those commands in this book, and you should become increasingly familiar with them as you progress through this book.

However, there are interesting and useful features in each of the various shells that are unique to that shell. One useful feature common to all shells is that you can write scripts in them. A *script* is a short program that executes one or more tasks. In Windows you can write batch files for the DOS or command prompt, but there's a limited number of functions you can write into a batch file. The term *batch file* stems from the fact that it's a batch of commands being executed in sequence. Linux and Unix administrators write scripts to automate repetitive tasks. With a Linux script, you can write either a simple script, quite similar to a DOS batch file, or a fairly complex script that's essentially a program. These scripts have all the options most programming languages do. We'll be writing some scripts in a later chapter, in the final section of this book.

There are multiple shells you can use, each with specific advantages. One of the oldest is the Bourne shell. This was followed by an updated version called the Bourne-again shell (often simply called *bash*). The bash shell is the default used in Linux. There are other shells, each with its own advantages and disadvantages. The most commonly used shells are summarized in Table 4.1.

TABLE 4.1   Linux Shells

Shell	Features
Bourne	One of the oldest shells for Unix or Linux. It was created in the late 1970s by Steve Bourne and was included in the seventh edition of Bell Labs' Unix.
Bourne-again (bash)	This is an updated version of the Bourne shell. It's the default shell used in most Linux distributions.
Korn	This shell was developed by David Korn at the AT&T Bell Labs. This shell is very popular with Linux administrators.
csh	This shell may be of interest to programmers since its syntax is similar to the C language.

The list of shells in Table 4.1 is not exhaustive. These are the most commonly used shells, and any Linux enthusiast should at least be aware of their existence. In this book we'll use the bash shell because it's the most commonly used Linux shell. Remember, however, that most of the basic commands and simple scripts work the same in all shells. It's only the more advanced techniques that are specific to certain shells. That means that what you learn about bash in this book can be applied to the other shells.

With Linux you have the option of having your machine start up in graphical mode or in shell mode. Even if you choose graphical mode, you can launch a shell, just as you can launch a command prompt in Windows 2000 and Windows XP. After you have a shell open, you can then type commands as you want. If you followed the installation instructions in Chapter 3, your machine starts up in graphical mode. Let's start by examining how you open a shell if your machine starts in graphical mode.

This chapter will mention the Windows command prompt several times and compare various Linux shell commands to the equivalent Windows command prompt commands. Many, but not all, Windows users have used command prompt commands. If you've never used a command prompt, it's found in Windows by clicking on the Start menu, choosing Programs, finding Accessories, and then clicking on the Command Prompt.

Assuming your machine starts up with a graphical interface, you'll have to start your shell manually. Before you can start working with shell commands, you must first start up a shell. At the bottom-left corner of your screen you should see a SuSE icon. It's a round, green button with the head of a gecko on it. (There's also an icon to the right of the SuSE icon that looks like a monitor with a stylized shell on it. It's a direct shortcut to the shell.)

The gecko is SuSE Linux's mascot, and his name is the SuSE Geeko.

This assumes you're currently using the KDE interface. If you're not, you should log out, and at the login screen change to the KDE desktop. It's also true that many distributions will put some other symbol here. In earlier versions of SuSE you saw a K in this location.

Clicking on the SuSE icon is much like clicking on the Start button at the bottom-left corner of Windows. When you click on the SuSE icon, you're given access to a number of options. You can see the Windows Start menu and the KDE Start menu in Figures 4.1 and 4.2.

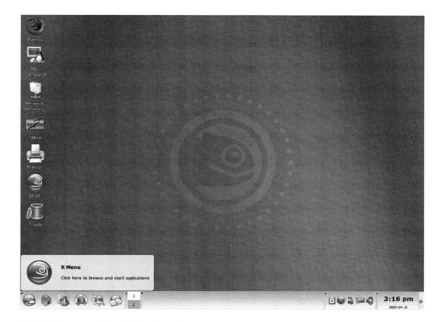

FIGURE 15.1 The KDE Start button.

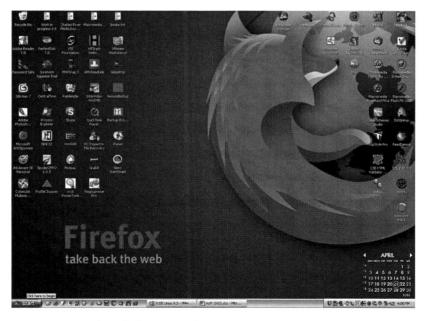

FIGURE 15.2 The Windows Start button.

You can see that the menus are very similar. This should give you some level of comfort. The KDE interface is not that different from Windows, and you should be able to get comfortable with it in a short time. We'll go into more depth on how to maneuver in KDE later in this chapter. For now, we just want to find the shell. Click once on the SuSE icon and then move up the options until you see System. If you let your mouse hover over this for a second or two, you'll see a sub-menu that's part of the System group. One of the items here is labeled Terminal. Hovering over the Terminal item will open another sub-menu that contains several shells. Click on the item labeled Konsole to launch a shell. It should look much like what you see in Figure 15.3.

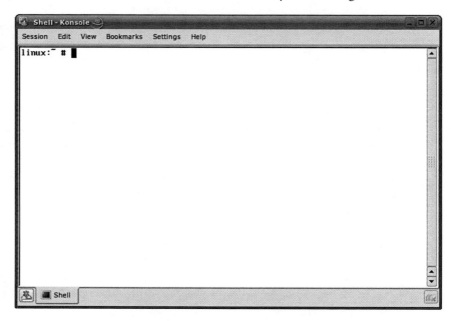

FIGURE 15.3 The shell, with the root user logged in.

As you can see, this looks a lot like a command prompt in Windows 2000 or Windows XP, or like a DOS prompt from Windows 95/98. This is to be expected, since a shell is basically a command-line interface. The next section will take you on a tour of some shell basics.

SHELL BASICS

The first thing you must do is get comfortable with a shell. You may have used DOS commands in a Windows command prompt, and this isn't going to be much different. If you never used any DOS commands, don't worry, this section will walk

you though the basics. First you should note the default command prompt shown in Figure 15.3. The default command prompt tells you who is logged in currently. The user's name and the domain he is logged in to are shown in the command prompt, such as *bhoff@linux*, or in another distro it might be *bhoff@localhost*. However, in our example since we're already logged in as root, it's just displayed as *linux:~* (it might be something like *root@localhost* in Fedora). This means that the root user is logged on to this local machine. Don't forget that the root user is the same as a Windows administrator and has full privileges to change anything in the system.

> *It's best not to log in as root unless absolutely necessary. For the examples listed throughout the book, you can log in as root, but get into the habit of logging in with your regular account, which you'll create during the installation process. This will help you avoid making accidental system-wide changes.*

As was previously mentioned, bash is the default Linux shell. Fortunately, all shells share many common commands. Now would be a good time to walk you through a few of these and compare them to DOS commands you might use in Windows. Keep in mind that these commands are case sensitive. That means that if you capitalize something you shouldn't, it will not be recognized. For example, the command to show who is currently connected to your Linux machine is done by entering who. If you enter Who, WHO, or wHo, it won't work. When in doubt, go with all lowercase.

One of the simplest commands is the command to list all the contents of your current directory: the ls command. This is very much like the dir command in Windows. Both commands list the contents of the current directory. You simply type ls, in all lowercase letters, and press the Enter key. You'll see the contents of that directory, as shown in Figure 15.4.

It was mentioned previously that the Linux shell is more versatile and robust than the Windows command prompt. You can see this in the ls command. When you use the equivalent DOS command, dir, you see a list of the directory content with no clue as to what types of files or subdirectories it contains. When you enter ls you might notice that some items are in different colors. All files are in black, all directories in blue, and all executable files or scripts are in green. This color-coding of items makes it easy to identify and use certain items. This is just one example, a simple one that illustrates some of the added features in Linux.

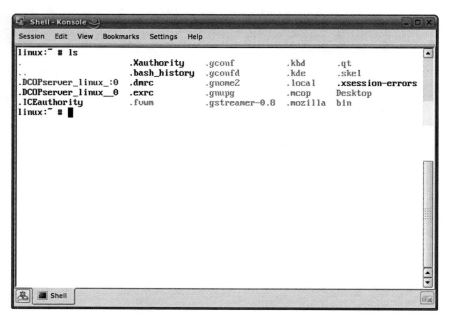

FIGURE 15.4   The ls command.

Now that you've seen how to list the contents of a directory, let's look at some other shell commands. This should help you get started with the basics of shell operations. This brings us to creating directories, changing directories, and moving files. Directories are designed to give you an organized way to store your files and programs. From time to time, you may need to create new directories, navigate through directories, or move files around. This is not much different from what it was in the Windows command prompt, where you create a file by typing md directoryname. For example, if you wanted to create a directory named stuff, you'd enter md stuff. In Linux you do this with the mkdir command (short for Make Directory) like this: mkdir stuff. Simply type mkdir stuff in the shell, and then run the ls command to see the content of the directory you are in. You should see a new subdirectory named stuff. You can see this demonstrated in Figure 15.5.

Changing directories isn't much tougher than that. Before we change to our new directory, perhaps we should put something in it. You may have noticed that when we ran the ls command, there was a file named .bash_history. This is a log of the last commands you typed into the shell. We're going to copy that file to our stuff directory. This is a simple process using the cp command. Simply type cp filename target directory (the name of the file you want to copy and the directory you want to copy it to). Enter cp .bash_history stuff, as you see in Figure 15.6.

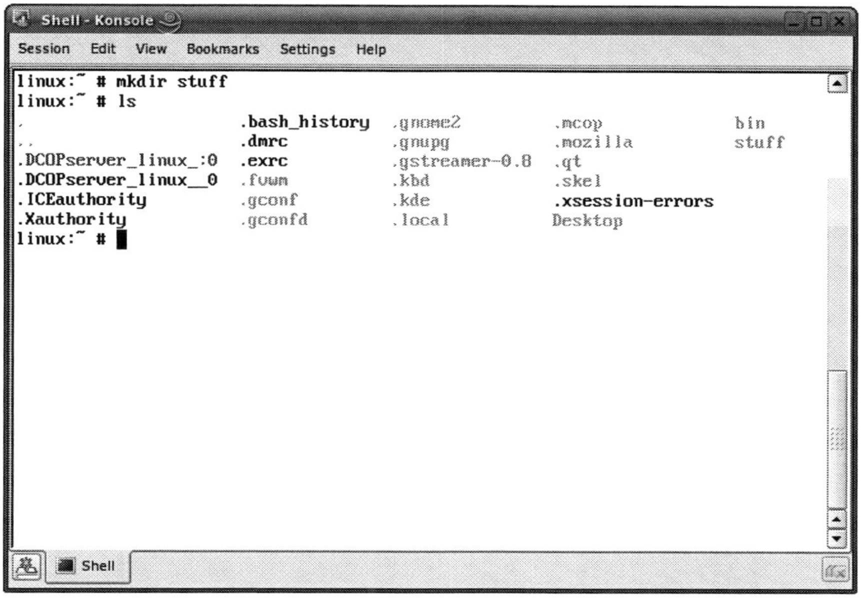

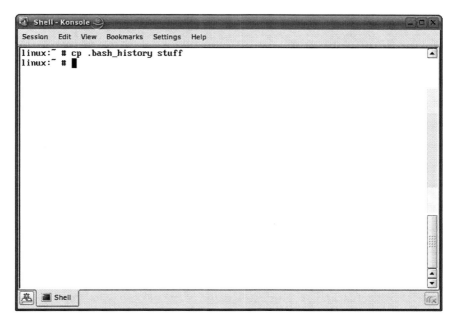

FIGURE 15.5 Using the mkdir command.

FIGURE 15.6 Copying files.

This command is very similar to copying files in a Windows command prompt, where you enter the word copy followed by the file and target directory. If we were performing this copy in Windows, we could enter copy bash_history stuff. (Windows won't allow the leading dot on the filename. In Linux, files with a leading dot are hidden, but as root you'll be able to see them.)

If you want to see if the file was actually copied to the directory in question, you'll need to change to that directory and run the ls command. You can change directories with the cd command by simply typing cd followed by the name of the directory. In our case, that would be cd stuff. Then enter ls and you will see that the file has been copied to that directory. This is shown in Figure 15.7.

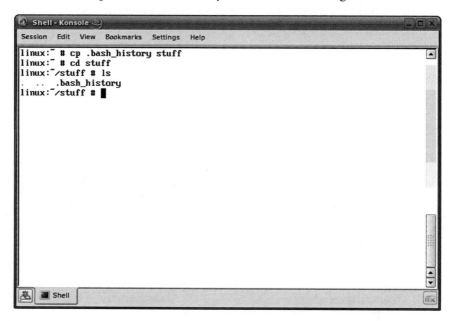

FIGURE 15.7   Changing directories.

The change directory command is the same as in Windows command prompts. You type cd followed by the directory name.

You'll note that in several instances we examine commands that are very similar or identical to Windows command prompt commands. It's important to remember that Unix existed decades before DOS or Windows, and Windows copied the commands from Unix, not vice versa. This is important because Linux beginners often wonder why Linux didn't simply use the same commands Windows uses.

You may have noticed that the previous commands are not displayed in the figures in this chapter, just the command being discussed. When you type this into your shell, you probably see everything you've entered so far. This may lead you to ask how to get rid of the old stuff you no longer want to view. Just type the word clear, and the shell screen will clear. The same thing can be done in the Windows command prompt by typing cls (short for clear screen.)

What happens when you want to get rid of a file or a directory? You must delete all files in a directory before you can get rid of that directory, so let's discuss removing files first. In Windows you probably used the del command, simply typing in del filename. The process is very similar in Linux, only the command is rm (for remove). You enter rm filename. In our case, we want to enter rm .bash_history. You'll then need to move out of the directory you were in, back in the root directory, to delete the directory stuff. In a Windows command prompt you'd enter cd\; in Linux, simply typing cd will take you to the root directory. So now you type cd, and you're back at the root and ready to remove that directory. In the Windows command prompt, you can use the rd (remove directory) command. In Linux, you use the rmdir command (remove directory). The format is rmdir directoryname. In our case, that would be rmdir stuff. The entire process, from removing the file to removing the directory, is shown in Figure 15.8.

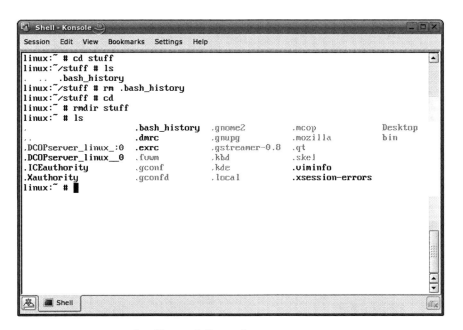

FIGURE 15.8   Removing files and directories.

Table 4.2 lists some basic Linux shell commands with an example of using each command, an explanation of the command, and the equivalent Windows command prompt command.

TABLE 4.2 Linux Shell Command and Windows Command Prompt Commands

Linux Command	Explanation and Example	Windows Command Prompt Equivalent
`ls`	List the content of the current directory. Example: `ls`	`dir` Example: `dir`
`cp`	Copy a file to another directory. Example: `cp filename.txt directoryname`	`copy` Example: `copy filename.txt directoryname`
`mkdir`	Create a new directory. Example: `mkdir directoryname`	`md` Example: `md directoryname`
`cd`	Change directories. Example: `cd directoryname`	Identical.
`rm`	Delete or remove a file. Example: `rm filename`	`del` Example: `del filename`
`rmdir`	Remove or delete a directory. Example: `rmdir directoryname`	`rd` Example:`rd directoryname`
`clear`	Clear the screen. Example: `clear`	`cls` Example: `cls`

This list is by no means comprehensive, but it does contain the basic shell commands you must be familiar with. It's recommended that you take some time to experiment with these commands and get comfortable with them. Part V, "Advanced Linux," deals extensively with using the shell. Chapter 18, "Linux Shell Commands," discusses a host of shell commands at some length. Chapter 19, "System Administration from the Shell," shows you how to perform administrative tasks using the shell. Chapter 20, "Basic Shell Scripting" teaches you the basics of writing your own shell scripts. For now all you need is a basic understanding of what a shell is and how to accomplish some basic tasks in the shell.

There's one last simple but very useful feature of the shell that needs to be covered before we continue. The shell has access to Linux manuals built into it. These are frequently called *man pages* (short for manual). Man pages enable you to look up the specifics for any Linux command. For example, if you forget how the `mkdir` command works, you can simply enter `man mkdir` at the shell, and you'll be shown

an entire section of the Linux manual on this command. Man pages are very useful, and no Linux aficionado would dream of not using them.

MOVING AROUND IN KDE

Shell commands are very useful, but frankly not that user friendly. You have to type them in exactly, and if you make any mistakes, even in capitalization, they fail to work. In addition, most Windows users want a cool graphical interface. Fortunately, Linux provides several to choose from. The two most popular are GNOME and KDE. For this book we'll use KDE because it's more commonly used and is the preferred graphical interface of the authors. However, in Chapter 8, "The GNOME Interface," we'll take some time to explore GNOME and some of the applications and utilities that ship with it.

> *You'll see several terms used interchangeably throughout this book, and throughout all Linux documentation. The terms* desktop, desktop environment, *and* graphical interface *are all referring to the graphical user interface you're using. This could be KDE, GNOME, or some other interface.*

You've already seen the KDE interface; it was used in the preceding section to locate and launch the shell. You might have noted that it isn't too different from the Windows interface you're used to. To begin with, on the desktop you should notice a taskbar at the bottom of the screen with a SuSE icon in the left corner. This is shown in Figure 15.9.

The bottom taskbar looks quite similar to the one in Windows. The icon on the left is a shortcut to Open Office, an office productivity suite that we'll examine in detail later in this book. On the right side of the taskbar you should see a clock displaying the current time. The shortcut icons in the taskbar are simply some common applications you might need. Let's examine how to add a shortcut or delete an existing one. Deleting is quite simple. You simply right-click on an icon with your mouse and choose Remove from the menu that appears. This is shown in Figure 15.10.

Adding a shortcut is not particularly difficult, either. Since there's no Open Office taskbar shortcut by default, let's add one. Right-click on the taskbar and choose Add to Panel. Then, select what you want to add. We'll explore all of these options later in this book, but for now the Application option is the only one we're interested in. You'll see a menu exactly like you see when you select the Start menu by clicking the SuSE icon. For the example, select Office and Office Suite. This is shown in Figure 15.11A.

FIGURE 15.9   The KDE desktop.

FIGURE 15.10   Removing an icon from the taskbar.

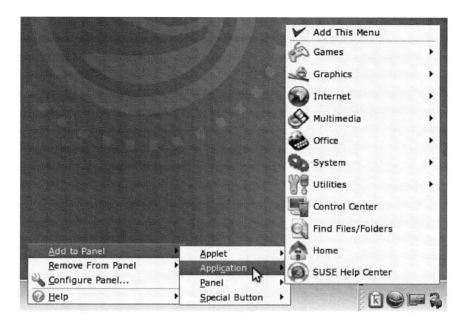

FIGURE 15.11A Adding a button to the taskbar.

Of course, you can create shortcuts only for applications you've already installed, and you'll want only the ones you use most frequently. How do you find other applications? What you need is a brief tour of KDE so you can find various programs easily when you need to later. Later in this book we'll explore many of these features and applications in some depth. Right now, let's just get comfortable.

When you click on the SuSE icon, you see a menu of items, much like what you're probably used to in Windows. Applications are grouped in sections based on their functions. The section on System Settings is shown in Figure 15.11B, and we'll explore that section in detail in Chapter 5, "System Configuration in KDE."

Each of these groups of applications contains logically related applications. For example, the Graphics group contains applications used to manipulate and generate various graphical images. What specific applications you have in each grouping will depend on what packages you chose when installing Linux. If you installed according to the instructions in Chapter 3, "Installing Linux," you should have all the applications we'll discuss in this and later chapters. Let's take a brief tour of each of these logical groupings and see what we have available.

At the very top you will see the applications you most recently used. In Figure 15.11B, that includes the Control Center and Konsole. On your machine, that would include any applications you've used recently. You'll then see a header that says All Applications, and beneath that are the various program groups.

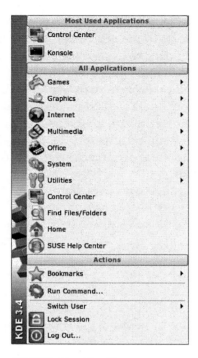

FIGURE 15.11B The menu.

The first group is Games. A number of games are included with Linux. It's beyond the scope of this book to explore and explain these games, but you should be aware that there's a plethora of amusing pastimes included with the standard installation of SuSE Linux.

This is one area where the various Linux distributions might differ. The number of games included varies from distribution to distribution

In many older versions of KDE, there was an Extras category. If you're using the very latest version of KDE, you won't see this category; it was folded into the other categories. In some distros, instead of seeing a separate Extras category, each category has a subcategory called Additional. In some distributions this is called More, rather than Additional. For example, there might be an Additional Graphics item under the Graphics category. If you're using SuSE Linux 9.3, you should have the more recent version of KDE. If you're using an earlier version, you might not. If you want to get the latest KDE, you can download it from *www.kde.org*. If you have an older version of KDE and want to stay with it, you should become familiar with the Extras section. This is a very interesting category. It contains applications that properly belong in one of the other categories but were added as extras.

Some readers might wonder why we spend time investigating Extras if that category no longer exists in the newest versions of the KDE interface. One reason is that many readers might be using older versions of Linux. Unlike Windows users, it's not uncommon to find Linux users sticking with an older version. New versions of Linux are not radical departures from previous versions. The changes are usually subtle and, therefore, there is often no pressing drive to constantly upgrade to the newest version. Another reason to discuss the Extras category is that every application in that category still exists with SuSE 9.3 but has simply been moved. They've been moved back to the appropriate categories; for example, Extras games are now found under Games.

One important tool that's been moved out of the Extras System Tools subcategory is a file manager known as Konqueror. It's been moved to the main menu and renamed Home (there's also a root version found under System > File Manager > File Manager > Super User Mode). This file manager is very much like the one that began in Windows 3.1 and was carried through subsequent versions of Windows. This tool will be of great importance in later chapters, so it bears exploration. When you launch Konqueror, it looks somewhat like a Web browser (because it is—more on that in Chapter 13, "Web Browsers, E-Mail, and Internet Applications"), and it begins by pointing to the home directory of the user who's currently logged in. If you're logged in as root, you'll be pointing to the root directory, as shown in Figure 15.12.

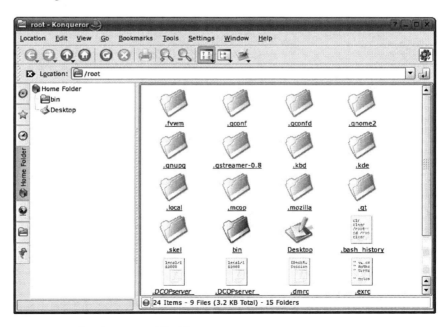

FIGURE 15.12 The Konqueror File Manager.

Standard practice is to not *work logged on as root unless you absolutely require administrative rights to perform a cetain task. Except for the chapters that deal directly with administrative tasks, it's recommended that while working through this book you log in as the user account you created in Chapter 3. It's recommended that you not proceed logged on as root.*

This brings up the question of what a home directory is. For that matter, some readers might be wondering what a directory is. Your computer has lots of files. If you save a document, that's a file. If you create a spreadsheet, that's a file. If you save a picture to your computer, that's a file. If you install a program, it probably has several files. These files are organized into *directories*. If you've ever used Windows Explorer to peruse the folders and files on your computer, keep in mind that looking through directories on a Linux machine using Konqueror is very much the same.

You can use the arrow keys on the left side of the toolbar to move up a level or down a level. The three keys farthest to the right change the way you view items in the File Manager. The view shown in Figure 15.12 is the icon view and is selected by the third button from the right. Selecting the second button from the right will choose tree view, which is shown in Figure 15.13.

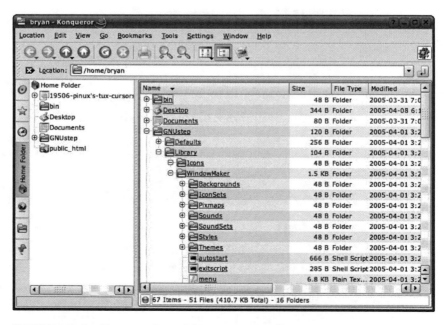

FIGURE 15.13   The tree view of the Konqueror File Manager.

The Konqueror File Manager shares some other features found in the Windows File Manager. One of the most useful features is the capability to bookmark a location. In any standard Web browser you can bookmark (or add to Favorites) any Web site you want, and then you have quick access to it later. Because the Konqueror File Manager operates like a browser, you can bookmark directories. You simply open that directory, select Bookmark from the drop-down menu, and click Add Bookmark. Figure 15.14 shows how to bookmark a folder, and Figure 15.15 shows that item in the File Manager Bookmarks.

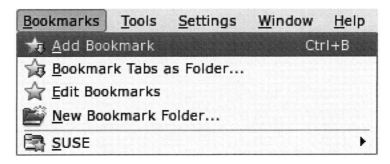

FIGURE 15.14 Bookmarking a directory.

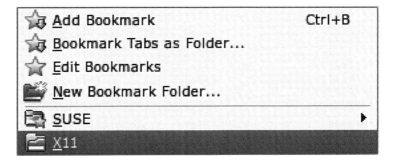

FIGURE 15.15 A new item in Bookmarks.

The Konqueror File Manager isn't the only item you might find interesting, but it's one of the most useful. It would probably be prudent for you to spend some time experimenting with Konqueror to make certain you're comfortable with it since you'll be using it in later chapters. However, there's one caveat you should keep in mind. If you're logged on as root, which you probably are at the moment, you could delete important system files. When you're experimenting with Konqueror, it's recommended that you adhere to the following rules:

■ Most of your experimentation should consist of simply moving around and finding things. You shouldn't be deleting any files.

■ If you want to experiment with deleting or moving files, first create a new directory and a couple of new files for that purpose. Then, you won't be hurting any system files.

■ If you're in doubt about what something is, or what it does, leave it alone.

If you follow these three simple rules, you should be able to take a rather extensive tour of the Konqueror File Manager without harming your system. An even better method is to log in with your regular account so you don't accidentally delete important files.

The category following Games is Graphics. In this category, you'll find some very useful applications, such as GNU Image Manipulation Program (GIMP). It's a full-fledged graphics program comparable to Adobe Photoshop. Chapter 14, "Moving from Adobe Photoshop to GIMP," is devoted to GIMP. One tool you'd also expect to find in the Graphics section is a screen capture tool (although it's in the right spot in Fedora). Instead, you'll find it under Utilities > Desktop. The program is called KSnapshot and was used to capture most of the images for this book. If you're using a different Linux distribution and GIMP wasn't included, don't worry. When we get to that chapter, you'll be told where to download it for free.

Most readers will probably find the Graphics section very useful. In this section you'll find several email clients, Web browsers, and instant messenger clients. All of these will be explored in detail in a later chapter. At this point, it's simply necessary that you realize they're there and where you may find them.

After the Internet category is Multimedia. This category has a number of useful applications in it. It has audio and video players, volume controls, and sound recorders, all of which you might expect because you find the same items in Windows. What you might not expect is the sound mixer program. It works just like a sound mixer on an equalizer for your home stereo, but it adjusts sounds you record or work with on your Linux computer. Another surprise not found in Windows is the inclusion of not one but several CD and DVD authoring tools.

One of the most commonly used categories is Office. This comes right after the Multimedia category and contains a rich suite of office programs. If you followed the installation instructions in Chapter 3, you installed Open Office (don't worry if you didn't; you'll be shown where to obtain Open Office for free). Open Office contains all you might need, including presentation programs, word processors, spreadsheets, and project management software—truly a complete suite of office products. Several chapters of this book are devoted to walking you through the intricacies of this software.

The next category is System. You're given a host of system, monitoring, and configuration tools for working with SuSE. Some of these include file management,

hardware, storage and network monitoring applications, and access to YaST and SaX2. You might remember that YaST is what we used to do the initial setup of SuSE's packages and device settings, while SaX2 was used to change screen resolution and color settings, plus monitor and video card selection. System is likely where you'll want to look if you need to change any of the aforementioned settings. YaST also offers access to various server settings, system tools, and system settings, which are used to perform various administrative tasks in Linux. These will be examined in detail in the chapters on Linux administration. Suffice it to say that there are a number of useful applications that make system administration much easier.

The final category is Utilities, where you'll find text editors, archiving tools, calculators, and print management utilities. As the category name implies, here you have everything that didn't fit in the other categories but has special utilitarian functionality.

After the category groups come direct links to important tools. The first is the Control Center, which is a convenient grouping of tools for personalizing virtually every aspect of your computing experience with Linux including networking and system administration setup, screensavers, and themes. You'll be walked through the basics of many of these applications later in this book.

The next link is Find Files/Folders, which is similar to the Windows Search Tool. Beneath that is the Home link, which will open Konqueror to the Home directory of the current user.

The last item we want to view is the SuSE Help Center. If you select this, you're provided with a rich array of helpful information and tips on how to use Linux and KDE. As you can see in Figure 15.16, there's an extensive array of documentation, including manuals for the operating system, KDE, and various commonly used applications. It also provides information on where to get technical support and how to find useful Web sites.

In addition to the wide assortment of applications you find in the Start menu, you probably noticed a few icons on the left side of the desktop. These are commonly used, essential shortcuts. These might include the Trash Bin, which works very much like the Recycle Bin you've used in Windows. It's a last chance to change your mind about deleting a file. You empty it by right-clicking on it with your mouse and choosing Empty Trash Bin. The CD/DVD-ROM and Floppy icons are shortcuts to your CD-ROM drive and your floppy disk (they'll only appear if there's media in the drives). They provide quick and easy access to these devices. Then there's Network Browsing, which is similar to My Network Places in Windows. You're also given shortcuts for printing, Open Office, the Firefox browser, and My Computer, another familiar shortcut for Windows users.

The taskbar (or panel) along the bottom of the screen provides shortcuts including the Home icon, which opens the Konqueror File Manager, beginning in

your home directory; Konsole, the Konqueror Web browser; and Kontact, which is similar to Microsoft Outlook. We'll look at these two in more detail in Chapter 13.

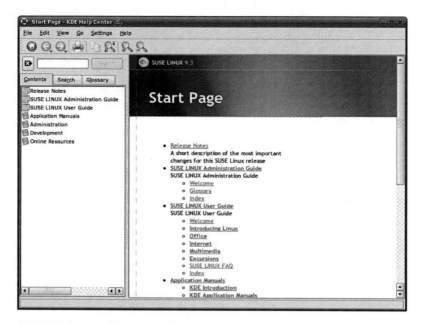

FIGURE 15.16   The KDE Help screen.

SUMMARY

As we've shown, there are two ways to approach using Linux. You can use the shell commands or you can use a graphical interface such as KDE. Most Windows users find that KDE has a familiar feel and is easier for them to adjust to. However, a basic working knowledge of shell commands is essential for many basic administrative tasks, which we'll delve into later in this book.

It's important that you be familiar with the material in this chapter before proceeding to subsequent chapters. Being comfortable with finding what you need in KDE, and at least a cursory familiarity with the shell, will be essential later in this book. It's recommended that you take some time now to go back and experiment a little with KDE and the shell, just to ensure that you're comfortable with both.

REVIEW QUESTIONS

1. What does the man command do?
2. What's the shell command to delete a directory?
3. What's the default shell used by Linux?
4. What's the Linux command to delete a file?
5. What's found in older versions of KDE under Extras?
6. What's the Linux equivalent of the Windows Recycle Bin?
7. The File Manager in Linux operates much like what other type of application?
8. What's the Linux command to view all the files in a given directory?

16 System Configuration in KDE

In This Chapter

- Desktop Preferences
- Setting Preferences
- Hardware Information
- Configuring Network Settings
- Internet Settings

INTRODUCTION

Any computer system you purchase will require some configuration. Whether it's a Windows system, Apple Macintosh, or Linux, you'll still need to configure it so it recognizes and uses your hardware. During the installation, most operating systems, including Linux, will detect and configure many types of hardware. However, you still might need to reconfigure certain settings at a later date. Reconfiguration can be required because you add new hardware, change your Internet connection, or simply want a different look to your interface. For these reasons, knowing how to configure your system properly is critical.

This chapter walks you through the essential configuration tasks you might need to perform in Linux. In this chapter, you learn to reconfigure your desktop settings, set up hardware, configure your network, connect to the Internet, and more.

This chapter focuses on using the graphical interface, KDE. If you followed the installation instructions in Chapter 3, "Installing Linux," your machine should boot up in KDE automatically. If you choose at some later date to use GNOME as your graphical interface, you'll find most of the same features, only they may be in different locations. Also recall that we discussed what to do if your machine has KDE installed but is booting to GNOME or some other interface. Go to the Start menu (the SuSE logo in the bottom-left corner of the screen) and log out. After you're logged out, you'll be at the login screen. Find the words Session Type at the bottom of the screen and click on it. You can then choose which of the installed desktops you want to use.

Throughout this book, the graphical interface we'll be concerned with is KDE. However, Chapter 8, "The GNOME Interface," will give you a brief overview of the GNOME graphical interface.

Before we get too far into our exploration of KDE, perhaps a brief history lesson is in order. The K Desktop Environment (KDE) project, which is the primary graphical interface used in this book, was founded by Matthias Ettrich in 1996. The first version was released in July 1998. The most recent version, 3.4.2, was released in July 2005. KDE is simply a modern, user-friendly, graphical desktop environment for Unix or Linux workstations. KDE seeks to fill the need for an easy-to-use desktop for Unix workstations, similar to the graphical interface PC users can find with Microsoft Windows or Apple Macintosh. You can find out more about KDE history and get the latest version of KDE at *www.kde.org*.

DESKTOP PREFERENCES

Configuring your desktop to be appealing and convenient is a task most computer users eventually have to undertake. The more you use your computer, the more important it will be to have it configured in a manner you find convenient and aesthetically pleasing. With earlier versions of Linux, those prior to KDE or GNOME, your graphical user interface options were limited. However, with recent versions you have a very rich graphical user interface, one you can easily reconfigure and adjust to meet your personal preferences. Inside KDE are a number of options for altering desktop appearance and behavior. We'll start with the simplest and most commonly used.

As in Windows, KDE enables you to right-click on the desktop and select Configure Desktop. This is one more thing that you'll find works almost exactly in Linux as it does in Windows. You can then adjust a wide array of settings. This is shown in Figures 5.1 and 5.2.

FIGURE 16.1   Right-clicking to configure the desktop.

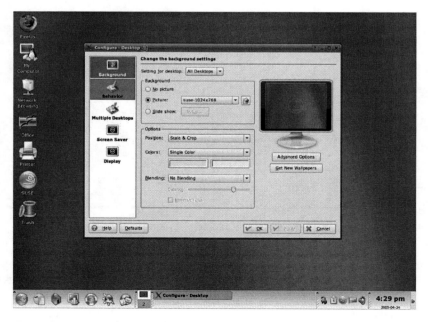

FIGURE 16.2   Desktop configuration.

As you can see, the first icon on the far left side of the dialog is Background. You probably noticed that you can set the background for the desktop. What you may not know is that KDE allows you to have multiple desktops, each with separate applications running on them, which is great for multitasking—but more on that later. There are two desktops by default but you can have up to 20. You can even set different backgrounds for each desktop. You simply select the name of the desktop in the Setting for desktop drop-down list and select a background, which can either be a background image (wallpaper) or a colored background. We'll set the backgrounds for Desktop 1 and Desktop 2 so you can see how it's done. Leaving Setting for desktop set to All Desktops will cause KDE to use the same background for all desktops, so select Desktop 1 first. For this desktop we'll use a color rather than an image. Click on the No picture radio button in the Background area, and then in the Options area select Pyramid Gradient from the Colors drop-down menu and choose a blue color by clicking on the left box below it, and a gold color for the box on the right, as shown in Figure 16.3.

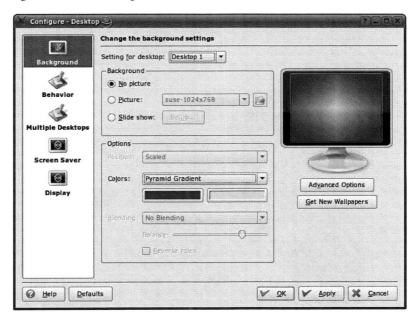

FIGURE 16.3 Setting the background for Desktop 1.

Now we'll set the background for a second desktop and examine how that looks. Select Desktop 2, and click the Picture radio button in the Background area. Then use the drop-down menu or Open file dialog button to find any appropriate image on your machine you like. Also make sure that Position in the Options area

is set to Scaled, unless you want to tile the image or otherwise alter its display. When you finish, it should look much like what's shown in Figure 16.4.

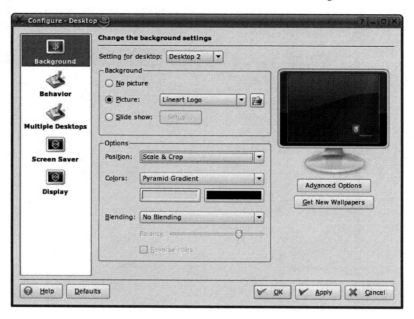

FIGURE 16.4   Setting the background for Desktop 2.

Now click the Apply button. You should see the background change behind your Desktop configuration screen. That should be the background for Desktop 1.

The next setting is Behavior, which enables you to set what occurs when a particular mouse button is selected, whether icons are displayed on the desktop, if a program might be used as a desktop background, and Menu Bar preferences. Most people will leave these with the default settings, but you can reconfigure them to behave in any manner appropriate or convenient for you. You've probably noticed that the Desktop section has several tabs. The second tab enables you to organize icons and how they're displayed. For example, enabling preview icons for certain files will show a mini preview of the file that's represented by an icon, which is useful for HTML and PDF files, among others.

The third tab in this section enables the dynamic display of mounted drives such as floppy drives, CDs, and DVDs. Enabling some of these is useful when you want quick access to a drive's contents.

One tab that used to reside in the Configure Desktop dialog has been moved to the Control Center under the Appearance & Themes heading. It enables you to select fonts and text size, as shown in Figure 16.5. This setting is very useful if you want to customize the look of your desktop, so even though it's moved it's worth

mentioning here (we'll take a closer look at the Control Panel next). While many users stick with the default settings, being able to change them is important. Not only can a different font make your desktop more appealing, it can also make it more readable if the default configuration is difficult for you to read.

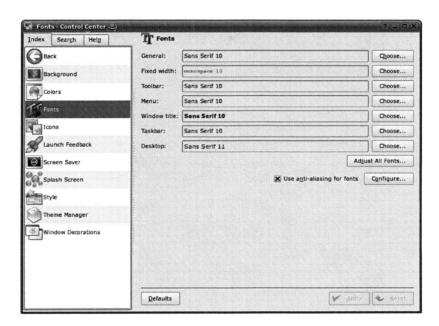

FIGURE 16.5   Font settings.

Setting fonts and icons is something you're probably familiar with from Windows. You can set all of that using KDE as well. However, KDE offers some features that Windows doesn't. One such feature is the use of multiple desktops, a feature that many Linux users find very useful. You can have more than one desktop and simply switch back and forth between them.

The third icon enables you to configure the number of desktops and name them. You probably noticed that in the taskbar is a pair of squares numbered 1 and 2; in fact, we used them briefly earlier when we were setting different backgrounds. These squares enable you to select the various desktops. You can see the number of desktop settings as well as the Desktop options in the taskbar in Figure 16.6. We'll explore setting different desktops in just a moment.

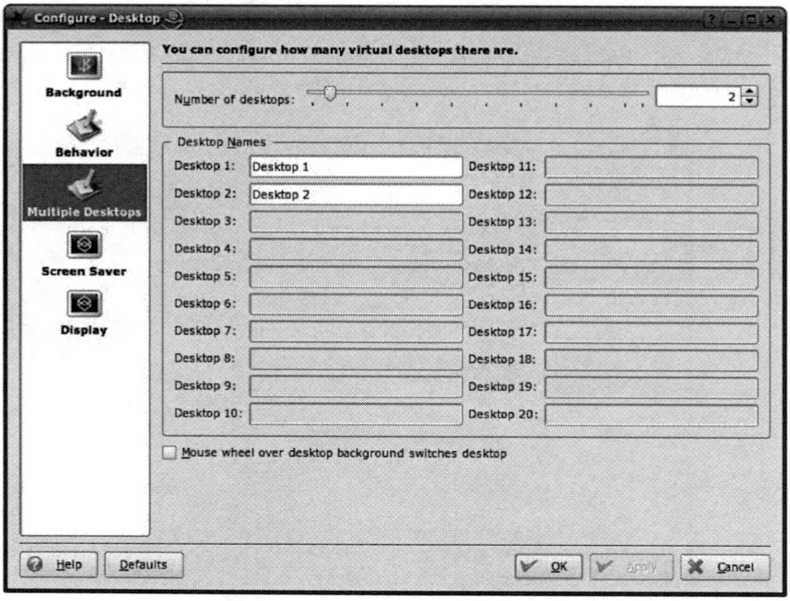

FIGURE 16.6 Number of desktops.

The next icon in the Configure Desktop dialog is Screen Saver. This is probably somewhat familiar to you because it's quite similar to selecting and configuring screensavers in Windows. You simply select the screensaver you want and the number of minutes KDE should wait before launching the screensaver. For our example, we'll pick six minutes. You then decide whether to require a password. At this point, your screen should look very much like the one shown in Figure 16.7. KDE has a number of different screensavers already in it, and you can find other screensavers written for Linux on the Web. Leaving the screensaver set to random is a good way keep things interesting.

At this point, simply click the Setup button to configure the individual screensaver you chose. Each screensaver has different options, depending on the type of screensaver you selected. For example, the Star Field screensaver enables you to select how many stars are displayed and how quickly they move.

The final icon is Display. It also contains multiple tabs, the first of which enables you to select screen size and refresh rate. The next tab allows you to change the gamma settings for your monitor, changing its overall brightness. Power Control allows you to control power management settings like powering off the monitor to save energy.

As you can see, you have all the options for configuring your desktop that you're used to accessing in Windows. You also have a few additional options you're probably not used to, since those options don't exist in Windows. One is the capability to use multiple desktops. You can now switch desktops merely by clicking on the number in

the taskbar. By default, you have two desktops to choose from. Imagine having one desktop for email and Internet applications and another for work. If you added a third, you might use that to place a console or a chat window.

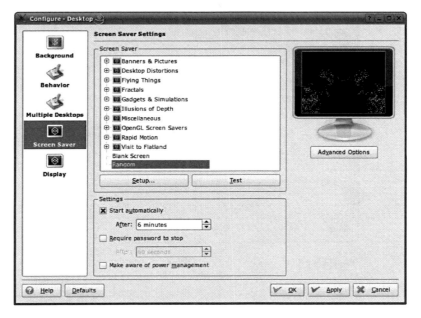

FIGURE 16.7 Configuring the screensaver.

Now you've seen how to configure your desktop preferences, establish screensavers, and even switch between multiple desktops. This information should enable you to configure your KDE desktop in the manner most appealing to you.

SETTING PREFERENCES

In addition to desktop settings, there's a variety of other preferences you might want to set. These preferences can be found under the Control Center in the Start menu. Under the Control Center you'll find numerous subcategories. The first of these is Appearance & Themes. You'll notice that under Appearance & Themes you can set some of the same settings you accessed by right-clicking your mouse on the desktop. You can set the desktop settings, backgrounds, and even screensavers. Under the second subcategory, Desktop, you can set even more desktop preferences. For example, if you select Taskbar, you have several options you can set regarding the look and behavior of your taskbar. These options can be seen in Figure 16.8. They include whether to group similar tasks, whether windows should be

shown on all desktops, and how the mouse behaves when a certain mouse button is clicked.

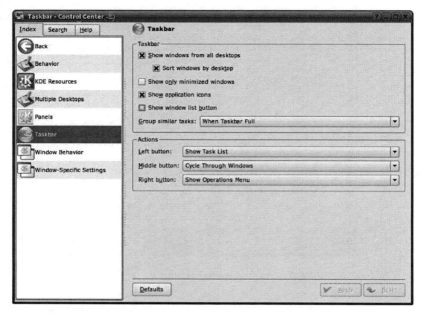

FIGURE 16.8   Taskbar settings.

The third subcategory is Information. This category provides a lot of useful information regarding various hardware devices in your computer. This will be dealt with in some detail in the next section.

In the File Browsing subcategory you can select what files are associated with what applications. For example, you might want all files ending in a .pdf extension to be opened with Adobe Acrobat Reader®. We'll be exploring the KDE Control Center more in Chapter 7, "Linux Administration from KDE."

HARDWARE INFORMATION

You can find all the detailed information you might need by looking in Hardware information, under the Hardware subcategory of YaST. You can see information about your system's hardware, as shown in Figure 16.9.

We won't delve deeply into these various settings because they depend on a thorough knowledge of PC hardware, and that's beyond the scope of this book. You can't actually change anything here, only view information about what's installed on your system.

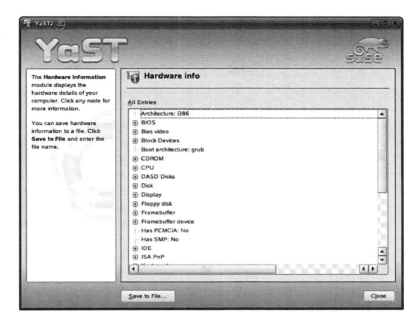

FIGURE 16.9   Hardware information.

You might wonder why this is even mentioned, since it's given such cursory treatment. The answer is twofold. First, should you ever be speaking to a technical support person over the phone, he'll probably ask about your hardware settings. You should at least know how to find them. Second, some readers will choose to expand their PC knowledge and learn more about PC hardware. The PC hardware is the same whether you run Windows or Linux. However, most PC hardware books have a strong bias toward Windows and will probably tell you where to find these settings in Windows but not in Linux.

CONFIGURING NETWORK SETTINGS

Configuring your network settings is something you'll probably have to do. Whether your PC is connected to a local area network (LAN) or simply connected to a cable modem or digital subscriber line (DSL) modem, you'll need to configure your network settings. In SuSE, you configure your network settings under YaST, as shown in Figure 16.10.

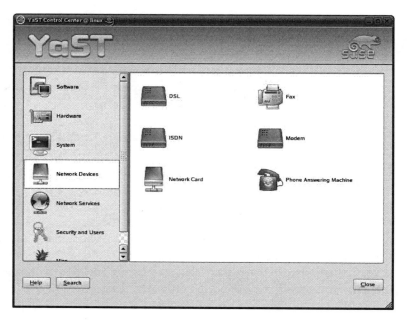

FIGURE 16.10   Network settings.

As you can see, you have several items to choose from, and the choices provided should allow you to configure any device you have connected to your system. YaST automates much of the network configuration process, so setup should be a breeze, but we'll explore how the process works and step you through it. We'll focus on Network Card and Modem, since they're the two most common methods of connecting to the Internet. Fax and Phone Answering machine aren't applicable here, and we also won't discuss ISDN because it's not very common in the United States, and if it's used in Europe you'll need to contact your Internet service provider to find out what settings to use. As for DSL (or cable for that matter), your computer is likely connected to a DSL or cable modem through a network card, so we'll look at configuring the network card itself.

Let's begin with the network interface card or NIC. Most NICs connect to a network via Ethernet. Ethernet is the most common type of network connection. Most office networks and virtually all home networks use Ethernet. The connection from Ethernet to a network card is an RJ-45 connection. RJ-45 connectors essentially look like rather large phone connectors. In fact, they are very much like the telephone connector, except that RJ-45 connectors have eight wires in them, whereas the standard telephone connector has four wires. Just for your information, the standard telephone connector is called an RJ-11. The RJ stands for *Registered Jack*. If you use a cable Internet connection, it probably comes into your home and connects with normal coaxial cable (the same cable used for television, round

wire about 1/4-inch thick with a connector that has a single needle-like protrusion in the middle) to a box, and then a network cable (also called CAT 5—category 5—cable) comes to a cable modem, and then connects from your modem to your computer's NIC via RJ45 connector. This means you have an Ethernet connection. You're also using an Ethernet connection if your PC gets to the Internet via a LAN such as in an office environment or a DSL modem.

If you're not familiar with these hardware terms, remember to look in Appendix E, "PC Hardware," which provides a basic crash course in PC hardware. It won't make you a trained PC service technician, but it will make you a computer user who understands basic PC hardware and terminology.

Selecting Network Card takes you to a list of the network cards that Linux has detected on your PC. You should see your card somewhere in the Already Configured Devices list, or possibly in the Network Cards to Configure list. If you don't, your card might not be supported in Linux. That means you'll need to contact your card's manufacturer to find out if it supports Linux and, if so, where to obtain the appropriate driver for the NIC. This screen is shown in Figure 16.11.

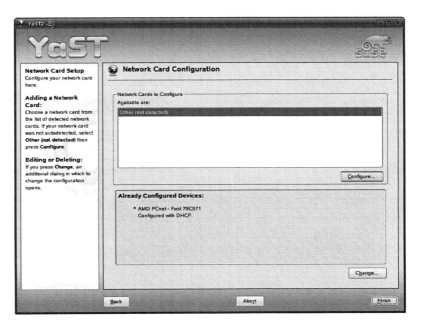

FIGURE 16.11   Selecting your Ethernet card.

You'll see the terms network card, NIC, NIC card, *and* Ethernet card *used interchangeably in most computer books. They all refer to the same thing.*

The next screen is used to configure your IP address, and you access it by selecting the Change button below Already Configured Devices and then selecting your card's name from the list that appears and clicking the Edit button. All computers on the Internet must have a unique IP address. Your ISP either assigns you an IP dynamically each time you log on or assigns you a static IP address that is always the same. If the former is true, simply select the option Automatic Address Setup (via DHCP, Dynamic Host Configuration Protocol). It means that when you dial up to your ISP or log on to your network, an IP address is assigned to your PC automatically from a pool of available addresses. If your IP address is permanently assigned, referred to as a static IP, then select Static Address Setup. You'll then need to set the two fields with information your ISP or network administrator gives you. Clicking the Finish button verifies and applies your settings, as shown in Figure 16.12.

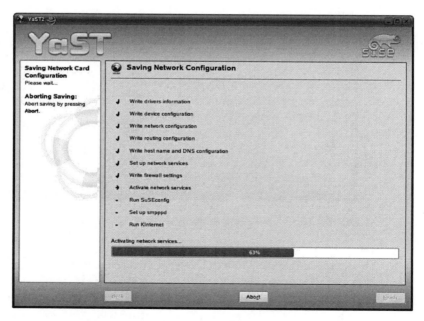

FIGURE 16.12   Saving Network Configuration.

That's it; your network card is set up and ready to go. Congratulations! That wasn't so hard, was it?

The next most commonly found connection type in homes and small offices is a modem. If your phone line plugs into the back of your PC, you're using a modem. When you select the Modem icon from the Network Devices list, you'll be presented with a list of modems detected on your PC. Like the Ethernet configuration, it's possible that your modem won't show. If that's the case, you'll have to contact the manufacturer of the modem to verify that your modem is supported by Linux.

The next screen asks you to set modem properties and is accessed by selecting the Change button below Already Configured Devices and then selecting your card's name from the list that appears and clicking the Edit button. This screen is shown in Figure 16.13.

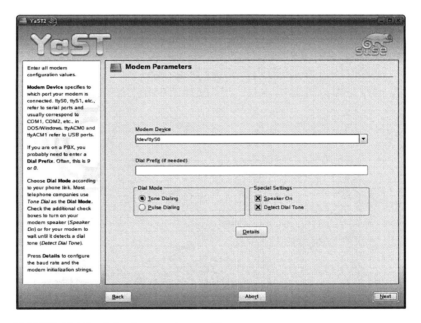

FIGURE 16.13   Selecting modem settings.

The first setting is the Modem Device. Linux refers to all modems as tty followed by a number. For example, your modem might be tty1. If you have two modems, you'll have tty1 and tty2. If you have more than one modem, you can select the one you want to use here. Clicking the Details button will allow you to set the baud rate and modem initialization strings for your modem. The box it came in or the owner's manual would have your baud rate information. Next, you set Speaker to on or off. Finally, you might notice under Dial Mode that Tone Dialing is selected by default. Very few people have rotary phones these days, but if you do, select Pulse Dialing.

Now press the Next button, and you're taken to information regarding your ISP. This is shown in Figure 16.14.

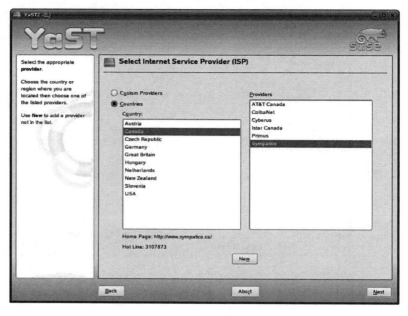

FIGURE 16.14   Your provider settings.

You can select a particular nationality here, if that's appropriate for your situation. Then, click Next and enter the phone number your ISP gave you to dial for Internet services. You'll then put in your provider's name, and the login name and password your ISP provided. This is shown in Figure 16.15.

Click Next two more times to step through the rest of the configuration screens and adjust the settings as necessary; then click Finish and you'll be taken to a screen identical to the final setup and verification screen of the Ethernet setup.

Another type of connection you might have is wireless. In the coming years, the odds of you using a wireless connection will increase. More and more businesses and even homes are going to wireless networks. Most consumer electronics stores now sell wireless kits for your home at a very reasonable price. For this reason, it's important that you know how to set this up in Linux.

You set up a wireless connection using the same interface you used for setting up your NIC, as you can see in Figure 16.16.

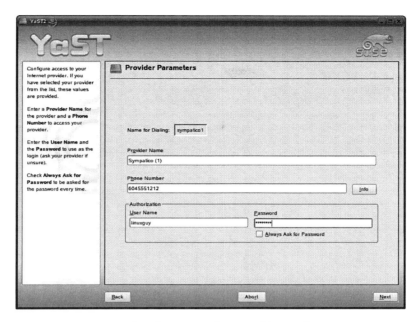

FIGURE 16.15 Entering the appropriate provider settings.

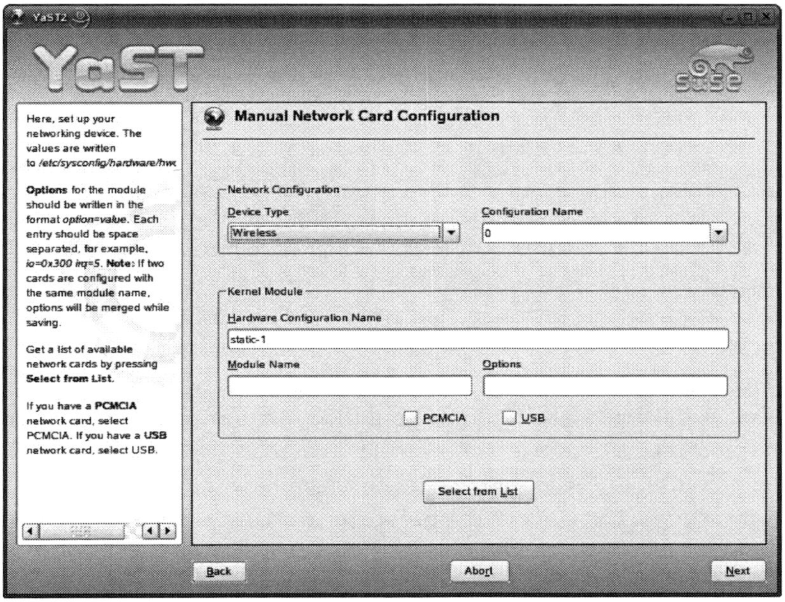

FIGURE 16.16 Preparing a wireless adapter.

Setting up your Internet connection, as you have seen, isn't particularly difficult. However, there are times when it's not sufficient. For example, if you purchase a new network card and install it, you'll need to configure it before you can connect to the Internet.

Fortunately, SuSE makes this easier by auto-detecting new hardware and allowing you to configure it through YaST. This is seen in Figure 16.17.

FIGURE 16.17   New hardware found!

You should have the Network Card Configuration dialog open. In the Network Cards to Configure area, select Other (not detected) and click the Configure button. On the screen that appears, select Wireless from the Device Type dropdown list under the Network Configuration section. Select Next and, if necessary, enter your static IP on the next screen.

All systems with Internet Protocol (TCP/IP) networking have what's called a loopback *address, which is 127.0.0.1 and allows you to connect to services on your local machine. Linux treats this address as an actual physical network card. That way, even if you have only one NIC in your machine, you'll see two Ethernet devices listed.*

Select Next again. Now you come to the Wireless Network Card Configuration screen shown in Figure 16.18. The plethora of choices might seem daunting at first, but don't worry, we'll walk through all of them.

The first setting, Operating Mode, allows you to choose whether your computer will be a part of a peer-to-peer network (Ad Hoc), connected to a network through an access point such as a wireless router (Managed, which is the most likely setting), or the connection point for other computers to access the network (Master). The second setting, Network Name, allows you to enter the name of the network you want to join. You may leave this empty for now to have SuSE offer you a list of likely networks in your area.

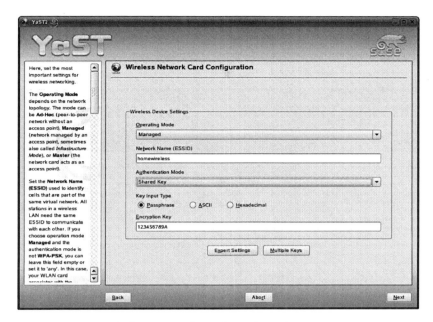

FIGURE 16.18   Wireless Network Card Configuration.

The last section, Authentication Mode, is where you can enter the settings necessary to connect to your wireless network. If you set up encryption on your router, you need to set Authentication Mode to match the type of encryption used by the router and then enter the encryption key you created in the Encryption Key field.

Choose Next and then Finish to apply your settings. SuSE may ask you for the DVD so it can install the appropriate packages, including network card drivers. Insert the DVD and follow the instructions. Note that not all wireless cards are supported under Linux, so check with the card's manufacturer or even some Linux forums for information on getting your particular card to work.

Your network card should now be configured. You can communicate on your local network, if you are on one. As you can see, this is not particularly difficult.

INTERNET SETTINGS

You might be thinking that we already covered this when we configured network settings in the last section. What network configuration did was set up your connection to the Internet. However, the various Internet software that you might want to use, such as a browser or an email client, will also need to be set. There are a number of Internet-related software packages that either ship with SuSE or can be downloaded for free. Many of these will be covered later in this book, but most

readers will want to be able to surf Web pages and check their email right away. With that in mind, we'll examine how to configure the default browser (Firefox) and the default email client (Evolution) that come with SuSE Linux 9.3. That way, you can start using the Web and email right away. However, keep in mind that what we cover here are just the basics for these Web applications, enough to get you started. There also are a number of useful Web sites in Appendix B, "Other Resources," that you can use to expand your Linux knowledge, but of course, your browser will be essential to accessing those sites.

If you're a Microsoft user, you probably use Microsoft Internet Explorer to visit Web sites. There's a plethora of other browsers you can use in Linux (Netscape, Mozilla, Opera), all of which are free. In this section, we'll examine the basic configuration of Firefox, a browser installed by many Windows users as a replacement for Internet Explorer, because it's far less prone to security issues.

If you use SuSE Linux 9.3 (or even an earlier version) and followed the instructions in Chapter 3, Firefox is already on your machine. You simply need to click on the Firefox icon on your desktop. When you first launch Firefox, it will look much like what you see in Figure 16.19. First, it displays Novell's Linux home page. It's probably a good idea to bookmark this page for later use. Bookmarks in Firefox work just like Favorites in Internet Explorer. You simply go to the Bookmarks menu at the top of the browser and select Bookmark This Page. You can also use the shortcut key Ctrl-D.

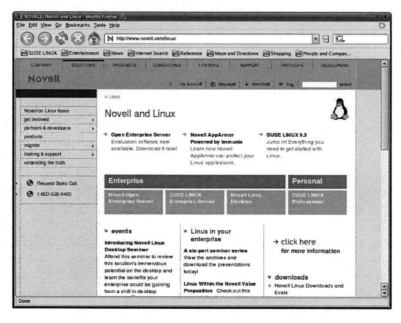

FIGURE 16.19   Firefox's opening screen.

The most important thing to learn is how to set up the browser's home page and make certain it connects to the Internet properly. With Internet Explorer, you accomplished this by going to Tools and then selecting Internet Options. The same thing is accomplished in Firefox by going to the Edit menu and selecting Preferences. You'll then see something like what's depicted in Figure 16.20.

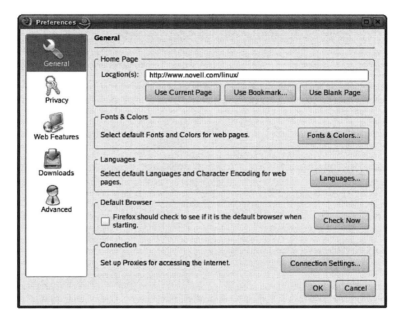

FIGURE 16.20   Preferences in Mozilla Firefox.

You can see that you have a host of settings you can configure through this dialog. We won't attempt to explore all of them, just the ones you'll most likely need. On the main Preferences screen you can set whether Firefox is your default browser, what home page is displayed, the fonts, the colors, and the default language. You select a home page simply by typing it in the Location(s) box in the middle of the screen. You can also use the page you are currently on by clicking on the Use Current Page button. This will cause the URL of the current page to be displayed in the location box. Checking the box under Default Browser will set Firefox as your default browser. Not that while Firefox is the default under GNOME, Konqueror is the default under KDE. Since we're going to use Firefox in many of the examples throughout this book, place a check there now.

If your PC is on a local area network, it's very likely that your network has a firewall and possibly a proxy server. A proxy server is a device that hides all the internal IP addresses from the outside world. You must go through it to connect to

any Internet resource. In essence, the proxy server is your one-way gateway to the Internet. You can select the Connection Settings button under Connection at the bottom of the Preferences dialog, and you'll be at a screen that looks like Figure 16.21, where you can enter the settings for your proxy server. Normally, you'll need to enter the IP address of your proxy server only into the HTTP Proxy and FTP Proxy boxes. You'll also need to enter a port number. You can get the IP and port numbers from your network administrator. Usually, FTP is on port 21, and HTTP on port 80.

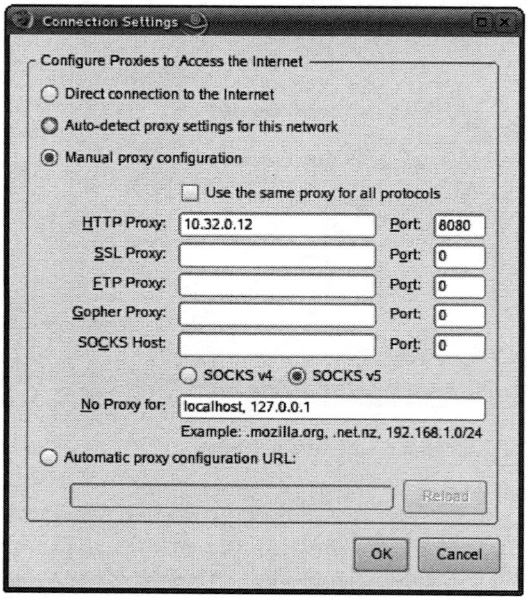

FIGURE 16.21   Proxy settings.

If you're not using a proxy server, you'll select the Direct Connection to the Internet button at the top of the screen. Of course, all this talk of proxy servers may be leaving some readers scratching their heads and wondering what in the world a proxy server is. A proxy server is a device that provides a barrier between a network and the Internet. You'll find a proxy server in many, if not most, business networks. A proxy server acts as an intermediary between a workstation and the Internet, passing your requests on and returning the results to you. The outside world can see only the proxy server and can't see the network behind it. The computers on that network get all of their external access through the proxy server and receive only the packets the proxy server lets through.

Another important setting you'll want to look at is the History setting. That screen is found by selecting Privacy and then History, and you'll see something similar to Figure 16.22.

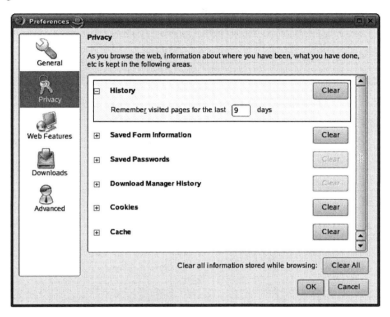

FIGURE 16.22 History settings.

At this screen, you can choose how long you want to keep sites you've visited in your history, clear the location bar of sites you've typed in, and clear your history. If privacy is a concern, set your History to one day and then clear the location bar and the history frequently. This will prevent others from determining sites you've visited.

If your company is using a proxy server, most proxy servers are capable of logging every site you visit. You won't be able to prevent that. This should make you reconsider visiting any illicit sites from your office computer; Big Brother may be watching.

You should now be able to use your browser to navigate Web pages. It's probably a good idea with this browser, or any software with which you're unfamiliar, to explore and experiment a little bit.

Configuring the email client is even easier. When you go to the Start menu, select Internet, select Email, and then Evolution Email—the Evolution Setup

Assistant will start. You should see something much like Figure 16.23. At this point, simply click the Next button and get ready to enter your email settings.

FIGURE 16.23   Starting the Evolution Configuration Wizard for email.

Of course, your email settings will be different from any other user's. However, to assist you in following along, this text used one of the authors' email settings as an example. This will also help should you want to email one of the authors. The first screen asks you to enter your full name and your email address. You can also choose to make this your default mail account and enter an optional return email address and company name. This screen is shown in Figure 16.24.

The next screen asks you to enter information about your incoming email servers. The email server is a machine at your ISP or in your company that handles incoming and outgoing email. The overwhelming majority of email servers use Post Office Protocol (POP) for incoming email, and it usually works on port 110. POP is simply the protocol that computers use to receive email. Some computers use a protocol called IMAP. Conversely, all computers use Simple Mail Transfer Protocol (SMTP) to send email, and that protocol works on port 25. You'll find that there's a protocol for every type of communication between one computer and another. The email server screen is seen in Figure 16.25. The screens for setting up your SMTP server and POP server are identical.

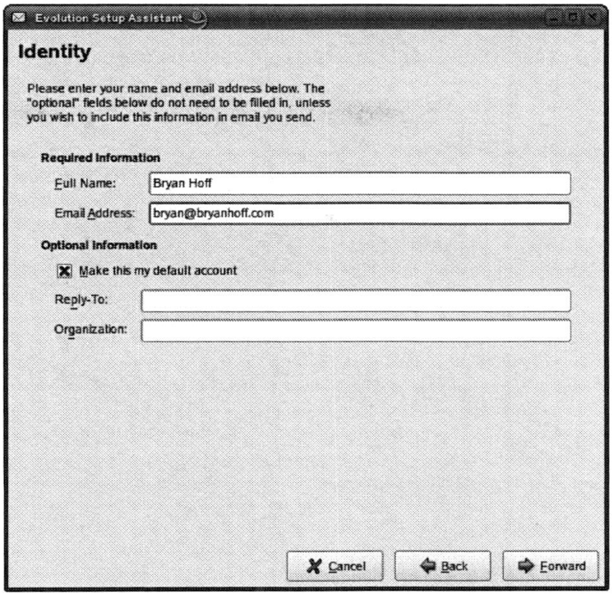

FIGURE 16.24 Entering your email address.

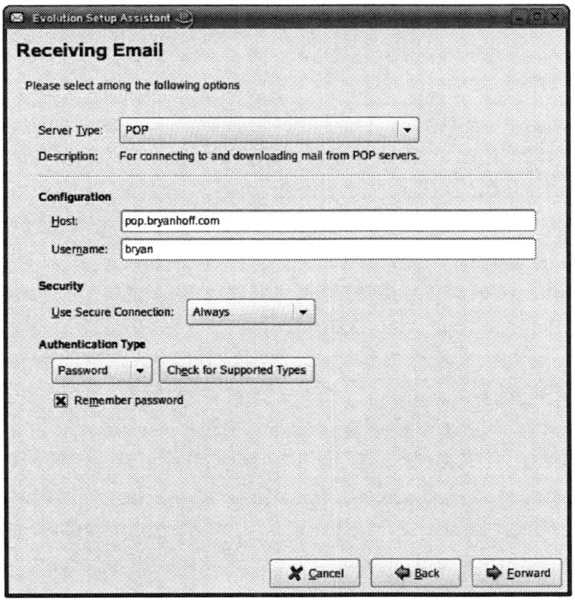

FIGURE 16.25 Your incoming email server.

The next screen, shown in Figure 16.26, asks your preferences regarding checking email. You're asked to indicate how often you want to check for new email and whether to leave a copy on the server. This means that even after you read your email, it's still on the server. This is usually preferred by people who might check their email from more than one machine. If you leave the email on the server, you can access it from any email client on any machine. Of course, if you get a large volume of email, this volume might exceed limits that your ISP or network administrator has set on your email inbox.

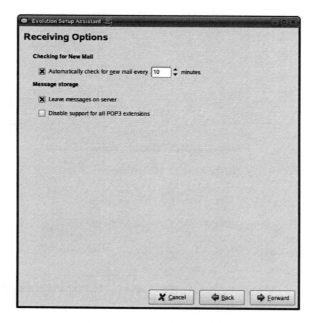

FIGURE 16.26   Preferences for receiving email.

The following screen, shown in Figure 16.27, is to set up your outgoing email. Recall that we previously mentioned that email is sent using SMTP, which usually works on port 25.

The next two screens have you enter your email address and select your time zone. You're now ready to start using the Evolution email client. In fact, you'll be taken to the main email client screen, shown in Figure 16.28. In the future, when you launch the email client, you'll go directly to this screen.

You can see that using Evolution for your email client is quite similar to using Microsoft Outlook® or Outlook Express®. In fact, the initial setup is considered easier by many people. This is just one of many alternative applications mentioned in previous chapters.

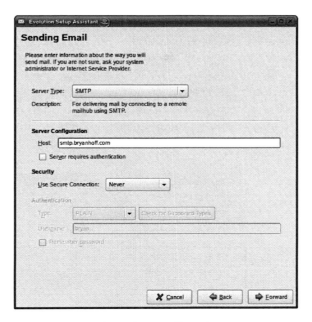

FIGURE 16.27   Outgoing email settings.

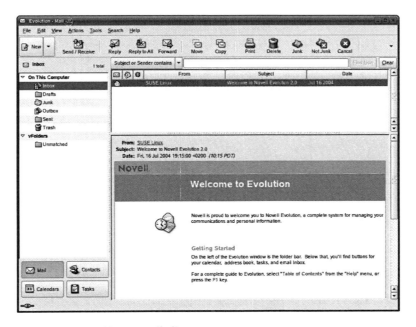

FIGURE 16.28   Your email client.

KMail is the default email client for KDE, while Evolution is the default for GNOME. However, we'll be working with Evolution for most of the examples in this book.

There's an option you may have noticed—Leave messages on server. This is just a little check box that you either check or uncheck. It simply directs the email software to leave the email on the server, even after you've read it. If you intend to check your email from more than one PC or email client, you may wish to leave the email on the server. If you don't, then when you log on with another email program, you won't see any of your emails. You might think they're gone! However, they were simply downloaded by the email client Evolution.

The option of whether to leave email on the server is hardly unique to Evolution. You're likely to find that option somewhere in almost any email client program you might choose to use.

SUMMARY

This chapter took you through the fundamentals of administering and configuring your Linux PC. You've seen how to get connected to the Internet, how to configure your browser, and how to configure your email. These are critical tasks because most people are particularly interested in Internet access.

In addition to establishing Internet access, you've also seen how to configure your desktop preferences, the look and feel of your desktop, and how to set up and use the multiple desktop feature of KDE. You've also been shown where to find hardware settings.

REVIEW QUESTIONS

1. What are the two most common means of Internet connection?
2. How many different desktops does KDE provide by default?
3. Under Background, what does the All Desktops setting do?
4. What is the default browser for KDE?
5. In Mozilla Firefox, what menu item do you select to set up your Internet connection settings?
6. What's the default email client for KDE?
7. Favorites in Internet Explorer are called what in Firefox?

17 Linux Administration from KDE

In This Chapter

- Managing Users and Groups
- Important System Tools
- Using the KDE Control Center
- System Administration
- Regional and Accessibility
- Scheduling Tasks
- AutoYaST

INTRODUCTION

By this point in the book you should be getting quite comfortable with Linux and the KDE graphical interface. You've installed Linux, configured Linux, and found out how to get on the Internet, and you've been introduced to several basic but highly useful applications. You should now be able to accomplish word processing, spreadsheet applications, use a calculator, and even do simple graphics with Linux. At this point, you should be a basically competent Linux user. However, Linux isn't always used for a single-user home environment. Many readers will want to use Linux in their small businesses. For this reason, in this chapter, we cover some basic Linux administration skills.

This chapter is aimed at showing you how to use Linux as a server, perhaps for a small office, and how to administer that server via the KDE graphical interface.

We explore how to add users and groups, schedule tasks, and monitor the system. All of this will be done with easy-to-use point-and-click applications (in a later chapter, you see how to perform many of these tasks with shell commands). Even if you're certain that you have no desire to use Linux as a server, it would still be a good idea to at least skim this chapter. It will give you some insight into how Linux works and perhaps a deeper understanding of computer systems in general.

You can use Linux to perform virtually every task that a Microsoft-based server is capable of; the main difference is that you can do it all at a fraction of the cost with Linux.

MANAGING USERS AND GROUPS

The purpose of a server is to provide services, files, or data to one or more people. In the information technology field, people who use a computer or system are referred to simply as *users.* This term is derived from the term *end users,* meaning the people on the end of the technology line, the ones ultimately using the product or service. For example, a Web server provides Web pages (data) to any user who can connect to that Web server via the Internet or a local network. The people accessing that data are the Web server's users.

Many offices, even small ones, use a server to store information. That way, all the authorized employees have access to the same data, since that data is located on a centralized server rather than on any individual employee's personal machine. In many if not most cases, you want some people on your network to have access to certain data and not to have access to other data. For example, you'd probably want human resources personnel to a person's personal records, but you might not want accounting or sales to have access to the same data. It's therefore necessary to restrict a person's access to only those items that are pertinent to the performance of his job. It's also probable that you wouldn't want general users to have access to system administration tools. They might accidentally or even intentionally change important system settings. This could be annoying, or could shut down your system.

With the Linux operating system, each time a user logs on, the settings in his user account determine which files and directories he has access to and which ones he doesn't. The place to start managing users and groups is with user accounts. Using the KDE interface, you'd go to System Settings and select Users and Groups. However, it's slightly different under SuSE. In SuSE, you'd open the YaST Control Center from the System group under the Start menu and then select Security and

Users and select Edit and create users. You should then see a screen that looks very much like the one in Figure 17.1.

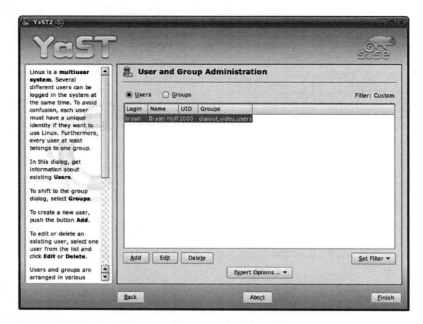

FIGURE 17.1   SuSE User and Group Administration screen.

The dialog buttons should be fairly self explanatory. There's also useful information on the left side of the dialog. At the top you'll see radio buttons to administer Users and Groups. Right now we're in User administration mode. Below these selections is a list of existing users and their info, and below that you'll see buttons to Add, Edit, and Delete users; a Set Filter button drop-down so you can display only certain users; and an Expert Options button that we won't worry about.

Let's add a user just to get the feel of how it's done. You begin by clicking the Add button at the bottom of the dialog. You should then see something very much like what's shown in Figure 17.2.

The fields under the User Data tab are all self-explanatory. In the first field, you simply enter the user's full name. After that, you enter a username for that person. What you select for a username is a matter of personal preference, but many organizations use the person's first initial and last name. For example, the username for one of the authors would be bhoff. Next, you need to enter a password. You'll be required to type this password twice to ensure that it is entered correctly.

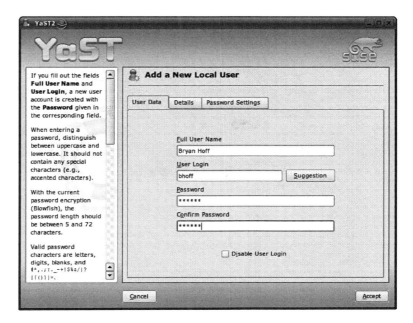

FIGURE 17.2 Add a New Local User screen.

If you want your system to be secure, there are a few guidelines regarding passwords you must follow. To begin with, there are programs freely available on the Internet that are used to guess passwords. For this reason your password should never be any common word or any word associated with you. It's foolish to use the names of your children or spouse, your anniversary, or other such items as passwords. Another good rule to follow is to mix letters and numbers. For example, if your password were *banana*, you should consider using something like *banana189* instead, or even *B4N4N4*, which looks like the word BANANA but replaces some of the letters with numbers. Finally, the longer your password is, the harder it will be to crack. Many system administrators make all users pick passwords between 5 and 20 characters long.

The next step is to click on the Details tab and check the home directory settings for this user. This is the default directory that user will have access to when he logs on. It's where he'll store files and data. All home directories are subdirectories of the directory home. It's common practice to name the user's home directory the same as the username. In fact, this user utility will by default create a home directory name that is the same as the username. So, for example, the default home directory for this user would be /home/bhoff. If you don't want to use the default name, you'll have to manually change it. You do that by typing in the alternative directory you want to use. You then have one field and a drop-down menu that need to be reviewed. One is labeled "User ID (uid)," and the other is labeled

"Default Group." We'll leave the Additional User Information field empty. The first field displays a unique user ID number for that user. That number is how the Linux system recognizes the person. Usernames are for people to read and understand. If you choose to create user IDs manually, you'll need to keep track of all user IDs and ensure that you never try to use the same one twice. It's far simpler to let Linux handle that. The Default Group setting allows you to add your new user to a user group (more about groups in just a bit). For now leave this setting at the default of users.

There's one more item on the Add a New Local User screen that we purposely left to last—the Login shell setting. Most users will want to use the bash shell, which you might recall is the most commonly used Linux shell and is selected by default. However, you can select from a list of shells, and any one of them can be the default shell for a particular user. When you're finished adding a user, the screen should look something like what you see in Figure 17.3A. All you need to do now is press the OK button, and you'll have created a new user account.

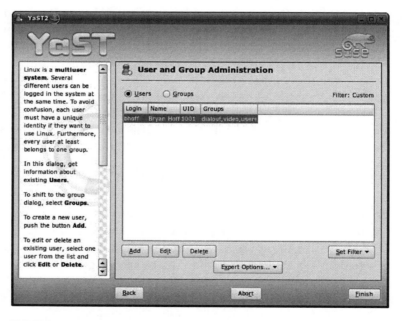

FIGURE 17.3A   A new user account.

If you restart the machine and log on with this username and password, you'll notice a few changes. The first is that your starting directory will be that user's home directory rather than the root directory. The only reason why root is your current starting directory is because you've logged on as root. The second change is that when you attempt to use many administration functions, you'll be asked to

supply a superuser password. *Superuser* is a term in Linux that denotes someone logged on to a regular user account who is using administrative privileges. To do this, you must have the root password. In short, superuser mode is being logged in as a normal user but using the root password to have temporary access to root privileges.

You've now established a user account, but what does this user have access to? The answer is, not much. At this point he'll have access to his home directory and not much else. In Linux, users are put into groups, and those groups are assigned access to certain resources. The access rights a user has depends entirely on which groups that user belongs to. When you double-click on a user account (or if you single-click on it and click the Edit button), you're presented with a Edit an Existing Local User screen. This is the same screen we saw earlier with the three tabs. The first is the account information you provided. This includes Full User Name, User Login, and Password. The second tab is where we'll determine important parameters about this account, including which groups that user belongs to. The third tab allows you to set Password Settings for the user.

The second tab of the Edit an Existing Local User screen is where we establish the groups a user belongs to. Select this tab, and you'll see the Default Group dropdown and Group Membership area, which are shown in Figure 17.3B. You can see a long list of groups; some might make sense to you, and others will make more sense as you move forward in this book. There are several groups listed, and some might seem quite obscure to you. In some Linux distributions, one group you might see and will probably make sense to you is the adm group. This group is for administrators. If you add a user to this group, that user will have some administration privileges. Contrary to what you might think, however, this group doesn't have the unlimited administration privileges of the root user. To practice, you might want to add the user you just created to the adm group. SuSE doesn't include an adm group, only a root group, and it's not recommended to add regular users to the root group. It's possible, however, to create your own adm group if you want. You can see that one of the easiest ways to grant a user access to certain items is to add him to the appropriate group. For example, if you want him to have access to the Web server, you add him to the apache group.

Apache is the name of the Web server that ships with SuSE Linux. Using Apache is covered in a later chapter. You might be interested in knowing that Apache runs as a daemon, which is a program that runs in the background and isn't visible to the user. In Windows, such programs are referred to as services.

In some cases, you'll want to create your own new groups. This is just as easy as creating new user accounts. To add a new group, click on the Groups radio button on the User and Group Administration screen and select Add. You'll then be prompted

to assign the group a name, as shown in Figure 17.4. It's usually a good idea to use logical names for your groups, names that indicate the type of group it is.

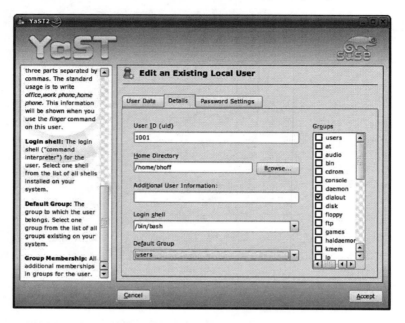

FIGURE 17.3B Adding a user to groups.

Next, you can opt to assign the group a password, and then click Accept when you're done. You'll arrive at a screen much like the one in Figure 17.5. You can see which users (if any) are assigned to the group under the Group members heading.

You'll notice that, in addition to the user you added, there's a number of users already on the list. Some of these users are actually applications. Many applications run as daemons. We previously said that a daemon is much like a service in Windows. Whether it's referred to as a daemon or a service, it's essentially just a program that runs in the background and has certain tasks it must fulfill. Usually, daemons handle system functions, things that the average PC user has no need to interact with. For this reason, daemons don't usually have a graphical user interface. For now, you need not be concerned with the other user accounts that are already loaded into the system. Simply find the username you added earlier by clicking the Users radio button, highlight the username, and click the Edit button. Now put a check by test group, as you see in Figure 17.6, and click the Accept button.

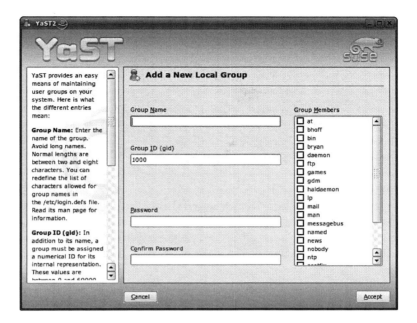

FIGURE 17.4 Adding a group.

FIGURE 17.5 Group properties.

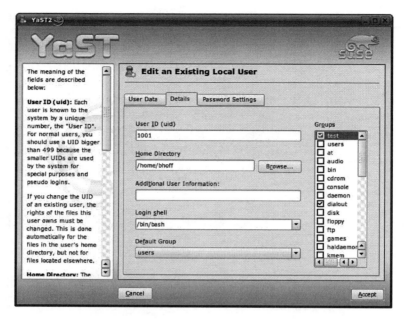

FIGURE 17.6   Adding users to a group.

The third tab contains information about a user's password. One important security precaution you can take is to require that users change their passwords periodically. In Figure 17.7, you can see the screen where you'd set the expiration date of the account if you wanted to. You'll want to set the Maximum number of days for the same password field's value to something a little lower than 99999, perhaps 90 or so. The user in question will get a warning that his password is about to expire every time he logs in for seven days preceding the expiration date. These are very useful features you'll probably want to turn on. Having the password expire after a given period of time definitely heightens security in your system. If you're going to force the user to change his password, you should remind him that his password's expiration date is drawing near. This gives him time to think of a new password. Many organizations have policies regarding acceptable passwords. These policies often include a minimum password length. A good basic password policy, if you don't already have one, is to require passwords to be at least five characters long and include both numbers and letters.

This tab also allows you to set an expiration date for the account. If you have a temporary employee, you definitely want to set an expiration date for that employee's account. Should you terminate an employee, you must immediately lock out his account.

Note that you can check the Disable User Login box on the User Data tab to lock out a particular account.

A few words about users and groups. A user is an individual given access to certain files on the computer. Each user is issued a username and password and has his own directory that contains files and settings relevant to that user. Users are given permissions to access certain files. Usually, these permissions consist of read, write, and execute privileges. Regular users don't have access to important system files. Groups give users access to files that would normally be off limits to them. For example, if a user is made part of the games group, he will be able to access all installed games.

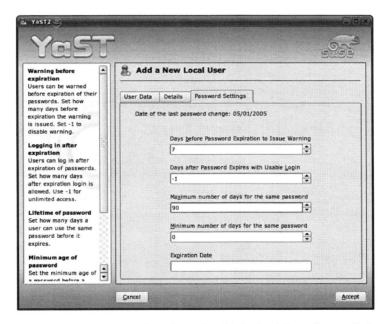

FIGURE 17.7   Password Settings; the third tab of the Edit an Existing Local User screen.

IMPORTANT SYSTEM TOOLS

You'll want to become familiar with a number of important system tools. These tools are of particular importance if you're using your Linux machine as a server for an office. However, several of these tools can be useful for the home Linux user as well. We examine the most important system utilities in this section.

The System Monitor

By going to System, clicking Monitor, and selecting GNOME System Monitor, you'll find the System Monitor utility, shown in Figure 17.8A. This is a very important system utility. It allows you to see how your system is performing.

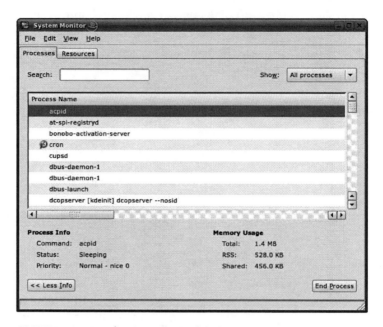

FIGURE 17.8A   The System Monitor screen.

If you didn't follow the install instructions in Chapter 3, "Installing Linux," you might not have the System Monitor installed on your system.

You might have previously used the System Information option in Windows to get similar information about your Windows system. If you haven't, you can go to the Start menu, select Programs, choose Accessories, and then select System Tools and click on the System Information option. The System Information screen, shown in Figure 17.8B, will then be displayed.

Although both the Windows System Information screen and the GNOME System Monitor provide access to similar information, their layouts are quite different. The GNOME System Monitor is displayed via tabs, with each tab representing a different group of options. The first tab shows you the processes that are currently running on your machine, how much memory they use, how much of the CPU's processor time, and what user initiated them. A process is any application, utility,

or daemon running on your machine. If your machine is performing sluggishly, you might want to see whether there are any processes that don't need to be running and can be shut down. System administrators often examine running processes of a system to look for telltale signs of a hacker attempting to infiltrate the system. Strange processes running might indicate some virus on your system or some malicious program that a hacker has loaded onto your system.

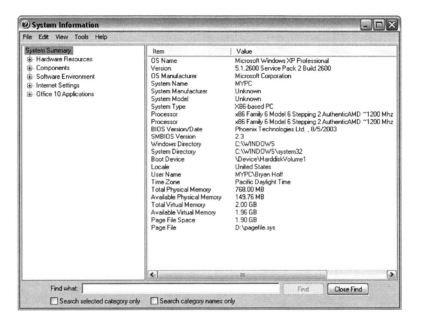

FIGURE 17.8B   The Windows System Information screen.

The second tab will be more useful. This tab is shown in Figure 17.8C and is labeled Resources. On this tab you see a neat little graph displaying the current CPU and memory usage. This is a very useful diagnostic tool. You can see whether your system needs more memory. As a rule of thumb, if you're consistently using more than 80 percent of your memory, you probably want to consider adding more memory.

At the bottom of this screen you can see how much of your hard drive space is being used. In Figure 17.8A we're using 3.4 gigabytes of a 4.4 gigabyte hard drive. Since we're using only 77 percent of our hard drive space, we don't need to consider a new hard drive quite yet. We're also using 102 megabytes of our memory, and we have 290 megabytes total, so we're in pretty good shape. However, it would probably be prudent to consider purchasing additional memory if we were using 200 megabytes or more.

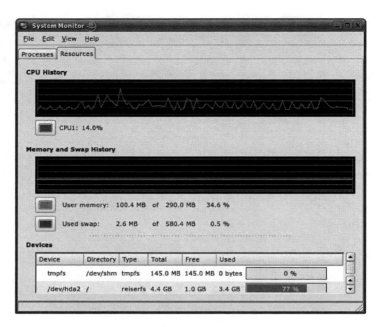

FIGURE 17.8C The second tab of the System Monitor screen.

Whether you're a system administrator for your organization or a casual home user, the System Monitor is an invaluable tool. It can be quite useful for diagnosing shortcomings in your system. Don't go out and invest money in more memory or a new hard drive if it's not needed. Use System Monitor to see whether your current memory, CPU, or hard drive is inadequate for your system's needs.

Hardware Information

One of the advantages to using SuSE is YaST. YaST puts most of the tools necessary for the proper operation of your system in one easy-to-access location. For example, if you want to work with your system's hardware, you can open YaST and then click on the Hardware icon on the left. Here you'll find tools to configure virtually every piece of hardware in your system. Right now we want to get an overview of the current system's hardware. To do this, select Hardware Information from the group of icons on the right side of the YaST dialog. You'll see an information box labeled "Probing." After a minute or so, you should see something like what's shown in Figure 17.9. This is a very important yet easy to understand and use utility. With the Hardware Information utility you can see what devices are on your machine. This includes disk drives, network cards, sound cards, and pretty much any piece of hardware you can put on a PC. In many cases, this utility will even display the specifications of the hardware, including manufacturer. This information can be critical to the PC novice and advanced system administrator alike.

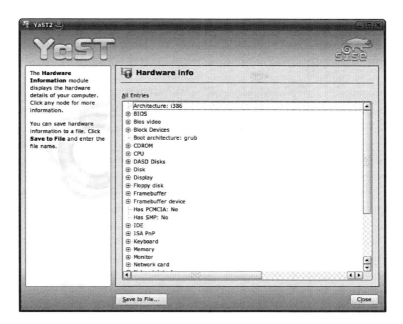

FIGURE 17.9 Hardware information.

If you're a novice user, there's a good chance that you'll find some occasion to contact a technical support representative. This might be technical support from your ISP, your PC manufacturer, or from SuSE Linux itself. Whatever the reason you contact them, technical support personnel often ask you questions about your system's hardware. These are questions that many novices can't answer. The Hardware Information utility will give you access to all of this information.

If, on the other hand, you're a technically savvy system administrator, you'll find a veritable gold mine of valuable data under the Hardware Browser. You can get specifications on every piece of hardware on a machine. You can then use that information in myriad ways. For example, you might take the manufacturer information from a video card, do a Web search to find that manufacturer's Web site, and look for the latest drivers for Linux that the vendor offers.

Under the device information for most hardware devices, the last item group is dev_names. You might note that all devices appear to be paths, just like the path to a file in a directory. Most also start with /dev/. Linux views devices as if they were files or directories within the /dev/ directory. Hard drives always start with hd, floppy drives with fd, and network cards with eth.

Firewall

Firewall configuration is so important that it would be a grave injustice not to introduce you to it. Once again, it's found under YaST, this time by clicking on Security and Users on the left side. When you were installing Linux, you had the opportunity to establish a number of configuration settings. Recall that you were admonished to leave the firewall settings at default. However, if in the interim since that installation you've picked up a little knowledge on the subject, you can now customize security for your system. Even if you haven't learned much more about network security, you should be aware of a few basics. Click on the Firewall icon on the right to see the Firewall Configuration screen as shown in Figure 17.10.

FIGURE 17.10   The Firewall Configuration screen.

Before we can discuss the security settings, it would be prudent to have a brief introduction to how networks and the Internet communicate. In short, data is broken down into packets that are sent using various protocols. A protocol is simply a standardized way of communicating. A number of protocols are used in networks and on the Internet, each with its own purpose. It's not necessary for a casual home user to memorize these, but since some readers might be their office system administrators, the most commonly used protocols are described in Table 7.1.

TABLE 7.1 Protocols

Protocol	Description
HTTP	Hypertext Transfer Protocol. It's the protocol used by Web browsers such as Netscape Navigator and Mozilla to communicate with Web servers and display Web pages.
FTP	File Transfer Protocol. This protocol is used to upload and download files. If you've ever downloaded a demo game, music, or any file from the Internet, it was probably done with FTP.
SMTP	Simple Mail Transfer Protocol. Used to send email.
POP3	Post Office Protocol. Used to retrieve incoming email from an email server.
DHCP	Dynamic Host Configuration Protocol. Used to get an IP address from a server.

To edit firewall settings you'd click on Allowed Services on the left and select the services you want to allow from the drop-down list on the right. You can also configure settings for your internal network here by selecting Internal Zone from the Allowed Services for Selected Zone drop-down. As you learn more about how networks work, you might consider customizing your security settings.

Adding and Removing Applications

From time to time you might find that you don't use an application you have installed, and you might want to remove it to free up more space on your hard drive. You might also discover that you forgot to install some application. The Install and Remove Software icon, found In YaST under Software, is what you need for either task. You might recall that in Chapter 3, you were told that if you forgot any applications, they could be installed later. This utility is how you go about doing that.

When you first launch the utility, it will take a moment to load. That's because it's checking your system to see which applications are already installed. While it's loading, you'll see a screen giving you the status of the process. This screen is shown in Figure 17.11.

After the utility is loaded, you'll need to choose how to list packages. You're met with a Filter drop-down that offers various ways of displaying the packages including Selections, Package Groups, and a Search utility. We'll go with Selections since that's how we installed software in Chapter 3. Choosing Selections shows a list of all available packages organized into common selection groups in the left pane. Entire selection groups can be installed by placing a checkmark next to their names. If you click on a selection's name, you'll see in the right pane that applications

FIGURE 17.11   Reading package information.

already installed on your system will have a checkmark beside them. Even if a selection group doesn't have a checkmark next to it, individual packages within that group might be checked. Packages that aren't installed won't have the checkmark. You might check the packages you'd like to install and uncheck packages you want to uninstall or remove. Then, simply click the Accept button. Depending on the choices you made, it might take several minutes to add and remove various applications. Also, if you chose to add applications, you'll be prompted to insert the appropriate installation disks. You can see the utility's main screen in Figure 17.12A.

KDiskFree

KDiskFree, shown in Figure 17.12B, is a rather simple utility that shows you various drives, including floppy, CD-ROM, and hard drives. In the display it will show how much space is still free, what percentage is in use, and the Linux device name and initial size of the storage device. KDiskFree is found under the Start menu by selecting System and then File System.

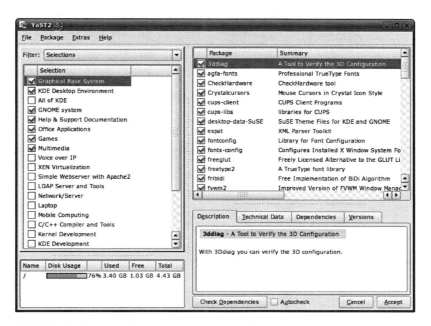

FIGURE 17.12A Adding and removing applications.

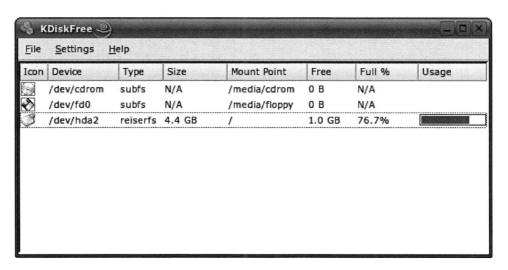

FIGURE 17.12B KDiskFree.

USING THE KDE CONTROL CENTER

The Control Center is found on the main Start menu. It is, as the name implies, a centralized location from which to control many important features of KDE. We looked at it briefly in Chapter 5, "System Configuration in KDE," but now it's time to explore it in more detail. When you first launch the Control Center, you'll see something much like what's shown in Figure 17.13. In the main screen on the right side, you should notice that it's telling you which version of KDE you're using, which user account is currently logged in, which operating system you're using (Linux or Unix), and which version of that operating system you're using. The release is the version of the Linux kernel you're using.

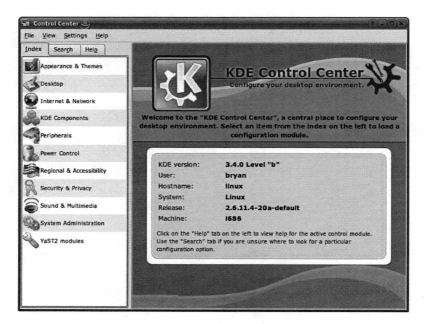

FIGURE 17.13 The opening screen of the KDE Control Center.

On the left side are three tabs. The first, Index, is a listing of all the various items you can control through the Control Center. The second tab is a Search tab allowing you to search for a particular item. The third is a Help tab where you can look up help on various KDE topics.

Many of the items you can control from the Control Center are items we previously covered, such as Appearance and Themes, Internet and Network, and Desktop. The Control Center provides a convenient single location from which to work with many of the various configuration utilities available with KDE. We won't cover the

items we've previously examined. They work exactly the same way from the Control Center as they did previously. However, we will look at a few interesting items in the Control Center that we didn't examine previously.

Power Control

If you look under Peripherals, select Display, and then click on the Power Control tab, you'll see something much like what's displayed in Figure 17.14. The settings shown here allow you to conserve energy. You can tell your PC to suspend operation after a certain amount of time or to completely power off after a given amount of time. That way, if you walk away from your PC and leave it running, it will eventually shut itself off.

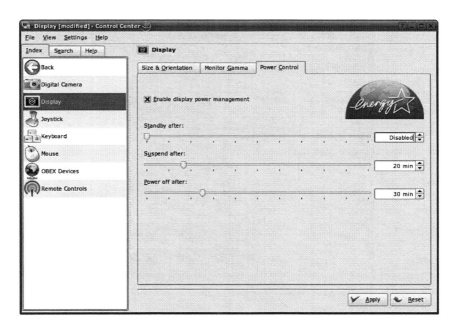

FIGURE 17.14   Power Control settings.

There's also a Laptop Battery section that is specifically for laptop users. It's found under Power Control. This section enables you to determine how to warn the user if his laptop battery is getting low. If you're installing Linux on a laptop, you'd be very wise to set up your laptop battery settings. This screen is shown in Figure 17.15.

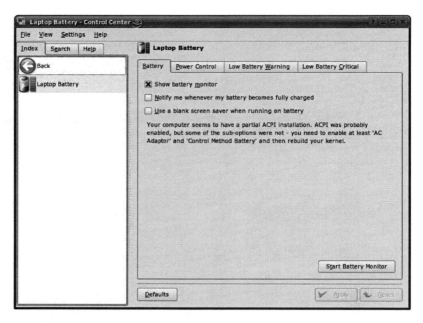

FIGURE 17.15   Laptop Battery settings.

The first tab establishes whether to display a battery status icon and how often to check the status of the battery. The second tab is very much like the Power Control settings we previously examined. It allows you to shut down the system power after a given amount of time. You can have a different amount of time selected, depending on whether your laptop is plugged into an outlet or running off battery power. This is a very useful setting and can prevent you from leaving your laptop running and running down your battery. The final two tabs determine how and when the user will be warned about a low battery. If you're using Linux on a laptop, it would be a mistake for you not to become familiar with these settings and to ensure that they're set up in such a manner as to maximize your use of the Linux operating system and your laptop.

SYSTEM ADMINISTRATION

This section is for some of the more common system administration tasks. We'll take a look at the ones that are most likely to be of use to you on a routine basis.

Login Manager

The Login Manager allows you to establish how the login screen is presented to the user when he logs in. This screen has six tabs that enable you to specify every aspect of the login process and appearance. You can see the screen in Figure 17.16.

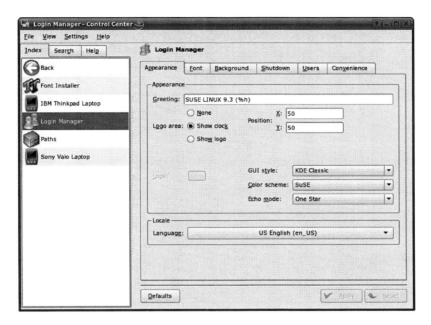

FIGURE 17.16 The Login Manager screen.

The first tab allows you to set the greeting, whether to show the logo (KDE), to show a clock, and what color scheme to use for the login screen. You can also change what character appears when someone is typing a password. Most people are used to seeing one asterisk appear for each character they type, so it's probably a good idea to stick with this format, but you can change it if you want. The next two tabs allow you to further customize the login screen by setting the font and the background. These tabs handle purely cosmetic properties of the login screen and should be set to whatever you find pleasing.

The fourth tab, labeled "Shutdown" and shown in Figure 17.17, isn't cosmetic at all. This tab deals with the options the user will be presented with when he gets to the logon screen and what he can do from this screen.

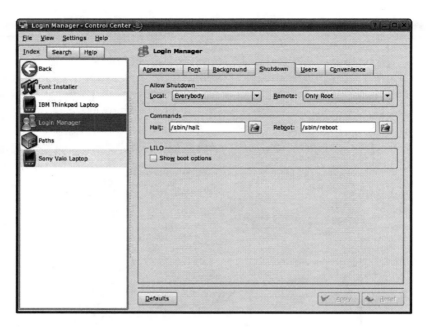

FIGURE 17.17   The fourth tab of the Login Manager.

As you can see, the first two settings allow you to determine which users can use the console/shell and which users can log on remotely. The second set of options, Commands, determines what happens when you halt or reboot. You should leave these with the default settings unless you have some compelling reason to alter them. The third section simply determines whether to show the boot options on the login screen. This will make very little difference unless your machine is set to dual boot with two or more alternative operating systems (such as Linux and Windows).

The Users tab allows you to select an image to display and to choose whether to show a list of users for the person to pick from. This would mean that instead of simply typing their usernames and passwords, they could pick from a list of users and then enter the appropriate password.

The sixth and final tab, Convenience, allows you to set some items you might find convenient. However, you should remember that convenience almost always comes at a price. On this screen you can choose to allow people to log on without a password. Unless the machine is a home machine, such an option would be very foolish. Even if it's a home machine, you should think very hard before choosing this option. Do you really want your 10-year-old to be able to log on as root and have complete system administration privileges?

REGIONAL AND ACCESSIBILITY

This section allows you to set some accessibility options, which we examined previously. However, it also allows you to reconfigure your machine for a given region. After you've chosen Regional & Accessibility, click on Country/Region & Language, and you should see a screen much like that in Figure 17.18.

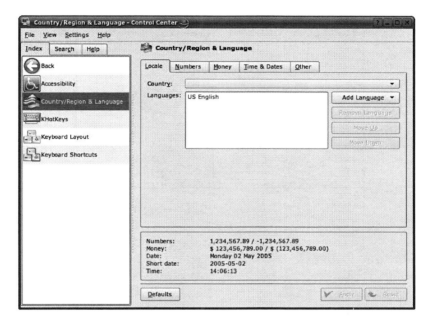

FIGURE 17.18   Country/Region & Language screen.

The first tab, Locale, allows you to set which nation and language settings to use. You can see at the bottom of this tab that your current settings are shown. The second tab determines how you'll display numbers. The third tab is probably the most important for setting up your machine for a different country. This tab allows you to change how money is displayed. Obviously, currency is quite different from one nation to the next, so this tab can be quite important. The fourth tab establishes how you'll display times and dates. This tab is more a matter of preference than regions. The final tab will allow you to choose paper format and measurement systems. If you're traveling abroad, you should remember that most countries use the metric system.

SCHEDULING TASKS

One very useful feature of Linux is the capability to schedule certain tasks to take place at some future date and time. If you'll recall, earlier we discussed programs that run in the background and accomplish tasks. In Linux and Unix these are referred to as *daemons*, and in Windows they're called *services*. The names of most daemons in Linux end in the letter d. The daemon that's responsible for handling scheduled tasks is called *crond*, for chronological daemon. You can completely manage crond via shell commands, and we'll visit that topic in Chapter 9, "Moving from Microsoft Word to Open Office Writer," but right now we'll see how to do this through the KDE interface. Like most tasks, scheduling tasks via the KDE interface is much easier and more user friendly than doing it via shell commands. To get to the Task Scheduler, go to System and then Service Configuration and select KCron. You should see something much like what's displayed in Figure 17.19.

You might need to install KCron. To do so, click Install and Remove Software under YaST. Set Filter to Package Groups and look under System > GUI > KDE for a package called kdeadmin3.

FIGURE 17.19   The Task Scheduler screen.

To schedule a new task, you simply select Edit from the menu and then click on New, as shown in Figure 17.20.

FIGURE 17.20 Selecting New tasks.

When you do this you'll see a screen like the one shown in Figure 17.21. On this screen you can decide when you want your task to run. You can pick months, days, time of day, even down to the exact minute when you want the task to run. Then use the Browse button to select the program you want to run.

That's all that's required to schedule any task. You can have any program you want run automatically at a certain time and date. This is very useful for system administrators who want particular programs or scripts to run while they're away. This allows you to have certain cumbersome administrative tasks take place when you're away from the computer.

FIGURE 17.21 Scheduling a new task.

AUTOYAST

Linux, being a descendent of Unix, was designed with a powerful high-end server in mind. For that reason, Linux, like many Unix variants, comes with a wide assortment of configuration utilities. Some of these, such as the System Monitor, have Windows analogs to which you can relate. However, some utilities, such as AutoYaST, don't have any close analog in the Windows world. AutoYaST is a very useful SuSE program. It's found in YaST under Miscellaneous with the name Autoinstallation, and the main screen is shown in Figure 17.22. The SuSE official documentation describes AutoYaST in this manner: "AutoYaST allows unattended and automated installation." This means it allows you to generate an XML configuration script via a very easy-to-use graphical interface. SuSE allows you to use this script later to reconfigure your system or a new system with all the options you set up in Chapter 3. It's often used by system administrators to create a single install script to be used for installs across an organization. From General Options in the basic configuration screen, you can change the language, mouse, keyboard, time zone, and other important settings.

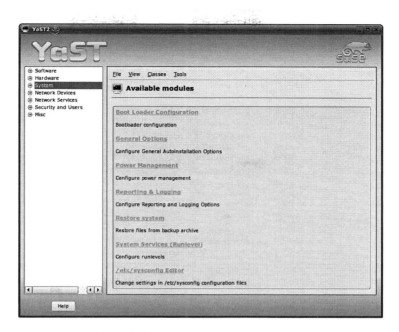

FIGURE 17.22 The AutoYaST screen.

The next section of particular interest to us is the Boot Loader Options screen, shown in Figure 17.23. You access it by selecting Boot Loader Configuration from the System section and clicking Configure. Among other things, this screen allows you to choose which boot loader to use. Even though GRUB is the newest boot loader, you don't have to use it; you can use LILO if you so desire. You can also choose to have a password on GRUB if you like.

Next, we'll discuss the Partitioning screen under Hardware, shown in Figure 17.24. Again, you must click the Configure button to get to the actual configuration area. This screen should be used to automatically create drive partitions.

The Network Devices and Network Services sections provide a way to configure options we've already explored. We've explored three different ways to configure your network card after installation, so you'd use those skills again here.

The Security and Users section includes a Firewall Configuration option. Like the two preceding sections, it provides a way to configure a particular part of your system. We mentioned firewall configuration during the initial install and noted that you could always reconfigure the firewall settings at a later date, as you learned more about networks.

The X11 Configuration screen, shown in Figure 17.25, and found under Hardware > Graphics Card and Monitor, is quite interesting. With this screen, you can pre-configure a system's screen resolution, video card, monitor, and default desktop. This section is likely to be of interest even to casual users. One setting that peo-

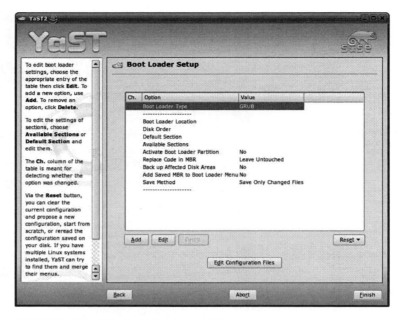

FIGURE 17.23   The Boot Loader Options screen.

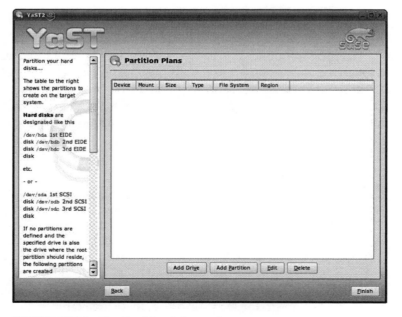

FIGURE 17.24   The Partition Information screen.

ple on any system (Windows, Macintosh, or Linux) seem inclined to change from time to time is their display.

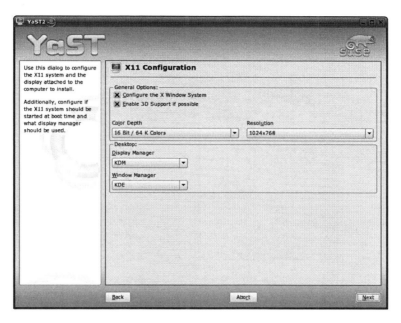

FIGURE 17.25   The X11 Configuration screen.

The Misc section of AutoYaST is used to alter how an installation proceeds. If, at some later date you want to install a new version of SuSE, you can follow the installation instructions to create an install script. If you plan on installing SuSE on multiple systems or think you might need to reinstall SuSE at a later date, AutoYaST might be of great use to you. If you just want to reconfigure your current system, use the YaST Control Center.

SUMMARY

This chapter showed you the essentials of system administration via the KDE interface. There are certainly many more tasks you can do in KDE, but these are some of the most common. After studying this chapter, you should be able to add new users, manage groups, use the System Monitor, add and remove programs, use the KDE Control Center, and schedule tasks. Whether you're a casual home user or the system administrator for your office, these are common tasks that you'll find yourself using with some frequency.

Of course, there are more system tools and administrative utilities in the KDE desktop interface that you might want to use. The utilities presented in this chapter are the most commonly encountered utilities. It's recommended that you take some time to experiment with these various utilities and become familiar with them.

REVIEW QUESTIONS

1. What's a daemon?
2. What daemon is responsible for scheduling tasks?
3. Why is your birth date not a good password?
4. What protocol is used for sending email?
5. What protocol is used for receiving email?
6. What KDE utility would you use to find out how much memory is being used by your system?
7. What's the purpose of the KDE Control Center?